D1613108

THE WEIMAR ORIGINS OF RHETORICAL INQUIRY

THE WEIMAR ORIGINS OF RHETORICAL INQUIRY

DAVID L. MARSHALL

The University of Chicago Press
Chicago and London

The University of Chicago Press, Chicago 60637
The University of Chicago Press, Ltd., London
© 2020 by The University of Chicago

All rights reserved. No part of this book may be used or
reproduced in any manner whatsoever without written
permission, except in the case of brief quotations in critical
articles and reviews. For more information, contact the
University of Chicago Press, 1427 E. 60th St., Chicago, IL 60637.

Published 2020
Printed in the United States of America

29 28 27 26 25 24 23 22 21 20   1 2 3 4 5

ISBN-13: 978-0-226-72221-4 (cloth)
ISBN-13: 978-0-226-72235-1 (e-book)
DOI: https://doi.org/10.7208/chicago/9780226722351.001.0001

Library of Congress Cataloging-in-Publication Data

Names: Marshall, David L., 1973– author.
Title: The Weimar origins of rhetorical inquiry /
David L. Marshall.
Description: Chicago ; London : The University of Chicago
Press, 2020. | Includes bibliographical references and index.
Identifiers: LCCN 2020001760 | ISBN 9780226722214 (cloth) |
ISBN 9780226722351 (ebook)
Subjects: LCSH: Heidegger, Martin, 1889–1976. | Arendt,
Hannah, 1906–1975. | Benjamin, Walter, 1892–1940. | Warburg,
Aby, 1866–1929. | Rhetoric—Germany—History—20th century. |
Philosophy, German—20th century. | Political science—
Germany—Philosophy. | Philosophers—Germany. | Germany—
History—1918–1933. | Germany—Intellectual life—20th century.
Classification: LCC DD239 .M374 2020 | DDC 320.01—dc23
LC record available at https://lccn.loc.gov/2020001760

♾ This paper meets the requirements of ANSI/NISO Z39.48-1992
(Permanence of Paper).

To the memory of my parents, Coralie Daniel and Peter Marshall

CONTENTS

I: THE WEIMAR WE KNOW AND THE WEIMAR WE DO NOT KNOW

POINTS OF DEPARTURE

A major topos in twentieth-century intellectual history has been that emigrants who left as the Weimar Republic became Nazi Germany had an incredible influence on a wide variety of fields of inquiry, and this topos has been especially prominent in political theory. Even a cursory scan of the terrain reveals a remarkable array of foundational concepts and modes of inquiry. One can lay out departures from the curve of Weimar history that have become foundational lines of inquiry for a host of investigative traditions. The sociological work of Max Weber on the rise and significance of communities organized by systems of rules established basic problematics around the nature of political leadership under modern conditions. Whatever his own reaction would have been to Mussolini, Stalin, Hitler, and Mao (had he not died in 1920), Weber's theorization of charismatic leadership made him seem prophetic as subsequent thinkers both explored and questioned his theorizations in the middle decades of the twentieth century. In turn, the juridical work of Carl Schmitt offered up a very particular vision of the relationship between any given legal order and what he thought of as the quite different extralegal political situation that surrounded it. Schmitt's decisionism not only gave conceptual cover to the Nazi seizure of power in 1933 but also became tremendously influential even in the post-1945 world for all those who wished to think about the "paper-thin" quality of democratic and constitutional foundations. Where Schmitt inherited the problematic of legal foundation from Weber, the political philosophical project of Leo Strauss took up the implicit nihilism of Schmitt's decisionism by reengaging with what he took to be antiquity's direct investigations into the good life and the good polity. And, in the North American continuation of his career, Strauss was able to build a significant coterie of collaborators engaged in a broad antimodern critique. If Strauss turned to ancient history in order to articulate a search for timeless values, then the Renaissance studies research of Hans Baron was a more historically invested and less politically overt attempt to discover in fifteenth-century Florence an ideology of republican citizenship that might speak to Weimar's republican moment. Baron's core statement of his position was published only once Weimar itself had become a lost possibility, but it became a core component of a variously civic humanist, neo-Aristotelian, or communitarian valuation of public life. In addition to these sociological, legal, political, and historical modes of inquiry, the Weimar emigration also included the Western Marxism of Frankfurt School critical theory. Indeed, the early work of Theodor Adorno was something like an age of capitalism critique of Baron's early modern fantasy of city-state life, for Adorno examined the material and imaginative dimensions of the metropolitan city dweller, who was more bourgeois than burgher. Doubtless, the précis ventured in the previous ten sentences is extremely selective, but it is also closely woven and ideologically diverse, which is both striking and interesting.

The Weimar origins of political theory just sketched have been tremendously influential, so influential in fact that one wonders whether we have now followed these lines of inquiry long enough. This book is written on the basis of twin convictions. First, accounts of these Weimar origins have indeed reached a late stage of conceptual saturation. Second, we can rejuvenate our reception of core elements in Weimar intellectual life by returning to some of those roots and reading them anew as part of a different intellectual history that I am calling "the Weimar origins of rhetorical inquiry." The core chapters of this book deal with the inference matrices of Martin Heidegger, Hannah Arendt, Walter Benjamin, and Aby Warburg. Taken together, these thinkers articulate a tradition of rhetorical inquiry. In this introduction, I will show how their work can be understood as inflecting and transforming problems set out by the departures proposed by Weber, Schmitt, Strauss, Baron, and Adorno. As I configure him, Heidegger offers an alternative to the account of human excellence given by Strauss. Arendt's prewar work—more than the famous initiatives of *The Human Condition* (1958)—develops an idiom for public life richer than Baron's civic humanism. In turn, I evoke a baroque-centered Benjamin who responded to Schmitt's decisionism with a topical theory and practice of what I call "indecisionism." Similarly, I discern in Warburg an inversion of the merely melancholic cosmopolitanism critiqued by Adorno, an inversion that generates new accounts of magnanimity and, indeed, freedom.

With the phrase "rhetorical inquiry" I specify a distinctive and eclectic zone between the more established fields of the history of rhetoric on the one hand and rhetorical theory on the other. Broadly put, my hypothesis is that the rhetorical tradition has been something like a seedbed of theoretical presuppositions. I contend further that these presuppositions have been capable of moving beyond the disciplinary bounds of rhetoric narrowly understood and have functioned as theoretical carapaces in other fields of inquiry. This book is disciplinarily promiscuous precisely because of the rich and cross-disciplinary afterlives of assertions that have discernable origins in rhetoric and yet achieve inferential depth in other fields in the sense that they become premises involved (either explicitly or implicitly) in a significant number of arguments in those fields. Each of the Weimar thinkers explored in detail in this book has brought fields of inquiry into being. Philosophy would be different today without Heidegger; the same goes for Arendt and political theory, Benjamin and literary theory, and Warburg and the history and theory of art. I claim that we miss major conceptual opportunities if we do not attend to the rhetorical aspects of the thought of these thinkers. I also claim that there is an opportunity to gather these origin points together in order to think of them as a series of potential trajectories.

My historiographic practice in this book is somewhat unusual and needs to be defended. I hold myself to strict philological standards and have spent considerable time with the oeuvres of the four core thinkers in this book. These collected corpora are the central facts of this inquiry, and I hold fast to them. I thus cite from German editions and make my own translations from the German throughout. (Readers who do not read German can find translations of some of the more frequently cited works listed at the beginning of the bibliography.) The book is not counterfactual as such, and I am not interested in asserting the existence of Heideggers or Arendts or Benjamins or Warburgs who never were. Nevertheless, I am interested in thinking dimensions of these thinkers that are, by and large, less often and less deeply thought. Taken together and seen together within the perspective of rhetoric, these thinkers invent a tradition. This is a tradition within which we can think today, and it is my explicit aim to lay out a history that can become a zone within which theoretical experimentation may be pursued in the future. As I practice it, intellectual history is a way of reenacting the inferential habits of individuals and the traditions to which they belonged such that one can run their arguments as scripts and gain, eventually, a capacity to improvise within their distinctive inferential repertoires. "Running" such scripts will be performative, and not all such performances will be labeled explicitly as paraphrases. When I am making an argument in my own voice, I shall make the change in speaker as explicit as possible.

Thus, the redescriptions of Weber, Schmitt, Strauss, Baron, and Adorno that I work up in this introduction are so many minority reports. I mean that the redescription I offer gives voice in each case to a less prominent version of the thinker in question. My suggestion is that these serialized minority reports motivate a broader investigation into the nature, viability, and conceptual richness of the Weimar origins of rhetorical inquiry. If there is a sense in which the future is counterfactual (because it does not exist and has not yet been "factuated"—that is, made), then there is a counterfactual dimension to the intellectual history I am writing here, but only in this sense. This way of proceeding contravenes some of the still-dominant presuppositions about what kind of work is legitimate in the history of thought (and the history of political thought in particular), and so I lay out a defense of my practices in the middle section of this introduction.

In order to state the problem to which this book is a response, I begin here in the introduction with a standard received version of the Weimar origins of political theory. I then defend my intellectual-historical practices. Finally, in the third part of the introduction, I redescribe the Weimar origins of political theory in terms of the hitherto occluded Weimar origins of rhetorical inquiry that I pursue in the rest of the book.

STANDARD RECEIVED VERSIONS OF THE WEIMAR ORIGINS OF POLITICAL THEORY

The analyses of modern politics written by Max Weber are influential to the point that they can anchor the series of Weimar inflections that I sequence and then redescribe in this introduction. Born in 1864, before the unification of Germany and during the decade of Bismarck's rise, Weber died in 1920. In no sense was he a product of the Weimar Republic, yet some of Weber's most acute political writings were penned immediately after Germany's defeat in the First World War, during the period of revolution that followed, and while the republic was establishing itself as a constitutional order in 1919. Perhaps the key founding sociologist of the twentieth century, Weber's sense of the ironic structures of modern life remains citable today. The paradox at the core of much of his political thought can be characterized succinctly. On the one hand, no modern political community will be capable of functioning efficiently if it does not establish a legal order cast as a system of rules. On the other hand, politics will remain a profoundly contingent affair because no one will ever be able to write a rule for every circumstance and because no political community founded on rules will produce leaders capable of responding adequately to the exception-to-the-rule judgments that circumstances will necessitate.

The constituent parts of Weber's ironic vision came together most compactly when he famously contrasted the three basic modes of legitimizing established power in "Politics as a Vocation" (1919). There, he spoke of "the authority of 'the eternal yesterday,'" namely, custom. He distinguished this from "the authority of the extraordinary personal gift of grace (charisma)," which he understood as "an entirely personal devotion to and a personal trust in the manifestations, heroism, or other characteristics of leadership in a single person." In turn, he differentiated rule by custom and rule by charisma from "rule by virtue of 'legality.'" This was rule "by virtue of belief in the application of legal statute and in a clinical 'competence' grounded in rationally fashioned rules."[1] Weber underscored the irony: neither custom nor the custom made explicit in the rule would obviate the need for charismatic individuals who might generate those customs and those rules in the first place by force of example.

One encounters the effects of Weber's paradoxical presuppositions about rules and leadership throughout his political writings. To be sure, said Weber (in his 1917 essay on "Parliament and Government in Germany"), "the future belongs to bureaucratization."[2] And "no differently than in the economy or in state administration," he thought, this tendency toward the bureaucratic rule of rules was "finally to be seen also in the political parties" that were forming in modern Germany.[3] The followers of Marx might perceive the beginnings of a prophesied dictatorship of the proletariat in the Russian Revolution. For Weber, though, "the dictatorship of the official rather than that of the worker" was clearly in the ascendant.[4] To him, this was true not only in the Soviet Union (which eventually became a party state to an extreme degree) but also in the capitalist world. For anyone who might live in "fear that the future will hold *too much* 'democracy' and 'individualism' and too little 'authority,' 'aristocracy,' and 'respect for office,'" Weber had the following advice: fear not, "it is already all too certainly taken care of that the trees of democratic individualism will not grow up into the heavens."[5] The age of the genuine individual that was a law unto itself had been eclipsed, Weber announced. The deadpan face of the functionary loomed over modern institutional life.

To Weber's way of thinking, Germany had been brilliantly confected as a nation-state of rules by Otto von Bismarck, but, when he died, Bismarck

---

1. Weber, "Politik als Beruf," in *Gesammelte politische Schriften*, 398: "die Autorität des 'ewig Gestrigen'" compared to "die Autorität der außeralltäglichen persönlichen *Gnadengabe* (Charisma), die ganz persönliche Hingabe und das persönliche Vertrauen zu Offenbarungen, Heldentum oder anderen Führereigenschaften eines einzelnen" and distinct from "Herrschaft kraft 'Legalität,' kraft des Glaubens an die Geltung legaler Satzung und der durch rational geschaffene Regeln begründeten sachlichen 'Kompetenz.'" I cite from an edition that was available to Weimar readers.

2. Weber, "Parlament und Regierung," in *Gesammelte politische Schriften*, 149: "der Bureaukratisierung gehört die Zukunft."

3. Weber, 143: "Nicht anders als in Wirtschaft und staatlicher Verwaltung steht es schließlich mit dem Fortschritt zur Bureaukratisierung nun auch: in den *Parteien*."

4. Weber, "Der Sozialismus," 508: "die Diktatur des Beamten, nicht die des Arbeiters, ist es, die . . . im Vormarsch begriffen ist."

5. Weber, "Demokratie in Rußland," 347: "es ist, nur allzusehr, dafür gesorgt, daß die Bäume des demokratischen Individualismus nicht bis in den Himmel wachsen."

"left behind a nation *without any kind of political education whatsoever.*"[6] Education here amounted to something like the production of judgment, and judgment was a capacity to work in the absence of easily or uncontroversially applicable rules. Naming an irony that some later historians would take up, it was as if the very success of German unification up to 1871 had laid the seeds of the nation-state's own arrested development or demise. Here, we encounter another of Weber's extraordinarily influential definitions—namely, his stipulation that "a state is the human community that, within a defined territory . . . , successfully lays its claim to a monopoly on legitimate physical force."[7] The creatures of the rule brought into being by Bismarck's efficient modern state would become oddly irresponsible as their moral energies became increasingly consumed by a desire simply to apply the rules *come what may.* The legitimacy of physical violence derived from its routineness.

We can understand the Weberian process of legitimation in terms of a transference from theology to politics. Applying the rules come what may amounted to the impersonal state's appropriation of what Weber termed an "ethic of conviction" (*Gesinnungsethik*). Paradigmatically, this had been an ethic in which "the Christian acts righteously and leaves the outcome to God." For Weber, such an ethic stood in fundamental opposition to an "ethic of responsibility" (*Verantwortungsethik*), according to which one had to "answer for the (predictable) consequences of one's actions."[8] Weber's inference was unmistakable: armed with their pristine rules, Christians had been politically immature. The modern state's appropriation of this "ethic of conviction" made it equally vulnerable to the same accusation. Rules would come to look like ends in themselves. Impersonal application of the rules became a theopolitical purity: proceduralism as danger. In reality (according to the counterargument), the blithe imperviousness of rules turned a blind eye to their consequences.

There was either a dearth or an oversupply of directives in the space between rules and cases, and, on Weber's account, only individuals qua individuals could negotiate this space. One might presume that with its various modes of anonymization and generalization the proper term

6. Weber, "Parlament und Regierung," in *Gesammelte politische Schriften*, 138: "Er hinterließ eine Nation *ohne alle und jede politische Erziehung.*"
7. Weber, "Politik als Beruf," in *Gesammelte politische Schriften*, 397: "Staat ist diejenige menschliche Gemeinschaft, welche innerhalb eines bestimmten Gebietes—dies: das 'Gebiet' gehört zum Merkmal—das *Monopol legitimer physischer Gewaltsamkeit* für sich (mit Erfolg) beansprucht."
8. Weber, 441: "Es ist ein abgrundtiefer Gegensatz, ob man unter der gesinnungsethischen Maxime handelt—religiös geredet—: 'der Christ tut recht und stellt den Erfolg Gott anheim,' oder unter der verantwortungsethischen: daß man für die (voraussehbaren) *Folgen* seines Handelns aufzukommen hat."

for giving birth to rules was "legislation." On Weber's account, however, the anonymization and generalization of the legislative process was itself essentially unreal. It continually forced legislators to pretend that they could do the impossible by writing rules that would be easily or eternally applicable. For him, the force and exemplarity of an individual's actions in the midst of contingency constituted the truer origin of rules. For this reason, he could say that "the big decisions in politics, even or rather most especially in democracies, are made by *individuals*," and, from this, he inferred a "Caesarist principle of leader selection."[9] Only the individual could grapple with the particular.

Weber determined that one had to reconfigure parliaments. One had to transform them from factories dedicated to the production of law into stages on which political individuals would be able to distinguish themselves. For him, "not a talking but only a *working* parliament can be the ground in which not simply demagogic but genuinely *political* leadership qualities grow and rise up in the selection process."[10] This turn toward "work," as distinct from "talk," entailed a shift from the legislative to the executive. It explains in part Weber's desire to import into Weimar the Caesarist components of the American Constitution with its directly—or somewhat directly—elected president. The disproportion between the populace as a whole and the president as an individual would be the strange amphitheater in which individuals equal to the tasks of political leadership would become visible—and the key figure here would indeed be, precisely, a *charismatic* individual.[11]

We can understand Carl Schmitt as a departure from the historical arc of the Weimar Republic in close relation to the Weber line just described. Born in 1888, completing his doctorate in 1910, then his habilitation in 1914, and serving as a volunteer in the First World War (but not at the front), Schmitt became one of the foremost legal scholars of the 1920s. Eventually, he joined the Nazi Party in May of 1933. Before he was sidelined in 1936, he justified both the purging of the Röhm faction in 1934 and the anti-Semitic Nuremberg Laws of 1935. A lawyer and a constitutional thinker, Schmitt took up Weber's pessimism about the rise of bureaucracy and its purportedly blind devotion to the proceduralism of the rule. As Schmitt put it in *Political Theology* (1922), "all tendencies in modern constitutional

9. Weber, "Parlament und Regierung," in *Gesammelte politische Schriften*, 213: "Die großen Entscheidungen der Politik, auch und gerade in der Demokratie, von *Einzelnen* gemacht werden"; "an das cäsaristische Prinzip der Führerauslese."
10. Weber, 169: "Denn nicht ein redendes, sondern nur ein *arbeitendes* Parlament kann der Boden sein, auf dem nich bloß demogogische, sondern echt *politische* Führerqualitäten wachsen und im Wege der Auslese aufsteigen."
11. Weber, "Politik als Beruf," in *Gesammelte politische Schriften*, 434.

development tend toward the marginalization of the sovereign." In his deliberately polemical response to ascendant proceduralism, Schmitt took the "sovereign" to be whoever "is responsible for the decision of whether the constitution can be suspended in its totality."[12] Schmitt responded to proceduralism by embedding the law in the pure decisionism of a newly differentiated sovereign that would take up something of the unpredictability function of Weber's charismatic individual.

Weber's postwar assertions about politics were available to Schmitt in the 1921 collected edition of Weber's political writings, and in Schmitt's citations of Weber we encounter a variety of decisive appropriations.[13] These appropriations reveal Schmitt's own intellectual trajectory. Where Weber hoped that one might transform German parliaments into venues for leader selection, Schmitt responded bleakly that "the development of modern mass democracy had turned argumentative public discussion into an empty formality," for "today parliament itself appears to be nothing but a giant antechamber standing in front of the offices or committees of invisible powerbrokers."[14] Where Weber spoke of a monopoly on the legitimate use of violence, Schmitt spoke of a "monopoly on decision" (*Entscheidungsmonopol*).[15] When Schmitt said that "the modern state seems really to have become what Max Weber took it to be—namely, a huge commercial operation," we have a droplet of Weber that monad-like reflects for us a great deal of the conceptual universe that Schmitt inherited from him.[16] The commercial operation is a set of habits, procedures, and rules. It is a system governed in the end by the imperative of efficiency. And this ultimate value has transposed itself under conditions of modernity from its rightful domain—the economy—to politics, a domain where properly speaking efficiency can have only secondary significance.

Schmitt specified Weber's account of politics by shifting attention from definitions of the state to a prior account of the political as such. In place of Weber's definition of the state as that which had successfully asserted

---

12. Schmitt, *Politische Theologie*, 10: the sovereign "steht außerhalb der normal geltenden Rechtsordnung und gehört doch zur ihr, denn er ist zuständig für die Entscheidung, ob die Verfassung in toto suspendiert werden kann. Alle Tendenzen der modernen rechtsstaatlichen Entwicklung gehen dahin, den Souverän in diesem Sinne zu beseitigen."

13. The lecture on politics as vocation had been available two years earlier: Weber, *Geistige Arbeit als Beruf*.

14. Schmitt, "Vorbemerkung," 10 and 12: "die Lage des Parlamentarismus ist heute so kritisch, weil die Entwicklung der modernen Massendemokratie die argumentierende öffentliche Diskussion zu einer leeren Formalität gemacht hat"; "heute erscheint das Parlament eher selbst als eine riesige Antichambre vor den Bureaus oder Ausschüssen unsichtbarer Machthaber."

15. Weber, *Geistige Arbeit als Beruf*, 10; Schmitt, *Politische Theologie*, 13–14.

16. Schmitt, *Politische Theologie*, 56: "Der moderne Staat scheint wirklich das geworden zu sein, was Max Weber in ihm sieht: ein großer Betrieb."

the legitimacy of its monopoly on violence, we have Schmitt's emphasis on an earlier distinction between friend and enemy. Before the task of legitimating violence came the scene of violence itself. One of the fundamental assertions of Weimar political theory was Schmitt's claim that "the specifically political distinction . . . is the distinction between friend and enemy."[17] One struggles to perceive the line clearly, so often has it been cited. Schmitt's extremism fetishized war. The "enemy" was not simply a competitor or an opponent in general. It was a *public* enemy threatening physical violence together with an existential destruction of the community. For Schmitt, politics was built on enmity of this kind.[18]

Schmitt's definition of the political was designed to permit twin declarations: first, that the categories brought into being by the law were not primordial; and second, that politics came before law and was essentially different from it. Politics did not deal with rules. It established and defended the possibility of rules and the possibility of a legal order as such. "The political" named the legitimacy of suspending the rule of law in the name of defending some future possibility of the rule of law. Characterizable as both a defender and a suspender of the constitution, Schmitt's sovereign might be associated with something like "the people." Under conditions of modern mass democracy, however, the people themselves could never be politically operative except in a derivative sense. The people might, for example, "acclaim" a dictator, and this dictator might then be said to embody a popular sovereignty in their person.[19] Modern democratic theory might presuppose that acclamation was a prelude to parliamentary representation, but for Schmitt "belief in parliamentarism belongs to liberalism and its world of ideas." He dismissed it as an unwarranted faith in government by discussion and went so far as to say that such belief "is alien to democracy."[20]

Schmitt is just simplistic enough to remain extraordinarily quotable, which is a matter of no small consequence for his intellectual legacy and for the degree to which even now he continues to structure discussions of the Weimar intellectual afterlife, especially in political theory. Schmitt lives on in his quotability, undead. "Dictatorship is not antithetical to democracy,"

---

17. Schmitt, *Der Begriff des Politischen*, 14: "die spezifisch politische Unterscheidung, auf welche sich die politischen Handlungen und Motive zurückführen lassen, ist die Unterscheidung von Freund und Feind."
18. Schmitt, 16: "Feind ist nur eine wenigstens eventuell, d. h. der realen Möglichkeit nach kämpfende Gesamtheit von Menschen, die einer ebensolchen Gesamtheit gegenübersteht."
19. Schmitt, *Parlamentarismus*, 21.
20. Schmitt, "Vorbemerkung," in *Parlamentarismus*, 13: "der Glaube an den Parlamentarismus, an ein *government by discussion*, gehört in die Gedankenwelt des Liberalismus. Er gehört nicht zur Demokratie."

Schmitt continues to say.[21] "In the most important matters, more important than *how* something be decided is *that* it be decided."[22] Simplicity of prose makes the radical blithe: "homogeneity belongs as a matter of necessity to democracy as does . . . the exclusion or annihilation of the heterogeneous."[23] In the context of such an underannounced—perhaps so much as even-tempered—turn to annihilation (*Vernichtung*), there is something both apposite and insufficient about the compact insult penned by the eminent German historian Hans-Ulrich Wehler, who said of Schmitt that he was "a fanatic of order in an epoch of turbulent confusion."[24]

Unlike the people taken as a whole, only a single individual would be agile enough to act, and so Schmitt's Caesarist dictator could protect the constitution from an extralegal political position—so went the argument. This was a generalization to the constitutional level of one of Schmitt's basic points about the legal order: "that legal ideas cannot implement themselves is clear already in the fact that they say nothing about who ought to apply them."[25] Jacques Derrida would take the point up later: "an *auctoritatis interpositio*" would always be needed.[26] Between 1930 and 1933, issues such as these were far from merely academic questions. The German parliamentary system was suspended in that period, and Paul von Hindenburg ruled by presidential decree. Schmitt's point was that Article 48 of the Weimar Constitution botched its attempt to make the directly elected and Caesarist office of the president into a defender of the constitution. Misled by their devotion to the principle of checks and balances, the framers had constituted a counterpower in the parliamentary system that, in turn, could suspend the suspension of the law effected by the president.[27] Who was sovereign here? Both *Reichspräsident* and *Reichstag*. Therefore neither.

In the extralegal and genuinely political foundation of the legal order, we encounter another of the quintessentially quotable and fundamental Schmittian assertions: "whoever decides upon the state of exception is sovereign."[28] To be sure, Schmitt had originally written the sentence in 1922,

---

21. Schmitt, 17: "Diktatur nicht der Gegensatz zu Demokratie ist."
22. Schmitt, *Politische Theologie*, 50: "es gerade in den wichtigsten Dingen wichtiger ist, daß entschieden werde, als wie entschieden wird."
23. Schmitt, "Vorbemerkung," 14: "zur Demokratie gehört also notwendig erstens Homogenität und zweitens—nötigenfalls—die Ausscheidung oder Vernichtung des Heterogenen."
24. Wehler, *Deutsche Gesellschaftsgeschichte*, 4.491: "Schmitt war ein Ordnungsfanatiker in einer Epoche turbulenter Wirren."
25. Schmitt, *Politische Theologie*, 31: "Daß die Rechtsidee sich nicht aus sich selbst umsetzen kann, ergibt sich schon daraus, daß sie nichts darüber aussagt, wer sie anwenden soll. In jeder Umformung liegt eine auctoritatis interpositio."
26. Derrida, "Force de loi": 924. The phrase was Schmitt's; the uptake, Derrida's.
27. Schmitt, *Politische Theologie*, 12.
28. Schmitt, 9: "Souverän ist, wer über den Ausnahmezustand entscheidet."

but his sentences are quotation ready and hence recontextualizable—1922 originated, 1932 applied. The state of exception for Schmitt was a kind of legally declarable vacuum in which the rule of law was suspended. It was not the same thing as a state of emergency. It was a political response to emergency that allowed a suspension of the law by saying that, for as long as the state of exception obtained, particular acts of the sovereign and its representatives would be precedents in no sense. The state of exception was thus a kind of generalization of the value of the exception for Schmitt. We have to understand that the power of the exception for Schmitt lay not simply in its being outside of the rule. It was not that the exception refused subsumption under any extant rule. More radically, the exception also insisted that it could not be read in any way as an action the maxim of which might be extrapolated into a new rule.

To sharpen our sense of the divergent trajectories of the Weberian and Schmittian departures, we must note a very precise distinction between charisma and the state of exception.[29] Weberian charismatic authority had been precisely rule generating. An *imitatio Christi* would be possible because one did not go around simply performing the precise deeds that Jesus was said to have performed. Each of those deeds was taken to have announced a principle that might be more broadly applied. Christ's life would become imitable in circumstances entirely unlike Roman Judea. "What would Jesus do?" would remain—or would aspire to remain—an omni-applicable question because Christ's being would be cultivated as a tissue of nascent rules embodied in particular acts. In contrast, the Schmittian exception refused principledness entirely. In Giorgio Agamben's formulation, Schmitt might have been willing to concede "that the sovereign be considered a living law," but he would have proceeded immediately to add that this "can mean only . . . that in him the life of the law coincides with a complete anomie."[30] The Schmittian sovereign would be anomic rather than autonomous. There would be no autonomic tension, no sense that a sovereign's own actions might generate limits in the manner of precedents on what sovereign power might do. As Schmitt put it, "the exception is that which cannot be subsumed."[31] And this was why Schmitt could also say that "the best thing in the world is not a law but a command [*Befehl*]."[32] After all, the command is precisely the rule that paradoxically exhausts itself in one case.

I am not fetching an idiom from very far afield when I speak here of the parables and miracles of Christ. These acts did not simply contravene

---

29. Compare Derman, *Weber*, 190.

30. Agamben, *Stato di eccezione*, 89: "che il sovrano sia una legge vivente può solo significare . . . che la vita della legge coincide in lui con una integrale anomia."

31. Schmitt, *Politische Theologie*, 13: "die Ausnahme ist das nicht Subsumierbare."

32. Schmitt, *Glossarium*, 274: "das beste in der Welt ist ein Befehl und kein Gesetz."

the laws of nature. More basically, they established moral laws by which human communities might live. And Schmitt, too, understood the exception in essentially theological ways. We sense this when Schmitt says that "considered normatively, the decision [underwriting exception] is born out of a nothingness."[33] The suspicion is confirmed by the explicit assertion that "for jurisprudence, the state of exception has a meaning analogous to that of the miracle for theology."[34] In Schmitt, of course, this analogy was simply one of the ways in which "all significant concepts of modern theory of state are secularized theological concepts."[35] In a sense that is anathema to the New Testament, the miracle becomes something like a model—or excuse—for purely arbitrary and capricious deployments of power.

We have departures from the Weimar arc, and I have called those departures "Weber" and "Schmitt." They announce the dilemma of a modernity in which an efficiency that is ever more legalized, normative, and rule bound threatens the very capacity of human beings to lead. Weber and Schmitt cast charisma or the exception as the manner in which this challenge of bureaucratization might be met. At this point in my rendition of the standard received version of the Weimar origins of political theory, I introduce a third departure: Leo Strauss. Having served in the First World War and having then studied at the University of Hamburg, Strauss worked at the Academy for Jewish Research in Berlin from 1925 until 1932, at which point he emigrated. Eventually, he arrived in the United States, where he taught political science at the New School for Social Research from 1938 to 1949 and then, more famously, at the University of Chicago from 1949 to 1968.

Leo Strauss understood himself to be working in the tradition of both Weber and Schmitt explicitly. Scholars argue about the degree to which, for Strauss, Weber was a relativist about value or simply someone who saw a multitude of values that could not be expressed in terms of each other. Either way, the Straussian inference was similar: empirical sciences aiming at the verification or falsification of hypotheses, trends, and laws of nature might inform policy analysts on how best to achieve certain ends once those ends had been chosen, but science would be incapable of telling policy makers anything about the ends toward which they should be working. A value-neutral science might inadvertently become political (or it might be blindly or covertly political from the outset). Regardless of the consequences it might generate, however, such a science could have no

33. Schmitt, *Politische Theologie*, 31: "die Entscheidung ist, normative betrachtet, aus einem Nichts geboren."
34. Schmitt, 37: "der Ausnahmezustand hat für die Jurisprudenz eine analoge Bedeutung wie das Wunder für die Theologie."
35. Schmitt, 37: "alle prägnanten Begriffe der modernen Staatslehre sind säkularisierte theologische Begriffe."

explicit politics other than a question-begging proceduralism because it had no way of speaking about what *should* be.[36] In Nasser Behnegar's account, "Strauss turned away from the 'value-free' social science of his time, which could not understand Hitler's and Stalin's regimes as tyrannies" and could only classify the manners of proceeding characteristic of these tyrannies.[37] As Behnegar goes on to say, there was for Strauss a sense in which the liberal United States of the postwar period was repeating the errors of the liberal Weimar Republic. "The new political science," he says (paraphrasing Strauss), "is part of the crisis of liberal democracy because it is unable to defend liberal democracy from its [Cold War] enemies."[38] Ascendant proceduralism, the argument went, phases out arguments for its own value.

We can characterize Strauss's break with Schmitt with unusual precision because Strauss reviewed the 1932 edition of Schmitt's *The Concept of the Political*. Referring to the review, Schmitt is reputed to have said to his assistant Günther Krauss, "You've got to read that," because "[Strauss] saw through me and X-rayed me as nobody else has."[39] Strauss's criticism of Schmitt amounted to a radicalization of the problem Schmitt had identified in Weber: Schmittian decisionism provided no way of valuing one norm above another. In what we might describe as Schmitt's proto-Luhmannian systems theory, "friend" and "enemy" constituted the constitutive binary for politics, "beautiful" and "ugly" for aesthetics, "good" and "bad" for morality, and so on. When Strauss examined this, he saw ways in which the friend-enemy distinction was colonizing morality. As Strauss put it, when seen from the perspective of Schmittian politics, the "bad" and the "good" became simply "the dangerous" and "the harmless" (*gefährlich* and *ungefährlich*, respectively). Inattentive to the good as such, Schmittian politics was self-consuming.[40]

Ultimately, Strauss came to the three-part conclusion that Schmitt's account of the political was merely a response to the crisis of liberalism in the early twentieth century, that Schmitt's polemic could only be understood in relation to that historical context, and that—as a result—there was nothing necessarily compelling about the case Schmitt made. The case could be compelling only locally in response to a historically particular problem.[41] Behnegar offers an incisive characterization of Strauss's response to Weber: "the aim of political science is the discovery of valid political judgments

36. Pangle, *Strauss*, 37–38.
37. Behnegar, *Leo Strauss, Max Weber*, 1.
38. Behnegar, 144.
39. The anecdote is relayed as personal communication from Krauss in Meier, *Carl Schmitt and Leo Strauss*, xvii.
40. Strauss, "Anmerkungen," 743.
41. Strauss, 733.

through the clarification of our understanding of human excellence."[42] The first supposition is that excellence is in and of itself good. Our political task is therefore to clarify the nature of human excellence and to cultivate it. As Joshua Parens adds, "such an inquiry studies the complete panoply of human possibilities, the various ways of living, the sorts of perfections available, and the fundamental problems faced by humanity," and thus "political thought is 'architectonic anthropology.'"[43] The multiplicity of these potential excellences underwrote a certain copiousness—"diversity" would certainly be the wrong word—in the great books tradition to which these attitudes gave rise. In the prewar period, some of these articulations of human excellence and the cultivation of "the great-souled man" sounded prototototalitarian (as with Werner Jaeger's classicizing *paideia* project).[44] In the postwar period, some of these articulations of human excellence became simply neo-Aristotelian.

To some, the Straussian political project that developed out of a rejection of Schmittian responses to the Weberian diagnosis of modernity seemed highly conservative and potentially authoritarian. At some point after the Second World War, Hannah Arendt—whose neo-Aristotelian project in *The Human Condition* was, after all, an antitotalitarian account of human excellence qua flourishing—is reputed to have said something like this to Leo Strauss: "we both know that, had it not been for the small biographical fact of your being Jewish, you would have been with them"—that is, the National Socialists. Was this insight or personal animus? Some interpretations have neutralized evidence that Strauss favored a right-wing response in 1933 and cast it as a tactical evaluation on his part that a right-wing response to the Nazis was more likely to halt Hitler's rise to power than anything from the center or the left.[45] In any case, once he became a founding figure in postwar American political theory at the University of Chicago, Strauss's politics became attached to different problematics and ironies. In the United States, his position came to seem both conservative and neoconservative. It seemed conservative because his emphasis on human excellence harkened back to a philosophical program that he saw most fully achieved in ancient Greece. And it has seemed neoconservative because the penumbra of Strauss's students (and students of his students) has been charged with transposing the "moral clarity" of the critique of totalitarianism into a twenty-first-century doctrine of preemptive war waged in the name of establishing and defending democracy—a kind of militant Wilsonianism.[46]

42. Behnegar, *Leo Strauss, Max Weber*, 207, emphasis removed.
43. Parens, *Strauss*, vii.
44. Consider the aspersions cast by Paul Oskar Kristeller, Ernst Abrahamson, and Erwin Panofsky as relayed in Schiller, "Baron's Humanism," 83–84.
45. Howse, *Strauss*, 20.
46. Zuckert and Zuckert, *Truth about Leo Strauss*, 6. Compare Howse, *Strauss*, 1 and 9.

The sequence of Weimar thinkers I wish to set out here as a background of received thoughts in the tradition of political theory against which a new tradition of rhetorical inquiry can be distinguished continues in a fourth departure with the work of Hans Baron. Baron was a historian of Renaissance Italy who left Germany in 1933. In the postwar period, he became a research scholar based at the Newberry Library in Chicago. Here, we encounter an anachronic appropriation that connects late modern to early modern republicanism and that asserts the value of republicanism in precisely the terms of human flourishing that we just encountered in the work of Leo Strauss. True, Baron was less tied to the Weber-Schmitt-Strauss line than they were to each other. His lineages were distinct. We can trace them back through Friedrich Meinecke and especially Walter Goetz, his mentors at Berlin and Leipzig, respectively. Nevertheless, Baron's story has become associated with the tremendously important received wisdom that Weimar was "a republic without republicans." This is the notion that the collapse of the Weimar Republic in the early 1930s is not to be attributed to some kind of Machiavellian genius on the part of the Nazis but rather to a kind of inherent weakness in the state, which—at its birth and during its various travails—was a kind of unstable compromise between figures on the left and right, none of whom believed in the legitimacy of the republic. According to the topos of an undefended Weimar, even moderates did not have much love for the republic, merely preferring it to the other possibilities they saw—namely, revolution from the left and revolution from the right. Scholars have subsequently cast doubt on the notion that Weimar was without defenders, but the revision had not come when Baron was working.[47]

In relation to what was called at the time "a tepid republicanism of the head rather than the heart" (*Vernunftsrepublikanismus*), Hans Baron's *Crisis of the Early Renaissance in Italy* has seemed like an attempt to provide Weimar with a heritage for the republican ideology that it lacked. To be sure, Baron's work was not published until 1955. Moreover, it was only in the subsequent decades that it became a foundational but much-disputed classic in the world of Renaissance scholarship. Nevertheless, Baron ventured south of the Alps in 1925 and discovered in the libraries of Florence and Rome what struck him as a treasure trove of resources for thinking about the importance of "civic life" (*vita civile*) to human life itself and to the life of the polity as well. In 1928 Baron published his first work on the quattrocento republican ideologue with whom he remained obsessed for decades—namely, Leonardo Bruni.

At times, Baron insisted on playing the dispassionate professional historian essentially unmotivated by contemporary political concerns, but not everyone has found that pose convincing. In a letter addressed to the Italian

---

47. See Gusy, *Weimar*, 370.

scholar Renzo Pecchioli (dated June 12, 1971), Baron claimed that the *Crisis* had been inspired "by the exciting intellectual and ethical problems" laid out by his intellectual mentors and that "the political upheaval of the Western world between 1935 [and] 1955 came second."[48] Eventually (in 1983), Pecchioli would publish a book on the myth of Venice as the enduring and quintessential republic. There, he would read twentieth-century histories of republicanism as ideologically motivated by republican failures, Weimar's chief among them.[49] We find that conclusion corroborated in some ways by James Hankins's assertion that Baron's dedication to the ideological work of Leonardo Bruni was so intense that "Baron's Bruni is a wooden puppet, an idealized projection of Baron himself, not a portrait of a man."[50] I would add that Baron's denial of political motivation prevented him from taking up the more urgent task, which was describing in a more forthright way the nature of his utilization of historical genres for political ends. The truth was simpler and should have been defended directly; Baron was looking for concepts he could use.

In some ways, Baron did acknowledge the contemporary resonance of his Florentine republican project, but he was neither willing nor able to defend the research as politically motivated and genuinely historical. He famously insisted that Florentine writers had quite suddenly discovered and articulated a defense of civic life in free republics as the city-state was locked in a struggle for survival with Milan between 1400 and 1402. In the *Crisis* of 1955, moreover, Baron stated explicitly that "one cannot trace the history of this explosive stage in the genesis of the states system of the Renaissance without being struck by its resemblance to events in modern history when unifying conquest loomed over Europe." Only those who have lived through such moments might "adequately reconstruct the crisis of the summer of 1402 and grasp its material and psychological significance for the political history of the Renaissance, and in particular for the growth of Florentine civic spirit."[51] Baron's debt to the work of his mentors similarly placed him in a Weimar context. Goetz sensitized Baron to the stakes of a claim that the Northern Renaissance in Germany was, in fact, highly influenced by the developments in Italy.[52] Such claims were themselves political in Weimar Germany, where they seemed antinationalist.

Despite Baron's tortuous and unresolved displacement of his ideological statement into early modern history, the intellectual components of the

48. Hans Baron to Renzo Pecchioli, June 12, 1971, Baron papers, folder "Dal Petrarca al Leonardo Bruni," as quoted and translated from the Italian by Schiller, "Baron's Humanism," 94.
49. Pecchioli, *Dal "Mito" di Venezia.*
50. Hankins, "'Baron Thesis,'" 320.
51. Baron, *Crisis*, 31–32.
52. See Weinstein and Zakai, *Jewish Exiles*, 38.

republican vision of political theory were potent and, indeed, influential. In effect, Baron was writing an early modern Renaissance alternative to Strauss's vision of ancient political philosophy as a response to the problematics of Weberian normalization and Schmittian decisionism recounted above. In place of a Straussian great books response to both Weber's value-neutral science and Schmitt's decisionist nihilism, Baron effectively articulated republicanism as an account of human flourishing under conditions of civic engagement. Eventually, in his epochal *Machiavellian Moment* (1975), J. G. A. Pocock would transform Baron's civic humanism into an Atlantic-world republican tradition culminating in an account of the ironic Americanization of virtue. This was a process in which "the theory of the polis—which is, in a certain sense, political theory in its purest original form—was cardinal to the constitutional theory of Italian cities and Italian humanists." As Pocock fashioned the narrative, this became an early modern inflection point for the retheorization of "dispersed" poleis in the modern world.[53]

It may seem that Theodor Adorno does not belong in a sequence running through Weber, Schmitt, Strauss, and Baron, but there is a real, live, and locomotive sense in which his trajectory—the fifth and final departure splintering off from the Weimar arc traced here—constituted a variation on the theme I have been laying out. We began with bureaucratization as an ideal type and sketched in brief the nightmare fantasy of a world increasingly predicted and hemmed in by rule procedures. In Schmitt's hyperbolic continuation of the Weberian line of inquiry, such proceduralism was transformed into the purportedly high drama of the sovereign who confirmed the rule afresh and quite arbitrarily at every moment. In Adorno, the landscape is radically changed once again. Authoritarian personalities in Adorno's postwar work were not banal or evil in the sense evinced by Arendt in 1963 in reference to the Nazi functionary, Adolf Eichmann. Nevertheless, an almost masochistic submissiveness and a "readiness to attack those who are deemed weak and who are socially acceptable as 'victims'" were components of the "potential fascist" described in that earlier work too.[54] Blithe application of a genocidal rule was at issue. And there is a sense in which *Dialectic of Enlightenment*—which Adorno coauthored with Max Horkheimer in the early 1940s—understood "enlightened" modernity as pathologically attached to rule procedures. That text's skepticism regarding the purported universality of concepts then became absolutely foundational for critical theory.

For Adorno, the increasing standardization of life practices that Weber had diagnosed found its most precisely observable expression in the field

53. See Pocock, *Machiavellian Moment*, 74 and "Machiavelli, Harrington," 114.
54. Adorno et al., *Authoritarian Personality*, 1 and 759.

of music. Adorno was not only a music critic and philosopher of music but also a practicing composer. For him, music was potentially at least a domain of release from the strictures of rhythmic and tonal form, as the twelve-tone method of musical composition in some ways demonstrated with its evisceration of key. That said, Adorno thought Kierkegaard's assertion that music "only exists in the moment of performance" was "completely absurd."[55] As Adorno saw things, music was also one of the preeminent domains of a nascent culture industry. This meant not only that art's commodity form was increasingly finely managed but also that reproducibility and predictability were managed in such a way that musical *performance* itself was increasingly immaterial. As Adorno lamented, "the text is now tagged down to the last note and down to the most imperceptible nuance in tempo, and the performer is transformed into the executor of the explicit will of the author."[56] Micromanagement of musical notation would be akin to a workplace Taylorism that itself expressed a characteristically modern and Weberian rise of bureaucracy along with its attendant management sciences.

The invocation of Kierkegaard is significant, because in his early work Adorno worked through the Danish philosopher in order to explore the aesthetic as a category. In place of Weber's charismatic individual, Schmitt's decisionist sovereign, Strauss's great-souled man, and Baron's civic humanist, Adorno gives us a superficially different but actually related vision of the Kierkegaardian melancholic. At issue here is Adorno's first published book, *Kierkegaard: The Construction of the Aesthetic*. The work appeared in March 1933, on the very day—so goes the topos—that Hitler seized dictatorial power.[57] We may say that the melancholic individual is a precise inversion of the magnanimous soul that Strauss sometimes eulogized. Magnanimity could be understood as something like having every excellence at one's fingertips, while melancholy (as portrayed by Adorno via Kierkegaard) was something like being overwhelmed by the sheer plenitude of realizable possibilities. Melancholy on that reading was a kind of aimless wandering among possibilities, or it was an inability to turn such imaginative life to account. Under such a description, melancholy became a bourgeois deliquescing in pseudopurposelessness.

In contrast to Baron's at times rather anodyne fantasy of the Florentine

55. Adorno, *Kierkegaard*, in *Gesammelte Schriften*, 2:31: "vollends widersinnig ist seine Behauptung, daß Musik 'bloß existiert, sofern sie wiederholt wird, . . . nur im Augenblick der Aufführung existiert.'"
56. Adorno, "Zur gesellschaftlichen Lage der Musik," in *Gesammelte Schriften*, 18:755: "jetzt ist der Text bis zur letzten Note und bis zur unmerklichsten Temponuance bezeichnet, und der Interpret wird zum Exekutor des eindeutigen Autorenwillens."
57. Adorno, *Kierkegaard*, in *Gesammelte Schriften*, 2:261.

citizen actively participating in the political life of the city-state, we have Adorno's gloss of the nineteenth-century metropolitan flaneur conjured by Kierkegaard. In that gloss, flaneur life had become so interiorized that "walking the city" (now not a city-state but a metropolis) was the twice-removed imaginativeness of a melancholic walking in his own parlor, at home, pacing out the cinematic screen of his own imagination. As Adorno paraphrased the Kierkegaardian idea, "the flaneur goes for a walk in his room; reality appears to him only as it is reflected from pure inwardness."[58] In Adorno's opinion, the idea was best expressed by Olaf Peder Monrad, Kierkegaard's biographer: "how [this pseudoflaneur's] fantasy developed, aided by the arts of disguise and imagery, during promenades in the parlor, how it ran wild!—In the parlor!"[59] Such flaneur life was to be understood as a particular moment in the history of material conditions. "Aestheticism is no 'attitude,' to be taken on at will," according to Adorno, because "it has its time and place—namely, the dawn of the metropolis."[60] Baron's city-state citizen (*Stadtstaatsburger*) had become a hyperimaginative shut-in. This human being had become a glorified and aestheticizing "retina" for the city as entrepôt.

Weimar Germany was an intellectually vibrant place. This, too, is one of the historiographic topoi. And the various emigrations driven by the Republic's demise—chief among them, the Jewish diaspora—meant that Weimar thinkers were unusually influential in the development of disciplines around the world. The standard received version of the Weimar origins of political theory précised here is only one way of organizing what could be many different narratives of the intellectual fertility of German thinkers in "the long 1920s." I have devoted considerable attention to the exposition of this series of departures because it structures a field of interests that are foundational to the tradition of rhetorical inquiry that I invent in this book. Weber's rule, Schmitt's exception, Strauss's exemplarity, Baron's *vita activa*, Adorno's bourgeois imagination—these are all constitutive elements of twentieth-century thinking. Others have thought this too, and my wager is that the lines of inquiry stemming from these points of departure have been rich but are now less productive. Equally, however, my claim is also that, for all the attention it has received, there are ways of remaking Weimar thought

58. Adorno, 2:61: "so geht der Flaneur im Zimmer spazieren; Wirklichkeit erscheint ihm allein reflektiert von bloßer Innerlichkeit."

59. Monrad, *Kierkegaard*, 30: "und wie entfaltete sich, von Vorstellungs- und Verstellungskunst begleitet, bei den Ausgängen in der Stube, wie wucherte seine Phantasie!—In der Stube!" The line is cited at Adorno, *Kierkegaard*, in *Gesammelte Schriften*, 2:61.

60. Adorno, *Kierkegaard*, in *Gesammelte Schriften*, 2:18: "Ästhetizismus ist keine 'Haltung,' die nach Belieben einzunehmen wäre. Wie seine Stunde hat er seinen Ort: die großen Städte in ihrer Frühzeit."

afresh by reading it in the context of an intellectual repertoire that is foreign to most of the scholars who have worked on the period. I shall begin the work of exploring that repertoire in the third section of this chapter. Before that, however, I need to legitimate my mode of proceeding, because some scholars will be suspicious of my desire to "invent a tradition" in Weimar intellectual history that we can use for our own purposes today.

METHODOLOGICAL PRESUPPOSITIONS AND CHAPTER OUTLINE

History—perhaps intellectual history in particular—is never a dead letter. Ever differently, history is a repertoire. Again now (but in new ways), Weimar is a precedent, both as the cautionary tale of how republics fail and as an ideological resource for ethnonationalism. The series of Weimar departures plotted in the first part of this chapter casts the history of thought as a prism that refracts possibilities. In each case, these iterations of Weimar thought took up earlier intellectual-historical moments. These Weimar iterations were themselves historical materials working with historical materials. Weber appropriated early Christian conceptualizations of charisma to contrast them with the distinctive quality of modern bureaucratic routinization. Schmitt turned to descriptions of ancient Roman dictatorship in order to develop an account of the classification. Strauss wished to resuscitate classical Greek political philosophy for the modern world. Baron turned from the collapse of the Weimar Republic to Renaissance Florence and its ideological self-defense. Even Adorno took up baroque initiatives in order to sketch a philosophical response to what he would call after 1945 the "damaged life" (*beschädigte Leben*) of the postwar world. In each case, these Weimar thinkers were appropriating historical material for purposes that historians would often describe as "presentist."

In the history of political thought, there is a fair amount of skepticism about presentist historiographic practices. The fear is that the imperatives of the present will overshadow the particularities of the past such that histories become as thin as they are ideologically motivated. The present that counts here is the present of the historical agents and not the various presents of historians themselves. "Select an ideology; then select historical materials supporting that ideology"—this is the worry. In the history of political thought, there is a particular version of this more general skepticism that builds, I think, on the intuition that political speech is the kind of historical phenomenon *least* amenable to presentist readings. Politics is intrinsically short term, the argument goes. Politics is so volatile and transient that deep pasts (nostalgic) and distant futures (utopian) are to be ruled out of court from the beginning. "A week is a long time," one says, and the political historiographic corollary emphasizes a kind of "eternal present" in political analysis. The default historical grammar privileges events, maneuvering, and short-lived victories.

From the notion that statements of political principle are tightly bound to immediate historical contexts one infers that there will always be a gulf between political theory and the history of political thought. It might appear as if political theorists engage in conversations across the ages and can be read therefore as a kind of sequenced and collected wisdom concerning particular transhistorical political phenomena, phenomena that may include rights or branches of government or processes of political foundation. In fact, the argument goes, such assertions are to be understood always only in terms of the particular affiliations to or defections from established convention as those conventions are understood in any particular place and time. In the moment when people become the audience for such political statements, all that they hear (or should hear) are the markers of loyalty or disloyalty to the established schools that are known to the audience—or known to be known to audiences that are known for being known.

The most articulate exponent of the view that political theory and the history of political thought are two quite different enterprises has been Quentin Skinner. In a 1969 article that became just one of a sequence of methodological interventions (the enduring success of which can be gauged by book series such as Ideas in Context or Cambridge Texts in the History of Political Thought), Skinner argued that "to demand from the history of thought a solution to our own immediate problems is . . . to commit not merely a methodological fallacy, but something like a moral error."[61] History is not an à la carte record of policy options or constitutional forms or political philosophical positions. Presentism, on this account, contributes to an erasure of the alterity of the past. The imagination unable to grasp or rearticulate such alterity would be doomed to live forever within its own narrow conceptions. Skinner used speech act theory in order to express the claim that only an extensive knowledge of past discursive conventions could reveal actual performances together with the intentions in acting that they inscribed. The task was to reveal such performances against the background of other performances that would have been intelligible at the time. Such knowledge of convention and departures from convention would retain the sheer alterity of the past, and historians might "ruminate" on that alterity and thereby hone an ability to defamiliarize their own particular presents.[62] On this account, we must always utilize history in order to defamiliarize ourselves from the present, but we may never treat that history as a resource for our own thinking.

In opposition to the scripts I have just run largely in the form of paraphrase,

61. Skinner, "Meaning and Understanding," 53.
62. Skinner, *Liberty*, 118.

my sense is that Skinner's historiographic strictures provide good reasons for doing some kinds of work—contextualist work that is highly valuable—but that these strictures have been weaponized inappropriately for the purpose of defining legitimate intellectual-historical practice more narrowly. Beyond rumination, for example, I wish to find ways of pursuing moments of discovered alterity as stimuli for different ways of thinking. I speak of "the Weimar origins of rhetorical inquiry" because I wish to gain new points of departure. In using the term "origin," I am not supposing that I can locate the headwaters of certain ideas or discern novelty without precedent. Such conceptions of the term are standard, received, and stultifying. Origins of this kind would be miracles (and just as rare). As a term of art, "origin" implies for me no ontology of the ex nihilo. An origin is simply a node that has many pasts and futures. What marks an idea as an origin is the kind of future it has rather than any miraculous relation of unprecedentedness to the past. The origin is distinguished from other nodes by the range of its potential futures and by the variety of pasts those various futures bring into focus.

Inspired in a certain sense by Skinner, I articulate the notion of an origin as a way of organizing the historiographic invention of a tradition in the idiom of a contemporary philosophical initiative. Here, the contemporary philosophical initiative is not speech act theory but rather the inferentialism of Robert Brandom.[63] Expressed in its most essential form, Brandom's basic claim is that meaning is not to be understood in terms of some relationship of reference between a sentence and a part of the world that the sentence picks out and to which it corresponds. Instead, meaning is to be understood as a virtual, forever changing, and exquisitely historical multiplicity of normative implications set out by inferential relationships among a sentence and those other sentences that are being or might be asserted alongside it by the same assertor (whether that assertor be an individual or a collective entity of some kind). The meaning of a sentence is to be understood in terms of its inferential entailments of commitment, entitlement, and disentitlement relative to other sentences. Having asserted "the skin is red," *must* I say something else, *may* I also say that "the skin is sunburnt," and may I *not* say that "the skin is also bluish-green"? As Brandom puts it, "to be conceptually contentful in the most basic sense is to play a role as premise and conclusion in inference."[64] Meaning *is* the legitimacy and illegitimacy of a sentence's inferential combinability with other sentences.

For intellectual history, one of the most important parts of Brandom's sometimes quite technical position is a quality of reasoning that he terms the nonmonotonicity of inference. Inferences are not monotonously either good or bad. When further assertions are involved, the same inference from

63. See Marshall, "Implications."
64. Brandom, *Tales*, 94.

one assertion to another may shift from good to bad. In Brandom's example we are asked to take a very simple inference: a "patient's fever is, by itself, a good reason to suspect bacterial infection." This is an instance of what C. S. Peirce referred to as hypothesis (or abduction as distinct from induction and deduction). That is, reasoning to infection from fever is the inference of a cause from an effect. It attempts to explain a striking or unusual circumstance. Other things being equal, a doctor will be perfectly justified in making the inference from fever to infection.

Reasoning from a fever to an infection seems relatively straightforward, but diagnosis is notoriously difficult. Why? Because the "other-things-being-equal" rider acknowledges that "other things"—that is, the concomitant circumstances surrounding the presentation of particular symptoms—will often *not* be equal. For example, "add the information that the patient was just administered the anesthetic halothane and the conclusion no longer applies." To prove the point, Brandom goes on to note that "if in addition the patient has a high white blood-cell count, the presence of infection again becomes likely—unless the patient is leukemic."[65] The difficulty of diagnosis is in large part due to the complexity of these kinds of inferential contextures. And this complexity exemplifies the connection between meaning and inferential implicature. If I assert "fever," may I infer that the *meaning* of this state includes "bacterial infection"? The point is that the meaning of any particular assertion is to be understood as a fluctuating and sometimes on/off-flickering phenomenon that changes as assertions appear in or fade from the domain of inferred relevance.

Brandom's account of meaning suggests that both making explicit and making implicit are fundamental historical processes in which coavowed assertions are brought to light or covered over. For the purposes of this book project, I wish to emphasize the four genres of inferentialist historiography that Brandom differentiates: *de dicto*, *de re*, *de traditione*, and phenomenological. The key distinction between *de dicto* and *de re* derives from Brandom's answer to the question of why languages possess individual terms. This is a problem that Brandom needs to resolve, because it is not only a fact about languages but also accounts for why many philosophers have presumed that we should invest in a referential (rather than inferential) account of truth. The individualizability of terms—not stone or stones in general but *that* stone—seems to provide an architecture in which truth is to be understood as a relation of correspondence between an assertion and a state of affairs in the world. The facts of the matter with regard to the utterance "that rock is porous" seem to lie very definitely in a quite particular vector of the world out there beyond utterance.

Brandom wishes to avoid in toto the descriptivism of referential accounts

65. Brandom, "Hegelian Model," 21.

of truth because his project is dedicated to revealing the normative status of meaning. Continuing the example, we are to understand the meaning of the utterance "that rock is porous" in terms of its implications of commitment, entitlement, and disentitlement for concomitant utterances such as "that stone is pumice." Meaning is not a matter of denotation or referring to things in a world outside of language; it is a matter of laying down normative and modal relations of commitment, entitlement, and disentitlement with regard to speech acts of assertion in the future. Commitment, entitlement, and disentitlement are deontic versions of the basic modal categories— namely, necessity, possibility, and impossibility. Languages possess individualizable terms both in relation to objects and the subjects who make assertions about those objects. And languages possess such terms so that we may track the inferential consequences of our assertions with precision.

Brandom appropriates the *de dicto* and *de re* distinction from Gottlob Frege's highly influential distinction between "sense" (*Sinn*) and "reference" (*Bedeutung*). This distinction allows Brandom to develop an account of why we should regard individual terms as pronomial anchors allowing us to regulate inferences of commitment, entitlement, and disentitlement. Clearly, the inferential implications of the assertion "the stone is hot" require us to decide *which* stone is hot so that we can monitor the other assertions that are made of this particular stone. One can certainly maintain both that "the stone is hot" and that "the stone is cold" if more than one stone (or time) is involved. A *de dicto* terminology allows us to speak about the logical objects to which many assertions may be attached within the discursive practices of a particular individual or community. All assertions utilizing the term "the evening star" may be read alongside each other in the process of inferring and judging inference that Brandom calls "deontic scorekeeping." I "keep score" of your assertions about "the evening star," and this means tracking your various commitments, entitlements, and disentitlements. When terms like "the evening star" are used consistently by an individual or a community, the anaphoric linking between various deployments of the term and its pronomial substitutes is relatively easy.

Differentiating diversities of logical objects covered over by a single homonymic term is one historical process in a Brandomian world, and its twin is establishing the intersubstitutability of different but synonymous terms. Equal and opposite to the homonym, but raising similar issues, is the synonym. In the synonym, several words are used in reference to the same logical object, whereas with the homonym the same word is being used to denote several logical objects. As Frege pointed out, there are situations in which language users deploy a number of terms to refer to the same thing. If I do not connect assertions about "the morning star" to those about "the evening star," then I will not be a good deontic scorekeeper. I need to intrude with an utterance such as this: "when people attribute characteristics to 'the morning star' and 'the evening star,' what they are really doing is predicating qualities of Venus." So far, so conventional—with Frege.

In his appropriation of Frege's distinction between sense and reference, Brandom infers the existence of two kinds of intellectual historiography. First, there is intellectual historiography of a *de dicto* kind in which historians use and respect terms as they have been deployed by a particular individual or community. Historians writing in this mode do not make judgments about whether different terms actually refer to the same (logical) object in the way that the locutions "the morning star" and "the evening star" both denote Venus. This is the kind of historiography that, for example, insists on utilizing the original language for key terms. Second, there is an intellectual historiography of a *de re* kind in which, even as we acknowledge the difficulty and dangerousness of construing different terms as denotations of the same logical object, we attempt to think the relationships between different terms by accepting that there are occasions on which we will fail as deontic scorekeepers if we do not take note of the shared function of terms such as "the morning star" and "the evening star."

Between *de dicto* and *de re*, there is a third form of Brandomian intellectual historiography—a *de traditione* kind. We can see why this would be the case for Brandom: claims for the intersubstitutability of terms in inference permit us to write longer histories of traditions that utilize an evolving set of terms laying out a set of related problems. Two distinct terms may be judged sufficiently synonymous to be subsumed as *de dicto* components within a larger *de re* history if those terms may be substituted into a variety of assertions without having inferential consequences for how those assertions combine with other assertions. No inference involving the term "the evening star" will be altered by inserting "the morning star" in its place. Initially, we wished to overcome the strictures of *de dicto* intellectual historiography because we wished to identify *all* the utterances concerning a particular logical object in order to score assertions appropriately. Now we see that in order to do this we need to track the ways in which vocabularies evolve.

The process of embedding in which an utterance is recycled from one moment to another takes place not only at the subsentential level of terms but also—perhaps more usually—at the properly sentential level of the assertion itself, and it is in the recycling of assertions that we can begin to grasp the fourth of Brandom's inferentialist historiographies, the phenomenological. One of the most important processes from the point of view of the intellectual historian will be, quite simply, quotation. After all, quotation is the mechanism that permits both the decontextualization of assertions from previously articulated inferential contextures and the recontextualization of those assertions into new discursive structures. For the inferentialist, disquotation is an equally crucial process in which a sentence is taken up from someone else in one's own voice. One encounters a sentence in the historical record. At first perhaps one quotes it; then one wishes to simply assert it. To be sure, its meaning is thereby transformed (because the tissue of assertions coasserted will be different), but the sentence will nevertheless take its place in a properly phenomenological historiography to the degree that the assertor narrativizes a sequence of de- and recontextualizations for that sentence.

In de- and then recontextualization, the meaning of a quotation may well be changed, and one might object that such mutability of meaning demonstrates the illegitimacy of such anachronic de- and recontextualization processes. The Brandomian response would be that, isolated from any context whatsoever, the meaning of a given assertion will be tremendously imprecise and essentially incalculable. The corollary here is not that first contexts—1651 for *Leviathan*, for example—are the only true contexts but rather that contexts will always be necessary in the course of determining meaning and that knowing the different implications of an assertion under different circumstances is nothing other than sensitivity to the historical contingency of that assertion. As Brandom says, "each set of further premises with which a claim can be conjoined is a further *context* in which its inferential significance can be assessed."[66] First contexts are important contexts, but they are one kind among many, and the more genuinely historical contextualization of an assertion will be the one that traces a multitude of contexts and thereby reveals contingency piecemeal.

The variety of ways in which textual fragmentation happens is tremendously important for intellectual historians. Even a simple history of aphorism—in its various modes—reveals processes to which intellectual historians should attend. The aphoristic phenomena generated by the pre-Socratics were, of course, a function of ancient citation practices. It was not that Protagoras et al. wrote only in epigrams but rather that other authors quoted their more epigrammatic formulations and that the texts of those authors survived where those of the pre-Socratics did not. When Heidegger eventually said that it would be a catastrophe if we were suddenly to chance upon the daily correspondence of the pre-Socratics, what he meant was that the fragmentary quality of the pre-Socratic corpus was essential to the intellectual-historical process in which he himself was engaged—namely, a stripping down and refashioning of the German philosophical vocabulary.[67] I have engaged with what we might call "aphoristic phenomena" at some

---

66. Brandom, *Tales*, 95.
67. Heidegger, *Überlegungen II–VI*, 390.

length elsewhere, and here it is most important to note that technologies of excerption are important structural dimensions of intellectual history as a process.[68]

My purpose in laying out the basic topography of Brandom's historiographic terminology is to prepare the ground for a characterization of the particular historiographic practices taken up in the different chapters of this book. I do not wish simply to descend magpie-like on particular sentences in order to collect them from their Weimar contexts and then deposit them as fragmented chunks in a new contemporary context. I do not pretend that the work of intellectual-historical "translation" can be effected quickly with nothing more than that collector's eye for an interesting item. Nor is it the aim of this book simply to perform the role of the aphoristic collector who appropriates a sentence not on account of its startling claim but on account of the complexity and unusualness of the inferential turning and hedging implicit in the arrangement of its clauses. In this book, I engage in five modes of intellectual historiography. I name them here: *de re* redescription, *de dicto* exercise, *de dicto* suturing, *de traditione* afterlife, and phenomenological surfacing.

I have been preparing the way for what I can now describe as a *de re* redescription of some of the basic terms and issues identified by and ascribed to core thinkers in the Weimar tradition of political theory—Weber, Schmitt, Strauss, Baron, Adorno. Thus, chapter 1 is a *de re* redescription of the Weimar origins of political theory in terms of an alternative tradition—namely, the Weimar origins of rhetorical inquiry. I wish to identify and articulate some of the core terms and concepts in the political thought of these five thinkers in such a way that we can recognize the imbrication of these terms and concepts in fields of analysis—specifically, *rhetorical* fields of analysis— that are quite different to those usually thought of as most relevant to their projects. Demonstrations of proximity to and presence in these other rhetorical idioms amounts to *de re* redescription. Such redescription means embedding a term such as "charisma" in the context of *ethos*, so that we can understand charisma as a particular species of arguing from the persona of the speaker. And it means tracing the progressive embedding of a term such as *metanoia* in rhetorical, spiritual, and then political domains. This at the subsentential level of terms; at the level of the sentence, such redescription means examining Adorno's use of a line from Augustine concerning the Christian orator. It means tracing Schmitt's denunciation of the political theological occasionalism embodied in the eternal conversational principle of democratic practice back into the defense of eternal conversation set out by Adam Müller. And it means thinking the significance of the different

68. Marshall, "Giambattista Vico, Aphorism."

discursive contextures for the *pathē* in, respectively, Aristotle, Hobbes, Heidegger, and Strauss.

With this beachhead into rhetoric established by the *de re* redescription to be laid out in the following section, chapter 2 is then what I call a process of "*de dicto* exercising." Having seen by the end of this chapter how political theory is embedded in rhetorical inquiry, we shall then need to establish that rhetorical tradition as a motley of assertions with an array of actualizable argumentative arrangements. Brandomian inferentialism asks us to understand the meaning of an assertion in terms of its implications of commitment, entitlement, and disentitlement relative to other assertions. In this spirit, I contend that the only way to prepare ourselves—myself as a writer, yourselves as readers—to understand both the actual and potential meanings of the rhetorical tradition is to stage its core assertions as argumentative clusters. I therefore epitomize the rhetorical tradition as received by German thinkers since about 1650.

At this point, some clarification of terms is helpful. Here, "epitomize" means extracting and then running the most frequently invoked or most deeply interconnected sentence-level scripts. *Running* a script means incorporating an assertion or assertions into an argument inferentially, and such incorporating involves a kind of inferential performativity. The frequency of a line's citation is simply how often it is invoked, but when I speak of a script's depth, I mean to distinguish a class of assertions that is explicitly cited—or functions implicitly—as a premise in an unusually high proportion of the arguments in a particular discourse community. If we may say that premises exist beneath conclusions, then deep premises are those premises that exist far back in a particular chain of reasoning. Understood thus, we can conceive of inference trees in which a large number of arguments can trace their inferences back to a small number of assertions.[69] When I use the term "exercising," I mean to suggest that all the parties to this book— writer and readers alike—are responsible for learning and rehearsing the rhetorical tradition to the point that its inferential implications in new contexts can be improvised. Integral to this capacity to improvise is intellectual imagination, for to perceive the mutual relevance of two assertions is to perceive their shared relationship to a middle term, which may be a *de dicto* element on the surface of the discourse but will also commonly be a more general category to which key terms belong as parts to a whole.

Having redescribed political theory in terms of rhetorical inquiry and having exercised the ability of writer and reader to improvise within the rhetorical tradition, the core of this book—chapters 3, 4, 5, and 6—will then consist of a series of *de dicto* suturings in which core trajectories in

69. Marshall, "Intellectual History, Inferentialism," 187.

the thought of Martin Heidegger, Hannah Arendt, Walter Benjamin, and Aby Warburg are identified and secured while weaving in the sentence-level and terminological awareness developed in chapter 2. It is here that the inferential imaginativeness exercised in that earlier chapter really comes into play. The task in each of those four chapters is to utilize the rhetorical tradition to flesh out lines of inquiry that are actualized somewhat but not fully in Heidegger, Arendt, Benjamin, and Warburg. These lines of inquiry cannot be adequately thought without bringing in supplements from the tradition to which these four thinkers did attach themselves but in ways that were too fitful to be easily visible or thinkable. In these chapters, I am very concerned to articulate my arguments in the terms developed by the authors themselves. The *de dicto* quality of these chapters is evident in the frequency with which I quote from the work of these scholars and relay the German terms or formulations. My task is essentially to clarify and dramatize the argumentative stakes of positions they themselves have taken up. I have read deeply in the oeuvres of these four thinkers, and I have published on each of them elsewhere.[70] I have not attempted to characterize all of the arguments or lines of inquiry that they pursued. I have very deliberately arranged their intellectual pursuits in ways that privilege their orientations to rhetorical inquiry. My claim is that the results are simultaneously selective and faithful.

Following the interweaving of Heidegger, Arendt, Benjamin, and Warburg into the rhetorical tradition (and vice versa), the book then pivots in chapter 7 to consider the post-1933 and post-1945 continuations of these thinkers by other authors. At this point in the intellectual-historical narrative, I am engaged in the specification of *de traditione* afterlives. If 1933, 1945, and all that happened between those two dates were shattering experiences, then—as Walter Benjamin said in a different way—we need to think of intellectual history as a process of the de- and recontextualization associated with fragmentation. Again, fragmentation is a profoundly generative intellectual process, and Brandom's inferentialism offers us a way both of understanding this and of pursuing it as an object of inquiry. Fragment sentences are quotations, and quotations are explicit recognitions of the ways in which an older intellectual legacy is being repurposed in the process of embedding that legacy in new circumstances, circumstances that can be most precisely understood as a different fabric of assertions endorsed alongside the quotation. Theodor Adorno's *Minima moralia* was an explicit thematization of this kind of fragmentation. It also remains a good example

---

70. See, for instance, Marshall, "Rhetorical Trajectories from the Early Heidegger"; "Origin and Character of Hannah Arendt's Theory of Judgment"; "Intrication of Political and Rhetorical Inquiry in Walter Benjamin"; "Warburgian Maxims."

of what "afterlife" means in a Brandomian *de traditione* sense. Adorno inherited his interest in the fragment from Benjamin, and, in turn, Benjamin's fascination for the quoted fragment derived in highly significant ways from Giambattista Vico's inflection of baroque rhetorical thought, which in turn had been developing accounts of *ingenium* that reworked elements of the classical rhetorical repertoire.

Connecting Adorno and Benjamin to Vico on down is "a dragging out of the past" that is synonymous with "tradition" when that word is understood literally. Such practices of tradition need not ignore transformation. We need to detach Adorno's practice from the context of baroque politics (with its revised Tacitean modes of dealing with the overly powerful and thus overly sensitive sovereign), and we need to insert Adorno's practice into the context of the postwar and post-Shoah world in which the bureaucratization of murder seemed to render all forms of reliable regularity suspect. Or rather, we need to fold the baroque revision of Tacitus in which *ingenium* became a kind of unvoiced conjectural virtuosity into a new consciousness of why we should fear the rule that seeks to apply itself indiscriminately to all cases. New contexts sharpen, distinguish, and articulate old lines of inquiry. In this way, we begin to intuit both how and why Vico was being put to work in *Dialectic of Enlightenment* as a theorist of a conceptuality that could exist in the absence of a rule.[71]

Finally, in chapter 8, I pursue the line of thinking that I have discerned in the course of this book by asking which elements of the Weimar tradition are intellectually most generative today. In order to do that work, I need to identify the basic assertions that we should acknowledge when thinking in the current age. I need to contrast these assertions with others that were maintained in the past but then given up in later contexts. And I need to identify the elements of the Weimar tradition I have articulated that take on a new life under these new conditions. In essence, this final chapter is a process of what I am terming "phenomenological surfacing." "Phenomenological" is Brandom's appropriation of a Hegelian term to distinguish a species of historiography that culminates in assertions made squarely in the voice of the historian. To be sure, in this moment the historian of thought is morphing into, simply, a thinker. This is a process of "surfacing" in my characterization because it is a moment at which the prolonged *oratio obliqua* that is characteristic of intellectual-historical prose is left behind. At a certain point, we all—writer and reader alike—have had enough of the "said Weber, said Schmitt, said Strauss, said Baron, said Adorno." Direct speech is one of the legitimate end stations of intellectual history, and, indeed, all of the *faux* direct speech instances in which the intellectual historian

71. Horkheimer and Adorno, *Dialektik der Aufklärung*, 39.

has elided locutions such as "Heidegger believed that" or "according to Warburg" are now revealed as so many preparations for the genuinely direct speech of an explicit position. These are not assertions that are set out in a newly emancipated state of splendid isolation from the lines of inquiry from which they have emerged and by which they were inspired. These are instead assertions that take up a place within the inferential contexture of the selective and selectively arranged lines gleaned from previous writers within the tradition that is both revealed and brought into being in this book. On the account given by inferentialism, the historian of thought and the thinker are much closer together than we might suppose. And this is why I have elsewhere come to a conclusion that I think is bracing and quite far reaching: "intellectual historical time and thought are the same thing."[72]

RHETORICAL REDESCRIPTIONS OF THE WEIMAR ORIGINS

This book began by running "a standard received version of the Weimar origins of political theory" in order to set the scene for the excavation of a different set of conceptual presuppositions that, at this point, are fresher and more generative (on account of that freshness rather than some intrinsic superiority). One of the largest wagers of this book is that an awareness of the rhetorical tradition allows us to rejuvenate theoretical debates stemming from the standard received version of Weimar origins. This rhetorical tradition is an intellectual lineage that is relatively unfamiliar to modern intellectual historians. It is an idiom of reference much more familiar to early modernists. (Indeed, I know that rhetorical tradition in large part because I began as an early modernist.) Nevertheless, in surprising and revealing ways, this tradition was in play—and in motion—in the Weimar trajectories traced through this book. Awareness of tradition need not be a form of intellectual nostalgia. Quite the reverse: awareness of tradition underscores innovation by way of contrast.

In the next chapter, I establish the aphoristic ecosystem that will nourish this inferential labor by epitomizing modern German receptions of rhetorical thought. Before that, in the remainder of the current chapter, I take up the challenge of redescribing the sequence of departures laid out above—the arc of departures leading from Weber through Schmitt, Strauss, and Baron to Adorno. I take them up again, in sequence, aiming to reveal this time their various intersections with the rhetorical tradition. By redescribing this standard received version in terms of rhetoric, I establish a problem addressed in the remainder of this book: what happens when

---

72. Marshall, "Intellectual History, Inferentialism," 195.

we cross-pollinate basic presuppositions in modern political thought with core elements of the rhetorical tradition? In response to this question, I reveal both that this work of cross-pollination was already happening in some of the major drivers of Weimar thought (together with their post-Weimar continuations) and that we may continue this work with profit ourselves.

One can stage debates in Weber scholarship so as to privilege rhetoric, but the more bracing rhetorical redescription of Weber's political categories runs through the concept of charisma.[73] As we have seen, for Weber, the only way out of a future of extreme bureaucratic efficiency combined with a gradual emaciation of political capacity is a mechanism for producing and offering leadership opportunities to charismatic individuals who will be able to renew the rules of the polity through the examples of their own persons. Immediately, the rhetorician will ask whether charisma is not essentially a form of persuasion by means of *ethos*. That is, does charismatic authority not function essentially by means of the performance of a particular mode of character in some public moment? To be sure, the sources for Weber's conception may have been a strange combination of German readings of the politics of early Christian communities with parts of an imperial British anthropology that translated and analyzed concepts like *mana*. And, no matter how relentlessly one points to the frequency with which the term *charis* (grace) appears in Aristotle's *Rhetoric*, philology will not compel us to conclude that "charisma" was originally a rhetorical term of art. Nevertheless, conceptual elective affinity combined with biographical portraiture supports the notion that we can understand Weber more profoundly if we read charisma rhetorically.

It is not surprising that charisma should involve rhetoric. In pursuing the concept, Weber was essentially concerned with the circumstances and nature of public speech or the kinds of public actions that might function as mute speech. Weber would lament that "speeches given by a representative are today no longer any kind of personal avowal; even less are they attempts to bring an opponent around." He would conclude that such speeches "are instead official statements of the party that are delivered to the country 'through the window'"—not so much heard as overheard.[74] And the Caesarist principles Weber attempted to invoke to counteract what he understood as a bureaucratization of political speech were themselves in part

---

73. Compare Mommsen, *Weber*, Kim, *Weber's Politics*, 12, and Ringer, *Weber*, 253, with Kelly, *State of the Political*, 58, and Breiner, *Weber and Democratic Politics*, 2.

74. Weber, "Parlament und Regierung," in *Gesammelte politische Schriften*, 163: "Reden, die ein Abgeordneter hält, sind heute keine persönlichen Bekenntnisse mehr, noch viel weniger Versuche, die Gegner umzustimmen. Sondern sie sind amtliche Erklärungen der Partei, welche dem Lande 'zum Fenster hinaus' abgegeben werden."

rhetorical. Thus, after Friedrich Ebert had been elected the first Reichspräsident of the Weimar Republic in 1919, Weber said that the Social Democrats should "consider that the much discussed 'dictatorship' of the masses calls for a 'dictator,' which is to say, a delegate elected by the masses themselves."[75] For Weber, the rhetorical sleight of hand that such a leader would need to perform involved striking the pose of a dictator who functioned as merely a "conduit" for populist sentiment. Charisma might distinguish itself from the routine and the everyday.[76] In time, it might come to be seen as capturing "the argument—increasingly popular in the 1930s— that mass dictatorship represented a form of secularized religion."[77] But it was also connected to *metanoia* understood as "the power of charisma to 'effect a subjective or *internal* reorientation.'"[78] In the Christian tradition, *metanoia* was conversion or repentance. In the older rhetorical tradition on which Christianity had been drawing, though, it was also an orator's about-face or self-revision when performing the replacement of one of their own statements by another. Orators began again in *metanoia*. More precisely, they would cannibalize a position of their own by subsuming or redescribing or overcoming it with another.

Some of the key concepts around charisma implied rhetoric, but was there a rhetorical dimension to Weber's examples of charismatic leadership? Yes. To be sure, with his parables of actions almost more eloquent than words, Jesus of Nazareth constituted a basic form of charisma. But there were contemporary examples too. One of Weber's biographers, Joachim Radkau, paints a picture in which Weber was tempted to take himself as the paradigm of the charisma concept. "At the end of the war," Radkau explains, Weber "made every effort to give himself the profile of a public speaker, and, as he himself soon came to realize with some pride, he possessed the makings of a demagogue." Further, "recent research has uncovered the zeal with which in January 1919 he threw himself into the election campaign of the left liberal German Democratic Party."[79] And Radkau goes on to hypothesize that Weber's exemplarity consisted in "the unusual extent to which [he] possessed the capacity to work himself into a rage against right

75. Weber, "Politik als Beruf," in *Gesammelte politische Schriften*, 391: "möchte sie doch bedenken, daß die viel beredete 'Diktatur' der Massen eben: den 'Diktator' fordert, einen selbstgewählten Vertrauensmann der Massen, dem diese so lange sich unterordnen, als er ihr Vertrauen besitzt."
76. Giddens, *Politics and Sociology in the Thought of Max Weber*, 38.
77. Derman, *Weber*, 179.
78. Weber, *Wirtschaft und Gesellschaft*, 2:658.
79. Radkau, *Weber*, 784: "dabei machte er nach Kriegsende alle Anstalten, sich als politischer Volksredner zu profilieren—wie er selber zuweilen nicht ohne Stolz bekannte, besaß das Zeug zum Demagogen. Erst durch neuere Recherchen wurde entdeckt, mit welchem Feuereifer er sich im Januar 1919 in den Wahlkampf für die linksliberale DDP stürzte."

and left alike."⁸⁰ Had Weber lived, extreme antiextremism might have been fertile rhetorical territory in the Weimar Republic.

The rhetorical scene of Weber's own charismatic potential can be described in registers that are both more performative and more personal. Again, Radkau makes the point: "at the same time that . . . he was attributing national 'masochism' to war-guilt acknowledgers such as [Kurt] Eisner, Max Weber luxuriated in desire for total surrender and submission to Else [Jaffé, née von Richthofen]"; "over and over again he reveled in the fantasy that Else, the 'beautiful despotic mistress' and 'slave-owner,' would come upon him from behind, shut his eyes, put a ring around his neck, and strip him of all his rights."⁸¹ Radkau is painting an ur-scene for Weberian notions of power on the basis of letters Weber exchanged with Else Jaffé—a former student, later a lover. And, on the basis of a letter dated January 15, 1919, Radkau relays that "while giving a lecture in which he once again attacked the revolutionaries [of 1918], chairs were flying across the room, and [Weber] gloried in the situation thinking of the 'dark gleaming eyes' of Else, whose attacks he also let wash over him with pleasure."⁸² If scholars of charisma stage debates about whether charisma's force is grounded in the speaker or the audience, Radkau's miniature suggests ways in which we might say, simply, "both." The point is not that Weberian sociology can be wholly redescribed in terms of sexual psychodynamic. The point is that the rule of rules leaves basic questions about power and its contingencies unanswered and that rhetoric is one of the idioms for characterizing power in, precisely, its contingency.

As is well known, Carl Schmitt's decisionist response to the Weberian diagnosis of increased regulation and decreased capacity for leadership was in significant part a rejection of what he called political Romanticism. Less widely recognized is the fact that Schmitt's exemplary political Romantic, Adam Müller, was a spokesperson for the rhetorical tradition. Schmitt cited the work explicitly in *Political Romanticism* on only a few occasions, but the decisive text for the position Schmitt was attacking was Müller's *Twelve Lectures on Eloquence and Its Corruption in Germany* (1816). For Müller, rhetoric

80. Radkau, 785: "in ungewöhnlichem Maße besaß Weber die Fähigkeit, sich sowohl in Wut gegen die Rechte als auch gegen die Linke zu steigern."
81. Radkau, 797: "Weber, der zur gleichen Zeit Kriegsschuldbekennern wie Eisner, ohne sie gut zu kennen, nationalen 'Masochismus' unterstellt, schwelgt Else gegenüber in der Wollust totaler Hingabe und Unterwerfung; immer wieder macht ihm der Gedanke Spaß, daß Else, die 'schöne Zwingherrin' und 'Sklavenhalterin,' die von hinten an ihn herankommt und ihm die Augen zuhält, ihm einen Ring um den Hals gelegt und ihn aller Rechte beraubt habt."
82. Radkau, 798: "als bei einem Vortrag, wo er wieder einmal die Revoluzzer attackiert, Stühle durch den Raum fliegen, genießt er die Situation in Gedanken an die 'dunklen schimmernden Augen' Elses, deren Angriffe er ebenfalls mit Lust über sich ergehen läßt."

was a kind of theory and practice of what he understood as an eternal conversation in which every discursive offering would be redeemed, in the long term, by the responses it occasioned. In Schmitt's reading, Müller's commitment to a dialogic principle between orator and auditor was actually the expression of an inflationary metaphysics in which "each flower, each image becomes the partner to a discussion and is now the listener, now the speaker." In this vision, "the entire world, the universe, is a conversation."[83] Romantics had a misplaced faith in history, Schmitt contended. Such persons thought of history as a novel-like process in which every detail would be "saved" by its incorporation into later stages of a character's (or a nation's) development.[84]

Lest we suppose that this nineteenth-century Romantic must have been a token enemy, we should note that Müller was a conduit for a rhetorical tradition that was newly alive and available for appropriation in Weimar Germany. As Schmitt put it, Müller held that "the speaker must think of himself as a listener, and the listener as a speaker, [for] one can exchange each role in the manner [of an alternating between] subject and object, positive and negative, etc."[85] Schmitt turned his response to Müller into a general criticism of parliamentary processes, which would be simply a form of failed "government by discussion." Schmitt's 1919 attack on Müller stimulated an immediate response from the sociologist Arthur Salz. Salz defended Müller because he thought Müller's inflection of the rhetorical tradition offered something like a theory and practice for the then nascent Weimar Republic.[86] If rhetoric were a purely republican art (as Nietzsche either supposed or reported), then the Weimar Republic needed a concomitant Weimar rhetoric.[87] On this account, republican life was dependent on a capacity to absorb and respond to the positions of one's opponents. Nor were Salz's efforts without effect, as we see in Hannah Arendt's 1932 discussion of a "Müller-Renaissance" in Weimar Germany.[88]

For Schmitt, political Romantics were a strange continuation of Weber's

83. Schmitt-Dorotić, *Politische Romantik*, 130: "jede Blume, jedes Bild wird Partner einer Unterredung, ist bald Hörer, bald Redner," and "die ganze Welt, das Universum ist ein Gespräch."
84. Schmitt-Dorotić, 13.
85. Schmitt-Dorotić, 129: "der Redner muß sich als Hörer denken, der Hörer als Redner, man kann beide Rollen vertauschen wie Subjekt und Objekt, positiv und negativ usw."
86. Müller, *Zwölf Reden*, v–xv.
87. Nietzsche, "Rhetorik," in *Gesammelte Werke*, 5:287. I say "either supposed or reported" because, as scholars have shown, Nietzsche's lecture notes are often compilations of unattributed quotations from other scholars, as if his practice was to sketch a scholarly domain for students. Even without a positively identified source, we should recognize that any given sentence may be reported speech when dealing with these lecture notes. See Most and Fries, "Die Quellen," 41–46.
88. Arendt, "Müller Renaissance?"

distinction between an "ethic of conviction" and an "ethic of responsibility." Seeing this, we become aware of the ways in which core elements of the
Weimar origins of political theory were part of larger debates concerning
the rhetorical tradition. Historical dialecticians would tend to be provi-
dentialists. They would tend to believe that "the truth never lies in what
the individual human being understands or wills."[89] This might sound like
humility. For Schmitt, though, such sentiment amounted to the following
politically Romantic instruction: Do either what you want or alternatively
what you think is right (the difference is more negligible than you think),
and do it without fear of consequence, because consequences are so often *unintended* that the true terminus of one's energies will always remain
essentially unknowable. The words are mine; the logic, Schmitt's. All ex-
penditures of energy are simply versions of what Schmitt, paraphrasing
Müller, called "sociability" (*Geselligkeit*). The crosscurrents of such energies will be incalculably complex, and it will be impossible to predict how
the interaction of these energies will play out ahead of time. All one can
do is smile, close one's eyes, and have faith that there will be what Schmitt
parodied as a "general tendency toward a 'higher third,' the true reality."[90]
Schmitt thought political Romantics profoundly dangerous on account of
their inordinate and cryptoreligious faith in the power of contradiction to
be resolved for the benefit of the whole. As for Weber before him, faith in
a dialectic that might be variously Hegelian, Fichtian, or sophistic was for
Schmitt the opposite of "responsibility" (*Verantwortlichkeit*).[91]

We may say that speakers are known by their interlocutors without
meaning thereby that the distinction between friend and enemy is the
constitutive binary of politics. In the case of Carl Schmitt, however, the
trajectory of his thought is precisely a denial of the first of these assertions
in order, eventually, to make the second. One of the conceptual models out
of which Schmitt's later conception of the political emerged was precisely a
kind of evacuated rhetorical situation. Before Schmitt's friend/enemy, there
was Müller's speaker/listener—and we may infer that before the distinction
between *Freund* and *Feind*, there existed a relationship between *Redner* and
Hörer. The enemy is precisely the conversation partner whose powers of
listening are now deemed foreclosed or negligible. The origin of Schmitt's
ideas in a denial of rhetoric is at times exceedingly obvious: "dictatorship is
the opposite of discussion," for instance.[92] In 1919, eight years before the first
version of his *Concept of the Political*, Schmitt observed the kind of similitude

89. Schmitt-Dorotić, *Politische Romantik*, 76: "die Wahrheit liegt . . . nie in dem, was der einzelne
Mensch begreift oder will."
90. Schmitt-Dorotić, 81: "allgemeine Richtung zum 'hohern Dritten,' der wahren Realität."
91. Schmitt-Dorotić, 117, 160.
92. Schmitt, *Politische Theologie*, 54: "Diktatur ist der Gegensatz zu Diskussion."

that can precipitate denial while paraphrasing Müller: "the orator can be thought of as being in a war with the listener even though he stands in a peaceful relationship with him, for otherwise the conversation would not be possible and the conflicts of interest [*Gegensätze*] would be immediately handled and overcome."[93] The listener is an enemy, a *constitutive* enemy whose function, in the first instance, is *not* to be immediately persuaded.

In the case of Leo Strauss, too, we can rediscover a constituent element of Weimar political theory by seeing it anew through the lens of rhetorical theory. Half a century after Strauss, Quentin Skinner would write a paradigmatic contextualist history of Thomas Hobbes arguing that we cannot understand the political theory of *Leviathan*—or, for that matter, the massive afterlife of this work in modern thought—without grappling with the fact that up until 1629, Hobbes was essentially a private tutor of the trivium and was thus immersed in the rhetorical tradition, completing (possibly) in that capacity a breviary of Aristotle's *Rhetoric*.[94] In 1936 (and without any of Skinner's speech act theoretical framework), Strauss had published a work that made a number of similar points about Hobbes's intellectual origins even as the overall aims of that book were radically different.

In that 1936 book *The Political Philosophy of Thomas Hobbes*, Strauss asserted that we can observe in Hobbes's work both the birth of modern liberalism and the demise of political philosophy. In his view, one could see that story in a transformation of the analysis of virtue into an analysis of the passions. As we saw above, Strauss believed that ancient thought had directly addressed questions concerning the good as such. He took his project to be a response to what he cast as the relativism and, thus, nihilism of modern historicism. As Timothy Burns has parsed the thought, historicism is to be understood as an assumption "that makes it impossible for anyone to ascend out of his time and place to grasp anything timeless" or anything of transcendent value.[95] Again, the postwar American liberal arts college looms. Like many others (some of whom he inspired), Strauss thought that good actions, good lives, and good polities could be examined as exemplars in the moments put on display by the best artistic records of the human spirit.

Leaving aside the questions begged by the liberal arts topos of "great books," we should notice that once again the rhetorical tradition supplied much of the conceptual material at the heart of Strauss's analysis. In this

---

93. Schmitt-Dorotić, *Politische Romantik*, 131: "den Redner kann man sich in einem 'Krieg' mit dem Hörer denken, er steht ebensosehr in einem friedlichen Zusammenhang mit ihm, sonst wäre das Gespräch nicht möglich, die Gegensätze werden sofort vermittelt und überbrückt."
94. Some doubts about Hobbes's authorship of the *Briefe* have been raised. See my discussion of the point in Marshall, "Afterlife of Rhetoric," 350n6.
95. Burns, *Companion to Leo Strauss's Writings*, 7.

case, the conduits were Aristotle's *Rhetoric*, Dilthey's *Worldview and the Analysis of Man*, and Heidegger's early lectures between 1922 and 1925 (at least some of which Strauss attended).[96] It is not altogether clear which of Heidegger's lectures he heard, but as Strauss later narrated it Heidegger made a fundamental impression on his sense of what a reinterpretation of ancient thought might do. Strauss's general conclusion was unequivocal: "Heidegger's interpretation of Aristotle was an achievement with which I cannot compare any other intellectual phenomenon which has emerged in Germany after the [First World] War."[97] As he demonstrated in his 1936 Hobbes book, the descriptions of the passions in part 1 of *Leviathan* were essentially cribbed from book 2 of Aristotle's *Rhetoric*. Strauss compared passages from Aristotle and from Hobbes, side by side, and he gave readers some sense of the itinerary of these receptions in the various redactions of Hobbesian theory in the *Elements of Law* (1640), *Leviathan* (1651), and *De homine* (1658).[98] This account of the passions was absolutely central to the razor-sharp pessimism of Hobbesian anthropology—and from a pessimistic anthropology, a pessimistic politics. Strauss inferred that "it would be difficult to find another classical work whose importance for Hobbes's political philosophy can be compared to that of [Aristotle's] *Rhetoric*."[99] Hobbes was crucial for the early Strauss. Aristotle's *Rhetoric* was crucial for Hobbes. Ergo, Aristotle's *Rhetoric* was crucial for the early Strauss.

What eventually became Strauss's fully antimodern project began in 1936 as a reading of the Hobbesian reception of Aristotelian rhetoric. To Strauss's eyes, what had been an analysis of virtue in Aristotle was transmogrified and betrayed in Hobbes as an analysis of the passions. As he put it, "whereas Aristotle discusses honourable and estimable passions with the same emphasis as base and blameworthy ones, the emphasis for Hobbes is from the beginning laid on the 'dissembled passions.'"[100] Strauss was proposing that we read Aristotle's *Rhetoric* as something like a phenomenology of Greek virtue. This was a sly gambit. Strauss was hoping that we might exploit the perceptiveness of Aristotle's account of the emotions in order to generate stories of human excellence. Hobbes and a good many other more recent readers have been more interested in Aristotle's depiction of the irascibility of the human soul—its hypersensitivity to "slight slights,"

96. There is some debate here, for which compare Husserl, *Briefwechsel*, 161 and Chacón, "Reading Strauss," 305. For his own account of how struck he had been by some of Heidegger's lectures, see Klein and Strauss, "Giving of Accounts," 461.
97. Strauss, "Living Issues of German Postwar Philosophy," 134.
98. Strauss, *Hobbes*, 41—where Strauss argues that, in these various iterations, Hobbes "studied Aristotle's *Rhetoric* afresh each time."
99. Strauss, *Political Philosophy of Hobbes*, 35.
100. Strauss, 131.

for instance. For Strauss, however, the most interesting component of Aristotelian virtue was magnanimity. As Strauss once put it, we may read magnanimity as courage, and then we must recognize that "courage is the only unambiguously unutilitarian virtue."[101] Courage looks to the good and the right rather than the advantageous. As courage, magnanimity is not simply a power of forbearance. Instead, it is a veritable greatness of soul. For Strauss, Hobbes's point was that "magnanimity is the origin of all virtue."[102] If contempt for the small was part of "greatness of soul," this for Strauss was part of its (natural) "aristocratic" attraction.

For Strauss, early modernity was the crucial scene of intellectual transformation; for Baron too, early modernity was the key, but for him quattrocento Florence was most decisive together with its civic republican ideology. The great irony of the Baronian departure in Weimar political theory articulated above was that although it set out an account of republicanism that was essentially built around a rhetorical core, that core was never installed. As Baron confected it, civic humanism emphasized the importance of active participation in public affairs. With significant numbers of citizens speaking and acting in public matters, the spiritual health of both citizens and the republic would be enhanced. In the early modern context that Baron was examining, rhetoric would be the theory and practice of such speaking and acting. Why, then, do we move from "religion of the ancient poets" to "Ridolfi, Lorenzo de'" in the index to Baron's 1955 masterpiece, *The Crisis of the Early Renaissance*? Why is there no entry for "rhetoric"?

Precisely why Baron neglected the rhetorical dimensions of Renaissance Florentine thought is unclear, but one hypothesis fits the facts rather closely: the drama of the story Baron wished to tell required a pivotal moment around 1400, and the long history of rhetoric was not amenable to that kind of grammar. To acknowledge rhetoric at the core of civic humanism would be to acknowledge that Renaissance Florentines did not invent this intellectual tradition in their face-off with the Milanese at the beginning of the fifteenth century. To acknowledge that would be to commit oneself to a complex intellectual history of variously Sicilian, Athenian, Hellenic, Roman, Christian, Arab, Medieval, and Byzantine receptions—to name only some of the iterations. James Hankins was suggesting this hypothesis when he said that "many of the republican ideas Baron claimed had emerged around 1400 in the writings of Italian humanists had, in fact, a long prehistory in the medieval scholastic and rhetorical traditions."[103] Baron's own historically resourceful response to Weimar's demise ought

---

101. Howse, *Strauss*, 32.
102. Strauss, *Political Philosophy of Hobbes*, 54.
103. Hankins, ed., *Renaissance Civic Humanism*, 8.

to have sensitized him to the ways in which experience makes intellectual history available and fresh.

For some Renaissance scholars, Baron's lack of attention to the rhetorical tradition constituted an opportunity to attack the hypothesis of civic humanism by contending that Baron had blithely misread a whole series of merely rhetorical performances as if they had been sincere attestations of political faith. The chief mover in this reaction, Jerrold Seigel, claimed that the writings of Baron's civic humanist protagonist, Leonardo Bruni, "like the programme of Renaissance humanism in general, must be approached as the products of a particular kind of culture: a culture which centered on rhetoric and eloquence."[104] Seigel went on to say that "Bruni spent his whole life as a practising rhetorician, whereas Petrarch did not."[105] His point was that we have to take Petrarch's words seriously in a way that we do not with Bruni's. Why? Because the rhetorician speaks on a particular day with a particular purpose to a particular audience and because principles cannot be articulated within the narrow focus of terms as short and shifting as these.

For other Renaissance scholars, however, attention to the rhetorical tradition constituted an opportunity to complete or complement Baron's project rather than reject it.[106] J. G. A. Pocock continued Baron's treatment of republicanism and then conceded to Quentin Skinner that he ought to have made the Ciceronian (and rhetorical) inheritance from classical antiquity more prominent.[107] For his part, Skinner has hammered home his advantage on the point about Cicero and the Roman rhetorical tradition with books articulating the rhetorical inheritances of Hobbes and, more recently, Shakespeare. Moreover, David Norbrook is right when he connects Skinner's Renaissance rhetorical investments to the Skinnerian historiographic initiative alluded to in the previous section, for "speech act theory . . . can be seen as a reinvention of rhetoric, that central art of civic humanism."[108] Renaissance scholars confirm the hypothesis that a Renaissance intellectual inheritance will be a rhetorical inheritance, but the deeper point that I wish to emphasize in this book is that high modern appropriations of early modern intellectual resources constitute opportunities for intellectual invention. And this is a gambit we have seen pursued to great effect in the works of Rocco Rubini, Victoria Kahn, and Nancy Struever.[109]

104. Seigel, "Ciceronian Rhetoric?" 10.
105. Seigel, "Ciceronian Rhetoric?," 38. We should also note that Seigel was relying heavily "on Kristeller's argument that the Italian humanists were essentially professionals, professional rhetoricians." See Schiller, "Baron's Humanism," 93.
106. See, for example, Hankins, *Renaissance Civic Humanism*, 167.
107. Pocock, afterword, 557.
108. Norbrook, *Writing the English Republic*, 11.
109. Rubini, *Other Renaissance*; Kahn, *Future of Illusion*; and Struever, *Rhetoric, Modality, Modernity*.

Like Weber, Schmitt, Strauss, and Baron, Theodor Adorno was no rhetorician, and yet in his case, too, we understand the oeuvre more fully and
more creatively when we see it in the broader intellectual context of the rhetorical tradition. In this last rhetorical redescription of a canonical Weimar
political thinker, I pay close attention to Adorno's interest in the fragment.
In the post-Auschwitz world that he lived to see and analyze, Adorno took
fragmented, disoriented, and damaged life as a point of departure. Kant's
theory of reflective judgment was one pertinent idiom, and both Adorno
and Horkeimer had an interest in it. In the paraphrase of Lars Rensmann
and Samir Gandesha, "rather than simply subsuming the particular auto-
cratically under an extant or false universal, such a form of judgment begins
with the particular, out of which it then generates a universal concept."[110]
Adorno was immediately suspicious of any new "universal concept," for
he saw there the undead return of the rule ready for application heedlessly
without exception. In contrast, he regarded the fragment as a kind of hope
precisely because of its generative capacity. And as we have seen the early
modern rhetorician Giambattista Vico was one of those licensing the
"philosophical fragments" genre of Horkheimer and Adorno's *Dialectic of
Enlightenment*. We may add that Horkheimer had studied Vico originally in
a Weimar context in his earlier book on historicism.[111]

Once again, rhetoric constituted a repertoire for thinking a twentieth-
century German problem. The rhetorical context into which we should
insert Adorno's interest in the fragment is aphorism, which, within the
rhetorical nomenclature laid out by Quintilian (among others), we may term
sententia. We are dealing here with the quotable phrase, the topos. This is
the line that can be inserted into a speech, the line that will be recognized
by an audience as a quotation. Initially, Adorno appropriated this interest
in the quoted phrase from Walter Benjamin. Benjamin's 1928 book on *The
Origins of German Tragic Drama* had been a brilliant reformulation of baroque rhetoric theory's obsession with the *concetto* (the witty and ingenious
conceit, the aperçu—again, the quotable fragment), and it was lurking in
the margins when Adorno relayed in 1933 that "Kierkegaard occasionally
refers to himself as 'the baroque thinker.'"[112] Now Peter Gordon may be
right that Adorno saw in Kierkegaardian existentialism "a paradigmatic but
unsuccessful attempt to realize what would become his own philosophical
ambition, to break free of the systems of idealism and to turn . . . 'toward the
concrete.'"[113] But Adorno had been giving classes on Benjamin's baroque
book at Frankfurt immediately after he joined the School for Social Research

110. Rensmann and Gandesha, *Arendt and Adorno*, 11.

111. Horkheimer, *Geschichtsphilosophie*, chap. 4.

112. Consider, for example, the connection announced by Adorno, *Kierkegaard*, in *Gesammelte
Schriften*, 2:91: "Kierkegaard nennt sich selbst gelegentlich 'der barocke Denker.'"

113. Gordon, *Adorno and Existence*, xi.

in 1931, and if we ignore the rhetorical patrimony inherited through Benjamin we miss opportunities to think Adorno's work in new ways.[114]

Heavily influenced by Benjamin, Adorno wrote a fair number of aphorisms himself, and we can perceive the relevance of rhetoric in these compositions. In the late 1920s, Adorno's music criticism often expressed itself within the genre constraints of aphorism, and I quote but one of those snippets: "the child trying to pick out a melody on the piano provides the paradigm of all true composition."[115] Picking out a melody is perceiving an immediate future, and it requires the sense of an ending. Such perception lays out possibilities in a state of approximate equidistance just as notes on a keyboard lie more or less equally within reach. Melody argues that only some continuations are true. In contrast, the keyboard loosens such stricture by implying that every note remains equally possible at every moment. Here in embryo, we have Adorno's obsession with the essay as a desultory and relatively undirected compositional form. Here, too, we find a point of departure for Adorno's interest in the paratactic. Refusing the hyperstructuration of, for example, the Ciceronian periodic sentence, parataxis loosens the bonds of an inferring that might be semantic or sensory and frees the writers and readers in its vicinity.

To fully appreciate connections between Adorno and the rhetorical tradition, we have to understand the individual fragment in terms of its potential arrangement in constellations of fragments—which both here and elsewhere I term "aphoristic machines."[116] Such machines isolate and arrange thought fragments. They arrange and facilitate the activation of fragments in the same way that a piano is a machine for arranging and facilitating the activation of an array of pitches. We need not jump to any conclusions when we hear Adorno saying in his Kierkegaard book that "the arrangement [*Anordnung*] of things in the apartment is called appointing [*Einrichtung*]." "Arrangement" may be a conjuring word for rhetoricians (connoting the second part of classical rhetoric), but, as *Anordnung*, it was almost certainly just another word for Adorno.[117] Yet the leapt-to conclusion, reined in as hypothesis, is given more weight when we hear on the same page that "the *intérieur* is the image incarnate of Kierkegaard's philosophical 'point'" in which "all that is real on the outside has collapsed to a single point."[118] This formulation will seem opaque, but the sense is this: just as piano keys are functionally

114. Müller-Doohm, *Adorno*, 137.
115. Müller-Doohm, 107–8.
116. Marshall, "Giambattista Vico, Aphorism."
117. Adorno, *Kierkegaard*, in *Gesammelte Schriften*, 2:65: "die Anordnung der Dinge in der Wohnung heißt Einrichtung."
118. Adorno, 2:66: "das Intérieur ist die leibhafte imago von Kierkegaards philosophischen 'Punkt': alles wirkliche Außen hat sich zum Punkt zusammengezogen."

equidistant for talented fingers, so domestic memorabilia put moods and narratives equally within reach for the housebound soul.

Rhetoric was lurking in Adorno's formulations, and this intuition is vindicated in the very next connection he made, which was unquestionably rhetorical in its provenance. Quoting Kierkegaard's *For Self-Examination*, Adorno relayed the thought that "just as in well-appointed apartments one does not have to go downstairs to haul water, since water pressure ensures that one has it upstairs and needs only to turn the tap, so must eloquence . . . be immediately at hand to the true Christian orator in every moment, because Christianity is his life."[119] Christian eloquence is a "water pressure" generated by a faith that is drawn both to and from every moment in a life. Turning back to the metaphor of the piano, we may infer that homiletic exegesis is, quite simply, an étude intended to place at one's fingertips a repertoire of quotations, glosses, and potential points.

In Adorno's postwar oeuvre, the interest in aphoristic machines would inform *Minima moralia*. In the prewar work that I am focusing on here, we find it expressed in Adorno's discussion of the *ars inveniendi* of Bacon and Leibniz in his "inaugural lecture" (*Antrittsrede*) of May 7, 1931.[120] In his 1931 debut at the School for Social Research in Frankfurt, Adorno offered up swift criticism of the various schools of German philosophy—Marburg neo-Kantianism; Simmel's *Lebensphilosophie*; Rickert's Southwest School; Husserlian, Schelerian, and Heideggerian phenomenology; Vienna Circle logical positivism. In response to what he regarded as these various failed initiatives, Adorno ventured a preliminary version of his later critical theory. In this early adumbration, we see not only the heavy influence of Benjamin's book on German tragic drama but also an en passant attempt to appropriate the baroque rhetorical material embedded in Benjamin's work by means of the *ars inveniendi*. In ways that are surprising and instructive, we can see how topical theory inflected the foundation of critical theory. In the *Antrittsrede*, the art of invention had been driven by the "exact imagination" (*exakte Phantasie*) that permits concrete exemplars to stand in for abstract concepts.[121] In "The Essay as Form" of 1958, the art of invention is sublimated. As Adorno put it, "the pleasures that rhetoric wants to provide to

119. Adorno, 2:66: "Wie man in wohleingerichteten Wohnungen keine Treppe hinabsteigen muß, um Wasser zu holen, da man es durch Hochdruck droben hat und nur den Hahn zu drehen braucht, so muß dem echt-christlichen Redner, weil das Christentum sein Leben ist, jeden Augenblick Beredsamkeit, gerade die wahre Beredsamkeit, gegenwärtig und gleich zur Hand sein."
120. Kierkegaard, *Entweder/Oder*, 1:138; quoted and glossed in Adorno, *Kierkegaard*, in *Gesammelte Schriften*, 2:198.
121. Adorno, "Aktualität der Philosophie," in *Gesammelte Schriften*, 1:341–42: "Organon dieser ars inveniendi aber ist Phantasie. Eine exakte Phantasie; Phantasie, die streng in dem Material verbleibt."

its audience are sublimated in the essay into the idea of the pleasure of freedom vis-à-vis the object, a freedom that gives the object more of itself than if it were mercilessly incorporated into the order of ideas."[122] It is as if for Adorno the diversity of audience receptions has been transmuted into a diversity of potential continuations of the object.

THE PROBLEM RESTATED

In this chapter, I have stylized a standard received history of the Weimar origins of political theory. I have then redescribed that standard received history in terms of a theoretical idiom—rhetoric—that is essentially absent from all scholarly discussion of that Weimar legacy. In addition, I have defended my historiographic and theoretical practices with warrants derived from the philosophical work of Robert Brandom. In this way, I have established the problem to which this book is a response: is it possible to reinvigorate problematics in the Weimar tradition of political theory that have been thought repeatedly and, quite possibly, too often by seeing elements of that lineage as part of a different story that I call the "Weimar origins of rhetorical inquiry"? My answer to this question is yes. If Weber constituted the base curve from which the trajectories of Schmitt, Strauss, Baron, and Adorno departed, then Heidegger, Warburg, Arendt, and Benjamin constitute glosses on these four departures. Heidegger offers an alternative to Strauss. Arendt enriches Baron. Benjamin utterly revises Schmitt. And Warburg takes the early Adorno in a quite different direction. Cobbling these four revisions together in this book, I invent a tradition that speaks to the ways in which presencing is a matter of distinguishing possibilities. This is a tradition attentive to the spaces and auditoriums that such presencings generate in a public world. It is also a tradition attuned to the ways in which genre can be a practice of retaining variety in such presencing in the midst of an unfolding moment of decision. Ultimately, this becomes a tradition that lays down essential preconditions for a theorization of freedom as a plenitude of capabilities within an individual or a community, capabilities that are in some sense equidistant to any particular action. In order to prepare ourselves for this work of creative intellectual-historical inflection, however, we have to exercise our minds in the rhetorical tradition, which is a lost continent of thoughts for many contemporary researchers. We shall sample that tradition in the next chapter by looking at the German reception of rhetoric in the centuries before 1933.

122. Adorno, "Essay als Form," in *Gesammelte Schriften*, 11:29–30: "die Befriedigungen, welche Rhetorik dem Hörer bereiten will, werden im Essay sublimiert zur Idee des Glücks einer Freiheit dem Gegenstand gegenüber, welche diesem mehr von dem seinen gibt, als wenn er unbarmherzig der Ordnung der Ideen eingegliedert würde."

2: IDIOMS OF RHETORICAL INQUIRY

THE NATURE AND PURPOSE OF CONTEXT

The problem has been stated: the Weimar Republic is recognized as a disproportionately significant point of origin for twentieth-century intellectual history (political theory in particular), but our sense of what that might mean has become repetitive, and there are unrecognized intellectual resources in Weimar for rejuvenating these lines of inquiry that are revealed by the rhetorical tradition. In this chapter, the task is to articulate traditions of rhetorical inquiry in such a way that they both retain their distinctiveness and also take on a new availability for use in the rejuvenation of our reception of Weimar thought. Rhetoric, understood comparatively and globally, has many sites of investigation. Here, "the rhetorical tradition" is understood more narrowly as a distinctive part of European and Mediterranean intellectual history developing, rejecting, and transforming inheritances from Greco-Roman antiquity. Before we can profitably investigate the creative receptions of rhetorical thought that I find in Martin Heidegger, Hannah Arendt, Walter Benjamin, and Aby Warburg, we need both a sense of the rhetorical tradition that was in play here and a sense of what it became in the context of German intellectual culture.

Thus, the task of this chapter is essentially contextual. It is very important to note, however, that I understand context in a distinctive way. My sense of the role and nature of historical contextualization is not identical with what is probably still the dominant school of thinking within avowedly "contextualist" intellectual history—namely, the Cambridge School. As I intimated in the previous chapter, Quentin Skinner's methodological arguments have been highly influential even though he is not the only leader of that school. For practitioners of the historical method framed by Skinner, "context" entails a commitment to reading beyond a canon of great works. Context there is not so much the social and economic conditions obtaining while an idea was being articulated. The context for the great works is the swathe of less conspicuous, less famous, and perhaps less brilliant works that bore witness to the conventional wisdom constituting a particular area of inquiry.[1] The interventions made by the "great works" become visible, so the argument goes, only when held up against the background of these contexts. In its purest form, this way of understanding context amounts to a pursuit of unavowed or perhaps even unavowable intentions. These are intentions that may be held by an author or that may alternatively be ascribed to an author by a reader. Here is the quintessence: the most beautiful, the most difficult to discern, the most lacerating interventions are the ones that occur in situations where authors and readers are saturated in a conventional wisdom to the point that interventions can call out and then destroy opponents without even mentioning them by name. The ambitious historian, so goes the line, pursues revelations of this kind.

Skinnerian contextualism constitutes one viable means of contextualizing a work, but it is not the only legitimate way of either staging or dramatizing context. Skinner's way of working can be exquisite, but actually its insistence on utterance occasions where parties to the utterance are saturated in a shared conventional wisdom narrows the range of its legitimate application quite significantly. Not all historical contexts offer up the same intensity of "utterance occasion" or, for that matter, the same kind. Distilled, this form of contextualism becomes something like a hermeneutic of inside jokes. This puts things a little uncharitably, but it clarifies the nature of the historiographic position that I am challenging. I conceptualize and pursue a different kind of context. As I understand it, "context" is to be understood as a topical cluster of positions around a problematic of some kind. The context for any utterance is the repertoire of available alternatives and available continuations.

I choose the word "topical" with care because I wish to mark and then explain the inventive function of context. The matrix of elasticities between similarity and difference that constitutes a topical cluster has a role to play in the emergence of originality. Arranged topically, these clusters call out new positions—sometimes because there is a space between positions that has not yet been taken up, sometimes because listing utterances together makes it clear which presuppositions are common to all and how one might blindside a discursive community with a new argument by rejecting what these ultimately local conflicts have taken for granted. As I conceptualize it, context is thus inferential. In order to elucidate the part of his thought that I am building on at this point, I repeat the specification of the term "context" offered by Robert Brandom that I deployed in the previous chapter. For him, "each set of further premises with which a claim can be conjoined is a

1. Thus, in its now quite old but still classic formulation, Cambridge School contextualism was articulated in *opposition* to contextualizations based on social or economic conditions. See Skinner, "Meaning and Understanding," 3.

further *context* in which its inferential significance can be assessed."[2] On my account, topical clustering is an arranging that makes interrelationships of inferential commitment, entitlement, and disentitlement explicit. That is, clustering arranges positions by articulating the senses in which—having adopted one assertion—one *has* to accept, *may* accept, or *may not* accept another.

I place particular emphasis on the inventive function of context because I do not believe that the only legitimate goal of contextualization is comprehension of the inside jokes of the past. Perceiving the complex inferential relationships that constitute clusters of positions around a problematic is essential to a mutually constitutive process of (1) understanding argumentative innovation in the past and (2) becoming argumentatively innovative in the present. If we wish to be able to stage the specific inventiveness of past thinkers, we need to learn to perceive opportunities for intervention alongside them. We need to perceive the ways in which positions held to be complementary are actually contradictory, the ways in which positions held to be contradictory may actually be complementary, and the ways in which the implications of particular assertions can be transformed when maintained in the context of new, hitherto unarticulated positions. The inferential capacity of the intellectual historian is thus very similar to the inferential capacity of the thinker. Above all else, we must understand that inference is not only—or even primarily—a formal armature of logical entailment but rather a kind of perspicacity in seeing the pertinence of assertions for each other.

I have learned the idioms of rhetorical inquiry available in Weimar Germany, and I distill those idioms here for readers of this book for two reasons. First, you and I, reader and writer of this book, are each more capable of reenacting the inferential dramas worked through by Heidegger, Arendt, Benjamin, and Warburg once we have exercised our own inferential imaginations in the collected stances of the rhetorical tradition, particularly as it was transformed in Germany from approximately the seventeenth century until the twentieth. Second, you and I, reader and writer of this book, are each more prepared to *continue* the lines of inquiry discovered in this book once we possess a rich sense of the variety of positions taken up in this rhetorical tradition. I think the rhetorico-political thought articulated in this book is both historically significant and intrinsically valuable. I want to be able to think in this tradition, and I want to create readers who can think in this tradition too. To write in this way places considerable responsibility on readers. They must read with an attention not only to what is being said but also to both what has been said and what could or could not be said under certain specifications. This chapter requires "plastic readers" both

2. Brandom, *Tales*, 95.

supple enough to take on the forms of the assertions they encounter and rigid enough to hold and explore the combinability of those forms.

Because the contexts explored in this chapter are potential as well as actual, I make no attempt to prove that topical clusters as I reconstruct them were taken up either by the protagonists of this book or by the audiences they called into being with their interventions. In this chapter, the contexts are the idioms of rhetorical inquiry. I call these "idioms" of rhetorical inquiry in the sense that they are loose clusters of assertions linked in a disheveled and underdetermined way on account of the relative frequency with which these assertions have been and can be brought together in inference. In this chapter, I operate in an intermediary space. On the one hand, there is "the rhetorical tradition" irrespective of its instantiation in particular places and times as a tissue of receptions and reinventions. On the other, there are the specific receptions and reinventions of rhetoric offered by particular Weimar thinkers. This intermediary space is the idiom of rhetorical inquiry available to a relatively impersonal "modern German rhetorician." I emphasize modern German refractions because I want thoughts that connect rhetorical patrimonies to modern German exigencies. And I interlace this predominantly German discourse with a number of key sentences from the classical and postclassical rhetorical tradition because the full implications of these refractions cannot be perceived (or continued) without them.

In this chapter, I am not attempting to represent a German rhetorical tradition that each of my protagonists possessed to the same degree. The task is not to prove that Heidegger or Arendt or Benjamin or Warburg possessed these languages of rhetorical inquiry *in toto*. It really does seem as if this would be a losing historical bet: when Nietzsche offered his best course on rhetoric at the University of Basel in the 1870s (following the negative reception of *The Birth of Tragedy*), he had two students.[3] This is not the way that intellectual foundations are laid. The task is to assemble these idioms of rhetorical inquiry for the writer and readers of this book so that they may stage the inventiveness of Heidegger, Arendt, Benjamin, and Warburg. This chapter does not trace intellectual-historical source and influence. It is a performance of a German reception of rhetoric, and the performativity here is primarily inferential. Run with alacrity, the scripts of this tradition call each other out inferentially, and I perform these scripts as a sequence of five issues: nature, topoi, context, trope, and belief.

WHAT IS RHETORIC?

We can begin with the most common responses: rhetoric is simply speech performance; rhetoric is language designed to persuade; rhetoric is one's

---

3. Consider, however, the ironies laid out in Porter, "Wilamowitz contra Nietzsche," esp. 79.

linguistic dealings with others where persuasion is the goal. True, in antiquity one might attempt to think this phenomenon through the institutions of oratory—the civic infrastructure of assembly, court, and festival dedicated to the persuasive performance of the spoken word. Indeed, a topos recorded by Aristotle and repeated many times since held that the first rhetor was Empedokles, who was not only a shaman, a magician, and a verse philosopher but also the founder of democracy at Agrigent.[4] Adjacent to this topos, in Nietzsche's rendition, was the thought that "speech" (*Rede*) is "the greatest instrument of power among equals."[5] This vision of speech among equals becomes a deliberative democratic truism. Witness the pared down and blanched version offered by the eighteenth-century Swiss thinker Johann Georg Sulzer, which bears almost no trace of historical specificity: eloquence "is clearly the most perfect means of making human beings more understanding, more civilized, better, and happier," and "in eloquence true politics finds the crucial means of making the state happy."[6] Still, fear is hard to banish. If it is the case that eloquence is a "means" (*Mittel*), then one may worry about the ends to which it may be put. Just so, Sulzer tempers his enthusiasm, for "the greater the power [of eloquence], the more harmful will be its misuse."[7] Power breeds fear.

Indeed, in the German reception of rhetoric, one notes a recurrent tendency to be suspicious of the persuasive urge, to see it as something liable to permeate all forms of cultural exchange—or, better, liable to cast all culture in the mode of exchange. Thus, the twentieth-century German literary scholar Max Kommerell declares that Friedrich Schiller—dramatist, lyricist, and aesthetician—was a "rhetor working with poetic means" (*Rhetor mit dichterischen Mitteln*). This led to a broader question: "how does one operate through poetry?"[8] The distaste is palpable. Striving for effect, the inference comes, is an addiction that spreads into culture more generally. Indeed, we may say that "mere rhetoric" is the language performance that betrays itself precisely in the degree to which it attempts to bring about change in an audience. On this account, rhetoric is the language performance that has no respect for itself. It regards itself always and only as a *means* to other ends. A narrative emerges that rhetoric is never undertaken for its own sake.

4. Aristotle cited in Diogenes Laertius, *Lives of Eminent Philosophers*, 8:57.
5. Nietzsche, "Griechischen Beredsamkeit," in *Gesammelte Werke*, 5:5: speech "ist das grösste Machtmittel inter pares."
6. Sulzer, *Theorie der schönen Künste*, 1:147–48: eloquence "ist offenbar das vollkommenste Mittel, die Menschen verständiger, gesitteter, besser, und glücklicher zu machen" and "in der Beredsamkeit findet die ächte Politik das wichtige Mittel den Staat glücklich zu machen."
7. Sulzer, *Theorie der schönen Künste*, 1:149: "je größer ihre Kraft ist, je schädlicher wird ihr Misbrauch."
8. Kommerell, *Der Dichter als Führer*, 177–78: "wie wirkt man durch Dichtung?"

Once raised, it is hard to shake the accusation of "mere rhetoric." The accusation returns again and again, recursive like an irony. This can be a self-hatred too. Nietzsche's late disavowal of Wagner becomes a substitute for his disavowal of his own earlier self.[9] "Wagner," Nietzsche came to say, "was not a musician by instinct." He was instead dedicated to a "theater-rhetoric" (*Theater-Rhetorik*). Of all people, *Nietzsche* disdains rhetoric? Look at his punctuation: was there ever a prose stylist so intent on having his readers synchronized alongside him in the stop, start, and crush of his own beliefs and antipathies? The man is hoisted on his own petard: Nietzsche has quoted Schopenhauer's description of rhetoric as an attempt "to lead the flow of our thoughts in the head."[10] Every Nietzschean em dash, every ellipsis, every exclamation mark—these are so many pacts with the devil. Nietzsche was deeply torn here. He was the greatest diagnostician of ulterior motive, which we may read as rhetorical purpose. He was deeply skeptical of the Kantian desire to connect beauty with disinterestedness. And yet he often enough distanced himself from rhetoric.

Here, what is more, is the other side of language as persuasion and of rhetoric as simultaneously the striving for effect and the cultural substrate left behind by such striving: language as performance becomes *a* language. The language forged by rhetoric is a language that does some things and not others. It facilitates some transactions but hinders others, and it freights a world of presupposition and predilection. Distinguished alternatively by a definite or indefinite article, "rhetoric" takes on particular cultural forms. Witness the Austrian writer Hugo von Hofmannsthal: "whoever substitutes 'language' in for culture is doing nothing but setting a richer and beyond that more effective substantive or definition in place of a tired and on that account now powerless artificial word."[11] Language is its own record of cultural transactions, past and possible. In making the assertion, Hofmannsthal was glossing Salz's 1920 republication of Adam Müller's 1816 lectures on eloquence discussed in the previous chapter. Hofmannsthal's point was that a language might be its own public sphere: language would be the stage on which speech might perform. Elsewhere, he spoke of the "sociability of forms" (*Soziabilität der Formen*) as a "circuit" (*Ring*) connecting poet and nation, writer and reader, speaker and listener: the forms of speech would be meeting places, spaces in which one might register the distinctiveness of a performance.[12]

9. Nietzsche, *Der Fall Wagner*, in *Gesammelte Werke*, 17:25.
10. Schopenhauer, *Die Welt als Wille und Vorstellung*, 129, cited by Nietzsche, "Rhetorik," in *Gesammelte Werke*, 5:288–89: "den Strom unserer Gedanken in ihren Kopf [zu] leiten."
11. Hofmannsthal, "Müllers Zwölf Reden," in *Gesammelte Werke*, 9:126: "wer für Kultur 'Sprache' setzt, setzt nur an Stelle eines übermüdeten und darum kraftlos gewordenen Kunstwortes ein reineres und darum wirksameres Wesens- und Hauptwort."
12. Hofmannsthal, *Das Schrifttum*, 12.

The language existing beyond its particular performances and conditioning them would become an entity or force in its own right, liable to be personified, feared, and celebrated. Thus, for the anarchist Gustav Landauer, a language is "a most highly conservative element and remains in place, so that even today it is necessary for science to fashion for its purposes new languages and new means of expression."[13] Equally (and in some ways contradictorily), a language would both resist innovation and need to be protected from it. If a word were not born out of some culturally (or, some might say, ethnically) specific experience, it would lack "authenticity" (*Echtheit*). Later, in 1937, the Germanist Ewald Geißler would say that Esperanto—for him, a rootless international invented language—was nothing less than an "un-language" (*Unsprache*), a language betraying the essence of language. To teach such an experience-neutralized artifice anywhere in the German school system would be a travesty, he concluded.[14]

In the midst of the sense that a language might be a law unto itself beyond the short-term intentions of its users, we encounter two of the holy dicta of modern German language awareness. A language is actually a monolog, the early Romantic poet and thinker Novalis had opined, and "nobody knows what is precisely the most characteristic aspect of language—namely, that it is simply concerned with itself."[15] We are therefore to speak of "moody language" (*launige Sprache*). This is language consumed with its own needs and remaining indifferent to the transient concerns of human beings. When Novalis asked in addition whether "a writer is really anything other than a language-enthusiast," he was not wondering whether a writer loves language. He was asking whether it is better to say that writers write language or that languages write writers.[16] Enthusiasts are so absorbed into that by which they are enthused that they become instruments. Just so, Friedrich Schlegel wanted to show "that words often understand themselves better than those by whom they are used."[17] Languages have lives and sensitivities of their own beyond their local deployment.

Of course (and here we come to one of the crucial hinges in this discursive structure), rhetoric cannot only be understood as speech performance for it is also—if not predominantly—some form of potential or power or possibility *with regard to* language serving the purpose of persuasion. Granted,

---

13. Landauer, *Ausgewählte Schriften*, 2:65: "ein äußerst konservatives Element und bleibt stehen, so dass die Wissenschaft schon heute genötigt ist, sich für ihre Zwecke neue Sprachen und Ausdrucksmittel zu erfinden."

14. Geißler, *Sprachpflege*, 18, 22.

15. Novalis, "Monolog," in *Schriften*, 2:672–73: "gerade das Eigenthümliche der Sprache, daß sie sich blos um sich selbst bekümmert, weiß keiner."

16. Novalis, 2.672–73: "ein Schriftsteller ist wohl nur ein Sprachbegeisterter?"

17. Schlegel, "Über die Unverständlichkeit," 364: "daß die Worte sich selbst oft besser verstehen, als diejenigen von denen sie gebraucht werden."

rhetoric's status as some kind of theory and not simply a practice was much debated in its ancient instantiations. In Greek and Latin, the terms used ranged from *empeiria* to *scientia*, via *technē* and *ars*, among others. In its post-seventeenth-century German receptions, however, the dominance of one of the Greek terms—*dunamis*—is clear. As a *dunamis*, rhetoric became a possibility, a potentiality, a power, a capacity. Speech performance itself was the act (which, for the sake of clarity, we might call "oratory"), while rhetoric was, more properly, the reservoir of what *might* be that lay around actuality and that took the world in its grip when forming that actuality. In English, it is prudent to sketch this domain with a number of words rather than just one. Similarly, we find a variety of translations in German: conceived of as a *dunamis*, rhetoric is *eine Kunst* (note the connection to *können*, to be able), *ein Kraft*, *ein Vermögen*, *eine Fähigkeit*, *eine Geschicklichkeit*, *eine Fertigkeit*—even *eine Gewohnheit*.[18] Of course, translating these terms is a fool's errand. The English "equivalents"—an art, a power, a faculty, a capacity, a dexterity, a skill, a habit—are not the semantic objects under discussion.

A *dunamis* for what, though? In the German tradition since the seventeenth century, one ancient inheritance once again stands out from the rest. In his *Rhetoric*, Aristotle had said "estō dē rhētorikē dunamis peri hekaston tou theorēsai to endechomenon pithanon."[19] Nietzsche glossed this as "purely philosophical and highly influential for all subsequent specifications of the concept" of rhetoric.[20] As specified by Aristotle in this passage, rhetoric was a capacity not so much to persuade as "to perceive" (*wahrnehmen*).[21] In some accounts, this would become a capacity to perceive "things" called "means of persuasion" (*Überzeugungsmittel*).[22] That version of the topos was recurrent and emphatic. Rhetoric had a "task" (*Aufgabe*), but it was neither "convincing" (*Überzeugen*) nor "cajoling" (*Überredung*); the task would be the perception or knowledge of *means* to the end of persuasion.[23] At one point, Nietzsche rendered this passage as "the power that Aristotle calls rhetoric, to discover in each thing what works and what makes an impression and to turn that to account." He goes so far as to equate this power with

---

18. The references here are too many to list, but take seven exempla for seven key terms, in the order of mention—Jaeger, *Aristoteles*, 45; Nietzsche, "Rhetorik," in *Gesammelte Werke*, 5:298; Gottsched, *Ausfürliche Redekunst*, 73; Gerber, *Sprache als Kunst*, 1:149; Volkmann, *Die Rhetorik der Griechen und Römer*, 4; Gottsched, *Ausfürliche Redekunst*, 76; Nietzsche, "Aus der Zeit der Morgenröthe," in *Gesammelte Werke*, 11:17.

19. Aristotle, *Rhetoric*, 1355b27–28.

20. Nietzsche, "Rhetorik," in *Gesammelte Werke*, 5:291: "rein philosophisch und höchst einflussreich für alle späteren Begriffsbestimmungen."

21. Gottsched, *Ausfürliche Redekunst*, 73.

22. Volkmann, *Die Rhetorik der Griechen und Römer*, 4.

23. Gomperz, *Griechische Denker*, 3:331; Kroll, "Rhetorik," 1058.

"the essence of language" (*das Wesen der Sprache*).[24] Speech deals not with things but with the impressions that things have made on human beings, and "there is simply no unrhetorical 'naturalness' to speech to which one could appeal." As a result, any power of speech worth the name would be an understanding of impressions, not simply "impressions" (*Eindrücke*) or "sentiments" (*Empfindungen*) but "irritations" (*Reizen*) that are "portraits of sentiments" (*Abbildungen von Empfindungen*).[25] At this point, we encounter an important twist in the topos. When Nietzsche went on to translate *to endechomenon pithanon* as "everything potentially credible and persuasive" (*alles mögliche Wahrscheinliche und Überzeugende*), we are alerted to the fact that the frequent translation of *to pithanon* as "means of persuasion" (*Überzeugungsmittel*) is an interpolation, for there is no equivalent in the Greek for "means" (*Mittel*). *To pithanon* is simply the persuasive, but the persuasive also in the mode of the convincing, the credible, the passable, the plausible, the verisimilar.[26]

Nietzsche's emphasis on impressions, sensations, and stimuli raised the question of whether regarding rhetoric as a *dunamis* entailed an assumption that rhetorical capacity would be a capacity to do, either primarily or exclusively. Holding to the purest Aristotelian flexibility with the term, Nietzsche—indeed, the German tradition more generally—remained aware that this would be a capacity, a *dunamis*, not simply to act but also to suffer. Nietzsche cast rhetoric as "an essentially *republican* art."[27] Why? Because to excel in rhetoric, "one must be accustomed to dealing with the most unfamiliar opinions and views, and one must even experience a certain pleasure in contradicting them."[28] Indeed, "one must listen just as readily as speak oneself, and one must as a listener be able to appreciate in approximate terms the art being demonstrated."[29] One develops sensitivities in such speaking and listening. When rhetoric is a "habit" (*Gewohnheit*), it is a practice "of only being moved in the vicinity of certain words and motifs" (*nur bei gewissen Worten und Motiven bewegt zu werden*).[30] We can say that possessing *taste* in one's irascibilities is a rhetorical talent.

24. Nietzsche, "Rhetorik," in *Gesammelte Werke*, 5:298: "die Kraft, welche Aristoteles Rhetorik nennt, an jedem Dinge das heraus zu finden und geltend zu machen, was wirkt und Eindruck macht." Note that here "turning to account" (*geltend zu machen*) is Nietzsche's interpolation.
25. Nietzsche, 5:298: "es giebt gar keine unrhetorische 'Natürlichkeit' der Sprache, an die man appelliren könnte."
26. Nietzsche, 5:291.
27. Nietzsche, 5:287: "eine wesentlich *republikanische* Kunst."
28. Nietzsche, 5:287: "man muss gewohnt sein, die fremdesten Meinungen und Ansichten zu ertragen und sogar ein gewisses Vergnügen an ihrem Widerspiel empfinden."
29. Nietzsche, 5:287: "man muss ebenso gerne zuhören als selbst sprechen, man muss als Zuhörer ungefähr die aufgewandte Kunst würdigen können."
30. Nietzsche, "Aus der Zeit der Morgenröthe," in *Gesammelte Werke*, 11:17.

Rhetoric would be a *commerce* in the exchange of perspectives. On the one hand, Schopenhauer would say that eloquence is "the capacity also in others to arouse our view of a thing or our attitude toward that thing"; it would be a capacity "to ignite our feeling about this thing in others and thereby to shift them into sympathy with us."[31] On the other hand (in a neat inversion), Adam Müller had said that rhetoric would be "the art of taking in foreign natures" (*die Kunst des Innerwerdens fremder Naturen*).[32] This is why the Baltic German essayist Carl Gustav Jochmann then said "lords and serfs are seldom good speakers."[33] Indeed, if we pursue the point, this is why Adolf Damaschke would then say in the early years of the Weimar Republic that "the greater the dissemination of the art of speaking (and, with and through that, civic education), the sooner will Stuart Mill's warning about the 'tyranny of the majority' and Proudhon's about 'the tyranny of the orator' lose their foundation."[34] Rhetoric's permeable membrane would permit both an importing and an exporting of perspectives. Facility in such traffic would prepare the way for rhetoric *as a defense*. The spiritually well-traveled rhetor is able to parry the blow as well as launch it.

As either the possibility of acting or the possibility of suffering, rhetoric lived in modality. It trucked in "possibility and actuality" (*Möglichkeit und Wirklichkeit*). These are "rhetorical ideas or categories" (*rhetorische Ideen oder Kategorien*), said the German Hugenot theologian Franz Theremin in 1814. We must retain that technical modal term "actuality" in order to render *Wirklichkeit*, because the obvious alternative—namely, "reality"—fails to anchor the real in the present. *Wirklich* specifies not that which is existent at any point but that which at present pertains or is in the process of activation.[35] As Geißler put it in 1914, eloquence and the arts of speaking deal with possibility and articulate the part of politics that we rightly term the "the art of the possible" (*Kunst des Möglichen*).[36] And we should be dogged at this point, because *Wirklichkeit* does indeed connote a "being-in-play" or "being-at-work." Partly a theory and practice of the possible, rhetoric is thus also a theory and practice of the actual. The orator oscillates between a world of possibility in which every action has been refracted into a thousand

31. Schopenhauer, *Die Welt als Wille und Vorstellung*, 129: "die Fähigkeit, unsere Ansicht einer Sache oder unsere Gesinnung hinsichtlich derselben, auch in Anderen zu erregen, unser Gefühl darüber in ihnen zu entzünden und sie so in Sympathie mit uns zu versetzen."
32. Müller, *Zwölf Reden*, 47.
33. Jochmann, *Über die Sprache*, 135: "Herren und Knechte sind selten gute Sprecher."
34. Damaschke, *Geschichte der Redekunst*, 320: "je weiter die Redekunst verbreitet wird und mit ihr und durch sie staatsbürgerliche Bildung, desto eher wird auch Stuart Mills Warnung vor der 'Tyrannei der Mehrheit' und Proudhons vor der 'Tyrannei der Redner' gegenstandslos."
35. Theremin, *Die Beredsamkeit eine Tugend*, 69.
36. Geißler, *Rhetorik*, 13.

possibilities and a world of actuality in which the emerging performance is entirely itself and nothing else. In the manner of an unrealized ideal, the orator approaches that German aesthetic fetish, the "beautiful soul" (*schöne Seele*). Such a soul casts no internal shadow. That is, there is no doubling between consideration and act, no contradiction between duty and enactment. Such pure actuality manifests itself in a certain kind of grace of gesture, unhurried, neither ahead of itself nor lagging behind.[37]

The shadowlessness of the beautiful soul is properly paradoxical, and this is instructive rhetorically. It is genuinely difficult to see how discerning, identifying, even practicing possibilities can contribute to the shadowless performance of particular possibilities when the crucial moment arrives. Think of the epithet "overprepared." Routinizing possibility develops scripts. The temporality of the gesture will not match the temporality into which it is being inserted. Opportunities do not present themselves as cutouts of actions that already exist somewhere in the soul of the orator in some shadowy potential. The actor who waits primed is an actor who hammers a cue like a nail. Overpreparation robs an action of the suppleness it requires to be itself. Who has made the point better than Heinrich von Kleist? Having finished a thought before giving voice to it actually poses a problem for speech performance. Better to let the thought come in the process of speaking.[38] Overpreparation leads to mannerism. Performance now casts the shadow of a consciousness of performance. And this is why Kleist was actually thinking seriously about the question he pretended to pose as a joke: can professional dancers learn anything from marionettes? Yes, they can learn about lightness, gravity, and the way in which the body finds its "center of gravity" (*Schwerpunkt*). The marionette is pure act. It does not second-guess, and it is not haunted by its own muscle memories.[39]

Here, we come to another key inflection point in the modern German account of rhetoric. Rhetoric is not simply either speech performance or an art of speech performance. It is also a kind of intellectual repository for the humanities writ large. In the modern German imagination, the claims of rhetoric to be more than simply an art of persuasion were already ubiquitous in Greek antiquity. For Theremin, eloquence did not pertain solely to dialectic but was "also related to the science of manners that is politics."[40] Indeed, for the twentieth-century classicist Werner Jaeger, rhetoric became "the dominant pedagogy in late antiquity" (*die herrschende Bildung der Spätantike*), where *Bildung* is not "education" in a narrow sense but rather

37. Kommerell, *Der Dichter als Führer*, 233–34.
38. Kleist, "Über die Allmähliche Verfertigung der Gedanken beim Reden," 534–40.
39. Kleist, *Über das Marionettentheater*, 5, 9, 12.
40. Theremin, *Die Beredsamkeit eine Tugend*, 19: "auch der Wissenschaft der Sitten, welche Politik heise, verwandt."

the "formation" of a citizen elite capable of engaging in properly public life.[41] This was "leader-formation" (*Führerbildung*), which was itself "simply the problem of nobility in a new form."[42] When Salz republished Müller's paean to and lament for eloquence and its corruption in Germany in 1920, he was fantasizing both about "eloquence" (*Beredsamkeit*) as a true and characteristic sign of the *Nation* and about politics as "a higher expression of the gathered potency and culture of the people" (*ein höchster Ausdruck der gesammelten Kraft und Kultur des Volkes*).[43] Similarly, when the philologue Georg Ammon reviewed Weimar research into the "riches" (*Schätze*) of Cicero's rhetorical writings, he did it in the name of "a knowledge of the demands of republican life and speech" (*die Kenntnis republikanischen Lebens und Redebedarfs*).[44] Rhetoric is political anthropology.

Even when the direct applicability of rhetoric to politics was passed over, the fable of rhetoric as a kind of ur-discipline or inquiry cornucopia was often close at hand. In 1940, the classicist Wilhelm Kroll argued that the importance of Aristotle's *Rhetoric* should be assessed not just in reference to the rhetorical tradition itself but also more generally in terms of "the history of ideas writ large" (*allgemeinen Geistesgeschichte*).[45] Indeed, according to Damaschke, no one could "exhaust" (*erschöpfen*) the history of rhetoric, and the history of rhetoric traces nothing less than "the history of human cultural development as such" (*die Geschichte der menschlichen Kulturentwicklung schlechthin*).[46] If we take up ancient rhetorical democracy as a paradigm, we can say with the classical scholar and art historian Adolf Philippi that "Greco-Roman rhetoric has prepared the ground for the entirety of modern culture."[47] According to Wilhelm Dilthey, moreover, rhetoric comes to be portrayed as a kind of theoretical treasure trove for early modern hermeneutics and anthropology. Karl Vossler made the same claim but in connection with modern sociology of language. And it was only because the idea had been articulated by others that Herder went out of his way to *deny* that rhetoric might be thought of as a kind of chrysalis for the emergent queen of the humanities in the eighteenth century—namely, aesthetics.[48] In pursuing rhetoric into the disciplinary domains of philosophy, political theory, literary criticism, and history of art, the present book exhibits an

---

41. Jaeger, *Paideia*, 399.

42. Jaeger, 368: "nur das alte Problem des Adels in neuer Form."

43. Müller, *Zwölf Reden*, viii, x.

44. Ammon, "Bericht," 58.

45. Kroll, "Rhetorik," 1057.

46. Damaschke, *Geschichte der Redekunst*, 1.

47. Philippi, *Die Kunst der Rede*, 31: "die griechisch-römische Rhetorik hat der ganzen modernen Kultur . . . den Boden bereitet."

48. Dilthey, *Weltanschauung und Analyze des Menschen*, in *Gesammelte Schriften*, 2:432; Vossler, *Gesammelte Aufsätze zur Sprachphilosophie*, 100; Herder, "Die Kritischen Wälder zur Ästhetik," 373.

affinity with this sense of rhetoric as ur-discipline. I do not mean thereby to suggest that rhetoric is not also speech practice or criticism thereof. I mean only to show that the theoretical rewards for such pursuit are substantial.

TOPICAL SURVEYING

Rhetoric may be understood as discovering, articulating, and performing possibilities, and a question follows from this: what architectures might facilitate such invention? Note that "possibility" does not entail some re-quirement for novelty. In calling the first part of classical rhetoric *inventio*, one did not presume that one was "inventing" new arguments. The better and more standard translation of that Latin term has been "finding." One *finds* arguments. One locates them, distinguishes them, and brings them to hand. Gathering arguments on a topic makes them surveyable. An orator's repertoire would be significant if all the arguments on a certain topic made in the past were simultaneously available. *Sensus communis* was the Latin term that discerned not so much the arguments that had been made in the past as those arguments that had been made and then retained in cultural memory. This meant that "common sense" was in fact a way of thinking about the inferential intersections (shared syllogisms) that defined com-munities.[49] Free indirect discourse was one literary marker of this sense of the common ("it is a truth universally acknowledged . . ."), and in mod-ernist German parlance this might be a sense for "recycled speech" (*Gerede*) too. Or, as the political sociologist Siegfried Landshut put it in 1925, the decisive gesture of the orator would be the rhetorical question. One invokes or stages the public undeniability of the commonplace by asking about it in a way that *advertises* an expectation of agreement.[50]

One might regard the commonplace as a thing that *could* be said because it *had* been said (and had become cultural code). In a related way, one might suppose that the more genuine topos was the space fashioned by a ques-tion that had provoked a multitude of answers. At a deeper, more complex level, one might also suppose that a variety of cultural initiatives posed alongside one another might well reveal themselves as answers implying the existence of a culturally pressing question. Here would be the genuine topos as question. And there are many topical arrangements that perform the role of aphoristic machines.[51] The ancient Roman rhetorician Quintilian had said that "maxims" (*sententiae*) were like the eyes of oratory.[52] These maxims were the opinions that would arrest a listener midspeech, as if the orator's gaze fell on each of the audience members at the end of a sentence

49. See Vico, *Scienza nuova*, §142–43.
50. Landshut, "Über einige Grundbegriffe der Politik," 64.
51. See Marshall, "Giambattista Vico, Aphorism," 324–47.
52. Quintilian, *Institutio oratoria*, 8.5.34.

and paused for a palpable half beat. Or, thinking the metaphor, they were the sentences that saw and organized the other sentences of a speech by investing them with meaning and relief and inferential power: a maxim was an oft-deployable premise. Detachability and deployability distinguished the maxim, and we can see a desire to create a reserve army of such sentences in the early modern phenomenon of the commonplace book, including its modern German variations—Lichtenberg's *Sudelbüchern*, Goethe's *Maximen und Reflexionen*, Jochmann's *Stilübungen*.

Considering it as an array of alternative possibilities implying a question, we may think the topos in visual terms. Consider what the sociologist Georg Simmel was saying of such clustering of visual exempla in 1890: "no single work of art is forthcoming that represents the sum of all available talent or the culmination of all hitherto achieved developments in the way that the Sistine Madonna or the Medici tombs [of Michelangelo] did" for the Renaissance. In the modern age, to assemble all art possibilities, one would need "to bring together the most various works, to convene every master imaginable."[53] The best exhibitions, one might conjecture, would give spectators a sense of the problem to which the gathered works were responses. And spiritual development was to be measured in terms of a combined intensity and range of feeling. Simmel was deeply suspicious of the psychology of the exhibition, and in response he wanted to moralize. For him, the phenomenon of the exhibition was related to the evanescent sensorium of the modern city with its fetish for individualized fashionability. Such embodied advertising both reflected and fostered a specialization that "produces a hurrying from one impression to the next, an impatience while savoring, a problematic striving after a condensate of the greatest possible diversity of excitations, interests, and pleasures in the smallest possible amount of time."[54] What was the result of this hurrying and striving—discernment? No, such visual scanning produced "a blasé attitude and shallowness" (*die Blasiertheit und die Oberflächlichkeit*) that alternated with an increased irascibility in the face of perceived "tactlessness" (*Taktlosigkeit*).[55] Shorn of Simmel's moralizing, however, the description remains arresting: "the greatest load

53. Simmel, "Über Kunstausstellungen," 46: "kein einzelnes Kunstwerk läßt sich angeben, das etwa die Summe des vorhandenen Könnens, den Höhepunkt aller bisher erreichten Entwicklung so darstellte, wie die Sixtinische Madonna oder die Mediceergräber es taten; darum bedarf es des Zusammenführens des Verschiedenartigen, des Zusammenkommens aller möglichen Meister, um die Kunst der Gegenwart kennenzulernen." I am grateful to Timothy Barr for making the connection to this part of Simmel.
54. Simmel, 46–47: "gerade das Spezialistentum unserer Zeit erzeugt das Hasten von einem Eindruck zum anderen, die Ungeduld des Genießens, das problematische Trachten, in möglichst kurzer Zeit eine möglichst große Summe von Erregungen, Interessen, Genüssen zusammenzupressen."
55. Simmel, 48.

of contemporary artistry is gathered together in the smallest point and unpacks in the viewer the most concentrated and most total spectrum of feelings that art as such is capable of awakening in him."[56] This is a potent topos.

Were there alternatives within the German reception of rhetoric to Simmel's skepticism? Yes—in, for example, Baumgarten's eighteenth-century transformation of rhetorical inheritances into (among other things) a nascent discipline of "aesthetics." The Baumgarten analogues for Simmel's exhibitions were "exemplars . . . of sublime writers or painters" (*exemplaria . . . sublimium scriptorum, pictorum*), or "the words and deeds of the noblest men of the ages" (*illustrium per omnes aetates virorum facta dictaque*) displayed "as in a mirror" (*velut in speculum*). In Baumgarten's version, the task—inherited from "Horace, Cicero, Longinus" but turned to his own purposes—was not simply to gaze on assembled variations. When confronted by actions, one's task would be to reenact them in one's own person, not so that one might "understand" them but so that one might *possess* them as possibilities for action. Where Simmel imagined the art exhibition producing an oscillation between irascible oversensitivity and numb overexposure, Baumgarten was hypothesizing a practicing in exempla that cast artistic topoi as so many spiritual gymnasia.

The mirror of great deeds might seem like an antiquated imaginary, but the topos can be rejuvenated. As Baumgarten himself pointed out, taking "history to be the instructor of life" (*historia magistra vitae*) meant assuming the past would provide examples to imitate because the future would not be different in any genuinely radical way. Baumgarten did not merely repeat the past, though. He subsumed and inflected it. In part, he was responding to Longinus's *Peri hypsous*. That work was a late antique investigation of the third of the basic rhetorical modes (low, middle, and high) that dealt with everyday, significant, and extraordinary occasions, respectively. At one point, Longinus had said we are to suppose that "sublimity is the echo of a noble mind."[57] Longinus did not give much by way of explanation. Indeed, he seems to have been quoting a part of his own oeuvre that is no longer extant. He gave only a single brief but famous example of such sublimity: the silence of Ajax.

Baumgarten was more forthcoming, and he gave an account of the capacity enacted in Ajax's wordless rhetorical performance. Baumgarten rendered Longinus's Greek phrase *hypsos megalophrosynēs apēkhēma* with the Latin *magnanimitas, cuius sublimia Longinus Echo dixit*. He evinced a

---

56. Simmel, "Kunstausstellungen," 47: "die größte Kraft des heutigen Künstlertums ist in einem kleinsten Punkt gesammelt und entfaltet im Beschauer nun in gleicher Verdichtung die ganze Fülle der Gefühle, die die Kunst überhaupt in ihm zu erwecken vermag."
57. Longinus, *Peri hypsous*, 9.2: "hypsos megalophrosynēs apēkhēma."

much sharper sense of what this "magnanimity" (*magnanimitas*) might entail.[58] Magnanimity—also "greatness of soul," recall—would be something like the condition of having taken into one's own person an array of exemplary actions witnessed in life or in art. Taking these actions "in" meant acquiring them as capacities. Magnanimity would thus manifest itself in the performance of great deeds.[59] Or, perhaps more interestingly, magnanimity might also manifest itself in nonperformance: a forbearing or underperforming that implied one's capacity for greater action would be "a remarkable proof of greatness of soul in meager things" (*singulare documentum animi magni in tenuibus*).[60] This was Ajax.

Baumgarten spoke of a sense in which one might acquire all the thoughts worth thinking by exercising in the gymnasium of exempla.[61] Magnanimity began in the collecting of exempla, and it proceeded by superimposing those exempla on a body by means of imagined or perhaps physical reenactment. The plastic reader, too, would embody *all* possibilities. Often *Großmut* in German, such "capaciousness" would produce "a state of calmness" (*status tranquillitatis*).[62] In point of fact, this kind of spiritual possession of great deeds would amount in each case to a kind of *persuasio*. *Persuasio* here was a being saturated by and therefore being at one with a deed. Baumgarten described such "persuasion" as the "supernatural complement and supplement of an internal and psychological freedom" (*supernaturale libertatis internae psychologicaeque complementum ac supplementum*).[63] Similarly, the "exhibition goer" capable of metabolizing the full range of visual and spiritual material on display would become something like a monad of timely capabilities to do and to perceive.

Perhaps Simmel's dyspeptic reaction to the art exhibition revealed the absence of a strong reception of the topical dimensions of the rhetorical tradition in fin de siècle German culture. Even in a figure like Nietzsche, who had a significant interest in both rhetoric and invention, we find no real investment in the *ars topica*, which after all had been, in various incarnations, the principal engine of the first part of classical rhetoric. Nietzsche relays that Aristotle's *dunamis* definition implied that he regarded "delivery" (*Vortrag*, the fifth part of classical rhetoric) as merely incidental to rhetoric, where "invention" (*Invention*, the first part) was essential.[64] Like a number of his contemporaries, however, Nietzsche was seduced by rhetoric's

58. Baumgarten, *Ästhetik*, 378.
59. Baumgarten, 370–72.
60. Baumgarten, 348.
61. Baumgarten, 372.
62. Baumgarten, 394.
63. Baumgarten, 392.
64. Nietzsche, "Rhetorik," in *Gesammelte Werke*, 5:292.

articulation of the tropes, and he was tightly focused on them as the rhetorical inheritance that should matter for modern readers. Moreover, although his perspectivism (a sophistic inheritance in some ways) performed topical functions, it was not strictly speaking topical.

Strange but true, one of the clearest topical inheritances in late nineteenth-century or early twentieth-century Germany was Eduard David's résumé of rhetorical tactics for the socialist orator, which appeared in eight editions between 1907 and 1947. If one were an aspiring member of the party, he counseled, then public speaking would be a skill one would need. To that end, one should acquire a sense of the chief dimensions of major political issues. David urged his readers to develop what we might call a kind of "commonplace book practice" for modern politics. The goal was a "surveyable ordering" (*übersichtliche Ordnung*).[65] The instructions: identify about twenty of the most prominent contemporary political issues, and procure an equivalent number of folders or envelopes.[66] Turn these folders into what David termed "files" (*Mappen*) by filling them with material collected from the daily press. Having divided them as necessary into more specialized "subfiles" (*Sondermappen*), take whichever constellation of files and subfiles is most relevant to the speech task at hand, excerpt the most pertinent parts of its contents, and distribute these excerpts on a single large piece of paper.[67] A speech is generated from this trove of points and potential connections. The desideratum is "a lightning-fast surveyable image that is clear to the eye."[68] Surveyability implies simultaneous or near-simultaneous presence, and simultaneity implies inference. It prepares the way for perceptions of similarity, entailment, cause and effect, contrariety, and other forms of potential relation. It becomes a seedbed of hypothesis.

The point of a topical array was not simply to lay out a variety of moves that might be made in a particular context. Inventiveness might be exercised by mimetic practices that emphasized taking on the forms of various exempla, but invention itself was often a matter of attunement to the possibilities of combination and recombination offered up by the array of "raw" materials constituted by previous incursions into the matter at hand. Thus, a good deal of the ancient rhetorical tradition had emphasized consciousness with regard to the forms of connection that might be observed if one paid attention to the synthetic work orators were doing when, for example, they combined the elements drawn from the files and subfiles just discussed. This is one of the reasons why the term "topical" has so many denotations. A topos might be a particular argument regarded as exemplary, but a

65. David, *Referenten-Führer*, 49.
66. David, 50.
67. David, 56.
68. David, 56–57: "ein furs Auge klares, blitzschnell zu überblickendes Bild."

topos might also be the form of argument exhibited in such an example. Exercising in received exempla might be a matter of acquiring particular arguments, or it might also be an accustoming of oneself to the kinds of move one might make in argumentation.

In essence, Frederick Solmsen was dramatizing a shift from exempla to the argumentative forms of exempla in 1929 when he argued that the history of logic had unjustly marginalized Aristotle's *Topics* by enthroning the *Posterior Analytics* (and to a lesser extent the *Prior Analytics*).[69] Solmsen saw that the "premises" dealt with in the *Topics* were "commonplaces" (*topoi*) and not, as one might have expected, "propositions" (*protaseis*).[70] Solmsen explained the significance: "in the *Topics*, we need to recognize a complete syllogistic method, indeed, not just a complete but also a self-sufficient and autonomous syllogistic method."[71] Taking up the commonplace arguments of the discursive culture in which he lived and distilling from those examples the *kinds* of arguments one might make, Aristotle had discerned a variety of forms of argumentation. In turn, one could use the list of forms that emerged in order to discover arguments.

Why might it be important to know the forms of Greek argumentation? Here is the crucial point: if one knew the forms of argumentation, one had places in which to *look* for arguments with regard to any particular subject matter. Most canonically, in Cicero, one might look for arguments in the following "seats of argumentation" (*sedes argumenti*): "definition, partition, etymology, conjugates, genus, species, similarity, difference, contraries, adjuncts, consequents, antecedents, contradictions, causes, effects, and comparison of things greater, less, and equal."[72] For centuries (if fitfully) the rhetorical tradition built on this insight. When Solmsen said that the history of logic had not recognized the importance of Aristotle's *Topics*, he meant that because of the institutional entrenchment of logic in departments of philosophy combined with the institutional atrophy of rhetoric there was no way to stage this point about topics for his contemporary German audience other than as the revelation of a long ostracism.

For whatever reason, Solmsen was unable to establish the point about this topical syllogistic broadly. Nevertheless, we can rehearse the moves of his argument to develop a sense of what topical inquiry had been in the European tradition and what it might become in Weimar Germany. Here are those moves. Aristotle's analytical works had privileged the kinds of necessary inferential connections that might connect and that might be derived from axioms that set out a specialized field of knowledge. The

69. Solmsen, *Aristotelischen Logik und Rhetorik*, 2.
70. Solmsen, 9.
71. Solmsen, 41: "wir haben also . . . in der Topik eine vollständige *methodos peri sullogismos* anzuerkennen, und nicht nur eine vollständige, sondern auch eine autarke und autonome."
72. Cicero, *Topica*, 18.71.

Topics, on the other hand, had dealt with probabilistic inferences that belonged to no particular field of inquiry and that drew on *topoi* and not *axiomata*.[73] Attending to topical inference meant attending to the nature of probability in logic, but this did not simply entail recognizing that logic would be interested in procedures beyond those in which "if the premises are true, the conclusion must *necessarily* follow." It is not simply that topical arrangement spurs induction and abduction (although it does that too). It is also that topical arrangement pays attention to the contingency or, better, nonmonotony of inference.

Solmsen's argument was subtle but worth following. He paraphrased Aristotle in the following terms: "conclusion and counter-conclusion . . . follow from the same topoi."[74] We should not satisfy ourselves with the easy gloss here. We should not rest in the commonplace that *topoi* sensitize us dialectically to denial because they are merely probable and can be rejected. The deeper point is that we may also think of the inferential relations between or among such propositions as necessary or contingent. We should strive to grasp the significance of the difficult gloss: contingency at the level of inference means nonmonotony, which means that the *same* claim or claims may yield different or even opposite conclusions when inferentially partnered with further supplementary claims. Here is the point in abstract form: "if A and B, then Y," and yet "if A and B *and* C, then not-Y." For Solmsen (who had studied with Werner Jaeger), the *Prior* and *Posterior Analytics* were built upon Platonic assumptions about the hierarchy and structure of being. On this account, the *Topics* was in fact the more genuinely Aristotelian innovation.[75] To be sure, Solmsen's was very much a minority report in the prewar German reception of rhetoric, but that does not mean we may not orient ourselves to it and gain from the encounter.

SPECIFICATIONS OF CONTEXT

The simple articulation of possibilities is an infinite and pointless task if those possibilities are not articulated as elements of a particular context. Context is rhetoric's province too. Witness two key topoi in the German reception. One can say that philosophy is "really homesickness" (*eigentlich Heimweh*). Alternatively, rather than the desire to make a specific home, one can describe philosophy as "the drive to be at home everywhere" (*der Trieb, überall zu Hause zu sein*). Often recycled, not least in Lukács's *Die Theorie des Romans*, I would argue that these *bons mots* from Novalis voice a desire to be capable of living in the rule without having to recognize the

---

73. Solmsen, *Aristotelischen Logik und Rhetorik*, 52.
74. Solmsen, 28: "Schluß und Gegenschluß . . . lassen sich aus denselben *topoi* vollziehen."
75. The point is clearer in Solmsen, "Aristotelian Tradition," 41.

specificity, relevance, and indeed creative power of particular contexts.[76] And, on such an account, context is merely a decoration that alters the look of a thing but not its substance. All of this on the one hand. On the other hand, recognizing that "the business of philosophy is determining the universal," one can add the antistrophe that "the particular passes to rhetoric" with the nineteenth-century classicist Leonhard Spengel.[77] Here, rhetoric does not share the desire attributed to philosophy of doing away with context-specific presuppositions. Rhetoric investigates the particular as such. Yet this last formulation is limp. When he says that "the particular passes to rhetoric," Spengel lists philosophy's other as an afterthought. Thus, the task remains: how may one *think* the project of "the particular" (*das Spezielle*) in a productive way?

In the first instance, we can say that sensitivity to issues of historicity was a thematic in the modern German afterlife of the rhetorical tradition. This was a sensitivity to the dependence of oratorical practice (and therefore rhetorical theory) on particular institutional platforms. Rhetorical forms and the exigencies requiring oratorical performance would all be historically variant. As Herder said (in a classic formulation of the thought), rhetoric's "fire was extinguished as *Greek freedom* declined." Or rather, rhetoric reached its peak at the point of political crisis. Thereafter, as democracy waned, rhetoric "crept into schools and narrow courtrooms, curled up in the dust, and fell silent."[78] In the historiography of rhetoric, this is a crossroads, and one faces a choice: one can channel one's polis envy (as many have done), one can say that ceremonial oratory was more primordial than the specific democratic institutions of early Greece (as some scholars such as Jeffery Walker have done), or—following the intuition of the "poetic to rhetoric" hypothesis—one can work on the transformation of rhetoric for different institutional contexts.[79] Indeed, one can say that once produced the apparatus of rhetorical theory *must* be transformed in order to remain alive intellectually. As Geißler put it in 1914, "rhetoric is no art that simply produces itself out of itself," for "it requires the stipulation of conditions."[80] The early modern "court" (*Hof*) will have its own invention, and

76. Quoted in Lukács, *Die Theorie des Romans*, 21.
77. Spengel, "Die Definition," 499: whereas "das Allgemeine zu bestimmen, ist Sache der Philosophie," "das Spezielle fällt der Rhetorik anheim." This is one of the passages that Nietzsche repeats in his lecture notes without attribution. Nietzsche, "Rhetorik" in *Gesammelte Werke*, 5:295.
78. Herder, "Ursachen des Gesunknen Geschmacks," 125: "mit der *Redekunst* eben also. Wie *Griechenfreiheit* sank, war ihr Feuer dahin: in *Demosthenes* war sie, wie in der letzten Not, eine auflodernde Flamme. Sie kroch in Schulen und enge Gerichtsschranken, krümmte sich im Staub' und verstummte."
79. See Walker, *Rhetoric and Poetics*, 3–41.
80. Geißler, *Rhetorik*, 8: "die Redekunst ist . . . keine Kunst, die sich nur aus sich selber entwickelt"—that is to say, "sie braucht Voraussetzungen."

eighteenth-century "homiletics" (*Homiletik*) will require its own eloquence. Always and ever again, "the present requires its own art of speaking."[81] And this is a matter of classifying new content, transforming old classifications, and inventing new ones.

True, one sometimes detects a paradoxical tendency in historical consciousness sponsored by rhetoric. On the one hand, language may be regarded as the most sensitive seismograph of historical inconstancy: language registers the difference between new and old with great subtlety. On the other hand, rhetorical attention to the modishness and transience of style may also erect transhistorical categories of stylistic and, by extension, historical analysis. In 1900, Ulrich von Wilamowitz-Moellendorff—a luminary of the philological establishment against which Nietzsche had struggled—spoke of the first-century BCE Roman debate between Atticists and Asiatics as both a contest of styles and a binary set of classifications for historical representation. This debate registered the Attic as a deliberately old-fashioned style—reactionary, yet somehow pure. Wilamowitz-Moellendorff also took it to be merely one facet in the rise of two great transhistorical categories—the classical and the baroque. For him, the hothouse verbal fecundity of the Asiatic was an "ancient baroque" (*antike Barocco*). The negative connotation of the phrase had to be blanched, though, and he declared that it would be the task of philology in the coming century to index—pinpoint and categorize—this "transhistorical baroque" in ancient guise, recognizing it as a "living language even in its neologisms and its noisy ornament."[82] Here, the paradox: a universal particular.

Nevertheless, the most basic engine of rhetorical sensitivity to matters of historical contingency remained the endless work of situating particular oratorical performances—whether in one's own staging of a performance (characterizing one's moment is a basic oratorical task) or in a critical exegesis of some past performance. Rhetorical situatedness in this sense required that Fichte had to begin by specifying his usage of "we" in contriving what in 1806 and 1807 was still very much a fictitious "German nation" (*deutsche Nation*). First person plural pronoun, first interpellation.[83] Discerning "situation" requires an ability to perceive and work with the coincidental and the ironic. Just so, one must be able to stage, for example, the bare fact

81. Weise, *Politische Redner*, in the opening letter to the reader; Herder, "Sollen Wir Ciceronen auf der Kanzeln Haben?" 513; Geißler, *Rhetorik*, 22: "die Gegenwart braucht eine Redekunst."
82. Wilamowitz-Moellendorff, "Asianismus und Atticismus," 50–52: "lebendige Sprache auch in ihren Neologismen und ihrem lärmenden Schmucke."
83. Fichte, *Reden*, ix: "wir stehen im Beginn des Winters von 1807 auf 1808, rund gerechnet fünf Monate nach dem über alle Maßen unglücklichen und grausamen Friedensabschluß zu Tilsit"; "die politische Existenz Preußens so wie die von ganz Deutschland sind lediglich bedingt durch den Willen und die Interessen Napoleons."

that the Siemens Studies Society for Practical Psychology listed exemplary speeches by *both* Vladimir Lenin *and* Adolf Hitler in the appendices to its 1933 publication *Supremacy through the Art of Suggestive Speaking.*[84] Indeed, staging a rereading of Adam Müller in order to establish a context for the topos "Hitler as Orator" is surely a sign of historical contextual weakness. One may advance the notion that German rhetorical culture was distinctive and distinctively vulnerable to an orator of Hitler's type, although Josef Kopperschmitt perceptively calls this a *Sonderweg* thesis for rhetoric. But is it really possible to bring in the early nineteenth-century writings of Müller as evidence for this absence of oratorical culture in the twentieth century?[85]

Historical sensitivity also took the form of a consciousness that rules promulgated in an earlier age might or might not be applicable in a later one. In some formulations, this thought continued the insight articulated earlier by Solmsen when he observed that the same topos might yield opposing conclusions in the context of different syllogisms. History, it might be added, was precisely one of the processes that accreted new premises to existing arguments, thereby transforming the conclusions they licensed. On this view, history was a process of de- and recontextualization. In other formulations, the notion was that although a rule might be thought of as teaching the conditions of dismantling and reconstructing an exemplar (to teach, that is, the "possibility" or "performability" of an exemplar), there would be cases in which the rule appeared to have no—or at least no *immediate*—purchase on the exemplar. Setting out the conventional vision, Fichte assigned a double function to the rule as it was *supposed* to function. The rule is there "in the first place, so that we can ourselves produce something by artistic means; and, in the second, so that we may strike upon appropriate judgments with regard to the works of others."[86] As Müller said soon after, however, if the normative quality of the rule is built on its pragmatic capacity to observe and direct the dynamics of sentence-level constructions, can we really say that "the rule of Cicero or Quintilian can be applied to this wholly differently constructed language?"[87] Why should the masters of ancient Latin prose have the right to tell me whether my German is or is not worthy of praise?

One response to the question of whether rules remained in force from

84. Gerathewohl and Siemens-Studien-Gesellschaft für Praktische Psychologie, *Überlegenheit durch Suggestive Redekunst*, 215ff, 218ff.

85. See Kopperschmidt, "Endlich Angenommen im Western," 455–79.

86. Fichte, "Regeln der Dicht- und Redekunst," 62: "einerseits, damit wir selbst etwas künstlerisch darstellen können, anderseits, damit wir über die Werke anderer ein richtiges Urteil zu fällen vermögen."

87. Müller, *Zwölf Reden*, 260: "die Regel des Cicero oder Quintilian angewendet werden [kann] auf diese ganz anders gebauten Sprachen?"

one epoch to another was to say that the exemplar might teach audiences about do-ability qua reenactability. In part, this was a repetition of the point made earlier by Baumgarten that examples of greatness (of whatever kind) might function as *exemplaria*. But it is important to add that one might conceptualize the mimesis involved in Baumgarten's magnanimity as a form of legislation. That is, the exemplar did not simply inaugurate performances that were imitations of the original. The exemplar might also function as a seedbed of rules. One master to another, Goethe was boasting about the power of genius when he said of Shakespeare's *Henry IV* that "if everything were lost that has ever been preserved to us of this kind of writing, the arts of poetry and rhetoric could be completely restored out of this one play."[88] The example was generative and did not need to be thought of as something that would be exhausted by rote imitation. Indeed, Schlegel turned the idea into something like a *criterion* for adjudicating the status of a work as a "classic." The classic qua classic "must never be entirely understood" (*muß nie ganz verstanden werden*).[89] The attraction *is* an "ever deeper rethinking" (*immer tieferem Nachdenken*).[90] And, in fact, this should change our attitude to "unintelligibility" (*Unverständlichkeit*) as such. In fact, unintelligibility is not something to be dreaded or shunned. It should be celebrated, for it marks a peculiar species of creative inexhaustibility. The unintelligible does not refuse all interpretation; it produces a cornucopia of readings.[91]

In the inexhaustibility of the exemplar that was an implicit and incipient rule, we are returned to the scene that so bewitched Carl Schmitt. Here we have the moment of arbitrary undecidability, the moment distinguished by the "absence" (*Mangel*) of any overarching rule to be applied, the moment that—in the Schmittian account—could only be overcome by the exercise of a purely sovereign and therefore entirely arbitrary will. Schmitt's was one response to what the Weimar sociologist Karl Mannheim called the point "at which as yet unmapped leeway begins, where unregulated situations demand decisions."[92] As Landshut understood it, this "leeway" *was* the space of governing, for "governing is . . . in fact a continual standing in the space of decision."[93] And when he added that "decision" (*Entscheidung*) is "the grasping of a possibility" (*das Ergreifen einer Möglichkeit*), we should

88. Goethe, *Sprüche in Prosa*, 169, #473.
89. Schlegel, "Über die Unverständlichkeit," 371.
90. Schlegel, 363.
91. Schlegel, 370.
92. Mannheim, *Ideologie und Utopie*, 74: "wo der noch nicht rationalisierte Spielraum anfängt, wo *nicht* regulierte Situationen zur Entscheidung zwingen."
93. Landshut, "Über einige Grundbegriffe der Politik," 73: "regieren ist . . . eigentlich das ständige in der Entscheidung stehen."

hear intimations of the word *Entscheidung* in its literal denotation as "de-splaying." The pun almost works in English, too, for "de-cision" is the neutralizing of a split, not an "in-cision" but rather the evisceration of multiple possibilities by choosing a path.[94]

In the context of the decision especially, one might understand possibility as the bane of humanity. Possibility was the mode of humanity's existence as a "being characterized by lack" (*Mangelwesen*), to use Herder's term. This term was taken up in the twentieth-century philosophical anthropologies of Arnold Gehlen and Helmut Plessner.[95] Their conception of lack constituted a studied inversion of the (perhaps ridiculous) notion that philosophy aimed to be equally at home everywhere. This concept of a being characterized by lack declared that homelessness was constitutive of the human condition. Exigency would never be domesticated by rules, and no home space of routinized everydayness would endure. Humanity's "capacity to make the absent present" (*Darstellungsfähigkeit*) would mean that the here and now could never be a total home.[96] And this became "eccentricity" (*Exzentrizität*), which was not so much oddness as a distance from "the"—or rather any—center.[97] "Habitat-free" (*Umweltfrei*) and "world-open" (*weltoffen*) might sound like compliments when bestowed as characteristics on humanity. In fact, these terms could be read as curses, as they were by Max Scheler.[98]

Within the German tradition, there were alternatives to the pessimistic gloss of "lack" (*Mangel*). As he was developing a hermeneutic account of the humanities, Wilhelm Dilthey had contended that understanding would always take the individual as its object.[99] Equally, one might argue that capturing and then transforming the particular was one of the basic aesthetic tasks. Aesthetic judgment itself might be understood as the generation of potential rules out of particular cases. The unavoidable commonplace here was Kant's delineation of reflective judgment in the third critique. This was "reflective" (*reflektierende*) as distinct from "determinative" (*bestimmende*) judgment. Instead of perceiving a particular under an already extant rule, reflective judgment took on the task of *thinking* the particular in its life as a potential rule.[100] In the Weimar context, we find Max Horkheimer arguing for the significance of reflective judgment because of its role in "discovery, deliberation, research, that is its *preparatory* work for determinative

94. Landshut, 72.
95. Plessner, *Die Stufen*, xiv–xv.
96. Plessner, 288.
97. Plessner, 291–92, 316.
98. Scheler, *Stellung des Menschen im Kosmos*, in *Späte Schriften*, 32.
99. Dilthey, *Aufbau der geschichtlichen Welt*, in *Gesammelte Schriften*, 7:212.
100. Kant, *Kritik der Urteilskraft*, 16.

knowing."[101] As a surprising denouement to that microhistory, we might also add that reflective judgment finds essentially no place in Horkheimer and Adorno's *Dialectic of Enlightenment* despite, as we saw in the previous chapter, that work's emphasis on the particular and its deep scepticism of the universal.

One could argue that genuine particularity might only ever be a function of serial and "individuating" (*bestimmender*) context. This was the logic of Adorno's critique of Kierkegaard and Kierkegaardian constructions of aesthetic life: aesthetes, even existential ones, would always ultimately be but connoisseurs of the moment. These connoisseurs delect the particular and luxuriate in its distinctiveness. Such delectation entails a slavery to the fleeting, for, in the words that Adorno relayed from Kierkegaard's *Either/Or*, "you live forever in the moment; your life falls apart into individual experiences lacking context, and accounting for it is impossible for you."[102] This is a retreat from genuinely historical, genuinely material, genuinely public life into an ever-narrower spiritual boudoir of minute and private sensations. Someone like Dilthey—who shared an interest in the lived experiences of individuals—would emphasize the "life horizon" (*Lebenshorizont*) as the kind of "context" (*Zusammenhang*) that might restore the privatized life of interior feelings to the world surrounding it.[103] In contrast, Adorno chose the "historical concretion" of Hegel and then claimed to have overcome the remnant idealism of the Hegelian project by reconsidering it within a more thorough conception of humanity's dialectical metabolism with nature.[104]

If, like Horkheimer and Adorno, one were suspicious of premature or overtidy attempts to bring the case into the orbit of a rule, one might alternatively say that the task of aesthetic judgment would be the ever-finer discernment of situatedness. Gustav Gerber, whose *Language as Art* was a significant influence on Nietzsche, was intent on confecting a lineage for himself at precisely this juncture. In 1871, Gerber said that for Aristotle poetry had been primarily an "imitating (or mimesis) of actions and situations" (*Nachahmung von Handlungen und Situationen*) that rendered their particularity in some sense communicable.[105] When Lessing took up this Aristotelian gambit in the eighteenth century, he emphasized that we

101. Horkheimer, *Kants Kritik der Urteilskraft*, 18: "Entdeckung, Überlegung, Forschung, also *Vorarbeit* für bestimmende Erkenntnis."

102. Adorno, *Kierkegaard*, in *Gesammelte Schriften*, 2:96: "du lebst immer nur im Moment; dein Leben zerfällt in zusammenhangslose Einzelerlebnisse, und es ist bei dir unmöglich, es zu erklären."

103. For various conceptualizations of context in Dilthey, see *Aufbau der geschichtlichen Welt*, in *Gesammelte Schriften*, 7:121, 195–97.

104. Adorno, *Kierkegaard*, in *Gesammelte Schriften*, 2:133: "historische Konkretion."

105. Gerber, *Sprache als Kunst*, 1:63.

should understand "action" (*Handlung*) in terms of the Greek term *praxis* and that, as a result, the zone specified as the grammar of the momentary or particular or case-like might be equally a "doing" (*Thun*) or a "suffering" (*Leiden*).[106] Speaking in his own voice, Gerber called the mediated articulation of these moments (whether in sculpture or in painting or in verse) the "self-explanatory" (*sprechend*). More basic than a search for regularity was this attention to the communicability of the particular, and this Gerber said was "the essence of the art of language" (*das Wesen der Sprachkunst*).[107]

Discernment, what is more, was not an end in itself. It might be a means to the end of refining the very organs of sense and articulation. When he said that the Greeks used to hold competitions to see who could bestow the most graceful kiss, Herder was attempting to ridicule the ancients. We were to think of such competition as aesthetic agon gone mad. Or, more precisely, Herder was attempting to ridicule not the Greeks themselves but rather the mindless forms of Grecophilia that existed in the eighteenth-century German academy. Any education system that prized "grace" (*Grazie*) above all else would produce "apes that imitate suavity, life-sized dolls hiding straw and wood under the clothing of beauty, or at most marionettes."[108] But, really, would an ability to distinguish and take note of a thousand different kinds of kiss not be in and of itself good? Would a world that practiced such differentiation not be richer, more perceptive, more capacious? Quite possibly, we might respond. And if such a world chose the regions of its emergent attending with care then such discernment might be essential to political capacity. Back to Aristotle, to glean from the *Posterior Analytics* the idea that "all living beings have a certain innate capacity to distinguish (*dunamis kritikē*) sensation (*aisthesis*)."[109] Forward to Nietzsche, where, in connection to rhythm, we are told that even the "subtlest sensation" will be "refined by rhetoric."[110] Cut to Gerber, for whom "differentiation [*Sonderung*] is the course of culture."[111] On these accounts, discernment is almost the opposite of a privately delectable connoisseurship.

Differentiation did not entail atomization, and genuine engagement with the particular did not necessarily mean fetishizing the moment to distinguish

106. Gerber, 1:64.
107. Gerber, 1:42.
108. Herder, "Grazie in der Schule," 30: "Affen, die Artigkeit nachahmen, Puppen in Lebensgröße, die unter den Kleidern der Schönheit, Stroh und Holz verbergen, oder höchstens Marionetten."
109. Aristotle, *Posterior Analytics*, 99b35–36; cited by Gerber, *Sprache als Kunst*, 1.149: "alle lebenden Wesen haben eine gewise angeborene Fähigkeit zu unterscheiden (*dunamis kritikē*) die Empfindung (*aisthesis*)."
110. Nietzsche, "Griechische Rhythmik," in *Werke*, 2:334: the "feinste Empfindung" will be "durch die Rhetorik gesteigert."
111. Gerber, *Sprache als Kunst*, 1:74: "Sonderung ist eben der Gang der Cultur."

it as simply an irreducible *unum*. Ways might be found to articulate the context or movement or background out of which such a moment might emerge. Thus, Nietzsche parsed rhetorical "conjuring images with words" (*enargeia*) as the "lively making present" (*leibhafte Vergegenwärtigung*) of an object against the background of merely "contingent circumstances" (*Nebenumstände*). Differentiation is also the work of distinguishing between figure and ground in an image. Howsoever economically one might render these two planes of the verbalized image, the action had to be seen to rise up out of a scene. More crucial was what techniques of perspicacity one might develop in order to deepen one's sense of "contingent circumstances" to the point that one's core concern might count as genuinely embedded—and therefore emergent.[112]

To understand the rhetorical approach to context, we can think of it as the piecemeal and serial removal of the blank *ceteris paribus* rider that is implicit in general theses. In classical rhetoric, three levels were usually distinguished, but an infinite number of gradations would be theoretically possible. In principle, there would be no necessary end to the circumstances accumulated by what we might call "rhetorical casuistic," but the ancient rhetoricians offer us three levels and three pairs of terms in both Greek and Latin, moving from most universal to least. The *thesis* or *propositum* might be "Is it wrong to kill?" The *hypothesis* or *causa* might be "Is it wrong to kill in time of civil war?" And the *peristasis* or *negotium* might be "Was it wrong for Cicero to kill Lentulus when he did?" In the eighteenth century, Johann Georg Sulzer reduced the gradation to two when he supplied the German translations *Allgemeine* and *Besonders* for *propositum* and *causa*.[113] Wilhelm Kroll returned to three when he specified *allgemeine Fälle*, *kommende Fälle*, and *Bedingtheit* for thesis, hypothesis, and peristasis.[114]

It is less important, however, to memorize terminological taxonomies than it is to recognize that the literary construction of "circumstance" was a function of parataxis and its management in grammar. With its elaborate hypotaxis, the Ciceronian period was exquisitely circumstantial. Its amalgam of grammars permitted the perception of relevant conditionalities in a kind of sequenced quasi simultaneity. Seriality would remain important because every turn of the sentence might itself also be turned, but the compositioning of the whole was decisive. In Dilthey's phrasing, the movement from a simple "experience" (*Erfahrung*) to an "adventure" (*Erlebnis*) was the embedding of, for example, a dominant present tense in a carapace of other tenses: pluperfects and future perfects, perhaps, together with ablative

112. Nietzsche, "Griechischen Beredsamkeit," in *Gesammelt Werkē*, 5:13.
113. Sulzer, *Theorie der schönen Künste*, 2:958
114. Kroll, "Rhetorik," 1095.

absolute proxies. In this way, one might generate a temporal manifold, a more or less tightly woven tissue involving narrative.[115]

Just so, elsewhere in the classical rhetorical corpus we encounter the startling assertion that *contextus* would be something like a measure of the tightness of a stylistic weave or the degree to which a speech might exhibit "of-a-piece-ness" and resist fragmentation. Per Quintilian's usage, *contextus* was the quality of hanging together that a speech might possess.[116] The opposite of "context" was, thus, fragmentation or atomization. *Contextus* would achieve hypotaxis by gathering together the fragments of parataxis. And, in parts of the German reception of rhetoric, we detect a similar concern for the degree to which a situation was describable as a matrix of torsional forces. Dilthey was echoing this idea when he cited Flacius's usage of *contextus* (not simply *circumstantiae* but also *harmoniae*) in order to think about the relationship between nascent Christian historiography in the German Reformation and the development of hermeneutics.[117] "Englished" in an early modern anthropology that Dilthey thought was part of the story he wanted to tell, *contextus* became Hobbes's "contexture," a quality of smoothness in speaking.[118]

THE SHIFT OF TROPE

I have been arguing that in its German reception, too, rhetoric was a power, a power to find possibilities and a power to find possibilities as dimensions of particular historical situations. Now I turn to one of the principal aspects of the German reception of rhetoric—namely, concern for tropes and figures. The German inflection of the classical rhetorical repertoire emphasized the sense in which tropes and figures were formal expositions of the various kinds of possible motion. Here is my core claim in this section, expressed in a concise and somewhat cryptic way: draping a possibility over an actuality generates a distension akin to the distance one travels when fusing together the parts of a trope or figure. The structure of that continuation out of actuality into distinct possibilities can be analyzed in relation to both rhetoric's figures and tropes.

Conventional definitions of the term "trope" are common enough in the German reception being considered here, but we can also detect echoes of rarer and finer conceptualizations achieved in antiquity that saw tropes as particular engagements with motion. Quite conventionally, the eighteenth-century German thinker Johann Christoph Gottsched repeated Quintilian's

115. Dilthey, *Aufbau der geschichtlichen Welt*, in *Gesammelte Schriften*, 7:140, 192–96.
116. Quintilian, *Institutio oratoria*, 10.7.26.
117. Dilthey, *Weltanschauung und Analyze des Menschen*, in *Gesammelte Schriften*, 2.128.
118. Hobbes, *Leviathan*, 19.

definition of a trope as *verbi, vel sermonis a propia significatione in aliam cum virtute mutatio*, rendering that phrase as "words taken in senses different from those commonly attributed to them."[119] Richard Volkmann was repeating and tweaking the topos in 1872 when he produced this same quotation from Quintilian but augmented it with what he regarded as the better formulation of the fourth-century grammarian Charisius, according to whom "trope" was "a word transferred from its own meaning to another comparison on account of necessity or cultivation."[120] The shift from difference to transfer encourages us to intuit the directionality that is important to the sense of tropic and figurative shift that I am emphasizing.

If we wish to remain in the conservative mainstream of the topos, then we should emphasize the phrase "its own meaning" (*propia significatione*), which is common to the definitions relayed by both Gottsched and Volkmann. On the other hand, if we wish to develop a minoritarian and more creative dimension of the topos, we should attend instead to the terms *mutatio* and *translata*. Decisive here is neither the "proper" signification (which, we assume, must precede the tropic usage) nor the particular context into which that signification is inserted. It is the shift that is generative. Indeed, Volkmann felt compelled to add that the Latin translation for the originally Greek term *tropos* was *motus* (motion).[121] Fleshing out the thought, we may add that Quintilian had said "the body when held bolt upright has but little grace" and "curve [*flexus*], I might almost call it motion [*motus*] . . . , gives an impression of action and animation [*adfectum*]."[122] For Quintilian, *motus* implied animation. It was not that the curved could capture the movement entailed by a verb. It was rather that the double exposition suggested by a trope encouraged a listener or reader to engage with the trope by shuttling backward and forward from one side of the trope to the other. The comparative dimension of a trope (similar to similar, part to whole, cause to effect, dissimilar to dissimilar, to name only some of those dimensions) created a distance that the recipient of the trope was to negotiate. One could think of animation here as something like the process of looking into a stereoscope, looking now with both eyes, now just with the left, now just with the right.

When he said in 1887 that "the real core of poetry, lived experience

---

119. Gottsched, *Ausfürliche Redekunst*, 272: "Wörter, die man in andern Bedeutungen nimmt, als die sie gemeiniglich haben"; Quintilian, *Institutio oratoria*, 8.6.1.

120. Volkmann, *Rhetorik der Griechen und Römer*, 354: "dictio translata a propia significatione ad non propriam similitudinem necessitates aut cultis gratia."

121. Volkmann, 354. For usage of *motus* in the sense of trope, see Quintilian, *Institutio oratoria*, 9.1.2.

122. Quintilian, *Institutio oratoria*, 2.13.9–11: "nam recti quidem corporis vel minima gratia est; nempe enim adversa sit facies et demissa brachia et iuncti pedes et a summis ad ima rigens opus. Flexus ille et, ut sic dixerim, motus dat actum quondam et adfectum."

[*Erlebnis*], entails a relation between inside and outside," Dilthey was reaching for an embodiment of the tropic as such in motion. This line of inquiry takes us to the heart of Dilthey's hermeneutic project. But "inside and outside" (*Innen und Außen*) are vapid words. Dilthey tried a second pairing, "spirit and cloak," and again, "ensoulment and sensualization," and yet again, "the meaningfulness of sequence in shape or sound and the imagistic conspicuousness of the fleeting mental state." Each substitution of one pair by the next is an example of the tropic shifting Dilthey was trying to specify. Each attempt to cast the idea in a specific verbal formulation was rejected, and each shift from one tropic suggestion to the next was an attempt to illustrate the serial dissatisfaction of a motive principle that cannot be captured by a single instantiation. "The eye of an artist," Dilthey said, "sees such things everywhere."[123] What is more, the doubleness of the "stereoscopy" here is conative impulse. It investigates the various ways in which a figure can pull against its own movement.

Dilthey certainly knew that rhetoric was the discipline that had done most to analyze the different forms of tropic stereoscopy. He said that rhetoric had in many ways done the work of poetics more thoroughly than poetics itself but that rhetoric "has unfortunately remained in the stage of development it achieved in antiquity." To his way of thinking, rhetoric had remained "an elementary morphology and method." It "has not yet made any progress toward becoming a knowledge of causes." That last phrase, "knowledge of causes" (*Kausalerkenntnis*), is both opaque and crucial.[124] Only considerably later in the same piece did Dilthey offer a glimpse of his true point. This "causal approach" was to take as its object the "imagistic richness" (*Bilderreichtum*) of a Shakespeare or a Calderón. This was an "imagistic richness" that sequenced "the unchecked flooding and streaming of this constant in-luster-and-light-bathed movement of the poetic imagination." What was the "point of origin" (*Ausgangspunkt*) for this causal approach? Nothing other than "the determinations of shape [*Formbestimmungen*] concerning the trope that the ancients have bequeathed."[125] In animation, motion itself is not represented but must

123. Dilthey, "Einbildungskraft des Dichters," in *Gesammelte Schriften*, 6:226: "wir erlautern dies zunächst an den *Tropen*. Der reale Kern der Poesie, das Erlebnis, enthält eine Beziehung des Innen und Außen, 'Geist und Kleid,' Beseelung und Versinnlichung, die Bedeutsamkeit der Gestalt oder Lautfolge und die bildliche Sichtbarkeit für das flüchtige Seelische: so sieht überall ein Künstlerauge."

124. Dilthey, 6:123: "die nächstverwandte Wissenschaft, die Rhetorik, ist leider auf dem Standpunkt stehen geblieben, den sie im Altertum erreicht hatte. Sie ist eine elementare Formenlehre und Technik. Sie hat noch keinen Schritt getan, der Kausalerkenntnis sich anzunähern."

125. Dilthey, 6:227: "der unseren Geschmack oft verletzende Bilderreichtum Shakespeares oder Calderóns ist ungehemmtes Fluten und Strömen dieser beständigen, in Glanz und Licht getauchten Bewegung in einer dichterischen Phantasie. Einer solchen Kausalbetrachtung

always be inferred in the gap between static images. Just so, the work of all tropes is properly inferential, for it is the formal quality of the unstated relation between components that drives the work of trope, which—as Dilthey was confirming here—is ultimately fundamental to the inferential life of poets themselves.

Whereas ancient rhetoric seemed to take great pleasure in discerning, naming, and cataloging an ever-larger number of tropes, modern rhetoric has often exhibited an almost too neatly inverted tendency to reduce this raft of categories to an ever-smaller number of "master tropes," but we should understand this inversion as an attempt to think of tropes as basic forms of inferential motion. We can elaborate variations on the topos. When he observed that rhetoric was not only a "science of speaking" (*Wissenschaft des Sprechens*) but also "a science of thinking" (*eine Wissenschaft des Denkens*), Sulzer was articulating a presupposition that is important to the assertion that the tropes are cognitive.[126] Even as he thought it natural that some should be dispensed with and others should be amended, Gerber was grateful for the quantity of classifications offered up by the ancient trope surveys.[127] Like his Neapolitan contemporary Giambattista Vico, Gottsched thought the tropes might be organized under four basic headings: metaphor, synecdoche, metonymy, and irony (and in this both may have been following Vossius.)[128] Perhaps such "master-tropification" dulled one's sense of the biodiversity inherent in tropic life. More often than not, however, these taxonomic simplifications were accompanied by a more explicit concern for the inferential and psychomotive work of tropes.

Others have pursued the issue more recently, but perhaps the sharpest articulation of the connection between tropes and inference came from Leibniz in the midst of his responses to Locke's *Essay Concerning Human Understanding*. In his *New Essays*, Leibniz contended that Locke had not thought his theory of the association of ideas deeply enough. If one pursued the point, it became clear that various associations of ideas could be cataloged and better understood by using the tropes as classificatory devices. Similarity, part/whole, cause/effect, contrariety—these were basic formal relationships with which to think the (inferred) association of ideas. The rhetorical armature thus offered a wealth of specifications and hypotheses.[129] While noting that the tropes could be theorized either by rhetoric or

---

können die Formbestimmungen über den Tropus, welche uns die Alten hinterlassen haben, Ausgangspunkte einer tieferen Erkenntnis werden."

126. Sulzer, *Theorie der schönen Künste*, 2:960.

127. Gerber, *Sprache als Kunst*, 1:v.

128. Gottsched, *Ausfürliche Redekunst*, 274.

129. Leibniz, *Nouveaux essais*, 135. According to Leibniz, people use the "figures … de rhétorique" (135) as templates to organize their perceptions. Compare Hume, *Treatise of Human Nature*, 45.

by grammar, the classical philologist Christian Karl Reisig referred almost without thinking to metaphor, synecdoche, and metonymy as "associations of ideas" (*Ideenassociationen*).[130] Gerber would quote this line from Reisig, and he would understand "association of ideas" as a process building on the "impulses" (*Reizen*) that stimulated thought in moments of impressed pleasure and pain.[131]

By the time we get to Nietzsche (for whom, recall, Gerber was an important source), we encounter the assertion that cognitive transformations performed in the processes of human understanding and occurring before language are already tropic in nature. As Nietzsche famously put it, "a nerve impulse, first translated into an image! First metaphor!" Thereafter, "the image further transformed into a sound! Second metaphor!"[132] In the Nietzschean reading, the tropes are absolutely protoconceptual. Indeed, as Nietzsche had put it earlier (in the *Birth of Tragedy*), "for the true poet, metaphor is not a rhetorical figure but rather a place-holding image that truly floats for him in the place of a concept."[133] Privileging metaphor, Nietzsche then declared that "each concept arises through treating as the same that which is not the same."[134] Tropes emerge not in luxury and choice but amid a paucity of concepts, and it is a physiologically embedded perceptual process.

To embed the tropes at the level of conception, thought, and inference was to reject an account in which tropes were a function of surplus. Predictably, therefore, one does encounter in the German tradition repetitions of the Ciceronian topos that "just as clothes were first invented to protect us against cold and afterward began to be used for the sake of adornment and dignity as well, so the metaphorical employment of words was begun because of poverty but was brought into common use for the sake of entertainment."[135] Thrice-boiled, we find the idea recycled in Adolf Philippi's conventional acknowledgment that "among all peoples, artful prose comes after poetry."[136] Commonplaces repeated without rationale do not always

130. Reisig, *Vorlesungen über lateinische Sprachwissenschaft*, 287.
131. Gerber, *Sprache als Kunst*, 1:258, 359 (where Reisig is cited).
132. Nietzsche, "Wahrheit und Lüge," in *Gesammelte Werke*, 6:79: "ein Nervenreiz, zuerst übertragen in ein Bild! Erste Metapher" and then "das Bild wieder nachgeformt in einem Laut! Zweite Metapher!"
133. Nietzsche, *Geburt der Tragödie*, in *Gesammelte Werke*, 3:60: "die Metapher ist für den ächten Dichter nicht eine rhetorische Figur, sondern ein stellvertretendes Bild, das ihm wirklich, an Stelle eines Begriffes, vorschwebt." See also Nietzsche, "Wahrheit und Lüge," in *Gesammelte Werke*, 6.82—where being able to "volatilize" (*verflüchtigen*) tropes into concepts is what differentiates humans from other animals.
134. Nietzsche, "Wahrheit und Lüge," in *Gesammelte Werke*, 6:80: "jeder Begriff ensteht durch Gleichsetzen des Nichtgleichen."
135. Cicero, *De oratore*, 3.38.155.
136. Philippi, *Die Kunst der Rede*, 9: "Kunstmäßige Prosa ist bei allen Völkern später als Poesie."

inspire enduring adherence, however. When Wilhelm Wackernagel felt himself duty bound to accept that poetry preceded prose, he could not resist adding that this could only have been true in literary history, because "of course" in ordinary everyday language-use prose would have come first.[137] Repeating the conclusions, he had forgotten the arguments.

We should not read what might otherwise look like distaste for ornament as a rejection of the tropic as such. Such distaste for ornament might, in fact, be a rejection of the merely decorative as a form that had become divorced from function. As Cicero had implied, the ornamental as such only developed once tropes had become unnecessary. Tropes became unnecessary when they were inserted to add flourish to a phrase rather than to advance some agenda that could not be expressed literally when a particular language possessed no tools for that particular purpose. Dilthey was gesturing toward this original indistinguishability between trope and purpose when he said, in reference to Goethe's way of expressing himself, that "in every case there is a situation, a feeling about his state, and a trope in which he expresses himself." Trope is psychodynamic because it is the product of "a feeling about a state." Similarly, Dilthey was rejecting the account of trope as mere accoutrement when he drew from Goethe's own performances the inference that "the image, the comparison, the trope do not enter the representation as clothing thrown over a body, for they are there more in the manner of skin."[138] If we find ourselves falling into the inference that a trope will be merely decorative because a poet like Goethe will add it for the benefit of a reader, we should consider the further hypothesis that a great many emotions are always already responses to representations of ourselves by and for others.

We must understand the rhetorical category of decoration in its double aspect as architectonic and as surplus. To do that, we would do well to recall—with Gottfried Semper, the nineteenth-century art historian—the homonymy performed by the Greek word *kosmos*. The word denoted both the cosmic and the cosmetic simultaneously. The stars would be both jewels to the world and indexes of a fundamental "lawfulness and world-ordering" (*Gesetzlichkeit und Weltordnung*).[139] Thus, when Nietzsche said that Cicero was "the ornamental man of a world empire," that his "political deeds were decoration," and that he was the discoverer of "beautiful passion," we should not get carried away by the exquisite viciousness of these insults. We should instead attend to Nietzsche's sense that Ciceronian excess establishes a type. "Task," Nietzsche told himself: "psychologically clarifying

---

137. Wackernagel, *Poetik, Rhetorik, und Stilistik*, 238.

138. Dilthey, "Einbildungskraft des Dichters," in *Gesammelte Schriften*, 6:227: "das Bild, die Vergleichung, der Tropus nicht in der Darstellung hinzutreten, wie Gewand, das über einen Korper geworfen wird, vielmehr sind sie dessen natürliche Haut."

139. Semper, *Gesetzmäßigekeit des Schmuckes*, 5.

the coming into being of such a nature."[140] We see once again the senses in which stylistic is more originally psychodynamic, for the sequence of displacements in a speech will reveal the structure of displacements in a mind.

When he called ornament a crime, we probably have no idea of whether the fin de siècle architectural radical Alfred Loos was responding in some way to Cicero's account of the double aspect of ornament (necessary at first, ostentatious later). Nevertheless, if we want to understand Loos's polemic, we must begin by grasping its ironic and apparently inconsistent quality. His core contention was *not* that all ornament is crime. His point was instead that "what is natural among the Papuan people and with children is a symptom of degeneration among modern peoples."[141] As we can see, this was not simply a manifesto declaring that form would follow function. It was a nascent cultural anthropology, complete with age-of-imperialism baggage. And, when Loos added that "cultural evolution is identical with the disconnection of ornament from use-objects," he was implicitly accepting the premise that originally ornamentation and use had been coeval.[142] And this was Siegfried Kracauer's position, too: fetishization of ornament was a late modern style, because it could pose as "*pure* dalliance" (*Selbstzweck*)—I translate for emphasis. For Kracauer, extremes of ornamentation amounted to a self-defeating pseudoescape "from the ruling economic system of aspired-to rationality."[143] The machine precision of Tiller-girl thigh—practically an uncountable noun in its hall-of-mirrors iteration—exceeded erotic function and was entirely without purpose. That was the rather deflating point.

ORIENTATION TO BELIEF

We learned earlier that it was possible to think of rhetoric as not simply a power of finding means of persuasion but also a power of identifying the believable as such. There was no talk of *Mitteln* in *to endechomenon pithanon* (no Greek term anchoring "means"). There was only the possible and the believable as such. In this section, I pursue the point that belief has been one of rhetoric's great preoccupations. We may understand the originally Aristotelian power of distinguishing the believable as an ability to locate a

140. Nietzsche, "Cicero," in *Gesammelte Werke*, 7:386: "der decorative Mensch eines Weltreichs," "politischen Thaten sind Decoration," "schönen Leidenschaft"; "Aufgabe: das Werden einer solchen Natur psychologisch zu erklären."
141. Loos, "Ornament und Verbrechen," 193: "was beim Papua und Kinde natürlich ist, ist beim modernen Menschen eine Degenerationserscheinung."
142. Loos, 193: "Evolution der Kultur ist gleichbedeutend mit dem Entfernen des Ornamentes aus dem Gebrauchsgegenstande" (emphasis removed).
143. Kracauer, *Ornament der Masse*, 52, 54: "von dem herrschenden Wirtschaftssystem erstrebten Rationalität."

position or positions that could hold firm at least provisionally within the shifting field of relevance that the tropes and their inferential fantasies might have brought into being. We may also understand this power as a capacity to discern the faces that might be worn as masks in particular situations. These "faces" would be the stances one might adopt without collapsing immediately under the weight of public incredulity.

Nietzsche's rendering of *to endechomenon pithanon* as "everything potentially verisimilar and persuasive" (*alles mögliche Wahrscheinliche und Überzeugende*) was unusual, but it was not idiosyncratic. We can locate similar accounts in other German sources. Taken together, these readings yield the sense that *to pithanon* was something like a plausible "stance" or "move." Volkmann was providing standard translations when he relayed Isocrates's injunction that one ought to keep things probable in matters of narration. The classical terms that he arranged around "probable" (*wahrscheinlich*) were *pithanē, verisimilis, probabilis,* and *credibilis.*[144] In his Erlangen dissertation of 1910, Friedrich Ackermann noted that one of the primary testimonies for Aristotle's usage of the term *pithanon* was the famous passage in the *Poetics* distinguishing between actions as represented on the one hand by historians and by playwrights on the other. The latter might attend more independently to matters of form, but whereas historians would be free to relay all manner of unlikely things that did actually happen, poets would remain bound by the always evolving rules of verisimilitude. Playwrights could not defend their creations by saying, "Well, yes, it does seem implausible, but truth is stranger than fiction." Ackermann alluded to a "law of the probable" (*Gesetz des eikos*) operating with regard to both "delineation of action" and "sketching of character." Indeed, Ackermann concluded, "the concepts *eikos* and *pithanon* were . . . in many instances used without distinction."[145] In its premodern meaning (before its radical statisticalization in the science of large numbers), "the probable" meant something like "the probe-able." With the improvised hyphenation, I mean to specify that which is "able-to-be-probed" or that which is "capable-of-withstanding-scrutiny" without appearing unbelievable.

Nietzsche went on to emphasize the aesthetic and even visual dimension of *pithanon*, and we, too, should focus on this point in order to unpack what Nietzsche was getting at when he said that *pithanon* was a way of standing with regard to something. In order to identify *to endechomenon pithanon*, one had to consider a matter's inscenation. A potential to be exhibited and to appear was already one of the distinguishing characteristics of the plausible, Nietzsche added, and every artifice in rhetorical performance

---

144. Volkmann, *Die Rhetorik der Griechen und Römer*, 113.
145. Ackermann, "Das Pithanon bei Sophokles," 1: "die Begriffe *eikos* und *pithanon* werden . . . auch vielfach unterschiedslos gebraucht."

ought to be made dependent on *pithanon*. *Pronuntiatio* was the rhetorical term of art he deployed here for "performance."[146] Nor did Nietzsche fail to incorporate *pithanon* into an agonistic account of performance. As he construed it, "wonder at the warrior is a core means of generating the credible, *pithanon*."[147] These are the contextual elements to bring to bear when deciding what Nietzsche was emphasizing when he relayed that "it is not things that enter into consciousness but rather the manner in which we stand to them, the *pithanon*."[148] In the first instance, to be sure, we should think of these stances as "belief" or "disbelief." We stand in relation to things primarily in terms of our credulity or incredulity. The performance offered up strikes us as probable or improbable, and we react not so much to the performance as to our reaction to that performance. We can love or hate ourselves for loving it. In reality, though, it seems as if Nietzsche wants to draw our attention to the full range of emotional reactions to "things." In addition to credulity and incredulity, we react to our reactions of desire and aversion, hope and fear—the whole zoology of irritability.

Thus, although "belief" might be a zero point with regard to a position, it would come with an array of emotional contours beginning with relief. Doubt is stressful; belief relieves. On this reading, "belief" is something like sinking into a position or the reception of that position without remainder. Belief is indistinguishability between agent and stance, whether that stance is being taken up in one's own name or is being modeled under the name of another. Nietzsche claimed that what passed for truth *did* have an emotional tincture, a pathos no less. In fact, he argued that this tincture was "believing" (*Glauben*).[149] There was no "drive to knowledge and truth" (*Trieb nach Erkenntniss und Wahrheit*). There was simply a drive to *believe* in a truth.[150] Belief might eventually be a *forgetting* of the tropic work that had gone into "cognizing" the world such that one's reactions to things came to appear simply as the things themselves.[151] The point was that belief qua credulity was a kind of anesthetic and that the somnambulism of belief was a kind of much-prized resting.

Indeed, elsewhere in the German reception of rhetoric we can discern moments at which the ratcheting up of disbelief into incredulity generated a much more precise emotional tincture, and at these moments it makes

146. Nietzsche, "Rhetorik," in *Gesammelte Werke*, 5:292.
147. Nietzsche, "Rhetorik," in *Gesammelte Werke*, 5:308: "die admiratio des Kämpfers ist ein Hauptmittel des *pithanon*."
148. Nietzsche, "Rhetorik," in *Gesammelte Werke*, 5:298: "nicht die Dinge treten ins Bewusstsein, sonder die Art, wie wir zu ihnen stehen, das *pithanon*."
149. Nietzsche, "Wahrheit und Lüge," in *Gesammelte Werke*, 6:99.
150. Nietzsche, 6:96.
151. Nietzsche, 6:84.

sense to infer that emotions can be understood more generally as imagined arrangements of stance. Take for example Theodor Gomperz's 1903 account of emotional life as described in book 2 of Aristotle's *Rhetoric*. Sitting, as he put it, "at the apex of the passions" (*an der Spitze der Affekte*), the first emotion examined by Aristotle was *Zorn*. This was "anger" or rage in the mode of spleen. As rendered by Gomperz, Aristotle's definition of this emotion was something like a painting that united multiple scenes in an unframed and interpenetrating way. This splenetic anger was actually "a passionate desiring" (*ein leidvolles Erlangen*) eroticized in the imagination of "a real or apparent vengeance" (*wirklicher oder scheinbarer Vergeltung*).[152] Imagining the scene of vengeance would place one in the midst of an array of postures.

Reading carefully, we can discern the embedding of scenes within the scene of retribution. Framing the tale, one visualizes another scene that depicts "a real or perceived slight" (*wirkliche oder scheinbare Kränkung*), equal and opposite—that is, responsive—to the specificity of the retaliation fantasy. Gomperz's emphasis on *wirklich oder scheinbar* here doubles what is in the Greek a single word (*phainomenēs*), and it coheres with Nietzsche's sense that we react to our own reactions. It is less important that there *is* a slight or that there *is* a revenge than that it *seems* so. And, farther in the background (one order of representation beneath the slight and its revenge), we have a third scene paired with a fourth that represents in diptych the character or position or history of the offender and then the offended. To both Aristotle and Gomperz, it was important to stage the *unearned* quality of this slight. As Gomperz rendered it, this was a slight "that one experiences from quarters that have no right to prepare such an action for us or for one of ours."[153] He was convinced that this account, which he called "a surpassingly exquisite acuity in the marking of affect" (*eine so erlesene Feinheit in der Kennzeichnung der Affekte*), had been one of Aristotle's greatest contributions to the history of thought. He also believed that it could explain why there would be emotions—like Nietzsche's metaphorically improvised "nobler brother of envy" (*edleren Bruder des Neides*)—that are named in one culture and not in another.[154]

It is necessary to add that emotions are imagined scenes that arrange stances or stage their failure. Just as belief has an emotional tincture, so too does its opposite, doubt, which is first and foremost an incapacity to adopt—or be at one with—a stance. But doubt is only one way of being at a distance from a pose. Irony is another. We should note two topoi. First

152. Gomperz, *Griechische Denker*, 3:342.

153. Gomperz, *Griechische Denker*, 3:342: "welche man von seiten solcher erfährt, die uns oder einem der Unserigen derlei zu bereiten kein Recht besitzen."

154. Gomperz, 3:344, 345. Gomperz was probably taking up the line from Nietzsche's *Menschliches, Allzumenschliches*, in *Gesammelte Werke*, 9:205.

topos: in a piece initially published in 1937, the classicist Wilhelm Kroll reported Quintilian's observation that although *pathos* would usually be understood as "passion" and *ethos* as "character" there existed a greater continuity between the two categories than was often assumed.[155] *Ethos* identified a milder emotional state of greater duration becoming a facet of a person's character. In contrast, *pathos* was brief, intense, and nonhabitual. In Quintilian's example, *amor* had been a *pathos* while *caritas* had been an *ethos*.[156] We may infer that the first two of the images embedded in the *Zorn* cycle just discussed depicted *pathē* (doings and sufferings taking place in particular times and places) while the second two depicted *ethē* (and were portraits of the protagonists alerting us to what is sudden or out of character or *unearned*). Second topos: in an earlier piece (published just after the end of the First World War), Kroll had also argued that *ethos* could mean not simply "character" but also something like "in character" in some circumstances. One spoke, as he put it, "jokingly" (*im Scherz*) or "sneeringly" (*spöttisch*).[157] To speak "in character" was like speaking *ironically*. Recognition of such speaking required a certain kind of prosopopoeic projection onto a displayed but not endorsed persona. There were always multiple positions one could take up relative to the stance one was wearing.

The ironist performs a kind of prosopopoeia entailing apostrophe as dog whistle. That is, ironists project characters or masks or poses and perform them in their own persons, but they do so in such a way that a retrenched authorial persona is implied (for some select audience members), and this implied persona is understood to be addressing the ironic target as a buffoon interlocutor. One can say with Thomas Mann that "the ironist is conservative."[158] After all, irony divides its publics into those who understand and those who do not. Moreover (so the implication went), radicalism can be said not to know its own actions, because history—qua irony writ large— always revises its achievements in unexpected ways. Or one can say with Friedrich Schlegel that "irony is the form of paradox." Once inaugurated, the hall of mirrors that is irony will lead the way to a radical undecidability in which mask and face can no longer be distinguished.[159] And indeed what *was* the speech act being performed by Gustav Herrmann in the two volumes of his *Art of Political Speech* published in 1920? The author was *posing* as someone saying that in a republic, "whoever has the floor [and claims the right to speak] has likewise the power." And this author seemed to be claiming that as a result one should excavate the rhetorical tradition in order

155. Kroll, "Rhetorik," 1059.
156. Quintilian, *Institutio oratoria*, 6.2.12.
157. Kroll, "En Ēthei," 470.
158. Mann, *Betrachtungen*, 571: "der Ironiker ist konservativ."
159. Schlegel, "Über die Unverständlichkeit," 368: "Ironie ist die Form des Paradoxen."

to learn how to speak.[160] But the "ideal orator" confected in this way is too ridiculous to be taken seriously. Stop. About-face. Yet Herrmann's own investment in the rhetorical tradition is too serious to be declared a farce. Turning this way and that, we are unable to pinpoint either his stance or our response. Irony, we conclude, is a facility with stance, a play with belief.

At this point in our extended précis of the German reception of rhetoric, there are some key terms that we can define with greater acuity. "Stance" denotes a compact position that can be extended or contracted as interrogation requires or opportunities allow. "Doubt" denotes an inability to align oneself with a position in this way or a fear that the position one assumes will in fact collapse at the slightest challenge. And "perspectivism" denotes a talent for articulating positions in the absence of belief. "Irony," it turns out, denotes one of many prosopopoeic practices giving voice to things or persons other than oneself. And this means that irony is a practicing in the borderlands of plausibility.

In both classical rhetoric and its modern German afterlives, the sharpest engagements with stance, doubt, perspective, and irony were sophistic. The reflexivity of sophistic is delineated *in nuce* in the famous Protagorean fragment concerning the human being as a measure. Of course, the fragment was radical not least for its own seductive "being in need of interpretation" (*Deutungsbedürftigkeit*). It was intriguing, so there were many opinions; it was ambiguous, so all opinions were different. Herrmann Roller read it as an assertion of the importance of the concepts that the human mind layers over the world.[161] Theodor Gomperz took it to be an empiricist claim that whatever appears nowhere in the collective human sensorium is nonexistent.[162] His son Heinrich Gomperz (modifying the father's conclusions), argued that we ought to read *metron* as "differentiator" (*Unterscheidungsmerkmal*) because human sensitivities would be a raft of different ways of distinguishing between what is greater than and what is less than the "mean" of the sense in its neutral or resting state. Gomperz fils added that there is no reason to suppose that different individuals would possess an identical set of statistical means between the more and the less. In this way, the son reasoned himself to the conclusion that the fundamental issue raised here was this: "on account of what are rhetoric and sophistic even possible?"[163] That is, Protagoras had implied that *each* human being would be a measure, and that led to the question of how persuasion would even be possible given diversity of opinion that had been built into our very senses.

A "stance" might expand into a "perspective," which we should understand as a congeries of "resting states" among the senses. These senses

160. Herrmann, *Die Kunst der politischen Rede*, 1:6: "Wer das Wort hat, hat auch die Macht."
161. Roller, *Die Griechischen Sophisten*, 20.
162. Gomperz, *Griechische Denker*, 1:362ff.
163. Gomperz, *Sophistik und Rhetorik*, 200ff, 273: "wie sind Rhetorik und Sophistik möglich?"

would always perceive the world in relation to its default settings (or fail to perceive if phenomena ran too close to expectation). The great philological factum undergirding this new consciousness of the sophistic project was Hermann Diels's *Fragments of the Presocratics*, first published in 1903. From the beginning, that compendium of quotations was equipped with a section on the "older sophistic" (*älterer Sophistik*) running from Protagoras through Xeniades, Gorgia, Prodikos, Thrasymachos, Hippias, Antiphon the Sophist, Kritias, and Anonymus Iamblichi to the Anonymi Dialexeis.[164] In this collection, readers had access to core articulations of a "relativist" practice. Not coincidentally, the likes of Karl Mannheim were also developing a sociology of knowledge that radicalized inherited notions such as "worldview" (*Weltanschauung*) by characterizing worldviews as "default settings" set by the social circumstances in which certain forms of knowing emerged. As Mannheim put it in the 1936 English edition, "were not the Sophists of the Greek Enlightenment the expression of an attitude of doubt which arose essentially out of the fact that in their thinking about every object, two modes of explanation collided"—one characteristic of a "dominant nobility already doomed to decline," the other expressing "an urban artisan lower stratum" that was "moving upwards"?[165] Sociology of knowledge, a reborn Weimar sophistic.

RÉSUMÉ

The languages of rhetorical inquiry sketched in this chapter did not constitute some storehouse of implicit presuppositions shared broadly by the educated writing and reading elites of Weimar Germany. The audiences for much of the material dealt with here remained academic—and specialized academic at that. The precise degree to which these ideas permeated Weimar intellectual culture more broadly is impossible to assess with any real precision. Or, rather, the intellectual gains promised by such a truth would not be commensurate with the labor required to establish it. Nor is it even clear that the thinkers who are the focus of the body of this book were unusually interested in or aware of the tradition laid out here in some breadth and depth.

The idioms laid out in this chapter were not seedbeds for the thought of Heidegger, Arendt, Benjamin, or Warburg, but the topical reveries sketched above can be engines of discovery for readers of this book as they work their way through the central chapters dealing with individual authors. In those chapters, the primary unit of analysis is the total oeuvre of the individual writer him- or herself. The writerly task is to identify rhetorico-political

164. Diels, *Die Fragmente der Vorsokratiker*.
165. Mannheim, *Ideology and Utopia*, 8.

trajectories in those oeuvres that run through much of the major work. My contentions will be that these trajectories have not been perceived clearly before and that they can help us think a lineage of rhetorical inquiry running out of Weimar. The *readerly* task in each of following four chapters is not simply to follow the argument and thereby discern new versions of these various famous thinkers. In addition to that, the task is to infuse the arguments made by those thinkers with new possibilities arrived at by creative transposition of *their* assertions and concerns into the languages of rhetorical inquiry described in the present chapter.

Thus, what I have presented in this chapter is a storehouse of potential premises ready for deployment in potential inferences. I have covertly organized those premises and inferential structures into topoi clusters that anticipate the principal concerns of each of the book's chapters. The Heidegger I pursue will be especially concerned with *dunamis*; Arendt, with proximities (that may be established by trope); Benjamin, with modes of belief and doubt; Warburg, with topical invention. By arranging the assorted topoi of this German intellectual tradition as I have, I have sought to make available a density of inferential weave. Nevertheless, all topoi quoted in this chapter may be treated by readers as potential premises to be deployed individually in as yet unwritten inferences confected in conjunction with the main contentions of the four core authors.

3: HEIDEGGERIAN FOUNDATIONS

A NEW ORIENTATION

The center of Martin Heidegger's oeuvre, I shall argue, is not *Being and Time*. It is a sequence of initiatives undertaken in and around 1924 when the essential components of his work began to take shape and before they were collated into and covered over by the formalism and terminological abstraction of the "masterwork" of 1927. Theodore Kisiel was brilliantly correct in his hypothesis that a genuinely phenomenological approach to Heidegger's phenomenology would trace the emergence of his project during the long period from 1916 to 1926 in which he published nothing. But Kisiel remained convinced that *Being and Time* was the apex of Heidegger's thought, the terminus ad quem.[1] We need not follow him in that, and I choose not to.

In order to show that there is nothing essential to the account of the Heideggerian foundations of rhetorical inquiry outlined in this chapter that one cannot get in the earlier texts, I do not cite *Being and Time*. Or rather, I make only one exception. I do consider one line from the magnum opus— namely, the assertion that Aristotle's *Rhetoric* was "the first systematic hermeneutic of the everydayness of being-with-one-another" (*die erste systematische Hermeneutik der Alltäglichkeit des Miteinanderseins*).[2] I make this exception to prove the rule: this assertion is foundational to *Being and Time*, and yet it is essentially unintelligible if one is reading the masterwork and only the masterwork. The line is a remnant or an index of how the project came to be, and it can only be understood via the earlier work. Indeed, because he was working in the 1960s without the manuscript material that has now appeared in the *Gesamtausgabe* of Heidegger's collected writings,

---

1. Kisiel, *Genesis*, 2: this "is basically a Book of Genesis of a great classic, perhaps the most important, of twentieth-century philosophy."
2. Heidegger, *Sein und Zeit*, 138.

one pities someone like Klaus Dockhorn, who was more or less marooned on that sentence. He insisted that there must be a rhetorical foundation for *Being and Time* and thence for Gadamer's *Truth and Method*. I think he was right, but without the earlier materials he had no means of either demonstrating or exploring his intuition.[3]

My position is that if Heidegger only genuinely became Heidegger in *Being and Time* then he was taking up residence in a mausoleum. After the fact, he certainly experienced the contraption of his *Being-and-Time* self as a kind of burden. It brought no great adversary. The long-delayed second part never appeared. He conceded he had no choice but to rewrite it continually from the beginning.[4] And the raft of neologisms coined in the work did not endure. Perhaps those terms endured for the Heideggerians; for Heidegger, they did not. "Murky" (*Trübe*) and "doubtful" (*zweifelhafte*) sources though they seemed to be to Heidegger himself, the lecture courses and public talks in the years leading up to the big book are fresher, more forthright, richer.[5]

At the heart of the creativity I am identifying in 1924 were Heidegger's engagements with Aristotle's *Rhetoric* and Plato's *Sophist*. These were, respectively, the two texts at the center of his Summer Semester 1924 and Winter Semester 1924–1925 lecture courses, given soon after his arrival at the University of Marburg in October 1923. In Heidegger's appropriation, these Greek texts were to be acid baths for the "basic concepts" (*Grundbegriffe*) encasing philosophical inquiry. These concepts—"nature" (*phusis*, *Natur*), "motion" (*kinēsis*, *Bewegung*), "reality" (*energeia*, *Wirklichkeit*), for example—had been received, refracted, and pirated countless times in the history of philosophy since the "beginning" of their etymological odyssey in Greece.[6] Inventive and excoriating, Heidegger's philological investments were designed to underwrite his rejection of the early twentieth-century German philosophical establishment: Marburg neo-Kantianism, Southwest philosophy of values, Husserlian phenomenology—all of them.[7] Having been Husserl's assistant at Freiburg, Heidegger began to disaffiliate from the founder of phenomenology as soon as he got to Marburg in 1923, and the method of choice was, in the first place, etymology. Throw off the German neologism *Phänomenologie*, he said. And return to the "appearing" (*phainō*) as "a self-showing" (*sich zeigen*).[8]

Did affiliation with the Greek version of philosophical inquiry entail an inherited enmity for rhetoric and sophistic? No. Enlisting Heidegger in the

3. Dockhorn, review of *Wahrheit und Methode*, 186.
4. Heidegger, *Überlegungen II–VI*, 9, 22, 184.
5. Heidegger, *Unterwegs zur Sprache*, 91, 147.
6. Heidegger, "Phänomenologische Interpretationen zu Aristoteles," 249.
7. For example, Heidegger, *Platons Lehre der Wahrheit*, 68, 70, 73.
8. Heidegger, *Einführung in die phänomenologische Forschung*, 6–7.

old war between philosophers and rhetoricians would occlude everything
that is new and creative and useful in his early work. To be blunt, the core
Heideggerian category of *Dasein* was a rhetorical category. When the term
is rendered as "being" (as it usually is), it is difficult to perceive rhetorical
edge. Here, I shall render the term somewhat unusually—but with justifica-
tion, I think—as "situated presencing." Neither being-here nor being-there,
Dasein was rather the matrix of tensions set out by the articulation of a
situatedness. And, of course, as we saw in the previous chapter, situating
is an exquisitely rhetorical task. As presencing, *Dasein* was a finding and
locating of oneself in a particular situation of speaking and listening. In
fact, Heidegger's project was to rewrite Greek ontology by recentering it
from the necessary to the possible, *to* that which could be otherwise *from*
that which could not. Those who have emphasized rhetoric's affiliation with
contingency have an ally in Heidegger. The core work of this chapter will
be to articulate a rhetorical Heidegger and a Heideggerian rhetoric centered
on the varieties of possibility he discerned.

This chapter establishes foundations for rhetorical inquiry by identifying
and clarifying key concepts around appearance that will be taken up and
developed further—sometimes in quite unexpected ways—in the remainder of this book. Absolutely central is the idea of the phenomenon that
defines itself in the moment of its appearance that I have taken up from
Heidegger. This formulation is a redescription of Heidegger's account of
truth as *alētheia*. In that account, truth becomes a process of disclosing in
appearance. This is a truth that is neither a correspondence between an assertion and a state of affairs in the world nor a coherence between one assertion and another. In subsequent chapters, this Heideggerian interpretation
of appearance will become first a concern for the space of appearance (in
Arendt) and then a focus on the dialectical self-splitting energies at work in
the moment of intensified appearance (in Benjamin). Finally (in Warburg),
it will become a hypothesis about how splaying the moment of self-defining
appearance into a number of images mounted on an image table sensitizes
sense, enables imagination to trace multiple potential continuations, and
lays out a new account of freedom.

Before taking up the challenges of interpreting Arendt, Benjamin, and
Warburg as inferential fabrics within the broader narrative of the Weimar
origins of rhetorical inquiry, we need to establish the Heideggerian foundation, and there are five key elements here. First, the Heideggerian account
of temporality is the grammar within which *Dasein* as situated presencing
happens, and in order to see that the situation of presencing is actually a
rhetorical process and talent we need to work through the initial formulations of Heidegger's rejection of previous philosophies of time. Second, to
appreciate how rhetoric's eclectic array of sensitivities to historical process

and emotional tincture are integral to the task of presencing, we need to recognize that the temporal manifold of past, present, and future emphasized in Heideggerian temporalization is actually a redescription of the Greek modalities of *entelecheia* (as duration qua achievedness), *energeia* (as activation or performance or unfolding), and *dunamis* (as potentiality). Third, turning explicitly to the Heideggerian reception of Aristotle's *Rhetoric* in Summer Semester 1924, we discover that rhetoric is intimately bound up with the faculties that are essential to the situation of presencing and that as a result rhetoric is inseparable from the kind of *epideixis* that sharpens Heidegger's phenomenology of self-definition. Fourth, in this 1924 reception, we find that rhetoric was more of a hermeneutic than a speech performance, and this allows us to see that—as a set of concepts and practices oriented to the presentation of complex situations, processes, and possibilities—rhetoric was intensively concerned with *Dasein* itself qua situated presencing. Pursuant to this emphasis, the term "rhetoric" in this chapter will predominantly mean "the tissue of theoretical insights penned in the name of rhetoric as an analytic practice." Fifth, because of the biographical and conceptual proximity of the trajectory for rhetorical inquiry identified here to the one that propelled Heidegger into the Nazi Party in the early 1930s, I work in the final section of this chapter to show how we can take up a sequence in early Heideggerian thought without becoming committed to the particular continuation the man himself chose.

THE TIME STRUCTURE OF SITUATEDNESS

We need to have the concept of "situatedness" (*Befindlichkeit*) at our fingertips if we are to reconstruct the trajectory that took Heidegger from time and modality through rhetoric to a historiography of the massification of means and potentialization. It is absolutely critical to understand that situatedness cannot be read as either a fundamental set of facts about a situation or an array of projections foisted on a pliant "nature" to generate a situation where none had existed "objectively." Time and space were not dimensions of being that existed somehow "outside" the world. Nor were they projections of the human imagination. Instead, both time and space were differentials in appearing that human articulation could sharpen and enrich. In this way, any reconstruction of something like a "situation" as a scene for rhetoric within the Heideggerian vocabulary needs to begin with a reenactment of Heidegger's thinking on space and—more especially—time.

Temporality was at the core of Heidegger's conceptions of situatedness, and as an indicative sample of his own most distinctive thoughts on temporality we may take up "The Concept of Time," a lecture he gave to the Marburg Theological Faculty on July 25, 1924. This talk condensed a manuscript bearing the same title that Friedrich-Wilhelm v. Hermann has called the "floor plan" (*Grundriß*) or even "originary draft" (*Urfassung*) of *Being and Time*.[9] In this talk, Heidegger's fundamental assertion was that "futurity endows time, it lays the present out and lets the past repeat itself in the mode of its having been lived."[10] Time itself was a spanning of tense—an orientation to the future, a pulling through the present, a repetition of the past as memory, as habit, as counterpoint against which a movement might distinguish itself. The present participle in my rendition of *Dasein* as "situated presencing" commits to this sense of spanning in tense itself—tense as tension.

One cannot grasp the subtle radicalness of Heidegger's conception of time without beginning with stark denials: the future does not and will not exist; the past does not and did not exist.[11] That is, the future may not be thought of as something like a place, existing already "out in front of us." Similarly, the past may not be thought of as a place, safely archived away, waiting to be dusted off and put on display. Look more closely instead at what Heidegger took from Henri Bergson: "we are always in the process of opening up before us space," Heidegger affirmed (using Bergson's words). We are always in the process "of closing up behind us duration."[12] Instead of past and future as preexisting but distant dimensions, one has possible motions marking out space and an array of endurances characterized by their quality of already being there at the opening of a scene. Past and future are aspects or modes of presentness. The past is that which endures in the present, and the future is that which is already in the present but indeterminately in the mode of possibility.

Along with conventional understandings of past and future, we must similarly eviscerate conventional understandings of the present. For Heidegger, the present was not a point. It could not be understood as a still life, tableau, or snapshot. Instead, the present would be a stretching, a collision and, as it were, a mutual rebounding of past and future. Past and future were the distinctive spanning, gathering, and interpreting capacity of a presencing that was a situatedness capable of inference. This would be the sense that Heidegger later lifted from Nietzsche, for whom the "moment" or the "blink of an eye" (*Augenblick*) was, in fact, the meeting of two timelines—one past, one future. But this "meeting" was not continuation but rather

9. Heidegger, "Der Begriff der Zeit (1924)," 132–33.

10. Heidegger, "Der Begriff der Zeit (Vortrag 1924)," 118: "Zukünftigsein gibt Zeit, bildet die Gegenwart aus und läßt die Vergangenheit im Wie ihres Gelebtseins wiederholen."

11. Heidegger, "Der Begriff der Zeit (1924)," 18.

12. Bergson, *Matière et mémoire*, 161: "Nous sommes en d'ouvrir toujours devant nous l'espace, de refermer toujours derriere nous la durée." Quoted by Heidegger, *Grundprobleme der Phänomenologie*, 1—see also 259.

collision. As Nietzsche imagined it, past and future were timelines that flowed in opposite directions, the future pushing back against the past.[13] In place of "the present," insert the *Da* of *Da-sein*. Not "being-here" or "being-there" but both at once, the *Da* was a stretching or dilation produced in encounter. And this spanning of the present by encounter was "experience" (*Erfahrung*). As the Heidegger of Winter Semester 1920–1921 put it, experience "does not mean 'to take note of' but rather a kind of setting-of-oneself-over-against, a self-reporting of the matrix of the experiencing."[14] On this account, waiting, too, was a motion (holding or resisting), and there would be many ways of being-stationary in presencing. The coiled quality of the sprinter at the start line was not the same stasis as a peasant woman kneeling at a wayside shrine. Pasts and futures extended through the "point" of the sprinter's motionlessness. The splay of the fingers was already a future.[15]

The present was not a point but a presence, or rather the present was a presencing with a variety of extensions, and here we are already on the way to the hypothesis that a phenomenon will define itself in the moment of its most extreme presencing. In Winter Semester 1920–1921, Heidegger was casting about for words with which to express the temporalization of this coming into presence. Eschewing a number of other philosophical vocabularies for expressing the relationship between "the temporal" (*das Zeitliche*) and "the supratemporal" (*das Überzeitliche*), he took up the idiom of Parousia.[16] The historical appearance, when it appeared intensively, simply *was* itself. On this account, the appearance did not represent or imitate or participate. It was. At first, this was an explicitly Christian Parousia on the model of the second coming.[17] What might this mean? It meant that if one wanted a definition of courage, one's task was to show the genuinely courageous act as it had manifested itself specifically in historical time. Definition, one might say, was not a semantic issue but rather a historiographic one. Only stories could genuinely define. Later, such presence denoted the span of the "phenomenon" (*Phänomen*) itself, which was "that which shows itself *as* a showing of itself."[18] This was the point that Heidegger would transform into a philosophical position on truth.

Attending to the presencing that might be its own definition, Heidegger's

13. Heidegger, *Nietzsche*, 1:311.
14. Heidegger, *Einleitung in die Phänomenologie der Religion*, 9: "[Erfahrung] heißt nicht 'zur Kenntnis nehmen,' sondern das Sich-Auseinander-Setzen mit, das Sich-Behaupten der Gestalten des Erfahrenen."
15. Heidegger, *Aristoteles, Metaphysik*, 217–18.
16. Heidegger, *Einleitung in die Phänomenologie der Religion*, 45.
17. Heidegger, 97.
18. Heidegger, *Ontologie*, 67: "das, was sich zeigt, als sich zeigendes."

Phänomenologie actively rejected the connotations of the German word, distanced itself from Husserl, and attempted to rejuvenate the concept through its Greek etymology. In the context of rhetorical inquiry, we should understand Heideggerian phenomenology as both the articulation of a rhetorical idiom for presencing and an account of the various faculties of the soul coinvolved in such presencing. Mind, or rather *psuchē*, was an array of sensitivities to motion that was indistinguishable from the world because it was part of the world's movements. Heidegger was emphasizing such sensitivity to the motions of presencing when he said that the Aristotelian analysis of the soul built up a concatenation of life capacities founded on "moving" (*kinein*) and "distinguishing" (*krinein*).[19] Alongside the significant investment that Heidegger made in *phronēsis* in the Winter Semester lectures of 1924–1925, we find also *krinein*, fashioned as a "distinguishing, a raising up of one thing over against another, or indeed against the background of the genus."[20] This process of raising up against the background of a genus by calling attention to certain aspects of an appearance was absolutely essential to the process of naming that I shall put close to the center of Heidegger's project. And this was more than a narrowly aesthetic project, because for the early Aristotelian Heidegger, all distinctions in sensation are sensitivities of the soul pertaining to possibilities for motion.

Heidegger's project entailed no commitment to a necessitarianism in which every effect was unavoidably and absolutely the slave of its cause. The project entailed neither a belief in the unity of a phenomenon involving multiple causes and multiple effects nor a concomitant phenomenology dedicated to the task of articulating such complexity. Heidegger was committed to an older, and in various ways Greek, account of change. The step toward necessitarianism becomes more difficult to resist when one treats change of place as the paradigm for all motion. For Heidegger (as for Aristotle), however, "sensing" (*aisthesis*) was itself a motion—not in the modern sense of a "change of location" (*Platzwechsel*) but in the sense of a "becoming other" (*alloiosis, Anderswerden*). Motion was simply "change."[21] For Heidegger, casting change of place as the essence of motion was characteristic of a post-seventeenth-century scientific worldview, which he read as a corruption or flattening out of the basic concept of *kinēsis*.

In his paraphrase of the Aristotelian program, motion qua *kinēsis*

---

19. Heidegger, *Grundbegriffe*, 30–31 and 44, where *krinein* was *Abheben und Bestimmen*. The point recurred during the next semester: Heidegger, *Platon: Sophistes*, 38–39.

20. Heidegger, *Platon: Sophistes*, 243: "unterscheiden, abheben eines gegen ein anderes, und zwar das genos." Heidegger also emphasized the relationship between *krinein* and *Urteil* in *Die Frage nach dem Ding*, 93.

21. Heidegger, *Einführung in die phänomenologische Forschung*, 29. See also Heidegger, "Der Begriff der Zeit (1924)," 78.

included all the various modes of change—"all versions of a capsizing from-to" (*alle Phänomene des Umschlagens von-zu*). *Kinēsis* was simply "becoming otherwise" (*das heteron*).[22] At the same time, *kinēsis* was also the "stubbornness" that might hold an appearance in a state of "achievedness" (*entelecheia*).[23] This was a being inured, coated, impervious, indifferent, or inert. In this way, change was an index of being susceptible. Here, the touchstone text was Aristotle's *Peri psuchēs*, where the metaphors of choice were wax and imprinting. For Heidegger, the title of this work became an impediment when translated as *Über die Seele*, as "On the Soul," or, for that matter, as *De Anima*. The preferable alternative—per the *Nachschrift* made by Helene Weiss and Herbert Marcuse from Heidegger's Winter Semester 1923–1924 lecture cycle—was "On Being in the World" (*Über das Sein in der Welt*).[24] More crucial was the tactical, local discerning of phenomena that were *processes* with a range of different scales, pacings, and media.

The account of change that Heidegger was attaching to his theorization of time might seem to suggest that his was a "temporal idealism" in which the individual conjures temporality into existence by remembering and projecting out from the perspective of the present, but—*pace* William Blattner—the account of temporality being rehearsed here was realist rather than idealist. Heidegger was not saying that time would be the mental life of memory and imagination pushing out from a particular point that we might term "attention." He rejected talk of what he called "the spheric" (*das Sphärische*), in which the world was pushed back and understood as a panoply of projections onto the IMAX screen of consciousness.[25] In his 1924 anticipations of *Being and Time*, Heidegger famously asked "am I myself time?"[26] He was not suggesting that time would be simply the recollections and anticipations that carved out an awareness that was in each case "mine." He was saying that time would be the motions passing through the in-each-case-mine that also, crucially, found some form of articulation. When he ventured the formulation that "time functions as a principle of individuation," Heidegger was arguing that time was the infinitely specifiable array of trajectories structuring a life: the repetitions of morning ablution; the pendula of commuting (or their absence); the work temporalities of shift and project and semester (or their absence); the affective attachments and protomovements of desire and aversion; sheer emotional sensitivity to the representations of others (irascibility, volubility, "shame-ability"); the public character that was being cast by the layering of conspicuous actions;

22. Heidegger, *Platon: Sophistes*, 541.
23. Heidegger, "Der Begriff der Zeit (1924)," 78.
24. Heidegger, *Einführung in die phänomenologische Forschung*, 293.
25. Heidegger, "Wozu Dichter?," in *Holzwege*, 278.
26. Heidegger, "Der Begriff der Zeit (1924)," 83: "Bin *ich* die Zeit?"

the public accelerations and decelerations of capital in inflation, interest, and wage; the biographical narration of a span between birth and death.[27] All of these were versions of an assertion that time was a structuring and calibrating of motions relative to each other.

The assertion that the primary constituents of time and space were differentials among processes rather than measurements generated by means of some exterior metric was subtle and difficult to grasp, but it was crucial to Heidegger's broader project, and we must secure the thought. To that end, we can compare the spanning of time and space to the scenes orchestrated by the film director George Cukor, in which bodies, exhibiting trajectories, move through shots and intersect at underdetermined angles. The effect conjured is at once disheveled and choreographic as the constellations of motion coalesce, for a time, into form before they deliquesce beyond gestalt. In this fantasy, fleeting alignment constitutes a center in time and space, a "present" complete with and extended into befores and afters. Like space, time might be constituted by the motions of the phenomenon that brought its own backgrounds into being. "Background" is a spatial metaphor, but the grammars of temporality— for instance, the tensings of pluperfect, imperfect, and future perfect—reinforce the fact of "emerging." As Heidegger would later characterize it, "sculpture" (*die Plastik*) was "an embodying activation of place and thus an opening of spaces, possibilities for human living."[28] All phenomena would structure their own time by means of the differentiation of their various calibrations of emergence. That is, the performed poem would have background temporalities in which it nestled qua event, and in its scansion that poem would generate a specific simultaneity of diverse motions. Scanning spans.

Understood as an interrelation among movements, the appearance of time itself in the emergence of a phenomenon would depend on "situated presencing" (*Dasein*), which was not something that would happen automatically given that it depended on forms of synchronization that would sometimes take the form of articulation. Motion's worldliness—its capacity to bring complex time spaces into being—would rely on sensitivities that could move along with it, trace its trajectories, and gather its complexities. Narrative would be a kind of selection making it possible to follow motions extending beyond the parameters of the most basic modes of being-in-the-world—namely, touch, taste, smell, hearing, and sight. As Rilke put it (in a line collected by Heidegger), "we [human beings] are the bees of

27. Heidegger, 82: "die Zeit gilt als ein *principio individuationis.*"
28. Heidegger, *Die Kunst und der Raum*, 13: "ein verkörperndes Ins-Werk-Bringen von Orten und mit diesen ein Eröffnung von Gegenden möglichen Wohnens der Menschen, möglichen Verweilens der sie umgebenden, sie angehenden Dinge."

the invisible."[29] The worlding effected by human beings was, in essence, a bringing into being of complex temporal manifolds.

As Heidegger maintained (even to the end of his life), "the fundamental thought in my thinking is simply that being [*das Sein*]—or, rather, the manifestation [*die Offenbarkeit*] of being—needs humans and that, by the same token, humans are only humans insofar as they stand in that manifestation of being."[30] "Manifestation" (*Offenbarkeit*) here stressed a kind of counter-positioning and reciprocal inscribing that emerged when a phenomenon stretched attention out beyond the boundaries of what we conventionally refer to as the "recent past" and the "near future." I both structure and am structured by the phenomenon to which I call attention. All souls would have their modes of "distinguishing" and "moving" (*krinein* and *kinein*), and all souls would have their own affordances—neither "material" nor "immaterial"—for participating in the articulation of being qua presencing as a motley of causes, actions, effects, and responses. Nevertheless, the wealth of human capacities for complex pasts, complex futures, and complex counterfactuals would make humanity's contribution to such articulation distinctive.

THE MODAL DIMENSIONS OF SITUATEDNESS

Ultimately, we cannot articulate the Heideggerian account of time without a robust revision of thoughts about modality. Conventionally enumerated, the modal categories are possibility, impossibility, and necessity. In Heidegger, we see that these categories—possibility especially—are constitutive of time itself. The possibility of an action in the future simply is the configuration of a particular "temporalization" (*Zeitigung*). We are now in a position to understand this temporalization as the spanning of presence qua coming into being and passing away. One of Heidegger's most crucial assertions is that being does not exhibit constancy. The totality of being in a world ebbs and flows without possessing any kind of absolute "quantity." Within a Heideggerian frame of reference, this conclusion derives from a rereading of "possibility" (*Möglichkeit*) as lack of specification. It is not that possibility *is* not. It is rather that possibility is a presencing that is vague such that it can still become many or at least several things. Again, situatedness is an articulation of temporalization (*Zeitigung*) that participates in the progressive determination of what will almost always remain a somewhat

29. Cited by Heidegger, "Wozu Dichter?," in *Holzwege*, 284: "wir sind die Bienen des Unsichtbaren."

30. Heidegger, *Martin Heidegger im Gespräch*, 69: "der Grundgedanke meines Denkens ist gerade der, daß das Sein beziehungsweise die Offenbarkeit des Seins den Menschen braucht und daß umgekehrt der Mensch nur Mensch ist, sofern er in der Offenbarkeit des Seins steht."

indeterminate field. Necessity happens rarely or never. The articulation of possibilities—and modality more generally—simply is the articulation of situatedness.

In order to develop his account of temporalization by expressing its connection to modality, Heidegger invested a great deal of intellectual energy in the basic modalities of Greek ontology, where the key terms were *entelecheia*, *energeia*, and *dunamis*. To trace his thought, we need to work through these modalities ourselves.

On the account fashioned by Heidegger, *entelecheia* was a being-in-a-state-of-finishedness (*Fertigsein*). This was a reading of the Greek term that Heidegger took up from Hermann Diels, although Diel's gloss is now disputed.[31] As a movement, *entelecheia* was a having come to an enduring halt, completion. It was "the entity that holds itself in the most proper possibility of its own being, so that its possibility is achieved" and thereby, in a sense, exhausted.[32] True, Aristotle's example had been the motions of the heavens. An ur-form of *entelecheia* was circularity or orbit. Such motions were not motionless as such, but they had come to a developmental halt in the sense that they had achieved—or were believed to have achieved—an enduring stability exhibiting itself as repetition. In Heidegger's Summer Semester 1924 paraphrase, "being [*das Seiende*] as *kosmos* is characterized by means of the presence of that which is always already there, Parousia."[33] And here *kosmos* is to be understood less in the sense of "universe" and more in the sense of "order" as an array of precise displacements constituting "ornament."

Crucially, *entelecheia* would actually have a much broader everyday character for Heidegger. The heavens were the primordial everyday—each and every day. But the workaday frames of the home, the studio, and the built environment had also come to an end, in the sense that they endured in the states that defined them. Having been constructed, they were "achieved" (*hergestellt*). Or, rather, their decay was gradual enough that it might look like stasis, their maintenance cyclical enough that care was constant or reliably seasonal. For this reason, pastness was very often an environment of everyday durations set out by fashioned matter. These were objects (the desk) and frames (the house) that marked out a kind of ersatz givenness on account of their relative immobility.

---

31. Heidegger, *Grundbegriffe*, 296, where he cited Hermann Diels, "Etymologica." Diels distinguished quite strictly between *energeia* and *entelecheia*, and Heidegger followed him in this. More recent scholars have disagreed. See Chen, "Relation Between the Terms *Energeia* and *Entelecheia*," 12–17, and Gonzales, "Whose Metaphysics of Presence?" 533–68.

32. Heidegger, *Grundbegriffe*, 90: "ein solches Seiendes, das sich selbst hält in seiner eigentlichen Seinsmöglichkeit, so daß die Möglichkeit vollendet ist."

33. Heidegger, 267: "das Seiende als *kosmos* ist charakterisiert durch die Gegenwärtigkeit dessen, was immer schon da ist, *parousia*."

If *entelecheia* named the ways in which the past might be a dimension of the present as duration, *energeia* named processes of emergence against the background of duration. *Energeia* was thus a "being-in-action qua activation" (*Im-Werke-Sein*). This was not an achieved form in the manner of *entelecheia*. *Energeia* was on the way to achieving form.[34] It was a reaching for form that emerged out of the background of achieved form, *entelecheia*. To call *energeia* the modality of the present would activate received and unhelpful understandings of time. It was instead a *commencing* of performance. Just so, in the later essay, "The Origin of the Work of Art," the rising out of a background that was the "work or working of art" was, precisely, an *energeia*.[35] Figure and ground relations in works of figural art were particularly evocative of the moment that Heidegger wished to isolate—namely, the moment in which an artistic process brought something into view.

Heidegger struggled with different ways of rendering the Greek term in German. He avoided the term *Wirklichkeit*, which did, in some ways, seem to be the most obvious candidate. Literally, the term denoted something like "work-li-ness" (the quality of being at work, in play, in process). Usage had overwritten the literal meaning of the term, however. To Heidegger's ear, it retained only an abstract philosophical status, denoting something in the vicinity of the English terms "reality" or "actuality."[36] For a time (in the earlier 1920s), Heidegger's German substitute for *energeia* was *Zeitigung* itself. This term denoted not only a "producing, yielding, or activating" but also—more literally—"the giving of a temporal structure to something, laying it out in time" or "possessing futurity." This was an impending future as form.[37] Heidegger's Summer Semester 1922 lecture course had been completely saturated in the term *Zeitigung*, where it meant not only "execution" or "implementation" (*Vollzug*) but also *energeia*.[38] This was an emerging from a background, but it was also the specifying of a temporal domain. *Energeia* as *Zeitigung* was a narrowing of focus between past and future.

As a performance that alluded to but had not yet specified form, *energeia* required the invention of *dunamis*, which became the specific time quality of a performance that could be but was not. In many ways, *dunamis* was the modality most difficult to think. To Plato, for instance, conceiving of *dunamis* appeared to entail speaking somehow of the being of nonbeing. This was a "being-in-a-state-of-nonactualized-possibility" (*Möglichsein*). Possibility, on this account, was not some raw logical or physical "compatibility-with." It was, instead, a kind of *indeterminateness* in being such that the range

---

34. Heidegger, 70.

35. Heidegger, "Ursprung des Kunstwerkes," in *Holzwege*, 28 (*Sich-ins-Werk-Setzen*), 68 (*energeia*).

36. Heidegger, *Grundbegriffe*, 70.

37. See, for example, Heidegger, *Phänomenologische Interpretationen ausgewählter Abhandlungen*, 76–77.

38. Heidegger, 42, 102ff.

of coming states for a given phenomenon was neither entirely open nor whittled down to one. That is to say—and this is a crucial point—possibility was an embedded and vague futurity. More precisely (in a better and more surprising formulation), possibility was the future that already existed in the present as vagueness.

As Heidegger had put it in "The Concept of Time" of 1924 (the manuscript, not the talk), futurity would be an inseparability of the "can" from the "is." That is, "so far as being-there"—facticity, embeddedness, situatedness—"is determinate on account of this 'I can,' the ensuing 'being-in-the-midst-of' [Insein] emerges as being-possible [Möglichsein]," and "a facticity always is—authentically or inauthentically—that which it can be."[39] The nonbeing of possibility was not a form of radical disappearance or nothingness. Its nonbeing was rather a limited explicitness, a being-in-a-state-of-partial-concealment. Possibility was an "absence" (Abwesenheit) but in the mode of "privation" (steresis). It was a darkness, but positively so, in the sense that it marked out the possibility of light. This was a blurriness that could sharpen into a number of different phenomena.[40] As Heidegger put it in Summer Semester 1924, such an "absence" (Abwesenheit) was "not simply nothing but rather a certain something in the manner of a deficiency" or lack of clarity.[41]

Dunamis was a corollary of energeia. One could not conceive of capacity without a concept of activity. Possibility was the nonactivity of an activity that was, in some sense, proximate. The possible was not something detachable from the actual because it could not be understood as a variety of scenarios out there in the future. The possible was already making its presence felt as an underdetermining of the world. Dasein simply was Möglichsein; "situated presencing" simply was "being-possible." Thus, "experience" (Erfahrung) itself was not quarantined in some time slice of the now. Experience was itself trajectory. As Heidegger had put it in Summer Semester 1921, "the direction of experiencing reveals: possibles unlock possibilities, but only when these possibilities are experienced as directions, that is, when the facticity of a life lives in directed execution—qua directed."[42]

39. Heidegger, "Der Begriff der Zeit (1924)," 44: "sofern das Dasein durch dieses 'ich kann' bestimmt ist, offenbart sich schon sein nächstes Insein als Möglichsein," and "es ist immer—ob eigentlich oder uneigentlich—was es sein kann."

40. Heidegger, Einführung in die phänomenologische Forschung, 10: "die Dunkelheit ist en dunamei on, etwas durchaus Positives."

41. Heidegger, Grundbegriffe, 33: "nicht einfach nichts, sondern es ist etwas da, aber in einem Mangel."

42. Heidegger, Augustinus und der Neuplatonismus, 253: "die Richtung des Erfahrens zeigt an: Mögliches, schließt Möglichkeiten auf; das aber nur dann, wenn sie als Richtungen erfahren werden, d. h., wenn die Faktizität des Lebens selbst in gerichteten Vollzugs—als gerichtetem—lebt."

Possibility might be a "horizon of expectation" (*Erwartungshorizont*), but experience and expectation were indistinguishable. They constituted the selfsame spanning.[43] "Life," Heidegger confirmed, simply "*is* its particular possibilities."[44] For this reason, it was impossible to distinguish being from nonbeing in a radical way. Where there was motion, there was nonbeing. Where there was capacity for motion, there, too, was nonbeing.

Although it is important to specify in sequence the conceptual fields of *entelecheia*, *energeia*, and *dunamis*, it is equally important to see that they must always be understood together. Just so, the temporality of activation did not overwrite those of the other modalities but instead depended on them. Indeed, activation was a change that could structure predication. The kind of "change" (*alloiosis*) that did not alter the identity of a phenomenon generated a distinction between "that which had already been present" (*hypokeimenon*) and "that which then appeared subsequently" (*to sumbebēkos*). Later, this distinction would be reduced to a logical separation of accident from substance in the context of predication. In this process of philosophical conceptualization, however, the "accidental" quality that could attach to a substance—but was not necessary to its nature—came to lose its temporal span. Contingency, that is, was not the future revisability of all commitments. Contingency was instead the stretching of a present state back through its previous metamorphoses. Not "substance" as such, the *hypokeimenon* was more like a background, an already there, out of which deeds, matters, or going concerns (*pragmata*) would emerge.[45] Substances were not absolute; they *were* insofar as there was change, for change was at base different rates of change and was therefore constituted by relations within the simultaneity of the nonsimultaneous.

Entelecheia, *energeia*, and *dunamis* were all complex modalities taking different forms, but *dunamis* qua possibility was particularly complex and complex in a counterintuitive way that we need to grasp. Possibility might structure a situation in a host of different ways. It was not simply the distinct possibility that gave a situation a very determinate structure in the mode of dread. Possibility was also a kind of oversupply of possibilities that shuttled between anxiety at permutations too numerous to follow and, crucially, a kind of jumble in which the capable-of-being-otherwise of an aspect glossed simply as lack of pertinence. Paraphrasing Augustine, Heidegger had described "possibility" (*Möglichkeit*) as "the real 'burden'" (*der eigentlich "Last"*).[46] But this burden was also an underdetermination in being

43. Heidegger, 207.
44. Heidegger, *Phänomenologische Interpretationen zu Aristoteles*, 84: "Das Leben . . . *ist* seine Möglichkeiten."
45. Heidegger, "Dasein und Wahrsein," 75.
46. Heidegger, *Augustinus und der Neuplatonismus*, 249.

that permitted multiple continuations. It was imprecise. Indeed, the greater the number of apparently unrelated characteristics attached loosely to a phenomenon, the greater was the sense in which that phenomenon *was* not and did not exist.

At a certain point, an oversupply of possibilities began to look like nothing in the sense of no-thing-in-particular. As Heidegger had put it in Summer Semester 1922, "that which is merely 'accessory' [*das Mithafte*] looks like something that approaches nonbeing."[47] The jumble was a loose bundle of the "accidental" (*sumbebēkos, Mithafte*), where the "qualities" coincident with a phenomenon could not double as its definition. Indeed, under such conditions, it might be difficult to pull appearance out of the flux as *a* phenomenon at all. Such contingency did not possess defined contours of "coming-into-being" (*genesis*) or "passing-away" (*phthora*).[48] There would be alternating periods of slackness and tautness in being. At one extreme, there were periods in which the greater part of the information being received would be deemed immaterial—"noise." At the other extreme, there would be moments of definition at which every aspect of a thing would appear to be essential to its being *that* thing and not another.

The "nothing" (*Nichts*) that was "being-possible" (*Möglichsein*) qua underdetermination and openness was the originary ground of affect, primarily fear but also its many species and configurations shading through dread and anxiety. Heidegger was appropriating this conception of "nothing" from ancient metaphysics, which, he argued, "understood nothingness in the sense of nonbeing, that is, the unformed matter that cannot fashion itself into a formed and thus appearance-offering being."[49] As he said repeatedly in 1924 (in "The Basic Concepts of Aristotelian Philosophy" and "The Concept of Time"), "fear is a finding of oneself in the presence of nonbeing."[50] Being-possible was a being-ambiguous. When Heidegger asked the apparently inscrutable question of why there was being and not much more nothing, he was actually pointing out that vagueness ought to be understood as a basic mode of being and that most vagaries are never tested. Testing a vagary would not mean finding out what that phenomenon had been all along but in an opaque way. Testing a vagary was in fact manipulating the circumstances of its existence such that it might be specified and rendered determinate for the first time. Heidegger was saying it is a wonder there is as much specificity in the world as there is.

---

47. Heidegger, *Phänomenologische Interpretationen ausgewählter Abhandlungen*, 251: "es sieht das Mithafte als so etwas aus, das nahe am Nichtsein ist."
48. Heidegger, 251.
49. Heidegger, *Was Ist Metaphysik?*, 25: "faßt das Nichts in der Bedeutung des Nichtseienden, d. h. des ungestalteten Stoffes, der sich selbst nicht zum gestalthaften und demgemäß ein Aussehen (*eidos*) bietenden Seienden gestalten kann."
50. Heidegger, "Der Begriff der Zeit (1924)," 42: "die Angst ist das Sichbefinden vor dem Nichts."

"Determination" qua *Bestimmung* could imply specification as distinct from the determinism that connoted necessity. In Heidegger, this denotation occasioned some surprising assertions about the nature of both "possibility" (*Möglichkeit*) and "necessity" (*Notwendigkeit*) that broke with earlier philosophical approaches. In the German philosophical tradition, there had been a particular sense in which *Möglichkeit* was *Notwendigkeit*. This was a species of possibility cast as the necessity that followed from autonomy. That is, per Kant, one could legislate a rule for oneself such that freedom and obligation coincided. In Heidegger's 1919 Summer Semester articulation of the "philosophy of values" (*Wertphilosophie*), this line of thinking surfaced in the formulation that necessity was not a "factical 'incapacity-to-do-otherwise'" (*faktisch "Nichtanderstunkönnen"*) but rather a "requirement of the ought" (*Notwendigkeit des Sollens*).[51]

Within the account that Heidegger was developing, however, necessity might be something that existed but only rarely in situations that had achieved an extraordinary degree of determinateness understood as extreme explicitation. In Summer Semester 1920, Heidegger identified "potency" (*Potenz*), which he thought of as the central tenet of psychology, as "the possibility of determination" (*die Möglichkeit der Bestimmung*) or the *specifying* of a rule in an act.[52] Possibility was that which lay between the fully determinate and the entirely indeterminate. This was the domain of the imagination, which, Heidegger argued, had been the decisive and conceptually unmastered heart of Kant's critiques. "Imagination" (*Einbildungskraft*) was both a power of immersion in the senses in the absence of an object (a power of "en-picture-ing") and a power of establishing rules.[53] Possibility was not an "empty conceptual—logical—possibility, understood as whimsy [*Beliebigkeit*], such that a body might be placed either here or there," unrelated to anything else and without consequence. Rather, "*dunamis* is a possibility that has a certain presketched quality, something that always carries with it a direction," and "this [moderate] determinateness of *dunamis* belongs to the *topos* [the place or particular space of possibility] itself."[54] In this way, possibility existed along the spectrum of determination. And, drawing on a different tradition in Summer Semester 1924, Heidegger also characterized "necessity" (*Notwendigkeit* qua *anagkaion*) as

<hr/>

51. Heidegger, *Phänomenologie und transcendentale Wertphilosophie*, 154.
52. Heidegger, *Phänomenologie der Anschauung und des Ausdrucks*, 106.
53. Heidegger, *Kant*, 121. Einbildungskraft was also *ein Vermögen der Regeln* (69, 142), the *Abbildung, Nachbildung*, and *Vorbildung* constitutive of time as spanning (166–67, 169), and a matrix of trajectories stretching out of the blurs of presence (178).
54. Heidegger, *Platon: Sophistes*, 109: "leere begriffliche—logische—Möglichkeit, als Beliebigkeit, so daß es dem Körper freigestellt wäre, da oder dort zu sein." Instead, "die *dunamis* ist eine Möglichkeit, die eine bestimmt vorgezeichnete ist, die immer eine Direktion in sich trägt," and "dieses Bestimmtsein der *dunamis* gehört zum *topos* selbst."

a "determination of being" (*Bestimmung des Seins*). In this appropriation of Greek thought, necessity was a narrowing of possibility and not simply its opposite. The *anagkaion* was the place of constraint, the prison, the bind.[55] The point carried two implications: first, absolute necessity might be rare or nonexistent; second, relative necessity—in which the range of possible motions was deeply but not absolutely restricted—was common.

RHETORIC, *EPIDEIXIS*, AND *ALĒTHEIA*

Heidegger's most intensive engagement with rhetoric came in his Summer Semester 1924 lectures, "The Basic Concepts of Aristotelian Philosophy." What we must notice there is the degree to which rhetoric was written into the very foundations of the Heideggerian project that we have been tracing in the previous sections on temporality and modality. As I am reconstructing it, this project was dedicated to the elaboration of a philosophical vocabulary apt to reveal how phenomena might name themselves in the course of appearing. This entailed a fundamental revision of the notion of "existence." Such existence would not be constant. Instead, it would fluctuate as a phenomenon approached and then overshot self-definition as it cycled through *dunamis, energeia*, and *entelecheia* in the course of its temporalization. As we have seen in the two previous sections, Heidegger's account of naming required a reconceptualization of time as a matrix of differentials structured by the narrativizations of such coming into being and passing away, and it required a repurposing of Greek categories of modality. It also required the construction of an account of truth as a being-true. In the current section, I turn to this account of being-true.

For Heidegger, truth would be a phenomenon in the moment of its self-definition. What is surprising about his 1924 "Basic Concepts" lectures, however, is the degree to which he recast rhetoric as the field of inquiry in which the life capacities essential to this process of unconcealing were themselves refined. In order to grasp this point, we have to overcome some remarkably stubborn misreadings of rhetoric's relation to "being-true." Having done that, we can understand how Heidegger could say, on a number of quite different occasions (and decades after 1924), that rhetoric stood at the core of naming. I am arguing that rhetoric was intimately related to the *epideixis* or "manifestation" project at the heart of Heideggerian thought. As Heidegger conceived it, rhetoric simply was one of the practices in which situated presencing happened.

We may anchor Heidegger's engagement with the rhetorical tradition in a newly available text, "Situated Presencing and Being-True according

---

55. Heidegger, *Grundbegriffe*, 3.

to Aristotle," which was published in an English edition and translation in 2007 and then in the original German in 2016 as *Dasein und Wahrsein (nach Aristoteles)*.[56] Heidegger delivered this talk on several occasions in late 1924. In reference to the lecture as it was given at the University of Cologne (hosted by Max Scheler, probably on December 3), Theodore Kisiel has done a great deal to contextualize the speech in the scene of the French occupation of the Ruhr from 1923 to 1925, calling it Heidegger's "Ruhr-Speech."[57] The lecture offers us early glimpses of the Heideggerian intuition that phenomena rather than representations "are true." Above all else, however, we must understand that "being-true"—or "presencing truthfully"—is something that only emerges out of and always in relation to "situated presencing."

On the account Heidegger was developing in 1924, the appearance of a thing genuinely as itself such that it might name itself took place in relation to the variety of other possible appearances of that thing. Recall that in its Aristotelian mode of *dunamis* rhetoric was for Heidegger a possibility. This was a major claim and not simply the imprecise repetition of a received topos. Heidegger was revealing a great deal about his own revision of Greek ontology when he said that "possibility" possesses a "greater worth than actuality."[58] Here, Heidegger was inverting an Aristotelian topos. He meant that possibility was more primordial than actuality, because moments of extreme self-defining presencing would be relatively rare and because such presencing would emerge as the progressive exclusion of possible alternatives constituting the ambiguity of possibility as nonpresencing. Possibility was the primordial ambiguity out of which all actualization emerged. Because rhetoric was a possibility of specifying possible adjacencies, it was intimately bound up with the project of presencing itself. The Aristotelian rhetoric Heidegger was parsing revealed the stances that could credibly be taken up around an issue. For Heidegger, the implication was clear: the speaking that contributed to the genuine showing forth of a thing was also the speaking that contradistinguished that understanding of the thing from all of the credible and received forms clustered around it. "Initial breakthroughs in the opening of beings" will come to pass, said Heidegger, "with compendia of the dominant viewpoints of them, given that in most cases an element of the true phenomenon is contained there."[59] Rhetoric, on Heidegger's

56. See Heidegger, "Being-There and Being-True," in *Becoming Heidegger*, 214–37; and Heidegger, "Dasein und Wahrsein," 57–101.

57. See especially Kisiel, "Situating Rhetorical Politics," 185–208.

58. Heidegger, "Dasein und Wahrsein," 97: "Möglichkeit—höhere Dignität als die Wirklichkeit."

59. Heidegger, "Dasein und Wahrsein," 67: "vorbrechendes Erschließen des Seienden am Leitfaden der herrschenden Ansichten von ihm, in denen zumeist ein Stück von echt Gesehenem beschlossen liegt."

account, was the diagnostic and descriptor of the domain of possibility out of which the presencing of being-true emerged. In the earlier 1920s, rhetoric was thus explicitly built into the foundations of Heideggerian inquiry.

We must notice and then avoid the trap into which one can fall while interpreting the lecture that Heidegger gave in Cologne. On account of its purposiveness, oratory would seem to be an other of "being-true" (*Wahrsein*), for in "being-true" the phenomenon would manifest itself. Because of Heidegger's frequent but never entirely sustained denunciations of the concealment of being in the everydayness of established habits, readers sometimes lapse into the supposition that his basic project was a moralization of individual distinctiveness followed by a progressive abandonment of this position in his later work. Indeed, even in Brian Hansford Bowles's preface to the English translation of the "Ruhr-Speech," we are told that "since Aristotle's *Rhetoric* deals not with philosophical statements but with the everyday mode of public discourse and its mode of concealing and unconcealing, Heidegger's focus on it is only preliminary."[60] To say this is to suppose that "facilitating by means of speech the appearance of a thing in its true form" (*aletheuein*) emerges from engagements with "philosophical statements" and not from engagements with "the everyday mode of public discourse." Received Heidegger overwhelms our ability to perceive the real thought. "Sound not like *hoi polloi*," we conjure Heidegger saying. "Fall not into the ways of the many, the mass, the average, the statistically generated (and degenerate), the indistinct, *the everyone and no one in particular*"—thus and so, the Heidegger of academic legend. These are Bowdlerized, received formulations that stand in the way of access to the novel Heideggerian position in 1924.

In order to identify and then reject the common misreading, we should take up a standard if usually implicit syllogism: Heidegger fetishized authenticity; rhetoric is the height of inauthenticity; ergo, Heidegger must have found rhetoric anathema. Yet he did not. To extract oneself from this mistake, one has to reconceive the relationship between authenticity and inauthenticity. Not simply an opposite of authenticity, inauthenticity was its condition of possibility. That is, authenticity only ever emerged out of inauthenticity. Rhetoric was more basically preoccupied with identifying newer, more original, more pertinent modes of articulation. We read Heidegger saying that "the greatest among [the Greeks] undertook a struggle for [unconcealment, *Unverborgenheit*], a struggle against sophistic and rhetoric" and that "we can scarcely any longer comprehend the scale of this spiritual confrontation of the Greeks with themselves and their situated

60. Bowles, "Introduction to the Cologne Address," in Heidegger, *Becoming Heidegger*, 217.

presencing [*Dasein*]."[61] Here, we must not fall into the trap of seeing just one more denigration of rhetoric, because the astounding fact in this particular construction is that Heidegger was aligning oratory with *Dasein* itself. Oratory is the embeddedness of "presencing" (*Sein*) in its "situatedness" (*Befindlichkeit*), and Aristotle's *Rhetoric* was the analytic of both.

"The possibility of an authentic speaking" (*die Möglichkeit eines eigentümlichen Sprechens*) emerged only on the basis of a received embedding of speech.[62] On this account, rhetoric staged a fundamental confrontation between "the speaking that revealed a phenomenon" (*Rede*) and "the received, homeless, tone-deaf hear-then-say that lacked pertinence to the matter at hand" (*Gerede*). "Idle talk" (*Gerede*) was not radically other than genuine speech. It was a once-genuine speaking in the moment of its being repeated out of place.[63] One had to *begin* in one's embeddedness and embark on the work of distinguishing there.[64] In a sense, such embeddedness was "the cluster of received opinions" (*endoxa*) that constituted an aporia, but aporia was to be understood in the potentially positive sense of an inability to mouth the assertions of others without arriving at a question.[65]

In order to disabuse ourselves of the common error that Heidegger the authenticity fetishist could not have had any real interest in rhetoric, we have to recall that oratory (speech performance) was not identical with rhetoric (speech analysis). In fact, given its orientation to the specific situation, rhetoric was an analytic of the possibilities for "being-true" (*Wahrsein*) under conditions of "presencing within a particular spatiotemporal elaboration" (*Dasein*). Thus, for Heidegger, the crucial document of Greek speech was not Demosthenes and his speeches but rather Aristotle and his *Rhetoric*. Ignoring at that point—and, indeed, for the most part—the Organon (the prior and posterior analytics combined with the topics), Heidegger declared that Aristotle's *Rhetoric* was "the fundamental doctrine of *logos*, the original 'logic.'"[66] Thus, in the now classic formulations of the Summer Semester 1924 lectures on the basic concepts of Aristotelian philosophy, Aristotle's *Rhetoric* was "a concrete documentation of the originality" (*der konkret Beleg für die*

---

61. Heidegger, "Dasein und Wahrsein," 67: "die Größten unter ihnen führten den Kampf um sie, ein Kampf [?] gegen Sophistik und Rhetorik. Wir vermögen uns kaum mehr ein Bild zu machen von der Größe dieser geistigen Auseinandersetzung der Griechen mit sich selbst und ihrem Dasein."

62. Heidegger, *Grundbegriffe*, 38.

63. Heidegger, "Der Begriff der Zeit (1924)," 35: "im Gerede verhärtet sich die Auslegung zu Ausgelegtheit."

64. Heidegger, *Grundbegriffe*, 63–64.

65. Heidegger, 367.

66. Heidegger, "Dasein und Wahrsein," 63: "Rhetorik—die Fundamentallehre vom Logos, die ursprüngliche 'Logik.'"

Ursprünglichkeit) of the Greek view of *logos*.[67] Possessing it was "better than having a philosophy of language" (*besser, als wenn wir eine Sprachphilosophie hätten*).[68] Here was Heidegger weaving the *Rhetoric* into his broader history of European philosophy and its progressive deliquescence.

I am claiming that even as he played the type often enough denouncing "the everyone and no one in particular" was not Heidegger's true project and that we should pay more attention instead to the points at which he said the indistinctness of the average had a positive role to play. As the Heidegger of Summer Semester 1923 had put it, "the indistinct and indiscriminate 'they' [*das Man*] actually has something positive about it; it is not simply a phenomenon of decadence; instead, it is a 'how' of factical being-there." The famous category of *das Man* is a casing and frame for situatedness.[69] Again, note the peculiarity of Heidegger's account of Aristotle: "this everyday speaking—and *this* is the true discovery made by Aristotle [!]—is not directed at *alētheia* [truth as unconcealedness] but has nonetheless a certain propriety, because it belongs to the meaning of everyday life in that it moves within a certain perimeter of appearance." Heidegger went on to say that "everyday speaking, which is not in any express way a form of *aletheuein* [disclosing or letting appear], derives its distinctive vindication."[70] Averageness was an indistinctness of being permitting many continuations. It was a tissue of habits—routines, pathways, infrastructures. As a background, it was a condition of possibility for a more distinct actualization.

Arbitrary, plenipotent, and creative, Heidegger declared that rhetoric was not simply "persuading" (*peithein*). With his classification of rhetoric, he proceeded to suture it into the account of temporality and modality that we examined in the first two sections of this chapter. Rhetoric was not persuading as such, nor was it "a practicing without knowledge of principles" (*empeiria*). Heidegger rejected Plato's handle on rhetoric as *empeiria* in the *Gorgias* as "really *quite* primitive." He was more interested in the sense articulated in the *Phaedrus* of rhetoric as a *psuchagōgia*, "a leading of the soul." And his imagination was fired in his Winter Semester 1924–1925 lectures on Plato's *Sophist* by the nonbeing of *technē*, "a power of bringing into being," which dealt with relationships between that which existed and that which did not yet exist. In the end, however, Heidegger affiliated himself most

---

67. Heidegger, *Grundbegriffe*, 61.
68. Heidegger, 117.
69. Heidegger, *Ontologie*, 17: "das *Man* hat etwas bestimmtes Positives, es ist nicht nur Verfallsphänomen, sondern als solche ein wie des faktischen Daseins."
70. Heidegger, *Platon: Sophistes*, 339: "dieses alltägliche Sprechen—das ist die eigentliche Entdeckung des Aristoteles—geht nicht auf die *alētheia*, hat aber doch ein gewisses Recht, weil es zum Sinn des alltäglichen Daseins gehört, daß es sich in gewissem Umkreis im Augenschein bewegt," and "von daher nimmt dann auch das Sprechen, das nicht ausdrücklich *aletheuein* ist, sein eigenständiges Recht."

basically with Aristotle on the question of rhetoric.[71] And for him, within the Aristotelian corpus, the authentic conception of rhetoric was as a *dunamis*, a possibility not a practice, not an art, not a "theory" (or, at least, not as that term is used today).

There is probably a sense in which Heidegger's preference for characterizing rhetoric as a *dunamis* was tendentious, but if anything this is evidence of Heidegger's desire to include rhetoric in his temporalizing account of the modalities and to revise that account by means of the preoccupations and interpretative possibilities he found in rhetoric. In Heidegger's translation of the key Aristotelian definition, *rhetoric* was "die Möglichkeit, am jeweils Gegebenen zu sehen das, was für eine Sache, die Thema der Rede ist, spricht, jeweilig zu sehen das, was für eine Sache sprechen kann."[72] Paraphrasing rather than translating, we can say that rhetoric was a possibility of seeing. It was a possibility of seeing in the midst of a particular given, or as Heidegger recast it in a subsequent variation amid what is on offer in a particular situation of being-with-one-another.[73] It was a possibility of seeing in a given situation what speaks or might speak for the matter that is under discussion.

We should notice three things about Heidegger's inflection of the Aristotelian account of rhetoric as a *dunamis*. First, in Heidegger's translation, *dunamis* was "possibility" (*Möglichkeit*) and not "capacity" (*Vermögen*). Heidegger was envisaging a rhetoric that was more of an undergoing than a mastering. On this account, rhetoric was the indeterminacy of seeing several potential ways of speaking in a particular circumstance. Moreover, possibility here was doubled. It was not simply that one might retreat from speaking into a position of seeing the possibility of speaking in a particular way. Possibility proliferated, and the *particular* thing that might be said came with alternatives, a netherworld of options. Second, Heidegger was more circumspect than those who translate *endechomenon pithanon* as "the available means of persuasion." His rendition—based on a grammar of *das, was spricht für oder für-sprechen kann*—was noncommittal, emphasizing credibility more than belief or the kind of coming into belief that might be persuasion. Third, what had been *peri hekaston* in Aristotle became *jeweilig* and *Situation* in Heidegger. In place of what has become the repeated and dimmed down English phrase "in any given case," we have a hovering between the stock occasion with its acceptable repertoire and the particularized moment with no obvious or uncontroversial set of precedents—an emergence of the new. Later, in the context of his lecture sequence on Plato's *Sophist*, Heidegger offered a supplementary fragment that may function as a kind of summation: "rhetoric: a being-capable-of

---

71. Heidegger, "Platons Phaidros," 104. Heidegger, *Platon: Sophistes*, 338.
72. Heidegger, *Grundbegriffe*, 114.
73. Heidegger, 117.

as presencing" (*Rhetorik: das Können als Sein*).[74] In this move, rhetoric was becoming the frame within which any radical differentiation between being and being-possible, present and future, would be untenable. As a manifesting of possible continuations, rhetoric simply *was* time. It simply *was* the process by which a situation came into being in conjunction with articulation as a complex amalgam of motions achieved, emergent, and possible.

As a *seeing* of possibility, rhetoric took up the accounts of temporality and modality that we examined earlier, but it also embedded those accounts in a tightly interwoven set of life capacities that Heidegger was appropriating from Aristotle and that came to define many of his own enduring interests: *theorein, aisthesis, krinein, phantasia, nous*.[75] At the intersection of these various life capacities, Heidegger was articulating what I am calling a rhetoric of *epideixis*. This was not an analysis of praising or blaming as such but rather an analysis of exhibiting, putting on display, calling out for attention. As Heidegger would say in his seminar on Plato's *Phaedrus* in Summer Semester 1932 (continuing his thoughts on Aristotle's *dunamis* definition), rhetoric was "a letting break through of appearing" (*das Aufbrechenlassen des Erscheinens*), or better, it was a "*letting*-appear of things" (*Erscheinen-lassen der Dinge*).[76] On this account, rhetoric was a kind of awareness of the ways in which a phenomenon might be cast within a particular community combined with an awareness of what might have the potential to enter that repertoire of received ideas with distinction. As I am using the concept here, something is distinct if it can take up and hold a place within the vocabulary of a particular community. Such a distinct appearance becomes a new name even before its arrangements of "accidents" can be articulated in the course of predication. Here, predication is not so much the process of adding qualities to a substance as it is the process of separating out and calling attention to aspects of a phenomenon that are already implicitly present in the appearance.

In Heidegger, the concern with *epideixis* eventually became a very basic concern with naming. Naming might seem like a timeless grammar because it deliberately avoids verbs and therefore tenses. In fact, it was one of the basic noetic acts and was anything but timeless. Thus, for Heidegger, "naming does not simply mean the giving of a name to a thing; it also means a bringing to attention, *dēloun*"—that is, "a rendering visible."[77] Indeed, "speech" (*logos*) simply was "rendering visible" (*dēloun*).[78] Like the

74. Heidegger, *Platon: Sophistes*, 625.

75. Compare Heidegger, "Wesen und Begriff der Phusis," in *Wegmarken*, 314.

76. Heidegger, "Platons Phaidros," 108.

77. Heidegger, *Platon: Sophistes*, 501: "Nennen meint nicht nur: einem Ding einen Namen geben, sondern auch: es zur Kenntnis bringen, *dēloun*."

78. Heidegger, "Diltheys Forschungarbeit," 164: "der *logos* ist *dēloun*."

painter, what the poet did was bring a phenomenon together and depict unity, but this was a unity constituted by tension or a set of tensions rather than a stasis.[79] Thus, in response to Hölderlin (whom he took to be a kind of metapoet), Heidegger defined poetry as "the instituting naming of being" (*das stiftende Nennen des Seins*).[80] Then, taking up Nietzsche's line that "language is rhetoric," Heidegger replaced one of the two substantives (either *Sprache* or *Rhetorik*) with *dichtend*.[81] Probably, he meant that "language is poeming." Conceivably, he was improvising with "poeming is rhetoric." We can say that both substitutions are meaningful and that both versions are in play here: poetry is the process of bringing language itself into being, and, by the same token, this process of contributing to the articulateness of the world by taking up some appearances and not others as definitions is the rhetorical project—the project of rhetoric as *epideixis*.

Rhetoric was intimately related to "unconcealment" (*alētheia*), because the processes of presencing associated with *epideixis* were essential to the Heideggerian account of truth. That which was most intensively in being—present, activated, not concealed or offstage—was most true. This meant that truth was not a relation of correspondence between assertion and world. Nor was it a normative relation of coherence between one assertion and another. Instead, truth was the phenomenon appearing as itself: named, delineated, uncovered.[82] In laying out the intellectual-historical deliquescence of this concept in its Latinization, Heidegger laid particular blame on medieval scholastic thought.[83] He emphasized a formulation from Thomas Aquinas in which "truth is 'a making equal' or 'a correspondence' of a thing and the understanding."[84] No longer a specification of a phenomenon's appearing, Acquinas was taking truth to be a characterization of the relationship of representation between mind and world.

Attending to the rhetorical epideictic quality of Heidegger's account of *alētheia* attunes us to a glitch in Heidegger's formulations that is otherwise easy to miss. Listening to the 1924 Ruhr speech, Max Scheler pointed out the irony that Heidegger's account of "being-true" (*Wahrsein*) was implicitly a gloss of the medieval transcendentals according to which being and truth and beauty were one. In response to Scheler's question, Heidegger could only gesture toward a tension in Thomas Aquinas between the insertion of a relation of *adaequatio* between thing and intellect and the supposition

79. Heidegger, "Andenken," 310.

80. Heidegger, "Hölderlin," 1073.

81. Heidegger, "Platons Phaidros," 108: "'*Sprache ist Rhetorik*' (Nietzsche), besser: *Dichtend!*"

82. Heidegger, *Vom Wesen der Wahrheit*, 7, 10.

83. Heidegger, "Platons Lehre von der Wahrheit," 119.

84. Heidegger and Scheler, "Discussion between Heidegger and Max Scheler," in Heidegger, *Becoming Heidegger*, 233–34: "veritas est adaequatio rei et intellectus."

that "every being is true."[85] Scheler had put his finger on something. Else-where, Heidegger had indeed utilized the convertibility of the medieval transcendentals (*unum, bonum, verum*) in order to articulate what he took to be the Platonic thought on the coincidence between truth and "being in the moment of its most intense presencing." We should not forget that this medieval philosophical mode of thinking had been particularly central to his habilitation. And Heidegger was working with convertibility of this order when he later declared that "beauty is the originarily unifying unity."[86] Again, we find the same dynamic in Heidegger's gloss of the final line of Edu-ard Mörike's 1846 poem "To a Lamp" ("Auf eine Lampe"). There, he argued that "beauty is . . . not a quality that attaches to an entity in the manner of an add-on." Beauty is not a predicate at all but rather "one of the highest modes of presencing," namely, "a pure emanating from itself and appearing."[87] As *epideixis* and as a skill with situated presencing, rhetoric is concerned with precisely these kinds of convertibility between truth and beauty and unity.

The appearance that could name itself in the manner of a definition by drawing attention to the predicates that distinguished it from other appear-ances was intense, but it was not stable. It was not simply that no organism could maintain itself at its moment of fullest maturation and expression indefinitely. Even a cosmos might be in flux and might tip beyond the sta-bilities of established orbits. More basically, however, naming was the pro-cess of bringing something out into the open, and bringing something out into the open was more essential to naming than holding it there. Naming was *energeia* rather than *entelecheia*. Here, we see the rhetorical dimension of naming most clearly. Naming as revelation and not classification was concerned with breaking a taxonomic schema by showing how it was that old received vocabularies covered over zones of potential attention and sensitivity. The performativity of rhetoric was its timeful awareness of the background of received names that dramatized the freshness and embodied freedom of the new name.

TOWARD A SYSTEMATIC HERMENEUTICS OF THE EVERYDAYNESS OF BEING-WITH-ONE-ANOTHER

We are now in a position to interpret the one sentence from *Being and Time* that is essential to the line of inquiry that I am laying out here—namely, the assertion that Aristotle's *Rhetoric* was the first systematic hermeneutic of

85. Heidegger and Scheler, "Discussion between Heidegger and Max Scheler," in Heidegger, *Becoming Heidegger*, 233–34: "omne ens est verum."
86. Heidegger, "Andenken," 310: "die Schönheit ist das ursprünglich einigende Eine."
87. Heidegger, *Der Satz vom Grund*, 102: "Schönheit ist . . . nicht eine Eigenschaft, die zum Seienden als eine Ausstattung hinzukommt. Schönheit ist eine höchste Weise des Seins, d. h. hier: das reine aus-sich-Aufgehen und Scheinen."

the everydayness of being-with-one-another.[88] As I have said, I do not think this sentence can be understood from within *Being and Time*. In order to reconstruct its connections and implications, one has to turn to the lecture materials, predominantly from earlier in the 1920s. In the previous section, we began the work of tracing the ways in which rhetoric was at the heart of Heidegger's phenomenological project. In this section, I pursue and confirm the point by arguing that in fact Heidegger was laying claim to Aristotle's *Rhetoric* as something like a first version of *Being and Time*. If "first version" seems too much, then we may think of the *Rhetoric* as a philological repertoire that Heidegger was metabolizing in order to generate his own distinctive set of concerns and practices. Aristotle's *Rhetoric* had been an analytic of *Dasein*. For Heidegger, it had been an analytic of the conditions of possibility for situated presencing. Thus, rhetoric was "nothing other . . . than the discipline in which the self-interpretation of situated presencing [*Dasein*] is explicitly achieved."[89] I proceed here by taking up the key terms of the *Being and Time* sentence, and I use them to reveal the intimate relationship between rhetoric and Heideggerian inquiry. Of course, the redescription works in both directions. It is not that I am simply claiming Heideggerian inquiry "for rhetoric." The project is not territorial in that way. Here as elsewhere, rhetoric cannot colonize without being itself fundamentally reconfigured. The Heideggerian category of "everydayness" (*Alltäglichkeit*) that emerges from this exposition is quite different from the standard received versions in most of the Heidegger scholarship, and the version of rhetoric that emerges is distinctive too. This is a rhetoric that sees everydayness as a condition of possibility for the appearance of a situation.

Heidegger did emphasize the Greek topos according to which "only insofar as he lives in the polis is the human being genuinely human," but we should not therefore conclude that the key Heideggerian category of "being-with-one-another" (*Miteinandersein*) denoted simply a coming together of persons in public spaces.[90] "Being-with-one-another" as it appeared in the *Being and Time* sentence on Aristotle's *Rhetoric* was not a being-together in that sense. Nor was it the obverse of being-alone. The *Sein*—"being," but as "presencing"—in *Miteinandersein* did not mean "coming-together" (*Zusammenkommen*). It meant the matrix of motions that was essential to temporality itself. *Being*-with-one-another was the class of ways in which the being of persons was their being-in-motions-with-others. It was their being-persuaded, their being-impressionable or -affected, their being-angry. It was their articulations of being in the world with others who were trying to put them in a particular place or who were

88. Heidegger, *Sein und Zeit*, 138.
89. Heidegger, *Grundbegriffe*, 110: "nichts anderes . . . als die Disziplin, in der die Selbstauslegung des Daseins ausdrücklich vollzogen ist," "die Hermeneutik des Daseins selbst."
90. Heidegger, 56: "sofern der Mensch in der *polis* lebt, ist er . . . eigentlich Mensch."

resisting the taking up of a particular place or stance. A degree of temporal synchronization was thus important for being-together, for it was a being-actualized in a particular place and time together. If *Dasein* were "situated presencing," then presencing-with-one-another was the myriad of ways in which one's relationship to others could become conspicuous, and it was the *manner* in which that relation became conspicuous. The *Da*, the time space of that becoming conspicuous, was a complex spacing of pronouns. It was a geometry of the you and the I complicated by routings through the he, she, and it, the they, we, and you plural. Confrontation was a locus classicus, but flanking was similarly crucial (isolation too), for the background against which one became conspicuous might be either a refuge denied or a prison escaped.

"Being-with-one-another," we begin to intuit, was essentially the emotional topography of human communities, and here the connection to rhetoric becomes more explicit, for rhetoric—especially in the Heideggerian reception—is very much an analytic of emotions. This was a central preoccupation in Summer Semester 1924. Indeed, Walter Bröcker's notes from the Summer Semester 1924 course were simply called *Rhetorik II*, because the lectures placed such emphasis on the second book of the *Rhetoric*, where Aristotle had concentrated on the *pathē*, the passions. In Heidegger's account, such "affects are not states of the soul; here we are concerned with an orienting [*Befindlichkeit*] of a living being in a world."[91] And, as we have seen, a *Befindlichkeit* was always a specification in space and time, a spanning of the *Da*, ahead and behind, drawing pasts and futures into being. Not bodily states, not physiological processes taking place under the skin (and not convulsions in individual souls), emotions were instead orientations to others, orientations to space, orientations to time.

Modality and emotion were deeply intricated, as we see in the example of fear. Like desire and aversion (the base categories out of which it was distinguished), fear was an orientation to being-possible. Fear related to a "nothing" (*Nichts*, a no-thing-in-particular or a *vaguely* perceptible something). It attached to a kind of indeterminate nonpresence that was the *possible* presence of something or several things.[92] If the *pathē* were exquisitely embodied (without being per se embodiments), that was because they were discriminations of motion and possible motion. The *pathē* were both the motions and possible motions of others and one's own motions and possible motions. Because rhetoric as an orientation to possibility incorporated all of the life capacities (from *theorein* through *aisthesis, krinein,*

91. Heidegger, 122: "*pathē,* 'Affekte,' sind nicht Zustände des Seelischen, es handelt sich um eine *Befindlichkeit des Lebenden in einer Welt*."
92. Heidegger, 192.

and *phantasia* to *nous*), the *pathē* were motilities in all life registers: ticks, feints, slights, irritabilities, continuations; poses, counterposes, imputed counterposes; reciprocations, mirrorings, fantasies, anticipated parryings; self-characterizations, character assassinations, inferred character assassinations; whole novel plots scripted ahead of time, in time, and after the fact. As Daniel Gross has argued, reading the Summer Semester 1924 lectures on the basic concepts of Aristotelian philosophy closely "suggests that emotions might be treated as structuring 'turns' that, like tropes, constitute a domain of mental perception that make language possible."[93] Emotion is the structuring and locomoting of scenes and their narratives.[94]

If "being-with-one-another" was a kind of conspicuous actualization of affective relations with others, then the "everydayness" (*Alltäglichkeit*) of these relations was a waning of their conspicuousness. Heidegger's move to everydayness constituted a deliberate displacement of theoretical attention from the moments of exception, of coming into consciousness, of framed uniqueness with which orators seem to deal. The move expressed an interest in the *repetitiousness* of the "in-any-given-case," which had been central to the Aristotelian definition of rhetoric that Heidegger privileged. Rhetoric had its scenes. It staged its own *tableaux vivants*, and it sketched its own characters. Indeed, Heidegger was struck by Theophrastus's caricature of the professional caricaturist that was the sophist, the "jawsmith" (*Schwätzer*), who traded in a knowledge of the clichés and *forms* of speaking that would float free of particular occasion.[95] To be sure, at times, Heidegger denounced such derivativeness, for the repetitions through which one cycled thoughtlessly were not awake to the places and times in which they were played like cards from a deck.

Everydayness, I am claiming, was a kind of temporality in which one was equidistant from a series of similar days, similar activities, similar scenes. Habit was something like being in many different times at once, present to them all, in a sense, and not to the time actually most proximate. Stock scenes were "everydaynesses" (*Alltäglichkeiten*) qua "trivialities" (*Trivialitäten*), as the Heidegger of Winter Semester 1919–1920 put it (rather absentmindedly).[96] Experiences of triviality were indexes of inabilities to attend, to be present. The more intensive redaction of everydayness from other resources came in Winter Semester 1921–1922, where the conceptual zone of everydayness entered the Heideggerian vocabulary by means of the dailiness of sin. There, Heidegger reported a base text transposed from Augustine: "our daily furnace is human language itself" (*quotidiana fornax*

93. Gross, "Being-Moved," 39.
94. Gross, *Secret History of Emotion.*
95. Heidegger, *Platon: Sophistes*, 302ff.
96. Heidegger, *Grundprobleme der Phänomenologie*, 103.

nostra, says the church father, is *humana lingua*). Usage is a daily kiln firing. It layers.[97] Life itself was a "taking care of the 'daily bread,'" and the everyday was difficult to see on account of the fact that it was omnipresent.[98] In Winter Semester 1924–1925, Heidegger argued that the *sophos*—the "wise person" not the "sophist" (*sophistes*)—should be identified as precisely the person who could uncover the most difficult to identify everydaynesses, the habits so habitual that they were usually impalpable and invisible.[99] The laminated, *overwritten*—overlaid and protostatistical—qualities of these scenes, characters, trivialities constituted their everydayness.

Everydayness, thus, was habit (and, indeed, the habitual virtues), but Nancy Struever was right when she said that everydayness was "timeful" (*zeitlich*) in addition to *alltäglich*. Decisive for her was Heidegger's assertion that "everydayness manifests itself in a fundamental basic structure—its timefulness."[100] That is, the habituation that was everydayness was itself fired by the strenuousness of temporal orientation. Such orientation was always a spanning into tense—future, past, imperfect, pluperfect, future perfect. Apt also is the pun proposed by tensing, which is both a linguistic process of placing in time and a physiological process of bracing for a future. "Repetition" (*das Öfter*) was that which characterized "the timefulness of presencing" (*die Zeitlichkeit des Daseins*).[101] The many-timed-ness of every-dayness was a kind of indexicality. As Heidegger said first in "The Concept of Time" (the 1924 manuscript version), "the desk over there, with its par-ticular number of places, indexes those with whom one sits at table daily," and, equally, "the instrument encountered in use carries with it a 'bought at' and a 'refined by,'" while "the book is a present from so-and-so," whereas "the umbrella in the corner has been forgotten by so-and-so."[102] Indeed, "habit" (*hexis*) was "a how of emotion" (*ein Wie des pathos*), which was, in turn, a mode of "being-brought-out-of-sorts" (*Aus-der-Fassung-Seins*).[103] Paradoxically, habit could become a routinization of being knocked out of kilter.

In the account that Heidegger was fashioning, habits were a form of

97. Heidegger, *Augustinus und der Neuplatonismus*, 228.

98. Heidegger, *Phänomenologische Interpretationen zu Aristoteles*, 90: "sorgen um das 'tägliche Brot.'"

99. Heidegger, *Platon: Sophistes*, 95.

100. Heidegger, *Grundbegriffe*, 131: "es offenbart sich die Alltäglichkeit selbst in einer funda-mentalen Grundstruktur: ihrer *Zeitlichkeit*."

101. Heidegger, 191.

102. Heidegger, "Der Begriff der Zeit (1924)," 24: "der Tisch dort hat mit seinen bestimmten Plätzen die Verweisung auf die, mit denen man täglich zu Tisch kommt," and "das in der Ver-wendung begegnende Werkzeug ist gekauft bei ——, ausbegessert von ——," while "das Buch ist geschenkt von ——," whereas "der in der Ecke stehende Schirm ist vergessen von ——."

103. Heidegger, *Grundbegriffe*, 185.

overwriting in which the repeated layings-down and imprintings of practice remained distinct and therefore capable of eliciting a multitude of subtly different responses to subtly different requests for performance. True, for Heidegger in 1919–1920, *Habitus* had denoted a "manner of reacting" made up of "passively and not spontaneously activating tendencies derived from whatever was available."[104] But the more pockmarked by impressions a habit was, the more it became a zone of unwitting but highly calibrated sensitivity. In Summer Semester 1924, the insistence came that "habituation" (*Gewöhnung*) was a result of "repetition" (*Wiederholung*) and not "exercise" (*Übung*). We must note that for Heidegger in this moment repetition did "not denote the bringing into existence of a sharply honed dexterity [*Fertigkeit*]." It denoted instead "acting afresh out of a corresponding decision in any given moment."[105] Habituation, that is, did not entail isolating a motion and working it over. It involved putting oneself in a situation of judgment and repeating the deciding. This implied that habituation was "not routinization but rather a holding of oneself free—qua capacity or possibility, *dunamis*—in the mean."[106] Never fully achieved, always an average (or an array of deviations from the mean), and nothing more than a possibility, habit was extremely time sensitive, liable to deterioration and forever in need of exercise.

When the distinctiveness of each near-perfect repetition became too fine to discern or remember, each-and-everydayness changed from the kind of habituation that Heidegger deeply valued to a specific form of absence akin to hiding in plain sight. Having achieved a kind of permanence in both form and use, everyday objects would disappear. As Heidegger put it in reference to interactions with "trusted objects," "I look past these things, for they have not the character of presence [*Präsenz*], they are much too everyday, and it is as if they vanish from my everyday living [*alltäglichen Dasein*]."[107] To perceive the true nature of Heideggerian "repetition," drop the metaphor "pockmarked." Take up instead the metaphor of "worn smooth," and visualize the adze-head worked clean into countless facets. In this way, the everyday became frictionless, tranquilized, without burr. Re-presenting that invisibility took work.

104. Heidegger, *Grundprobleme der Phänomenologie*, 68: habit was a "Weise des Re-agierens" derived "von passiv (nicht spontan) wirkenden Tendenzen, die aus der Verfügbarkeiten entwachsen."

105. Heidegger, *Grundbegriffe*, 189: "Wiederholung besagt nicht: Ins-Spiel-Bringen einer festsitzenden Fertigkeit, sondern *in jedem Augenblick neu aus dem entsprechenden Entschluß heraus Handeln*."

106. Heidegger, 190.

107. Heidegger, 32: "ich sehe darüber hinweg, sie haben nicht den Charakter der Präsenz, sie sind viel zu alltäglich, sie verschwinden gleichsam aus mein alltäglichen Dasein."

In establishing a spectrum between the habituation that was continued presencing even under conditions of intensive repetition, on the one hand, and, on the other, the everydayness in which repetition became a mode of camouflage, Heidegger was performing a very precise inversion of some basic Greek presuppositions concerning ontology and modality. Ancient Greek ontology had privileged the necessary as that which always was, as that which did not deviate and could not be otherwise. If Heidegger took from the Greeks the presupposition that "being" (*Sein*) was "presence" (*Präsenz*), then he inverted the meaning and consequences of that presupposition. *Präsenz* for him was not the full achievedness of *entelecheia*. It was the coming into form of *energeia*. For the Greeks, "being means being-completed."[108] For Heidegger, being-finished was an acme that predicted disappearance. It was a "death mask" (*Totenmaske*).[109] For Heidegger, presence required spanning out of a plastic here and now. In contrast, "it would never even occur to a Greek person to see the genuine 'Da' in a particular here and now."[110] In a Greek reading, the *Da*, the "there," would be the distributed and enduring temporality of the entity brought to its good form, a form that was, is, and would be. Heidegger first came to this insight in the 1924 manuscript on "The Concept of Time," where, ventriloquizing and betraying Greek idioms, he claimed of any phenomenon that "only when it is what it can be will it be graspable as a totality." That is, only "in its having-come-to-an-end is it fully there for the first time." But then, "in its being-completed qua being-finished it is actually no longer there."[111] Repetition does not evince a natural order; it poses a challenge to presencing.

The conspicuousness that Heidegger was drawn to in his sketch of being-with-one-another as a kind of affective synchronization was covered over by the many-timed-ness of the everyday. In turn, however, the task of the *hermeneutic* of this everydayness of being-with-one-another—which was rhetoric itself—was to render conspicuous the work of obfuscation completed by everydayness. My claim, thus, is that Heidegger's account of Aristotle's *Rhetoric* effected a double reversal: turning the conspicuousness of affective synchronization into habit, then turning the inconspicuousness of habit into an object of inquiry. Hermeneutic for Heidegger, recall, was most basically a laying-out, spanning, "tensing" (*Auslegung*). Thus, rhetoric was "the laying-out of situated presencing [*Dasein*] with regard to the basic possibility of

108. Heidegger, 12: "Sein heißt Fertigsein."
109. Heidegger, *Kant*, 88.
110. Heidegger, *Grundbegriffe*, 223: "der Grieche kommt gar nicht darauf, in diesem hic et nunc das eigentliche Da zu sehen."
111. Heidegger, "Der Begriff der Zeit (1924)," 46–47: "erst wenn es das ist, was es sein kann, wird es als Ganzes erfaßbar." That is, "in seinem Zu-Ende-gekommen-sein ist es erst voll da," but then "in seinem Fertig-sein ist es doch gerade nicht mehr."

speaking with one another"[112] This characterization cast rhetoric as a basic life function. But, above all, as the Heidegger of Summer Semester 1923 had insisted, hermeneutic was a *practice* and not a theory of interpretation. Thus, "the term *hermeneutics* ought to denote the patchwork of activities of exerting, assessing, approaching, interrogating, and explicitating facticity itself."[113] The problem, as he identified it, was that "hermeneutics is now no longer the practice of interpretation itself and has become instead the doctrine dealing with the conditions, the objects, the tools, the communication and practical application of interpretation."[114] For Heidegger, hermeneutic was in fact a form of "vigil" (*Wachsein*).[115] *Auslegen* was a spanning of the *Da*. As such, "the first principle of all hermeneutics" was historicization, which meant placing oneself in a particular present that traced itself out of a past and *thereby* brought into being a particular specification of nonbeing—namely, the possible.[116]

LIQUIDATING *DUNAMIS*

I have been arguing that there was an intimate connection between rhetoric and core elements in the Heideggerian philosophical project. For Heidegger, neither time nor space were prior to motion. In fact, time and space were produced by motions, the differentials among motions, and by the articulation of those differentials. This contention established "situatedness" (*Befindlichkeit*) as the first—rhetorical—task of all presencing. One of the corollaries of this position was that presencing itself was not constant and that some moments of presencing were more involved than others in the naming of the world that was the rhetoric of *epideixis*. When Heidegger was most intensively involved in excavating this project in the early 1920s, he turned to Aristotle's *Rhetoric* and found there an exploration of the modalities and life capacities most tightly entangled with these processes of presencing. And the sentence that Heidegger used to mark the burial of this line of inquiry at the center of *Being and Time* recorded the role played by rhetoric in the articulation of such presencing against the background of an averaging of experiences that was very basically emotional in character. In

112. Heidegger, *Grundbegriffe*, 139: "die Auslegung des Daseins hinsichtlich der Grundmöglichkeit des Miteinandersprechen."
113. Heidegger, *Ontologie*, 9: "der Ausdruck *Hermeneutik* soll die einheitliche Weise des Einsatzes, Ansatzes, Zugehens, Befragens, und Explizierens der Faktizität anzeigen."
114. Heidegger, 13: "Hermeneutik ist jetzt nicht mehr die Auslegung selbst, sondern die Lehre von den Bedingungen, dem Gegenstand, den Mitteln, der Mitteilung und praktischen Anwendung der Auslegung."
115. Heidegger, 15.
116. Heidegger, "Der Begriff der Zeit (Vortrag 1924)," 123.

this final section, I seek to confirm the hypothesis that engagements with being-possible were central to Heidegger's thought by tracing the modality of possibility into his later work. In addition, however, I argue that the earlier rhetorical articulations of possibility are more useful and more compelling.

Not long after his 1947 rejection of Jean-Paul Sartre's appropriation of his work in the *Letter on Humanism*, Heidegger would claim that "the resolution conceived of in *Being and Time* is not the decided upon action of a subject but rather the opening of presencing." This was a key moment in a long campaign on Heidegger's part to insist on the continuity of his thought amid radically changing historical contexts.[117] The "turn" (*Kehre*) so often spoken about in relation to Heidegger denoted not a change in his thought but rather a change in the disclosures of presencing—or so he maintained.[118] I wish to shift the point of inquiry and will argue that we see a philosophical and historiographic flattening of the concept of presencing that was deleterious to both Heidegger's thought and his politics.

In the later 1930s, when Heidegger began redescribing National Socialism as just another symptom of what he cast as a basic problem called "modernity," he was also developing a critique of this modern age as a "total mobilization" (*totale Mobilmachung*) of resources. This was a phrase that Heidegger had taken from a piece originally published in 1930 by Ernst Jünger, where it denoted the complete mobilization of energies in a wartime economy. In Heidegger's recently published notebooks from the 1930s, we see variations on this way of speaking as he sought to develop a critique of modernity so complete that it would consume even his former belief in National Socialism.[119] The story I have told thus far in this chapter is continued here because under this description of modernity, energy and capital became the twin hypostases of *dunamis*. Energy and capital became maximally vague placeholders for possibility as such. Heidegger came to understand them as nonbeing at the furthest degree of its indistinctness. In energy and capital, possibility was a fetishized capacity to become anything at all.

Ironically, Heidegger's own thinking about *dunamis* became increasingly affected by the tendency to reduce a phenomenon to all the things it *could* become that he associated with modernity. In place of the hermeneutically adroit articulation of a phenomenon by means of the relatively limited range of its immediately realizable possibilities, Heidegger became increasingly

117. Heidegger, "Ursprung des Kunstwerkes," in *Holzwege*, 55: "die in 'Sein und Zeit' gedachte Entschlossenheit ist nicht die decidierte Aktion eines Subjekts, sondern die Eröffnung des Daseins aus der Befangenheit im Seienden zur Offenheit des Seins."
118. Heidegger, *Platons Lehre der Wahrheit*, 72.
119. Jünger, "Die totale Mobilmachung," 11–30; Heidegger, "Über 'Die Linie,'" 12.

oriented to the description and denunciation of the kind of commodification that understood a phenomenon in terms of its liquidation into energy or capital. The stronger Heidegger's denunciations of modernity became, the more he fell victim to his own diagnosis. Although pure liquidity will remain a kind of dream even under conditions of advanced capitalism, Heidegger himself was becoming more successful in liquidating his own conception of possibility by treating each distinct technology indiscriminately. In this respect, "The Origin of the Work of Art" and "The Question Concerning Technology," two of Heidegger's most famous post-1933 essays, were closely connected initiatives, focusing respectively on the past and the future of *dunamis* and its various modes of production.

Heidegger's affiliation to National Socialism in the early 1930s seems to have been underwritten by precisely the sense of world-historical mission encapsulated in his diagnosis and rejection of "modernity." Perceiving oneself in a world-historical context was part of his early commitment to "history," and this commitment underwrote his palpably grandiose political allegiance between 1930 and 1934 to the possibility of a radically new beginning. No longer the achievement of *nous*, "historicity" (*Geschichtlichkeit*) was becoming the potentialization of life as such. And this, I would warrant, was what Heidegger was getting at when he proposed, opaquely (and, it would seem, before his purported break with National Socialism in 1934), that "the metaphysics of presencing must deepen itself in accordance with its own innermost microstructure and broaden into a metapolitics of—the genitive is both objective and subjective—the historical people."[120] "Metapolitics" was a simultaneously grand and weak gesture, for it attempted to embed the political sphere in a conception of the academy's role in thinking the historicity of a people. In the infamous "Rector's Address" (*Rektoratsrede*) of 1933, Heidegger put whatever intellectual impetus he commanded in the service of the National Socialist cause. In that speech, he cast the historicity of a people in terms of "the highest form of the *energeia*, of the being-in-activation, of humanity" (*die höchste Weise der energeia, des 'Am-Werke-Seins,' des Menschen*).[121] We see his modalities being put to political work.

Ultimately, however, Heidegger betrayed his own commitment to historicity. In his case, commitment to historicity came to entail an extreme judgmentalness on the basis of an increasingly slim archive. In the end, this preacher of historical contextualization did not really practice. Even in his own self-exonerating accounting, the same inflationary historical consciousness that underwrote his philosophical adherence to National

---

120. Heidegger, *Überlegungen II–VI*, 124: "die Metaphysik des Daseins muß sich nach ihrem innersten Gefüge vertiefen und ausweiten zur Metapolitik 'des' geschichtlichen Volkes."
121. Heidegger, *Selbstbehauptung*, 10.

Socialism drove his eventual and *still merely philosophical* rejection of it. Witness the articulation from the private notebooks from the 1930s: "thinking in a purely 'metaphysical' (that is, being-historical) manner, in the years from 1930 until 1934, I held National Socialism to be the possibility of a transition into another beginning and gave it that gloss." Hiding in the passive voice, Heidegger went on to say that it was in this way that "this 'movement' was misunderstood and underestimated in both its true powers and inner necessity as well as its nature and kind." In reality, this movement was simply a vehicle for the "the consummation [*Vollendung*] of modernity." For Heidegger, it was the consummation of a process that was "Romantic" in its origins, geared to "the humanization of humankind in self-assured rationality," and radicalized by a "decisiveness of the historical-technical" dedicated to "a complete mobilization of all the powers of a humanity turned upon itself."[122] In the later 1930s, Heidegger would argue that "the new politics is an inner and essential consequence of 'technics'" and is "in itself the scheming organization of the people to the highest possible performance, in which regard the people is understood in terms of its biological constitution, essentially 'technical' (scheming), which is to say, understood from the point of view of breeding."[123] To be sure, the history of biological theory and practice, not least in racialization, is one of the fundamental stories of modernity, but Heidegger's attempt to swiftly absorb those complexities into his overall narrative exhibits an overweening synthetic ambition.

Whatever else it was, the later Heideggerian pseudopolitics of "equanimity" (*Gelassenheit*) was also a response to this hypertrophy of "possibility" (*Möglichkeit*) into a "complete 'mobilization' of all capacities" (*vollständige "Mobilisierung" aller Vermögen*). It amounted to a new fetishization of powerlessness. In his private notebooks, Heidegger transformed "the foundational experience of my thought" (*die Grunderfahrung meines*

---

122. Heidegger, *Überlegungen VII–XI*, 408: "rein 'metaphysisch' (d. h. seynsgeschichtlich) denkend habe ich in den Jahren 1930–1934 den Nationalsozialismus für die Möglichkeit eines Übergangs in einen anderen Anfang gehalten und ihm diese Deutung gegeben. Damit wurde diese 'Bewegung' in ihren eigentlichen Kräften und inneren Notwendigkeiten sowohl als auch in der ihr eigenen Größengebung und Größenart verkannt und unterschätzt. Hier beginnt vielmehr und zwar in einer viel tieferen—d. h. umgreifenden und eingreifenden Weise als im Faschismus die Vollendung der Neuzeit—; diese hat zwar im 'Romantischen' überhaupt begonnen—hinsichtlich der Vermenschung des Menschen in der selbstgewissen Vernünftigkeit, aber für die Vollendung bedarf es der Entschiedenheit des Historisch-Technischen im Sinner der Vollständigen 'Mobilisierung' aller Vermögen des auf sich gestellten Menschentums."

123. Heidegger, *Überlegungen II–VI*, 472: "die neue Politik ist eine innere Wesensfolge der 'Technik'" and "in sich selbst ist sie die machenschaftliche Einrichtung des Volkes zur höchstmöglichen 'Leistung,' wobei auch noch das Volk hinsichtlich der biologischen Grundbestimmung wesentlich 'technisch'-machenschaftlich, d. h. züchterisch begriffen ist."

Denkens) into a sense of "the superiority of Being before all beings—the powerlessness of beings, that from Being an origin might arise."[124] Presencing as such was beyond the control of the particular conduits of that presencing. At this point, though, even Heidegger's humility was grandiose. Witness the ahistoricity of the assertion that "only in 2300 at the earliest may history be possible again."[125] One cannot say *precisely* when Heidegger wrote this—either just before or soon after the beginning of World War II. The fact is that Heidegger, the theorist of datability, did not date the entries in his so-called intellectual diaries (*Denktagebücher*). I am arguing that these developments are all of a piece: total mobilization produced total equanimity, which produced an obliviousness to the particularity of the present historical situation that could be devoured endlessly anew without discrimination by the narrative of "modernity."

Granted, some of Heidegger's most intensive philosophical labors in the 1930s were concentrated on the question of how to think concepts in the vicinity of *dunamis* afresh. There was, for example, something both ingenious and spent in his reconciliation of the twin ideas that for him were at the center of Nietzsche's intellectual project—namely, the ideas of "will to power" (*Wille zur Macht*) and "eternal recurrence of the same" (*ewige Wiederkunft des Gleichen*). Heidegger emphasized what he took to be a fundamental tension between the power of origination embedded in the will to power and the exhaustion of creativity embodied in the Nietzschean "yea-saying" to an endless recurrence of the same sequence of life and lives. His move in the Nietzsche lectures that he gave originally between 1936 and 1940 and then published in 1961 was to argue that will to power and eternal recurrence were instantiations of the same idea of being as a process of infinite and infinitely repeated differentiation. Will to power was a creativity that realized every possibility, and eternal recurrence was the vindication of this process even in the moment of its exhaustion. As Heidegger put it, "that everything recurs is the most extreme proximity of a world of becoming to a world of being—and this is the apex of the thought."[126] To Heidegger, recurrence reinstated the version of Greek ontology in which the orbit of the heavens was an emblem of *entelecheia* qua fully achieved motion and fully achieved presence.

Nevertheless, despite his desire to differentiate and renew the idiom of possibility, what we really see in the Heidegger of the 1930s is a thinker wandering in a no-man's-land of his own creation between "total mobilization"

---

124. Heidegger, 362: "die Übermacht des Seyns vor allem Seienden—die Ohnmacht des Seienden, daß aus ihm ein Ursprung komme."
125. Heidegger, *Überlegungen XII–XV*, 225: "frühstens um 2300 mag wieder Geschichte sein."
126. Heidegger, *Nietzsche*, 1:466: "Daß Alles wiederkehrt, ist die extremste Annäherung einer Welt des Werdens an die des Seins:—Gipfel der Betrachtung."

and "equanimity," attempting to find a conceptual rapprochement for his commitments. For Heidegger in 1931, theorizing "force" (*Kraft*) entailed a philological project of separating the various usages of "ability" (*Fähigkeit*), "art" (*Kunst*), "talent" (*Begabung*), "capability" (*Vermögen*), "capacitation" (*Befähigung*), "aptitude" (*Eignung*), "skill" (*Geschicklichkeit*), "violence" (*Gewalt*), and "power" (*Macht*).[127] But this taxonomy was left unpursued. Similarly, Heidegger expended considerable energy trying to read Nietzsche in terms of the modality of "basic concepts" he had excavated from Aristotle. Thus, "agency [*Kraft*], the in-itself-gathered and coiled capacity, the standing-ready-to . . . is that which the Greeks, and Aristotle above all, termed *dunamis*." In contrast, "power [*Macht*] . . . is a being-potent in the sense of command enactment, a being-at-work of agency—and in Greek this would be *energeia*." Further, "power [*Macht*] is will as willing-beyond-oneself, but it is equally a coming-to-oneself, a finding and reporting of oneself in the closed simplicity of essence—for the Greeks, *entelecheia*." Yet what had been differentiated was then simply lumped together again: "for Nietzsche, power [*Macht*] is all of these things at once: *dunamis, energeia, entelecheia*."[128] Self-defeating, Heidegger was replicating his commitment to a taxonomic differentiation of modalities and then casting it aside.

We should read "The Origin of the Work of Art" (delivered as a series of lectures in 1936 but first published in 1950) in the context of the matrix of tensions set out within Heidegger's thought by the extremes of "total mobilization" and "equanimity." Although he emphasized that "the great artists prize artisanal ability above all else," Heidegger insisted even more vehemently that the handwork arts of the artist could never be thought of as a form of "operation" (*Tätigkeit*).[129] The activity of pushing out the bounds of a world by means of artworks that *were* the truths of that world, he claimed, was a process much more profound than the mere "exercise" of skill. The *technē* of a *technitēs* (the "fashioning" or "bringing-to-the-fore" of the "artist") might be understood as a participating in the founding and articulation of a world (*Welt*) by working with what are now called the "affordances" of the "earth" (*phusis, Erde*) qua materialities with their own

127. Heidegger, *Aristoteles, Metaphysik*, 72.
128. Heidegger, *Nietzsche*, 1.76–77: "Kraft, das in sich gesammelte und wirkungsbereite Vermögen, das Imstandesein zu . . . , ist das, was die Griechen, vor allem Aristoteles, als *dunamis* bezeichnen. Macht ist aber ebenso das Mächtigsein im Sinne des Herrschaftsvollzugs, das Am-Werk-sein der Kraft, griechisch: *energeia*. Macht ist Wille als Über-sichhinaus-wollen, aber so gerade das Zu-sich-selbst-kommen, sich in der geschlossenen Einfachheit des Wesens Finden und Behaupten, griechisch: *entelecheia*. Macht heißt für Nietzsche dieses alles zugleich: *dunamis, energeia, entelecheia*."
129. Heidegger, "Ursprung des Kunstwerkes," in *Holzwege*, 47–48: "die großen Künstler schätzen das handwerkliche Können am höchsten."

distinctive life cycles and tendencies to fall into both form and chaos. But this had to be presented as a very particular kind of potentialization of nature. Why? Because modernity as a "total mobilization" of natural and human resources was lurking in the background. Heidegger insisted that once it had been removed from its cultural context, inserted in an exhibition, or visited from afar (by the tourist at Paestum, for instance), the work of art would no longer be capable of achieving itself as an event and as a truth. And in this he was profoundly conservative. The minoritarian Heideggerian report is that, in fact, works of art build worlds precisely because they are radical and name something previously unnamed. Conservativeness was in part a response to a radicalism that Heidegger had only just disowned, but contradictions lay strewn all about the text. Despite Heidegger's purported disavowal of the National Socialist historical mission, the work of art essay still listed "the historical people" (*das geschichtliches Volk*) as the vehicle of the world of artworks.[130]

Many of Heidegger's most famous post-1945 statements extend the hypothesis that Heideggerian historiography was becoming increasingly indiscriminate. The notorious Bremen lectures of 1949 were clearly histories of the present. Cast as an "insight into that which is" (*Einblick in Das Was Ist*), this sequence of four lectures proposed a massive historical thesis about the processes underlying recent events, and it was the astounding historiographic *immodesty* of the project that readers have found most offensive. That is, in one of his very few semidirect public references to the Nazi crimes of extermination, Heidegger infamously proposed a historical connection between the "fabrication of corpses" (*Fabrikation von Leichen*) in the death camps and the rise of a "mechanized food industry" (*motorisierte Ernährungsindustrie*). Both were to be understood simply in terms of a massified attitude toward "life" characteristic of "modernity." What we have here is an omnivorous historiography of the now, one that was insisting that all developments were simply aspects of a single deeper process.[131]

Thus, the late critiques of technology would themselves be jeremiads against the technologization of possibility that set all technological innovations in the lockstep of modern decline on the basis of snippets of evidence and massive projection. Radio was the possibility of a mass production of soul-states in isolation. For Heidegger, it was "the emblem of an interdependence between the planetary and the idiotic" (*das Sinnbild der Zusammengehörigkeit von Planetarismus und Idiotismus*).[132] In the "Equanimity" essay, collected later in the *Heimat*-focused volume dedicated to Heidegger

130. Heidegger, 37.
131. Heidegger, *Einblick in Das Was Ist*, 56.
132. Heidegger, *Überlegungen XII–XV*, 265.

by his home city of Messkirch on his eightieth birthday, the complexities of "The Question Concerning Technology" were simplified into a very flat assertion: "nature is being transformed into one single and gigantic gas station, into an energy source for modern technics and industry."[133] Heidegger was appropriating just enough Marx to make himself citable by historians of technology and what has become the environmental humanities, but the truer history of this claim within Heidegger's own corpus is a history of growing imperviousness to differentiation. Technics was becoming an all-consuming concept.

When we read Heidegger's assorted denunciations of modernity together with its modes of "manufacture" (*Herstellen*), we should be suspicious, because in the denunciation of technological modernity there is a proximity between Heidegger's thought and his anti-Semitism. The reserve armies of possibility qua "inventory" (*Bestand*) stored by modern technological capitalism, the reconceptualization of "technology" (*Technik*) not as a means to an end but as "a mode of unconcealing" (*eine Weise des Entbergens*), the insistence that "technology" (*Technik*) transformed the world into a series of "calculabilities" (*Berechenbarkeiten*) fostering necessitarianism in *The Principle of Reason*, the distancelessness of the distance media (the televisual, the telephonic) that made all things equally presentable in any given place and time, the deracination of peoples rendered "homeless" (*heimatlos*), stripped of "down-to-earth-ness" (*Bodenständigkeit*)—all of these critiques of possibility run amok had a precedent. In Heidegger's words, "one of the most hidden forms of the gigantic and perhaps the oldest is the hard-bitten scheming of the counting and huckstering and mixing all together upon which the worldlessness of the Jews is based."[134] Heidegger's anti-Semitism was built into his account of the blank stare of an omnipossibility embedded in capital. The irony is shocking and should give us pause: the critique of technologized modernity that was supposed to drive Heidegger's disowning of National Socialism was itself conceptually of a piece with his anti-Semitism.

No one can say anything about Heidegger without confronting the man's politics between, at least, 1930 and 1934 together with his either cowardly or unrepentant failure to address his political mistakes publicly once the scale of the crimes with which they were complicit became clear after, at the latest, 1945. My position on this point is that Heidegger's phenomenological, temporal, and rhetorical investments before 1927 were neither

133. Heidegger, "Gelassenheit," 23.

134. Heidegger, *Überlegungen VII–XI*, 97: "eine der verstecktesten Gestalten des Riesigen und vielleicht die älteste ist die zähe Geschicklichkeit des Rechnens und Schiebens und Durcheinandermischens, wodurch die Weltlosigkeit des Judentums gegründet wird." For the man's sense of the connection between modernity and Jewry, see also Heidegger, *Überlegungen XII–XV*, 46.

determinative of his political positions in the 1930s nor immaterial to them. If a story ends this way, we might wonder, why trace its beginnings? Because beginnings are not destiny, and because history contains points of no return before which things could have been otherwise. Aristotle was not always already infected with the bacillus of National Socialism, and the Heideggerian transposition of Aristotle into Weimar Germany was not always already fated to yield either the *Rektoratsrede* of 1933 or the anti-Semitic critique of modernity's gigantism. As I am endeavoring to do here, we can build a book on the basis of Heideggerian materials dating from the 1920s because those materials themselves provide the beginnings of a criticism of the direction Heidegger himself pursued in the 1930s and beyond.

THE AFTERLIFE OF HEIDEGGERIAN CONCEPTS

The transformation of *dunamis* into "total mobilization" that I have been tracing remains indicative of a broader problem in the work of Martin Heidegger. As my emphasis on his Summer Semester 1924 evocation of the basic concepts of Aristotelian philosophy demonstrates, Heidegger was a thinker engaged primarily in the reevaluation of basic investigative terms. If successful, a thinker working at this level will become the author of an oeuvre with implications extending across the disciplinary map, but that kind of success is dangerous because the work of *applying* those basic concepts in particular zones of localized inquiry will remain tremendously difficult and, indeed, creative work. As the inferentialist historiography that I have elicited from the work of Robert Brandom attempts to confirm, there is no application of a concept that is not itself a development of that concept. Just so, there is no application of the basic concepts forged by Martin Heidegger that is not a development of those concepts. Heidegger's own "application" of the forms of modal analysis that he developed in the 1920s to the forms of possibilization he saw around him in the 1930s, 1940s, and 1950s were certainly developments. As I argued in the previous section, however, the specific development that we see in those applications was profoundly ironic because the *dunamis* of the later period became a kind of all-consuming and for that reason paradoxically emaciating concept.

I have called the basic Heideggerian concepts on temporality, modality, life capacities, and hermeneutics "foundations" of rhetorical inquiry, and the task in the next chapters of this book is to develop these categories of thought by giving them specificity in particular zones of investigation. To embark on a historiography of this kind is not to suppose that Hannah Arendt, Walter Benjamin, and Aby Warburg can be thought of as instruments of a more basically Heideggerian project. The afterlife of concepts may be understood as their more genuinely creative moment. And, in fact, this stands in stark contrast to the Heideggerian impulse that wishes at each moment to fetishize what came first—as the pure and primordial and pristine. In the chapters that follow, I shall pursue Heidegger's intuition that an appearance may name itself. In (respectively) Arendt, Benjamin, and Warburg, this appearance that names itself will become a process in which an appearance calls into being and is called into being by a space that surrounds it. It will become a moment exhibiting dialectical tensions. And it will become a moment that can become free and generative once fractured into something like an image table that clusters the "moment" in the variety of its distinguishable aspects and potential continuations. These thoughts do develop a basic Heideggerian insight on truth as *alētheia*, but they transform it almost beyond recognition. What is more, they improve it decisively.

4: HANNAH ARENDT AND THE RHETORICAL CONSTITUTION OF SPACE

REALIZING A MISSED OPPORTUNITY

Hannah Arendt was one of the most significant political thinkers of the twentieth century, but there is a glaring absence at the center of her project: rhetoric. After all, Arendt emphasized the absolute centrality of acting and speaking in a public realm to the flourishing of both human individuals and human communities, and this emphasis was crucial for her critique of politics under modern conditions, but she paid almost no sustained attention to the ancient *artes rhetoricae*, which had dealt with precisely this kind of acting and speaking. Thus, *The Human Condition* of 1958 has captivated generations of readers with its breathtaking analysis of the basically antipolitical nature of modern societies characterized by public fixation on the household matters of maintaining, conditioning, and reproducing bare life and by a relentless reduction of human questions to technological issues of means and ends. For Arendt, modernity involved massive depoliticization, and this depoliticization helped her to explain how radical political movements in totalitarian states like Nazi Germany and the Soviet Union had functioned by means of a kind of thoughtless bureaucratic acquiescence. Her response to these problems was to champion politics itself. Hers was a radical democratic politics, and this was her wager: a community's ability to resist totalitarianism would depend on the proportion of its citizens who were actively involved in politics. If people were directly involved in the words and deeds of democratic self-rule, then, as in effect she argued in 1963, they would learn to resist the kind of abdication of decision that led to Adolf Eichmann, the Nazi functionary of mass murder. Knowing that "words and deeds in the public realm" were so crucial to Arendt, one has to expect that hers would be a rhetorical account of politics. Yet the index to *The Human Condition* lists only one reference to "rhetoric." Following the reference, one finds that the word itself is not even used. How could this be?

Arendt was aware of and not particularly interested in the art of persuasion as a set of speech practices, and what she lacked was an account of rhetoric as the ability to think the now as an actualized moment that was nonetheless always in motion amid an array of more and less proximate possibilities. In a text on the relationship between philosophy and politics originally drafted in 1954 (which, according to Jacques Taminiaux, was a disguised dialogue with Heidegger), Arendt was working with an empty category when she declared that, for the Greeks, "rhetoric, the art of persuasion," had been "the highest, the truly political art." "Rhetoric" for her was only ever a husk word, one that she would use occasionally without ever really sensing what it might mean.[1] She had not metabolized in any deep way the Aristotelian account of rhetoric as an ability to see possibilities clustering around a particular situation that we have encountered in previous chapters. On this account, rhetoric did not simply refer to utterances aiming at persuasion. Indeed, properly speaking, rhetoric was not the speaking itself. One might refer to that as "oratory." Rhetoric was instead an analytical power or possibility (*dunamis*) to perceive the motions ending in belief (*pithanon*) that were attached as contingencies (*endechomena*) to a particular actuality, a given case.

It is not historically far-fetched to say that Arendt "lacked" the Aristotelian account of rhetoric as a *dunamis*. This account of rhetoric is not some retroactively imposed and presentist theory. It was there for her to find if she had looked for it. As we saw in the previous chapter, probably the foremost twentieth-century theorist of this account of rhetoric was none other than Arendt's mentor, Martin Heidegger, and he had lectured on "The Basic Concepts of Aristotelian Philosophy" in Summer Semester 1924. For Heidegger, "situated presencing" (*Dasein*) was always to be understood in relation to "actuality" (*energeia*) and "possibility" (*dunamis*). Indeed, one might say that the ultimate indistinguishability of the actual and the possible was "movement" (*kinēsis*). In turn, "speech" (*logos*) was to be understood not as logic but rather as the capacity to make present in words what was absent in fact. Speech, thus, was intimately connected to "imagination" (*phantasia*), which Arendt understood in terms of making the absent present. Visualizing that which could be but was not was the core of human *kinēsis*, both as "acting" (*prattein*) and "suffering" (*pathein*), because such visualizing was always also a matter of desire and aversion. Rhetoric was both the analysis of dispositions to possible motion in human beings and an awareness of the articulations that might make the possibility of those motions more distinct and more prepossessing.

History, however, is a massive concatenation of contingencies (being available does not necessitate being taken up), and this is true also of

1. Arendt, "Philosophy and Politics," 73–74. Taminiaux, "Platonic Roots," 24ff.

Arendt's possible reception of Heidegger's Summer Semester 1924 lectures. She arrived in Marburg to study with Heidegger only in Winter Semester 1924–1925, the semester immediately following the lectures on Aristotle and rhetoric. "Notes" (*Nachschriften*) from the Summer Semester lectures were circulating in Marburg in the student groups to which Arendt belonged. The edition of the lectures that eventually appeared in the Heidegger *Gesamtausgabe* in 2002 drew on a number of these detailed sets of student notes. Arendt could have read these notes, but I see no direct evidence that she did so in the 1920s, and I think it unlikely that she ever worked through them in a concerted way. There is a record of her engagement with Aristotle's *Rhetoric* in some of her diary entries in the *Denktagebuch* from 1953. Nothing in those notes suggests an awareness of Heidegger's sophisticated earlier gloss. Moreover, in 1972, when Heidegger indicated that he had neither the manuscript nor any copies of what he referred to as "the important Summer Semester 1924 lectures concerned with book 2 of Aristotle's *Rhetoric*," Arendt could only report that these lectures were unfortunately not among notes that had recently surfaced.[2]

What Arendt did receive from Heidegger was the much more truncated treatment of rhetoric and sophistic offered up in his Winter Semester lectures of 1924–1925 on Plato's *Sophist*. In the published record of Heidegger's thought, almost all that Arendt had to go on was the one sentence in *Being and Time*, where—as we saw in the previous chapter—Heidegger summed up the three-hundred-odd pages of his Summer Semester 1924 lectures with the following words: Aristotle's *Rhetoric* is to be understood as "the first systematic hermeneutic of the everydayness of being-with-one-another."[3] Despite the intensely cryptic nature of this encoding, Arendt nevertheless intuited that there was a political theory to be written at precisely this juncture. That is what she was getting at, I warrant, when, at the 1954 American Political Science Association meeting, she said that among "the prerequisites for a new political philosophy" was "Heidegger's analysis of average everyday life."[4] Here we have a provisional answer to the conundrum of how Arendt could have overlooked rhetoric: she saw that the "everydayness of being-with-one-another" was a protoscience of politics, but she did not see that rhetoric was an analytic of everydayness.

Here comes the crucial move that I make in this chapter: as scholars, we can do more than throw up our hands in frustration at this missed opportunity. That Arendt did not go more deeply into the Heideggerian account of rhetoric was a matter of extreme historical contingency. There

2. Heidegger to Arendt (April 19, 1972), and Arendt to Heidegger (June 18, 1972), *Briefe 1925 bis 1975*, 231–36.
3. Heidegger, *Sein und Zeit*, 138.
4. Arendt, "Concern with Politics," 445.

is no historically significant reason why Arendt could not, by chance, have arrived at Marburg one semester earlier. And when history does not present intellectual historians with good reasons, they are not duty bound to obey its lacunae by remaining silent. Indeed (and as I suggest in the introduction to this book), the historian of thought qua thinker has something like a duty to continue the line of inquiry that could have been but was not. In this case, what is more, the pursuit of possibilities that were not fully realized does not entail a wholesale writing from scratch at the center of Arendt's oeuvre. Instead, it will be the task of this chapter to generate an only somewhat counterfactual account of Arendt's political thought with Heideggerian rhetoric now a key point of departure. The chapter is only somewhat counterfactual because it continues thoughts that were for the most part actualized in her work before the publication of *The Origins of Totalitarianism* in 1951. In fact, Arendt's work in her doctoral dissertation on Augustine, her habilitation project on Rahel Varnhagen, and her journalistic writings in the 1940s had been precisely a series of investigations into the everydayness of being-with-one-another in the world. Hence, the core claim of this chapter is that the early Arendt remains, potentially, a new beginning for Arendtian rhetorical inquiry.

The implicit rhetoric that I find in Arendt's early work is concerned with the question of how political space emerges. More particularly, it is a rhetorical analysis of how political space is to be understood. It does not emphasize the preexistent dimensionality of the public stage on which political acts can be performed and witnessed. It is a rhetorical analysis that inquires into how acts and stances and orientations to others generate the exemplary, bipolar, and multipolar spaces within which political actions appear. The task will be to construct an alternative genealogy for what Arendt eventually called "the polis." Usage of that term is very often just as blanched as the ancient Greek statues that were once painted but are now bone white. Here my task is to prepare the way for a reinvigoration of the term, together with the space of political appearance for which it stands, by tracing continuities through Arendt's examination of "love of neighbor" (*dilectio proximi*) in Augustine, her impersonation of Rahel Varnhagen's salon performativities, and her generation of political space in her early journalistic writings before the publication of *The Origins of Totalitarianism* in 1951 by fracturing the "we" of community into a concordance of possibilities and multipolar oppositions.

ELISIONS OF DISTANCE IN THE CONCEPT OF LOVE IN AUGUSTINE

The basic issue in Arendt's dissertation on the concept of love in Augustine—completed in 1928, published in 1929—was how one might conceptualize the process of establishing a distance *from* the world that nonetheless left one firmly rooted *in* it. Even as the political dimension of the project was left largely implicit in the original version, I would argue that this was a basically political issue: what analytical language might describe my being alongside others without dissolving myself into them? In general, one might describe Arendt's *Der Liebesbegriff bei Augustin* (*The Concept of Love in Augustine*) as a somewhat unachieved book. Indeed, in his official evaluation (*Gutachten*) of the work, the chief supervisor of the project, Karl Jaspers, described the work bluntly as unfinished.[5] In turn, Arendt's Weimar reviewers found the book's essentially paraphrastic style difficult to decode.[6] Later, Arendt herself decided that her pre-1933 work had been hopelessly apolitical. Nevertheless, my contention is that it is both possible and worthwhile to reread the Augustine book with greater attention to its implicitly rhetorical categories.

Arendt was interested in the Augustinian conception of love because it brought together three quite different kinds of movement. "Love" (*Liebe*) was "appetite" (*appetitus*), it was "care" (*caritas*), and it was "love of neighbor" or "solidarity" (*dilectio proximi*). Crucial here was the understanding of love as an affect implying motion. The passions were the beginnings of motion. "Passion" (*pathēsis*), the motion of suffering an impression, had been at the very center of Heidegger's 1924 lectures. As we have seen, this was why some of the notes from those lectures were called, simply, *Rhetorik II*. What is more, there was a fundamental continuity between these two projects: in both Heidegger's Summer Semester 1924 lectures and in Arendt's Augustine book, passions were to be understood in terms of their worlding and world-articulating functions. Heideggerian "emotions" (*Affekten*) were modes of being-with-one-another not because one could not be emotional while alone but rather because he came to understand emotions as ways in which one's presencing was structured by narratives stretching through past, present, and future emplotments that involved other human beings. Similarly, love was a way of world building in the final analysis for Arendt. Love was able to lay the world out as a series of distances to neighbors whose being was affirmed in the *dilectio proximi* beyond the twin motions of desire in *appetitus* and subsumption of difference in *caritas*. I am thus claiming that Arendt's work in *The Concept of Love in Augustine* ought to be understood as a student's detailed working through of a mentor's general project in a particular case. Heidegger on emotion becomes Arendt on love.

Perhaps we are now so saturated in the alternately sentimentalized and

5. Jaspers, "Gutachten," in *Hannah Arendt–Karl Jaspers Briefwechsel*, 723–24.
6. Hessen, review of *Der Liebesbegriff bei Augustin*, 175; Zepf, review of *Der Liebesbegriff bei Augustin*, 101–5.

sexualized accounts of love that it is difficult to work our way back into the conceptual domain that Arendt was exploring in this Weimar dissertation. With regard to *appetitus*, Arendt connected the Augustinian concept with the Aristotelian account of "conation" or "desire" (*orexis*).[7] For her, this implied that Christian abstention from *appetitus* was a radicalization of what she termed the "doubtfulness" (*Fragwürdigkeit*) or contingency of "action" (*praxis*) in the Aristotelian tradition.[8] To enter into the world of action was to give oneself over to a multiplicity of potential outcomes. The Stoic retrenchment from a life in the world that one could not control (to an inner life that, it was said, one could) might prove to be only a temporary victory. The inner world of the emotions might turn out to be as recalcitrant and uncontrollable as the exterior world of events. The worlds of conation, both interior and exterior, constituted specific distensions between that which senses and that which is sensed. In fact, however, the Christian conclusion remained the same: conation would render one powerless.

Qua *appetitus*, love was the inclination of a subject toward an object in such a way that the distinction between subject and object began to break down. Perception of an object of desire was itself conation, a kind of beginning to lean into that object. Thus, *appetitus* was a distension of perception in both space and time. It was a "distension" (*Spannung, extentus*) toward that which might be grasped or enacted. As a contingent and neighboring phenomenon, such an object of desire might be understood as an *endechomenon*, as something that could be grasped and as something that had to be grasped before it changed or became otherwise.[9] Indeed, although conation was something begun in the senses, it was also something that was simultaneously underway in the imagination. As movement, conation was already living in its own anticipated future, and this living in the future was something like an explanation for movement in the present. The conative quality of desire as that which might begin a motion in acceleration (or end it in deceleration) was something like a zone of indistinction between the actuality of a thing and its possibility in the occupation of desire qua futurity. The caress is always both in advance of and behind itself, always beginning or ending, luxuriating in a temporality spanning out from the moment in a desire for experience (hungering) and in a desire for more prolonged experience (lingering).

Because the world of perceptions was a world of the fleeting and the manifold (in Arendt's reconstruction of the affective topography of Augustinian thought), the distension of *appetitus* was always also a "scattering"

---

7. Arendt, *Der Liebesbegriff*, 29–30.
8. Arendt, 29.
9. Arendt, 18. Compare Arendt, *Willing*, 14–15.

(*dispersio*). That is, *appetitus* was also a scattering of the perceiving node into the variety of its potential objects.[10] At first, this kind of hyperstimulation might look like a state of enhanced attention. Channeling Augustine, Arendt nevertheless said that dispersion would overwhelm attention and that the result was, in fact, "habit" (*consuetudo*).[11] The speed and ubiquity of desire would necessitate habituation, which could be understood as a state in which motions were undertaken in the absence of attention. Paradoxically, the world of desire was thus a world of numb disattention. The eyeball constantly straining to take in all available beauties is eventually and paradoxically victorious in its quest to colonize objects and call them its own. This would be a visual sensitivity dulling its own powers of delectation. Using a term that did indeed connote Jaspers's characterization of the contemporary Weimar context, Arendt saw this Augustinian world of desire ending in an exhaustion or "leveling" (*Nivellierung*).[12] Just as Heidegger had predicted, all motions were to be understood as differentials always only on the path toward the generation of time and space as historically specific senses of dimension. Repetition, what is more, entailed something like a statistical reversion to the mean even as that mean would only be something emergent in the process of repeatedly differentiating more incremental passions.

Such a statisticalization of emotion implied the coming into being of a quite different relationship to the topography of affects—away from "desire" (*appetitus*) and toward "care" (*caritas*). For Arendt, *caritas* was something that made it possible for the Christian to accept God's offer of liberation from the tyranny of the here and now. *Caritas* reciprocated "grace" (*gratia*). And grace—which was divine love—might be understood as something like an intervention in the stream of consciousness permitting one to decouple oneself from the immediately intruding world. Affect would be topographical if desire were held to set out a range of objects that in the first place remained describable by the intensity of the attraction and, perhaps more so, by the narrativization of the time space to be negotiated in the fulfilment of the desire to go from a "here" to a "there." And repetition of such orientation would imply a quite different relationship, because it would arrange such directionality in a folder of comparables treating each as the same even as the specificity of each would be—for a time and in some way—retained. The constitution of a world would entail the erection of such multidirectionality. And a world constituted in this way would itself appear and disappear in relation to presencing or absencing in repetition.

10. Arendt, *Der Liebesbegriff*, 33.
11. Arendt, 58–59.
12. Arendt, 59. Compare Jaspers, *Die geistige Situation*, 74.

We should not be at all surprised that the birth of a "philosophy of existence" (*Existenzphilosophie*) in Germany in the 1920s was accompanied by renewed interest in Christian theorists of the autobiographical everyday (such as Augustine and Kierkegaard). Indeed, Arendt's dissertation project was very much an expression of this preoccupation. Within this discursive frame, habit was something like a direction. Just so, Arendt averred that for Augustine, "alienation from the world is essentially an alienation from habit."[13] Alienation or abstention from the world would be an abstention or distance from habit. If imagination were the domain of desire, its twin, memory—qua *anamnesis*—would be the vehicle of a remembrance of something more encompassing, less transient. Imagination could narrativize the path from here to there, and memory could file away the collected works of such imagining as well as keep them equidistant or equally accessible in the manner of a library. The utterly washed out and mathematized senses of space and time as pure dimensionality against which Heidegger railed in *Being and Time* were hypostases of the potential motions carved out by actions recorded in memory.

As "care" (*caritas*), love became a concern for the finite creatures of the world that took up the standpoint of an infinite creative being. *Caritas* was the emotional topographic equivalent of ubiquity or its cognate omniproximity—namely, equidistance. This was ultimately distinct from both a moving *into* the world and a destruction of one's distance from it by means of a thoroughgoing and quotidian habituation. This was, instead, a moving *away* from the world in order to become equidistant from all of the world's constituent parts. The greatest degree of equidistance to objects that remained stubbornly distinct could only be achieved from a great distance. To love creation in the manner of its creator was to love it from afar. This was a kind of indiscriminate care for creation as a whole that did not differentiate between the close and the distant or, for that matter, the past and the future. *Caritas* was a removal from all particular relationships of appetite. It was an extinction of being-in-the-world as a matrix of more and less proximate possibilities.

We are in the process of decoding how it was that Arendt developed a sense of worldliness by articulating various conceptualizations of love in the Augustinian tradition, and we can understand what Arendt was trying to do with the concept of *caritas* more precisely by seeing how she was disagreeing with her contemporaries. Against Max Scheler, she was contending that Augustine did not simply effect an "inversion" (*Umkehrung*) of human relationships to the world and the desires that constituted it as a

---

13. Arendt, *Der Liebesbegriff*, 61: "die Entfremdung von der Welt ist wesentlich eine Entfremdung von der *consuetudo*."

matrix of proximities and distances. Augustine, she said, had argued for an "annihilation" (*Vernichtung*) of this matrix in "the abjuration of the world" (*die Lossagung von der Welt*).[14] This was a denial that *caritas* (which took the eternal as its object) could be understood within the categories of *appetitus*. It was a denial that one might understand the distinction between the Greek theory of "conation" (*orexis*) and the Christian account of love as an inversion of a striving for that which was higher into a care on the part of that which was higher for that which was lower. In arguing in this way, Arendt was exploring the implication that Scheler had been wrong to conceive of love as something like a power of attending to *telos* or the value implicit in the purpose of one's being as created by someone else—namely, God.

Within the Augustinian concept of *caritas*, there was an equidistance from all creatures that articulated the beginning of a political theory of equality. Here, too, the contrast between Arendt and Scheler is instructive. Implicit here was the argument that Scheler had invested unwisely in the Nietzschean category of *Ressentiment*. Whereas Nietzsche had seen Christian love for the lowest and the most humble as a kind of perverse and indirect retort to the Greek admiration of excellence, Scheler viewed the modern love for humanity—egalitarianism as a principle—as a perverse and indirect retort to the Christian specification of care on the part of the higher for the lower, the noble for the ignoble, the healthy for the sick, the rich for the poor, the beautiful for the ugly, Christ for the sinner, God for his creation.[15] For her part, Arendt was insisting that *caritas* was not the inversion of any of these worldly relationships. It was a complete but, in her reading, temporary abstention from all such fallings into the world.

In Arendt's analysis, both *appetitus* and *caritas* were movements of the soul that destroyed worldliness as such. Active in this inference was the presupposition that worldliness was a matrix of more and less proximate possibilities. Worldliness would be modal, because asking about the kind of world in which one lives is tantamount to asking about the laws constituting some local game, constituting it as a sometimes more and sometimes less specific list of necessities and possibilities. Appetite might dissolve itself into possibility by losing track of the tension between specific heres and theres, like a fantasy in which the subject and the object of desire become interchangeable or where the doing and the being done to become indistinct. Similarly, care might distance itself from all possibilities in such a way that nothing appeared merely possible anymore because from the divine perspective adopted by care, all eventualities were encountered simultaneously. Beheld from the great distance of a god and appearing from that great distance as simply a creation, the modal categories of worldliness would dissolve into one, for the distinction between possible and actual would fade, and the sum total of all possibilities would become a version of the necessities characteristic of one world as distinct from another.

Ultimately, within the Arendtian political topography of affect, the world and love could only coexist in *dilectio* when that term is understood in the very precise Christian context of "love of neighbor" or "solidarity" (*dilectio proximi*). The task of solidarity was to understand oneself amid a series of relationships with persons and communities that simply happened to be nearby without dissolving oneself into them. One neither abandoned those persons and communities wholly nor assimilated into them. As Arendt was motivated to write it, the cycle of immersion in, abstention from, and return to the world—in the *appetitus, caritas, dilectio* sequence—transformed the proximate human being from "the other" (*Der Andere*) to "the next" (*Der Nächste*).[16] The celebrated notion that "I love" (*amo*) would equal "I am willing in order that you might be" (*volo ut sis*) was not simply a commitment to the distinct being of the other. It was also a commitment to contexture as such together with the tissue of dispositions brought into being by the proximity of the one to the other.[17] Love of one's neighbor was thus a principled love of contiguity as such. Understood from the perspective of the tropological theorizations of the rhetorical tradition, *dilectio proximi* was a kind of pleasure in the diversity of adroit neighborly attendings. This solidarity was something like a sheer interest in contexture and every kind of proximity. It was a response to the challenge posed by the proximity of differences that abutted each other. Indeed, one might say that *dilectio proximi* was the condition of possibility for complex perceptions of simultaneity. It was a commitment to "sequence" (the *Nacheinander*) as well as "proximity" (the *Nebeneinander*). It was attention to contingency.[18]

As Arendt appropriated it, Augustinian *dilectio proximi* was Heideggerian *Dasein*, "presencing" with an emphasis on "situatedness" (*Befindlichkeit*). Both "solidarity" and "situated presencing" were specific forms of thrownness into a world of preexistent contiguities. More than that, however, both were also attentions to the particular way in which such attending to local distance would be a form of activation and presencing of those distances qua distances without wishing to annul them in the no-space and no-time of possession that was at once the consummation and extinction of desire. One found oneself adjacent to things and persons and possibilities for use, action, or passion, and one found oneself able to articulate the presencing of those things and persons and possibilities. We can trace this transposition

---

16. Arendt, *Der Liebesbegriff*, 90.
17. Arendt, 71.
18. Arendt, 40.

of interests in the footnotes to Arendt's Augustine book. Whereas *caritas* had denoted an orientation to a Greek conception of "cosmos" (*kosmos*), "solidarity" (*dilectio proximi*) existed within a Christian conception of the "world" (*mundus*). To shore up this distinction between cosmos and world, Arendt turned to "The Eschatology of the Gospel of John" (1928), where Rudolf Bultmann—one of Heidegger's Marburg colleagues—had argued that the Christian understanding of *Welt* was to be categorically distinguished from the Greek conception of the *kosmos* as a "totality" (*Gesamtbestand*). In fact, he had claimed, "the world is humanity in the mode of 'one.'" This was, indeed, an invocation of the account given by Heidegger in *Being and Time* of *das Man*, of holding oneself with respect to a phenomenon in the concealed, derived, safety-in-numbers way that in any given place and time "one" holds oneself to that phenomenon.[19]

In turn, Arendt criticized Heidegger's account of the Augustinian conception of "world" (*mundus*) in his 1929 work *Vom Wesen des Grundes* (*On the Essence of Reasons*). She accepted that Heidegger spoke of a double meaning in the term *mundus* as deployed by Augustine. Sometimes it was "creation" (*ens creatum*). At other times, it was "living in one's heart in the world" (*habitare corde in mundo*). In this second usage, *mundus* denoted the structure of one's affective embeddedness in matrices of desire and aversion. Arendt claimed that Heidegger only interpreted the second of these two meanings. He remained blind, she concluded, to the creative tension within Augustine's work between falling into the world and abstaining from it. On her reading, the concern for contiguity that was love of one's neighbor emerged from this tension.[20] Heidegger saw *appetitus* and its efflorescence in habit, but the obsession with finitude prevented him from taking up the Augustinian conception of *caritas* as infinitude in orientation qua equality. A politics of the neighbor as an exercising with orientations was stillborn in Heidegger, consumed by the merely double move of everydayness as presencing and habituation.

I would argue that Arendt's sheer commitment to contexture, the motley of the world in which the least congruent things find themselves juxtaposed without mediation, was most visible at the very beginning of *The Concept of Love*. The ostensible cause of the book's existence, she noted, was a curiosity sparked by "the proximity [in Augustine himself] of the most diverse traditions of thought" (*das Nebeneinander verschiedenartigster Gedankengänge*).[21] Arendt was referring to the way in which particular strains of Greek

19. Bultmann, "Die Eschatologie des Johannesevangeliums," 6: "die Welt ist die Menschheit im Sinne des 'man.'" Bultmann was citing Heidegger, *Sein und Zeit*, 126–30.
20. Arendt, *Der Liebesbegriff*, 42. Heidegger's position was not so different from Arendt's; see Heidegger, *Wesen des Grundes*, 86, 88, 89, 91, 95 (for the various meanings of *Welt*), 102 (for *stiften*), 110 (for *Hörenkönnen*).
21. Arendt, *Der Liebesbegriff*, 1.

philosophy, Roman rhetoric, and Christian theology were woven together in Augustine. One had to think those proximities together in order to understand the whole. Augustine's *On Christian Doctrine*, the dominant source alongside the *Confessions* in Arendt's treatment of *appetitus*, had itself been an argument for the legitimacy of using rhetorical means for Christian ends. Rhetoric on that account was comparable to Christ's incarnation. That is to say, both were communicating by means that were appropriate to the human constitution. Just so, engaging with metaphorical speech did not amount to reveling in the flesh for Augustine. On the contrary, to adopt metaphorical ways of speaking was to recognize the carnal index that might point to spiritual meaning. Attention to contingency was thus a kind of training in the perception of ironies, and the Arendtian inquirer might ask the following question: "within an Augustinian frame of reference, how could rhetoric and Christianity imply each other?"

As Heidegger had himself argued in his lectures on Augustinian religiosity, one of Augustine's distinctive contributions to rhetoric had been his relocation of the *artes rhetoricae* into an analysis of the "everydayness" of desire as it deliquesced into habit. Indeed, the version of Heidegger that Arendt did receive directly by way of the Winter Semester 1924–1925 lectures on Plato's *Sophist* was the one in which her mentor sought to give an account of Socratic dialectic as a kind of transposition of rhetorical capacity beyond the institutions of assemblies, courts, and festivals (in which it was formally situated) to—as Heidegger put it—"speaking in each moment."[22] As we saw in chapter 2, every historical epoch could be thought to need its own rhetoric. And sophistic was actually an essential engagement with Greek ontology, as I relayed in chapter 3. The nonbeing of possibility qua *pseudos* was the essential alternative to a world of constant and manic presencing qua *energeia*. Similarly, such possibility solved the philosophical puzzle in which the world—achieved as *entelecheia*—was resistant to all forms of motion qua change not in the sense that nothing could move but in the more refined sense that having achieved its cycles and law-abiding repetition no phenomenon could develop and become genuinely historical.

Like the Augustinian *Confessions* itself (one might say), rhetoric—considered as a hermeneutic—could be understood as a practice in which a gap or buffer or distinction emerged between oneself and the world. In relation to that formulation, my claim is this: for Arendt "solidarity" (*dilectio proximi*) was a rhetorical capacity to attend to possible motions without immediately succumbing to them. Love of neighbor was a recognition of a complex array of orientations toward others—their hopes, their interests, their deeds, their misdeeds. This was a form of recognition capable of

---

22. Heidegger, *Platon: Sophistes*, 319: "es bezieht auf das Reden in jedem Augenblick."

representing to itself a diversity of possibilities that could be realized in the relatively near future. That is, solidarity was a conscious simultaneity of desire and aversion, hope and fear, acceptance and rejection. This, in turn, was a kind of rewriting of the Heideggerian gloss of *phronēsis*, which was not an anodyne "practical wisdom" so much as a mode of "disclosing" (*aletheuein*) that would be distinguished by its—emphasis added— "*circumspective* insight."[23]

NONASSIMILATION IN *RAHEL VARNHAGEN*

On the surface, Arendt's second book project on the early nineteenth-century salonnière Rahel Varnhagen was very different from the Augustine book. This was a habilitation, drafted for the most part between 1930 and 1933. It was a historical and primarily biographical study spanning the Jewish emancipation decree issued in 1812 that had normalized the citizenship status of Jews in the Kingdom of Prussia. In this work, Arendt made the ironic observation that, born in 1771 and dead in 1833, the daughter of a successful Jewish dealer in precious stones might have had a better chance of integrating into society before 1806 in what Arendt described as "the short and genuinely tumultuous interval between ghetto and assimilation."[24] What could possibly connect a late antique North African Father of the Christian Church and a Jewish salonnière almost a millennium and a half later living in Berlin in the age of the French Revolution? If the two projects had been written by two different authors or anonymously, it is hard to believe that any historian or literary critic or philosopher would ever have intuited enough of a connection between them to warrant further investigation. How can one think the sheer contingency that, having finished with the Augustine project, Arendt went on almost immediately to deal with Rahel?

My gambit in this section is to claim that in fact one can only fully understand these two works if one sees them as radically different approaches to the same basic problem. I constitute that problem in the following terms: where Augustine's difficulty had been how to understand the achievement of a distance from the world, the work of Rahel's life was overcoming the arm's length at which Prussian society held her on account of her Jewishness. Assimilation had been Augustine's fear, but it was Rahel's task. (I call her Rahel rather than Varnhagen—or any of the other names she

23. Heidegger, 47: "die *phronēsis*, die Umsicht, die umsichtige Einsicht."
24. Arendt, *Rahel Varnhagen*, 17: "in der kurzen und recht stürmischen Zwischenspanne zwischen Ghetto und Assimilation." The original English edition bears the copyright date 1957; the German, 1959. One of the Weimar-era manuscripts survives as Hannah Arendt, "Rahel Varnhagen/Manuskript" under Jaspers: Prosa, Hannah Arendt: Rahel at the Deutsches Literaturarchiv, in Marbach.

took on—in order to mark the single constant standing at the center of her various performances of personae inflected by the surnames of others.) Augustine's attempt to think a category of neighborliness in which one neither fell into the world nor removed oneself from it was—roughly speaking—a success. In contrast, Rahel's attempt to gain entry to Prussian society was a series of failures, howsoever irreducible and memorable those failures may have been. For Arendt, though, the result was the same from a conceptual point of view. What she gained in both cases was a capacity to describe and analyze specific distances from the others with whom one shared a world. Indeed, one might even say that Rahel's failures mapped out more brilliantly than Augustine's successes the kinds of nonidentity that generate protopolitical distances between persons and that might be articulated and discovered by rhetorical means.

For contemporary readers, the historical pertinence of this problem of falling, or assimilating, into the world is far more easily grasped in the context of *Rahel Varnhagen* than in the *The Concept of Love*. This is true for "contemporary" readers today as well as for the potential "contemporary" readers Arendt was thinking of in the early 1930s. The events of 1933 confirmed the timeliness of the Rahel project, but it robbed that project of its most immediate audiences. That year, Arendt was forced to flee Germany. Heading to Paris, she abandoned the habilitation, which was almost complete. In 1938 (encouraged by Walter Benjamin and her husband, Heinrich Blücher), she added what now constitute the final two chapters of the work, although it was not until the 1950s that the project finally emerged as a book. A genuinely ingenious translation by Richard and Clara Winston appeared first in 1958, followed closely by the German original in 1959. By that point, Arendt felt that events had rendered the book largely obsolete. Indeed, in a letter to Karl Jaspers in 1956, she toyed with the notion that having missed its moment as an investigation of the problematic of assimilation the project might find a historical valence as *ein Frauenbuch*, a book focused not on "the Jewish question" but on "the issue of women."[25] Perhaps Arendt meant the joke to be wry, but it indicated a certain unease in relation to matters of sex and gender. In fact, Arendt had already established the possibility of such a transition in her 1933 review of Alice Rühle-Gersetel's *The Women's Question of the Present Age*. There, she saw in the victories of the women's movement precisely the same kinds of merely formal equalities that had been produced by the Jewish emancipation of 1812.[26] In any case, the reviews *Rahel Varnhagen* received in the 1950s displayed a certain confusion. Unable to speak to the book as largely an artifact of pre-1933 Germany,

25. Arendt to Jaspers (September 7, 1956), in *Hannah Arendt–Karl Jaspers Briefwechsel*, 332.
26. Arendt, review of *Das Frauenproblem der Gegenwart*, 177–79.

reviews of the German edition written by Hilde Spiel and Reinhard Buchwald concentrated more on the nature of the interpretative lens separating Hannah from Rahel ("sociological," they concluded), or, alternatively, the nature of the identification between author and subject.[27]

The Rahel book dealt with the ways in which racialized identity might structure access to and appearance in a public sphere, and in this section my principal contention is that we should understand this project as the beginning of a mode of inquiry that runs through *The Origins of Totalitarianism* and into *The Human Condition*. In a way that was actually subtler than anything in either of those two much more celebrated works, the Rahel book inquired into the performative and historically emergent qualities of publicity itself. In laying out this position, I am developing arguments made in earlier feminist work on Arendt. In 1995, by emphasizing the ways in which the salon Rahel built "contradict[s] the agonal model of the public sphere of the polis that predominates in *The Human Condition*," Seyla Benhabib attempted to locate an alternative and affirmative genealogy of modernity in the Rahel book.[28] In the same volume, Bonnie Honig countered that we cannot so easily perform a Habermasian rehabilitation of Arendt's purported Grecophilia, not least because the "feminine" salon is no less agonistic than the "masculine" polis and also because in fact it offers up just as many opportunities to theorize the performative dimensions of politics.[29]

My response to the debate between Benhabib and Honig attempts to develop and synthesize their arguments. I make two claims. First, the salon is the better model of what would become the Arendtian "space of appearance" not because it is more affirmative of modernity but because it offers richer descriptions of the relationship between performance and the reception of performance. Second, the performativity of the salon is to be understood in terms of the ways in which an action becomes *itself* the condition of possibility for the appearance of subsequent actions in a community of gesture. Words and deeds are the lingua franca of publicity in *The Human Condition*, but in the Rahel book words and deeds are themselves the stages on which subsequent words and deeds appear. In 1958 Arendt indicated that the Rahel biography had been "written with an awareness of the doom of the German Jews (albeit naturally without any inkling of the scale that the physical annihilation of the Jewish people in Europe would take)."[30] This

27. Spiel, "Rahel Varnhagen." Buchwald, review of *Rahel Varnhagen*, 142–43.
28. Benhabib, "Pariah and Her Shadow," in Honig, *Feminist Interpretations*, 99.
29. Honig, "Agonistic Feminism," in Honig, *Feminist Interpretations*, 156–60.
30. Arendt, *Rahel Varnhagen*, 11: "die vorliegende Biographie ist zwar schon mit dem Bewußtsein des Untergangs des deutschen Judentums geschrieben (wiewohl natürlich ohne jede Ahnung davon, welche Ausmaße die physische Vernichtung des jüdischen Volkes in Europa annehmen würde)."

was a retrospective assertion that the Rahel project was an attempt to think the conditions of possibility for political appearance in the context of crisis.

In order to pursue the goal of tracing interrelations of identity and publicity, we can consult other materials dating from the early 1930s that permit us to develop a more precise historical contextualization of the Rahel book. There were, for example, the obvious contexts. In March 1930, Arendt defended herself against Jaspers, who had read an early version of the book, by denying that she had reified Rahel's Jewishness. Arendt said that she was simply reporting the habits of self-objectification exhibited by Rahel, who used her own performances to frame herself publicly and forge thereby a very specific space of appearance. Jaspers thought that Arendt was removing Rahel too quickly from Germanness, but we may read this as an indication of how quickly one could be found to have "seceded" from the German nation. We may instructively compare the kind of identifications Jaspers himself was making in his own biography of Max Weber. That biography appeared in 1932, and it constitutes a kind of contemporary pendant piece to Arendt's work on Rahel. More striking than any "self-objectification" on Arendt's part, I would argue, was Jaspers's identification with and nostalgia for Weber as variously a great man, a great German, and a great politician capable of seeing contemporary history in terms of its genuine possibilities.[31]

We begin to grasp the subtlety of Arendt's analysis of identity and publicity when we read that she had indeed written the Rahel work out of a Zionist critique of assimilation (as she put it) and when we understand that in 1932 this position entailed criticism of the Enlightenment for its fixation on questions of merely juridical equality.[32] Public spheres are not legislated; they are performed. The specific texture of a public sphere's archiving of past performances will be integral to the constitution of that sphere as "public." Arendt believed that assimilation entailed a certain dissimulation. It asked people to pretend not to know things that, in fact, they thought they did know. In turn, such dissimulation facilitated a certain fetishization of "the enemy within" as a discourse of fear. In the period between the Enabling Act of March 1933 and her arrest (then flight) in July of that year, Arendt published an article marking the hundredth anniversary of Rahel's death. There, she argued that Rahel had been early proof of the failure of assimilation as a project in Germany (something that was now plain for all to see, she thought). After all, the most viable escape from Jewishness had not been the post-1812 marriage to Karl August Varnhagen, the Prussian

31. Jaspers to Arendt (March 20, 1930), Arendt to Jaspers (March 24, 1930), in *Hannah Arendt–Karl Jaspers Briefwechsel*, 46, 47–48; Jaspers, *Max Weber*.
32. Arendt, "Aufklärung und Judenfrage," 65–77.

bourgeois, set against the background of Jewish emancipation. The most viable escape from Jewishness had actually been offered by the salon before 1806.[33] Perhaps on account of a certain received classicism, we tend to think the salon transgresses the categories of "household life" (*oikos*) and "civil world" (*polis*). For Arendt, however, the salon was distinguished by its capacity to facilitate what she called an "objectification of the personal" (*Objektivierung des Persönlichen*), which transformed the personal into an object available for public scrutiny.[34]

There were also less obvious contexts for the habilitation project, contexts that confirm how Arendt's interests in the constitution of worldly space were transposed from Augustine to Rahel. Indeed, in the final years of the Weimar Republic, Arendt was practically obsessed with what I would call "the tactics and facts of distantiation." Like Rahel's salon, Augustinian confession had been a means of objectifying the personal. In 1930 (on the fifteen-hundredth anniversary of Augustine's death), Arendt made a case for a forgotten Protestant inheritance of the *Confessions* that moved through Luther into Karl Philipp Moritz's *Anton Reiser* and the Goethean personal history of *Wilhelm Meister* (a novel from which, Arendt noted elsewhere, Rahel learned tactics for establishing herself as a publicly performed persona).[35] Moreover, in reviewing Hans Weil's history of the concept of "formation" (*Bildung*) in 1931, Arendt found a heritage coming out of the bildungsroman that stressed the role of taste not simply as a social differentiator for the bourgeoisie but also as a capacity to establish oneself as an individual standing at a specific and distinctive distance from a cultural patrimony.[36] Alternatively, the Augustinian inheritance might also resurface in Kierkegaard. In Arendt's interpretation, Kierkegaard had spoken of himself as a "witness to his own namelessness." Here there was a split or a contradiction between the inescapability of his experiencing of the world through the lens of himself in his own specific here and now on the one hand and, on the other, the nothingness that was his self when beheld in the presence of God.[37] Rahel's performances of herself also had this paradoxical quality of witnessing her own namelessness, and we begin to see that the connections between Rahel and Augustine were to be articulated along the axis of performative autobiography. Whereas Augustine's had been something like a displacement of rhetorical ethos into a performative autobiography to be witnessed by God, Rahel's was an implicit reconfiguration of rhetorical ethos into a performance of illegitimacy that interpellated and called into

33. Arendt, "Originale Assimilation," 143.
34. Arendt, "Berliner Salon," 178.
35. Arendt, "Augustin und Protestantismus," 1.
36. Arendt, review of *Die Entstehung des deutschen Bildungsprinzips*, 200–205.
37. Arendt, "Søren Kierkegaard," 2: "Zeugnis seiner Namenlosigkeit."

being a very particular kind of eclectic audience. At the core of both projects was the constitution of particular conditions of possibility for appearance.

Beyond context and within the book itself, Rahel was most essentially a salonnière. Her task was not to perform in a space of appearance but rather to be the condition of possibility for the appearances and performances of others. Salons like the one that Rahel created were, Arendt noted, spaces in which "those who had learned to represent what they were in conversation might meet."[38] Until Napoleon defeated Prussia at Jena in 1806 (that is, until a reactionary nationalism changed the tone of Prussian public life), salon culture was a kind of historical anomaly. In Arendt's estimation, this was a historical anomaly in which representatives of the old world (members of the nobility) could interact with individuals of no certain social standing (actors and Jews, for instance). These were people who could be bound together by the belief that one ought to be defined simply by who one was and not by what one had, a belief that Arendt attributed to the Grecophile and antimodernist Junker Alexander von der Marwitz.[39] We should assess this belief carefully. In some ways, the emphasis on who one was rather than what one had was the opposite of "progressive," but it did open up a line of possibility in which one might perform into existence "who one was" even if that persona were not the activation of ready-made scripts one had inherited from one's reserve cultures of privilege. Not only a space for the nobility (Prince Louis Ferdinand of Prussia and his mistress, Pauline Wiesel, for example) and the artists (such as Jean Paul, Clemens Brentano, Friedrich and Ludwig Tieck, Adelbert von Chamisso, and Friedrich de la Motte Fouqué), Rahel's salon also drew most of the leading Berlin intellectuals of the day: Schlegel, Schleiermacher, Wolf, the brothers Humboldt. Performing "who one was" could be in a sense diverse, because not all of these identities were exhibitions of aristocratic privilege.

The core argument of this section is the argument around which the chapter as a whole is structured: in her very person, Rahel was the earliest incarnation of what would later become the celebrated "space of appearance" of *The Human Condition*. What is more, Arendt's depiction of that space in the person of Rahel is more nuanced and more useful than its more famous revisions. Making this argument entails suggesting that the original analogue for the polis was not the Pnyx (against the backdrop of which, say, a Pericles might shimmer) nor even the Homeric tales of council and combat in which Achilles might distinguish himself in word and deed. Elsewhere, I have devoted considerable attention to the question of what

38. Arendt, *Rahel Varnhagen*, 45: "im Salon treffen sich die, welche gelernt haben, im Gespräch darzustellen, was sie sind."
39. Arendt, 127, 205ff.

analogues we may draw into the orbit of the Arendtian polis in order to flesh that vision out.[40] Here, I am arguing that the original analogue for the polis was Rahel herself.

In order to grasp the argument that Rahel constituted a space, we have to think carefully about what we mean by phrases such as "political space" and "space of appearance." Heidegger's point had been that like time space cannot be understood in the first instance as abstract dimensionality. Continuing the Heideggerian initiative, we may add that space will always be constituted by motions, differentials in motion, and by possibilities implied in the continuations of actualized motion. In the context of these contentions, we can see that Arendt's point was similar: political space is not the abstract geometry underlying, for instance, the built environment of architectures dedicated to political tasks. What is more, "political geography" in the case of someone like Rahel did not consist simply in the material conditions of possibility for the salons in which she participated—their fabrics and chaises and lighting. The salon was also these things, to be sure, but it was more fundamentally concerned with the ways in which past performances might make certain forms of repetition and deviation meaningful. The constitution of such space as a matrix of differentials between not simply motions but verily actions was a simultaneously literary-critical and art-historical process of discrimination. It was a transdisciplinary political aesthetics most capaciously developed by rhetoric.

My contention that Rahel was something like a polis qua space of appearance is licensed in the first instance by Arendt's emphasis on Rahel's characterizations of herself as an "auditorium" (*Sprechsaal*), a "battlefield" (*Schlachtfeld*), and a "theater" (*Schauplatz*) for others.[41] Again, this salon was a literal space: it was a set of attic rooms in Rahel's residence at Jägerstraße in central Berlin. But, more especially, this space of appearance was the sequence of invitations, introductions, dispositions, and postures generated in Rahel's performances. The true space of the salon was simply the matrix of glances and jokes and veiled attacks that constituted conversation. This matrix included Rahel's letters recounting tales of the salon and the persons, arguments, and love affairs that flourished there, and Arendt's representations of Rahel's letters continued the work of articulating the matrix. This is a space in which every memorable action was the presentation of a persona in a particular mode. Memorability here meant that the action committed to memory became the background out of which subsequent actions did or did not emerge. Subsequent actions were performances that disappeared into the silhouette of the previous performance, shifting

40. Marshall, "Polis and Its Analogues," 123–49.
41. Arendt, *Rahel Varnhagen*, 61, 82, 89.

Heideggerian *energeia* into an *entelecheia* that might be constitutive of the space itself or, alternatively, either forgettable or a means of hiding in plain sight. Repetition would structure regulation; it would also fade into the past as a particular kind of habit.

Perhaps Arendt herself did not build on the foundations she laid in the Rahel book by developing a subtler account of the space of appearance, but this should not stop us from pursuing the point. Later, Arendt appears to have concluded that the Rahel book was preoccupied with apolitical performances and that she could not draw directly on that work in the more classical thematizations of *The Human Condition*. Nevertheless, in the context of the Weimar origins of rhetorical inquiry brought into focus by *Rahel Varnhagen*, we begin to see that Arendt's interests continued a line of inquiry into presencing by means of emotional narrativization in ways that exceeded the bounds of her own considerable powers of self-awareness. The analysis of Rahel's performances was nothing other than rhetorical analysis of the everydayness of being-with-one-another. The earlier, Rahel-inspired analysis of the space of appearance was better and less burdened by a need for eulogy. Eventually, Arendt's concept of the polis became burdened by normative expectations that have been hard to ignore, and it has been difficult to translate that normative vision into practical contexts on account of the relative absence of thick descriptions of action in the polis. The Rahel book anchors a different reading of the Arendtian polis.

Arendt insisted that Rahel saw her role as a kind of spectator, a passive recipient of the actions of others who by means of that passivity provided opportunities for others to distinguish themselves. Arendt found here a deeply fetishized language of subjection. We are told that Rahel, the Jewess, had to draw her suitor, the nobleman von Finkenstein, out of his life of good social standing and convert him into a nullity before she could love him. She had to begin from a foundation of equal effacement.[42] Insofar as the Rahel book possessed a plot, moreover, it was a narrative of a failed engagement to Karl von Finkenstein, a feigned affair with Friedrich von Gentz, a real affair with Don Raphael d'Urquijo, and a friendship with Alexander von der Marwitz culminating in a marriage to Karl August Varnhagen. Overall, the book was an investigation of feigned passivity. The fetish was catching, and Gentz turned the language of subjection back against Rahel: "you are an *infinitely productive* being; I, *infinitely receptive*," he said to her, adding that "you are a great *man*; and I am first among all the women who have ever lived."[43] Elsewhere, we find that such transposability of role was decisive. Referring to interactions between Wilhelm von Humboldt and Caroline von

42. Arendt, 49.
43. Arendt, 88–9: "Sie sind ein *unendlich produzierendes*, ich bin ein *unendlich empfangendes* Wesen; Sie sind ein großer *Mann*; ich bin das erste aller Weiber, die je gelebt haben."

Dachröden (later Humboldt's wife), Arendt—or rather Arendt impersonating Rahel—observed that there was a strange doubleness. On the one hand, there were "his letters to his bride-to-be in which he constantly cast himself as the one needing protection and as the subordinate one." On the other hand, there was "his diary, in which he had her speaking to him in precisely the same ways that in fact he spoke to her."[44] The fantasy of such positions of inferiority and superiority simply overwrote the assignation of roles.

Fantasies of passivity were more than simply a fetish, and Rahel was wishing to become something like a conduit, the function of which might be to condense and thus reveal. As Arendt cast it, this salonnière's purpose was "to expose herself to life to such a degree that she might encounter it—Rahel's words—'as a storm without protection.'"[45] This was a deliberate self-negation, an electing neither to choose nor to act, "because choice and action would themselves already be anticipations of life thereby distorting pure happening."[46] The Augustine book recognized that being born into a context made by others and by history was a structural element of the human condition as such. In the Rahel book, this became a kind of indistinction between happenstance, fate, and luck. To be born Jewish, Arendt said, was to be born into a story already seventeen centuries old (a quite particular dating of Jewish origins, one may note). And, as presented in the book, escape from such a fated context—in the form, say, of marriage to someone ostensibly inappropriate—could only come in the manner of chance.[47]

Arendt relayed that, at a certain point, Rahel grew tired of being a stage on which others might appear, but in Arendt's representation she had never really been simply a condition of possibility for others.[48] In the paradox that Arendt depicted, one might attempt to assimilate into society by constructing oneself as a person of such extreme individuality that one's Jewishness ceased to be one's overriding distinguishing mark in the eyes of others. In the first instance, such individuality might take the form of a kind of capaciousness of soul that bordered on incoherence. The pose of passivity had, in fact, been simply preparation for a kind of articulateness that would demonstrate the power of an individual voice to master even the most purportedly random stimulations. The task was "to become a

44. Arendt, 68: "seinen Briefen an die Braut, in denen er sich ständig als den Anlehnungsbedürftigen, als den Unterlegene hinstellt" and "seinem Tagebuch, in dem er sie mit akkurat den gleichen Worten zu sich sprechen läßt, mit denen *er* faktisch zu *ihr* spricht."
45. Arendt, 10: "sich dem Leben so zu exponieren, daß es sie treffen konnte 'wie Wetter ohne Schirm.'"
46. Arendt, 10: "weil Wahl und Handeln bereits dem Leben zuvorkommen und das reine Geschehen verfälschen würden."
47. Arendt, 49.
48. Arendt, 89.

mouthpiece for every occurrence, to transmute everything that occurred into something that could be said."[49] The supposition was that Rahel's very passivity accounted for her inimitable expressive capacities. Being a space for the performance of others also meant fashioning a self out of the fragments of one's responses to them.

As it was presented by Arendt, the coherence of Rahel's person was something like the movement of a chess champion playing dozens of opponents simultaneously: they always took the first move, Rahel's genius lay in responding, and perhaps she also had to lose. Yet her rhetorical style was the discontinuous circumference described by the poses she struck at each board as she moved around the circle of her challengers. Rahel's genius was purely tactical, according to Arendt, who added that Rahel had "no real consciousness of what words belonged together and what did not." The game was a combinatorial of moves, and her ignorance was a certain unorthodox strength. Her ability was simply to "bring together in an act of wit the seemingly most unrelated things," a capacity—we should recall—that the rhetoricians had called *ingenium*.[50] Similarly, Rahel's talent consisted in a complementary capacity to "reveal the incoherence in things that appeared to be most tightly integrated."[51] This, we may add, was the equal and opposite faculty of *iudicium*, the power of discrimination. Rahel's exchanges were brilliant and somewhat isolated. In this way, the "space of appearance" built by this protopolis was also the matrix of distances *from oneself* that salon performance brought into being. The more diverse the society in which one moved, the more capacious—or, potentially, incoherent—one's person would become.

In the absence of habit, the play of similarity and difference was reset, and Rahel's passivity was therefore quite different from the "vacuity" of her eventual husband, Karl August Varnhagen. Varnhagen took up the passivity fetish as well and characterized himself as "a beggar by the wayside," as someone who was unable "to grasp connections as a system" and unable "to discern the most particular thing in an individual life as wit."[52] In Arendt's rendition, Karl August was a machine seeking impetus; Rahel, a protean imagination. But the point was not simply to achieve individuality by turning oneself into an utterly singular poem. The point was to become distinct to such an undeniable degree that all those in one's presence would have to take up a position relative to one's specificity. In part, this was what Rahel

49. Arendt, 10: "ein 'Sprachrohr' des Geschenen zu werden, das Geschehene in ein Gesagtes umzuwandeln."

50. Arendt, 42: "sie kann das Entfernteste im Witz zusammenbringen."

51. Arendt, 42: "sie kann im Zusammenhängendsten die Zusammenhanglosigkeit aufdecken."

52. Arendt, 141: "ein *Bettler am Wege*"; "weder den Zusammenhang kann ich darstellen als System, noch das Einzelste heraussondern in ein individuelles Leben als Witz."

was saying when she declared that true conversation could only be conducted on the basis of an absence of the interlocutor in the medium of letter writing. In the letter, there was an intimacy guaranteed by the uniqueness of the distance that had opened up between two individuals.[53] Because of the material absence of the other, one had to pay closer attention to the construction of that interlocutor in one's epistolary—but, of course, still rhetorical—performance.

Arendt was analyzing the rhetorical concept of style in its indistinguishability from ethos: what would it be to remain somehow constant in the midst of myriad dealings with others? The genius of her depiction went deeper, however. She was in fact proposing that language use in the world exhibits at least two extremes. There are those who are so insensitive to the demands of particular places and times that they remain always themselves and take on the static self-identity of a walking and talking corpse. But there are also those who are so highly sensitive to the demands of the moment that they begin to disintegrate. They become no more than a jumble, a miscellany of masks. Rahel was somewhere between these two extremes, tending perhaps toward disintegration in Arendt's presentation. The threat of gracelessness, discombobulation, inconstancy of style was ever present. Arendt was thus willing to grant that Wilhelm von Humboldt was merely being candid when he said that, in the course of one romantic humiliation or another, Rahel had lost her "inner grace."[54] Rahel accepted this insult (Arendt noted), saying that episodes of coming apart and finding spaces of disorganization within oneself could be something like "beautiful parentheses belonging neither to us nor to others."[55]

Arendt herself was experimenting with the kind of inconstancy of style that she found modeled for her in Rahel's literary remains. In a way that is rare in Arendt's work, the Rahel book is paraphrastic to the point that readers lose their sense of there being an author in control. In the book that I myself am writing here, the problem of paraphrase is endemic, and I deal with the frequency of my recounting the words of others not by continually attributing each sentence to Arendt (or whomever) but by leaving most of those attributions implicit and by marking more unmissably those sentences in which I appear in my own voice with the shamelessness of the academic idiom "I am claiming" (and the like). Elsewhere, Arendt is almost always speaking in her own voice such that self-assertion is less material. Readers of the Rahel book have often struggled to distinguish the points that Arendt wished to make from the endless reportage and inhabitation

53. Arendt, 32.
54. Arendt, 73: "innere Grazie."
55. Arendt, 95: "das sind schöne Parenthesen im Leben, die weder uns noch anderen gehören."

of opinions and reactions. That Walter Benjamin had been looking at the text over Arendt's shoulder in Paris makes a good deal of sense, because the text was something like a weaving together of quotations that did not quite cohere. The Austrian novelist Hermann Broch was showing a good deal of literary-critical perspicacity in 1947 when he described the Rahel manuscript as "woven" (*textilisch*).[56]

If one could not expose oneself to the world without running the risk that the contiguities, juxtapositions, and non sequiturs of that world would overwhelm one's ability to domesticate both similarity and difference as unity, it followed that one might be forced to shore up the stability of one's distance from the world—one's stylistic equipoise—by metabolizing the language of a genius. According to Arendt, this is what Rahel did with Goethe. Rahel had distinguished herself as one of the first to understand Goethe, but it was he who "conveyed to her the language that she could speak."[57] Arendt argued that without his novels Rahel would not have been able to see her life from the inside. Without his idiom, that life would have remained but a sequence of unmastered happenings, one thing after another without what Hobbes (following Quintilian) had called "contexture."[58] Rahel may have detested Goethe's *Elective Affinities*, but in Arendt's depiction of her Rahel was at her most Goethean in those moments when she, in effect, took up the thematics of that novel while detecting the strange oscillations and ironies that characterized what I am calling the spaces established by human relationships, their fields of force.

Perhaps like Rahel before her, Arendt was aware that there was a fiction at work in the figure of the genius, for Goethe's own stylistic unity, his capacity to be always himself and to force others ever and again to take up positions relative to him, was naturally itself a deeply literary conceit. One might strike the pose of stylistic serenity. And one might successfully feign a release from the anxiety of influence if one's imagination were more capacious than one's immediate interlocutors. Disaffiliation might be disguised for a time. Such a pose might imply a kind of deep and complete assimilation into oneself without remainder. In this way, Goethe could become a literary historical topos precisely because he was not a space at all and was instead a singularity that others could only copy, countenance, or ignore. He was the somewhat mythical model of what it would be to remain always oneself even as one was responding adroitly to the challenges of any given situation. He could be understood as a center—a point and not a space—because the totality of forces that constituted the historical epoch in which he lived was said to be both fully present and fully mastered in his person. The myth

56. Broch to Arendt (December 14, 1947), in *Hannah Arendt/Hermann Broch Briefwechsel*, 65.
57. Arendt, *Rahel Varnhagen*, 113: "Goethe vermittelt ihr die Sprache, die sie sprechen kann."
58. Arendt, 112.

might even imply that he could not betray himself, for every aberration would be reread as the unpredictability of a genius whose acts were to be retroactively legislated into a rule.

If Goethe metabolized his precedents so thoroughly that they became unrecognizable in the "flesh and blood" of his creations, other lesser lights might perform a comparable assimilation into or identity with the zeitgeist that would be legible not as the achievement of individuality but the complete abnegation of it. These contraries were not as far apart as one might suppose. Among the merely minor geniuses of the age, Humboldt wanted to be a "tinkling cymbal" moving in the breeze of history, Gentz desired to be a clearinghouse of information, and Schlegel sought to approach the spirit of the age in "a participatory thinking-with." And all were simply versions of Hegel's notorious fantasy of Napoleon in 1806—there strides history, encapsulated. Said Varnhagen, the fantasist, "destiny itself is the sole acting person."[59] For her part, Arendt took the notion that an individual might embody the world-historical forces of an age to be an artifact of the Romantic imagination, and her sustained critique of assimilation counted as a rejection of, among other things, what we might call this principle of the genius. In part, this may have been a rejection of the cult of genius she found expounded in Heidelberg when she began to think of a habilitation on Romanticism. There, she was in the ambit of Friedrich Gundolf, whose work on Shakespeare (1911) laid down a palette of thoughts on the subject of genius.

Of course, it was not by metabolizing Goethe that Rahel came closest to annulling the arm's length at which she was held by Prussian society on account of her Jewishness. The closest she came to assimilation was marriage to Karl August Varnhagen, a type Arendt described as "a bourgeois journalist in waiting." Rahel was never successful in achieving assimilation. She never became, as it were, an achieved parvenu. Referring to the period immediately before the marriage, Arendt noted that Rahel "did not now and never would renounce her desire to be included in the society of parvenus; but she began to employ different means." That is, "rather than let herself be pulled up by someone already at the top, she sought now to let herself be taken up by someone still at the bottom."[60] Assimilation here did not take the form of assuming Varnhagen's last name and disappearing

59. Arendt, 70, 86, 185: "das Geschick ist die einzig handelnde Person."
60. Arendt, 171: "anstatt sich von irgendeinem, der schon oben ist, heraufheben, versucht sie sich von einem, der noch unten ist, mitnehmen zu lassen." By the time that Arendt added the two final chapters, "Between Pariah and Parvenu" and "One Does Not Escape Jewishness" in 1938, a new series of contexts had intervened, occasioned by the rupture of 1933 and the transfer to Paris. She had appropriated the terms "pariah" and "parvenu" as a shorthand for the poles of ostracism and assimilation that she had been working on for some time. "Pariah" and "parvenu" were part of a new analytical language appended to the Weimar-era corpus.

legally behind the public person of a husband. It occurred in the collection of Rahel's letters edited and published by her husband.[61] Prior to publication, the letters had to be assiduously rewritten. Jewishness had to be retrospectively expunged, marginalized, or recast. Arendt observed that the manuscripts bore two sets of revisions, only one of which seemed to belong to Rahel herself. Assimilation, for the parvenu and for those working on the parvenu's behalf, was an endless task.

The Rahel book was the autopsy of a series of failures, but—as I have been arguing—failure can entail its own distinctive exemplarity. From the point of view of rhetorical inquiry, the failure ever to reach absolute assimilation was an advantage. Failing in this way involved a continual awareness of the specific distances setting one apart from one's neighbors. The gap could never be closed for Rahel, something that was not the case for Augustine. As Arendt put it, one could not escape Jewishness. In sum, we can see that the Rahel book explored four means of leaving the pseudospace of identity difference: becoming a space for others; achieving individuality; metabolizing the language of a genius; and entering into couverture beneath a neutral identity. All failed. Nevertheless, in the broader history of the constitution of space in the thought of Hannah Arendt, these failures played an important role. They constituted not only an indictment of the whole project of assimilation but also a series of prototypes for existing in the world but at a certain distance from it.

The space of differences in which Rahel existed was not experienced as a political space, but that does not mean it did not function as a prolegomenon to the explicitly political work in Arendt's later essay, "The Jew as Pariah." The purpose of Rahel's salon had never been the kind of discussion that ended in decision and took decision to be its purpose. Its raison d'être was simply "wit" (*Witz*), brilliance in composition and conversational performance. Indeed, Arendt insisted that Rahel remained so apolitical that only once politics and history had intervened in and after 1806 did she realize that there had been any kind of political dimension to the salon experience at all.[62] Nevertheless, we can say that the salon was a condition of possibility for the objectification—which is to say the distinction—of individuals. Suddenly independent of background and insulated from concerns for the future by the pointlessness of the exercise, performance was supposedly all that counted. Action, witticism primarily, began and ended with itself. It was atelic, brilliant, and without purpose. Thus, there is a sense in which the acutely rhetorical awareness of situations and persons and passions and possible futures that Arendt concentrated on in the Rahel book could—and,

61. Varnhagen, *Rahel: Ein Buch des Andenkens für Ihre Freunde.*
62. Arendt, *Rahel Varnhagen*, 118.

in my opinion, should—have been transferred to the space of differences that was politics as Arendt theorized it in her later works. In short, Arendt's depiction of Rahel was far more textured, insightful, and politically sharp than her merely Olympian depiction of Achilles.

ANTAGONISM AND TRIANGULATION UP TO *THE ORIGINS OF TOTALITARIANISM*

To this point, I have made the following claims. First, Arendt's account of politics as a distinct form of human activity—exceeding both the cyclical routines maintaining bare life and also the means/ends trajectories involved in building a world of objects—was brilliant but lacking in a rhetorical consciousness of what it might mean to take up a particular position in a particular moment. Second, such a rhetorical consciousness had probably been available to her when she first came to Marburg in the form of notes taken in Heidegger's Summer Semester lectures on the basic concepts of Aristotelian philosophy, but Arendt only arrived in the Winter Semester of 1924–1925 (missing the *viva voce* exposition), and she never worked through Heidegger's reading in detail. Third, Arendt nevertheless expressed interest in Heidegger's rhetorical analysis of the everydayness of being in the world with others as the potential foundation of a political theory, and this interest can be understood as the remnant of an indirect reception of Heidegger's rhetorical analysis. Finally, one can reread Arendt's early works on St. Augustine and Rahel Varnhagen as a working out of this indirect reception. As a result, there are conceptual resources available within Arendt's oeuvre for thinking about a rhetorical account of politics.

The task in this final section is to ask whether there were traces of this rhetorical account of politics in Arendt's explicitly political writings in the 1940s and whether there are therefore opportunities to flesh out the account of distances in and from the world given in the works on Augustine and Rahel in a manifestly political context. My claim in this section is that there were. Given that this is a book concerned with the Weimar origins of rhetorical inquiry, one may ask why it is legitimate to extend this examination of the "early" Arendt into the texts of the later 1930s and early 1940s before the publication of *The Origins of Totalitarianism* in 1951. How can artifacts from two decades or so after 1933 contribute to an articulation of *Weimar* origins? As I argued in the opening chapter of this book, I do not use the term "origin" to denote some kind of unanticipated point before which nothing. The word does not entail an ontology of the ex nihilo. As I understand it, an origin is distinguished not by its lack of a past but rather by the futures it comes to take on. An origin is a past that calls a multiplicity of futures into being, but it is these futures that retroactively give that past focus and form. This means

that the beginnings I identify in *The Concept of Love* and *Rahel Varnhagen*
are known to a significant degree by the narratives that incorporate them
into later developments. In this final section, I engage texts from the later
1930s and early 1940s, in order to continue the work of tracing the trajectory
between Arendt's first two books and to establish continuities between the
prewar and postwar works. Of course, these continuations do not characterize "Weimar" as such. Nevertheless, they do characterize the Weimar
origins of rhetorical inquiry on which this book is focused.

Arendt came to regard the Rahel book as politically naive in hindsight.
She did not change her mind about the impossibility of assimilation as Rahel
had encountered it, and in 1952 Arendt agreed with Jaspers when he said
that the book might lead readers to conclude that "a person could not in
point of fact live properly as a Jew at all." She had said it was impossible to
live within the particular intersection of historical processes that Rahel encountered.[63] Jaspers raised the issue because he feared that such a depiction
of the impossibility of Jewish assimilation might, paradoxically, be taken up
by anti-Semites.[64] Arendt declared herself unconcerned with them as an
audience. She did continue to insist that such a book could have had its uses
before 1933 (and even in pre-1938 contexts). Nevertheless, in the postwar
environment, she worried that "people of good will might see a connection
between these things and the extermination of the Jews that in fact is not
there." And, thus, she confessed that the book had grown out of the Zionist
critique of assimilation that, while correct in itself, was "politically witless"
(*politisch ahnungslos*).[65] Understood in purely political terms (we can interpolate), the book appeared to take up precisely the nonassimilationist
position that Zionists and German anti-Semites had shared: the Jews cannot
remain in Germany.

Understood in purely political terms, however, the problem with the
Rahel book was not simply that it played into the mutual constitution of
Zionism and anti-Semitism. It was also built on an assumption that Arendt
had inherited tacitly from Rahel—namely, that exiting the pseudospace of
racialized otherness was a matter for individuals and not for groups. This
was a well-known paradox: one could not exit Jewishness as an individual

63. Jaspers to Arendt (August 23, 1952) and Arendt to Jaspers (September 7, 1952), in *Hannah Arendt–Karl Jaspers Briefwechsel*, 230, 234: "ihr Buch kann die Stimmung erwecken, als ob ein Mensch als Jude eigentlich nicht recht leben könne," and "ich bin auch heute noch der Mei- nung, daß Juden unter den Bedingungen der gesellschaftlichen Assimilation und staatlichen Emanzipation nicht 'leben' konnten."
64. Jaspers to Arendt (August 23, 1952), in *Hannah Arendt–Karl Jaspers Briefwechsel*, 232.
65. Arendt to Jaspers (September 7, 1952), *Hannah Arendt–Karl Jaspers Briefwechsel*, 233: "ich befürchte, daß gutwillige Leute zwischen diesen Dingen und der Ausrottung der Juden einen Zusammenhang sehen werden, der de facto nicht besteht."

without entangling oneself in the dilemmas of pariah or parvenu, yet exiting Jewishness together with other Jews would be understood as reinscribing the Jewishness one was attempting to exit. Speaking in the idiom that Arendt herself made famous in her essay of 1944, the pariah would stand on the ground of otherness with a variety of different forms of recalcitrance, whereas the parvenu would attempt to show that identity was nothing other than the distinctiveness of scripts that could be run. Neither pariah nor parvenu would exit identity politics as individuals, and, even as it might aim at the abolition of identity political distinctions, collective action in any form would underscore the identity that was to be legislated away. So run the arguments.

I contend that Arendt's journalistic writings up to the publication of *The Origins of Totalitarianism* in 1951 constituted her attempt to overcome the paradoxes of "exiting" identity politics. This was an attempt that dealt with the problem of how to bring into existence a "we," the most political of pronouns. Equally, it demonstrated the need to construct a tradition setting out a space of alternative possibilities for any given "we." And, as was particularly evident in her *Aufbau* essays between March 1943 and April 1945, Arendt's attempt to overcome the paradoxes of exiting identity politics required ceaseless attention to discernment, specification, and revision of actuality and possibility in politics. This implied an understanding of politics as nothing more and nothing less than discursive negotiation, a space, I am arguing, dilated by the array of differences emergent in a community charged with leaving the state of collective indecision. The point to emphasize once again is that "space" is something more than architecture (although it is that too), for the space of appearance is the record of differences in a cultural topos where the accumulation of versions of an action or gesture lay out the "dimensions" along which divergence may appear.

Of course, Arendt's sudden politicization in 1933 was produced by what she termed a declaration of war against the Jews issued by Nazi Germany. She was politicized by a suspension of politics. The bipolar distance brought into being by the Nazi state's interpellation of Jews after 1933 was indeed a space, but it was meant to be a space existing between communities and not within a single community. As such, this was a rhetorical space of poses and threats and acts of violence, but it was not a political space of collective indecision. Arendt herself used a Schmittian language of friends and enemies in order to state the nature of her politicization. As she said repeatedly during the Second World War, the formation of a Jewish army was to be regarded as "the beginning of Jewish politics." And, as she said in *Aufbau* in November of 1941, "one truth as yet unknown to the Jewish people, a truth that they are now beginning to learn, is that one can only defend oneself as the person one was attacked as."[66] In reality, however, Arendt's sense of the political was already radically different from Schmitt's. It was not the "international" relationship between communities at war with each other that Arendt took to be political. Indeed, she observed that the importation of foreign policy categories into domestic politics was one of the fundamental dangers of modern politics. It constituted one of the basic moves of Nazi biopolitics.[67]

Arendt objected to the extension of Schmittian friend-enemy modes of constituting political space into situations where war was not underway or at hand. It might well be exceedingly difficult to make judgments about the clearness and presentness of danger. Pace Hobbes, however, the distinction between war and peace had to be made because for Arendt, Theodor Herzl's supposition that "a nation is a group of people . . . held together by a common enemy" made for bad bilateral politics.[68] In the postwar context surrounding the declaration of the state of Israel in 1948, this meant that "a general hysteria" might impose "all-or-nothing policies upon a moderately friendly world." To be sure, Arendt immediately conceded that "the right distinction between friend and foe will be a life-or-death matter for the State of Israel."[69] But the "we" ought not to be so monolithic, she contended, that any attempt at negotiation would be denounced as "collaboration."

Ultimately, what Nazi interpellation brought into being was a new consciousness of a Jewish "we," and it was this Jewish "we" that was political because it could be—and was—collectively indecisive. One of most profound shifts in Arendt's thought between the fall of the Weimar Republic and the beginning of the war was the sudden transposition of interests from the first person singular to the first person plural. No more of the Augustinian "I" and its analogues; in its place, questions of the "we." Arendt's implicitly rhetorical conception of politics was visible in her desire to investigate the decision taken by Jews in the Warsaw Ghetto in 1943 to fight against the Germans. Indeed, she doubled down on rhetoric: in her first article on the uprising, published in the New York Jewish magazine *Aufbau* in April 1944, she wanted above all to mark the moment, to commit it to memory as a monument. In a second follow-up article published in July, though, she went on to describe in more detailed way precisely how it was that the decision to fight had been taken. In the two articles, she moved from a rhetoric of *epideixis* to one of deliberation.[70]

66. Arendt, "Die Jüdische Armee," 1: "eine dem jüdischen Volk unbekannte Wahrheit, die es erst zu lernen beginnt, ist, *dass man sich nur als das wehren kann, als was man angegriffen wird.*"
67. Arendt, "Zionism Reconsidered," 180.
68. Arendt, 180. Arendt attributed the line to Herzl without citation, but she may have been thinking of the definition of a nation that he gave in *The Tragedy of Jewish Immigration*, 26.
69. Arendt, "About 'Collaboration,'" 56.
70. Compare Arendt, "Für Ehre und Ruhm," 1–2, and "Die Tage der Wandlung," 16.

For Arendt, the Jewish "we" was first and foremost a set of constantly changing and specific differences. Her experience of this collective was always an experience of precise, pertinent, political disagreements about what was happening, where tensions came from, and how one might respond. One needed a very thick skin to live in this space of continual differentiation, and Arendt's practice of drawing distinctions was at times so caustic that others refused to share it with her. One should understand this "thickness of skin" as a rhetorico-political capacity to see the moves made in one's immediate vicinity in the context of a broader problematic. "Thickness of skin" was thus a kind of rhetorical equipoise amid a multitude of developments and possibilities. Conversely, "thinness of skin" was a kind of Augustinian falling into the world. It was a kind of subsumption—not into love but into pain, aversion, fear, hate, self-pity, and the varieties of narrativization in which these emotions and their like were axial.

Displaying apparent imperviousness would be rhetorically risky, and this quickly became one of the characteristics of Arendt's public performances. Long before she published her analysis of Adolf Eichmann and became persona non grata for some members of the Jewish community, she interpreted the suicide of Stefan Zweig in Brazil in 1942 as a kind of demonstration of his political stupidity. She accused Zweig of having been a snob and too much in love with the adulation he had received in prewar Austria to recognize the obvious—namely, that his flight from the Nazis was a political and not merely personal matter. There was a polemical force in Arendt's denunciation that was, indeed, equal and opposite to her own prewar acquiescence in Rahel's refusal to understand her inability to assimilate into German society as anything more than a biographical fact. Suicide was an Augustinian "annihilation" (*Vernichtung*) of worldly relations but without any possibility of thereby returning to the world or a community. Zweig "the I," she was arguing, never "the we."[71]

Arendt attacked Zweig (a dead man who could not respond), because she believed that his case was emblematic of a kind of apolitical and merely personal despair that characterized some parts of the Jewish refugee community. She took it as part of her journalistic task to diagnose moods and habits and locutions in the political community to which she belonged. She did so for the purpose of bringing that community to a state of greater self-awareness and in order to prepare it for more adroit action in the world. This amounted to a rhetorical critique of what one might call the quotidianization of political languages. Published in the *Menorah Journal* in 1943, "We Refugees" was an exemplary article in this regard. Narrated in a faux first person plural, Arendt's piece impersonated her refugee

71. Arendt, "Portrait of a Period," 307–14.

peers. She was mocking what she performed as their brittle cheerfulness, and the unannounced paraphrastic quality of the performance reproduced elements of the style in which the Rahel book had been written. In her rendition, this cheerfulness exhibited a parvenu psychology. It expressed an inauthenticity produced by moving in circles that were not one's own. "We lost our language," she had her token refugee say, "which means the naturalness of reactions, the simplicity of gestures."[72] No matter (here Arendt was sneering in the background), give us a year and we'll have learned the repertoire—assimilation is our talent. But, she implied, brittle cheerfulness was to be understood alongside the increasing rate of suicide among Jewish refugees. Both reactions, she charged, were indicative of an inability to respond to a political situation in a political way. At moments such as this, Arendt was engaging the powers of paraphrase together with an understanding of the discourses of assimilation that she had honed in the Rahel book, and she was applying them to a new form of rhetorico-political critique. The task was to represent her own readers to themselves in the mirror of caricature. In this way, one might jolt them out of language habits that, in Arendt's opinion, were either eroding Jewish political capacity or impeding its development in the first place.

In the crosshairs of genuine political debate during the 1940s, Arendt remained highly sensitive to the most recent political developments. Characteristic in this regard was a piece from February 1943 on "The Crisis of Zionism," which remained unpublished until 2007. In that piece, Arendt noted that "during the last weeks, we had to add two other very critical signs of immediate political danger," both pertaining to Palestine. "The first and the more important," she said, "is the well-known Magnes declaration" calling for the formation of a binational Jewish-Palestinian state situated within an Arab federation that would itself be embedded in "a kind of Anglo-American alliance." After the war, Arendt supported a reformulated version of this proposal, but during the war she saw it as dangerously weak. Arendt continued: "the second bad news from Palestine during the last weeks was the formation of a new party, the so-called Aliyah Hadashah, the party of new immigrants," which marked a fracturing of the Jewish community in Palestine, something that Arendt deplored in the context of war.[73] As an actualizing that is inseparable from the multiple possibilities surrounding it, politics was short term. Indeed, it was the unpredictability of politics that made Arendt say that it was an activity beyond the calculus of means and ends. One could only act on principle (or rather, one always had to be able to redescribe one's actions in terms of principles retrospectively), because

72. Arendt, "We Refugees," 69.
73. Arendt, "Crisis of Zionism," 332–33.

the machinations of history were always superior to the machinations of particular persons. If something had at one time been desirable but was now impossible, she simply named and then rigorously ignored it.

The rhetorico-political histories that Arendt wrote in the 1940s were always explicitly presentist. They were narratives designed to inform one's understanding of the now. This was what she would try to do in *The Origins of Totalitarianism* in 1951. And, in 1954, she was similarly concerned to set out some basic presuppositions of her presentist historiography in a manuscript on "Understanding and Politics," most of which was published in *Partisan Review*. "Causality," she claimed, "is an altogether alien and falsifying category in the historical sciences." In history, "effects" would very often be completely out of proportion with the "causes" from which they sprang. (Think of the First World War, she proposed.) One could not say that the effect was contained in the cause. History forced one continually to reassess the moment. And, in a reversal of the historical linearity that one might suppose led from the past into the future, Arendt proposed that in fact it was always the event—the unpredictable, calamitous event—that brought new pasts into being. In her words, "whenever an event occurs that is great enough to illuminate its own past, history comes into being."[74] This was an appropriation of Heideggerian "situatedness" (*Befindlichkeit*) as originally rhetorical consciousness. It was also a basic transposition of the rhetorical focus on the contingent, the that-which-could-have-been-otherwise, to the realm of historiography.

Arendt was intimating that consistency was a relatively minor virtue in politics. This was not because expediency counted most in political calculations. It was because history transformed situations so rapidly that the fully consistent person would be subsumed by history's "cunning." One had to act on principle because it was history and not the individual that did the instrumentalizing, but one could not always act on the same principle because unimaginative consistency would be no match for the ironies discovered by situations. One needed many principles. In this way, I would argue, the Arendtian politician was more Rahel than Goethe. That is, the task of politics was not to achieve a kind of consistency of style that might distinguish the individual, even by virtue of the range of their potential performances. The task of politics was the extreme, adroit, swift adoption of a pose relative to emergent possibility, whether that be the swift and dramatic possibility of a national security threat or the sometimes slow and sometimes fast but always fundamental processes of socioeconomic change.

Adroit responsiveness to situation implied change or redescription of position, and for Arendt there was a sense in which multipolarity as distinct

74. Arendt, "Understanding and Politics," 318–19.

from bipolarity was a chief means of exercising such an adroitness. Despite her wartime insistence on the importance of creating a Jewish army, she emerged after the war as an ally of Judah Magnes and the Ihud proposition that Jewish and Arab populations in Palestine should be joined in a larger federation of peoples in Palestine, Transjordan, Syria, and Lebanon.[75] To turn the Yishuv, the Jewish "we" in Palestine, into a nation-state would run the risk of reinscribing into an Israeli state the principles of racial nationalism that had made its establishment such a vital necessity in the first place. Moreover, to expect either the Jews or the Palestinians to live as a minority in a state controlled by the other community was to ignore the bankruptcy of international guarantees of minority rights, as demonstrated in the interwar period. The solution, as Arendt (and others) saw it, was to multiply the number of minorities in the state to the point that no single minority could threaten any other. Arendt saw the United States of America as one example of this kind of federal principle in action, and on multiple occasions she also argued for the proposition that only a federally organized Europe could engineer an exit from the debacle of the European nation-state system.[76] Arendt believed that, in order to found a lasting political space in the Near East, one had to move beyond bilateral antagonisms by engineering a state in which a multiplicity of crosscurrents existed.

Arendt's shift from bipolarity to multipolarity in the postwar environment was part of a growing tendency to triangulate political disputes. Thus, already in 1945 she was willing to grant that, where Zionists were right to propose that assimilation was a kind of willed self-destruction, assimilationist groups in the global Jewish community were also right to point out that Zionists had never seriously addressed the question of how Jews outside of an Israeli state ought to deal with accusations that they owed a double loyalty—one to the state in which they lived and another to a Jewish state.[77] And, of course, the idea of federation itself was an attempt to finesse the either/or of a Jewish-controlled Israel or an Arab-controlled Palestine. Arendt's advocacy of these policies was calculated on the basis of the particular (and changing) situation on the ground, but they were also indicative of what to her mind was a basically Augustinian problem of how one ought to go about constructing relationships with neighbors. After the war she insisted repeatedly that the appropriate response to the German habit of feeling ashamed to be German was to say that after 1945 one had to be ashamed to be a human being. Similarly, Arendt was expressing a basically Augustinian notion of solidarity—of being-alongside—when she noted that

75. Magnes, "Toward Peace in Palestine," 243. Arendt, "Peace or Armistice," 78–82.
76. See Arendt, "Approaches to the 'German Problem,'" 93–106.
77. Arendt, "Zionism Reconsidered," 166.

the Jews in the Warsaw Ghetto had at times flown the Polish flag alongside their Jewish one and when she feared that Jewish fascists might do to the Palestinians what German fascists had done to the Jews.

In order to facilitate a flexibility and creativity of thought within the various "we's" to which she belonged immediately after the war, Arendt paid particular attention to the constitution of traditions. In her understanding, a tradition would gather together under a single heading a variety of different ways of doing some particular thing. A tradition was, in this sense, a space opened up by the specific distances between particular exemplars. In Rahel's case, past actions might become a stage on which to perform future actions (for appearance would be a matter of conforming to or deviating from silhouettes that had become characteristic), or one's responsiveness might become a way of holding open a space of appearance for others. Such spaces would be spaces of potential creativity. Whereas the exemplars only indicated a particular number of ways of addressing an issue, the gaps *between* the exemplars, or alternatively the ways in which they faced off against each other, became opportunities for taking the tradition to be a line of inquiry that might be further developed or reinvented.

It was on account of the intuition that exemplars opened up spaces that, even following the war, Arendt wanted to include the case of Rahel in a tradition of what she now called "conscious pariahs." This was a lineage in which she also included Heinrich Heine, Scholem Aleichem, Bernard Lazare, Franz Kafka, and Charlie Chaplin. Each iteration of the tradition specified a different possibility in the array. Thus, in Arendt's treatment, Heine transformed the *schlemihl*, the cheerfully hapless person to whom accidents were always happening, into a kind of laughing pariah who was capable of the common man's joie de vivre and who was not like the parvenu who was both trying and failing to join "society." Lazare politicized this character, Arendt said, by claiming that one could not remain aloof from the world and that there would be times and places when a collective political response would be the only possible one. Chaplin was the figure of the 1920s for Arendt (but not the 1930s), because he represented the outsider, the small man, under suspicion by the authorities and because he became a kind of popular hero. Hapless and also somehow cunning (but in an unwitting way), the Chaplin character routinely escaped the complications in which he became entangled. Finally, especially in *The Castle*, Kafka represented the pariah as the man of good will, the outsider—from neither the Castle nor the Village—who succeeded in showing the small people of the Village that they were living a false life in thrall to the whims and capricious demands of the important persons and their bureaucrats in the Castle.[78]

78. Arendt, "Jew as Pariah," 99–122.

The tradition of the conscious pariah (and others like it) constituted what rhetoricians had called a topos. As we have seen, a topos might be a place in which one could search for a particular kind of argument. By means of a metonymic substitution, a topos might also be the specific argument that either gave birth to a particular kind of argument by force of its own exemplarity or, alternatively, occluded that region altogether. In turn, the collection of lines qua topoi might constitute another space one could consult in order to find arguments, and Arendt's traditions were topoi in this last sense. Traditions constituted topoi, for they were matrices of exemplars that rendered the perception of new—and different—exemplars possible. These were zones of sensitivity to difference, distinction. From the multipolarity of Arendt's immediately postwar politics came an interest in the topos as a matrix of connected differences that would eventually underwrite her late interests in judgment and common sense.

If one examines the Arendt of the period in and around *The Human Condition* (a book that remains the most canonical statement of her political theoretical positions), one finds that her conceptualization of the polis as a space of appearance for political action was, in fact, intimately related to the notion of the topos. As I have been saying, she imagined topoi as public domains in which past actions would themselves be conditions of possibility for future action. The notion was that past actions would constitute the public domain as a rhetorically inflected space. I have made that argument in detail elsewhere with a fairly exhaustive survey of the usage of the term "polis" in Arendt's works.[79] In a companion piece, I have also explored the ways in which Arendt's famous account of judgment as a political capacity augmented this account of the polis as a space of appearance constituted by past performances.[80] The argument in the second article was that to Arendt's way of thinking the faculty of judgment was not simply a kind of practical wisdom permitting political agents to pick their way among the various traps and opportunities of political life; more basically, judgment was a capacity to distinguish phenomena that appeared closely related or identical. Judgment was *krinein* as well as—or more basically than—*phronēsis*. Expressed within the rhetorical idiom explored in this book, Arendtian judgment became a practice of *iudicium* (distinguishing in sensation) that was integral to the work of *ingenium* (connecting in inference). What I am suggesting here is that distinctions among the "we," multipolarities with various neighbors, and diversity within tradition were all lines of inquiry consonant with highly significant developments in Arendt's later work.

79. Marshall, "Polis and Its Analogues," 123–49.
80. Marshall, "Origin and Character of Hannah Arendt's Theory of Judgment," 367–93.

A NEW WEIMAR ORIGIN

There is no sense in which the books Arendt wrote before 1950 were "better" than those that came later. The classic texts—*The Origins of Totalitarianism, The Human Condition, On Revolution, Eichmann in Jerusalem, The Life of the Mind*—were all more complete, more learned, and above all more significant in their various historical moments than the little Augustine book and the, in some ways quite odd, biography of Rahel. Jaspers was right not to give the Augustine work the highest possible evaluation. And Arendt was right when she described the Rahel book as politically naive in the 1950s. In depicting how it had been impossible for Rahel to escape Jewishness, Arendt had run a version of the Zionist argument against assimilation, and she had ignored the sense in which Zionists and anti-Semites shared a presupposition. As for the political writings of the 1940s, they were overwhelmingly addressed to particular moments in time, and so their ability to speak to and inform historically distant audiences is necessarily limited. Thus, my argument in this chapter has certainly not been that we should simply shift our focus from Arendt's later works to the early ones. No one would heed such an argument. No one should.

My claim has instead been that the rediscovery of the rhetorical dimension of Heidegger's early thought makes it possible for us to reread and redescribe Arendt's early work in a way that gives it a new unity and a new edge. The Rahel book inverted the Augustine book's focus on paraphrasing a Christian anxiety about living in the flesh and transformed it into a paraphrase of a Jewish desire for assimilation. The political writings of the 1940s then took up the accounts of solidarity and distantiation together with possibility and contextualization that had been forged in the earlier texts. In this process of rereading and redescribing, we also gain an ability to project a new line of inquiry into the later works as a hypothesis concerning intellectual-historical development that can be fleshed out in the course of verification.

In the end, I am claiming that this new account of Arendt's assembled points of origin enables us to see the categories of her mature thought with new eyes. Two of the chief aspects of this revisionism would be new conceptual contexts for the core Arendtian ideas of action and judgment. Seen through the emphasis on modality in Heidegger and Arendt's early works, the category of action becomes a retooling of the concept of "actuality" (*energeia*) that cannot be fully understood without its conceptual twin, "possibility" (*dunamis*). Indeed, whereas the later Arendt appeared always to want to gloss politics as action (and action, in turn, as *energeia*), the line of inquiry given to us by the early Arendt suggests that politics may be understood alternatively as a *dunamis*, a faculty that has its being in a certain way of orienting oneself to possibility. The much closer descriptions of Rahel's various appearances lay out her distinct public personae, and so do her assorted attempts to specify her appearances beyond the strictures of identity politics as they obtained in the worlds through which she moved. The variety of her possibilities *was* the space in which any given actualization appeared.

In turn, these arguments about the space of appearance entailed corollaries in Arendt's work on judgment. One of the tasks of the faculty of judgment was precisely to discern the interest or distinctiveness of a particular performance in the midst of comparable performances. This also explains why the Kantian account of the relationship between judgment and *sensus communis* was so important to Arendt. The ability to compare one's own judgment to the possible judgments of others would be, once again, a capacity to locate actuality in the midst of a properly topical range of possibilities. When one can grasp the particular as a tension between the actual and the possible, it becomes clear that judgment as the faculty of thinking the particular is in fact a capacity to generate a space of possibilities around that particular. Hence my claim: a new early Arendt means a new Arendt, and a new Arendt means a new account of the Weimar origins of rhetorical inquiry.

5: WALTER BENJAMIN AND THE RHETORICAL CONSTRUAL OF INDECISION

A CONSTITUTIVE DENIAL

On December 9, 1930, Walter Benjamin wrote to Carl Schmitt from Berlin to say that a copy of his *Origin of German Tragic Drama* would arrive soon. The Heidelberg sociologist Albert Salomon had suggested gifting the book, and Benjamin predicted that Schmitt would recognize the debt owed to *Political Theology*. Important in Schmitt's *Political Theology*, Benjamin said, was the "the doctrine of sovereignty." When he added that Schmitt's later work *Dictatorship* had also been relevant, Benjamin may well have been referring to the second edition of that work (published in 1928), which included an appendix setting out an expansive reading of the power of the president to declare a state of emergency and suspend basic rights per Article 48 of the Weimar Constitution. According to Benjamin, the approach in his *Origin* was "art-philosophical" (*kunstphilosophisch*) where Schmitt's approach was "state-philosophical" (*staatsphilosophisch*), but they were both investigating the same phenomenon—namely, sovereignty.[1]

December 1930 was very late in the day for Benjamin to be writing to Schmitt in this way, and this historical context forces us to consider the ways in which a work ostensibly centered on seventeenth-century drama might have had a properly contemporary Weimar context. By late 1930, the political situation in Germany was becoming increasingly delicate. The second cabinet of Hermann Müller had fallen in March, and the republic had entered another period in which the president, Paul von Hindenburg, issued emergency decrees under Article 48. As the political situation in Weimar grew more acute, a raft of reviews of Benjamin's book on early modern German tragic drama (*Trauerspiel*) appeared. The volume was often reviewed as a pair with Benjamin's "aphorism book," *One-Way Street*, which had also appeared in

---

1. Benjamin, *Gesammelte Briefe*, 3:558–59. See also Benjamin, "Lebensläufe," in *Gesammelte Schriften*, 6:219.

1928 and explicitly addressed the contemporary moment. Although many reviews were complimentary, almost none inquired into the *Trauerspiel* book's potential relevance for Weimar. In sending the book to Schmitt, Benjamin was selecting a Weimar contemporary as interlocutor, opponent, or enemy. Citing his own diary from April 21, 1930, Benjamin cast the relationship thus: "Schmitt / agreement hatred suspicion."[2] The dialectic with Schmitt established the possibility of a Weimar frame for the *Trauerspiel* book.

No immediate response from Schmitt to Benjamin's letter has yet surfaced, but Schmitt attempted to use the connection to specify his own position at various points after the war. Schmitt's *Leviathan in the State Theory of Thomas Hobbes* forged no explicit link to Benjamin when it appeared in 1938. In 1973, however, he described the work as a covert and unrecognized response to the *Trauerspiel* book.[3] Only after the war, in 1956, did Schmitt respond to Benjamin openly with a work titled *Hamlet or Hecuba*. In that work he argued that on the Shakespearean stage the queen—Hamlet's mother, Gertrude—who married a man suspected of murdering her former husband could not be read as anything other than a reference to Mary Stuart (mother to James I). This was something like an argument that history contained or even dominated fiction. Putting this work in dialogue with Benjamin's treatment of early modern drama in the *Trauerspiel* book, we may infer that this wished to be a realpolitik response to Benjamin's aesthetic investments.

Somewhat uncertain on how to proceed, scholars have dealt with the apparent proximity between Benjamin and Schmitt in a variety of ways. In his 1955 edition of Benjamin's writings, Adorno omitted the three references to Schmitt in the *Trauerspiel* book. In their 1966 edition of Benjamin's correspondence, Adorno and Gershom Scholem then also excluded the December 1930 letter from Benjamin to Schmitt. A number of German articles did discuss the letter in the 1970s, but the matter only became a controversy in the mid-1980s.[4] At that point, Jacob Taubes declared the relationship "a land-mine that completely explodes our sense of the intellectual history of the Weimar period."[5] The implication was that one would have to construct a model for the ideological spectrum of Weimar politics in which Schmitt the decisionist authoritarian and Benjamin the Marxian anarchist were adjacent. A lively debate then emerged between Ellen Kennedy, Alfons Söllner, Ulrich K. Preuss, and Martin Jay.[6] More recently,

2. Benjamin, *Gesammelte Schriften*, 2:1372: "Schmitt / Einverständnis Haß Verdächtigung."
3. Schmitt to Viesel (April 4, 1973), in Viesel, *Jawohl, der Schmitt*, 14.
4. Rumpf, "Radikale Theologie"; Güde, "Der Schiffbrüchige"; and Turk, "Politische Theologie?"
5. Taubes, *Ad Carl Schmitt*, 27: "eine Mine, die unsere Vorstellungen von der Geistesgeschichte der Weimarer Periode schlechthin explodieren läßt."
6. Kennedy, "Carl Schmitt," 380–419; Söllner, "Jenseits von Carl Schmitt," 502–29; Preuss, "Anmerkungen," 400–18; Jay, "Les extrêmes," 542–58.

scholars have attempted to deflect the suggestion that extreme right and radical left were in some category-exploding dialogue by demonstrating that Benjamin's "debt" to Schmitt was more antagonistic than even the caustic tone of his diary implied.[7]

In the context of my attempt to invent a tradition by tracing the Weimar origins of rhetorical inquiry, the proximity between Benjamin and Schmitt constitutes a real opportunity to think rhetorical inquiry as an alternative to the Weimar origins of political theory sketched in the introduction of this book. The wager of that introduction was that we can grasp the value of this narrativization of rhetorical inquiry by distinguishing it from a tissue of received thoughts. Schmitt remains a key component in the standard received version of the Weimar origins of political theory, and Benjamin's "response" to him shows us how rhetorical inquiry is a very specific turning away from a dominant line of inquiry in political theory. As we saw, that line of inquiry understood systems of rules to be essentially weak—merely legal rather than political. Schmitt's conception of sovereignty was centered on an ability to suspend legal order combined with an ability to redescribe that suspension as having the interest of the legal order at heart. The sovereign existed behind legal systems that were only capable of structuring the polity in moments that did not constitute emergency or existential threat. This sovereign was a miraculous ex nihilo force that consumed its own actions in the moment of performance itself by insisting that no sovereign action undertaken in the state of emergency could be understood as a precedent.

In the introduction, we saw that there were ways to connect Schmitt's work to a repressed history of rhetoric in the German tradition, but my task in this chapter is to sketch a sequence of initiatives for rhetorical inquiry with material from the oeuvre of Walter Benjamin. Benjamin's *Trauerspiel* book described a genre of early modern drama exploring the space of intrigue, prevarication, and dictatorship in and around the baroque sovereign. The sovereign that Benjamin described via this aesthetic material was anything but a Schmittian decisionist. Benjamin's sovereign was overwhelmed by crisis. In part, his response to Schmitt emphasized a pessimistic depiction of sovereign *incapacity*. The point of counterposing these two thinkers here, however, is not simply to mount a critique of decisionist fantasy. As I cast it, Benjamin's role is not that of the critic who says that the maximalist sovereign is actually weak. It is tempting but oversimple to suppose that Benjamin's criticism amounted to the prediction that centralizing the power to declare a state of exception in the person of an individual sovereign would simply render that sovereign pathological and debilitated. The *indecision*

---

7. Weber, "Taking Exception," 18. Similarly, Bredekamp, "From Walter Benjamin to Carl Schmitt," 260.

of Hamlet, a son who might be sovereign, was, to be sure, a challenge to Schmitt's decisionism, but it is not the core of the point I wish to make.

The heart of the claim in this chapter is that the real genius in Benjamin's response to Schmitt lay in his reevaluation of the category of indecision. Indecision for Benjamin, I shall be arguing, was a mode of paying attention to the moments in which a multitude of actions seemed possible and might be taken to constitute not so much a dilemma as a surfeit of possibilities for action. On this account, the moment of indecision was potentially a moment of invention, and I shall be paying close attention to the ways in which Benjamin drew on the traditions of invention within rhetoric and, indeed, contributed to them. It is the contention of this chapter that a red thread runs through practically the entirety of Benjamin's oeuvre, marking his contribution to the invention of a tradition of rhetorical inquiry. Of course, Benjamin was such a brilliant, oracular, and polyvalent thinker that many such sequences may be inferred from his work. That a multiplicity of such construals is possible does not mean that the lineage of rhetorical inquiry traced here did not exist. Nor does it mean that I present this lineage as a minority report for a merely specialized audience of Benjaminian rhetoricians.

The hypothesis I present speaks to a great variety of Benjamin's preoccupations and weaves them together. Sovereign indecision in the *Trauerspiel* book, it turns out, was but one of many iterations of an interest sustained throughout Benjamin's oeuvre. We find the theme reprised in a rich variety of ways and through a rich array of terms: "standstill" (*Stillstand*), "paralysis" (*Starre*), "hesitating" (*Zögern*), "indecision" (*Unentschloßenheit*), "decision-incapacity" (*Entschlußunfähigkeit*), "a simultaneity of the necessity and impossibility of making a move" (*Zugzwang*), "tension" (*Spannung*), "vacillating" (*Schwanken*), "mirroring" (*Spiegelung*), "infinity" (*Unendlichkeit*), "duck/rabbit images" (*Vexierbilder*), "state of uncertainty" (*Schwebezustand*), "contrapposto" (*Kontrapost*), "debate" (*Debatte*), "dialectic" (*Dialektik*), "alarm-readiness" (*Alarmbereitschaft*), and "mental readiness deriving from equipoise" (*Geistesgegenwart*), for instance. My proposal is to constitute this sequence of interests as a trajectory from Benjamin's early work through the *Trauerspiel* book itself into the political works of the late 1920s and early 1930s and up into the classic late theoretical works until 1940. Reading this sequence of interests more or less chronologically facilitates the work of transposing Benjaminian conceits into new domains.

TRAUERSPIEL AS EARLY THEMATIC

The 1930 Schmitt context for Benjamin's *Trauerspiel* book was only one of many, and in this opening section I prepare the way for the construction of a lineage within Benjamin's work for the Weimar origin of rhetorical inquiry that I am identifying in this chapter. The 1930 context was late arriving, and we should not try to make it determine the text completely. The book was published in 1928, but it had been submitted and then withdrawn along with Benjamin's abortive habilitation application at Frankfurt in 1925. Moreover, even as the published text of 1928 indicated that it had been "composed" (*verfaßt*) in 1925, it gestured also to an earlier origin by indicating that it had first been "outlined" (*entworfen*) in 1916. Similarly, in a letter to a friend dated March 23, 1923, Benjamin indicated that he had left behind his copy of Schmitt's *Political Theology*, adding that he needed it for his *Trauerspielarbeit*.[8] Benjamin's work on *Trauerspiel* is datable in a variety of ways.

Benjamin himself understood an "origin" (*Ursprung*) not as the beginning but as the center of a phenomenon. Pursuing that intuition, I treat the *Trauerspiel* book as an origin standing in the middle of a longer series of developments before and after 1928. A quick précis of the work itself allows us to trace its history. Ostensibly, it was focused on a critical differentiation of the genre of the "mourning play" (*Trauerspiel*) from that of "tragedy" (*Tragödie*). Benjamin took the seventeenth-century works of Gryphius, Lohenstein, Haugwitz, Hallmann, and others, positioned them alongside the oeuvres of Shakespeare and Calderón, and vindicated the genre as an analysis of high baroque politics. Nietzsche's intuition that the protagonists of classical Greek tragedy were less articulate in speech than they were in action stood at the core of Benjamin's conception of the distinction between classical tragedy and the early modern "mourning play." The notion was that "[ancient] heroes speak more superficially than they act," for, "the myth does not find in the spoken word anything like an adequate manifestation of its nature."[9] The cultural afterlife of the paradigmatic acts contained in tragedy was rich precisely because of the need to give voice to these relatively mute deeds.

What Benjamin found interesting in the *Trauerspiel* genre was the inversion of the relationship between action and word. As he understood it (and in stark contrast to the mute eloquence of tragic heroism), *Trauerspiel* characters were creatures of the word more than the deed. A tension emerged here between speech and action, between deliberation and *inaction*. Take Hamlet as the central exemplar. Was there a need for Hamlet to avenge his father? If so, how? In the play, action takes second place to hypothesizing about potential action. For Benjamin, this amounted to a delaying of the moment in which an agent might sum itself up in a particular act. To his

8. Benjamin, "Walser," in *Gesammelte Schriften*, 2:327.

9. Cited in Benjamin, *Ursprung*, in *Gesammelte Schriften*, 1:287: "Helden sprechen gewissermaßen oberflächlicher als sie handeln; der Mythus findet in dem gesprochnen Wort durchaus nicht seine adequate Objectivation."

way of thinking, the desire for characters to sum themselves up in decisive but unarticulated actions expressed an aesthetic preference for symbol over allegory that ran through the dominant schools of German aesthetics. German aesthetic theory had taken up the relationship of particular and universal as one of its constitutive issues, and many had either assumed or argued that aesthetic perfection was to be understood as the moment of absolute decisiveness in which the conceptual value of, say, a character was indistinguishable from the *manifestation* of that character.

The ur-example of self-summation was the tragic character that achieved completion by dying in a certain way, but Benjamin rejected both the ontology and the aesthetics of culmination implicit in such a preference. He was more interested in nonidentities of type and instantiation, which he understood in terms of "allegory" (*Allegorie*). Where symbol encouraged a submersion of the reader into the text that mirrored the submersion of the character into its most characteristic moment, allegory held the reader at a kind of distance, for a thing never was its appearance. For Benjamin, most crucial was the space of indecisiveness opened up within such nonidentity. This was akin to a space that opened up in the concept of genre itself when Benjamin described it as bounded by a constellation of opposed extremes. Genre was nonidentity. It was a complex of proximate tensions that brought new possibilities into being by leaving certain spaces empty.

Benjamin did not wish to argue that disproportion between speech and action was simply an effect of the political structure of early modern Europe, but there was a real sense in which the object of his analysis existed in a post-Machiavellian moment—that is, a moment in which "fate" (*fortuna*) had made a clear mockery of "human endeavor" (*virtù*).[10] Just so, in one of the examples of the *Trauerspiel* genre to which Benjamin attended closely (namely, Gryphius's *Leo Arminius*), the play's core human endeavor, the action of "regicide" or "tyrannicide," was almost completely elided. Fated, as it were, to a life of unintended consequence and misconstrual, the play was almost entirely preoccupied with descriptions of dishonors perceived and avenged. It was a theatrical world that existed without—but perhaps with a perceived need for—Leviathan.

If we wish to understand what Benjamin was suggesting when he said that his work was an "art-philosophical" antistrophe to Schmitt's "state-philosophical" investigations, we should attend to the contrasts between his accounts of early modern sovereignty and Schmitt's. Schmitt had analyzed this world in *Dictatorship* with an excursus on Albrecht von Wallenstein,

---

10. The terminology of *Virtus* and *Fortuna*, *Kairos* and *Tyche* occurred elsewhere in Benjamin's oeuvre, but the four terms are used simultaneously in 1928. See Benjamin, "Portrait eines Barockpoeten," in *Gesammelte Schriften*, 3:86.

a Bohemian general during the Thirty Years War. In his treatment, this had been a digression in which the tense, uncontrollable, barely nameable relationship between sovereign dictatorship and delegated commissarial dictatorship was never settled, save in assassination.[11] Where Schmitt analyzed the tension between the sovereign and his military representative in terms of the contracting that took place between independent or quasi-independent powers, Benjamin saw the relationship through the lens of Friedrich Schiller's trilogy of plays—as a nest of emotions. The art-philosophical dimension of such work consisted in the by turns ekphrastic and enargeiac reading of body form and imagined body form in reference to motive. The indeterminacy of such postures accounted for a proliferation of words combined with an attenuation of actions. For each action, for each image of an action—a thousand words.

In Benjamin's 1928 retrojection, the *Trauerspiel* book had first been sketched in 1916, and, although we do indeed possess short drafts from 1916, the dating was nevertheless too precise, for in fact a host of even earlier concerns were being woven together in that book. Among the earliest extant records of Benjamin's thought, we have the notion that Hamlet had been a kind of marker for youth as such—a marker for being born into a world not of one's own making.[12] Like a genre, a school ought to be full of empty and realizable spaces: both dealt with "propagation" (*Fortpflanzung*).[13] A genuine genre would be forever finding variations within itself. For Benjamin, this potential infinity was analogous to religiosity itself. In this early period, he characterized religiosity as a kind of asymptotic consciousness of the unattainability of a rule or commandment: religiosity was an "endless striving" (*unendliche Arbeit*) driven by "skepticism" (*Skepsis*) and "a despair structured by doubt" (*Verzweiflung*).[14] Equally, in this early period, history was something like a dissatisfaction with habit, a never-ending tension between "the enlivened" (*die Begeisterten*) and "the laggards" (*die Trägen*) in which "we would not be able to name the law under which we stand."[15] After all, "the young stand in the center where the new manifests itself."[16] Moreover, in a kind of miracle of the infinitesimal (where further precision would always be possible), the new, understood in the case of poetry as a

11. Schmitt, *Die Diktatur*, 79–96.

12. Ardor-Berlin [pseud.], "Das Dornröschen," in Benjamin, *Gesammelte Schriften*, 2:9.

13. Eckhart, phil. [pseud.]. "Die Schulreform, eine Kulturbewegung," in Benjamin, *Gesammelte Schriften*, 2:13–14.

14. Benjamin, "Dialog über die Religiosität," in *Gesammelte Schriften*, 2:24.

15. Ardor, Freiburg [pseud.]. "Gedanken über Gerhart Hauptmanns Festspiel," in Benjamin, *Gesammelte Schriften*, 2:60: "wir ... werden das Gesetz, unter dem wir stehen, noch nicht nennen können."

16. Benjamin, "Dialog über die Religiösität," in *Gesammelte Schriften*, 2:72–74: "die Jugend steht im Zentrum, wo das Neue wird."

constant renewal of language, had been a process of naming experience in such a way that it might be rendered more "determinate" (*bestimmt*).[17]

This emphasis on spaces into which new generations might move without simply taking on the established codes of the cultural system they inherited articulated a more basic idea concerning tragedy that Benjamin was anticipating in this very early work. When he spoke of rendering something more determinate, Benjamin was not presuming that some ultimate state of determination was reachable or desirable. Indeed, it was at this point that he took up the basic presupposition of tragedy according to which "the definition of hubris is to give form unto oneself."[18] What tragedy denied to its protagonists (the power to sum themselves up) it illegitimately bestowed on itself. We can very easily infer a continuation of this definition into the later preference for allegory over symbol. Similarly, Benjamin had pointed out that, insofar as Germany's teachers thought they had an achieved cultural inheritance to pass on to the young, they too were guilty of a kind of *hubris*. Belief that a culture had been achieved would be a false faith in having epitomized oneself once and for all. The opposite of such a pose had been, indeed, "a veritable academic or sophistic culture of conversation."[19] *Sophistische Kultur*—the phrase denoted a desirable tension within tradition.

When one gets to 1916 (the year of the first sketch of the *Origin*), one finds the discursive frame of the *Trauerspiel* book already in motion, and the more explicit specifications of "tragedy" and the "mourning play" came into focus quickly. That is, tragedy committed the sin of acculturating audiences to the belief that reality would offer up a series of climaxes in which being and act were simultaneous. The messiah-cum-ego would bring time to an end, but history, as Benjamin understood it, was not tailored in this manner. It did not end. History was infinite. It was a never-ending series of tensions with its accumulated pasts.[20] Just so, the "possibility of arriving at an end" that was characteristic of tragedy glossed as a kind of exhaustion, and it manifested itself in the speech modes of the Greek tragedians. Whereas modern scholars such as Jacqueline de Romilly have argued for a connection between rhetoric and early Greek tragedy, Benjamin perceived something like a "paralysis" (*Starre*) in the words of the tragic heroes that makes us ask questions about the relationship between rhetoric and tragedy.[21] In contrast, *Trauerspiel* was distinguished by a constancy of worry about the

17. Benjamin, "Zwei Gedichte," in *Gesammelte Schriften*, 2:105.
18. Benjamin, 121: "sich selbst Gestalt geben, das heißt *hubris*."
19. Benjamin, "Leben der Studenten," in *Gesammelte Schriften*, 2:81: "eine wahrhaft akademische oder sophistische Kultur des Gesprächs."
20. Benjamin, "Tragödie und Trauerspiel," in *Gesammelte Schriften*, 2:133–37.
21. Romilly, *Les Grands Sophistes*, 39. Benjamin, "Bedeutung der Sprache," in *Gesammelte Schriften*, 2:140.

adequacy of verbal overlays on action. Every verbal description of an action was provisional, requiring further investigation, iteration, correction.

The infinite and infinitely inventive work of giving but not achieving form was the task of "art criticism" (*Kunstkritik*), according to Benjamin. Alienated by those Weimar critics who assumed the duty of judging a work of art either "good" or "bad," Benjamin argued instead—in his dissertation of 1920—that only something that continued a work of art constituted genuine "criticism" (*Kritik*). We are coming up against another moment in which there is a certain proximity between critical and topical theory. On the Romantic account being relayed by Benjamin, the critical task would also be the inventive and properly topical task of finding continuations. Here once again we have the irony that I observed above in reference to Adorno. Indeed, I would also hypothesize that Benjamin was the source of Adorno's interest in the *ars inveniendi*. When he said that genuine criticism would continue the work of art, Benjamin meant that a critic should be able to identify the fragments in a work that marked it as distinct from others in its vicinity in the same genre or constellation. He meant also that the genuine critic—having judiciously identified such fragments—would propose or perform ways in which the work could be remade or taken further in a direction implied by the fragment.

Benjamin's position on art criticism took up the Romantic dictum that the only true reader would be a writer (a rewriter), and, for that reason the position entailed a rejection of the Goethean notion that the genuine work of art was beyond critique.[22] Goethe had been arguing that completion was a quality of the genuine work of art *by definition*, but Benjamin was implying that this was merely Johann Wolfgang's Olympian pose.[23] Both "art" (*Kunst*) and "criticism" (*Kritik*) were endless tasks. Given the proximity of Benjamin's *The Concept of Art Criticism in German Romanticism* (1920) to Schmitt's *Political Romanticism* (1919), it is not too much to see in Benjamin's first book the beginnings of a dissent from Schmitt's critique of politics as an "eternal conversation" (*ewige Gespräch*). The infinite task of recalibrating the finite models legislated by the human mind to the sublime infinities of nature was not the same thing as the faith in dialectics of positioning and counterpositioning that Schmitt detested in Adam Müller. Nevertheless, the willingness only ever to advance a position as a hypothesis made the two comparable.

22. Benjamin, *Begriff der Kunstkritik*, in *Gesammelte Schriften*, 1:11–122: "Kritik ist also gleichsam ein Experiment am Kunstwerk" (1:65); "der wahre Leser muß der erweiterte Autor sein" (1:68); the opposite of "criticism" (*Kritik*) is "evaluation" (*Beurteilung*) (1:78); criticizability is a *sign* of something being a work of art (1:79); "Kritik ist die Darstellung des prosaischen Kerns in jedem Werk" (1:109).

23. Benjamin, "Goethes Wahlverwandtschaften," in *Gesammelte Schriften*, 1:146.

Dissenting from the Romantic view of totality (which was at ease with the notion that history would manifest itself *eventually*), Benjamin found himself joining with the sophists. As Friedrich Schlegel had framed it, the sophists were precisely those thinkers who denied that "any link in this sublime weave of the human spirit could equally be the whole."[24] Beyond the limit of symbol, allegory. Benjamin was supposing that sophistic antilogies were inexhaustible. Assertion would never cease to be answered with denial even as that denial would often come at an angle. Or, as Benjamin would put it, the denial would arrive "left-handed"— improvised and without preparation.[25] This was the problem with *Kompromiß* as Benjamin analyzed it, drawing on Erich Unger in his "Critique of Violence." As practiced by democratic parliaments, for instance, compromise was more often than not a mathematical business of splitting differences and horse-trading, arriving thereby at solutions that were in a sense maximally equidistant from all opinions and yet identical with none of them.[26] Benjamin emphasized instead that the ingenious intervention was the one that finessed standoffs and that exchanged the rigor mortis of established and calcified disputes for new proposals.

Read against the background of these articulations, the *Trauerspiel* book of 1928 begins to look much less like an achievement and much more like a process or installment, and the task of this chapter is to trace that process more fully through the course of Benjamin's life. Amid these early formulations of ideas that would be repeated and renewed in subsequent iterations of Benjamin's rhetorical inquiry, we must note one point in particular: the infinity of the endless task need not be understood within the logic of the sequence. That is, pursued variously in the field of art criticism, in the ethical determination of a rule, and in the reproduction of culture in the education of the young, the infinite task did not need to be understood in terms of a one-dimensional sequence akin to the production of whole numbers under the function, "the last number in the sequence + 1." Infinity was also the infinitesimal, and the infinitesimal might be understood as "interpolation," which we may define as a process generating a distance between two points. When we refract Benjamin's notion of the endless task of culture through Arendt's conceptualization of the topical and rhetorical construction of political space, we begin to see that the cornucopia of exemplars is itself a generative space of discovery. Infinity is the work of discovering and bringing into a state of explicitation an instance located

24. Benjamin, *Begriff der Kunstkritik*, in *Gesammelte Schriften*, 1:115: "jedes Glied in diesem höchsten Gebilde des menschlichen Geistes zugleich das Ganze sein [kann]."
25. Benjamin, *Einbahnstraße*, in *Gesammelte Schriften*, 4:89: "In der Improvisation liegt die Stärke. Alle entscheidenden Schläge werden mit der linken Hand geführt werden."
26. Benjamin, "Kritik der Gewalt," in *Gesammelte Schriften*, 2:179–203.

between two exemplars that are themselves grasped within the cultural matrix of a genre. Benjamin's concern to understand the idea of the genre of *Trauerspiel* in terms of a splaying of extremes was a concern precisely to discover *spaces* amid those extremes, spaces that could be explored for the purposes of cultural and political innovation.

TRAUERSPIEL AS TRANSPOSED RHETORIC

Rhetoric was the analytic of an indecision that for Benjamin was characteristic of dramatic representations of early modern sovereignty. Indeed, indecision was itself a kind of hyperrhetorization because it derived from hyperconsciousness of possibilities fracturing out from a point of crisis. Scholars have paid little attention to the rhetorical origins of Benjamin's analytical frame in the *Trauerspiel* book. Yet confirmation of the rhetorical nature of those origins was explicit. Benjamin cited the historian of literature Werner Richter's assertion that the success of early modern drama was driven by its inheritance of "rhetorical artistic means, which in the last analysis are always derived from antiquity."[27] In response to Richter, Benjamin agreed that the verbal pyrotechnics and extreme artifice of baroque theater were intensifications of rhetorical skill in "wordplay" (*Wortstile*), but he argued against Richter's supposition that stylistic complexity meant that these plays would have been effectively incomprehensible to the mass of ordinary theater goers. For Benjamin, extreme verbal acuity in dramatic representations of high politics was something like political education. The stylistic taxonomies of ancient rhetoric were not simply nomenclatures with which critics might reveal and categorize the workings of drama. Rhetoric made available "artistic means" (*Kunstmitteln*) that were themselves critical frames with which audiences might think about how politics operated. Time, crisis, confrontation, possibility, affect, anticipation, finesse, ordering—all of these were frames that a public might learn in the theater and then use in the analysis of political life.

It would be a mistake to think that Benjamin's immersion in the early modern reception of classical rhetoric was something comparable simply to learning the language in which the subjects of his analysis thought and wrote. As I argued in the methodological section of the introduction to this book, learning the language of others often involves learning to run their scripts in one's own voice. Strictly policing the boundary between assertion and paraphrase is difficult and, in the end, self-defeating. At times one's

27. Richter, *Liebeskampf*, 170–71, cited in Benjamin, *Ursprung*, in *Gesammelte Schriften*, 1:381: these "rhetorische Kunstmitteln . . . in letzter Linie immer auf die Antike zurückgehen." Rhetoric's antique dominance is attested to also at Benjamin, "Autor als Produzent," in *Gesammelte Schriften*, 2:687.

position relative to the boundary will be clear. But this is not always the case. Disquotation is a series of "points of equilibrium and undecidability" (*Schwebezustände*) in which reportage and assertion lose their radical distinctness. Benjamin both colonized and was colonized by the classical rhetorical idiom in which he immersed himself in the course of researching and writing.

We see Benjamin colonizing and being colonized by rhetoric in the "Epistemo-Critical Prologue" to the *Trauerspiel* book. There, Benjamin took up the ancient quarrel between philosophy and rhetoric. In his rendition, philosophy was a field of inquiry that defined itself in opposition to a rhetorical other. Where philosophical style embodied a desire for not only "universalism" and "polemic" but also a "chain of deduction" (*Kette der Deduktion*) and the "sustained quality of a treatise" (*Ausdauer der Abhandlung*), the rhetorical mode from which it was differentiating itself represented an "art of counter-posing in contradiction" (*Kunst des Absetzens im Gegensatz*), an emphasis on the "gesture of the fragment" (*Geste des Fragments*) as well as "the repetition of motifs" (*Wiederholung der Motive*) and a "cornucopia of teeming positivity" (*Fülle der gedrängten Positivität*).[28] Benjamin was appropriating the rhetorical critique of philosophy for his own purposes. "Contradiction" (*Gegensatz*) was the constitutive concept for his interest in genre as a constellation. "Gesture" (*Geste*) was to become one of the most sustained of his critical interests, and it played a key role in the analysis of *Trauerspiel* too. "Repetition" (*Wiederholung*) in the mode of iteration was precisely his interest in the generation of topoi through the continual refashioning of cultural objects. And "cornucopia" (*Fülle*) was something like his sense that variations on a theme—*copia* in the early modern idiom that Benjamin was parsing—constituted a distribution within which the new might emerge.

In Benjamin's appropriation, rhetoric's repertoire of analytical techniques was focused on the moment of indecision. Indecision was the moment in which human animals found themselves dithering between two or more objects of desire or aversion that could not be easily ranked in terms of their respective attractiveness or hatefulness. Sovereign indecision in the *Trauerspiel* book was emblematized by Dürer's famous engraving *Melencolia I*, and Benjamin's sources of inspiration for thinking about the extreme sullen, paralyzed, distended tension captured in that image were indeed Fritz Saxl and Erwin Panofsky.[29] Even as the body posture in Dürer's image might denote an exaggerated and showy contortion (a being stuck),

28. Benjamin, *Ursprung*, in *Gesammelte Schriften*, 1:212.
29. Benjamin, *Ursprung*, in *Gesammelte Schriften*, 1:327. See Panofsky and Saxl, *Dürers "Melencolia I."*

the mind of the baroque sovereign that Benjamin saw depicted in German *Trauerspiel* was a whir of conjecture—conceived, dismissed, returned. As Saxl and Panofsky had rendered it, melancholy was to be understood as an indetermination between genius and illness, for fecundity of imagination was the common cause of genius and illness alike.

Just so, and in a sense that is difficult to explain without an awareness of the vocabulary of baroque rhetoric, Benjamin's term for "mind"—here and elsewhere in his oeuvre—was *Ingenium*.[30] In classical Latin, the term had also denoted "innate quality, nature, temperament, constitution" (an influence or "flowing in" of the stars). In the early modern Latin of the baroque rhetoricians, the term denoted above all a capacity to perceive connections among things that were distant one from another. (And note that, although he never completed it, Benjamin had intended to write a piece on Balthasar Gracián, the author of an *Art of Ingenium* [1642].)[31] Because it perceived the *tertium comparationis* that generated figurative expression, *ingenium* was the basic poetic faculty. As Benjamin deployed it in the *Trauerspiel* work, however, the term also denoted what one might call a faculty of madness.[32] It was the source of conspiracy theory or the power of conjecture in a melancholic state that could not find rest and could not stop itself from producing ever-new explanations or possibilities. Decoding never ceased, and neither did the kaleidoscopic mutations of the affective states that accompanied such decoding.

In the political anthropology of sovereign indecision that Benjamin was articulating, the moment was always a fragment, and the moment of indecision could dilate itself into an enduring state of debilitation because the fragments to which a sovereign might be exposed were always different, never quite calculable. Just so, Benjamin emphasized that *Trauerspiel* dialogue was something like training in the perception of "fragments" (*Bruchstücke*). The character that one encountered on stage was never an adequate embodiment of the abstraction for which it stood. The character was allegory rather than symbol. Therefore, one always had to find one's way within a space where things were not identical with the signs they wore. The basic cognitive demand was enthymematic. As Benjamin said, "allegories are in the realm of thought what ruins are in the realm of things."[33] Allegory demanded supplement, continuation, and the involution of a supplement suturing itself to the outline of the fragment.

30. Benjamin, *Ursprung*, in *Gesammelte Schriften*, 1:229, 325. See also 1:566, 674, 680, 689; 2:258, 274, 328, 649; 3:58, 94, 254, 514; 4:17, 498, 601, 613; 5:54, 277; and 6:78–79 (where Benjamin goes so far as to speak of "Leib und ingenium" as if they constituted a dyad).

31. Benjamin, "Projekte," in *Gesammelte Schriften*, 6:157.

32. Benjamin, *Ursprung*, in *Gesammelte Schriften*, 1:325.

33. Benjamin, 1:354: "Allegorien sind im Reiche der Gedanken was Ruinen im Reich der Dinge."

In Benjamin's account of baroque power, the state of sovereign indecision was fundamentally inflationary. Because of a hyperconsciousness
that information was always only fragmentary, the sovereign was forced
into an endless practice of inferring, extrapolating, projecting. And for this
reason, ideas forced themselves on the sovereign as *Einfälle*—not just "conceptions" but also "attacks" or "incursions." Moreover, because such ideas
would often come in the form of visions of possible futures (vivid imagistic
portraits of betrayal, revenge, or preemption), Benjamin characterized
them as moments of "image-eruption" (*Bilderuption*). The mental life of
the sovereign was a state of constant agitation in which things were always
metaphors—which is to say indexes of something else. This was the "style"
(*Stil*) of "the sublime" (*das Erhabne*), as Benjamin put it. The speech practice, the "expression" (*Ausdruck*) of the sovereign under such circumstances
of stress was, thus, a form of "condensate" (*Niederschlag*) produced by inner
affective concoction.[34] Against this background of emotional turmoil, Benjamin's comparison of the dictator to the Stoic was something like a joke.

The time of sovereign crisis was a time of compaction, and "crisis" indicates here a situation requiring decision, denoting therefore indecision. The
rhetorical style appropriate to this temporal compaction was the laconic. In
particular, Benjamin focused his attention on the baroque form of speech
compressed into the maxim. The maxim was an "aphorism" (*Sentenz*). It
was an enthymeme, a conceit, an aperçu (above all, pithy). In the guise of a
returned tacitism, the *Sentenz* had been one of the central preoccupations of
the early modern rhetoricians. Benjamin compared the maxim's function in
Trauerspiel to the role performed by lighting in baroque painting: "the equivalent of lighting in Baroque painting here is the maxim; it flashes dazzlingly
amid the gloom of allegorical plaiting [*Verschlingung*]."[35] How ought one to
speak to the sovereign enveloped in the chaos of indecision? Understanding
such indecision as a complex of equally balanced and mutually opposed
hypersensitivities, one might—as Benjamin supposed (citing Herder)—
think of "high-political maxims" (*hochpolitschen Maximen*) as a form of
"asylum" (*Asyl*) "for those thoughts that one certainly would not wish to
name in the presence of the prince."[36] In the event that such a maxim came
across as too pointed, one could always neutralize such reported speech by
clarifying that of course this was just "what others might say" and "certainly
not what I would say to you in my own voice in this situation, now." The
maxim never said too much or was, at least, disavowable.

34. Benjamin, 1:349.
35. Benjamin, 1:373: "was in barocker Malerei der Lichteffekt, ist hier Sentenz: grell blitzt sie in
dem Dunkel allegorischer Verschlingung auf."
36. Benjamin, 1:348: "für manchen Gedanken, den man vor Fürsten klar nicht habe nennen
wollen."

Even as the maxim was a form of discursive prophylaxis, it was also deeply ensconced in theories and practices of invention. When he spoke of the motive qualities of the maxim, Benjamin was invoking conceptions of aphoristic collections as reserve armies of premises. If politics was the state of collective indecision, then the center of such a politics was the point at which different visions of the future existed in mutually distinct equipoise. Advising the sovereign, thus, would entail the extraordinarily delicate business of inserting new forces into a balanced complex of tensions. As Benjamin relayed it, the maxim was the mode of speaking in which such advice was couched. "Howsoever staccato the referred to matter halts in that moment," he explained, the *Sentenz* nevertheless had also to propose "motion" (*Bewegung*). This was "a technical exigency of pathos," Benjamin added.[37] The maxim was stimulus to action, and it was embedded in the imaginative narratology of emotion as a rhetorical proof.

When analyzing the portrait of sovereign indecision conjured by baroque *Trauerspiel*, Benjamin's covert and perhaps only partly conscious debt to rhetoric was so extensive and so close to complete that we may catalog the multiplicity of his appropriations under the five basic headings of classical rhetoric. "Invention" (*inventio*), "arrangement" (*dispositio*), "style" (*elocutio*), "memory" (*memoria*), and "delivery" (*pronuntiatio*) sort Benjamin's transpositions. His use of elements of *elocutio* has already been discussed with reference to the *ingenium* that generated figurative language, the sublime style, and the maxim. Benjamin's examination of *inventio* took a distinctive form. The laconism of the *Sentenz* functioned as a cue to *inventio*. It sparked the process of looking for an argument that would explain the maxim's cryptic prompt. As Benjamin put it, allegory—the *tension* between an idea and its instantiation—taught artists "discovery" (*erfinden*).[38] And because allegory was a kind of arranging of available cultural codes in such a way that those codes might themselves be brought into question (or rendered dubious in some way), Benjamin declared that within the baroque frame of reference "poetry must be understood as an *ars inveniendi*, an art of discovering."[39] Baroque composition was such ostentatious discovery that it taught *inventio* to its audiences.

In the context of *Trauerspiel*, rhetorical invention became a kind of continual and performative catachresis mapping out the disjunction of words and things and signaling to audiences that they needed to hypothesize. Benjamin favored a theater practice in which word and image, action and descriptions of action, stood in a tension with one another. For this reason,

37. Benjamin, 1:380: "so stationär auch die von ihr getroffene Handlung im Moment verharrt"; "eine technische Notwendigkeit des Pathos."
38. Benjamin, 1:348.
39. Benjamin, 1:355: "'Ars inveniendi' muß die Dichtung heißen."

the torrent of rhetorical devices deployed in *Trauerspiel* was also to be put on display by means of a disconnect between their apparent meaning and the slight inappropriateness of their deployment in a particular situation. Locating such disconnections was the shared task of dramaturge, actor, and audience. The result was a veritable gymnasium of perspicacity. The desideratum was a kind of stylistic overdetermination with language—a showiness, or gesture of showing—that called attention to the medium of communication itself.[40]

Ostension of a topos—Benjamin's term was *Ostentation*—relied on highly developed cultural memory. The sense of dislocation between a commonplace and the deployment of a commonplace might be generated only if a public could be relied on to recognize the commonplace for what it was—namely, a cliché or received content. For this reason, Benjamin went out of his way to emphasize the sense in which the baroque was distinguished by its immense consciousness of semiotic repertoire. As he put it, the emblem books, *ars heraldica*, and physiognomic studies of early modernity organized a massive cultural repository of conventions.[41] Especially in its *deliberately* derivative handbook tradition, rhetoric was a study of the variety of conventional solutions to conventional problems. Unlikely as it may seem, we have here in effect a continuation of Heidegger's interest in rhetoric's sensitivity to everydayness qua the repetition of a topos. We do not need to propose any specific debt that Benjamin owed to Heidegger. Such a debt is quite unlikely. I am hypothesizing instead that Benjamin offers a specification of Heidegger's interests that we may take up within a lineage of Weimar origins for rhetorical inquiry.

In the mourning plays analyzed by Benjamin, the repetition of baroque motifs took the form of stockness in the rendition of character, and we should understand this as a kind of early modern topics. Such derivativeness was something like working with a shared cultural alphabet or system of writing. As Benjamin explained, this was a practice of writing with topoi, "thing-images," instead of letters.[42] Instead of increasing an audience's acquiescence in similarity, such topical practices accentuated powers of distinction: the very proximity of characters to clichés generated a heightened attention to small differences. These differences were breaches between what one was actually seeing and what one had been told one would be seeing. Nothing other than topical repertoire made such sensitivity possible, and this repertoire was a "pool" (*Fundus*) that was closely related to the "cornucopia" (*Fülle*) of which Benjamin had spoken in the "Epistemo-Critical Prologue."[43]

40. Benjamin, 1:355, 361.
41. Benjamin, 1:339.
42. Benjamin, 1:345: "statt mit Buchstaben mit Dingbildern (rebus) zu schreiben."
43. Benjamin, 1:404.

In Benjamin's appropriation, the first and last parts of classical rhetoric took on a new similarity. That is, there were connections between the *inventing* of arguments and the *delivery* of a speech with all the appropriate gestures, body postures, and performative dimensions. As we have seen, the dominant source of *inventio* was simply consternation or puzzlement stemming from this sequence of questions: Why does that character *say* this thing when in fact it is *doing* something else? What sense could that have?" Relatedly, the overwhelmingly dominant form of "delivery" (*Pronuntiatio*) was "pointing" (*deixis*). Expressed in the terms that Benjamin took up, the "swing and bombast" (*Schwulst*) of baroque composition was an "Asiatic style" (*asiatische Wörter*) constituting a "gesture" (*Geste*) that was self-interpellating: "Look here (at me)!"[44] On the account that Benjamin was giving, the function of *Trauerspiel* was not to mirror reality or to permit an audience to slip unseen into an identification with the action on stage. Like the deictic figure in baroque painting (who was embedded in pictorial space but looked out through the frame at the spectator in a theatrical fashion), the self-awareness of staged performance hailed audiences and involved them. Such self-awareness reminded audiences they were at a performance and thereby intensified the work of the stage as semiotic training ground.

Benjamin emphasized the deep investment of early modern culture in the semiotic dimension of the natural world. The most conspicuous example was astrology. Natural events were signs, signs that were to be decoded. Even in the midst of this semiotic activity, however, what nature lacked—according to Benjamin's paraphrase—was a power of "delivery" (*Pronunciation*). That is, nature lacked a power of gesturing at a particular individual in a particular moment in order to indicate that this was a message tailored to the who, when, and where of a given situation. The Latinity of Benjamin's usage of the term was conspicuous enough to count as an invocation of classical rhetorical idiom. In this incarnation, the word *Pronunciation* was itself deixis. It was a selecting by pointing and a speaking not of but to. Such a deictic capacity, Benjamin relayed, was so distinctive that it "must have come from somewhere else and been gifted."[45] We may recall that—as manifestation or pointing out—deixis had a close and, indeed, etymological relationship to one of the three principal oratorical genres: epideictic. This was praise and blame as distinct from deliberative or forensic speech. Expressed more primordially (as in the Heidegger chapter above), *epideixis* was displaying. In Benjamin's presentation, *epideixis* had a more concrete and finely observed theatrical moment. It was a "rhetorical apostrophe" (*rhetorische Apostrophe*). It was the "Look how . . ." (*Schau*

44. Benjamin, 1:384.
45. Benjamin, 1:360, citing Franz von Baader: "anderswoher gekommen und gegeben sein müßte."

wie...) verbal description that a character might lay over scenes playing out silently elsewhere on stage.[46]

If Renaissance art theorists had understood pictorial composition through the lens of rhetorical "arrangement" (*dispositio*), then Benjamin was arguing for the transferability of that rhetorical sensibility to drama as well. The most famous example of what Benjamin called *rhetorische Apostrophe* probably remains Iago's counseling of Othello on how to interpret the interaction—visible but not audible—of Cassio and Desdemona. Iago was "the schemer" (*Intrigant*). He therefore stood under the sign of one of the stock *Trauerspiel* characters. The schemer was one such character; the sovereign, the martyr, the courtier, and the fool were others. In what did the distinctive doomed-to-fail talent of the schemer really consist, though? In another creative reallocation, Benjamin effectively transposed the category of *dispositio* into the field of machination. Classically, *dispositio* was the process of arranging the order of a speech. It identified ways of beginning, continuing, transitioning, and ending. Analogously, as Benjamin analyzed it in *Trauerspiel*, machination—the schemer's forte—was simply a knowledge of the order in which human affairs would unfold. The schemer possessed what Benjamin called a properly "choreographic" (*choreographisch*) capacity. This was a capacity to organize persons, actions, and exchanges ahead of time. It was a capacity to direct.[47] The *Intrigant* used people as the painter might use colors, setting up not simply *tableaux* but *tableaux vivants*.

As Benjamin presented it, the schemer's talent was a rhetorical talent: it was a capacity to identify and to work on those moments that could be redescribed most readily and with greatest consequence. What the schemer understood were the ways in which human actions, right down to their embodied silhouettes, might be used for purposes other than those for which they were undertaken. This was something like a "visual paradiastolic talent," which we may describe as an eye for identifying *Vexierbilder* (duck/rabbit visual homonyms). In turn, this was an act of visual *iudicium* that might be sharpened by a rhetorical practice of arguing "on both sides of the case" (*in utramque partem*). Calderón's schemers were the most accomplished in this regard, Benjamin noted. Exercising as it were a highly trained sophistical capacity to perceive the world in terms of its potential for being turned to different purposes, these were characters who treated dramatic action like a game. They were able to handle dramatic action like a ball they could turn about in their hands, considering it now from this angle, now from that.[48] The schemer was a would-be theater director,

---

46. Benjamin, 1:369.
47. Benjamin, 1:274.
48. Benjamin, 1:263.

ultimately a failed puppet master, skilled in but ultimately overcome by the task of sequencing.

   The sources of Benjamin's sensitivity to baroque iterations of the classical rhetorical inheritance are less clear than they might be. Some of Benedetto Croce's work on aesthetics was conspicuous in the epistemo-critical prologue, but the Crocean position had been notoriously antirhetorical. Similarly, one of Benjamin's other authorities, Herbert Cysarz (whose *German Baroque Poetry* had appeared in 1924), defined the baroque phenomenon as something more like an epiphenomenon, an effect that had lost contact with its causes and was not itself a cause. What was the baroque, according to Cysarz? "Nothing other than a systematic imitation of ancient speech-arts," viz, rhetoric, "that are not orientated to kindred forms of life."[49] Similarly, in Paul Hankamer's *Language* (1927), rhetoric was a kind of Renaissance fetish for Roman prosody—grammatical, therefore, more than anything else. Hankamer's work had focused on the concept and interpretation of language as such in the sixteenth and seventeenth centuries. Benjamin had reviewed it for the *Frankfurter Zeitung,* citing it also in the 1928 version of the *Trauerspiel* text. On the account given by Hankamer, the humanist champions of ancient rhetoric could be great writers, but they could never be poets because they had cut themselves off from the living development of language with their veneration of the old authorities. Cicero was the dead hand hanging over them all.[50]

   In the sources Benjamin cited, perhaps only Friedrich Gundolf's *Andreas Gryphius* (1927) corroborated his notion that rhetoric was a constitutive feature of both the worlds that *Trauerspiel* represented and the world out of which it came.[51] Benjamin was not simply running a received script, however, and this makes his appropriation of rhetoric all the more striking. Benjamin used this rhetorical vocabulary to focus attention on the central problem of baroque politics as revealed in its plays—namely, sovereign indecision. Again, Benjamin was not content to use rhetoric as a diagnostic power for revealing the pathological state of the sovereign individual, who proved physiologically incapable of handling the cognitive, affective, and choreographic pressures angling within the monarchical or pseudomonarchical distribution of power. In fact, depicting such failed attempts to focus power at a single point was a means to the end of exploring situations of paralysis in the midst of crisis. That moment of "equipoise, stasis, or

---

49. Cysarz, *Deutsche Barockdichtung,* 40: "Vorerst nichts anderes als ein systematisches Nachahmen antiker Wortkunst [namely, rhetoric] das nicht von kongenialer Lebensform gesteuert wird."
50. Hankamer, *Die Sprache,* 5–10.
51. Compare Friedrich Gundolf, *Gryphius,* 23.

immobility" (*Gleichgewicht*) in the eye of the storm of power was to prove an enduring interest in Benjamin's ongoing research. And in time this moment would lose its pathological connotations and begin to approximate the process of politicization itself. Interest in this moment would structure Benjamin's inquiries into the politics of Russian art in the post-1917 world. Eventually, it would drive his investigation of the sensorial possibilities introduced by new media, film most especially. I turn to these dual inflections of Benjamin's baroque rhetorical investments in the next two sections.

BENJAMINIAN SOPHISTIC IN LATE WEIMAR

On July 4, 1930, Benjamin published a piece titled "Russian Debate in German."[52] Only a couple of pages long, the piece reported on a talk given by the writer and literary critic Osip M. Brik in Berlin at the Gesellschaft der Freunde des neuen Rußland (Society of Friends to the New Russia).[53] Brik had been the keynote speaker, and debate had ensued. As Benjamin relayed the scene, Brik attacked absent enemies such as Isaak Babel, the Bolshevik playwright and author of *Red Cavalry*. Brik's purpose? To assert "that art may put itself in the service of propaganda without reservation."[54] The German publisher and writer Wieland Herzfelde responded to Brik and argued for the value of the "the objective novel" as distinct from the "tactically understood propaganda-narration" (*taktisch visierte Propaganda-Erzählung*).[55] To this, Brik responded by proposing that the alternative to the objective novel was not "a primitive suggestion- and buzzword-literature" (*eine primitive Suggestiv- und Schlagwörterliteratur*) but rather "an authoritarian literature" (*ein autoritäres Schrifttum*).[56] Finally, the Hungarian writer Béla Illés spoke in a way that Benjamin described as "the orator" throwing "the lasso of its argument to its mark": "is perhaps . . . the objective reality of the Soviet state something that one must hide, something that in and of itself could be damaging to propaganda?" Illés continued: "is the objective representation of our life not the very best mode of propaganda?"[57] Here, the basic components of Benjamin's brisk mis-en-scène.

52. Benjamin, "Russische Debatte," in *Gesammelte Schriften*, 4:591–95.

53. See Brik, "Selected Criticism, 1915–1929," 74–110.

54. Benjamin, "Russische Debatte," in *Gesammelte Schriften*, 4:592: "daß Kunst sich restlos in den Dienst der Propaganda stelle."

55. Benjamin, 4:593.

56. Benjamin, 4:593.

57. Benjamin, 4:594: "ist vielleicht—hier wirft der Redner das Lasso seiner Argumentation zum entscheidenden Fang aus—die objektive Wirklichkeit des Sowjetstaates etwas, was man verbergen muß, was der Propaganda schädlich sein könnte? Ist nicht die objektive Schilderung unseres Lebens das allerbeste Propagandamittel?"

We find in this inconspicuous piece of journalism an emblematic displacement of Benjamin's rhetorical *Trauerspiel* interests into European debates about art and politics as they were intertwined around 1930. Sovereign incapacitation amid distending moments of indecision had been at the center of the *Trauerspiel* book. At the center of this piece of reportage, we find precisely the same figure of indecision. Benjamin was extremely careful to represent the debate just recounted as a kind of set-piece antilogy. Antilogy was the rhetorical exercise, or historiographic depiction, of speaking on both sides of a motion. On the one hand, there was the opinion that art was an important part of a politically revolutionary process. Those who wanted to further the cause of a revolution ought to think of art as a means to that end. On the other hand, there was the opinion that a genuinely just revolution would never be capable of finding an enemy in the transparent representation of its own activities.

A persuasive case could be made on both sides of the issue, and Benjamin was not interested in responding to the antilogy with something like a public adjudication. Instead, he focused on options for representing the inconclusiveness of such debates. He was pointing to one of the necessary aspects of politics, revolutionary or not, namely, the centrality of issues on which persuasive arguments could be found on both sides. With the democratization of political action (or at least with the aim of such democratization having been raised), sovereign indecision had been displaced from the prince to the people. No longer did the art that represented (and analyzed) politics center and fixate on the private psychomachy of the sovereign individual. Into that absent center stepped the public debate. Debate itself, indecision in motion as one might describe it, was the object of Benjamin's interest.

Whereas the dissent from Schmitt's decisionism had been relatively explicit in the *Trauerspiel* book, Benjamin's rejection of Schmitt in the piece of Russian debate was more implicit. He contended that interest in debate itself constituted a rejection of the contempt for discussion that was so conspicuous in the work of one of Schmitt's heros, the conservative nineteenth-century Spanish author Juan Donoso Cortés. Specifically, Benjamin seems to have adapted his paraphrase of Donoso Cortés's account of the bourgeoisie as "the endlessly discussing class" (*die ewig diskutierende Klasse*) from Schmitt's discussion of the point in *Politische Theologie*.[58] To Schmitt's citation of Donoso Cortés's phrase *clasa discutidora*, Benjamin appended the adverb "eternally, endlessly" (*ewig*), a term that echoed throughout Schmitt's 1922 work but that derived more originally from his 1919 work on *Political Romanticism*, as we have seen. On Schmitt's account,

58. Benjamin, "Russische Debatte," in *Gesammelte Schriften*, 4:591. Schmitt, *Politische Theologie*, 54.

Romanticism in the political sphere was a kind of risible posttheological faith in the impossibility of making errors at the end of prolonged discussion. As long as one kept the question open for long enough and allotted time to the airing of all possible opinions on an issue, the response, understood as a kind of averaging of the sum total of opinions voiced on the topic, could not be wrong. *Ewig* was Schmitt's retort to this simultaneously democratic and conservative (Burkean) vision. Holding discussion of a motion open in perpetuity, refusing ever to call it to a vote, was simply a vision of democratic self-incapacitation: democratic sovereign indecision.

"Eloquence" (*Beredsamkeit*) and its analogues were at stake in the historical relationship between aesthetics and politics that Benjamin was specifying. As Benjamin explained it, Donoso Cortés's definition of the bourgeoisie expressed a "disparaging opinion of discussion" (*abschätzige Meinung vom Diskutieren*) that in point of fact "had become one of the characteristic features of the postwar period."[59] This was part of a broader process that Benjamin described as "the corruption of eloquence." It is very difficult to read this phrase—the German was *Verfall der Beredsamkeit*—without hearing echoes of one of the chief objects of Schmitt's scorn in *Political Romanticism*. We have encountered Adam Müller's *Twelve Lectures* several times above. Here, we should note that Müller spoke on *Eloquence and Its Corruption in Germany* (the key German phrase here is *Beredsamkeit und deren Verfall*). Originally delivered in Vienna in 1812, the lectures had bemoaned the absence of a genuine public in the German-speaking lands of the Napoleonic era.

As we saw in chapter 1, Arthur Salz had published a new edition of Müller's *Twelve Lectures* in 1920, and we may legitimately hypothesize that Benjamin thought the publication ineffectual. We know that Benjamin was familiar with the work: he included Müller's lectures on the list of books he had read (although he did not specify which edition).[60] Salz had republished the work as a direct response to Schmitt. For Salz, Müller claimed "eloquence" (*Beredsamkeit*) on behalf of the *Nation* as "one of the highest expressions of the collected power and culture of the people" (*ein höchster Ausdruck der gesammelten Kraft und Kultur des Volkes*).[61] In Benjamin's gloss of this intellectual-historical topos, the corruption of eloquence contributed to a postwar distaste for discussion. He also pointed to a nascent "equality of and indifference toward" (*Gleichgültigkeit*) all private opinions. This amounted to a decline in political tolerance in his narrativization, and it was aligned with a resurgent "affinity" (*Sinn*) for authority.[62]

In Benjamin's reaction to this putative and lamented "corruption of

59. Benjamin, "Russische Debatte," in *Gesammelte Schriften*, 4:591.
60. Benjamin, "Verzeichnis," in *Gesammelte Schriften*, 7:448.
61. Salz, "Vorwort" and "Anhang," in Müller, *Zwölf Reden*, vii, x, 273–74.
62. Benjamin, "Russische Debatte," in *Gesammelte Schriften*, 4:591.

eloquence," we encounter a fundamental twist in his relationship to rhetoric. For him, the kind of corruption of eloquence hypothesized by Müller was in fact a process to be encouraged and celebrated rather than lamented. Müller's eloquence aimed at "persuading" (*überzeugen*) or "coming to an agreement with one another" (*miteinander sich zu verständigen*). Interpolating, one might say that for Benjamin such conceptions were mistaken because they assumed the point of rhetoric was simply persuasion or mutual reconciliation. To assume this was to assume there was no real difference between rhetoric and oratory, as if the only possible attitude toward politics—that is, difference of opinion in the shadow of a possible decision—was "how can we escape this state of nonidentity?" In this account, persuasion was not so much the moving of others from one opinion to another as it was the process by which individuals might coalesce to the point of indistinction.

Crucially, however, we should not read Benjamin's rejection of "persuasion" (*Überzeugung*) as a simple rejection of rhetoric in all its forms. In fact, this rejection announced Benjamin's distinctive reception and reinvention of the rhetorical tradition that I have been tracing and reconfiguring in this chapter. In encouraging an obsolescence of eloquence, Benjamin was seeking a rebirth or "a volte-face in the nature of discussion" (*ein Umschwung im Wesen der Diskussion*).[63] He offered the public and collective indecision of the Brik-Herzfelde-Illés debate as an example of the transformation he had in mind. Benjamin wanted questions such as "what is the relationship between art and politics?" And he wanted these questions more than he wanted answers because he valued attention to such moments of indecision together with a greater perspicacity in perceiving, characterizing, and addressing oneself to them. For this reason, the genuinely enlightening aspect of the evening at the "Club of Friends to the New Russia" was, for Benjamin, simply a recognition that "the Russian Revolution has to deal with one basic circumstance, a circumstance that distinguishes it as an exception within Europe—that, namely, what is thought has consequences."[64] Ideas had to be cross-examined, the simple mantra ran, because the court proceeding was and would remain "a scene in which words were falling on the scales" (*ein Vorgang, in welchem Worte in die Waagschale fallen*). And, as so often, Benjamin sought to capture his thought in the ekphrasis of a verbalized image (which we may now understand as a displaced early modern emblematic): the genuine motif of the evening was simply the sight of the scales of Justice being held by the figure of Revolution.[65]

Attention to debates on Russian aesthetic politics was not some statistical

---

63. Benjamin, 4:591.
64. Benjamin, 4:595: "die Russische Revolution hat mit einem Umstand zu rechnen, der für Europa zu den Ausnahmen zählt: daß nämlich, was gedacht wird, Folgen hat."
65. Benjamin, 4:595.

outlier in the vast array of Benjamin's pursuits. This interest was intimately connected to the dominant research priorities that drove his work forward in the period of Weimar's extended crisis in the years before 1933. One finds a sophistic concern for indecisive argumentative counterposing in a raft of different initiatives dating from the late Weimar period. In his "Disputation at Meyerhold's" from 1927, for example, Benjamin reported on another debate focusing on political aesthetics. The Russian theater director Vsevolod Meyerhold had convened a debate in order to discuss his staging of Gogol's *The Government Inspector*. Benjamin was particularly struck by the *Rowdy-Intelligenzler* style of Vladimir Mayakovsky's oratory—polemical, abrupt, enthymematic. Yet the evening was a dialectical failure, he concluded. Meyerhold spoke last, "toward midnight," and all trace of dialectical tension was suddenly dissipated: the host was on show.[66]

The meticulous observation of debate performance was one of the central thematics in Benjamin's work in the late Weimar period, and we see this again and again in his various "sociological" treatments of the writer, the intellectual, and the critic. What distinguished not just the group of writers Benjamin encountered at Meyerhold's but the Russian writer as such, he thought, was the saturation of their work in "publicness" (*Öffentlichkeit*). Benjamin was particularly interested in the work of Mayakovsky and Meyerhold, Sergei Tretiakov and Mikhail Bulgakov. The publicness of the Russian writer, he contended, was a politicization in which the recognition of "color" (*Farbe*)—or what we might term "political tincture"—was "a pivotal issue" (*Lebensfrage*). Censure was the obverse of all utterance.[67] Similarly, it was the *Schwebezustand* of French intellectuals that struck Benjamin in 1927 in the French equivalent of the Society of Friends to the New Russia. This *Schwebezustand* was not simply the "poise" or even "independence" of these intellectuals but most properly their "balanced uncertainty."[68] On this account, *Schwebezustand* was the achieving of a state of public indecision, debate. Weighing assertions that were somehow "in the balance" was the core concern.

To be sure, as Benjamin imagined it, the role of the intellectual did not consist in achieving some kind of position "above the fray." The point was to facilitate the fray. Thus, in his 1930 article on "What a Russian Theater Hit Looks Like," Benjamin commented on the fact that the Russians had produced no great arbiters of public taste (no superstar *Feuilletonkritiker*). Benjamin's explanation was that in Russia the role of the critic was simply to organize discussion of the piece in the theater itself immediately after

66. Benjamin, "Disputation bei Meyerhold," in *Gesammelte Schriften*, 4:481–83.
67. Benjamin, "Russischen Schriftsteller," in *Gesammelte Schriften*, 2:743–47.
68. Benjamin, "Verein," in *Gesammelte Schriften*, 4:486.

the performance, a discussion to which the writer might also be party.[69] And this was not just a culture of orality, for it had literary components too. The constructivist Sergei Tretiakov was of particular interest to Benjamin because of his theory and practice of the "operative writer" (*operierende Schriftsteller*). The role of an operative writer was to facilitate the writing of others rather than focus on putting pen to paper oneself. The task was to organize communities of proletarian writers.[70]

I am arguing that Benjamin's statements on the sociology of authorship gave voice to concepts that had captivated him earlier in the *Trauerspiel* work, where the theater was the organ of political education, and there is evidence of this continuity of interests in Benjamin's observations about twentieth-century theater too. For him, theater was a space dedicated to the analysis of human gestures. Analysis of gesture, as distinct from its mere representation, became possible when a distance opened up between word and image. A kind of dissonance had to emerge between the lines given to an actor by a script on the one hand and the staging of those lines that was acting itself on the other. There had to be either a hesitation or an excessive haste, an emphasis that was either too great or too slight. Actors, that is, had to appear to be bound to the lines they uttered as if by a somewhat elastic rope. Theater became analytical when it manifested this counterbalancing between script and performance. The state of indecision was thus transposed onto the stage as a wavering equilibrium.

Such concern for precise disequilibrium informed the *Trauerspiel* work itself (with its theory of allegory), but the notion found a more direct expression in Benjamin's responses to dramatic theories and practices emerging in the 1920s. As Benjamin put it while reviewing the French dramaturge Gaston Baty's *The Mask and the Censer* (1927), a perfect synchronization between word and image, script and performance, was simply a form of tiresome repetition, as if one were watching two identical versions of a play simultaneously.[71] In Benjamin's account of the Italian director Anton Giulio Bragaglia, the emphasis was on a state of continual "alarm readiness" (*Alarmbereitschaft*) among actors who were prepared to "resist the invasion of the playwright."[72] The point was to represent every instruction as the aperture of a moment of indecision: if the writer orders me to "say this," I must represent to the audience my consideration of how to respond to this order by deflating it into a mere request.

Benjamin's most perceptive consideration of theater came in the

69. Benjamin, "Russischer Theatererfolg," in *Gesammelte Schriften*, 4:561–63.
70. Benjamin, "Autor als Produzent," in *Gesammelte Schriften*, 2:686–87.
71. Benjamin, review of Baty, *Masque*, in *Gesammelte Schriften*, 3:67.
72. Benjamin, "Bragaglia," in *Gesammelte Schriften*, 4:522: "um der Invasion der Stückeschreiber sich zu erwehren."

"Manifesto for a Proletarian Children's Theater" that he cowrote with Asja
Lacis as a theorization of her theater practices. Written during late 1928
and early 1929, the "Manifesto" set out an account of how theater might
be utilized as an educational instrument for the new generation that was
emerging in the Soviet Union. Benjamin and Lacis were thinking of children aged between four and fourteen; this was the generation that would
determine the success or failure of the revolution. In the years following
1917, Lacis had worked in the city of Orel (located between Moscow and
the Ukraine), where she had established a school-cum-theater troop for
children orphaned by the revolution. In her 1971 autobiography, Lacis
recalled establishing the theater company in the house made famous by
Turgenev's *A Nest of Gentlefolk*, expecting perhaps fifty children and dealing
with hundreds.[73]

In the "Manifesto," the question of "persuasion" (*Überzeugung*) and
its place in modern politics resurfaced. We see Benjamin fleshing out his
answer to the question of what might take the place of an older rhetorical
tradition of eloquence attached to the elimination of differences in belief
by means of persuasion. In the account given by Benjamin and Lacis, all
initially and provisionally successful proletarian movements would face a
dilemma posed by the advent of a new generation: "oratory"—the German
term was *Phrasen*, and the metaphor relied on the notion of overcrafted
and overintended sentences—"has absolutely no power over children."[74]
One might be able to get children to recite mantras, and those language
fragments might persist as habits for a while, but such indoctrination would
fail in the long run. The task was to replace the visions of parliamentary
democracy against which such proletarian movements would define themselves with a kind of theater practice in which all statements opened up
spaces in which one could respond in an indeterminate variety of ways.

In place of handbooks and the like, the rhetorical education Benjamin
envisaged for contemporary politics focused on developing a capacity for
improvisation that could be honed on the stage. In the vision that Benjamin
and Lacis worked up together, children orphaned by the Russian Revolution
were to be reared within theater itself, with workshops for making "stage
props, painting, recitation, music, dance, and improvisation."[75] Thus,
before proletarian children were exposed to "eloquence" (*Beredsamkeit*),
alongside "engineering" (*Technik*) and "class history" (*Klassengeschichte*),
they were to receive a training in *Improvisation*. Such improvisation entailed
practicing a capacity to read all utterances as gestures. Each gesture was

73. Lacis, *Revolutionär im Beruf*.
74. Benjamin and Lacis, "Programm," in *Gesammelte Schriften*, 2:763: "über Kinder . . . haben
Phrasen gar keine Gewalt."
75. Benjamin and Lacis, 2:767.

an implicit "order" (*Befehl*) or "cue" (*Signal*).[76] Equal and opposite to such a hermeneutic capacity was a performative capacity to set oneself against this request in a state of angled noncompliance. Such noncompliance did not necessarily constitute explicit, open, or merely negative dissent. Improvised, such noncompliance implied a creative capacity to identify ways of responding to the request as a request but in new, unanticipated, nonhabitual ways. The result of such an education, Benjamin believed, would be an enhanced power of "observation" (*Beobachtung*) together with an enhanced capacity to turn such perspicacity into a response. "Presence of mind" (*Geistesgegenwart*) would be the chief quality to emerge from such a school. For Benjamin, only this kind of acuity could continue to revise the rules thrown up by revolution in such a way that revolution might, over time, survive.

In this late Weimar moment, Benjamin was thinking of theater through the lens of his engagements with the work and person of Bertolt Brecht. The relation between Benjamin's rhetorical reading of baroque theater and Brecht's "alienation effects" (*Verfremdungseffekte*) was close. In both instances, one was to understand the theater as a space of political education and experimentation, for it was a moment in which the codes of a community might be displayed and interrogated. The task of epic theater was to halt the stream of human actions in order to focus attention on the tensions of particular motions, to isolate the "framed enclosedness of each element of an action" (*rahmenhafte Geschlossenheit jedes Elements einer Haltung*).[77] The task was to turn such an action into a "gesture" (*Geste*) that could be quoted. Quoting a gesture in this way put it on display and analyzed it as the expression of a particular physiological process or exchange. In my reading, this amounts to an argument that Benjamin was placing Brecht in a topical tradition practiced and theorized in baroque art.

Traditionally, one has supposed that in Benjamin's 1931 depiction of Brechtian epic theater as "dialectics at a standstill" (*Dialektik im Stillstand*), the "dialectic" at issue was essentially Marxist. Of course, Benjamin was Marxian, and such a response would not be entirely wrong. Nevertheless, there were important ways in which this interest in Marxist dialectic went back through Hegel and through Adam Müller's *Doctrine of Opposites*.[78] Müller's sense that rhetoric might be an "art of taking in foreign natures" was itself based on an ontology of contradiction. We need to acknowledge that behind Marx (and in Marx), there was a tradition of rhetorical, indeed, sophistical antilogy. For this reason, "dialectics at a standstill" was also a

76. Benjamin and Lacis, 2:766.
77. Benjamin, "Epische Theater," in *Gesammelte Schriften*, 2:521.
78. Benjamin, "Porträt," in *Gesammelte Schriften*, 3:87.

kind of psychophysiology in which any given "phenomenon" (subject or not) was to be understood as a *complexio* of countervailing forces, all of which might be modulated through the tropic narratology of the emotions.

Once again, we can understand Benjamin in a different and more precise way by translating him into a rhetorical idiom. *Stillstand* was not simply "standstill"; it was also stasis in the classical rhetorical sense of a question on which a case might turn. Rhetoric had taken the term from wrestling, where *stasis* had meant "clinch." In this way, the image of *Stillstand* is to be understood as an intersection of temporarily counterbalancing forces depicting neither the absence of motion nor some delicately engineered inertia. *Stillstand* was instead precisely the possibility of multiple motions each of which was running through the same set of coordinates. It was possibility qua indeterminacy incarnate. To perceive the captured potential of the concept, we need to understand that for Benjamin *Stillstand* was also "rendering present" (*Vergegenwärtigung*) as practiced by the French novelist Julien Green. That is, it was also the description of a moment with such an eye for detail that a character's passion—his *Passio*, his suffering of a particular action or process or interpellation—could appear as an *Indifferenzpunkt*, that is, "a point of perfect, arrested, debilitated confusion."

Stillstand or indecision was something like the "equiproximity" of alternative possibilities, and the best example would come from one of Green's novels—namely, *The Strange River*. Here is the scene constructed by Green that interested Benjamin most: a man is walking in a city; a woman cries for help; "should I intervene," the man asks himself, "or should I refuse to get involved?" The question constituted a dithering to which Green attended in the novel. In his interpretation, Benjamin reread this prevarication in terms of a question he believed the novelist was implicitly asking himself: "should I make my protagonist's failure to respond to this cry for help *because the woman's accent was lower class* a central scene in my novel?"[79] Green's failure, in Benjamin's opinion, was something like an inability to halt the moment definitively enough. The novel did not effectively identify or underscore its own center. If one were already walking (or, for that matter, writing), inertia entailed carrying on and remaining "on course." Like that of his character, Green's nondecision was an inability to alter a motion that was already underway.

In 1931 Benjamin published an account of the polemical practices of the fin de siècle Viennese journalist Karl Kraus, and there as well we encounter a continuation of Benjamin's baroque rhetorical interests in the displaying of gesture. Kraus, too, had been a practitioner of *Geste*, which in this instance

---

79. Benjamin, "Green," and "Zum gesellschaftlichen Standort," in *Gesammelte Schriften*, 2: 329, 790.

we may parse as a painting of portraits by means of stances taken up against the utterances of others. It was not simply that Kraus hated everything and wanted to make an exhibition or *Pronunciation* of his misanthropy. In Benjamin's account, it was that he wanted to display antagonism. This was the constitution of a very specific kind of "humanness" (*Menschlichkeit*) that could come alive only in an oscillating between "malice" (*Bosheit*) and, precisely, "sophistry" (*Sophistik*).[80] In the same way that Julien Green was displaying his interest in representing an individual character in a state of indecision, Karl Kraus was establishing a public stage on which to direct scenes of pose and counterpose in moments of polemic.

I am trying to establish the tenacity with which Benjamin pursued the problematic of the *Stillstand* as an embodied and argumentative stasis, and I now underscore that tenacity by pursuing the topos beyond both theater and literary criticism into Benjamin's radio work. Although Benjamin never refered to the *Dissoi Logoi*, a "radio play" (*Hörmodell*) that Benjamin composed with Wolf Zucker in 1931 displayed the same basic structure of "argument/counterargument" (*Beispiel und Gegenbeispiel*). Here, I refer to one of the eighty-odd radio pieces to which Benjamin contributed in the years immediately preceding the collapse of the Weimar Republic— namely, "You Want a Raise?! What Are You, Crazy!"[81] Benjamin cast the piece as an experiment in performativity, thereby making a virtue of earning a living through radio and the newspapers, which he referred to as *Brotarbeit* (literally, "bread work").[82] Ostensibly a comparison of how to ask—and how not to ask—for a raise, this particular antilogy contrasted the failure of a Herr Zauderer and the success of a Herr Frisch. The aim was not, however, to educate listeners on how they might conduct such negotiations with greater success. The point, I suggest, was to sensitize listeners to differences in how tensions in such negotiations might be channeled. The objective was simply, as Benjamin put it, to present the *Konfrontation*.[83]

We see, thus, that the insistence on decision that Benjamin had appropriated from Schmitt and that he had redescribed as indecision with the aid of rhetoric in the *Trauerspiel* book had now been transformed again. It

80. Benjamin, "Kraus," in *Gesammelte Schriften*, 2:348.

81. Benjamin's radio work is collected under four headings in the *Gesammelte Schriften*: "Vorträge und Reden," 2:635–83; "Hörmodelle," 4:627–720; "Rundfunkgeschichten für Kinder," 7:68–249; and "Literarischen Rundfunkvorträge," 7:250–94. See also Tiedemann's summary of the work at Benjamin, *Gesammelte Schriften*, 2:1440.

82. For the *Brotarbeit* characterization, see Benjamin's letter of January 25, 1930, to Scholem, in Benjamin, *Gesammelte Briefe*, 3:507.

83. Benjamin, "Hörmodelle," in *Gesammelte Schriften*, 4:629; Benjamin and Zucker, "Gehaltserhöhung?!," in *Gesammelte Schriften*, 4:629–40.

had been transformed from something that appeared to be a pathology of monarchical sovereignty into something much more like the beginnings of a political program. To be sure, the seeds of this transformation had been present in the *Trauerspiel* book. After all, that book was not ultimately an analysis of early modern sovereignty. It was an analysis of representations of such authority within baroque drama. The implication had been that drama was itself a form of political analysis, that drama could educate its audiences. This notion of a pedagogical drama recurred in the "Manifesto" written with Lacis. The political analytic that was being advanced there was one focused on indecision. Or rather it was an analytic focused on collective indecision in moments following on the dethroning of—for example—the director or teacher as an essential authority figure. The desideratum was, ultimately, the development of skill in avoiding a premature sealing of the tear in the social fabric that was the essence of such collective indecision. But Benjamin's interest in the problematic of indecision did not find its culmination in these various scattered artifacts of late Weimar journalism. Indeed, the continuations of this line of inquiry ran directly through Benjamin's major achievements after 1933, the "Work of Art" essay included. I make the case for this claim in the next section.

REGENERATING THE MOMENT OF INDECISION IN EXILE

On December 17, 1933, Benjamin wrote to the art historian Carl Linfert. By this point, Benjamin had left Germany, and he was writing from Paris. He thanked Linfert for three things: for letting him hold on to "the visual material pertaining to 'Daphne'"; for Linfert's comments in response to his essay "Experience and Poverty" (which had appeared ten days earlier); and for Linfert's enclosure of an article of his own concerning the Apollo and Daphne myth. In that article, Linfert had underscored what he took to be the "the positive conception of barbarism" (*positive Begriff des Barbarentums*) presented by Benjamin in "Experience and Poverty." In response, Benjamin emphasized how struck he was by Linfert's presentation of Giambattista Vico in the "Apollo und Daphne" piece. This was a Vico, Benjamin said, "whom I've never seen so well construed."[84] In that piece, Linfert had been reviewing the "visual material pertaining to 'Daphne'" that Benjamin was happy to have a little while longer—namely, Wolfgang Stechow's *Apollo und Daphne* (1932), a study of the modern afterlife of the Greek myth. Benjamin had been captivated by the cinquecento Italian painter Dosso Dossi's *Apollo and Daphne*, the last image included in that work. The next thought

84. Benjamin, *Gesammelte Briefe*, 4:318–19: "den ich noch nie so gut dargestellt gefunden habe."

Benjamin recorded was this: Linfert would be just the person with whom to visit the Hubert Robert exhibition, then on display at the Orangerie Gallery in Paris. In recording this thought, Benjamin was marking out a stream-of-consciousness interval between Dosso Dossi and Hubert Robert that it is also the historian's task to assess. What was at stake here? How should we parse this cryptic and hypercontextualized exchange between Linfert and Benjamin? I submit that this apparently incidental back-and-forth was actually something like a coded summa of Benjamin's late political interests. Moreover, it continued the inquiry sequence begun in the *Trauerspiel* book and advanced in "Russian Debate in German" together with its related texts. I make my case for these twin assertions in the remainder of this section.

In "Experience and Poverty," Benjamin had addressed the perceived exhaustion of the categories that had structured experience in the prewar world, an exhaustion that he thought of as one of the basic issues of postwar European civilization. For him, "experience" (*Erfahrung*) was something like a language inheritance in which distribution of terms constituted a training ground for attention. If something had a name within a given community, then that something was preformed within the community's sensorium and would be more easily perceived as a result. This was force of habit, which for Benjamin was not simply *Gewohnheit* but also the Greek quasi homonym *ethos/ēthos* (habit/character). This was the accretion of past experiences around the particular constitutive conjunctions of world and mind that had taken on the force of signs.[85] Habit was a practice of perceptual shortcutting or inference in the absence of decision: "Situation X; Action Y." Benjamin believed that the First World War had eviscerated great swathes of such habit. It constituted a radical caesura in European tradition, which Benjamin termed "transmissibility" (*Tradierbarkeit*).

We can understand the Benjaminian category of experience in relation to the Vichian conception of *sensus communis*. Both concepts emphasize the "judgments without reflection" freighted by cultural terminologies. These are terminologies that facilitate attending to some phenomena while ignoring others. *Sensus communis* denoted not so much "common sense" (or a library of received truths) as the sum total of perceptual sensitivities shared by a group, a nation, or a species. In putting the matter thus, I am channeling Vico's definition of *sensus communis* as "judgment without reflection" (*giudizio senza riflessione*).[86] In the Vichian scheme of things, this was a theory of how the cycle of fables making up Greek mythology, for example, might emerge progressively as the work of a community of writers.

85. Benjamin, "Zwei Bücher," in *Gesammelte Schriften*, 3:163.
86. Vico, *Scienza nuova*, §142.

By distinguishing a particular epithet or passion or micronarrative, each of those writers was adding a facet to poetic characters that were held in a common store.

Thinking "Experience and Poverty" alongside Vico allows us to understand the sense in which Benjamin's essay was articulating a *positive* conception of barbarism. "Barbarism" (*Barbarentum*) here is to be understood as an inarticulateness that derives from the inapplicability of old terminologies to new experiences. This barbarism constituted a kind of new poetic age in which expressions might be invented instead of simply being recycled. As Linfert had seen, however, this erasure of precedent—whatever its causes—was not wholly negative for Benjamin. The "poverty" (*Armut*) that it brought into being was indeed a barbarism. It amounted to a culturelessness or inarticulateness. But this barbarism was also a kind of cognitive denuding in which everything became possible once again. The breaking of experience on the lips of language, as it were, would be an opportunity for creative and originary expression.

My hypothesis is that the "positive barbarism" Linfert was imputing to Benjamin's "Experience and Poverty" was—or ought to have been—what Vico referred to as a second returned "barbarism of sense" (*barbarie del senso*). Neither Benjamin nor Linfert were entirely explicit on the point, but they did gesture to Vico, and we can certainly reconstruct a compelling version of the point by importing more of Vico's argument than they supplied. In the eighteenth-century Neapolitan's opinion, one basic historical process entailed what he called the supplanting of a "barbarism of reflection" (*barbarie della riflessione*) with a renewed "barbarism of sense."[87] Concepts that had been rendered overly explicit through constant use in a community lost their force. In an idiom more native to Benjamin, we might say that concepts evincing no tension between their denotation and their invocation were no longer capable of convincing their users that they were in a serious normative situation while deploying these concepts. Above all, the "barbarism of reflection" was abstract and flippant. Such a corruption of concepts led eventually to the deaths of entire conceptual systems. A new process of concept formation would eventually begin at the moment when an experience was so searingly intense that, for instance, the visual memory of it became an index of an ur-situation for the organism that had undergone it. Visual memory became a word. As Benjamin had said in the *Trauerspiel* work, early modern *Emblematik* echoed the origin of language. As Vico conceived of it, this barbarism of sense was a cyclical *reemergence* of language as such.

Benjamin expressed a preference for Linfert's Vichian gloss of the Apollo

---

87. Vico, §1106.

and Daphne topos over the treatment provided by Stechow in his book, and we should understand this as a preference for the Apollo and Daphne cycle of fables as a miniature world of imaginative universals brought into being by what Vico had termed "poetic logic" (*logica poetica*). According to Vico, Apollo's pursuit of Daphne—the Olympian god's lust for a wood nymph ending in the transformation of Daphne into a laurel bush—was in fact a kind of primordial history of the moment at which family lineages (that is, family trees) emerged together with laws of inheritance. Published in the Studies of the Warburg Library, Stechow's work was a historical reconstruction of the evolution of this topos in European art. It specified an interest in "afterlife" (*Nachleben*) as a tension between repetition and invention. He was tracing the embedding of this topos in a visual *sensus communis*, and Benjamin was interested in such topoi. In this case, however, it was not the sequence that captured Benjamin's imagination but rather a single image (Dosso Dossi's): Apollo at the center, Daphne distant in the background and on the periphery. This was an Apollo who had been cut off at the torso, an Apollo who had become a kind of fragmented torso elided into vegetation in the area of his reproductive organs. Half there, half not—Apollo was himself caught in the moment of indecision, "lyre" falling from his shoulder as if entering a trance.

The sensory barbarism that Benjamin was exploring stripped away cultural routines across a variety of domains, and he saw this historical process at work in numerous ways in interwar Europe with renovation of cultural memorizing in architecture, poetry, and the visual arts. Dada "word-salad" (*Wortsalat*) poems and photomontage compositions contributed to a kind of decomposition of centuries of accreted linguistic and visual habit. Similarly, the glass and steel architectures that he saw as a new reality in the European built environment generated spaces for human life in which it was more difficult to leave traces. Such architectures required new muscle memorizing, and their slick surfaces resisted the accretion of cultural habits.[88] The various affordances of these new materials also opened the way to an exploration of new forms, idioms, and juxtapositions.

Even as the conceit of "positive barbarism" could be read across a wide variety of art-sensory domains, Benjamin explored this positive valence for barbarism most intensively in the visual-kinetic domain of film. For him, Dada avant-garde aesthetic practice was simply an anticipation of the rise of film, which opened up vast new perceptual territories for precise observation and fresh habituation. Film transformed montage into the cut. Cultural old age thus became a renewed cultural youth with the cineaste cast as new poet. Perhaps the most striking example came from Osip Brik. We know

---

88. Benjamin, "Erfahrung und Armut," in *Gesammelte Schriften*, 2:217–18.

how to film a romantic kiss, Brik said. We have analyzed it endlessly and have little trouble capturing it with a camera. Yet we do not know how to represent someone leaving a political meeting in disgust. The particular biomechanics of this gesture are still foreign to us.[89] Benjamin was inferring that the absence of such an understanding was a form of poverty. At the same time, however, he was also saying that such absence was an opportunity.

Capturing a gesture as a fresh word in a new medium such as film for a positively barbarized community of sense was a matter of excerpting or paring down to the point of portability. Given that excerpting functioned by means of imaginative reenactment and continuation, there was a sense in which photography was culturally more advanced than film, even as it was technologically prior. Benjamin was obsessed with the ways in which moments could be excised from the flux of their first appearance and transposed as fragments into new perceptual environments where they could function as the principles—that is to say, the beginnings—of new movement. When he observed that the French photographer Eugène Atget pictured empty streets in Paris like the scenes of a crime in the "Work of Art" essay, Benjamin was saying that, excised from their quotidian environments and put on display, these photographic time slices generated new narratives and new hypotheses in viewers.[90] The radical isolation of the photographic image required supplement. It required the enthymematic continuation in a before or an after. It staged the procedural. Narrativizing the moment might begin a process of embedding in a new perceptual habitat, but Benjamin did not want to relinquish the assertion that excising a moment from one context and inserting it into another transformed such a moment into questions.

The Vichian Benjamin that I am constructing here is a hypothesis that finds further verification in the late conceptualizations of language, where processes of excision akin to those in photography were absolutely fundamental. In a 1935 review essay "The Sociology of Language," this process of extraction began as deixis, pointing. Picking up on the work of the psychologist Karl Bühler, Benjamin found an origin for language in a mimicry that consisted in pointing. Onomatopoeia was the imitation that picked a phenomenon out of the perceptual flux amid which it originally appeared. Such imitation constituted an "object." One could say, in fact, that such imitation *named* that object.[91] Whenever he used the term *Geste* (in reference to Brecht or Chaplin or Kafka), what Benjamin really meant was not so much "gesture" as deixis, a pointing out or putting on display. The positivity of

89. Brik, "Selected Criticism, 1915–1929," 103.
90. Benjamin, "Kunstwerk," in *Gesammelte Schriften*, 1:485.
91. Benjamin, "Sprachsoziologie," in *Gesammelte Schriften*, 3:477.

barbarism consisted in an ability to believe in the exhaustion of a cultural idiom to the point that one could lay one's senses on the polyform flux of any given moment and discern in that flux miniature gestalts that might be framed. And here "framing" means "putting in quotation marks to save for later as a name."

The interest in excerpting that I am attending to here was very often visual, but Benjamin was deeply interested in processes and cultures of quotation with regard to literary constructions as well. Here we encounter Benjamin's *Arcades Project*, the dreamt of but never finished magnum opus approaching the "perfection" of being a book composed entirely of quotations. This, too, contributes to the verification of the Linfert-Vico hypothesis that I am examining and arguing for in this section. Quotation, we must understand, was essentially "photographic": it tore an object (a sentence) from its context and reproduced it elsewhere for other purposes. On this account, quotation marks and picture frames were functionally the same. The *Arcades Project* was an inventory of the wreckage of European civilization. It was a collection of fragments and was the beginning of what, improvising, we might call a renewed barbarism of inference. That is, the project was an assemblage of premises separated from the arguments in which they had emerged, and they were organized in such a way that inference might once again weave them together into lines of inquiry. Like the photograph, the literary fragment both demanded continuation and resisted completion. Like the commonplace book, the *Arcades Project* was an aphoristic machine built for the production of argument.

Analogies between the visual structure of a painting and the grammatical structure of a sentence had been structurally important in the *Trauerspiel* work, and those analogies were again at work in Benjamin's exchange with Linfert. In that exchange these analogies suggested a relationship between Vico and the paintings of Hubert Robert exhibited at the Orangerie in Paris. Robert was a painter of ruins, and ruins were to be understood as "quotations" from ancient architectures that had been "excerpted" by historical processes of decay, demolition, and reuse. Once again, this was positive barbarism, because the fragments were old and incomplete to the point that they could not be reused without being, in effect, reinvented. Benjamin wanted to see these paintings in the presence of Linfert because he knew that Linfert was a man capable of imagining into incomplete architectural spaces. After all, Benjamin had reviewed Linfert's dissertation, which in turn drew on Benjamin's *Trauerspiel* book in order to think through early modern architectural reveries.[92]

The decontextualizations achieved by film, photography, quotation, and

---

92. Linfert, *Die Grundlagen der Architekturzeichnung*, 244. Benjamin, "Strenge Kunstwissenschaft," in *Gesammelte Schriften*, 3:363–74.

ruin generated "attention" (*Aufmerksamkeit*), and such attending entailed a sensing of the almost impossibly small beginnings of motion. In a kind of covert reengineering of the baroque conception of conatus (defined by Hobbes as motion across a point), Benjamin defined "the faculty of imagination" (*das Vermögen der Phantasie*) as "the capacity to interpolate into the infinitely small" (*die Gabe, im unendlich Kleinen zu interpolieren*). This was a capacity "to discover in any given intensity its new crowded cornucopia qua extension, in short, to take each image as if it were a closed fan that first takes breath in its unfolding."[93] Interpolation here was something like the magnifying effect of attention in which new spaces could be discovered between points that had previously seemed identical or continuous. We can see that Zeno of Elea was being transposed into the world of art history. For Benjamin, moreover, this had been the basic mode of Proustian composition. Benjamin had translated some of Proust's works, and he made his point by relaying an anecdote: it was said that, upon receiving his proofs from the printer and without correcting a single error, Proust would insert new sentences into what he now saw were spaces or gaps between the sentences of the proof text.[94] In this way, his texts were composed as a series of lateral agencies.

It would be a serious mistake to think of Proustian composition as a model for the writing process only. In fact, such composition prototyped a much more fundamental presupposition about creativity. In this context, the most basic point I want to make is that where Schmitt emphasized emergency, Benjamin was emphasizing emergence.[95] Schmitt and the political theorists who have followed him have focused on the moment as a point of closure, of decision, of an exception that would never be a precedent. They have thought of the most distinctively political moment as, precisely, the moment of *depoliticization*: "I suspend the rule, here is my decision, the matter is closed and has no future." In contrast, Benjamin thought of the moment in terms of its capacity for beginning motion. "Momentariness" for him was something like focusing to the point that something became an open question for a community. He thought of the moment in terms of its capacity for indecision, for—in short—*politicization*. And this is the context in which we should understand the famous couplet with which the "Work of Art" essay ended. In what may well be the most cited passage in his entire corpus, Benjamin said that communism was developing a "politicization of art" (*Politisierung der Kunst*) in response to "the aestheticizing of politics

93. Benjamin, *Einbahnstraße*, in *Gesammelte Schriften*, 4:117: "jeder Intensität als Extensivem ihre neue gedrängte Fülle zu erfinden, kurz, jedes Bild zu nehmen, als sei es das des zusammengelegten Fächers, das erst in der Entfaltung Atem holt."

94. Benjamin, "Zum Bilde Prousts," in *Gesammelte Schriften*, 2:312.

95. Here, I am endorsing and adding to an idiom fashioned in Honig, *Emergency Politics*.

that fascism practices" (*die Ästhetisierung der Politik, welche der Faschismus betreibt*). Here the ABBA schema was a paradiastolic chiasmus securing a distinction between two ostensibly similar processes.[96]

I make two claims with regard to Benjamin's chiastic inversion of the aestheticization of politics into the politicization of art. First, the politicization of art was precisely the enhanced opportunity of large numbers of people to become producers of art. As producers rather than simply consumers, people were now able to use art's capacity to "quote" by placing parts of the world within a frame. New technologies made it simpler to deploy such "quotation" in particular contexts in order to raise questions and provoke indecision. Second, the mirroring of "the aestheticization of politics" and "the politicization of art" was itself a kind of "duck/rabbit" (*Vexierbild*), the purpose of which was to distinguish what might appear merely identical. These phrases specified alternative possibilities that were equidistant from what Benjamin took to be a post-1933 actuality in which Europe was dithering. This was a kind of revision of the debate between Brik and Illés in which the decisive innovation was a greater insistence on democratization of the means of reproduction. Yet the question this posed was neither as rhetorical nor as easily answered as scholars have sometimes presumed. After all, Leni Riefenstahl's *Triumph of the Will* and Slatan Dudow's *Kuhle Wampe* shared a certain visual interest in representations of massed assembly (qua political rally and athletic meet, respectively). It was in their representations of oratory that these Nazi and Communist films differed: acclamation in Nuremberg contrasted decisively with debate in the Berlin U-Bahn.

Conspicuous in the first draft of the "Work of Art" essay but less so in the last version (where the thought appeared only in the footnotes) was Benjamin's interest in radical transformations in the representability of political debate under modern conditions. As Benjamin put it, "the crisis of democracies can be understood in terms of a crisis in the conditions of exhibition for political personage."[97] Parliaments could be made to appear outmoded because film could generate simulacra of apparently direct interactions between leader and people. Film made the fiction of "direct" democracy plausible. Once again, however, it was moments of indecision that interested Benjamin more. In the "Work of Art" essay, indecision appeared as the "stations of movement" (*Bewegungsmomenten*) that film could isolate.[98] Film was a technical enhancement of the human sensorium. It could keep pace with speech, but it also excelled in enlargement,

96. Benjamin, "Kunstwerk," in *Gesammelte Schriften*, 1:508.
97. Benjamin, 1:454–55, 7:369, 1:491: "die Krise der Demokratien läßt sich als eine Krise der Ausstellungsbedingungen des politischen Menschen verstehen." The paragraph was excised altogether in the French version of 1936.
98. Benjamin, 1:488.

deceleration, excision, reproduction. As such, it fundamentally altered the human relationship to time. The "tenth of a second" (*Zehntelsekunde*) took on a new reality, and here we may observe a continuity between Benjamin in his early baroque rhetorical and late media historical phases. In the *Trauerspiel* book, the sovereign melancholic's resignation was precisely a resignation from the extreme time sensitivity of crisis. In the "Work of Art" essay, the fraction of a second was a new zone for potential interpolation. It led to the inventive work of revealing the panoply of potential trajectories implicit in an only apparently smooth motion.

We begin to see that the Linfert-Vico line runs directly through the "Work of Art" essay. Film subjected human action to a series of optical tests (as Benjamin put it), and the film editor's job was to splice these moments together so as to imply totalities to the film audience. This was a form of cinematic enthymeme in which sequences were abbreviated into fragments. Moreover, the cut could literally fracture the moment of indecision and represent it from different points of view. Perhaps nowhere in Weimar cinema was this "film sophistic" more palpable than in the *Kuhle Wampe* scene where a brother and a sister faced each other through a silence produced by family quarrel. We cut to her face, burgeoning warmth; to his face, utter impassivity. The camera lingers in the diptych long enough to make it a question. Then it is gone. The sister leaves, and the brother— unemployed, exhausted, and bullied by the father—commits suicide. Elsewhere, Benjamin had said that the peculiar talent of *Berlinisch* as a dialect was its manifold ways of exhibiting "astonishment [*Staunen*], such that one is immobilized by one's transfixed stare, goggling."[99] As the scene from *Kuhle Wampe* showed, film, too, could be a mode of being brought up short by astonishment. Benjamin said that film was to ordinary visual experience what Freud's *Psychopathology of Everyday Life* (1901) had been to ordinary speech—and the slips of the tongue that abounded in it. In making this claim, he was licensing a shift in the filmic political imaginary from "the exhibition of political personage" to what amounted to a visual rhetorical analysis of everydayness.[100] The research program implied thereby was a rich one.

CODA

Quoting André Gide, Benjamin maintained in 1928 that "it is only when we take leave of a thing that we name it."[101] The topos organizes our attention

99. Benjamin, "Wat Hier Jelacht Wird," in *Gesammelte Schriften*, 4:541.
100. Benjamin, "Kunstwerk," in *Gesammelte Schriften*, 1:498.
101. Benjamin, "Gide," in *Gesammelte Schriften*, 4:506: "ce n'est qu'en quittant une chose que nous la nommons."

here too. The account of Benjamin's work that I have staged in this chapter is rooted in the rhetorical dimensions of the *Trauerspiel* book. It follows the interests specified there into the public critical work that he did in the last years of the Weimar Republic. And it traces the enduring and fundamental importance of these interests for the classic late essays too, which I have characterized as another transposition of baroque rhetorical sensibilities—in this case, Giambattista Vico's—into twentieth-century European contexts. As Gide predicted, the most explicit verification of the hypothesis I have been articulating came at the very end of Benjamin's life.

On April 6, 1940, Benjamin wrote to Max Horkheimer from Paris, responding to a letter in which Horkheimer had relayed an accusation of plagiarism made against Benjamin by Werner Kraft. The accusation focused on a piece that Benjamin had published the previous year on Carl Gustav Jochmann, an early nineteenth-century Latvian writer whose anonymous publications in German had been almost entirely forgotten. The oblivion of those publications remains extreme to this day, although they did appear in chapter 2 of this book on account of their place in the modern German reception of rhetoric. Benjamin had been particularly interested in Jochmann's work on "the regressions of poetry" (*Die Rückschritte der Poesie*).[102] An old acquaintance of Benjamin's from the days before Weimar, Kraft was a fellow German-Jewish émigré living in Paris in the 1930s who had also been working on Jochmann. Kraft felt he had been first.

Benjamin was captivated by Jochmann's thesis that in human affairs progress and decline very often coincided. In its most basic form, this irony replicated Vico's sense of a continual oscillation between the barbarism of sense and the barbarism of reflection. Benjamin defended himself against the charge of plagiarism by saying that, although the interest in Jochmann was common to both scholars, his own treatment distinguished itself from Kraft's on two counts. First, Benjamin believed he had discovered a fundamental continuity, ignored by Kraft, between Jochmann and Vico. Second, he believed there was a "genealogy" (*Filiation*) running back from his own work—the "Work of Art" essay, in particular—to Jochmann's ideas on the regression of poetry. Elsewhere, Benjamin interpolated this genealogy through Jugendstil, Henry van de Velde, Joseph Maria Olbrich's Düsseldorf school, Vienna Werkbund, Neue Sachlichkeit, and Adolf Loos.[103] Thus, deep within the "Work of Art" essay, there was a lineage spanning the sequence "Vico—Jochmann—Benjamin." Here was the inference that Benjamin was putting to Horkheimer: what is most intimately my own could not have been plagiarized.

102. Benjamin, *Gesammelte Briefe*, 6:426–31; "Rückschritte," in *Gesammelte Schriften*, 2:572–98.
103. Benjamin, "Rückschritte," in *Gesammelte Schriften*, 2:581.

Almost no one has explored the potential lineage running through Vico, Jochmann, and Benjamin.[104] This is a missed opportunity. In this lineage, we encounter one of the most enduring continuities in Benjamin's intellectual interests. To be sure, Vico, Jochmann, and Benjamin shared a common concern for the potential utility of rhetorical analysis in societies that did not possess the classical oratorical institutions that gave rise to formalized accounts of rhetoric in antiquity—the Pnyx in Athens and the Forum in Rome, among others. There are obvious ways in which this hypothesis is correct. Vico asked openly about the analytical utility of rhetoric for societies, like eighteenth-century Naples, in which free political debate did not exist.[105] Jochmann was explicitly concerned with the early nineteenth-century argument that German was a weak language precisely because it lacked the democratic institutions that (so the argument went) continually renewed English and French as so many oratorical crucibles. And, as we have seen, Benjamin's "Work of Art" essay also emerged from his recognition of a fundamental new reality: modern communicative technologies had transformed the way in which leaders might appear before peoples.

The fundamental point was a different one, however: above all, what Benjamin took from Vico was the supposition that imagination was the basic capacity of the human soul.[106] For Vico, imagination had been *ingenium* at its core. It was a capacity to perceive similarity in phenomena that were distant one from another (in all the myriad senses of "distant"). At base, imagination was *Phantasie* for Benjamin. It was the capacity to interpolate distances between points that might seem identical or continuous. In the relation between the two concepts, we notice a very particular shift. In a quite precise sense, Benjaminian *Phantasie* was the obverse of Vichian *ingenium*. As we have seen, such *Phantasie* was constitutive for the process of politicization itself, which—as Benjamin understood it—required opening a gap between habit and the moment. This opening up of the moment of indecision was one of the core leitmotifs in Benjamin's work.

To understand Benjamin's interest in the breadth and depth of indecision, one has to move beyond the obvious context with which this chapter began—namely, Schmitt's *Political Theology*. One has to reconstruct the less obvious but ultimately richer series of contexts that Benjamin's work constituted for itself, a series of contexts that incorporated but never quite became identical with the rhetorical tradition in a variety of its historical

---

104. The few exceptions are Mali, "Retrospective Prophets"; Meyers, "Notes on 'Now'"; Meyers and Struever, "Esquisse"; and Struever, *Rhetoric, Modality, Modernity*, 84–86.
105. Marshall, "Transformation of Rhetoric," 123; see also the broader argument in Marshall, *Vico and the Transformation of Rhetoric.*
106. Benjamin, "Rückschritte," in *Gesammelte Schriften*, 2:584, where Benjamin traced Jochmann's notion of "Phantasie als das 'urprüngliche Seelenvermögen'" back to Vico.

instantiations. In Benjamin's revision of this rhetorical line of inquiry, political criticism became a practice of locating the points of greatest possible redescribability within any given community. These were the moments of potential indecision, and they were the points on which a community's most acute attention was to be focused. That idioms of redescribability could also become the discursive fields of greatest repetitiveness was thus a fundamental political problem. Repetition in moments of indecision rendered indecision itself habitual and pathological. This was a bad infinity. Precisely where attention was required, there was habit.

6: WARBURGIAN IMAGE PRACTICES

RÉSUMÉ AND PRÉCIS

In a way that is both surprising and illuminating, this chapter functions as a kind of interim culmination of the lines of inquiry traced in the previous three chapters. In chapter 3, we saw how Martin Heidegger's Summer Semester 1924 metabolization of Aristotle's *Rhetoric* into his renovation of the fundamental terms of Greek philosophy generated a theory of *epideixis* in which the presencing of a phenomenon was understood as a temporal spanning expressing relations among the modalities of its finality, potentiality, and activation. *Entelecheia* as a final achievedness might be both rare and then ambiguous (because for Heidegger, everydayness was both the many-timed-ness of habit and an absencing in repetition), but it underwrote interest in *energeia*, which was to be understood as appearances of activation in which a phenomenon implied the coming of a presence that could function as a definition. In chapter 4, we then saw how Hannah Arendt's early work was an exploration of the conditions of possibility for appearance. As I argued in that chapter, one of the through lines from the Augustine book to the Rahel book and from the Rahel book to the early political writings of the late 1930s and early 1940s was precisely a concern for worlding as an opening up of cultural distances in the midst of a community. This was something like a geometry of political or protopolitical space, and I argued that in Arendt's depiction of the oratorical and "auditorical" performances of Rahel Varnhagen, we had the first (and actually more vivid) description of what eventually became her theorization of the polis. In that treatment, I emphasized the "topical" role that performances played in creating a space of appearance for the agent exhibiting those performances, and this emphasis on performances as topoi was then something that I perceived also in the early work of Walter Benjamin. Other scholars have emphasized the importance and fecundity of Benjamin's interest in "dialectical images." In my interpretation, however, this focus on images pulling apart became just one articulation of a thematic that was broader, deeper, and more explicitly rhetorical. Benjamin's *Trauerspiel* book had been saturated in rhetorical terms and problematics, and the interest in allegory parsed there echoed throughout many of the later works on theater. In those works on theater, Benjamin revealed the ways in which a character could carry its own name with a heaviness implying that a stage might become the most indispensable classroom in any political education.

It is precisely here, with the emergence of carrying one's own name with a certain kind of "heaviness," that the work of Aby Warburg inflects the line extending through Heidegger, Arendt, and Benjamin. Warburg, I shall argue, wished to combat precisely the moments of appearance in which a phenomenon might serve as its own definition. Unlike Heidegger (who desired presencing even as he underscored the importance of absence), unlike Arendt (who focused on the fundamental role played by the ground or scene or space in which appearance might happen), and unlike Benjamin (whose imagistic preference was for the *Vexierbild*, the image that was equidistant between two interpretations), Warburg was explicitly concerned with the kind of fragmentation of an appearance that might occur in the medium of what we should call "visual topoi."

The visual topos, I shall be arguing in this chapter, was a space in which the vicissitude and variety of appearances might be recorded, and this was not only a rejection of the dream of self-defining presence but also the beginning of a certain kind of very important imaginative training. Warburg's assemblage of visual topoi in his last project, the *Mnemosyne Image-Atlas* (unfinished when he died in 1929), was comparable to Benjamin's collections of quotations in the *Arcades Project* (and both were analogues of early modern commonplacing). Yet Warburg's chosen media—photography and photographic montage—were more effective than Benjamin's scholarly quotations at pursuing questions of embodied continuation and its imaginative variegation.

Pursuing the Weimar origins of rhetorical inquiry through Heidegger, Arendt, and Benjamin has taken us through philosophy, political theory, and literary theory. In turn, working through Warburg entails engagement with the history and theory of art. Warburg, too, was a discipline-founding figure. Once again, however, it is the ur- or para- or "interdiscipline" of rhetoric that organizes my analysis in this chapter. To be sure, these four thinkers remain fundamentally diverse. Reading them as part of a sequence of rhetorical inquiry in this book does nothing to alter that irreducible diversity. But diversity within sequence is a strength. In Warburg's case, the appearance that might constitute its own name was most closely approximated by what he called the "gods of the moment" (*Augenblicksgötter*). There, the notion of constituting one's own name in appearance took on a new precision.

For Warburg, self-defining appearance occurred when every quality of an appearing could be included in a definition of the phenomenon. Crucially, however, Warburg's god of the moment was something to be feared and overcome. Why? Because such self-defining appearance interpellated subjects and diminished their abilities to discover variety of response.

At the point where Warburg rejected the advent of the *Augenblicksgott*, rhetoric intruded. One of the titles Warburg considered for his unfinished masterwork was "The Restitution of Eloquence" (*restitutio eloquentiae*). In a line from his manuscripts that scholars seem to have passed over, Warburg elaborated the meaning of this phrase. Describing his image atlas as a restitution of eloquence meant the image atlas would be preoccupied with issues of pathos, ethos, style, and—he added—magnanimity. All four of these terms have long and complex histories within rhetoric. In my reading, though, it is the last that is the most surprising and the most instructive. As I reconstruct the notion, Warburgian magnanimity becomes something like a plasticity and thus potential adroitness of body-imaginative response. Exercising such magnanimity would enable subjects to diminish the subjection worked on them by Warburg's gods of the moment, because such magnanimity consisted in a perspicacity that transformed moments of would-be self-definition into pluriform invitations for continuation.

Ultimately, I shall be arguing, exercising such magnanimity implied a theory of freedom based in the faculty—or facility—of imagination rather than in some putative faculty of will. Warburg's invocation of *magnanimitas* implied that certain forms of imagined and embodied motion were in fact practices of freedom. For Warburg, freedom was the achievement of something approaching equidistance in relation to a variety of proximate, realizable, and richly imagined possibilities. Indeed, as Warburg used the words, "freedom" (*Freiheit*) and "inhibition" (*Hemmung*) were basically the same, because one could understand "in-hibition" as "a projecting internally," equal and opposite to "an ex-hibiting that projected externally." But such inhibition was not simply suspension. Freedom would not be synonymous with inaction. The image-atlas-stoked multiplex of the mind was a preparation for action, a readiness for acting into moments that would appear in the world, moments at which previously imagined continuations might become themes on which one improvised.

I can epitomize my argument in an anecdote. While campaigning in 1928 for the retention of the philosopher Ernst Cassirer, Warburg described the foundation of the University of Hamburg after the First World War as "a symptom of the will to rebirth through spiritual deed" (*ein Symptom des Willens zur Wiedergeburt durch geistige Tat*).[1] At the recently founded uni-

---

1. Warburg, "Cassirer," in *Werke*, 700.

versity, Cassirer was an important figure, a monumental writerly amalgam of neo-Kantianism, Renaissance and Enlightenment intellectual history, and the history and philosophy of science. He was considering an offer from another university. With perhaps an exaggerated sense of what a single individual at a single institution might mean for a city, Warburg was desperate to keep Cassirer. In speaking of rebirth, he was attempting to bind Cassirer to the larger calling of the university, which he cast against the backdrop of Germany's defeat in the First World War.

One can construe Warburg's assertion as a commonplace if one wishes. We can transform the assertion into an innocuous expression that exemplifies larger discursive formations. There are, for example, elements of German parochialism here. And at times during the war Warburg had been extremely parochial. One could also gloss the sentence in such a way that it read like a typically—thus, sociologically neutralizable—intellectual account of politics as a matter of "spirit" (*Geist*). Warburg's brother Max administered the affairs of the family bank, and we can say that he would have a much more realist sense of the daily life of politics. Aby, the older brother, had given up his patrimony for the life of the mind, the life of the independently wealthy scholar and founder of a research institute. "Of course a man like Aby Warburg would suppose that the domain of politics is spirit," we infer. In this mood, we perceive traces of a rather weak, received, hard-to-rearticulate-with-conviction version of the topos "Enlightenment."

I sense something different, though, and this chapter excavates the inquiry sequence that in my opinion runs through Warburg's 1928 appeal. For Warburg, the "spiritual act" (*geistige Tat*) was in fact something like a response to interpellation that displaced energies from an immediately inferred counterposition into an array of imagined stances. Among other things, post-Versailles Germany was an array of defensive counterpositions being organized rhetorically by right-wing political groups. For Warburg, "defense-fantasy" (*Abwehrphantasie*) would be a central analytical term. We grasp the core of that term when we render it as "the defensive imagination" or "the phantasmagoria of imputed threat." It connoted obsession with and scrutiny of the small detail. It entailed scrutiny of absence, absence as a sign, and waiting-amid-absence as a basic quality of time itself. Rooted in the nonnegotiability of the either/or, *Abwehrphantasie* was an incapacity to think beyond a very limited range of possibilities. I shall be arguing that "spiritual act" (*geistige Tat*) was an antonym of and therapy for such phantasmagoria. "Spiritual act" also denoted an imaginative practice, but it multiplied possibilities, and it exercised a multiplicity of response positions. Many gambits, many responses.

I pursue my argument in three phases. First, I work through Warburg's projected 1917 talks on superstition and their iteration up to publication in 1920 as "Pagan-Antique Divination in Word and Image in the Age of Luther." There, the concept of "conjunction" (*Konjunktion*) underwrote investigation of the state of spiritual tension brought about by an intensified impinging of context on life. Second, I examine Warburg's 1923 talk "Images from the Region of the Pueblo Indians in North America," where the perception of "ornamentation" (*Ornament*) secured a victory over the *Augenblicksgötter*, a term I will translate as "deities of extreme interpellation." That is a less literal translation than "gods of the moment," but I prefer it because it conveys the deeper logic of Warburg's thinking. Warburg's inference was that whoever perceived ornamentation was seeing that not all the predicates of an experience were essential to the definition of a phenomenon. Ornamentation was a mode of and fillip for freedom because it could be seen through, rerouted, and changed. In this way, contingency was balm to necessitarian fantasy. Such fantasizing fell into the belief that any given manifestation must happen precisely as it does and may come to pass in no other way. Third, I reinterpret the remnants of Warburg's famous 1929 talk on the Mnemosyne project at the Biblioteca Hertziana in Rome. One of the most pivotal terms there was once again "restitution" (*Restitution*), and I read it as a particular form of displacing the fetish power of any one image or scene by viewing it alongside an eclectic variety of alternative visual narrativizations.

THE CONJUNCTIONS OF 1917 AND THEIR CONCEPTUAL IMPLICATIONS

As we saw in chapter 2, rhetorical inquiry is preoccupied with context, and we find this thematic at the core of Aby Warburg's work as well. In rhetoric, context had been important not only because the occasion of speech required a thick description drawing on all the tools of the historian but also because once begun a speech would function as its own background. A speech drew its moves out from the beginnings it had made. Within the rhetorical tradition, *contextus* denoted tightness in the weave of a speech. There were moments at which feigned discombobulation—the *metanoia* of breaking off and beginning again, for instance—would be the better way of responding to some particular oratorical challenge. The "tightness" of extreme hypotaxis was not always optimal. In this section, I shall be arguing that in Warburg, context consisted of more than just the relative clauses supplied by, for instance, the numismatic assiduousness that might inform art-historical inquiry of the Florentine quattrocento. In a manner analogous to Quintilian's specification of *contextus*, Warburg was also interested in how a situation might be described as "all-of-a-piece." The tightly woven fabric was the fabric that having begun in a certain way had to be continued in a certain way. Tightness of weave approximated a necessitarianism that one might associate with fate. In this section, I begin by highlighting Warburg's investigations of astrological constructions of fate around 1917. I use that moment as a point of departure to establish and explore one of the basic constitutive tensions in Warburgian thought: an image will often emerge in the midst of tensions between figure and ground, but sometimes those tensions slacken to the point that figures separate from their grounds and mark trajectories that can be de- and recontextualized across vast swathes of historical time.

On November 18, 1918, a week after the armistice that brought the First World War to an end, Aby Warburg took up a revolver. He intended to kill his wife, his two daughters, and then himself. In words attributed to him on August 10, 1921, and recorded in his medical file at the Bellevue Sanatorium in Kreuzlingen, Switzerland (where he convalesced from 1921 until 1924), Warburg explained that his actions were motivated by a concern for his family—"you know, because Bolshevism was coming."[2] No attempt to account for this avowed intention will be made here, but we should place it—as others have—in the context of Warburg's obsessive collecting and cataloging of newspaper materials pertaining to the war between 1914 and 1918. The "card file of war materials" (*Kriegskartothek*) that he built has not survived, but it is reputed to have grown to twice the size of the famous "card catalogs" (*Zettelkästen*) of research notes that now line one wall of the Warburg Institute Archive in London. Almost every day during the war, it seems, Warburg scanned the press for items of interest. Over the years, massive files of press clippings accumulated under topics such as "Iconology," "Modern Superstition," and "Aphorisms." Here is the essence: Warburg wanted to know how a fate mechanism like the First World War changed human attitudes to vicissitude.

In 1916, Warburg accepted invitations to give lectures the following year in Leipzig and Hamburg on "Superstition and Conceptions of History in the Late Middle Ages." Fuel shortages in February and March meant that lecture halls could not be heated, and the talks were canceled. Nevertheless, the line of inquiry stimulated by those opportunities led to an extended article that eventually appeared as "Pagan-Antique Divination in Word and Image" in 1920, after the beginning of Warburg's convalescence. The article was a dense treatment of the role of astrology in the politico-religious rhetoric of the early German Reformation. There was a contemporary point of reference too, though, and the opening words of the article made that clear: "The also as yet unwritten scientific investigation into 'The Renaissance

2. Binswanger and Warburg, *Die unendliche Heilung*, 49: "Weißt du, weil der Bolschewismus kam."

of Demonic Antiquity in the Age of the German Reformation' must precede the missing handbook, 'On the Unfreedom of Superstitious Modern Men.'"[3] Warburg wanted to understand what we might call the cultures of "psychological necessitarianism": what are the scenes and modes of a lassitude stemming from the belief that one is either indistinguishable from or entirely at the mercy of fate?

In the article, Warburg examined sixteenth-century debates about the significance of Martin Luther's nativity, and behind this lurked early twentieth-century questions about human beings caught in the meshing of two or more great power systems. In the Reformation context, that question had taken the form of asking whether Luther had been born in 1483 or 1484. Mathematical calculations of the orbit of Jupiter and Saturn made it possible to predict the conjunction of major planetary systems retrospectively. Fate began to look like coincidence under such circumstances, for the necessitarian workings of one system simply *happened* to mesh with the necessitarian workings of another system to produce a particular result. Just so, systems of prognostication attempted to explain things that appeared to be resolutely unpredictable, such as the monstrous births of donkeys, calves, or sows with eight feet and almost two bodies. Micro- and macrocosm were so closely intertwined that the leap from farmyard accident to world-historical portent was but a short step. "Conjunction" (*Konjunktion*), in short, was the coincidence of systems, and this was a coincidence that randomized mechanism in a paradoxical way.

The power of astrological actions at a distance was not to be understood purely in terms of the occult influence that astral objects might have on human beings, for the "influence" here could be understood as an expression of human power rather than weakness. As Warburg parsed early modern astrology, "imitation" (*Nachahmung*) was essential to the process of astral influence. Falling under the influence of something was, in fact, a capacity to identify both its forms and its characteristic modes combined with a capacity to reproduce those forms and modes in oneself. Imitation was thus a kind of suggestibility. It might also be a kind of feigning, though. When we find Warburg emphasizing the rhetorical *choices* offered by the astrological body of knowledge, we should not be surprised. After all, one could choose Luther's date of birth for the purpose of giving him a particular meaning. One bestowed nativity in order to choose a narrative. The imitation of astrological belief adopted a range of parameters established by astrological science. One could play by its rules even as one chose the inputs.

Imitation was only one form of response, however, and it is meaningful

3. Warburg, *Heidnisch-antike Weissagung*, 4: "dem fehlenden Handbuch 'Von der Unfreiheit des abergläubigen modernen Menschen' müßte eine gleichfalls noch ungeschriebene wissenschaftliche Untersuchung vorausgehen über: 'Die Renaissance der dämonischen Antike im Zeitalter der deutschen Reformation.'"

to say that imitation existed *between* alternatively active and passive re-sponses. On this account, imitation was actually a kind of receding into a state of indifferentiation between an active offensive posturing and its pas-sive defensive antistrophe. Warburg expressed the thought provocatively in his *Grundlegende Bruchstücke*. This was the collection of "fundamental fragments" constituting his evolving miscellany of principles, a collection that has only recently been published. Warburg said that "imitation" (*Nach-ahmung*) ought to be understood as existing midway between "lashing out" (*angreifend*) and "covering up" (*deckend*).[4] As he put it in another of the foundational fragments, "imitation is a relationship to the object that stands between carrying and being carried."[5] Mirroring stood between attacking and recoiling, and this mirroring was a choice of inconspicuousness in re-sponse to threat. Camouflage was the *tertium quid*, we might say, between fight and flight.

All three modes of response expressed extreme sensitivity to environ-ment, a sensitivity brought into being by failures to decontextualize. This, we can say, was Warburg's debt to the aesthetician Robert Vischer. Accord-ing to Edgar Wind (a Warburgian historian of art and science), Vischer's work "offers the best approach to the study of Warburg's conceptual system as a whole."[6] Sensitivity to environment was an inference deriving from Vischer's rejection of an easy distinction between what he termed "undi-rected gazing" (*blosses Hinsehen*) and "interested scrutinizing" (*Zwecksehen*). Vischer was motivated to make this distinction on account of his rejection of the apparent nonchalance with which Kant had distinguished between interestedness and disinterestedness in his *Critique of the Power of Judg-ment*.[7] The forms of interest were many. Not all appeared in the guise of an intense captivation. Empathy might be a subtler form of interest, and Vischer made mimicry one of the prototypes of empathy when he coined the neologism *Einfühlung*. As if anticipating Roland Barthes's brilliant line that "meaning is above all a cutting out of shapes," Vischer understood imitation to be a mirroring of the world that both distinguished and named it.[8] Kinesthetic quotation began as camouflage, and imitation was in fact attentiveness to context.

The problem was that if one did manage to overcome the paranoid style

4. Warburg, *Fragmente zur Ausdruckskunde*, §46 (January 15, 1890).
5. Warburg, §302 (March 13, 1896): "die Nachahmung ist ein Verhältnis zum Objekt das zwischen Tragen u. Getragenwerden steht."
6. Wind, "Warburgs Begriff der Kulturwissenschaft," 170: "Von hier aus [Vischer's essay, "Das Symbol"] ist daher auch am leichtesten ein Zugang zu seinem Begriffssystem als ganzem zu finden."
7. Vischer, *Über das optische Formgefühl*, 1–4 (for the opening discussion of *Hinsehen* and *Zweck-sehen*), 34 (for the allusion to Kant's third critique).
8. Barthes, *Éléments de sémiologie*, 130.

in which everything became of interest because everything was either a declaration of war or an opportunity for exploitation, the alternative seemed to be simply a lassitude in which one's distinction from the world faded. This would be a lassitude in which the only possible achievement became a purposeless observation of one's cooption by the laws of the cosmos. Lassitude itself became something like a concession that one was subject to these laws. The laws might then write themselves on such a "modest" subject in one of two ways: either by an astrological magic or an astronomical mathematics. There appeared to be no third alternative. Warburg had appropriated the irony from a formulation in Goethe: "a great part of that which one usually terms 'superstition' develops out of an inappropriate application of mathematics."[9] In Warburg, this irony became an oscillation. The history of an astrological attitude toward the conjunction of forces was to be narrated as a pendulum swing "from cultic practice to mathematical contemplation—and back again."[10]

We often find it difficult to think cult and mathematics together, but Warburg was insistent on the interpenetration of the two, and we should understand this in reference to his perception of the relevance of Luther for the generation of World War I. Warburg's emphasis on the concepts of fortune and fate and fatalism is to be understood against the background of increasing mechanization. That is, we can grasp the point against the background of an apparent rise in lawfulness. In the context of the machine processes that were emblematic of nineteenth-century industrialization brought to a horrific crescendo in World War I, one could no longer ignore the indistinguishability of necessity, fate, luck, chance, contingency, coincidence, and dumb proximity. Fate was thus (pace the intellectual legacies of ancient Rome) also a quintessentially modern idea. Indeed, it was a corollary of technical and scientific achievement. In the age of the machinic, law and luck were twins.

In a deeply paradoxical way, powerlessness existed at both extremes of a spectrum that Warburg extended from "cultic idolizing concatenation" (*kultlich verehrender Verknüpfung*) to "mathematical abstraction" (*mathematische Abstraktion*).[11] Regardless of whether one was bound into the movements of music in a corybantic fervor, for example, or set apart from a process by one's mathematical calculation of the laws underpinning it, the abnegation of voluntary motion was the same. On this reading, "concatenation" (*Verknüpfung*) and "abstraction" (*Abstraktion*) were oddly similar

9. The line appears in Goethe's work on the history of color theory and is cited in Warburg, *Heidnisch-antike Weissagung*, 71: "ein großer Teil dessen, was man gewöhnlich Aberglauben nennt, ist aus einer falschen Anwendung der Mathematik entstanden."
10. Warburg, "Orientalisierende Astrologie," in *Die Erneuerung*, 2:565.
11. Warburg, *Heidnisch-antike Weissagung*, 5.

in that they both involved a moving under the rule—even if this "moving under" was quite different in each case. With concatenation, moving under the rule was an embodied performance of the "case." With abstraction, one moved under the rule in attempting to state it. Thus, we see that Warburg's inheritance of the Dionysian-Apollonian distinction made famous by Nietzsche was structuring his sense of the ironies embedded in Renaissance astrology.

At this point in my paraphrase of Warburg's position, we must note the body habits of the Dionysian and the Apollonian. Elision of self into dance on the one hand and forgetfulness of self as a case sacrificed to the rule on the other—both were instances of self-abandonment. Even as they were radically different in a host of ways, both extremes of this spectrum extending from magic to mathematics depended fundamentally on a principle of equalization. Concatenation was a meeting the object halfway either by entering into a zone of indistinction with it by imitating it or, alternatively, by articulating oneself as its enemy, a counterforce, opposite but also equal to it. Such articulation of an enemy position was a stance taking, either defensive or offensive, attaching oneself to it. Warburg seems to have understood mathematics here primarily in terms of astronomical calculability, and such mathematics was an analysis of the systems of equilibrium structuring the cosmos. Planets circled the sun as soldiers circling an enemy. Orbit was encampment.

As we rehearse the grammatical presuppositions of the Warburgian gaze, we must note his strong impulse to trace and reveal tendencies to fall into good form, whether by means of imitation or by means of mathematical calculation. Warburg fetishized equilibrium and could claim that "an organization comes into being only when one will counterposes [*gleichsetzt*] itself to the will of another, constituting thereby a constancy of direction for the community."[12] This was a fetish in which the being of the community simply was the *complexio oppositorum* that contributed to "directional constancy." To look at art with Warburg, therefore, was to exercise sensitivities to the most complex *contrapposti* among human figures. Gestural reciprocity began to look like a leaning of wills, one against another, or a mirroring in which two appeared to become one. Such reciprocity might seem abstract, but it is there to see quite plainly in myriad Renaissance figural images where gestures balance or repeat each other. Images sutured themselves shut by depicting accumulated and synchronized response arrays.

The line of inquiry that led to regarding images as so many *complexiones*

---

12. Warburg, *Fragmente zur Ausdruckskunde*, §383 (March 24, 1899): "jede Organisation kommt nur dadurch zustande daß man sich mit dem Willen eines Anderen gleichsetzt und dadurch eine Richtungsconstante für die Gemeinschaft erhält."

oppositorum was a striking program, but the development of that perspicacity was not the heart of Warburg's project: beneath his fascination with equilibrium, Warburg was obsessed with captured and fleeting disequilibrium. The body convolutions of motions both proximate and incompatible, the almost-but-not-quite replication of similar but not identical gestures and poses, the refusal to reciprocate an offer squarely—these were the visual descriptions of imbalance in which Warburg was interested. Take the clearest example: Michelangelo's *Moses*. What oxymoron did Warburg choose while summarizing the piece? Answer: "the dynamics of rest" (*die Dynamik der Ruhe*). Warburg emphasized something like an interposed ego function: what Michelangelo had captured in the San Pietro in Vincoli Moses was "the individual detention of an encroaching moment, the pause between stimulus and action being saturated with a goal-setting tension."[13] Two actions—remaining and departing—were represented in the same body. This was a visual zeugma, for the leaving was sutured onto the staying like the staccato continuation that latches serially onto a verb's alternate significations.

In 1928, Warburg characterized the San Pietro in Vincoli *Moses* as the superimposition of two movements on one body, and we can understand his claim more precisely by reading it as a response to or a continuation of positions articulated by Erwin Panofsky about four years earlier. In his recently rediscovered habilitation on the principles of formation in Michelangelo and Raphael, Panofsky had reported the commonplace that Michelangelo was only really interested in representing "either 'constrained' or 'ratcheting' actions" (*entweder "gehemmte" oder "anhebende" Aktionen*). To that, Panofsky added a claim about how Michelangelo's *Moses* both constituted and broke out of a cubic space. Examining the sculpture, a rectangular column rises up in our imaginations from the base on which the sculpture sits. The right-angled volume of this column is confirmed by the shoulders and right knee of the seated figure. At the same time, however, the Euclidean space thereby conjured is disrupted and broken by the receding left leg. We find the index toe of that left leg wrapped around the plinth on which the artwork rests, as if the figure were trying to pull itself out of the composition. Our inferences should be that space itself is produced by the motions implied by body forms and that such endeavor can be understood as a contest between spatial grammars.

Moses was one conspicuous example of Warburg's developing notion that complexes of motion could be understood as intricate *staseis* (or "clinches") as well as constructions of space out of which new topographies might

---

13. Warburg, *Tagebuch*, 370: "die persönliche Beschlagnahme des nächsten Augenblicks; die Pause zwischen Antrieb und Handlung wird mit zielsetzender Spannung erfüllt."

emerge, but there were other such examples, each carving out its own concept. The Swiss psychiatrist Eugen Bleuler may have being coining a term in 1911 when he used the word *Ambivalenz* ("ambivalence"), but the body shot through with divergent desires for different imagined futures was also an established topos.[14] Warburg cited Medea. Ernst Gombrich, one of Warburg's successors as director of the Warburg Institute after World War II, added Ovid's famous phrasing of Medea's ambivalence: "I see the better, but I follow the worse."[15] We can add the beautiful ancient ekphrasis of Callistratus: "one could see the marble [of a Macedonian statue of Medea] now flashing passion in its eyes, now wearing a look sullen and softened into gloom."[16] Sullenness softening into gloom—here we have a momentous and massively subtle in-between. It evinces the faintest relaxing of a clenched jaw. As Warburg would say, self-separation was a specific cultural achievement. When he was thinking in this direction, he was revising a sentence he had taken from Vischer: "movement," which is to say initiation-of-motion and not simply being-in-motion, "always appears as a relationship between the forms of an individual body."[17] Animation often uses but does not in fact require multiple images. An image can animate a figure by combining multiple movements within a single frame.

To be sure, Medea was an extreme case, but a visual interest in the gaps between the various attributes predicated of a pictorial subject was common to representations of both the most extreme "struggle of the soul" (*Seelenkampf*) and the most subtly off-kilter "tightness in arrangement" (*concinnitas*). One might moralize the distance between *Seelenkampf* and *concinnitas*. One might, for instance, privilege the "naturalness" of Renaissance depictions of motion over the explicit, overexplicit, or mannerist quality of baroque gesture. Warburg's interest was more subtle than this, though. He looked to the absence of selfsameness that conjoined an entire spectrum of phenomena all the way from the soul riven against itself to the ensemble that was almost of a piece. If *concinnitas* was a rhetorical capacity to connect words and clauses skillfully, the painting that rejected such contexture or tightness of weave made a show of its cobbled-together and cento qualities: a collage of figural fragments drawn from different sources almost-but-not-quite woven together against their new background. One could render such a disheveled or motley variety either at the level of the individual figure or at the level of the ensemble of figures.

Subtler, certainly, than the riven Medea end of the spectrum was the

14. See Schoel-Glass, "Warburg's Late Comments," 637.
15. Ovid, *Metamorphoses*, 7.19–20: "video mediora proboque deteriora sequor."
16. Callistratus, *Descriptions*, 437.3–14.
17. Vischer, *Über das optische Formgefühl*, 49: "die Bewegung ist immer die Form der Beziehung zwischen den Formen der einzelnen Körper."

splay of attitudes toward conspiracy rendered in Rembrandt's *Claudius Civilis*, which Warburg categorized alongside the "the hesitating Medea" (*zögernde Medea*) as an icon of "the eternal Hamlet-problem of the riven conscience" (*ewigen Hamletproblem der Gewissensqual*). In Rembrandt's visualization of the Tacitean account of the first-century CE Batavian rebellion, a palpable reluctance to elide oneself into the common gesture of swearing an oath was worn on the bodies of the figures in the painting that pulled away from the center of the group portrait. This reluctance appeared in the diversity of eyes that were lowered and raised, focused and wan.[18] A species of *concinnitas* was achieved in the swords thrust together, but this motif of centralization underscored that overall the image resisted unification around that focal point. More conspicuous was the dislocated, splayed, privatizing effect produced by a loose and lopsided center of gravity that anchored the painting's great variety of orbits—some stable, some not.

Between the two worlds of equilibrium theorized by Warburg ("cultic idolizing concatenation" and "mathematical abstraction"), there existed imagination. More precisely, this imagination was *Witz*, a faculty allowing human beings to intuit connections—or rather motions—between the dissonant body positions one encountered in *Moses*, *Medea*, and *Claudius Civilis*. At one extreme, there was a state of indistinction between subject and object. This was imitation, mirroring, or camouflage. At the other extreme, one had a state of absolute distinction between nature and a mathematically informed knowledge of nature. This was the Apollonian antistrophe to Dionysus. In his specification of the term (which Warburg took up from the Romantic novelist Jean Paul's *Introduction to Aesthetics*), *Witz* was a capacity to find "relationships of similarity (that is, partial sameness) hidden beneath a greater difference [*Ungleichheit*]." In Cassirer's *Conceptual Form in Mythical Thinking* (published in 1922 among the Studies of the Warburg Library), this was "the true dialectical art" (*die eigentliche dialektische Kunst*), namely, "the art of cutting and connecting" (*die Kunst des Schneidens und des Verknüpfens*).[19] Once again, we are in the world of *ingenium* that Benjamin encountered in the baroque *Trauerspiel* redaction of rhetoric. *Witz* was "wit." Rather than humorousness itself, however, it was more essentially the quickness of mind that produced humor.

Witz was also, eventually, an engine of self-awareness. In the original version of a line from Jean Paul that Warburg cited and improvised on repeatedly, "constitutive wit" (*bildende Witz*) was a faculty that extended the characteristics of body to soul and the characteristics of soul to body.

18. Warburg Institute Archive (henceforth WIA), III.101.2.1, "Italienische Antike im Zeitalter Rembrandts," 1926, lecture held at the Kulturwissenschaftliche Bibliothek Warburg, May 29, 1926, 106.

19. Cassirer, *Begriffsform*, 1.

Originally, at a time "when 'I' and 'world' were still fused together" (*sich noch Ich und Welt verschmolz*), such *Witz* did not explicitly compare dissimilar things. Instead, it proclaimed sameness in a kind of metaphoric shorthand.[20] "You are nymph!" The nonliteralness of the trope would not be visible, and self-consciousness would then be in part a function of the realization that one's tropes were indeed tropes. *Witz* would eventually open up a space between I and world. And here we should invoke Christopher Johnson's excellent metaphor: Warburgian wit is "stereoscopic vision."[21] In a metaphor, two words qua images offer slightly different angles on the same phenomenon, and the images are laid over each other in such a way that the difference yields depth. On this account, self-consciousness is something like a capacity to close one eye at a time so that the stereoscopically generated image with depth and solidity can be understood as two separate elements intersecting at a certain distance.

In Warburg's opinion, Albrecht Dürer's engraving *Melencolia I* was to be perceived at a point of extreme ambivalence where falling into the world of actions at a distance combined simultaneously with recoiling from that world. In this ambivalence, one hovered between a consciousness of and an obliviousness toward one's own metaphorical identifications. Indebted to the art historian Karl Giehlow (who had been in play for Benjamin too), Warburg viewed this image through a motif of "the power of concentration" (*Konzentrationskraft*) that was both physical and spiritual. In Dürer's image, he saw a physical drawing back from an object combined with a compacting of the physical apparatus of the thinker that accompanied a spiritual gathering together and then explosion of imaginative forces.[22] On the one hand, *Witz* was emblematic of the human mind's impressionability, its weakness, and its liability to be overwritten by the similitudes of the world. Here, *Witz* was the kind of thing that might be diagnosed. On the other hand, *Witz* also marked the human mind's capacity to redescribe such impressionability as its own genius.

In taking up Dürer's copper engraving as an emblem of *Witz*, Warburg was in effect—if unintentionally—attaching his research program to the topoi of melancholy and magnanimity as imaginative and topical domains that we have seen Warburg's Weimar contemporaries exploring in a number of ways. In their famous 1923 treatment of *Melencolia I*, Erwin Panofsky and Fritz Saxl articulated how Dürer's image brought together in a single frame the bipolar extremes of a melancholy that was simultaneously "gloom and

---

20. Paul, *Vorschule der Aesthetik*, 2:295.

21. Johnson, *Memory*, 84.

22. Consider Warburg, "Planetenbilder," in *Werke*, 369. And compare one of the texts from which Warburg took a great deal of inspiration—namely, Giehlow, "Dürers Stich *Melencolia I*," 37.

creative arousal" (*Trübsinn und schöpferische Erwecktheit*).[23] Indeed, on account of this paradoxical self-possessed impressionability (said Warburg in the Luther essay), we should think of Dürer's *Melencolia* as a "symbol of the humanist Renaissance."[24] Warburg claimed that "the essence of the process of renewal" (*das Wesen des Erneuerungsprozesses*) was itself visible in Dürer's engraving because of its extremely acute attention to adopting past and received modes for the purpose of transforming them.[25] Creativity, the script ran, must risk extreme derivativeness if it is to do something genuinely new. It must begin by exercising in a culture's topoi.

By emphasizing the point in Warburg where imagination mediated between Dionysus and Apollo (that is, between elision into embodiment and the abstraction of forms), I am seeking to make the moment of Warburgian freedom available for further scrutiny. How was this freedom figured? Was it a decision? An action? An autonomy? None of the above. Freedom was "a power of finding or discovering" (*Erfindungskraft*). After all, when the Renaissance art theorist Leon Battista Alberti had recommended that painters keep company with poets and orators, he had been arguing that painters would thereby learn invention and composition. When Warburg's teacher and Alberti's nineteenth-century editor Hubert Janitschek commented on this, he emphasized Alberti's choice of "grace" (*Anmut* or *Gratia*) over "mere agreeableness" (*blosse Gefälligkeit*) as the core element of "beauty" (*Schönheit*).[26] According to Janitschek, Alberti had turned to Cicero at this moment: beauty was both *gratia* and *dignitas*, the one more feminine, the other more masculine.[27] All—and this is a crucial point—were issues of inventive compositioning. Flat-footed concepts of freedom as a simple choice to absent oneself from immediate causal intrication must be avoided when paraphrasing Warburg. After all, his precisely *contextual* method of art-historical inquiry was an alternative to what he called "the conventional account of genius [as] a willed turning away from present context."[28] There were neither simple "freedoms from" nor simple "freedoms to." There were instead complex "variations of relation with."

The account of freedom in terms of *Erfindungskraft* that Warburg was offering might seem paradoxical. The alignment of freedom with imagined possibility and not, for instance, with decision meant that freedom began

23. Panofsky and Saxl, *Durer's "Melencolia I,"* 71–72.

24. Warburg, *Heidnisch-antike Weissagung*, 63.

25. Warburg, 62.

26. Janitschek, introduction to *Kleinere Kunsttheoretische Schriften*, xviii.

27. Cicero, *De officiis*, 1.36.

28. WIA, III.75.3.1, "Einführung in die Kultur der florentinischen (in die italinische) Frührenaissance," lectures, Hamburg, WS 1908–9, Lecture III, "Donatello/Pollaiuolo," 34–35: "die landläufige Doktrin vom Genie" as "das gewolte Abkehre vom realen Zusammenhang."

to look like confusion. Dürer's freedom, after all, was no happy, joyous, or ecstatic moment. And Warburg's counterposition of "classical unrest" (*klassische Unruhe*) to the Winkelmannian topos concerning "classical repose" (*klassische Ruhe*) expressed a concern with something that genuinely was at the limits of representability.[29] Both stasis and kinesis could be modes of "rest" (*Ruhe*). As we saw above in the discussion of Michelangelo's *Moses*, only the *beginning* or the *ending* of motion genuinely represented "unrest" (*Unruhe*). Genuine unrest was only the changing of a speed, a direction, or a state. It was not a new direction peacefully achieved and then predictable in its now established trajectory or rhythm. In this way, if it had phased out improvisation, even dance could be rest.

One can parse Warburg as proposing that the true purpose of art was to practice (and make publicly available) a form of attention that would reveal moments of freedom understood as the simultaneity of multiple visualized possibilities. Warburg had encountered ideas like this in the work of Robert Vischer. There, the topos was expressed in the following terms: "art encounters its highest purpose in the depiction of a deeply moved conflict of forces."[30] And the baseline corollary in Vischer was the simple assertion that "art is a potentialization of sensuousness."[31] It was not that art would provide the exemplars for a mind to use when snapping its experiences into good form. "Potentialization" referred not only to an equipping of the senses with exemplars. It referred also to a capacitation of the senses in which multiple different, conflicting, mutually exclusive continuations might be simultaneously attached to a particular visual field.

The visualization of multiple possibilities was sensitivity, and it was also freedom from the apparent strictures of the well-made context. In reality, the well-made context would not be one in which fate demanded only one outcome. Intensity of context actually registered plurality. And intensity of context was the coexistence of multiple scenes in one. As Warburg once put it (when articulating his contextual art-historical method), such multiplicity was like a position in chess that could only be understood as the overlaying of multiple possible future games.[32] For this reason, Warburg had been fascinated by the means of specifying context in his Luther essay. Conjunction was an astrological shorthand for the concatenation of influences, like so many chess pieces threatening a particular square. *Witz* was a commitment to perceiving the greatest possible number of influences for any given conjunction. The task was to make oneself as vulnerable as possible to external

29. Warburg, "Eintritt des antikisierenden Idealstils," in *Die Erneuerung*, 1:176.
30. Vischer, *Über das optische Formgefühl*, 48: "die Kunst sieht aber ihr höchstes Ziel darin, einen bewegten Conflikt von Kräften darzustellen."
31. Vischer, 48: "die Kunst ist . . . eine Potenzirung [*sic*] der Sinnlichkeit."
32. WIA, Family Correspondence, Aby Warburg to Max Warburg, June 30, 1900.

influence so that one might take up those powers, subsume them, and then turn them to one's own purposes by naming them in new ways. It is to naming that we turn next, but, somewhat unusually, we shall have to examine it in the context of ornamentation. Why? Because ornament spurred Warburg to push further into the superimposition of two images that was metaphor. Strange as it may sound, this too will be essential to the account of freedom being articulated here.

ORNAMENTATION IN 1923 AND ITS SIGNIFICANCE

When he said that "style" (*Stil*) informed the phrase *restitutio eloquentiae* (which as we saw he was considering as a title for the image atlas), Warburg was implying that variability of presentation was at the core of his interests. Style was not only the mode of composition that was recognizable from one expression to another—as "personal style." It was also the variety of ways in which a particular performance might be executed, and rhetoricians had traditionally analyzed this phenomenon under the heading of *elocutio*. "Style" was literary formalist code for shapeshifting, and facility in variation sometimes appeared to be the same thing as treacherousness. Ornamentation came to be understood as something that could be thrown on or thrown off like a garment. For this reason, it seemed opportunistic and potentially faithless. In this section, I lay out a sequence of thoughts mapping Warburg's interest in how phenomena might or might not exhibit ornamentation. As I read his thought, an extreme absence of ornamentation had a divine purity that was ultimately dangerous. Something lacked ornament if it was purely itself. Expressed in terms I have used before, whatever lacked ornamentation of any kind defined itself in appearing. This, to repeat, was the "deity of extreme interpellation" (*Augenblicksgott*). Warburg was fearful of the necessity in appearance that led to necessity in response. For him, ornamentation was something like the achievement of a cognitive and spiritual freedom. The engine of this achievement was iterated recognition of potential vicissitude in a phenomenon's appearance. I shall argue that ultimately this freedom was a function of what Warburg termed *Denkraum*. Rendered literally, this term denoted "thought-space." In my heterodox reading, *Denkraum* qua freedom was generated by recognizing a series of spaces within an appearance itself—between, that is, the qualities of that predication. Once again, in order to prepare the ground for laying out this argument, I situate my line of inquiry in a very particular moment within the life and thought of Aby Warburg. I begin in that moment, and I build from there.

On September 26, 1923, the day that Germany called off passive resistance to French occupation of the Ruhr, Aby Warburg wrote to his wife, Mary, from the Swiss sanatorium in which he had been living for over two years. Initially, Warburg had been diagnosed as suffering from dementia praecox, or schizophrenia. In February 1923, the German psychiatrist Emil Kraepelin offered a revised diagnosis of "manic-depressive mixed state."[33] Warburg said that he felt his life was ebbing away and that his personal situation was connected with the broader political one.[34] It can be tempting to see Warburg's feeling as an example of exactly the kind of "astrological" thinking from which he had been trying to distance himself in the Luther essay. Perceived similitudes between microcosm and macrocosm raised potentially nonsensical questions of causality. "Weimar and Warburg seem to be falling apart," the hypothesis might begin. The inferences might continue with questions such as "Has the one caused the other?" and "If so, which is the cause; which, the effect?" At issue would be the indistinguishability of historical process and individual circumstance. Either the misplaced conceit of a microhistorian or the projection of a megalomaniac, Warburg's comment might seem to represent a potentially paranoid underside to his famous (perhaps cribbed) dictum "God is in the details." In July 1921 (a few months after having been admitted), Warburg described his illness in a letter addressed to the administrator of the Bellevue Sanatorium. There, he relayed that he had lost "the capacity to make connections between things in terms of their simple causal relations."[35] He did not mean that everything had disintegrated into a chaos of mutual indifference. He meant instead that his desire to perceive cause was overwhelming. It was as if the category of the "the accidental" (*zufällig*) had been evacuated and as if, as a result, a deep-set cause had to be discovered for every coincidence.

Whatever the status of his observation (and irrespective of whether we regard it as an insight, a symptom, or both), the point to underscore here is that one of the backgrounds against which Warburg's famous 1923 lecture on Pueblo Indians delivered in Kreuzlingen can be understood was the Ruhr crisis and the generalized experience of crisis that the collapse of the German mark precipitated. The point is not to fantasize about causal relationships between crisis and talk. Nor is it important here to ask whether Warburg himself consciously intended his talk to be a response to contemporary German circumstances. There is some evidence of that, but it is relatively generic and chiefly consists of oft-quoted statements, such as talk of "the duty" of "even the weakest" to strengthen "the will to cosmic order" in "the present age of chaotic disintegration."[36] More crucial

33. Binswanger and Warburg, *Die unendliche Heilung*, 76.
34. WIA, General Correspondence, Aby Warburg to Mary Warburg, September 26, 1923.
35. Binswanger and Warburg, *Die unendliche Heilung*, 99–100: "ich die Fähigkeit, die Dinge in ihren einfachen Kausalitätsverhältnissen zu verknüpfen, verliere."
36. Warburg, "Reise-Erinnerungen," in *Werke*, 573: "in dieser Epoche eines chaotischen Untergangs auch der Schwächste verpflichtet ist, den Willen zur kosmischen Ordnung zu verstärken."

for me is the following question: what could others reasonably have taken Warburg's lecture to mean within the context in which it appeared?

The Kreuzlingen talk took place on April 21, 1923, and it dealt with Warburg's memories of a journey he had taken to the United States in 1895–1896 with particular attention to his time in Oraibi, Arizona. Soon after his return to Europe in early 1897, Warburg had spoken about the trip to audiences in Hamburg and Berlin. He had said that "what led me, as an art historian, to visit [Arizona] was the sense that nowhere was the connection between pagan-religious representations and artistic activity so specifiable as here."[37] This aspect of Warburg's thought has to be read against the background of European colonial practices in the late nineteenth and early twentieth centuries. Equally, we can see here that Warburg's approach to art was not high connoisseurial but rather anthropological, for he sought to think through the broader implication of art practices for life and for the organization of community.

Twenty-six years later in 1923, Warburg's situation was very different. At that point (the story goes), giving the talk was to be part of demonstrating that he had recovered and might leave Bellevue. Recalling the talk in a letter from April 1924, Warburg said that he spoke extempore for an hour and a half. There does not seem to be any genuinely verbatim record of the event, but there are two quite distinct typescripts with manuscript corrections that give us a sense of Warburg's thoughts.[38] (The two texts appeared in print side by side for the first time in 2010.[39]) By 1923, Warburg's articulation of his motivation in making the journey to Arizona had changed. This time, "as a cultural historian," he was fascinated that "an enclave of primitive pagan humanity could survive" in "the middle of a land that had made technical culture into an amazing precision-weapon in the hands of intellectual men."[40] This phrasing is close to colonial anthropological boilerplate, but Warburg quickly specified the interest further: "to us this proximity of fantastical magic and sober instrumentalization seems like the symptom of a fissure." And he went on to say that "for the Indian, however, [the fissure] is not a 'schizoid' but, on the contrary, a freeing and self-evident experience

37. Warburg, "Reise," in *Werke*, 508: "was mich, als Kunsthistoriker, nun gerade die Gruppe der Pueblo Indianer in New-Mexiko und Arizona zu besuchen veranlaßte, war daß der Zusammenhang zwischen heidnisch-religiösen Vorstellungen und künstlerischer Thätigkeit nirgends besser erkennbar ist, als bei den Pueblo Indianern."
38. See WIA, III.93.1, "Bilder aus dem Gebiet der Pueblo-Indianer in Nord Amerika," and WIA, III.93.4.1.
39. Compare Warburg, "Bilder" to "Reise-Erinnerungen," in *Werke*.
40. Warburg, "Bilder," in *Werke*, 525: "Was mich als Kulturhistoriker interessierte, war, dass inmitten eines Landes, das die technische Kultur zu einer bewundernswerten Präzisions-Waffe in der Hand des intellektuellen Menschen gemacht hatte, eine Enklave primitiven heidnischen Menschentums sich erhalten konnte."

of the boundless interrelatability of man and environment."[41] Here we see the beginning of the problem that I wish to explore in this section. The task of the symbolic was to forge a space between "man and environment" (*Mensch und Welt*). The symbolic was a function of the ornamental. In turn, the ornamental was an antonym of necessity and a species of the accidental.

Once again (as in the Luther essay), one of Warburg's basic concerns was oscillation between, on the one hand, a complete coincidence of two phenomena that fell somehow into a kind of lockstep with each other and, on the other, a partial dislocation of two phenomena such that they could establish a relationship of counterbalance. In one of the subtitles to the Kreuzlingen talk, Warburg's terms for these two processes were "embodiment" (*Verleibung*) and "conflict" in the mode of an originally embodied "setting-out-against-one-another" (*Auseinandersetzung*). We may visualize this distinction by appropriating one of the earliest objects of Warburg's art-historical interest—namely, "animated accessory" (*bewegtes Beiwerk*). This was the phrase Warburg had used in his 1893 dissertation on Botticelli's *Primavera* and *Birth of Venus*. It carved out an interest in motions registered by seemingly inconsequential addenda such as hair or clothing. On the account Warburg was giving in 1923, "conflict" (*Auseinandersetzung*) was the pendulum sway recorded by clothing that hung loose on the limb. This might be, for example, the ancient nymph in her diaphanous garb; the pendulum sway was the movement of her clothing. At first, in the motion of a limb, loose garb would be left behind. Then, when the limb decelerated and came to a halt, the fabric would spill over and reach out "ahead" of the limb. "Animated accessory" was, thus, a marker of acceleration and deceleration.

An apparent isomorphism of garment and limb would reemerge when motion ceased and as the garment eventually settled back into line with the limb, and this apparent isomorphism was "embodiment" (*Verleibung*), or a state of indistinction between body and ornament. One level deeper, this was an indistinction between spirit and body qua potentiality and actuality. Such indistinction might become conspicuous in the nude figure that was entirely and seamlessly of a piece. This would be a figure devoid of the slightest trace of being ahead of or behind itself. Here, for instance, we have the sheer vertical simplicity of the sixth-century BCE kouros at the Cleveland Museum of Art, which is complicated only by an almost imperceptible turn of the hips. Alternatively, we have here the perfect unhurried and unhesitating rhythm of Myron's *Diskobolus*. As Warburg understood it,

41. Warburg, 525: "uns erscheint dieses Nebeneinander von fantastischer Magie und nüchternem Zwecktun als Symptom der Zerspaltung, für den Indianer ist es nicht 'schizoid,' im Gegenteil, ein befreiendes selbstverständliches Erlebnis der schrankenlosen Beziehungsmöglichkeit zwischen Mensch und Umwelt."

there were three basic possibilities with regard to motion: one could be out in front of it, one could be behind it, or one could be alongside and identical with it. As we saw above, "imitation" (*Nachahmung*) was "a relationship to the object that stands between carrying and being carried," and we may add here that "carrying" will emerge under conditions of acceleration while "being carried" describes the part of a body fighting to decelerate the whole.

For Warburg, this distinction between "embodiment" (*Verleibung*) and "setting-out-against-one-another" (*Auseinandersetzung*) underwrote a further distinction between "imitation" (*Nachahmung*) and "symbolism" (*Symbolismus*). Imitation aimed at replication allied with an inability to differentiate between original and copy. Following the word's Greek etymology, *symbolism* was something like a collision. It was a dissonance or distance between an occurrence and one or more of its features. In symbolism, some aspect of a motion took on a distance from the context in which it appeared. This aspect raised itself up as a question posed to the faculty of attention. "Conspicuousness" occasions attention. Such symbolic appearance had a way of saying, "Yes, you see me here, but what is it, do you think, that I am saying to you?" In this way, the symbol or the symptom or the tell was above all else a question.

We begin to grasp Warburg's understanding of symbolism when we take up the example that fascinated him in the Kreuzlingen talk—namely, the snake, a symbol with several denotations. As a lightning bolt snaking down from the heavens in a way that was maximally in motion and maximally targeted, the snake form might pinpoint and thus represent the singularity of an event.[42] Alternatively, the snake devouring its own tail might figure time not as event but as cycle, standing in as a "symbol for the rhythm of time."[43] Yet the snake shedding its own skin might also dramatize a primordial act of self-separation, representing thereby ornamentation itself. After all, ornament was a certain conspicuousness of being superfluous. It isolated the merely contingent and thus optional elements subjoined to a more fundamental entity. Whatever was extraneous and ready to be shed was ornamental. One might even say that this was a special case of "setting out against" (*Auseinandersetzung*). Ornament was an *Auseinandersetzung* that seemed to have become incongruous, detached, superfluous, slack, or limp.

Just so, Warburg was conjuring the Native Americans of his talk as "palimpsests."[44] That is, to him they were surfaces or screens on which one could differentiate distinct layerings of text, like the double set of markings

---

42. Warburg, "Reise-Erinnerungen," in *Werke*, 574: "ein Maximum der Bewegung und ein Minimum der Angriffsfläche."
43. Warburg, "Bilder" in *Werke*, 536: "das Symbol für den Rhythmus der Zeit."
44. Warburg, "Reise-Erinnerungen," in *Werke*, 572.

one might perceive on a snake in the process of shedding its skin. In the Warburgian imagination, the people of Oraibi were human beings whose very surfaces and movements bore witness to different substrates. These substrates were historical ages (the primordial, the modern) or educational inheritances (traditional, early modern Catholic, modern American). Native Americans were not Myron's *Diskobolus* but rather Euripides's Medea in Warburg's account. They were, precisely, *not* selfsame. Among (and, indeed, within) these people, *concinnitas* had been riven and was at odds with itself. This was what Warburg was getting at while discussing an observation made by the American anthropologist Frank Hamilton Cushing. They had met before Warburg's visit to Oraibi, and Cushing had relayed to Warburg what he cast as the Native American belief that human beings were distinguishable from other animals precisely on account of their *imperfection*. Where the human being—one might say—would be adorned with a variety of merely average, motley, and alienable attributes, the antelope simply *was* running (*ist nur Laufen*).[45] The antelope's perfection, on this account, lay in the indistinguishability of its being from its performance. The antelope simply was one of the living definitions and visible names of running.

Indistinguishability between being and performance had characterized the concept of *Augenblicksgott* that Warburg took from the German philologist Hermann Usener. Warburg had studied Usener's concept closely, but the degree to which he was aware of its longer history is unclear. Nevertheless, that intellectual history is highly instructive. It went back through Usener to the nineteenth-century Italian thinker Tito Vignoli and through Vignoli to none other than, once again, Giambattista Vico. Indistinguishability of being and manifestation at this juncture constituted a certain kind of necessitarianism. Expressed in a philosophical idiom, this form of necessity implied "analyticity" (where a predicate expresses no more and no less than what is contained in the concept of a subject). The moments of greatest necessity would be the moments at which all the predicates of an appearance were analytic rather than synthetic so that each and every quality took its place in the definition of the entity appearing. In the Luther essay, planetary conjunctions had been the moments at which necessity was greatest. Just so, Warburg described these fleeting intersections of the stellar cycle as *Augenblicksgötter*.[46]

Warburg's conception of these "deities of extreme interpellation" was the creative confection of several different instantiations of the idea. In Usener's classic account, the *Augenblicksgott* had named the point at which

45. Warburg, 573.
46. Warburg, *Heidnisch-antike Weissagung*, 28.

"the momentary sensation of a thing before us . . . measures out the situation in which we find ourselves, the force-matrix that surprises us, and the magnitude and power of a divinity."[47] Whatever appears as itself, without remainder and without need of supplement—this would be divinity. Analyticity was a feature of divinity, which could do nothing in its acts other than state unequivocally the nature of its being. In turn, when Ernst Cassirer glossed Usener's formulation, he denied that the *Augenblicksgott* appeared "as part of a power that can manifest itself here and there, in various places, at various times or in various subjects, manifold and yet simultaneous." He asserted instead that the *Augenblicksgott* was something that is "present before a single subject only here and now, in the single undivided moment of experience."[48] This, he said, was "a necessity of the moment" (*Not des Augenblicks*).[49] What this established in Warburg was a kind of notional limit case: the moment of absolute selfsameness was a name and definition, but it was also a personalized name and definition that would function in the manner of an interpellation.

In another sense, however, the overwhelming presence of the *Augenblicksgott* implied not only the indistinguishability of being and performance but also paradoxically its opposite—namely, absence. That is, presence that overwhelmed the parameters of the senses implied the existence of domains in which that presence was continued. These were domains that, at the crucial moment, absented themselves from the senses. Paradigmatically, overwhelming presence raised the question of causation for Warburg. The outsize event occasioned the question, "Why, what lies behind the event, as its cause, and what lies in front of the event—as its effect and its potential purpose?" This was an idea that Warburg confected from Vignoli's *Myth and Science*. Like Vignoli, Warburg insisted on an originary unity between myth and science, because the *Augenblicksgott* was simultaneously an expression of extreme presence and a movement beyond presence that raised the question of causation. For Vignoli, anthropomorphic extensions of human desire and purpose to natural processes was the original cognitive

47. Usener, *Götternamen*, 280: "wenn die augenblickliche empfindung dem dinge vor uns, das uns die unmittelbare nähe einer gottheit zu bewusstsein bringt, dem zustand in dem wir uns befinden, der kraftwirkung die uns überrascht, den werth und das vermögen einer gottheit zumisst, dann ist der augenblicksgott empfunden und geschaffen" (unusually, the German eschews capitalization here).
48. Cassirer, *Sprache und Mythos*, 15: "steht vor uns in unmittelbarer Einzelheit und Einzigkeit; nicht als Teil einer Kraft, die sich hier und dort, die sich an verschiedenen Orten des Raums, die sich zu verschiedenen Zeitpunkten und in verschiedenen Subjekten vielfältig und doch gleichartig offenbaren kann, sondern als etwas, was nur hier und jetzt, in dem einen ungeteilten Moment des Erlebens dem einen Subjekt gegenwärtig ist und das es mit dieser seiner Gegenwart überfällt und in seinen Bann zieht."
49. Cassirer, 51.

genius. To him, this meant that science as a disciplined process of inquiry was a "depersonalization of myth" (*spersonificazione del mito*).[50]

Fear was the great protoscientific emotion in Vignoli's account, and this meant that interpellation and research were twins. Earlier, the ur-event had been thunder and lightning in Vico. Indeed, the lightning bolt was the first word, because it was the first sign in the Neapolitan's conjectural history of human origins. In Warburg's nineteenth-century sources, the archetypal semiotic events that called such metonymic imagination into being were rather more mundane. Not the lightning bolt but the dog startled by the parasol that seemed to flutter of its own accord was the moment that awoke life to the question of causation. This was Darwin's example. Vignoli's was the horse spooked by a handkerchief flickering above a hedge.[51] Warburg himself took up the door that slammed in a draft.[52] The isolated effect required a cause. The imagination underwrote the effect with a purposive will. And scientific hypothesis could then develop its varieties of impersonalization. Warburg's thought was structured by an oscillation between interpellation and impersonalization. The lightning bolt, the parasol, the handkerchief, and the door were so many interpellation machines exercising "defensive imagination" (*Abwehrphantasie*). Such machines captivated their human marks, saying to those credulous souls continually, as it were, "I am an event that expresses a purpose, and somehow you are a component of that purpose."[53]

We encounter a crucial turn in the argument right here, for equal and opposite to "defensive imagination" (*Abwehrphantasie*) was the fundamental Warburgian concept of "thought-space" (*Denkraum*). Because any translation of *Denkraum* would already be a specific hypothesis and because I need to hold open a space for an original interpretation, I refrain from translation and simply use the German term. Paraphrasing the concept, we can say that *Denkraum* was a power of resisting the urge to respond to every stimulus as exclusively either a threat or an opportunity. Ventriloquizing the impersonalization machine of *Denkraum*, we can have it say in response to *Abwehrphantasie*, "This purpose you pretend to announce is not the unique effect of some consciously conceived action; it is instead one of many such effects patterned and sculpted by forces that display a regularity and indifference to individua that is characteristic of law." According to Warburg, escaping an infinite repetition of the question "How does that threaten me?" was in fact one of the fundamental tasks of civilization.

50. Vignoli, *Mito e scienza*, 171. In turn, Vignoli's account of the anthropomorphic imagination was fundamentally Vichian. Vico's *fisica poetica* is cited on the same page.
51. Darwin, *Descent of Man*, 1:67. Vignoli, *Mito e scienza*, 49.
52. Warburg, "Reise-Erinnerungen," in *Werke*, 578.
53. Warburg, 578.

We are bordering on received thoughts here, and we have to think *Denkraum* both carefully and afresh. Traditionally, scholars have spoken about the concept of *Denkraum* in terms of the opening of a "gap" (again, an *Auseinandersetzung*) in perception between subject and object.[54] A fair number of sentences written by Warburg do license this reading. This gap is said to be a space "between human being and environment" (*zwischen Mensch und Umwelt*), "between subject and object" (*zwischen Subjekt und Objekt*), "between stimulus and response" (*zwischen Antrieb und Handlung*).[55] *Denkraum* is like the space implied by "a severed umbilical cord" (*durchschnittenen Nabelschnur*). Alternatively, it may be a "center of hesitation" (*Centrum der Verzögerung*) located fitfully in the various sense spaces opened up by hand (the reachable), eye (the seeable), and mouth (the nameable).[56] On this account, *Denkraum* overcame fear by establishing a distance between event and subject such that not every happenstance connoted imminent danger.

Let me press the point, however. What kind of space is really being called out by the term, *Denkraum*? We need not say that a subject backing away from an object by which it feels interpellated has opened up a *literal* space. I propose that we speak of decontextualization rather than the opening up of a gap. This seems like a non sequitur. It is not. As the newborn is separated from its mother, so the "I" absents itself from its immediate environment. The interpenetration of circulatory systems is ended, and the infant is established as a distinct entity. It becomes *absent* in some important way. Barely at first, increasingly with time. More than hand and more than eye, mouth effects decontextualization. That is to say, beyond the kinesphere of locations a body can reach and beyond the "eyeshot" of things a body can see, the mouth and its words fill hand and eye with imagined sensations of absent things.

My suggestion is that we read the "space" in Warburgian *Denkraum* as an expanding of the distances between the qualities of a phenomenon. Expansion here is an unraveling or decoupling of these qualities. There was an important sense in which the distance being created with *Denkraum* existed not between the subject and object but rather between the predicates registering in the object of perception itself. If it were nonessential to the

54. Surveying the field, consider the following paraphrases of *Denkraum*: Wedepohl, "'Wort und Bild,'" 44: "Distanz zwischen Individuum und Außenwelt"; Wedepohl, "Pathos, Polarität, Distanz, Denkraum," 17: "ein gewisses 'Ferngefühl' zwischen dem Menschen und seiner Umwelt"; Hensel, *Wie aus der Kunstgeschichte*, 64: "die Folge eines Schaffens von Distanz zu den Phänomenen"; Efal, *Figural Philology*, 85: "the manner in which artworks serve as a distancing instrument between man and the forces of nature."
55. Warburg, "Bilder," and "Reise-Erinnerungen," in *Werke*, 561, 575; *Tagebuch*, 370.
56. Warburg, "Reise-Erinnerungen," in *Werke*, 575; *Tagebuch*, 548.

definition of the whole, then a quality would become "distant" from the other qualities with which it was being predicated. If a being were identical with a performance (in the sense that the antelope *was* running), then the being and the performance would not so much represent each other as *be* each other. *Denkraum* was a form of freedom because it permitted human beings to escape the kind of impressionability that insisted every aspect of a sensory experience was essential to the being of the *Augenblicksgott* manifested therein. *Denkraum* was a freedom to decree some or all aspects of an appearance merely incidental, contingent, and therefore not immediately pressing. *Denkraum*—and I cannot emphasize this enough—was an achievement of the feeling that an experience was underdetermined. Like the *Moses*, the *Medea*, and the *Claudius Civilis* discussed above, it layered predicates whose relevance for each other was somehow open: woven but loosely so.

How can one account for the double meaning of the term, *Denkraum*, as a space between subject and object on the one hand and as a space between the predicates of an appearance on the other? The response emphasizes Warburg's description of "embodiment" (*Verleibung*) as the "logical act of primitive culture."[57] Rendering oneself indistinguishable from an object was a way of understanding that object. That is, replicating the aggregate of an object's qualities—confecting its *concinnitas* as best one could—was a form of "reverse engineering" that allowed one to comprehend something. Each reenactment would be a hypothesis about how a phenomenon works. Embodiment was comparable to the bringing into being of a simple sentence: "This here is that there." Alternatively, we might make that sentence more explicit as "Witness my performance, for I am the object." In its original version, this sentence would have possessed an entirely implicit copula. That is, there would be no verb of predication. All one would have would be two phenomena resembling each other. Indeed, at the most primitive extreme, one would have simply a single undifferentiated phenomenon. This would be the wide-reaching and distributed resonance of dance.

Dance exemplified the way in which predication might take place in the absence of the kind of discursive move heralded by verbs of predication. Dance would be a zone in which the differentiation of individual figures or individual exchanges of call and response would be a late, relatively inessential, post-Dionysian move. Insertion of the copula would be a serial and (as metaphor became simile) ultimately figurative recognition of the difference between the imitating subject and the imitated object, resemblance notwithstanding. For this reason, the process of *Denkraum* was achieved in the moment of registering the nonidentity of imitating subject and imitated

57. Warburg, "Reise-Erinnerungen," in *Werke*, 590: "logischer Akt der primitiven Kultur."

object. Insofar as *core* functions of the object could be more or less successfully replicated by recalcitrantly nonidentical subjects, one began to see that there was a distinction between essential and nonessential qualities. In the context of moderately successful *Verleibung*—say, the embodiment that was a reenactment—the difference between subject and object *was* the distance between the object and its nonessential qualities.

As we have seen in a number of different ways in this book, the systole and diastole of thought was *ingenium* and *iudicium*, which we can now read as a capacity to perceive connections among qualities paired with an equal and opposite capacity to liberate oneself piecemeal from those imputed identities. This was Cassirer's genuinely dialectical art, and it was what Warburg was getting at when he described the human being as both "an animal that handles" (*ein hantierendes Tier*) and an animal that finds its "actualization" (*Betätigung*) in "connecting and dividing" (*Verknüpfen und Trennen*).[58] One picked up tools, one partook in particular activities, one adorned oneself in particular ways. And one could divest oneself of this "predicative accoutrement" too. Indeed, we can say that Thomas Carlyle's *Sartor Resartus* was one of Warburg's core texts precisely because it presented modernity as a massive oscillation between the adorned and the unadorned. For Carlyle (the great nineteenth-century polemicist), modernity was something like an endless process of accruing and eschewing qualities. On the one side (as he put it), there was "the Dandy," a being who was predicated and outfitted with every possible exorbitance. On the other side, there was "the monster UTILITARIA," which Carlyle was figuring as a historical force constantly at work in stripping a thing down to its purest and merest functioning.[59] Glossing Carlyle, Warburg said that the human being was not simply a "wielding" (*hantierendes*) animal but also "a 'carrying' animal" (*ein "tragendes" Tier*). That is, the human animal not only "handles" but also "accessorizes."[60] After the collecting came the lugging. Just so, periods of accretion would be followed by periods of evisceration—and vice versa. One hoards, one clears out, and then one hoards again.

"Ornament" (*Schmuck*) was a figure for possibility in Warburg. In ornament, one recognized that there would be a corresponding array of attendant possibilities for presentation for any given particular. Here we have the beginnings of a thought that is essential to rhetorical inquiry. And if we never find any discussion of the rhetorical office of *elocutio* among the records of Warburg's thinking that we possess, the pertinence to rhetorical inquiry is not reduced. Fleshing out these beginnings, we have the following

58. Warburg, "Reise-Erinnerungen," in *Werke*, 580.
59. Carlyle, *Sartor Resartus*, 163 (for Utilitaria), 188 (for the Dandy), 191, 198 (for the struggle between "Dandyism and Drudgism").
60. Warburg, *Fragmente zur Ausdruckskunde*, §162 (March 22, 1891).

insight: *elocutio* is not an essentially paradiastolic practice of making the black seem white and the white seem black; *elocutio* is freedom qua indeterminacy. Within the Warburgian frame, ornament was antinecessitarian by its very nature. Ornament was a category denoting all that which could be taken on or thrown off even as a thing remained essentially itself. True, Gottfried Semper, the preeminent nineteenth-century theorist of *Schmuck* (whom Warburg read closely), emphasized the identity in Greek of the cosmic (the perfect and circular motions of the heavens) and the cosmetic (the ornamental), as if to stake a claim for the intrication of being and beauty.[61] But not all theories of the rule would insist that the rule must precede the case, and not all theories of the case would insist—in the manner of the *Augenblicksgott*—that all individua are paradigms.

To Warburg's way of thinking, ornament revealed itself in the variability of mimetic performances. Paradigmatically, ornament was the variety of masks one might wear in a multitude of rituals, but it also revealed itself in invariability. Continuing to wear a mask inappropriately from one ritual *into* the next would be a way of calling attention to the mask as a mask. Within the bounds of art history proper, ornamentation would be distinguished by repeatability: with its reproducible geometric patterning, the frieze was ornament in one of its purest forms. This is why we might more ordinarily assume that a Semper line of inquiry would think of repetition as an antonym of freedom. After all, the frieze connoted machinic repetition. How could this be an emblem of freedom? Warburg's finessing of the paradox was unusually precise. As he put it, "the repetition of a movement in itself fixed and framed [*einer an sich characterischen Bewegungsfixation*] without connection to the real individual leads to ornament."[62] Knotwork, one might say, was a kind of material mathematization of dance in which all trace of individual dancers had been effaced. And on this account the accoutrement gestures of social posturing were so many moments of decorative embroidery.

Social situations might be infinitely variable, but the social codings of those situations would not be, and this was the lesson taught by the core Warburgian concept of "pathos-formula" (*Pathosformel*). Static representations of dynamic states such as passions would contribute to the recognizability of emotions by encoding a certain "specification of perimeter" (*Umfangsbestimmung*). Yet the pictorial encoding of such affective exposures tended always toward mannerism because the specification of range, volume, or perimeter (*Umfang*) was *as a matter of necessity* a process of decontextualizing an object from the situation that, in point of fact, defined it. In Warburg's

---

61. Semper, *Gesetzmäßigkeit des Schmuckes*, 5ff.
62. Warburg, *Fragmente zur Ausdruckskunde*, §161 (March 21, 1891).

ingenious formulation, the pose brought into being by one situation and then deployed with less than perfect appropriateness in another was itself a kind of performed ornamentation. Under these conditions, "the action turns into something lugged around—into ornament."[63] Ornamentation as a form of mannerism thus became the bedrock of a theory of social masks.

In a quite paradoxical way, personal identity was produced by the rigidification of response possibilities. As we saw also in Hannah Arendt's rendition of Rahel Varnhagen (but in a different idiom), absolute adroitness of response might inhibit the development of an ego. For Warburg, therefore, the equivalent of the frieze in matters of human action was actually play. In turn, play qua repetition was a constitution of self. "In biological terms," Warburg argued, "play denotes the peaceful growth of self-awareness through the perception of the successful and willed mastery of a reflex movement made possible by means of hypothesizing the identity of two separate impressions."[64] In the German, "self-awareness" was *Ichgefühl*, which we may also understand as "coenesthesia," or the medley of sensations coursing through an individual body. The *feeling* of oneself derived from the distinctive kind of set of weightings brought about by an ornamental gesture played at a moment described as felicitous by the rules of some particular game.

For Warburg, the visual arts increased one's capacity to balance and to choose between decontextualization and its opposites. Rife with various anxieties of influence, art was a constant attempt to escape itself. For this reason, while he was distinguishing the features of "art as process" (*Kunstprocesse*), Warburg said that "the predicate steps into the space of appearance at the same moment as the subject." On the one hand, "the greater the power of the artist, the more powerfully elicited will be the predicate." On the other, "as the power of the artist declines, so the conspicuousness of the subject will increase."[65] A genuinely art-historical image will not shrink behind the title bestowed on it. The difficult work of distinguishing the central attributes of an image from its more peripheral elements ensured that the collage of qualities presented by that image would not be easily overwritten by the name of the subject thereby represented. If the work of art was

63. Warburg, *Fragmente zur Ausdruckskunde*, §127a (February 5, 1891): "die Handlung wird zu einem Getragenen zum Ornament."
64. Warburg, *Fragmente zur Ausdruckskunde*, §371 (February 16, 1899): "das Spiel bedeutet biologisch das friedliche Anwachsen des Selbstbewußtseins (Ichgefühls) durch die Empfindung der erfolgreichen willkürlichen Beherrschung einer Reflexbewegung, ermöglicht durch die Hypothese der Identität zweier Eindrücke."
65. Warburg, §107 (November 11, 1890): "das Praedikat gleichzeitig mit dem Subjekt in die Erscheinung tritt," and "je stärker die Künstlerkraft desto stärker das Praedikat ausgebildet, je schwächer, desto mehr das [umschriebene] Subjekt."

genuinely a "potentialization of sensuousness" (as Vischer had proposed), then works of art would name themselves. Cutting out their own shapes, those works of art would specify their own meaning, carving themselves out from the formless chaos of the hitherto unnamed—or, alternatively, the derivatively "overnamed."

All artistic representations of motion were attempts to resolve a dilemma that Warburg derived from a "principle of insufficient reason" (*Prinzip des mangelnden Grundes*). In its clearest—borderline banal—form, this principle was an incapacity to decide, in the absence of further contextual information, whether hair streaming back from a person's head indicated a strong wind or, alternatively, decisive forward motion. At a deeper level, this involved the question of whether a particular motion was carrying or being carried (*Tragen* or *Getragenwerden*), and this raised the issue of whether an action should be understood as a threat or as a happening. This was the question of whether an event was the product of a site-specific intention or was instead the working out of a process that was already underway and that was obeying all relevant laws. What was crucial here, however, was once again the partially implicit and partially explicit redescription of freedom. The question was not so much, "Is there a will at work here?" Instead, the question was, "Is there a distinctive recognition of *this* here and now as a contexture of particular adjacent possibilities?" The question of being ahead of a motion or being behind it, carrying it or being carried by it, was thus, at base, a question of perspicacity.

When Warburg said that "a retreat from the real locus of the object is effected by means of attention to the *momentary expression* of the object," he was not arguing that the task of art was to attend to the ways in which a particular gesture or a particular figure might break free of the context in which it appeared.[66] Such excision from context was certainly one of the ways in which visual memory worked, and the Warburgian reception has rightly emphasized this a great deal. But the task of art was to recognize *complex* objects rather than simple ones. The task was to draw attention to *Gestalten*, that is, "circulations of carrying, being carried, and mirroring." On this account, Warburg was fascinated by Botticelli's representation of the three graces alongside Mercury in the *Primavera*. Seneca had pointed out that a god of eloquence was proximate to the visual logistics of giving and receiving as well as their synthesis (namely, reciprocity), but he had not explained why.[67] We may supply an inference: eloquence is excellence in rendering palpable the value of speech acts as deeds of giving and receiving

66. Warburg, §322 (August 2, 1896): "durch Aufmerksamkeit auf den *augenblicklichen Ausdruck* des Objects wird eine Abkehr vom realen Milieu des Objects erzeugt."
67. Seneca, *De beneficiis*, 1.3; Warburg, *Sandro Botticellis "Geburt der Venus" und "Frühling*," 24.

and reciprocating. When Warburg described "attention" (*Aufmerksamkeit*) as the faculty underwriting these gift processes, he was casting attention as a practice of discerning a compositum of forces in terms of the several (but not infinite) ways in which its possible futures could be paradiastolically differentiated.

The space of indeterminacy between carrying and being-carried was an intersection of what Nietzsche had told Warburg were the two great countervailing forces of Greek antiquity—namely, Apollo and Dionysus. Students of the rhetorical tradition should pay attention when they find Warburg describing these countervailing forces in terms of *ethos* and *pathos*. Varying the topos he had appropriated from Jean Paul, Warburg insisted that "Apollonian ethos grows alongside Dionysian pathos as two branches sharing the *same* trunk."[68] Art, as Warburg understood it, was constantly posing the question of when "character" (*ethos*) might be said to tip over into the more sudden, more fleeting affective states that were "passion" (*pathos*). *Ethos* here denoted those subtle but enduring affective states that were both character and a cluster of predispositions to motion. For Warburg, the sense in which a life might be a work of art was not tied to the question of whether that life was of a piece, artificial, and perfect in its *concinnitas* (or "hanging together"). A life was a work of art insofar as it oscillated between the extremes of Apollo and Dionysus, form and its disruption. And perhaps this explained why Warburg was so struck by Ernst Bertram's 1922 work on Nietzsche, which had begun with the insight that Nietzsche was for Weimar Germans what Socrates had been for Nietzsche—namely, "a caricature, overloaded with qualities that could never have come together in one single person."[69] Such an individual might embody not so much the minting of a new form as the most compact intersecting of an overriding cultural anxiety.

For Warburg, ornamentation would be a hard-won achievement. This is the point to repeat and underscore. To perceive the ornamental accoutrement of a phenomenon, to perceive the difference between what a phenomenon was and what it might be, to perceive (that is) the gestalt of everything currently present to the senses in terms of a series of distinctions

---

68. WIA III.88.1, "Der Eintritt des antikisierenden Idealstils in die Malerei der Frührenaissance," lecture held at the Kunsthistorische Institut, Florence (April 20, 1914), 92: "das apollonische Ethos wächst mit dem dionysischen Pathos gleichsam als Doppelzweig aus *einem* Stamme hervor." This passage is a variant of the paragraph that one finds in Warburg, "Eintritt des antikisierenden Idealstils," in *Die Erneuerung*, 1:176—where the pairing of Apollo with ethos and Dionysus with pathos is not to be found.

69. Bertram, *Nietzsche*, 8: "eine Karikatur, . . . überladen mit Eigenschaften, die nie an einer Person zusammensein können." For Warburg's interest in the book and its author, see WIA Kopierbuch VI, 383, Aby Warburg to Ernst Bertram, September 9, 1918.

between what was and was not essential—all of this amounted to a victory over the *Augenblicksgott* that stood for the assumption that every last detail of a presencing revealed singularity of purpose. "Out of necessity, into contingency." This, we might say, was one of Warburg's mantras. If this seems unconnected to the historical situation in which the citizens of Weimar Germany found themselves in 1923 as Warburg gave his talk on the Pueblo Indians of Arizona in Kreuzlingen, Switzerland, then let us consider this simple question: in what ways might Versailles—and everything associated with it in the German imagination—have become a deity of extreme interpellation? As we shall see in the next section, escaping imaginative capture in scenes of radical defeat and subjection (or their opposites) was a significant Warburgian theme.

THE RESTITUTIONS OF 1929

One of the fundamental facts about Aby Warburg is that his published work was philologically scrupulous and tightly focused on historically particular questions even as his unpublished work gave voice to a series of theoretical presuppositions that were extremely ambitious and highly speculative. He was both an art historian and an art theorist. Meticulous as he sometimes was, his account of visuality's place in the world was tremendously expansive. For him, genuinely encountering a figural painting entailed responding to it with a series of body positions. Some of those body positions would be identical to those depicted in the image. Others would reciprocate the gestures made within the frame with a counterpositioning that might be defensive, aggressive, or complementary. And still others would be imagined continuations plotting trajectories from the moments in which a single image captured the differential between two or more motions in one body. In their body responses, viewers might produce an elasticity or play in the "weave" of an image. I examine the nature of this play in this final section by taking up the question of what Warburg could have meant in saying that the "restitution of eloquence" entailed magnanimity. Magnanimity, I shall suggest, was a plasticity and agility of soul exercised by the motive imagination that Warburg saw in the silhouettes and trajectories of figural art. This was the beginning of a theory of freedom. In order to understand that theory in the kind of political context to which it could have been applied, I begin my exposition by establishing a context in 1929, the last year of Warburg's life.

On January 19, 1929, in the middle of a lengthy Italian research trip that had begun the previous year, Aby Warburg held what was to become probably his most famous set of lectures at the Biblioteca Hertziana in Rome. Warburg lectured on "Roman Antiquity in the Workshop of Domenico Ghirlandaio" in a room equipped with approximately two hundred reproductions of images "that were to illustrate a substantial work on the importance of ancient imprints [*Vorprägungen*] on the artistic form-language centered on the representation of animated life [*bewegten Lebens*]."[70] The set of images that Warburg displayed in Rome was arranged into nineteen tables, a redaction—it seems—of what has come to be known as the first version of the Mnemosyne photo series.[71] There are manuscripts of the lecture that survive in London, so we have some sense of what he said that day. The texts are skeletons of the event, however, for the lecture was a performance (inspiring for some, trying for others).[72] In a letter written the next day, the librarian Axel von Harnack reported that the lecture lasted about two hours, with Warburg reading at times from prepared notes and speaking at other times extemporaneously while moving among images that were displayed on three sides of a large space.[73]

A few weeks later (on February 11), Warburg was still in Rome as the Catholic Church and the Italian State signed the Lateran Accords, thereby regularizing a relationship that had remained uncertain since Italian unification. Accompanied by Franz Alber (his personal aide) and Gertrud Bing (his research collaborator), Warburg went to St. Peters to witness Pope Pius XI's celebration of mass marking this "conciliation" (*conciliazione*) of church and state. In Bing's description, Pius XI was "so tightly swaddled in his heavy white and sumptuously gold-embroidered vesture that he [was] unable to make any large blessing motion over the crowd." To these anthropologists of the gesture, it was significant that "only hand and underarm tap[ped] the cross as the mouth repeat[ed] the benediction."[74] As Alber and Bing went into St. Peters itself, Warburg remained in the piazza outside, fulfilling—as he put it—his duty as a "historian-psychologist of the symbol" (*Historiker-Psychologe des Symbols*).[75]

On February 18 (a week after the signing of the Lateran Accords), Warburg reported that he had also "experienced" (*miterlebt*) the "day of conciliation" at the cinema, and the next day he wrote to his wife to recommend the film. A number of things in the film struck Warburg as particularly interesting. On the day in question, he noted, "Mussolini appeared nowhere

70. WIA, III.103.1.1, 1: "die zur Illustrierung eines umfangreicheren Werkes über die Bedeutung antiker Vorprägungen die künstlerische Formensprache bei der Darstellung bewegten Lebens zeigen sollen."
71. WIA, III.105.2. The version of the Mnemosyne image tables now published in the Akademie Studienausgabe is the so-designated third and last version.
72. WIA, III.115.1.1–3, "Die römische Antike in der Werkstatt des Domenico Ghirlandajo."
73. WIA, General Correspondence, Axel von Harnack to E. Jaffé, January 20, 1929.
74. Warburg, *Tagebuch*, 407: Pius XI "ist in seinem weißen schwer und prächtig goldbestickten Mantel so eng eingehüllt, daß er keine große Segensgeste über die Menge hin machen kann: nur Hand und Unterarm schlägt das Kreuz, während der Mund die Benediktionen wiederholt."
75. Warburg, 408.

in public." He drew attention to the cinematic representations of Cardinal Pietro Gasparri and Mussolini via their rise to prominence from ordinary beginnings—"humble villages appearing as their birthplaces." He spoke of "lip-play" (*Lippenspiel*) on the face of Mussolini, who had "a Caesarian mouth, at once evil and beautiful," and he observed how Gasparri sat during the signing "unaware of being watched, like an imposing and old and wizened village mayor."[76] A film print of the day's events still exists. Looking over Warburg's shoulder at Mussolini's "lip-play," one sees Mussolini accepting genuflections as he enters the Palazzo Apostolico Lateranense before he turns away, casts a glance up at the Vatican architecture around him, and either smacks or licks his lips. The performance plays as a feigned, perhaps successful, nonchalance.[77]

As I read it, this sequence of lecture, event, and representation presents an opportunity to think through the implications of Warburg's Mnemosyne project for rhetorical inquiry. The *Bilderatlas* project culminated a life's work, so it would be wrong to suppose that the immediate Italian political context for the Hertziana lecture can *exhaust* its meanings. Moreover, the nature of the context I am sketching here is distinctive. It is not that the Hertziana lecture emerged out of, in response to, or in dialogue with the signing of the Lateran Accords. The sequence of events speaks plainly against that: lecture preceded signing. I am claiming instead that we can specify what Warburg's work would have meant in that contemporary context. The task here is to render the conceptual implications of Warburg's Mnemosyne project more explicit by thinking them through terms, problems, and artifacts that were associated with the signing of the Lateran Accords.

What are we to make of Warburg's interest in the staging and cinematic representation of the *conciliazione* between the Italian State and the Catholic Church? In 1986, the great historian of historiography Arnaldo Momigliano provided a suggestion in his essay "How Roman Emperors Became Gods." There, he told a story relayed to him by Gertrud Bing about the events of February 11, 1929. Separated from his colleagues on the crowded streets of Rome, Warburg did not reappear that evening for dinner as expected. His

76. Warburg, 410: "Mussolini erscheint am 'Versöhnungstage' nirgends in der Öffentlichkeit"; "ärmliche Dörfer erschienen als Geburtsstätten"; "Lippenspiel—ein böser schöner caesarischer Mund"; "unabhängig vom Bewußtsein des Beobachtetwerdens, wie ein monumentaler alter gewiegter Dorfschulze." See also WIA, General Correspondence, Aby Warburg to Mary Warburg, February 19, 1929.
77. Istituto Nazionale L.U.C.E., *La Conciliazione fra l'Italia e il Vaticano* (1929). The film is available for viewing online via the European Film Gateway, and the scene in question occurs following the 4:47 mark (reckoning by the timer displayed in the film print itself). Some of the details correlate with Warburg's observations; some of the things that Warburg mentions are not in the version currently available. Warburg may well have seen a different cut of this same film.

colleagues became so worried that they eventually called the police. Later that night, Warburg turned up, and—in Momigliano's version of Bing's paraphrase—he chastised his companions in the following terms: "You know that throughout my life I have been interested in the revival of paganism and pagan festivals." Then, "today I had the chance of a lifetime to be present at the repaganization of Rome, and you complain that I remained to watch it." For Momigliano, this anecdote was a way of framing the fact that between 1929 and 1934 a number of seminal works had appeared on the Roman imperial cult.[78] We can double down on this intuition: Warburg's interest in repaganization was one response to a theological fetishization of political leadership characteristic of his historical moment.

Following Momigliano's terms of analysis, one comes to the hypothesis that Warburg's own 1895 essay on Florentine *intermezzi* was not only a kind of rewriting of Nietzsche's interest in the "total work of art" (*Gesamtkunstwerk*) but also a kind of rewriting of ancient rhetorical analyses of epideictic—the oratorical performance of praising and blaming. For Momigliano, the classical interpreter of the genre par excellence had been Menander Rhetor, who began his treatment of *basilikos logos* by pointing out that whoever took on the task of praising an emperor was in the unenviable position of being able to say nothing surprising: when praising power, the display of perspicacity would always be suspect.[79] In Warburgian terms, such capacities to unpack the *Gesamtkunstwerk*, to decode the *intermezzo*, or to read the Emperor's "presence" (*adventus*) became so many strategies for distancing oneself from the manifestation of an *Augenblicksgott*.

I am claiming that we can understand the Mnemosyne project as a continuation of Warburg's work on the *Augenblicksgott* transposed via rhetoric into the realm of politics. The *Bilderatlas* certainly was concerned with more than representations of secular power in the figure of Mussolini in the late 1920s. Visual representation of Mussolini constituted a tiny sliver of the *Bilderatlas* image tables. We find images of him in table 78 only, and no more than one of the photographs displayed there (78.1³) presents him with the sharpness of profile that a viewer might find interpellating. Nevertheless, our ability to think Warburg's project is greatly enhanced when we understand it as a kind of therapy for what we might call "Mussolini captivation." It is instructive to recast the *Bilderatlas* as a decentering of Mussolini and what we might call "the Mussolini class of authoritarian political artifacts." In Warburg's opinion, the affective stances captured by the photographs of the *conciliazione* embodied not so much a "reconciliation"

78. Momigliano mentioned works by E. J. Bickerman, L. R. Taylor, Andreas Alföldi, and A. D. Nock.

79. Menander Rhetor, *Division of Epideictic Speeches*, 368.

between church and state as the Catholic Church's submission to the authority of fascist Italy.

If the figure of Mussolini in the moment of Rome's repaganization desired to be an *Augenblicksgott*, then the *Bilderatlas Mnemosyne* was an inoculation against fascination with singularity in leadership. Such fascination was the fantasy of a Mussolini who symbolized a political power so centralized in an individual that the individual assumed the role of a god among men. In the *Bilderatlas*, however, Mussolini's image was submerged among a flood of others. In those tables, one encountered a multiplicity of stances that might be rehearsed. These were stances in relation to fortune and chance. They were also stances in the midst of a wide variety of human schemes. The task of the viewer was to assume in their own person a variety of affective positions that mirrored, reciprocated, or continued the positions represented in the *Bilderatlas*. For a soul that had become expansive and elastic in the course of such exercise, the late apparition of *il Duce* would be but one of many requests for affective response. Implied requests for ingratiation, obeisance, and wonder recorded in Mussolini's body were therefore merely provincial requests located in a particular zone of affective capability. In my reading, the *Bilderatlas* reversed apotheosis by denuding the would-be god.

I am also claiming—and here we come to a crucial step in my argument—that we should understand Warburg's consideration of the phrase *restitutio eloquentiae* as a potential title of the Mnemosyne project in the context of Mussolini captivation and its dissolution. As Momigliano implied, Mussolini was an eloquence. Appearing in the atlas as a stock-still, hands-clasped, eyes-down, chin-up figure captured photographically on February 11, 1929, Mussolini was a nexus of tacit requests for deification. This was a would-be Parousia. Casting the camera in the role of orating sycophant, we can say that Menander was the rhetorician with whom to analyze such *epideixis*. To be sure, Mussolini was no god, but he was the emblem of a political leadership that wished to assume the aesthetic form of one. In contrast, Warburg's analytical desire was properly rhetorical. Rather than offering up instances of eloquence, he wished to subject those moments of performance to "restitution." Just so, he mounted the figure of Mussolini in the *Bilderatlas* in the manner of a trophy.

The "restitution" in *restitutio eloquentiae* did not denote simply an innocent or antiquarian resuscitation of what had once been. As Warburg once put it, restitution was not "re-presentation" (*Wiederherstellung*).[80] It was a fully analytical process focused on the achievement of contingency. In Warburg's extremely rich definition, *Restitution* was "an act that negotiated

80. Warburg, "Planetenbilder," in *Werke*, 350.

a spiritual space for artistic genius between driven self-abandonment and conscious restrained formal composition (that is, between Dionysus and Apollo), an act in which one could, in fact, take a most personal language of forms to the level of a minting of oneself."[81] Restitution, that is, was an affective topics of the soul, a variety of responses through which one could run (habitually, to the point of unconsciousness) before actualizing a possibility in a particular situation. Moreover, the distances between the possibilities that one possessed were gaps into which one could create. That is, stock memorized responses generated new possibilities.

Warburg's term for what I am calling "an affective topics of the soul" did not appear in any of the introductory materials attached to the Mnemosyne project (although he did call that project an *Inventar*, an "inventory"). Nor did the term for "affective topics" appear in the diary passages in which Warburg wondered whether the project might be titled *restitutio eloquentiae*. In those passages, Warburg had concluded that, although restitution of elo-quence "would work very well in its broader signification ('pathosformula' for example) . . . , the act of cosmic ordering—that is, sphereology—would not be included." On this account, *restitutio eloquentiae* might name a part but not the whole of the *Bilderatlas* project. We might hypothesize a line of inquiry in which eloquence would be "taking up a position" and in which sphereology could be understood as a broader geography of stance taking, but this was not a line that Warburg himself pursued. In the end, Warburg concluded that "The Restitution of Eloquence" would "only [be] adequate as a chapter title." The "better general title," Warburg concluded, would be "Mnemosyne."[82] This is the title that has remained, and rightly so.

Nevertheless, it is crucial that we pursue the question of the title into a manuscript fragment penned on the same day as the diary entry just discussed, because it is there that we encounter Warburg's term for what I am calling an "affective topics of the soul." There, we encounter *Magnanimitas*. On December 22, 1927, Warburg asked himself the following question: what aspects of the classical rhetorical tradition were implicit in the phrase *restitutio eloquentiae*? Style, pathos, ethos, and magnanimity, he responded.[83] We might say that for Warburg, *Stil* was the distinctiveness of

81. Warburg, "Mnemosyne Einleitung," in *Werke*, 634: "ein Akt, der zwischen triebhafter Selbst-entäusserung und bewusster bändigender formaler Gestaltung, d. h. eben zwischen Dionysos-Apollo, dem künstlerishen Genius den seelischen Ort anwies, wo er seiner persönlichsten Formensprache dennoch zur Eigenausprägung verhelfen konnte."

82. Warburg, *Tagebuch*, 170: *restitutio eloquentiae* "würde im weiteren Sinn ('Pathosformel' zum Beispiel) sehr gut passen . . . , der Akt kosmischer Ordnung, die Sphärologie wäre nicht drin." Rhetoricians have not paid much attention here, but see Knape, "Gibt es Pathosformeln?," esp. 124 and 127.

83. WIA, III.113.5.2, "Bilder Disposition zur Schlussübung," 23: "Drin 'Stil' 'Pathos' 'Ethos' 'Mag-nanimitas' beschlossen."

a person, a mode, or an age. It was an unpredictability of response to visual inputs that, in time, came to be understood as characteristic. That *pathos* should have appeared while explaining the meaning of *restitutio eloquentiae* is entirely unsurprising. After all, Warburg has become famous as a theorist of "affective archetypes" (*Pathosformeln*), and, from Aristotle's *Rhetoric* on down, *pathos* has been regarded as one of the basic modes of persuasion. *Ethos*, another of the Aristotelian modes of persuasion, is perhaps a little more surprising. Like *pathos*, it was also one of Warburg's terms of art, but *ethos* is found more often in the notes than in the publications. One may add, however, that it is important to read *pathos* and *ethos* together within the Warburgian frame of reference. Together, they formed a constitutive binary, and they took their place alongside other constitutive binaries such as Apollo and Dionysus and the manic-depressive.

Of the four terms that Warburg used in this manuscript to gloss the phrase *restitutio eloquentiae*, it is *Magnanimitas* that is the least expected and the most interesting. Read against the background of intellectual histories that map "magnanimity" together with its cognates, Warburg's usage remains distinctive. Postclassical conceptions of the term had deliquesced from the striking and controversial depiction of the *megalopsychos* offered by Aristotle in book 4 of the *Nicomachean Ethics*. Aristotle had meant to delineate a kind of greatness of soul that looked down contemptuously on ordinary doings in the world. When translating the Greek term into Latin as *magnanimitas* in the *De officiis*, Cicero had then spoken of a kind of independence or bodily spiritual balance that was essential to the conduct of public business. In times of crisis, he had said, one has to avoid being "thrown off one's feet" (*de gradu deici*). One had to live with a kind of equanimity in a variety of possible futures, minimizing the chances that one would be forced to confess, after the fact, "I had not anticipated that possibility."[84] In contrast to these intensive ancient glosses, modern European languages have for the most part reduced magnanimity to an anemic kind of generosity. "Magnanimity" itself has become a ten-dollar word—pointlessly fancy, merely a synonym. Almost no one uses it.

In contrast, the Warburgian invocation of the term *magnanimitas* was a kind of brilliant (and probably unwitting) reinvention of what Aristotle was suggesting when he described *megalopsychia* as a kind of *kosmos* of all the virtues. Here, *kosmos* meant "ornament" or "crown" or "gathering-together."[85] Within an Aristotelian frame of reference, such gathering together was to be understood as the building of an array of capabilities. Virtue, for Aristotle, was a power of striking a balance—a mean—between extreme variants of an action. For any given action, virtue lay between the

84. Cicero, *De officiis*, 1.23.80–81.
85. Aristotle, *Nicomachean Ethics*, 1124a1.

too much and the too little. *Megalopsychia* was a kind of accumulation of extremes contributing, in turn, to the calculation of means. Within a Warburgian frame, such processes of averaging into habit had a less normative and more topical role. But the basic gesture of describing an organism in terms of its accreted and arrayed potentialities for action was remarkably similar. Here, potentialities for action were being laid down by past performance qua habit understood as a form of memory. Indeed, Richard Semon, one of the theorists of biological memory taken up by Warburg, defined *Mneme* as the "quintessence of the mnemic capacities of an organism," which we may paraphrase as the repertoire of its memorized motions.[86]

It is not clear that Warburg's invocation of the magnanimity topos had an immediate or decisive Weimar context. Werner Jaeger (with whom Warburg's son Max Adolph was studying) did translate an excerpt of Aristotle's treatment of the *megalopsychos* from the *Nichomachean Ethics*. He appended a short coda explaining that it was so difficult to translate *megalopsychos* (which he rendered as *der Großgesinnte*), because it stood for a kind of personality that emerged from the center of Greek culture and *Bildung* (which, of course, is yet another term that resists translation).[87] Elsewhere, the Marburg philosopher Gerhard Krüger cast modern philosophy as a mode of inquiry founded on Descartes's account of freedom as *générosité*, which had been the Frenchman's term for *magnanimitas*.[88] And, most suggestively for the American afterlife of Weimar conceptions of the political (as we saw in the introduction to this book), Leo Strauss picked up on Krüger's work and paid significant attention to what he thought of as Hobbes's brief and fleeting theorization of "magnanimitie" as the origin of all virtue in *Leviathan*. Strauss characterized magnanimity as a summing up of the "virtues of the free superior individual."[89] All of these initiatives postdate Warburg's invocation, however. Because his use of the term *Magnanimitas* occurred in unpublished material, moreover, there is no reason to speak of Warburg as the source of these ideas. If there was a relationship between Warburg and these other initiatives, it appears to have been indirect.

We are on firmer ground when we say that for Warburg the artistic topos pushing most explicitly into the conceptual terrain of *magnanimitas* was the "the continence of Scipio" (*Großmut des Scipio*). A host of early modern artists had construed the topos, and the early modern visual topoi these artists produced played an important role in table 52 of the image atlas.[90]

86. Semon, *Die Mneme*, 15: "den Inbegriff der mnemischen Fähigkeiten eines Organismus bezeichne ich als seine Mneme."
87. Jaeger, "Der Großgesinnte," 97–105.
88. Krüger, "Die Herkunft," 225–72.
89. Strauss, *Political Philosophy of Hobbes*, 51.
90. See, for instance, Civai and Caciorgna, *Il tema della* Magnanimitas.

Deriving in large part from a story told by Livy, the originally literary version of the topos had imagined Scipio Africanus returning a woman captured in the course of a military campaign to her betrothed, the Celtiberian leader Allucius. Scipio's was a performance of sexual honor, and Livy's account specified that the Roman general transformed "a considerable weight of gold" (brought by the woman's parents to ransom their daughter) into a dowry that he, in the name of the woman's parents, gave to Allucius. But the calculation in this exchange was also political: "what I request in return," Scipio was in effect saying to Allucius, "is only this: be a friend to the Roman people."[91]

Warburg included eight different versions of the continence of Scipio topos in the *Bilderatlas*.[92] Crucial for Warburg in these images was the process of transforming poses of supremacy into poses of forgiveness. As described in the subtitle appended to table 52 of the *Bilderatlas* by Gertrud Bing (perhaps in collaboration with Warburg), the continence of Scipio was a kind of "ethical inversion of victor-affect" (*ethische Umkehrung des Siegerpathos*). It was not *magnanimitas* in the mode of *clementia* that was crucial here. More crucial was *magnanimitas* as the distance traversed between victory and establishing the possibility of a new political beginning. Deep in the etymology of *continenza* and *continence* (the Italian and English terms for *Großmut* in this context), there perhaps existed the metaphor of continuance: magnanimity might also be the continuity or seamlessness of a transition (which was actually a rupture) from mortal combat to political friendship and reciprocity. Of course, as I intimated above, this was in no way a merely academic issue in Weimar Germany. This was the existential question of the republic: "How does a community begin to live again with its enemies?"

The act of "returning" a woman to her betrothed might be deeply ambiguous, and to fix that ambiguity visually one may consult Nicolas Poussin's visualization of the scene. In Poussin's version (not included in the *Bilderatlas*), Scipio's gesture is extremely precise. The gaze is intent and not so very far from vindictive. The betrothed, her status as a possession emphasized by Scipio's invocation of her as an article of commerce, affects displays of chasteness; the situation and Scipio's action has called her virtue into question. And Allucius cannot look on Scipio directly. He has lowered his gaze. His hands, moreover, affect genuflections of gratitude in an exaggerated fashion. He knows he has to offer such tokens, but his lips are pursed. This theater is being played out not for him but through him and on his body. Indeed, this is theater at his expense. After all, in this image, it is Scipio who

91. Livy, *Ab urbe condita*, 26.50.
92. Warburg, *Die Bilderatlas*, tables 52 and 74.

is being crowned. And, in the most minutely displayed mannerism of his gestures, Allucius attempts to register—for whom, himself?—his awareness that he is being coopted for political purposes.

In the *Bilderatlas*, the visual thematizing of magnanimity continued through the legend of the "justice" (*Gerechtigkeit*) of the Emperor Trajan.[93] The visual topos centered on a moment that had been framed vaguely by an episode in Cassius Dio's history of Rome, developed and transformed in the Middle Ages, and then fixed in the popular imagination by Dante's description in *Purgatory*, canto 10. While leaving Rome on his way to war, the story went, the Emperor Trajan's horse had been brought up short by a woman calling for justice on behalf of her murdered son.[94] Visualizations of the gestures in this scene—a person, arm raised, almost under hoof—were fundamentally ambiguous. The scene might show a moment in which a rider was acquiescing to an appeal. Alternatively, it might record the moment before someone is trampled to death in a cavalry charge. That is, depending on its continuation, it might stand for either mercy or mercilessness. Warburg presented this legend as a kind of finessing of the either/or proposed by "pride" (*superbia*) and "dutifulness" (*pietas*). He said that this finessing had been accomplished in the Middle Ages by means of (paradiastolic) "reinterpretation" (*Umdeutung*).[95] In the medieval period, retellings of the fable of Trajan's justice transformed mercilessness into mercy. And, in this version, magnanimity was a traversing of the distance between refusing an appeal for mercy and accepting it. For Warburg, there was no reason to suppose that such a traversing from mercilessness to mercy might not also move in the other direction. In this way, magnanimity was folded into an account of how a visual image might be a "station . . . in contradictory interpretation" (*Vorgang . . . der konträren Sinngebung*).[96] Paradiastole, we can add, would be a capacity to produce the differences that a capacious soul might traverse.

Thought in the midst of these particularities, Warburg's *Bilderatlas Mnemosyne* becomes a kind of therapy for the soul. The image atlas was a kind of prophylactic or vaccine. It was a controlled exposure that prepared one for more dangerous exposures. Changing the metaphor, one can say that the image atlas was a shield of Perseus on which the head of Medusa might be hung. As Warburg intimated in 1925, "in the Perseus grip on the head of Medusa, one finds a most illuminating symbolic specification for the

93. Warburg, tables 7, 44, 45, and esp. 52, where the topos was linked visually to the *Großmut des Scipio*.

94. In what may be the original topos (or one of them), the emperor in question is Hadrian and not Trajan. See Cassius Dio, *Historiae Romae*, epitome of 69.6. See also Boni, "Leggende," 31, who hypothesizes a medieval accretion of "justice-attributes" around the figure of Trajan.

95. WIA, III.115.1.2, "Die römische Antike in der Werkstatt des Domenico Ghirlandajo," 7.

96. WIA, III.115.1.2, "Die römische Antike in der Werkstatt des Domenico Ghirlandajo," 8.

energetic imperturbability of heroic humanity."⁹⁷ We should gloss "imperturbability" (*Unerschrockenheit*) as a readiness for many eventualities rather than a lack of sensitivity to context. Now frozen in book form, the panels of the image atlas were visual exercises. It is not simply that each panel posed a challenge to the viewer's powers of *ingenium*. To be sure, "What on earth holds this motley of images together?" was certainly a question that such a viewer might ask, but each panel was also a means of empowering the faculty of *iudicium*. That is, variations on a theme sensitized one to the possibilities contained within, as it were, the family resemblances of an affect grouping. Variation was a move from necessity into contingency, because nonidentical repetition implied that a thing could remain itself even as its qualities varied. Taken collectively, the panels amounted to, precisely, a visual and affective exercising that produced magnanimity. This was a complex of distances and a capaciousness marked out by the movements between affective states displaying polar opposites.

Magnanimity was a continuation into the *Bilderatlas* project of a thought that Warburg had expressed in his "Foundational Fragments" in the following terms: "art is a particular faculty of reacting against the images to which one is exposed."⁹⁸ I would add that this is a sentence to be read in the context of the Renaissance art-theoretical tradition of contrapposto, which was itself a rhetorical inheritance (according to David Summers).⁹⁹ Classically, contrapposto had been a kind of embodied rhetorical antithesis, where hips and shoulders implied quite distinct and even contradictory motions that were to be continued by leg and arm. In order to comprehend it, one cannot think of Warburgian contrapposto simply as a relationship of balanced opposition among parts of a body (or among persons in an image). Warburgian contrapposto was also a relationship between images and real human beings beyond the frame. Magnanimity could be understood as an awareness of the standard exercises of bodily and affective reciprocation. On this account, magnanimity would be an essential precondition of originality in such reciprocation. To take up a position at an angle to the commonplace, one had to know one's topoi. As E. R. Curtius would later show when he dedicated the foundational text of twentieth-century *Toposforschung* to Warburg, Warburg was an essentially topical thinker.¹⁰⁰

Responding adroitly to visual input was also a task for artists and not just

97. WIA, III.94.1.1, "Die Einwirkung der Sphaera Barbarica auf die kosmischen Orientierungsversuche," 30: "im Perseus-Griff nach dem Haupte der Medusa findet die energetishe Unerschrockenheit heroischen Menschentums ihre einleuchtendste symbolische Auspraegung."
98. Warburg, *Fragmente zur Ausdruckskunde*, §48 (February 7, 1890): "die Kunst ist eine besondere Art wie man gegen die eingedrückten Bilder reagirt."
99. See Summers, "*Maniera* and Movement: The *Figura Serpintinata*," and "Contrapposto: Style and Meaning in Renaissance Art."
100. Curtius, *Europäische Literatur*.

for persons studying the *Bilderatlas*, according to Warburg. For him, the quattrocento Florentine painter Domenico Ghirlandaio was the individual who mostly clearly exhibited what we may call the "spiritual exercises" of magnanimity. Ghirlandaio was an exponent of performative *magnanimitas*. Here, Warburg spoke of "the oscillation-span of a soul" (*seelische Schwingungsenge*). In the case of Ghirlandaio, such capaciousness of soul took the form of a prodigious ability to both assimilate and innovate on visual topoi taken up from classical antiquity and the Northern European Renaissance. This was range, and it amounted to something like a visual sovereignty as well. As Warburg put it in his Hertziana lecture, the painter as "sovereign surveyor" (*der souveräne Augenmensch*) was capable of remaining an adroitly reflective spectator in the presence of "the entire range of still and moved life without itself experiencing the oscillation between stasis and kinesis as something like a tragic foundational experience."[101] In Warburg, sovereignty was both a kind of quoting at will and a capacity to identify quotations with ease.

Crucially, magnanimity was not simply something to be exercised in a visual topos or possessed by visually sovereign artists: it was also a political virtue. Perhaps it was even *the* political virtue. For Warburg, Lorenzo de' Medici embodied this virtue most clearly. In the Lorenzo of Warburg's imagination (we need not assess the claim's historical veracity), the crucial characteristic was "balance" (*Gleichgewicht*). Before we assume that "balance" can only ever be something anodyne, consider this: balance is a radical illegibility of proclivities to future motion. As Warburg put it, "the personal preeminence of Lorenzo the Magnificent consisted in his capacity to hold in balance the strong receptive and generative powers of his soul."[102] This was, Warburg specified, a "brilliant capacity to achieve equilibrium" (*geniale Ausgleichsfähigkeit*). That which is balanced may initiate motion in a number of different directions.

Implicit in the notion of equilibrium are the extremes that balance mediates. Warburg expressed the thought with great precision in the early 1902 essay on "The Art of Portraiture and the Florentine Bourgeoisie." There, Lorenzo's specificity was his *seelischer Umfang*. This was not simply his "spiritual outline" or "girth" but fully his spiritual *range*, and it "surpassed the average measure in terms of its amplitude of oscillation [*Schwingungsweite*], and also, above all, in terms of the intensity of those oscillations."[103]

---

101. WIA, III.115.1.2, "Die römische Antike in der Werkstatt des Domenico Ghirlandajo," 4: "der ganze Fülle ruhigen und bewegten Lebens, ohne aber selbst den Pendelgang z[w]ischen Ruhe und Bewegung etwa als tragisches Grunderlebnis zu empfinden."
102. Warburg, "Florentinische Wirklichkeit," in *Werke*, 229: "die persönliche Überlegenheit des Lorenzo Magnifico beruht darauf, dass er befähigt war, seine starken empfänglichen wie schöpferischen Seelenkräfte im Gleichgewicht zu halten und in den Dienst des Lebens zu stellen."
103. Warburg, "Bildniskunst," in *Die Erneuerung*, 1:110: "durch die Schwingungsweite und vor allem durch die Intensität der Schwingungen das Durchschnittsmaß phänomenal überschreitet."

Lorenzo's capaciousness of soul derived from his ability to take up extreme and contrary positions. Warburg emphasized the ambivalence of Lorenzo's gesture in the Ghirlandaio fresco depicting the confirmation of the Franciscan Order by Pope Honorius III. He saw in the gesture a kind of indistinction between motions of beckoning and waving off. This was something like a play on the words of power because it took up a position that was equidistant to the squarely opposed commands, "Come forward!" and "Remain there!" We may compare this ambivalence to the paradiastolic redescribability of the justice meted out by Trajan.[104] A man with the power to do anything, a man who was *capable* of anything, had to be perceived—and therefore represented—as a duck/rabbit *Vexierbild*. And this is instructive politically: power is precisely the genuine possibility of multiple future movements.

The most striking icon of the divergence that Warburg was imagining with the concept of *Denkraum* can be found in a book that on September 23, 1928, Warburg said he wanted to read—namely, *Possibility* by Scott Buchanan (the founder of St. Johns College in Annapolis).[105] Having stated his desire to work through the book, Warburg died a little over a year later, and it may be that he never actually read what Buchanan wrote. Nonetheless, we may use Buchanan's sentences to think through the implications of Warburg's intuitions. In Buchanan's book, Warburg's imaginative divergence was the point at which possibility dissected the actual in the same way that a prism refracted light: "just as sunlight is broken up into a manifold of colour by passage through the prism," we may say (using Buchanan's words), "so experience is referred to the concept of possibility and spread out into a thousand and one possible worlds."[106] Refraction was the work of the *Bilderatlas*, and it was the work of magnanimity too.

One cannot say that magnanimity as a capaciousness of soul was merely an incidental Warburgian interest; it was central to his work. Witness how he described the purpose of the Warburg Library. Founded in Hamburg as the Kulturwissenschaftliche Bibliothek Warburg and relocated to London in the 1930s where it became the Warburg Institute, this research institute was designed to facilitate examination of "European culture as the product of confrontation, as a process in which we . . . are to search neither for friend nor for foe but are instead to look for symptoms of a soul-oscillation that swings between distant poles but is in fact a unitary process: from cult practice to mathematical contemplation and back."[107] The task, Warburg

---

104. This representation of Lorenzo was reproduced in the *Bilderatlas* (table 43).

105. Warburg, *Tagebuch*, 344.

106. Buchanan, *Possibility*, 117.

107. Warburg, "Orientalisierende Astrologie," in *Die Erneuerung*, 2:565: "die europäische Kultur als Auseinandersetzungserzeugnis, als ein Prozeß, bei dem wir, soweit die astrologischen Orientierungsversuche in Betracht kommen, weder nach Freund noch Feind zu suchen haben, sondern vielmehr nach Symptomen einer zwischen weitgespannten Gegenpolen pendelnden,

was saying explicitly, was not to chart a progress from cult to mathematics. The task was not to "befriend" a mathematical Enlightenment. The task was instead to commit to memory the full range of possibilities actualized in European culture between extremes that Warburg identified with cult and mathematics, between, that is, a complete immersion in and a complete detachment from the motions in the midst of which one lived. To Warburg's way of thinking, "magnanimity" was one of the terms that captured this sense of a range of possibilities.

CONCLUSION

If—pace Hobbes—one wishes to deny that freedom is simply "the absence of external impediment," and if one wants to say (actually, with Hobbes) that imagination is "the first internal beginning of all voluntary motion," then one encounters a difficulty in describing the emergence and status of nonnecessity in human action. Such action looks either caused or uncaused. If caused, then unfree; if uncaused, then random (and not free in any meaningful sense). My chief claim in this chapter has been that the writings of Aby Warburg constitute an alternative line of inquiry into this problematic— and a sophisticated one. By means of the concept of "conjunction" (*Konjunktion*), Warburg ratcheted up the pressures exerted by contexts that were angling in from different quadrants on the nodes of perception at which they appeared to intersect. Then, in the concept of "ornamentation" (*Ornament*), he explored ways of differentiating a thing from all the modes in which it might appear together with the ways in which one might thereby neutralize the particular way in which a context would confront a node of perception. Finally, under the heading of "restitution" (*Restitution*), Warburg developed a series of visual and mnemonic exercises designed to increase both the perspicacity with which nodes perceived the interpellations of context and also the range of possible counterposes those nodes might adopt in response. At this point (and here I am not so much paraphrasing Warburg as pointing out a continuation of his positions), freedom emerged as a term describing the fineness with which a perceptual apparatus distinguished its sensations and the suppleness with which it imagined varieties of possible continuation. Here, then, is another Weimar origin for rhetorical inquiry: Warburg's restitution of eloquence as a practice of freedom.

As my recurrent emphasis on "continuation" indicates, this book presupposes that ideas themselves are inseparable from their histories and that the histories of ideas will be narratable as a series of points at which premises

---

aber in sich einheitlichen Seelenschwingung: von kultischer Praktik zur mathematischen Kontemplation—und zurück."

are transposed and new inferences are licensed, occasioned, and at times rendered newly urgent. Implicit in this approach to intellectual history is the notion that thinkers can be understood as broadly underdetermined fabrics of inference. Each assertion is a potential premise in an argument, and every argument is a fabric that can be unraveled and restitched. Much of this working and reworking of the fabric of inference will have been undertaken by thinkers engaged in historical analysis, and the work of the intellectual historian in such moments will be to give accounts of what has changed and how that change came about. Are we, for instance, speaking of the continued effect of old premises, the transformed effect of those premises under new circumstances, or new assertions either taken up from elsewhere or newly minted within a space mapped out by the intersection of assertions that already existed within a thinker's repertoire? The permutations continue.

As I argued in the first chapter of this book, there need be no clearly demarcated or heavily policed line between thought and the history of thought. The work of articulating a tradition of inquiry shades into simply working in that tradition under one's own name. I challenge the notion that one must be either paraphrasing the ideas of others or asserting ideas in one's own voice, and crucial here is the interstitial domain in which one follows the consequences of a particular thinker's thought into a line of inquiry that eventually became something like a tradition. To build a tradition is to exercise in the line of inquiry that one is preparing to continue—or it can be. I have been building up something like a sequence from Heidegger through Arendt and Benjamin to Warburg, and this chapter on Warburg has been an interim culmination of that sequence. I say interim only because the ultimate aim of this book is to work the Weimar origins of rhetorical inquiry into the present. So as to prepare the ground for that eventual transition from paraphrase to assertion in the last chapter of this book, I turn in the next chapter to the largely post-1933 and post-1945 afterlives of the Weimar origins that I have discerned to this point.

7: NEW POINTS OF DEPARTURE IN THE WEIMAR AFTERLIFE

EMERGENT PATTERNS

The modes of inquiry employed to this point have been topical, expository, and inferential. I have surveyed a standard received version of the Weimar origins of political theory to distinguish its rhetorical aspects. I have organized a repertoire of the rhetorical tradition as it was received by German speakers in the centuries before 1933, and I have interwoven this material into new inferential complexes. My claim continues to be that we recognize Weimar to have been an incredibly influential moment for the generation of twentieth-century and contemporary thought, but we have passed over an alternative tradition in Weimar rhetorical inquiry. In the course of this book, I have been engaged in excavating and dramatizing the logic of this rhetorical constellation. Although they each represent investigative traditions that remain in many ways radically divergent, Martin Heidegger, Hannah Arendt, Walter Benjamin, and Aby Warburg have constituted points of origin within that constellation.

In this chapter, I turn to the afterlife of patternings that I have perceived in the work of Heidegger, Arendt, Benjamin, and Warburg. The inferentialist account of intellectual historiography I sketched at the outset and have been practicing throughout emphasizes that meaning is a function of the changing inferential consequences of premises as those premises are embedded in more parsimonious, more elaborate, or simply different inferential structures. Pursuant to what Robert Brandom has called the nonmonotonicity of inference, the same assertion incorporated as a premise in different arguments also takes on new meanings. "Afterlife" is thus a particularly important category within inferentialist intellectual historiography. To be sure, that category was also at work in the four central chapters of this book. After all, new circumstances can help or force an author to discover the implications of their own assertions. Nevertheless, if one is attempting to think about the nature of a tradition and not simply the implications of a particular author's positions, then the *fortuna* of positions asserted by earlier authors and taken up, combined, and applied by other authors in subsequent contexts will be especially important.

The four sections of this chapter investigate the afterlives of inquiry sequences set out in each of the four preceding chapters, but there is no attempt to limit the afterlife of each chapter to the specific uptake of Heidegger, Arendt, Benjamin, and Warburg. All four of these authors have been prodigiously influential, and recounting the reception history of any one of them would be in itself an overwhelming task for any chapter-length exploration. Here, I propose something more targeted: I derive a problem from each of the preceding four chapters, and I then follow the afterlife of that problem across thinkers influenced variously by Heidegger, Arendt, Benjamin, and Warburg. The principle of selection for sources in this chapter was a specifiable inheritance of the thought of one or more of those thinkers, but I have drawn from Heideggerians, Arendtians, Benjaminians, and Warburgians promiscuously as I chart the variety of responses to each of these four problems. Thus, specifiable derivation from one or more of these Weimar thinkers is the criterion of entry to the chapter, but once a source qualifies, I allow myself to deploy it as seems analytically best. I can state each of the four problems developed in this chapter in the form of a question. First, how was the problematic of decisionism inherited and inflected by writers influenced by these four thinkers? Second, how may we think the rhetorico-political faculty of judgment in this afterlife? Third, in what ways was the issue of modality, especially everydayness, taken up within this tradition? Fourth, what forms of topical practice emerged in the wake of the Weimar origins of rhetorical inquiry that I have identified? In the sections that follow, I pursue each of these questions, and I show that they constitute a sequence.

INDECISIONISM

Where Carl Schmitt articulated a decisionist theory of sovereignty, rhetoricians have emphasized instead something like "undecidability," but the line of inquiry excavated in this book gives voice to a different possibility that focuses on the generative potential of moments of indecision. The Schmittian lineage in Weimar political theory insists that politics is a zone of secularized divinity, where something like a half-god, half-beast sovereign inserts itself as a miracle or law unto itself into the moment of decision. This vision of the role and nature of political leadership has been highly influential. The reception of Schmitt's gambit within the field of rhetoric has articulated an alternative to this explicitly dictatorial fantasy in which the fetish for Schmittian resolution encounters an endless process of displacement nourished by the polysemy of words. This book locates an alternative to this alternative. The "alt-alt" here focuses on indecision itself. Indecision will often be experienced as anxiety. It may be an oscillating of desire and aversion, fear and hope, and it may end in frustration, inaction, or the sense of missed opportunity. Those truths notwithstanding, indecision may also be understood and then practiced as a domain of potential creativity.

Some of the early receptions of Heidegger took up decisionism. In order to think beyond the standard received version here, we can rehearse and then marginalize those receptions. One of the most important early articulations of the connection between Heideggerian "existentialism" and Schmittian decisionism came in the 1935 article "Political Decisionism," written by Heidegger's former student Karl Löwith. In the immediate wake of Heidegger's decision to join the Nazi party and his appointment as rector at Freiburg University, Löwith argued that there was a similarity between "Schmitt's analysis of the political" and "Heidegger's Dasein analytic." Heideggerian "facticity" (*Faktizität*) dramatized itself in the extreme circumstance of what Schmitt had referred to as "the political emergency [*Ernstfall*] of war."[1] As we saw in chapter 3, "facticity" emphasized the senses in which presencing was always already embedded in a particular situation. Löwith repeated the point that the now-or-never historicity of *Dasein* facing the possibility of its own finitude was to be understood in opposition to the endless and utterly impersonal displacements of a political Romantic historiography oriented to what Schmitt found in Müller— namely, a blind faith in "eternal conversation."[2]

Löwith's response may well have been the right one in 1935, but our moment is different, and we are freer than he was to pursue alternative formulations of the Heideggerian trajectory. Putting ourselves in the original 1935 context, in the wake of Heidegger's *Rektoratsrede*, we are indeed dealing with a moment in which, as Löwith put it, "the transition from freedom-unto-death to the sacrificing of life was possible at any time."[3] Repeating the argument in 1946, Löwith made the point that the zero hour of "being-unto-death" in the extreme case of being-at-war did not specify a being in its authenticity or distinctiveness. On the contrary, such a zero hour marked "the passing of a *Dasein* that was always particular and individual into a *Dasein* that was always general."[4] In this immediately postwar

1. Löwith, "Politischer Dezisionismus," 110.
2. Löwith, 104.
3. Löwith, 111n1: "der Übergang von der Freiheit zum Tode . . . zum Opfer des Lebens jederzeit möglich ist." In connection to "Freiheit zum Tode," Löwith refers us to Heidegger, *Sein und Zeit*, 266.
4. Löwith, "Les implications politiques," 354: "le passage du Dasein toujours particulier et individuel à un Dasein toujours général."

context, Heidegger himself would reject Jean-Paul Sartre's appropriation of his work in the *Letter on Humanism,* but Christian Graf von Krockow would still include Heidegger in his treatment of decision in 1958.[5] While Löwith was rejecting a still evolving trajectory in his former teacher's work, we are surveying the Heideggerian corpus of texts with something approaching a greater equidistance to each of its parts. Heidegger's most recent work was legitimately most important to Löwith (since it indicated directions in Heidegger's thought that might be pursued or cast aside), but for us "earliest" and "latest" are less determinative characterizations because each actualization of Heideggerian thought possesses its own array of future perfect potentials.

In the 1960s and 1970s, a significant number of political thinkers broke with the version of decisionism that Löwith had attributed to Heidegger and Schmitt. They were attempting to develop a variety of classicizing alternatives instead. As the postwar philosopher and political theorist Hermann Lübbe put it in 1971, "the concept of decision is compromised."[6] In a provocative inversion, Lübbe went on to characterize the Schmittian account of decision as "Romantic." According to Lübbe, prewar decisionism could not be taken up in the postwar period, and yet "decision" (*Entscheidung*) was still unavoidable in politics. For him, politics simply was "the practice of constructing a will capable of deciding and acting in the midst of the battle of opinions and interests through the production of readiness to consent."[7] Voting was the prosaic but crucial decision-procedure that would end "eternal conversation" (*ewige Gespräch*), a phrase that—like Löwith— Lübbe recycled from Schmitt.[8]

For Lübbe, rhetoric became a *Technologie* that could be inserted precisely where discussion and voting intersected, and one of the traditions on which he was drawing was the *ars topica*.[9] He was not alone in this. Ludwig Landgrebe had studied phenomenology with Husserl before the war (and later became one of Hans Blumenberg's mentors), and two years earlier in 1969 he had been making many of the same points as Lübbe. In his attempt to recover other conceptual resources to supplant "decision" (*Entscheidung*), Landgrebe had invoked the Aristotelian concept of *prohairesis* (choosing one thing before another).[10] Six years before that, moreover, the political theorist Wilhelm Hennis had been setting the scene when he sequenced

---

5. Krockow, *Die Entscheidung,* 89.

6. Lübbe, *Theorie und Entscheidung,* 7: "der Begriff der Entscheidung ist kompromittiert."

7. Lübbe, 55: "Politik ist die Praxis, im Streit der Meinungen und Interessen durch Erzeugung von Zustimmungsbereitschaften einen entscheidungs- und handlungsfähigen Willen aufzubauen."

8. Lübbe, 29.

9. Lübbe, 55; for invocations of topos, see 61, 144, and 167.

10. Landgrebe, *Philosophie der Politik,* 12, 39.

three key assertions: that Weber's purportedly value-neutral power politics was precisely the kind of political theory one would expect in an age of empire; that Arendt's *Human Condition* underscored an important distinction between "making" (*poiēsis*) and "acting" (*praxis*); and, most crucially, that the rhetorical topical tradition could enrich one's description of probabilistic domains such as those traversed by *praxis*.[11] In Hennis's work, we find something like a license to pursue the topical tradition in postwar German intellectual history. Hennis defined topics as "the art of finding the right, which can only mean the better reasoned [*begründete*], answer."[12] In the end, however, even as he reported the scale of the art's ambition, Hennis's sense of its history and practice was not as rich as it needed to be to achieve his project of reconceptualizing decision within topical theory.

We may also count Hans-Georg Gadamer's continuation of the Heideggerian initiative into a theory of hermeneutics among the postwar attempts to mobilize older resources for redescribing indecision. Gadamer had studied with Heidegger, and he had been present at the Summer Semester 1924 lectures that I emphasized in chapter 3. Three quarters of a century later, he was setting out a position that was consonant with the 1924 Heideggerian emphasis on rhetoric as *dunamis* when he denied that rhetoric might be understood as essentially goal directed and resisted instrumentalist readings of the disciplinary formation. He asserted instead that rhetoric dealt simply with the realm of the "probable" (*eikos*, the verisimilar as "true-like" or *Wahr-ähnlich*). He insisted that "the concept of rhetoric" active in his own writing "is initially a very formal one," for rhetoric would simply be "speeches [*Reden*] that are not demonstrable" in the sense of logically incontrovertible.[13] Gadamer resisted Habermasian calls for a theorization of the ideal speech situation and defended rhetoric as precisely a tradition that, like hermeneutics, would deal with the "domain of persuasive—as distinct from logically compelling—argument."[14] In doing so, Gadamer was reiterating both his commitment to the nondemonstrability of rhetoric and its pertinence in moments that called for decision but that did not provide the conditions of possibility for uncontroversial decision. Merely probabilistic argument made for a domain of possibility or indecision.

In turn, Gadamer's initiative had been in dialogue with a variety of other

11. Hennis, *Politik und praktische Philosophie*, 17 and 116. See also topoi added in the expanded edition of 1977 at 136 and 187.

12. Hennis, 93: "die Kunst, die richtige, und das kann nur heißen: besser begründete Antwort zu finden, ist die Topik."

13. Gadamer, *Die Lektion des Jahrhunderts*, 62: "der Begriff der Rhetorik ist zuerst ein ganz formaler; und es ist der: solche Reden, die nicht beweisbar sind."

14. Gadamer, "Replik," 314: rhetoric deals with a "Bereich der überzeugenden Argumente (und nicht der logisch zwingenden)."

rearticulations of rhetoric. These alternatives included programs set out by the literary scholar Klaus Dockhorn and the metaphorologist Hans Blumenberg. In his review of Gadamer's *Truth and Method* (1960), Dockhorn had criticized the book for its relatively thin treatment of the rhetorical tradition. In that review (which appeared in 1966), Dockhorn himself characterized rhetoric "as the second-chance educational path [*zweite Bildungsweg*] of antiquity over and against philosophy."[15] Earlier in 1949, Dockhorn had claimed that "for rhetoric, the irrational is not simply one problem among several and is instead its motive principle."[16] In setting rhetoric and philosophy apart in this way and in casting rhetoric as an analytic of the irrational, Dockhorn was dividing the two disciplines in a way that Gadamer did not accept. One can imagine Gadamer countering that a decision may be made in the absence of logically compelling reasons without being on that account "irrational." Gadamer's point had been that there are plenty of reasons that are nonbinding without giving up their status as reasons.

Perhaps the most incisive rhetorical response to decisionism in the postwar period came from Hans Blumenberg. In a captivating 1971 formulation published originally in an Italian translation, Blumenberg argued that "the fundamental presupposition [*assioma*] of all rhetoric is the principle of insufficient reason [*principium rationis insufficientis*]."[17] Insufficiency of reason existed in the midst of a "freedom" brought into being by the combination of an absence of evidence and the unavoidability of action. Working with the more canonical 1981 German edition, we see that Blumenberg was situating rhetoric in a realm defined by both "lack of evidence" (*Evidenzmangel*) and "pressure to act" (*Handlungszwang*). "Acting" (*Handeln*) emerged out of an "indeterminacy" (*Unbestimmtheit*) in human being that was redescribable as "freedom."[18] My contention is that these formulations correctly specify the insufficiency of decision (which cannot justify itself fully) but that they do not give us ways of conceptualizing or practicing this distance between reasons and initiatives without once again representing decision as a miracle.

As I argued in chapter 5, we can respond to the decisionist problematic developed by the likes of Weber, Schmitt, and Heidegger by shifting the domain of investigation to the work of Walter Benjamin. There, we get the beginnings of an account of creative indecision. In this chapter, I continue that gambit by taking up more recent receptions of the Benjaminian

---

15. Dockhorn, review of *Wahrheit und Methode*, 169.

16. Dockhorn, "Die Rhetorik als Quelle," 112: "für die Rhetorik steht das Irrationale nicht als Problem neben anderen Problemen, sondern ist ihr bewegendes Prinzip."

17. Blumenberg, "Approccio antropologico all'attualità della retorica," 64: "l'assioma di ogni rhetorica è il *principium rationis insufficientis.*"

18. Blumenberg, "Anthropologische Annäherung an die Aktualität der Rhetorik," 117.

investigative program. Consider, for example, the kind of indecisionistic possibility space of the aphoristic collections that Benjamin assembled. As the resolutely Benjaminian Susan Sontag once intimated, Benjamin's sentences "do not seem to be generated in the usual way." That is, "they do not entail." She relayed a line from the *Trauerspiel* book: "a writer must stop and restart with every new sentence." Again, we have a pointillist style of composition in which each dot establishes a principle of extension—the utterance as potential premise, sprouting continuations, inferentially. In Sontag's gloss, Benjaminian writing became a practice in which "mental and historical processes are rendered as conceptual tableaux." She came to the conclusion that his "style of thinking and writing" is "incorrectly called aphoristic" and "might better be called freeze-frame baroque."[19] On the one hand, such fragmentation would constitute a surfeit of possibilities: "slowness is one characteristic of the melancholic temperament," and Sontag added that "blundering" about is another such characteristic, deriving "from noticing too many possibilities."[20] On the other hand (we may infer), interpolated possibilities would be conative. We can understand the distance between the constituent parts of a dialectical image as a distance pulled open by trajectories laying out potential discoveries.

When she emphasized the baroque and topical dimensions of Benjamin's work, Sontag was not only continuing a line of inquiry described above in chapter 5 but also bringing Benjamin closer to the Warburg discovered in chapter 6. Given his considerable and innovative investment in both Benjamin and Warburg, the contemporary Italian theorist Giorgio Agamben is a fertile site for continuing this line of inquiry. For a time in the 1980s, Agamben coordinated the Italian Einaudi edition of Benjamin's collected works. Earlier in the mid-1970s, he had spent a fruitful period at the Warburg Institute that yielded an essay on "Aby Warburg and the Nameless Science" and that laid the foundation for later works (such as *Nymphs* and his methodological essay *Signatura Rerum*). Inverting the order of the continuation that I have been proposing in this book, Agamben confirmed in 1975 that "it is in a heterodox research program like that centered on Benjamin's dialectical image that we will be able to identify fertile continuation of the Warburgian legacy."[21] This will be "an outcome of Warburg's legacy" only if we ourselves develop the Benjaminian line of inquiry in this direction, and this is work that I am doing both in this chapter and in this book.

It is important to both agree with and then dissent from Agamben's attempt to wrestle Warburg's "nameless science" free from the reception that

19. Sontag, *Under the Sign of Saturn*, 129.
20. Sontag, 114.
21. Agamben, "Warburg," 66: "è in una ricerca eterodossa come quella di Benjamin sull'immagine dialettica che potremmo riconoscere un esito fecondo del lascito warburghiano."

he saw stabilizing around him during the mid-1970s. There is something both brilliant and obtuse in Agamben's assertion that Warburg's *Bilderatlas* project conceived of the image as a place in which "the subject takes off the mythic and psychosomatic consistency that . . . had been conferred on it by a theory of knowledge that was in truth a concealed metaphysics in order thereby to recover its original and—in the etymological sense of the word—speculative purity."[22] In the first instance, "speculative" is a conjuring word here given its intimation of a pun on "mirroring." In the second instance, however, the last word in the passage just quoted announces a radical mistake, for there is nothing "pure" about Warburg's image tables. If these tables were mirrors, they were smashed mirrors fragmenting visual sociality and making the stations of such sociality available for investigation. They were not the "mirror of Narcissus" that Agamben went on to hypothesize.[23] Pursuing the metaphor, these image-table mirrors were so many shards strewn about on an uneven surface. Rather than reflect a single scene, they evinced a range of actions now displayed—or simply splayed—from a host of angles. Once again, the pun is something more than a pun: etymology helps us remember the sense in which display is in fact the unfolding of a phenomenon into its variegating fullness.

We find a further way to mine the Benjaminian seam if we turn to Agamben's work in *Infancy and History*, originally published in 1978. There, Agamben has inserted a rather cunning rapprochement between Heidegger and Benjamin by focusing on what he has called the experience of language itself. Picking up on a line from Heidegger's lectures on the essence of language, Agamben argued that we have an experience of language (as distinct from an experience of particular objects or processes or events) "only where we lack names, where speech breaks on our lips." Such inability is illuminating because "this breaking of speech is 'the backward step on the road of thought.'" Indeed, the wager is that "infancy [speechlessness] is staked on the possibility that there is an experience of language which is not merely a silence or a deficiency of names, but one whose logic can be indicated, whose site and formula can be designated."[24] Alternatively, invoking Benjamin's "Experience and Poverty" (and changing it by means of a Heideggerian concern with everydayness), Agamben contended that experience (as nameability) may be destroyed not only by catastrophe but

22. Agamben, 66: "poiché proprio l'immagine . . . è il luogo dove il soggetto si spoglia della mitica consistenza psicosomatica che, di fronte a un altrettanto mitico oggetto, gli era stata conferita da una teoria della conoscenza che era, in verità, una metafisica travestita, per ritrovare la sua purezza originale e—in senso etimologico—speculativa."

23. Agamben, "Warburg," 66.

24. Agamben, "Experimentum Linguae," 6. Written in 1988–89 and added to the English edition, this preface had not appeared in the original Italian work.

also by repetition—by dailiness.[25] As we saw in chapter 5 (in the Vichian gloss on Benjamin's sense of experience), both experience and naming are a function of a novelty cast as freshness. Inarticulateness in the face of "coincidences" is the experience of language making names possible.

In my own alternate sequencing, I am suggesting that Warburg can be understood as a continuation of Benjamin at precisely the point where the dialectic image became an image table. I am suggesting further that both the dialectical image and the image table were contributing to a theorization of indecision as generative, but we should not presume that being a Warburgian inoculates against the Romantic mythologization of decision.[26] Just so, in his 1925 essay on contemporary German philosophy (undertaken in conjunction with Cassirer but also within the broader ambit of the Warburg Library in Hamburg), the polymath art historian Edgar Wind was repeating the topos that the role of the philosopher would be to reveal the arbitrariness of decisions. Invoking Weber explicitly, Wind repeated a version of the topos that science can decide on appropriate means only once ends have been established by some extrascientific power. This was supposed to be a proof that decisions "cannot be based on reason," and Wind parsed the Weberian idea with a classic articulation of the eventually Schmittian decisionist topos: "Reason says: You cannot decide on my ground. Life says: You must decide for my sake."[27] Skepticism breeds decisionism, and, ironically, philosophy becomes the training ground of a certain kind of irrationalist commitment.

Edgar Wind would become one of the most influential Warburgians of the twentieth century, but precisely here where will has no reason our Warburgian response should be that "arbitrariness" is a thin concept unless it is understood in an essentially philological way. Arbitrariness is not a decision produced out of nothing by a faculty of will in the manner of a small miracle. Arbitrary things are simply the various products of human ingenuity instantiated in such a way that they can be received and taken up by others. Understood as a tissue of received gestures, the Warburgian image table *is* arbitrariness incarnate. It is willfulness qua conation. Wind understood this but not fully. At times, he did emphasize the sense in which one might hand oneself over to the incompatible arbitrarinesses of others in the course of empathizing with their decisions. This was something like a failed and incomplete intuition of the magnanimity line of inquiry that I sketched in the previous chapter. For Wind, though, such exercising was most basically a kind of risk. In his famously excoriating—perhaps resentful—review of

25. Agamben, *Infanzia e storia*, 5.
26. Didi-Huberman, "*Dialektik des Monstrums*," 634.
27. Wind, "Contemporary German Philosophy," 518.

Ernst Gombrich's 1970 intellectual biography of Warburg, Wind invoked the commonplace that Warburg "knew the dangers of excessive empathy" and that "having entered deeply, as a witness of contemporary political history, into the spirit of a whole cluster of quite calamitous decisions that left the comity of nations in a shambles, this good European went out of his mind in 1918."[28] In this gloss, a "magnanimous" capacity to enter into narrative continuations of the decisions of others led to a madness in which the assembled and mutually incompatible scripts of a schizoid war culture progressively colonized and then consumed their human host.

In his purely skeptical attitude toward empathy (I would argue), Wind was recognizing the Dionysian side of Warburgian magnanimity without taking its Apollonian antistrophe into account. The more genuine Warburgian practice had been an oscillating in which one shuttled between, on the one hand, identifying oneself with body postures in order to understand them and, on the other, attending to the Apollonian revision of this practice in which such body positionings once taken up in one's own body then became elements of a shared vocabulary that one might deploy as social tokening rather than impersonation. To be sure, Wind had not been entirely wrong in 1931 when he took Warburg to have been saying that "any attempt to excise the image from its embeddedness in religion and poetry [or] cultic practice and drama amounts to cutting off its very lifeblood," but in framing matters thus he was neglecting to emphasize the middle ground between complete identification and intellectualized alienation.[29] As I argued in the previous chapter, the construction and negotiation of this middle ground had been one of the prime tasks of Warburg's *Bilderatlas*.

One can capture indecision in the dialectical images of painting and photography (where figures are captured in moments of genuine divergence), and there have been Warburgians who have developed this line of inquiry. Reading Masaccio's fifteenth-century fresco *Expulsion from Paradise* alongside the conventional signs adopted by the Benedictine Order for communicating during periods of silence, Michael Baxandall—another Warburgian art historian—argued in 1972 that we see Masaccio's painting "as combining in the paired figures two inflections of emotion." In Baxandall's reading, "it is Adam (*lumina tegens digitis*) who expresses shame, Eve (*palma premens pectus*) only grief."[30] Masaccio's pairing of figures raised the possibility that alternatives were being articulated. We may add that Eve covers not only

28. Wind, "Biography of Warburg," 111.

29. Wind, "Warburgs Begriff der Kulturwissenschaft," 168: "es ist eine der Grundüberzeugungen Warburgs, daß jeder Versuch, das Bild aus seiner Beziehung zu Religion und Poesie, Kulthandlung und Drama herauszulösen, der Abschnürung seiner eigentlichen Lebenssäfte gleichkommt."

30. Baxandall, *Painting and Experience*, 61.

her breast but also her sex, and perhaps this argues against Baxandall's hypothesis that this figure is minting a socially communicable sign of grief but not shame. In any case, my deeper point holds: the alternatives available to a single body may be displayed and made available for use on multiple bodies.

At the point where images conjure alternatives, we encounter anthropologies of the image that have been developed in the late twentieth and early twenty-first centuries. These were initiatives pursued by the likes of the art historian Hans Belting. Here, too, the Warburgian heritage is very much in play. As Belting put it in the preface to the English reader added to his *Anthropology of Images* in 2011, "Warburg would have developed his own anthropology of images had his thinking not been narrowed [in reception] by the iconology of Erwin Panofsky and Edgar Wind."[31] There are moments of real insight in Belting's appropriation of Warburg. He observes how "one can go as far as understanding portraits generally speaking as masks that have become independent of bodies and have been shifted into a new carrier medium."[32] In this reading, heraldry "produced *de jure* persons," and death itself turns a being into a mask.[33] Here Belting is showing his readers how artworks contribute to the formation of a semantic economy of expressive and gestural exchange. Furthermore, we are witnessing a very specific Warburgian afterlife when we hear Belting relay the story of the contest between Marsyas and Apollo that Ovid told in his *Metamorphoses*. "Why do you tear me from myself?" Marsyas the satyr asks as he loses both his hide and his life. Because, we might respond, it is the very essence of the Apollonian to inaugurate social tokening by, as it were, skinning the phenomena that appear in the civil world.[34] The trophy pelt is a social token par excellence because the scene of death stretches so compellingly into its own narrativization.

I am suggesting that one of the tasks of criticism is to locate fault lines within dialectical images of all kinds and mark potential continuation. Benjamin's reading of Brecht finds an unwitting but potent continuation in Belting's analysis of the moments at which expression is separated from life-form in such a way that it takes on both the appearance and the function of a masking that has its being in social tokening. As we saw in chapter 5 and see again now, Brecht was experimenting with a kind of modernist

31. Belting, *Anthropology of Images*, 2.

32. Belting, *Bild-Anthropologie*, 37: "man kann wohl so weit gehen, Porträts überhaupt als Masken zu verstehen, die vom Körper unabhängig geworden und auf ein neues Trägermedium übertragen worden sind."

33. Belting, 122 and 143ff. The language of "*de jure* persons" is taken up from the Austrian philosopher Walter Seitter.

34. Belting, 209.

prosopopoeia. This was a mask making that did things to social codes by manifesting those codes consciously and performatively on a physiognomy or a body. Belting's anthropology of images is an exploration of what I described earlier as the "somewhat elastic rope" structuring Benjamin's reading of actorly theory and practice. Only when the mask is "wooden" enough that it pulls free of a body does it begin to signify in a more complicated way as ornament.

In the classic Schmittian formulation of decisionism, the moment of decision's punctum had neither past nor future (for it supplied no reason and considered no consequence). In the Benjaminian and Warburgian exit from this imaginary, however, the moment of decision itself was dilated and splayed. The body caught in the moment of indecision would be itself a body caught up in a multiplicity of motions and narrativizations. The French thinker Georges Didi-Huberman was both right and perceptive when he inserted into this Warburgian line of inquiry the Freudian presupposition that "the symptom represents the realization of two contradictory desires."[35] As Benjamin had suggested, the point would itself divide, revealing an extension between two poles, and such interpolation was an imaginative attention to the mix of conations tracing out from the nexus of indecision. As Warburg had suggested, this was not simply the enumeration of different possibilities; it was also the arrangement of a series of persuasions from one movement to another such that the image table became a topos agglomerating a variety of hypotheses in which one might experiment with the shift from one narrativization to another. That we find versions of these hypotheses in a variety of postwar thinkers influenced by these Weimar "rhetoricians" is both a verification of this book's prediction and a repertoire of potential refinements.

JUDGMENT

Sometimes we call indecision "crisis." Such crisis may be prolonged or brief, but in essence it is "a bracketings of nested possibility." When we say that someone is in crisis, we mean they face choices and cannot decide, and we possess a vocabulary with which to express the winnowing down of options as possibility shades into necessity. Beyond "trilemma" and "dilemma," there is "Hobson's choice," where the appearance of alternatives is a sham and there is only really a single option. The Bielefeld historical semanticist Reinhart Koselleck had placed issues of crisis and decision at the heart of his 1959 book *Critique and Crisis*, which dealt with what he described as the "pathogenesis of modernity." In his subsequent 1982 theorization of

35. Didi-Huberman, *"Dialektik des Montrums,"* 634.

crisis, Koselleck developed the twentieth-century German interest in decision. On the basis of a historicization of the older medical and theological
conceptualizations of the term, he then concluded that "'crisis' turns into a
structural signature of modernity."[36] The wager was that modernity was a
hyperconsciousness of history turning every socially transactable moment
into a moment of potentially systemic change.

If we read the post-Weimar Arendtian line of thought in a standard received manner, we will eventually come to the conclusion that judgment
is the key faculty exercised in the midst of crisis and that judgment is to
be understood as something like practical wisdom allowing human beings
to negotiate circumstance. On this account, judgment becomes a kind of
renovated and originally Aristotelian *phronēsis*. That is, judgment would
be a practical capacity both to see the consequences of actions responding
to the call for decision and then to choose among them in ways that do
indeed promote desired goals. In the conventional reading, Arendt spliced
this Aristotelian inheritance together with a Kantian one in which the practical wisdom of *phronēsis* would participate in a kind of "broadened manner
of thinking." *Erweiterte Denkungsart* was the Kantian phrase that Arendt
emphasized here.[37] In this process, one brought the perspectives of others
into play for the purpose of seeing one's situation more fully and constituting that situation as a kind of public sphere characterized both by difference
of opinion and by a process of giving reasons for one's perspective.

Scholars have calculated trajectories issuing from the Arendtian position largely on the basis of unpublished materials. In a story that has
often been repeated (because it gestures so evocatively to the task and
temptation of continuing her work), we are told that Arendt died in 1975
with a sheet of paper inserted in her typewriter bearing only two epigraphs
together with the words, "Life of the Mind, Part III, Judging." The inference has been that had she lived longer Arendt's next project would have
been a volume on judging and that this would have completed a would-be
trilogy that appeared in partial form in 1978 with the publication of *Thinking* and *Willing*. Since Ronald Beiner's 1982 edition of materials used in
classes that Arendt offered at the New School in 1970 under the title *Lectures on Kant's Political Philosophy*, scholars have addressed themselves to
the question of whether these notes offer us the best anticipation of how
Arendt would have finished *The Life of the Mind*. Synthesizing what has
become a large literature, we can say that these scholars tend to believe
that Arendtian judgment is a capacity to articulate one's own position in

36. Koselleck, "Krise," 626: "'Krise' wird zur strukturellen Signatur der Neuzeit." See Koselleck,
Kritik und Krise, 146: "die Krise wird zum moralischen Prozeß."
37. See, for instance, Beiner, "Hannah Arendt and Judging," 134ff, where Beiner emphasizes the
tensions involved in thinking Aristotelian *phronēsis* and Kantian *Urteilskraft* together.

such a way that one recognizes the perspectives of others even as one expresses and advocates for one's own. As Linda Zerilli has parsed it, the problem was this: how should we think about judgment "in contemporary democratic societies [that are] characterized by deep value pluralism"? In such societies, the argument goes, judgment cannot be thought of as the application of shared principles.[38] Arendt's specification of judgment becomes an important capacity in diverse political communities because it permits citizens to articulate their perspectives in ways that do not presume agreement about first principles.

There is an alternative to the interpretation just relayed. The Arendtian minority report that I extrapolate now builds on different unpublished sources and proposes that we may understand Arendtian judgment less in terms of either Aristotelian *phronēsis* or Kantian *Urteilskraft* and more in terms of a process of discerning that in her own thought Arendt anchored with the Greek term *krinein*.[39] The 1970 New School course on judging was tremendously important (and its contents have constituted a treasure trove of thoughts), but the archival sources attesting to Arendt's position on judging are more complex and more widely distributed than Beiner's important edition suggested. We can develop a sharper account of judgment and what it might mean to a political community if we attend more closely to some of these other sources. In particular, material from the *Denktagebuch*—Arendt's intellectual diary, first published in 2003—can give us a quite different sense of what judgment actually does. In that diary, she often attached the English term "judgment" not to the Greek word "practical wisdom" (*phronēsis*) but rather to "distinguishing" (*krinein*).

If we connect the usage of "distinguishing" (*krinein*) to her readings of Hegel's *Science of Logic* (in 1952), Aristotle's *Rhetoric* (in 1953), and Kant's *Critique of the Power of Judgment* (in 1957), we discover that for Arendt the term denoted a process of "synthesizing differentiation" that was integral to perception as well as predication itself. The essential idea was that any attribution of a predicate to a subject was something like pulling a quality or qualities out of a sensory manifold. To judge would be to discern a characteristic and to distill that characteristic in some public assertion. We should understand this in relation to the Kantian account of reflective judgment. Kant had distinguished between "determinative" (*bestimmende*) and "reflective" (*reflektierende*) judgment, and this distinction underwrote a contrast between subsuming a particular case under a rule and eliciting a rule from a case. The *Denktagebuch* reveals Arendt engaging with Hegel's

38. Zerilli, *Democratic Theory of Judgment*, xii.

39. Arendt, *Denktagebuch, 1950 bis 1973*, 1:408, where Arendt was working from Aristotle, *Rhetoric*, 1354b29–1355a1.

intimation that reflective judgment—where the case produces and is not subsumed—was judgment in its truest form.[40]

At first, the examples of judgment that Arendt took up were banal. When we say "the sky is blue," she maintained, we are not merely predicating the quality "blue" of a subject named "sky." We are also eliciting "blueness" from an evental substrate. If we make the "is" in that sentence transitive rather than predicative, we see that—in the originally poetic occasion of this utterance—the sky was manifesting blueness and sharpening the being of that color by making it conspicuous and utterable in a new way: not "the sky is blue" but rather "the sky manifests and thus exemplifies blueness." This was a double movement of binding and separating that Arendt termed "the origin of all abstract thought."[41] "Cicero is a great orator" was the example that she took up from Hegel in order to demonstrate how one might elicit a quality from a subject. This was not a particularly good example, however, precisely because of the hackneyed quality of the criticism.[42] No one needs to be told that Cicero is exemplary for oratory.

The early examples were banal, but the later examples were explosive. In fact, Arendt's account of "distinguishing" (*krinein*) made sense of what in the context of this book we may call her properly "topical" style of political criticism. The better example of *krinein* in Arendt's political criticism is her 1963 book *Eichmann in Jerusalem*. Eichmann is better than Cicero as an example of *krinein* because Arendt genuinely did something new in her elaboration of the meaning of "Eichmann" as a topos. Whatever we think of the politics of the Eichmann book (whether it was a courageous or deeply problematic effort), we should recognize that the form of Arendt's argument turned on the properly critical work of distinguishing a quality from a subject. The book was remarkable not simply for its politics but also for its literary process. Eichmann was evil but in a banal way. "Evil but banal" was not an already differentiated quality that Arendt attached to Eichmann. It was, on the contrary, a quality that Arendt elicited from the horrific exemplum of Eichmann. The quality is not thinkable except, at first, in the context of its case. The quality emerged from the "background" of Eichmann.

In theory, Arendt's account of *krinein* can take its place in a broader argument concerning the importance of articulateness for the possibility of community. Arendtian judgment was intimately bound up with the process of naming. Perhaps the primary function of such practices of judging

---

40. Kant, *Kritik der Urteilskraft*, 15–16; Hegel, *Wissenschaft der Logik*, 2:280; Arendt, *Denktagebuch, 1950 bis 1973*, 1:286 and 571. I cite the Kant and Hegel editions that Arendt used.

41. Hannah Arendt Papers, Box 58, "Political Theory of Kant," course at University of California, Berkeley, 1955, ms. 032308.

42. Arendt, *Denktagebuch, 1950 bis 1973*, 1:286. Compare Hegel, *Wissenschaft der Logik*, 2:279.

would be the development of a rich vocabulary anchored in exempla. Such exempla would be naturally occurring or artistically occasioned phenomena taken up and shared by a community. Framing this analysis are the claims that a community's arguments will be contoured by a perceiving together (or apart) and that—on average—a community possessing a richly articulated vocabulary will conduct its political affairs more capaciously. Care for and attention to the shared intelligibilities of phenomena that name is political work. In the account I am working up here, terms such as "beautiful" do not genuinely name qualities at all. They are instead a kind of intersubjectively important punctuation. Pseudopredicates such as "beautiful" tag a phenomenon and express before a public the contention that subjecting this particular phenomenon to aesthetic and political criticism will enhance that community's powers of articulation.

The work of distinguishing that I am describing here in an Arendtian key is distinct from the work of unmasking that is also sometimes associated with "criticism." For example, the "revolutionary criticism" that Terry Eagleton confected from the Benjaminian corpus aimed at ascribing to rhetoric "the function of unmasking all power as self-rationalization, all knowledge as a mere fumbling with metaphor." It sought to turn rhetoric into a "vigorous demystifier of all ideology."[43] This is a venerable and still viable line of inquiry, but it is distinct from the Arendtian line I am distinguishing here. As I have been arguing in the course of this book, naming is related to a process of differentiating that fixes and secures possibilities. The task of a "criticism" based on *krinein* is a topical articulation of the stations of change. Such a criticism accepts that motion exists in continua. It accepts that any given name may well be in the process of pulling apart amid the kind of interpolation that Benjamin hypothesized. Nonetheless, it emphasizes the importance of securing particular calibrations of difference in the interim.

When Arendt emphasized *krinein* in her reading of Aristotle's *Rhetoric* in 1953, she was directly or indirectly picking up on one of the lines that Heidegger had appropriated from Aristotle in Summer Semester 1924. To specify Arendt's thinking here, we need to distinguish her approach from other Heideggerian treatments of judgment. As we saw in chapter 3, Heidegger took up the supposition that "moving" (*kinein*) and "distinguishing" (*krinein*) were the two basic principles of the Aristotelian soul. Arendt's distinctiveness within the Heidegger penumbra emerges when we can compare her case to that of the Italian scholar Ernesto Grassi. Grassi had also studied with Heidegger during the prewar period, and in the aftermath of the war he became a significant figure in the history of twentieth-century rhetoric. In

43. Eagleton, *Benjamin*, 108.

the present context, we should attend to the ways in which Grassi was very basically preoccupied with what he termed "differentiation" (*Differenzierung*). Indeed, it was precisely in the vicinity of this concept that in 1942 Grassi discovered both rhetoric and—I do not grow tired of pointing out these connections—the neo-Latin rhetorical project of Giambattista Vico. At this moment during the war, both rhetoric and Vico seemed to Grassi like potential continuations of the Heideggerian program that he in some ways shared with Arendt.[44]

For Grassi, "differentiation" was one of the others of, or contraries to, modern massification. Following Heidegger, he saw massification at work in both the Soviet and American alternatives to the Italo-German lineage that he worked to recover and advance both during and after the Second World War.[45] One of the key texts here is Grassi's *Defense of Individual Life* (1946). As he was at pains to point out, Grassi wished to defend individuated rather than individualist life. The life he championed was differentiated and thereby individuated in the sense of achieving distinctiveness in heroic performance.[46] It was less important that an individual be forged in such moments of heroism than that individuated names be seared into the cultural memory—as agents or qualities or processes. This, too, amounted to a political defense of a certain kind of aesthetics. Some performances achieved a distinctiveness that one had to capture for a community in the semiosis of a language. Art—in all media—had to fix a hero against the background of its historically specific scene. Beauty had to be articulated.

The degree to which individuating beauty was a shared task for Grassi remains a question, and there is a related question about whether he ever genuinely specified the scene of his own heroic writerly deeds at this point in his career. In precisely this moment, Vico was becoming central to Grassi's research, and yet we cannot specify how he stood in relation to the Neapolitan's core point about Homer as a collective rather than individual author. In approximately 1946, when Grassi said "we win all the possibilities of our language through the poets and not through the babbling of the many," he was channeling Heidegger on Hölderlin more than Vico on Homer.[47] In the original, what I am rendering here as "babbling" was the Heideggerian term of art *Gerede*. If *Gerede* is first and foremost a speaking that has come loose from its original situation, then it characterizes the quotation from Grassi that I just reproduced: Grassi was participating in the *Gerede* idiom in a generic fashion, "as any Heideggerian might." The genericness of this utterance is underscored by the fact that we do not know precisely

44. Grassi, "Über das Problem des Wortes," 21 and 60.
45. Grassi, *Verteidigung*, 11.
46. Grassi, "Über das Problem des Wortes," 9.
47. Grassi, *Verteidigung*, 33: "durch die Dichter gewinnen wir alle Möglichkeiten unserer Sprache, nicht durch das Gerede der vielen."

when these words on poets and *Gerede* emerged. "In Germany, sometime between 1942 and 1946" is probably the best approximation. As any reader can see, this is a very particular kind of indeterminacy, and it raises basic questions about Grassi's project.

Grassi's *Defense of Individual Life* (*Verteidigung des individuellen Lebens*) was fundamental to his entire intellectual trajectory in the postwar period, but he gave us no way of individuating the precise place and time of its original context. It was written during World War II and published after the defeat of the Axis powers. The preface specifies "Rome, December 1945"; the colophon, 1946. Yet the book displayed no consciousness whatsoever of radical changes in the world-historical situation that emerged between 1942 and 1946. We should recall that Grassi operated as Benito Mussolini's cultural ambassador in Adolf Hitler's wartime Berlin. In that capacity and in the eye of the storm in 1942, Grassi founded the Institute for the Study of Humanity. The revisionist scholarship that has emerged in recent years has not established whether Grassi clearly compromised himself during the war.[48] We may hypothesize that the same caginess and political acumen that allowed Grassi to navigate this treacherous situation also made it difficult for him to situate his project with the degree of individuation that he, in principle, valued. Was Grassi's work during the war an attempt to write a Latin and Italian version of the Heideggerian Teuto-Greek alternative to the massifications of American capitalism and Soviet communism? Or was it a covert critique of totalitarian society? Grassi does not seem to have said clearly what kind of situation he took himself to be in during this period. For these reasons, his *Defense of Individual Life* remains deeply ambiguous.

The more we lay out Grassi's intellectual position as it emerged in the early 1940s, the more we become aware of the comparative obscurity of his historical position. From Heidegger he took up the basic point about truth as "unconcealedness" (*alētheia*). Expressing himself in an idiom taken very directly from his former teacher, Grassi said that "the problem of truth remains . . . wholly determined in the question concerning the being of the self-disclosing [*Sich-Zeigen*] of something."[49] Truth is the manifestation of a definition, and, as we move through the argument, we see that individuated life is the appearance of "the objective" in the sense of a phenomenon that shows itself in such a way that it can function as its own name. The manifestation that can function as a name is the *first* appearance of a thing, and the humanistic arts are to be organized as modes of philological attention to such moments of primordial naming.[50] The discussions of Vico, the

48. Büttemeyer, *Ernesto Grassi*, 301–3, 318–20. And compare Rubini, review of *Ernesto Grassi*, 540.
49. Grassi, *Vom Vorrang des Logos*, 42: "das Problem der Wahrheit bleibt . . . ganz allgemein bestimmt als die Frage nach dem Wesen des Sich-Zeigens von etwas."
50. Grassi, "Vom Wahren und Wahrscheinlichen," 61.

ars topica, and the power of images that were to occupy so much of Grassi's later work all emerged as versions of this basic concern with naming.

In Grassi's inflection of the Heideggerian tradition, rhetoric itself became an orientation to the moment and its contexts considered as occasions and occasionings of the name. In ways that I wish both to compare and to contrast to the Arendtian lineage discerned here, the Grassian orator was to give birth to names. In descrying situations, that orator would open a space for the appearance of a phenomenon against its proper and fullest background. The orator was thus distinguished by an unusual and, in Grassi's figuration, elite capacity for "passion" (*Leidenschaft*). Such an individual would become a *scene* for the visitation of the phenomenon naming itself in the orator's speech.[51] Within that broader frame, the "rhetorical" faculty that took pride of place within Grassi's project was, once again, *ingenium*. As Grassi later described it in 1968, *ingenium* was not simply a capacity to perceive similitudes between distant or apparently unrelated things but also "the faculty that takes the primordial, the 'archaic,' as its object."[52] In Grassi's rendition, "topics" was very much a field of originary sensing.

As I am construing it, Arendt's project was both related to and distinct from Grassi's. To secure the difference, we need to create a distance between her emerging sense of judgment as distinguishing and the superficially similar articulations of someone like Walter Bröcker. Bröcker, too, had studied with Heidegger. His notes on the Summer Semester 1924 lectures are some of the most detailed, and they played an important role in the reconstitution of those lectures in the *Gesamtausgabe* edition of 2002. Bröcker's dissertation focused on Kant's critique of aesthetic judgment. It appeared in 1928, a year before Arendt's on Augustine, and it is a testing ground for the construction of judgment within the Heideggerian tradition. In that dissertation, Bröcker offered up the doctrinaire notion that "intelligibility belongs to the beautiful essentially."[53] On the surface, this formulation appears to be related to my emphasis on the role of Arendtian *krinein* in the development of articulateness. From this connection between beauty and intelligibility, however, Bröcker inferred that the activation of the work of art would be primarily conceptual because it would instantiate and thereby communicate a concept by embodying that concept in some way. Paraphrasing Kant but revealing his own perspective in the process, Bröcker stipulated that the work of art would communicate "a concept that is enlarged in its representation on account of such presentation." In this gloss, "that which is communicated" (*das Mitgeteilte*) will be "a concept"

51. Grassi, *Verteidigung*, 168.
52. Grassi, "G. B. Vico," 507: "die Fähigkeit, die das ursprüngliche, das 'Archaische' zum Gegenstand hat."
53. Bröcker, *Kants Kritik*, 110: "zum Schönen gehört wesentlich Verständlichkeit."

(*ein Begriff*).[54] Here we have the beginnings of a Bröckerian trajectory for the early Heidegger of the 1920s.

We can distinguish Arendt more clearly by placing her within a Heideggerian aesthetic tradition alongside both Grassi and Bröcker. Bröcker diverges from the Arendtian tradition I am distilling here by insisting that the work of art cannot be a "communication" (*Mitteilung*). For him, the genuine work of art does not communicate; for her, it contributes to the coming into being of language itself. This prior move is crucial in the Arendtian turn of the argument, and it is consonant with the common intuition that works of art are not rhetorical and cannot be said to stage direct oratorical appeals to beholders. Art makes communication possible. It does so by staging the *appearance in time* of something that names a new phenomenon or quality. Equally, Arendt and Grassi share Heideggerian presupposition about the topical work of naming achieved by poetry, but they part ways when it comes to the degree to which each articulated the historical situation of their political criticism: Arendt did a great deal of this; Grassi, not much. Excavating the banality of evil from the appearance of Eichmann could happen only once, and the literary-critical performance of excavation was integral to the process.

If in the previous section interpolation appeared like a deux ex machina descending on an image in order to save it from becoming its own definition, we find now that, in the guise of *krinein*, Arendtian judgment would be the faculty making such interpolation possible. As we saw in chapter 6, predication may be understood as a form of interpolation. The appearance that seems singular and unitary in the first instance comes apart in a logical operation. Only in retrospect can that predication seem to be the suturing together of two distinct things—namely, a subject and a quality (or set of qualities). Articulating into being an extension between "Eichmann" and "evil but in the aspect of banality" amounts to an interpolation of his apparition. If this manner of speaking seems radically different from the standard received Arendt (famous for her conceptualizations of "action" and "natality"), then we should reassess our understandings of those concepts, because—as we began to see in chapter 4—performance establishes its own spaces of appearance. Just so here, exemplarities begin the cultural historical work of constituting topoi, and these topoi are so many spaces of appearance for future actions.

MODALITY AND EVERYDAYNESS

Within the tradition I am inventing, the emphasis on attending to moments of actualization and exemplification that we have been dealing with

54. Bröcker, 110.

motivates investigation of processes of accumulation in zones demarcated by exempla. In the previous section, I was eliciting a line from within the Arendtian tradition of thinking about judgment. That line emphasized both the identification of moments at which something new had presented itself to a community and the critical work of articulating that novelty in such a way that it might be captured in an expressive idiom. In the current section, I am shifting from this set of arguments to another related set of arguments that pick up from the moment in which exemplification has happened. These arguments attend to the zones of topical accretion that such exemplification makes possible. *Eichmann in Jerusalem* brought a category of analysis into being that has to be articulated further with reference to other exempla because "Eichmann" does not exhaust the category of "evil but in a banal way." In the current section, I explore the variety of approaches to this process that are discernable in the Weimar afterlife. In particular, I emphasize receptions and construals of the Heideggerian concept of everydayness. As we saw in chapter 3, Heideggerian everydayness may also be understood topically as a modality in which phenomena accrete.

As with the other strands of the reception history being woven in this chapter, there are angles on Heideggerian "everydayness" (*Alltäglichkeit*) that have to be registered and described so that they can be questioned or decentered. As I contended in chapter 3, Heidegger himself contributed to a dulling of the concept of the everyday. We can detect these tendencies in the earliest appropriations of his work. In his 1928 investigation of *The Individual in the Role of Fellow Human Being*, for example, Karl Löwith— who participated in Heidegger's Summer Semester 1924 lectures along with Gadamer and Bröcker—rendered Heideggerian "being-with-one-another" (*Miteinandersein*) as a merely dialogical and highly personal spacing between "I" (*Ich*) and "you" (*Du*). This construal effaced much of the suppleness of the German formulation "with-an-other" (*mit-ein-ander*). It constituted a turning away from the earlier versions of Heidegger's thought because it did not attend to the timed and spaced appearance of a dialog against the background of "received speech" (*Gerede*).[55] The modality of performativity only functions in reference to a modality of everyday ersatz necessity. Indeed, when Löwith punctuated the thought with references to the merely generic pronouns "we" (*wir*) and especially "one" (*man*), we can detect precisely the banalization of everydayness as a concept that remains characteristic of *Being and Time*. When "everydayness" becomes simply a term of abuse or distaste or condescension, it loses the analytical precision it possessed when it pointed out the writing and overwriting or sedimentary quality of "every-day-anew" practices. In turn, disparaging the

55. Löwith, *Das Individuum*, 55.

everyday produces a kind of reactionary desire to justify the everyday, the noneventual, the peripheral in and of itself. As so often, the bifurcations of rejection and vindication are unhelpful here.

A teacher is not responsible for a student's thoughts, but the intellectual history of construal within a pedagogical context can tell us how an idea may lose its promise in the course of its repetition as a commonplace. As we have seen, Walter Bröcker was tremendously important in the capturing and passing on of Heidegger's 1924 lectures, but philological scruple is only ever half the battle. In this case, the student tended to fail at the task of thinking his teacher's thoughts in new and creative ways. In Bröcker's Aristotle book (first published in 1935 and republished many times since), we find a flattened commitment to "wonder." It is a commitment that shortchanges— indeed, misconceives—the role of everydayness in Heideggerian ontology. Bröcker could say that "wonder [*das Staunen*] disturbs human beings from their dormancy [*Ruhe*]" and that "wonder brings with it the discovery of not-knowing."[56] Yet the more genuinely Heideggerian point would be that the everyday does not simply disappear in the presence of wonder. The unusual comes into focus surrounded by the continued presence of an everyday that the unusual nonetheless displaces. The unusual deviates from the mean. The more intensively Heideggerian reception of Heidegger is one that resists the statisticalization of relationships between the usual and the unusual. What this means is that we should not understand "deviation" in terms of number but instead in terms of the twist or askance readiness of particular displaced body actualizations and their immediate possibilities.

In the reception of Heideggerian thinking on modality, there has often been something of a flat overemphasis on "actuality" (*energeia*), as if actualization might be separated wholly from the "possibility" (*dunamis*) out of which it emerges and, similarly, from the "completedness" (*entelecheia*) to which it is, perhaps, destined. Arendt's beautiful but actually relatively empty emphasis on the *energeia* or performativity of action in and after *The Human Condition* of 1958 is less evocative for rhetorical and political criticism than the early topical spaces explored in the book on Rahel Varnhagen. And Ernesto Grassi was contributing to a similar dimming down, or "marble-ization," when he argued that rhetoric was the fundamental mode of inquiry because it attended to moments of the greatest hereness and nowness—the moments of greatest performativity.[57] Witness his repetition in 1950 of the standard received version of the Heideggerian everydayness topos together with his refusal to think the value of fragmentariness:

56. Bröcker, *Aristoteles*, 19, 20: "das Staunen stört den Menschen aus seiner Ruhe auf," and "das Staunen bringt die Entdeckung des Nichtwissens."
57. Grassi, *Vico and Humanism*, 164–65.

"everyday life in contrast to drama is only fragmentary."[58] Presence implies or even requires something like hypotaxis—namely, a suturing together of all parts.

Heidegger had his obsessions, and presencing was certainly one of them, but if we attend as much to his practice as to his pronouncements, then we find—especially in the early lectures—a basic orientation to fragments and an underdetermined interest in their serial extrapolation. Before, in his name, we fetishize the culminating moment or the moment that is able to organize all others as subordinate clauses, we should recall Heidegger's line on the beautiful discontinuity of the pre-Socratic fragments.[59] Those fragments were saved by quotation, and it was precisely their self-contained and radically polyvocal, irreducible, and paratactic quality that made them so inexhaustibly quotable. Nor should the issue of "quotability" strike us as a merely ivory-tower pursuit with little influence in the world. After all, thought more deeply, quotation is actually something like the conative proposal of a beginning. Quoting an aphoristic fragment is a process of taking up a principle as a license for—and spur to—action.

Much closer to the generative heart of early Heideggerian thinking that I have been evoking in this book was Helene Weiss's gloss of what she transliterated into English for an Anglophone audience as "being-able-to-be." This phrase denoted both potential as such and also underdetermination. Weiss had worked with Heidegger in the early 1930s, and we see the beginnings of an intimate reading of power in her 1941 insistence that "man 'is' always some of his potentialities . . . even if they will never in any future 'now' actually be present."[60] Being is also ability-to-be, and there is no need for a particular future to be realized for it to structure a present in the manner of a possibility: a power never exercised may nonetheless exert influence. Temptation is a sweet guilt cultivated by enduring—even purposeful—inaction. A threat is both more purely itself and more effective when it has not been carried out, and there is a sense in which power always destroys itself in actualization. Power is potential-to-be. One orients oneself to power not simply out of masochism but also and more basically because power is a point around which many different futures gather. The corollary would be that the psychodynamics of power are most precisely legible in the radiating paths of known unknowns.

Weiss's emphasis on chance helps us reinforce the arguments made in chapter 6 concerning Warburg's treatment of ornament, and her emphasis helps us prepare the way for continuations of that line of thinking in the Warburgian afterlife. Given the centrality of "chance" (*Zufall*) in her 1942

58. Grassi and Uexküll, *Geisteswissenschaften und Naturwissenschaften*, 87: "das alltägliche Leben ist eben im Gegensatz zum Drama nur ein fragmentarisches."
59. Heidegger, *Überlegungen II–VI*, 390.
60. Weiss, "Greek Conceptions," 185.

dissertation, we should not be surprised by the richness of Weiss's work on modality.[61] The essence of her point in that work had been that we can only begin to understand the Aristotelian and broader Greek conception of chance (and enrich our own abilities to conceive of these things in the process) if we understand those conceptions as iterations of the topos that a phenomenon may define itself in the process of its appearance. Attending to chance is attending to times of less intense "presence" because chance is a name for the ways in which the elements of an appearance appear mutually indifferent and do not coalesce into form or narrativization. Weiss's intuitions are more helpful than Bröcker's (and more helpful than Grassi's, too) precisely because she did not immediately gravitate toward the moments in which truth qua self-definition "happened."

As Weiss pointed out in 1942, we may read the Greek term for "chance" (*tuchē*) through the pun suggested by its German translation (*Zufall*). The German suggests that, in reality, chance is nothing more than a falling together, a "happening-alongside." (As "co-inciding," the pun works with the English equivalent "coincidence" too.) On this account, what we ought to focus on when we speak of "chance events" is not what (if anything) caused the coincidence of two things. We should focus instead on how we are unable to think them together as part of a broader self-disclosing process. Given the Heideggerian context in which Weiss was continuing to work, the antonym we should set out in opposition to "chance" is precisely "presencing"—in the sense of a phenomenon characterized by *energeia* (being-at-work, being-in-play, actualizing). *Tuchē* is not identical with *sumbebēkos*. That is (more or less), "coincidence" is not synonymous with "accident." But the difference is actually rather subtle. At base, it may be nothing more than a distinction between nonrelation among predicates attributed to separate phenomena (*tuchē*) and nonrelation among predicates attributed to the same phenomenon (*sumbebēkos*). Chance, thus, is a jumbled, chaotic, fractured, paratactic field of experience—a form of nonpresencing. This is "nothing," but it is a nothing in the sense of being "no-thing-in-particular."

In contrast, we have long known that some of the most creative receptions of the Heideggerian initiative insisted on more complex relationships between presence and absence, actualizing and chance, hypotaxis and parataxis. Jacques Derrida was being unusually forthright when he said that "*ousia*, as *energeia* in contradistinction to *dunamis* (movement power), is presence." With this simple articulation and decentering, an entire economy of absences was put on the agenda.[62] Agamben was working on the same problematic when he declared that potentiality could not be

61. Weiss, *Kausalität und Zufall.*
62. Derrida, "*Ousia et Grammē,*" 239: "l'*ousia* comme *energeia* par opposition à la *dunamis* (mouvement, puissance) est présence."

understood simply as nonbeing and that in fact potentiality was the much more paradoxical and much more interesting "presence of an absence."[63] Even a reader as unsympathetic as Adorno was offering us ways of using the Heideggerian account of ontology when he described the Hölderlin poetry that so obsessed Heidegger as essentially paratactic.[64] Parataxis makes absence present by making the nonspecifiability of the fragment palpable.

I am suggesting—and this is a crucial part of my argument here—that when we understand it as many-timed-ness, everydayness approximates a kind of topical collecting in which fragments of appearance are not statisticalized and do not disappear into a mean. This emphasis suggests that—visceral and acute as it may have been—it might be better to put aside Adorno's famous critique of Heidegger in *Jargon of Authenticity* (1964). Setting aside that critique, we can investigate the aphoristic power of the fragment—which precisely refuses context and resists contextualization. If hypotaxis spans the here and now, then parataxis narrows the frame. The hypotactic Ciceronian period asks readers to wait for a discursive phenomenon to come more fully into view. In contrast, the paratactic fragment says, "this is all there is; begin again." A motley of quotations becomes something like a raft of potential beginnings where questions of mutual exclusion have been suspended because there is an operative assumption that beginning is *continually* an issue. When we attend to the paratactic gaps between items on aphoristic lists, we see that aphorisms breed aphorisms.

One of Giorgio Agamben's thought experiments shows us how coincidence, potentiality, actualization, and everydayness have to be dealt with as an ensemble. The experiment in question is simply a form of slow motion, but it is handled in such a way that it becomes an analytic of everydayness. Experiments with speed reveal modality in especially perspicuous ways. Acceleration reveals diurnal or seasonal patterns as the presencing of these phenomena is made consonant with the scales of human motion and pattern recognition. Similarly, deceleration also reveals the clustering of phenomena that exist in the vicinity of an actualization and that give it structure in the mode of background alternatives. In fact, extreme slowness generates potentiality. Take, for example, Agamben's interpretation of *The Passions*, a film-photographic sequence created by the contemporary video artist Bill Viola.[65] These were visual explorations at the boundary between photography and film. Viola slowed down his filmic representations of emotional states to the point that glancing at those images at any given moment they seemed to show a static pose. At the same time, however, more sustained

63. Agamben, "On Potentiality," 179.
64. Adorno, "Parataxis," 15–46.
65. Agamben, *Ninfe*, 7–10.

attention revealed to viewers that these images were in a glacial but perpetual motion. This radical deceleration produced what Agamben felicitously termed "kairological saturation" (*saturazione cairologica*).[66] Every moment in these glacial flows was a time when a microemotion came into and then passed out of focus. If the movement of the entire sequence was an arc, then each moment in that arc proposed a trajectory continuing the motion but in a way distinct from the course eventually taken.

Agamben explored the problematic of kairological saturation by retrojecting it onto *On the Art of Dancing and Moving* by Domenico da Piacenza, the fifteenth-century Italian dance theorist. In Domenico's idiom, dance was to be understood as the serial isolation of poses. Thus, "at each interval you seem to have caught sight of Medusa's head" with the result that "the movement completed, you are to appear made of stone in one instant, before—in the next—you take flight like a falcon moved by hunger."[67] The point was that alternations of speed and slowness would reveal the extreme "knobbliness" of being, which was constantly coming into and passing out of focus. Here, "focus" is to be understood as the presence of a phenomenon that raises the question of whether it is a name. As taken up by Agamben, Domenico's interest in presencing assumed a topical form, because the multiplicity of forms recast the stage as a repertoire of potential poses. In this respect, the schemas of Domenico were akin to both the allegories of Benjamin's *Trauerspiele* and the shattered mirrors of Warburg's image tables.

Agamben's point in accentuating how Viola and Domenico cycled through form was to decenter actualization as naming without remainder by localizing a diversity of names, and a similar resistance to actualization was conspicuous in the examination of "detachment" (*iki*) conducted by the Japanese Heideggerian Shūzō Kuki. We should not presume that any given thoughts in his 1930 work *The Structure of Detachment* constitute specific continuations of his interest in and time with Heidegger. Nevertheless, we can explore Heideggerian thematics for ourselves by attending to Kuki's insights. We recognize the idea that modality saturates the passions when we find him noting that "the main concern of coquetry—and the essence of pleasure—is maintaining a dualistic relationship, that is to say, protecting the possibility as a possibility."[68] This overly familiar idea was being differentiated and empowered, however, when Kuki went on to specify that "detachment" (*iki*) would be a kind of compound affective stationing

66. Agamben, 9.
67. Agamben, cited at 12: "a cadauno tempo che pari aver veduto il capo di medusa, como dice el poeta, cioe che facto el moto, sii tutto di pietra in quello istante e in istante metti ale come falcone che per paica mosso sia." See Smith, trans., *Fifteenth-Century Dance and Music*, 12.
68. Kuki, *Structure of Detachment*, 19.

drawing on "*bitai* 'coquetry,' *ikiji* 'pride and honor,' and *akirame* 'resigna-tion.'" At this point, we must pay attention to the multiple temporalities embedded in these various components, for resignation would depend on an infinite deferral of coquetry's possibility.[69]

Consummation would be a very particular achievement and dissolution of sexual "actualization" (*energeia*), and "detachment" (*iki*) could be un-derstood as a manner of holding actualization at bay by approaching and then denying it. The asymptotic unachievability of such possibility would be spatial and tactile, too, as we may infer when Kuki says that "the wearing of very thin fabric" expresses *iki* via the entire body.[70] The desired body would never quite be where it was, and this displacement informed Kuki's observation that the body that had just completed bathing would possess *iki*. Similarly, it informed his observation that if *iki* had a color, it would be the various shades of brown resulting from "loss of brightness." In this account, "browns embody *iki* because the opulent characteristic of a color and the loss of saturation express a sophisticated sensuality and a coquetry that knows resignation." For Kuki, such colors captured the sense in which "*iki* lives in the future, holding the past in its arms."[71] *Iki* would be a diver-sity of tenses and modalities, and it opened up possibilities for thinking repetition, postponement, and the kind of everydayness that is richer than any recursion to the mean.

One must hold the Heideggerian conception of everydayness at a dis-tance from the banality of its indistinct repetitions and rejuvenate it by holding up a variety of the concept's most distinct iterations. Wittingly or unwittingly, Jean-Luc Nancy was pointing back to earlier 1920s iterations of everydayness when he proposed in 1996 that "Heidegger confuses the everyday with the undifferentiated, the anonymous, and the statistical." Again, in a way that is remarkably insightful given his lack of access to the unpublished lectures of the 1920s in which Heidegger developed his conception of everydayness in quite similar ways, Nancy proposed that the undifferentiated, the anonymous, and the statistical "are not less impor-tant but can only constitute themselves in a relation to the differentiated singularity that the everyday already is by itself: each day, each time, from day to day."[72] The differentiated singularity that is collected, made part of a series, or given a place within a topical domain—these are the iterated and decentered exemplarities that give everydayness its nonstatisticalized form.

69. Kuki, 22.
70. Kuki, 36.
71. Kuki, 48.
72. Nancy, *Être Singulier Pluriel*, 27: "ceux-ci n'en sont pas moins importants, mais ne peuvent se constituer que dans un rapport avec la singularité différenciée que le quotidien est déjà par lui-même: chaque jour, chaque fois, au jour le jour."

To be sure, the tool is precisely the object that possesses a statisticalized and intangible everydayness written into it from the beginning. In 1986, the computer scientist Terry Winograd and the philosopher Fernando Flores were certainly right to say that designing architectures for use would be designing forms of repetition that contour, sculpt, and shape being in ways that would become, every day, less visible. Channeling Heidegger explicitly in *Understanding Computers and Cognition*, Winograd and Flores claimed that "we encounter the deep questions of design when we recognize that in designing tools we are designing ways of being."[73] Theirs was simply an early version of a sequence of claims that have become almost axiomatic both among media analysts and technology boosters alike—namely, that "the programmer designs the language that generates the world in which the user operates," that "this language can be 'ontologically clean' or it can be a jumble of related domains," and that "a clearly and consciously organized ontology is the basis for the kind of simplicity that makes systems usable."[74] In this direction, a whole suite of procedural and ambient rhetorics awaits. Design architecture collects the modality of possibility by recording and rendering visible the pathways discovered and secured in the process of iteration.[75] Similarly, repetition, habituation, and a concomitant decentering of presence and its forms of highly focalized attention make it possible to dilate the parameters of attention and broaden the parameters of ambient awareness.[76]

Nevertheless, there are *practices* of everydayness that keep habituation visible by structuring it in certain ways. Take Victor Klemperer's daily practices of recording Nazi language practice in *LTI*, for example. Imagining it in an athletic idiom, Klemperer called the diary his "balancing pole" (*Balancierstange*).[77] And we find something similar in the art historian Roger Hinks's characterization of his journals as a "gymnasium of the mind."[78] Somewhat surprisingly, the person to interject quickly here is once again Michael Baxandall, whose late "memorybook" is especially pertinent. In that autobiographical but theoretically meditative book, Baxandall examined memory as a process of sedimentation. Memory for him was the repetition and iteration of stories. An event became a topos when its stories were told and retold. To take up his analogy, memory would be the laminating process by which dunes are produced.[79] Baxandall was a Warburgian, but the idea here informs the Heideggerian interest in modality. Specifically, it

73. Winograd and Flores, *Understanding Computers and Cognition*, xi.
74. Winograd and Flores, 165.
75. See Bogost, *Persuasive Games*.
76. See Rickert, *Ambient Rhetoric*.
77. Klemperer, *LTI*, 15.
78. Hinks, *Gymnasium of the Mind*, 33.
79. Baxandall, *Episodes*, 17–21.

illuminates for us a tactic for laying down topoi. Cultivating topoi is cultivating everydayness, many-timed-ness. In this reading, one is not simply turning toward an account of ethics (or politics) as habit; one is developing a political cultural store of points of departure. As I would put it when glossing Mireille Rosello's brilliant book *Declining the Stereotype*, the topos is a zone of repetition that facilitates and potentializes deviation.[80]

The most relevant renovation of the Heideggerian project at the juncture between repetition and practice comes from the contemporary German thinker Peter Sloterdijk. Sloterdijk advertised this renovation in his *Spheres* trilogy, which he described as a kind of sequel: *Being and Space* rather than *Being and Time*. For him, "sphere" circumscribed a spatializing metaphorics with which to rewrite the temporal preoccupations of Heideggerian *Dasein*.[81] The "Da" of Sloterdijk's "Sein" was not so much the accordion inhalations and exhalations of a temporal manifold composed of past, present, and future. The Sloterdijkian "Da" was a wild miscellany of forms including bubble, globe, and foam; amniotic sack; and what he called "interfacial space."[82] "Sphere" became an extraordinarily fecund metaphoric zone demarking the horizon of a genuinely lived or inhabitable space. As Sloterdijk has put it, "spheres are configurations of space that function as immune systems for ecstatic beings who are worked on by the outside," where "ecstatic" denotes precisely a projection out from a central point.[83] But this ec-stasis would not be preoccupied solely with determining the borders of an everyday life. It also had to do with distributions of the soul into an array of artifacts (or naturalia taken up as artifacts). The being of an organism and the materiality of its systems extended out beyond the wall of its skin. In this way, "for the lifespan of the bubble, the bubble-blower will have been outside of themselves."[84] A spanning of the now is transposed into the spanning of a here. In terms that inflect the topical receptions of Heideggerian ontology effected by Otto Pöggeler and Helmut Kuhn, Sloterdijk has characterized his *Spheres* project as "ontotopology."[85]

Given the emphasis on modality in my reading of Heidegger, the most pertinent part of the Sloterdijkian corpus is his 2009 book *You Must Change Your Life*. Here we find the array of Heideggerian modalities set out together as so many dimensions of an anthropotechnics, which was a range of

80. Rosello, *Declining the Stereotype*.
81. Sloterdijk, *Blasen*, 345—where Sloterdijk says this continues an *early* Heideggerian project "entombed" by the later work.
82. Sloterdijk, 152: "interfaziale Raum."
83. Sloterdijk, 28: "Sphären sind immunsystemisch wirksame Raumschöpfungen für ekstatische Wesen, an denen das Außen arbeitet."
84. Sloterdijk, 17: "für die Lebensspanne der Blase war der Bläser außer sich gewesen."
85. Sloterdijk, 336: "Ontopologie."

practices oriented to what—conscious of the Nietzschean resonance—we might call "self-overcoming." A statue of the god Apollo had spoken to the poet Rainer Maria Rilke and said, "You must change your life," and Sloterdijk founded his obsessions with both everyday practice and actualization on that line. The line is apostrophe followed by prosopopoeia as the poet, whose position anyone can occupy, interpellates himself by putting a command into the mouth of the art work. The ancient statue survives only as a torso. For that reason, it is an incomplete potentiality continually hinting at completion and thus presence. Such continuation would be a motion that does not simply copy the supple glory of this Apollo but completes it in a creative imitation. The work of such completion is many timed, for it is not the single imitation that constitutes capacity. Completion is a function of a distributed, honed, endless imitation—namely, practice.

Sloterdijk was working toward a synthesis of the early Heidegger and the late Foucault in *You Must Change Your Life*, and we can perceive a continuation of the topical regimes proposed by everydayness in the practices of training that Sloterdijk explores there. Care of the self attaches itself to, and then rewrites, the account of freedom précised in my treatment of Warburg in chapter 6. Routinization need not be simply the bureaucratic writing of one's crimes and punishments into one's habits in the manner of "rehabilitation." It is also a kind of curation of the gallery of the self. Practice distinguishes and retains possibilities, making them available for subsequent deployment. Again, this is an aphoristics, perhaps embodied. It is a concern, perhaps gymnastic, for the cultivation of an array of beginnings. And Sloterdijk's treatments here are as bracing as they are simple. First, "the possibility of faciality is conjoined with the process of anthropogenesis itself."[86] That is, faces are screens that recognize ab initio the possibility of being read. They are always already plural rather than one. Here Sloterdijk iterates two of the most basic gestures of his work: individuality is a late-arriving phenomenon (not primordial), and individuality is the last stage of a process of differentiation, not the first point of departure for socialization.

Sloterdijk's choice of example in discussing anthropogenesis is significant. In Giotto's fourteenth-century *Kiss of Judas*, he maintains, "the viewer encounters a painting in which the space between two human faces is charged with extreme and antithetical spheric tensions."[87] We paint the faces of Judas and Christ onto the, as it were, "concave" curvature of the sphere in which we are immersed, and in so doing we find ourselves projected

---

86. Sloterdijk, 166: "die Möglichkeit von Gesichtlichkeit ist mit dem Prozeß der Anthropogenese selbst verbunden."

87. Sloterdijk, 152: "Mit der Szene des Judaskusses begegnet der Betrachter einem Gemälde, in dem der Raum zwischen zwei menschlichen Gesichtern mit extremen antithetischen sphärischen Spannungen aufgeladen wird."

onto an exchange of glances. We should pay attention to the—advertently or inadvertently—topical quality of the "alphabet" idiom Sloterdijk uses. In the frescoes of the Scrovegni Chapel in Padua, he finds, "Giotto wrote down an alphabet of interfacial configurations."[88] Here we find Sloterdijk collecting faces as so many masks, and his obsession with spatialization becomes an interest in topics. The everydayness that collects exempla and does not resolve them into a mean treats them as so many concrete instantiations of a nonstandardized deviation. Such collecting then becomes an exercise regime for anthropogenesis—namely, the coming into being of the human. In ways that have been quite controversial in Germany, Sloterdijk adds that one can act on the coming into being of the human via an anthropotechnics understood as a congeries of operations on the human.[89]

Although the reception of Heidegger's thought looms unusually large in the panoply of afterlives following on from Weimar theorizations of modality, this section has not been an attempt to trace an alternative Heidegger reception. That would be a massive and controversial task. Instead, I have been attempting to lay out some possibilities for the modality of everydayness. Repetition has been crucial here, but I have not been emphasizing the kind of repetition that has a mathematical precision or a mass-produced industrial scale. At the heart of this inquiry, we have a repetition that gathers subtly differing responses. The presupposition is that practicing anew every day produces not stock response but rather a tissue of modulations. In order to theorize how the collecting of such modulations happens, it has been important to take account of modalities at a distance from the extreme presencing or activation that would be the phenomenon naming itself in appearance. Weiss's chance, Agamben's kairotic saturation, Kūki's detachment, Nancy's each-and-every-day-ness, and Winograd and Flores's design space are all modes of engaging with modality without insisting on extreme actualization. And they point to pursuits of layered, differentiated, topical everydayness that are continued in the practices of Klemperer, Hink, and Baxandall. Sloterdijk's anthropotechnics is the most extreme philosophical articulation of this position. In order to pursue this line of inquiry further, though, I turn now to topical practices articulated in a broadly but not exclusively Warburgian tradition.

TOPICAL PRACTICES

Amid the Arendtian practices of *krinein* that I have been developing, connoisseurship expresses itself in as many registers as there are faculties of

88. Sloterdijk, 145: "Giotto hat in diesem Fresken . . . ein Alphabet interfazialer Konstellationen aufgeschrieben."
89. See the exchanges between Thomas Assheuer, Habermas, and Sloterdijk in *Die Zeit* issues 36, 37, and 38 from 1999.

sense. In the present context, "connoisseurship" denotes something like a capacity not to be saturated by sensation in its various singular instantiations. This is a rather unusual formulation. I mean to specify a process in which a sensor—any kind of sensor—may become so consumed with actualizing the quality of an appearance that all attendant possibilities surrounding that actualization become impossible and, thus, disappear. As I am constructing it, connoisseurship entails knowing something by means of its origins and alternatives. This stands in opposition to being overwhelmed by the sheen of a sensation's immediate presence. In this way, connoisseurship distances. It renders the patina of the work of art intelligible and knowable by revealing its various cultural overlays and mediations, its prototypes, successors, and alternatives. Or, expressed in a rhetorical mode, connoisseurship is something like an enhanced reality device capable of overlaying all speech acts with knowledge of an audience's customary alternatives.

As we saw in the previous section, everydayness is deceptively mundane. Even in Heidegger's own work, the concept deliquesced quickly into a kind of denunciation of the merely average. There, "averageness" was construed as a mean that was in a sense the "sum" of previous phenomena. In reality, however, this Heideggerian construal of averageness failed to represent those phenomena with even the most basic sense of how various statistical representation may be. That is, Heidegger did not go on to conceptualize varieties of everydayness within the metaphorics of statistics. As we know, "averageness" is an ambiguous term, one that effaces the specificities of "mean," "median," "range," and "deviations from the mean," among others. When we pursue this metaphorics more doggedly, we begin to see everydayness as the abstract quality produced by a selecting that is repeated and aggregated. Under the specification of "deviations from the mean," this aggregation takes on forms that are reminiscent of Aby Warburg's image tables, which map distances between particular body inhabitations. The image tables ask questions about what kind of motion would take a body from one posture to another. If one interpolates that simple change of posture with a reason, one is already within narrativization. The sensory topos developed by the daily practice of collecting becomes something more akin to an inference infrastructure where concatenations of if-then clauses map deviations in plot continuation, motive, and consequence. Under this description, Heideggerian "everydayness" begins to morph into Warburgian "memory."

I am arguing that the critical capacity announced by "distinguishing" qua *krinein* and collected in the mode of everydayness may be specified by "connoisseurial" but not with the narrow, elite, or conservative connotations usually accompanying that term. Moreover, we can characterize this critical practice as an *ars topica* in disguise, because the art of distinguishing produces constellations of similars that facilitate invention. As I argued earlier, Warburg's *Bilderatlas Mnemosyne* was an essentially topical project built on topical practices with all the qualities of copiousness one would expect. When we turn to the afterlife of these Warburgian ideas, we find the hypothesis confirmed. How did Carlo Ginzburg understand the Warburgian pathos formulas when he was charting the history of art-historical method from Warburg to Ernst Gombrich? As so many *topoi figurativi*.[90] Here, "figural topoi" are visual topoi, and they are topical in at least two senses. First, they are visual commonplaces. That is, they are images embodying "judgment without reflection shared by an entire class, an entire people, an entire nation, or the entire human race."[91] Even in the absence of attention, these images freight the assumptions, commitments, and unwritten rules that structure culture. Second, clustered in image tables, these figural topoi constitute what Vico called "a sensory topics" (*una topica sensibile*).[92] That is, within the image-table frame, such image collections function as names that draw attention to and delineate new zones of sensitivity.

Now, images do freight scripts (and as "judgments without reflection" they certainly may generate conformity), but the power of images lies also in their ability to induce desires and abilities in beholders to complete those scripts variously. Images produce counterparts, not just mirror images. Desire for an image when it wears its desirability like an invitation can be something like falling into an image or completing it. Such falling or completing is a phantasmagoric resuturing of that image into a rhetorical situation of stimulus and response. In this situation, a desirer standing initially outside the frame is brought into the scene pictured within the frame, and that desirer is thereby changed from a beholder into a participant. Bouncing—as it were—its desire off the object on which it is fixated, this beholder becomes an object of desire for the object within the image, which imagination has transformed into a desiring subject in its own right. In this way, a new dimension has been projected: from delimiting a two-dimensional pseudoworld, the image now constitutes a kind of imagination-infused virtually real volume. I transform myself into a hologram when I complete the desire script that an image introduces into the world by configuring my body and my desire as a kind of pendant piece or antistrophe to some element of that image. Sexuality is clearly one domain in which imaginative circuits of this kind run, but the point holds for desire more generally. Here we should understand "desire" broadly as "desire to narrativize": I desire something when I wish that the thing and my own self be coinvolved in a narrative.

90. Ginzburg, "Da A. Warburg a E. H. Gombrich," 1019.
91. Vico, *Scienza nuova*, §142: "il senso comune è un giudizio senz'alcuna riflessione, comunemente sentito da tutto un ordine, da tutto un popolo, da tutta una nazione o da tutto il gener umano."
92. Vico, *Scienza nuova*, §495.

One can characterize the desire to narrativize as a desire to foreclose possibility by fixing a single outcome for a process, but this is only one of several options, and one can choose instead to investigate narrativization as itself a practice that pluralizes continuation. As W. J. T. Mitchell (another occasional Warburgian) has proposed, if we are being seduced by the desires we ourselves have projected onto images, then "What Do Pictures Want?" should become the unashamedly more anthropocentric "What Do We Want from Pictures?"[93] According to Hans Belting, the answer to this second question is simply that "we want them to be alive even though we know very well that it is we who are lending them a life."[94] In reality, it is less interesting to insist on the undecidable question of cause than it is to pursue the oscillating practices in which images come alive or are said to come alive. And it is here, rather than in some intuition of the distinction in the realm of the visual between locutionary and illocutionary force, that we find the origin of Horst Bredekamp's *Image Acts*, which follows the life practices in which works of art are indistinguishable from or exchangeable for human beings.[95]

We are now in the vicinity of what I think is a characteristic error in the reception of Aby Warburg's work. Warburgian *Denkraum* is predominantly understood as a force of negation specializing in detachment or distantiation. On this reading (précised in chapter 6), the purpose of *Denkraum* is to establish distances between subject and object, input and output, call and response. Contemporary scholars often cast *Denkraum* as something like a prophylaxis against image-inaugurated conformism or script completion. We encounter this kind of mistake even in such rich and wonderfully informed projects as the *Handbook of Political Iconology*. That volume represents the culmination of a massive collaborative research project molded by such eminent Warburgians as Uwe Fleckner, Martin Warnke, and Hendrik Ziegler. They declare that the aim of the project is to "conduct research into the fascination of political image strategies not in order to succumb to this fascination but rather—and quite contrarily—to transform this fascination into the wholly unemotional object of art-historical inquiry."[96] More than some workaday academic commitment to objectivity, this is a quite specific privileging of the Apollonian side of the Warburgian inheritance over its Dionysian counterpart. In their repetition of the word

93. Mitchell, "Pictures," 71–82.
94. Belting, *Anthropology of Images*, 130; the line occurs in the English edition.
95. Bredekamp, *Theorie des Bildakts*.
96. Fleckner, Warnke, and Ziegler, *Handbuch der politischen Ikonologie*, 8: "die Faszination politischer Bildstrategien zu untersuchen, dieser Faszination dennoch nicht zu erliegen, sondern sie—ganz im Gegenstil—zum nüchternen Gegenstand kunsthistorischen Forschungen zu machen, ist das erklärte Ziel des Handbuchs der politischen Ikonographie."

"fascination" (*Faszination*), these authors are recognizing the danger of a human desire for images. Here, this is a desire to be a participant—heroic, compliant, exploited (it matters not)—in the narrative suggested and partially actualized by an image. My response is to say that despite their erudition these scholars are making a very specific mistake. They seem to assume that refusing the invitation is the only way to respond to an image that invites a beholder to play its game. They urge us to inoculate ourselves against the appeal or, as it were, to lock the image away in some kind of academic quarantine.

I am making a contrary point: there are ways to embrace and then take up the stored and potentializing energy of an image without becoming its mug. The wholly unemotional response to an art-historical object may be like impassivity in the face of Medusa—indistinguishable from paralysis. I have been arguing and shall be arguing again here that the truer Warburgian trajectory for rhetorical inquiry appears in a topical agglomeration that stages the proximity of alternative movements. On this account, one has left the task only half-completed when one says that unsophisticated viewers have little or no access to the derivativeness of any given performed gesture and that, as a result, such viewers find it difficult to avoid conformism or script completion. One has to say at the same time that for connoisseurs (as I am characterizing them) images will dramatize movements in ways that highlight the possibility of multiple continuations. If one supposes that an image will permit only one kind of participation, then one has ceded all imaginative power to the image. Such supposition assumes that in inviting the beholder to play its game the image provides space for only one kind of supplement. To play the game suggested by an image under such conditions is to become its puppet. On the other hand, if an image is held to permit many continuations, then it is much more genuinely a game because its visual dispositions constitute a play space that may be explored.

In making the point about multiplicity of continuations, I am rejecting among other things Kenneth Clark's attempt to channel Warburg in his 1956 study *The Nude*. Clark had been present at and deeply impressed by the Hertziana lectures given by Warburg that I discussed in the previous chapter. He claimed a Warburgian filiation and recognized the essentially rhetorical dimensions of the pathos formula as worn, for example, by the Laocoön sculpture group that, when it was rediscovered in 1506, became a paradigm for Renaissance artists of the ways in which motion and passion might be represented. Nevertheless, Clark understood rhetoric in terms of persuasive power, and he understood the power of the Laocoön in terms of necessity. As he expressed the thought in 1956, the Laocoön group "contains no movement that cannot be justified by necessity as well as art."[97] Clark

97. Clark, "Pathos," 230.

was supposing that a great work of art would be intentional to the point of unalterability.

We may compare Clark to the writer—I confess, I have been that writer on occasion—who pretends that Myron's *Diskobolos* will be a visual manifestation of necessity on account of the fact that change in any one part of the composition will require change in the others.[98] This is a writer who is ignoring the fact that, actually, we do possess very localized alternatives for the angle of the discus thrower's head. When Clark qualified his assertion about the "necessity" of the Laocoön group, he added the caveat that there were motions diverging from those of the original that had been introduced "owing to [the work's] restoration in the sixteenth century." Alternatives begin to seem inauthentic or merely a function of botched reassembly. Pursued to its conclusion, the line proposes that necessity is authentic and that the authentic will be necessary. Those presuppositions may be noxious; they are certainly optional. The point about the topos function of the pathos formula that I am making in response to Clark is not so much that the articulation of an image's figure can be altered but more that the viewerly task with any given image in fact consists in a serial reconfiguration of the artwork. In this way, "contingency" becomes something like sensitivity to the points at which body positioning can become otherwise.

An array of gathered possibilities may be understood as something like the burden of genius, but there are alternatives to this way of thinking. In this vision-cum-nightmare, we are faced with "genius" agents paradoxically slouched passively before the riches of their manifold options. These genius "patients" become overburdened luxuriants. To think in this way, however, is to misunderstand the relationship among possibilities. Possibilities are not simply mutually exclusive alternatives. They are instead components that may be combined, projected one onto another, or sequenced in the manner of animation. Once again, the slipstream of Warburgian thought can help us power this line of inquiry. This line was in motion when Erwin Panofsky spoke of the sense in which "different creative possibilities illuminate one another in the artist's mind." Yet Panofsky went on to bury this intuition under twin presuppositions in his famous and discipline-influencing article on "artistic volition" (*Kunstwollen*) in 1920. First, he assumed that only something definite can be willed. Second, he presupposed that the research projects focusing on "artistic volition" that he was announcing would reveal a priori preconditions of compositional possibility.[99] Rather than say that one iteration of a topos can reveal possibility in another, Panofsky committed himself to the project of asking of the cluster of comparable productions only what its shared optical preconditions might be.

98. Marshall, "Warburgian Maxims," 367.
99. Panofsky, "Der Begriff des Kunstwollens," 325, 326, 336.

Similarly, we can say that Panofsky was both entrenching and blunting his neo-Kantian concerns for conditions of possibility when he combined them with some received Heideggerianism in his 1932 essay on "description" (*Beschreibung*) in the visual arts.[100] It was no coincidence that Panofsky took up precisely Heidegger's reading of Kant; similarly, it was no coincidence that the Heideggerian account produced in Panofsky was a kind of flat and merely portentous drama. We see this blanching at work in Panofsky's summative assertion: "in the final analysis, the greatness of an artistic achievement is dependent on the quantum of 'worldview energy' that has been introduced into the formed matter and radiates from there over the viewer."[101] The decisive word here is "worldview" (*Weltanschauung*). For Panofsky, "worldview" was impersonalized "metempirical subjectivity" (*metempirischer Gegenstand*), a phrase he had deployed in 1925 while rearticulating his conception of artistic volition. The phrase drew attention to the ways in which the conditions of possibility for one's own cognition of the world might be projected out into that world.[102] In the account Panofsky was giving here, the task of art criticism was to see how particular visualities might be structured by a historical a priori.

The Panofsky route has been tremendously influential, and that route is both proximate to and crucially distinct from the Warburgian line that I have been proposing. As I intimated earlier in this study, one of Panofsky's most important early interests—melancholy itself—can be understood in relation to Warburgian magnanimity. In my pursuit of the Weimar origins of rhetorical inquiry, the surfeit of possibilities has become a leitmotif, and melancholy is one way of organizing such abundance. In the 1923 first edition of their Dürer book, when Panofsky and Saxl said that "the true being of Saturn is . . . *to theōrētikos*," they were stranding themselves between the sense that saturnine melancholy was a place of theoretical *inaction* and the sense that such melancholy was a state of pure observation or an openness to perceptibility that recalled and laid out past perceptions of phenomena now absent.[103] Just so, they did not pursue the basic point they made about Dürer's famous *Melencolia I* engraving—namely, that it succeeded in conveying simultaneously both the depressive-overwhelmed and the creative-original tendencies of melancholy. I say that this was a point announced but not pursued because Panofsky and Saxl did not address how an oversupply

100. Panofsky, "Zum Problem der Beschreibung und Inhaltsdeutung," 103–19.

101. Panofsky, 116: "die Größe einer künstlerischen Leistung letzten Endes davon abhängig ist, welches Quantum von 'Weltanschauungs-Energie' in die gestaltete Materie hineingeleitet worden ist und aus ihr auf den Betrachter hinüberstrahlt."

102. Panofsky, "Über die Verhältnis der Kunstgeschichte zur Kunsttheorie," 129.

103. Panofsky and Saxl, Dürers *"Melencolia I,"* 26: "das eigentliche Wesen des Saturns ist wie bei Proklos und Macrobius: *to theōrētikos*."

of possibilities might be transformed into a cornucopia of options.[104] There is another parallel project, hitherto merely potential and yet to be extracted from Panofsky's early work, that can fertilize the better Warburgian line of inquiry. This would be a project attending to works of art not simply as representations of freedom but as manifestations thereof.

Having identified a magnanimity sequence in the Warburg project, we can now continue that trajectory by drawing on elements of the Warburgian afterlife. In the book on Michelangelo and Raphael, Panofsky had been saying quite brilliantly that movements generate the space in which they themselves appear. Our task now is to see that Panofsky's position entails a rich cache of suggestions. He was not simply telling us to deny the priority of abstract, empty three-dimensionality. To be sure, he certainly was interested in showing that a figure might generate space with its own motions because it revealed that the essence of space was nothing other than the possibility of motion. That was one project. Nor was Panofsky urging us to anticipate the point that performance beats a path for habit (or legislated norm). Granted, he did employ a Kantian idiom of autonomy to express concern for the action that was being undertaken for the first time and that might legislate repetition. That was another project. What I wish to underscore in place of these two plausible alternatives is that Panofsky was actually making it possible to understand space as an infrastructure carved out by the pluripotentiality of gesture. Space was a covering over of the concept and the practice of freedom insofar as it generated an abstract void by smoothing over the multitude of particular and precise motions carved by the configuration of limbs, weights, and balances.

There was an extreme delicacy in Panofsky's conceptualization of space as an infrastructure of potential movements. Witness Panofsky's sublime phrasing of the point when he spoke of his interest above all else in the realization "of a new concept of the essence of living presencing itself."[105] As Panofsky parsed the point, he conjured Ghirlandaio's late fifteenth-century *Birth of the Baptist* in his mind's eye, focusing on the way in which motion stood next to motionlessness in the various parts of its rightmost figure, expressing haste. It was "not that from now on the forms [of these corporeal figurations] *have space* enabling them to perform arbitrary movements or allowing them to take up arbitrary positions."[106] No, the point was rather that "the movements they perform and the positions they take up seem to issue from a power of free self-determination and seem thereby themselves

104. Panofsky and Saxl, 71.
105. Panofsky, *Die Gestaltungsprincipien*, 101: "es handelt sich vor allem um die Realisierung eines neuen Begriffs vom Wesen des lebendigen Daseins überhaupt."
106. Panofsky, 101: "nicht, daß die Gestalten von jetzt an *Raum haben*, um beliebige Bewegungen ausführen und beliebige Stellungen einnehmen zu können."

in some sense *to produce space*."[107] The pluripotentiality of particular gestures and movements and purposes would be space or would constitute it in the first instance before it could be sanded down and geometrized into dimensionality. Crucially, though, space here would not be simply the single gesture in its carved out before and after. Instead, space would be the cascading plenitude of potential motions radiating out from the inscenation proposed by a work of art. On this account, the work of art becomes the life phenomenon that has been captured, intensified, and made prismatic by artistic attention.

Pursuing the parts of Panofsky's project that were most "Warburgian" (as I reconstruct that term in this book), we should say that among its several kinds there will be a distinctly filmic species of magnanimity. Panofsky was making investigation of this filmic magnanimity possible in 1936 when he spoke of the optical mobility of cinemagoers who were encouraged to and indeed did identify themselves with the lens of the camera. As he put it, "in a movie theater the spectator has a fixed seat, but only physically, not as an aesthetic subject," because, "aesthetically, he is in permanent motion, as his eye identifies itself with the lens of the camera which permanently shifts in distance and direction."[108] We can improve on this already arresting formulation by pushing into the vague and imprecisely expressed idea of permanence in the phrase "permanently shifts." Recently emigrated from Germany, Panofsky was still learning the nuances of a new language, and he means not so much "permanently" as "continually." Equipped with the Warburgian presuppositions excavated earlier in this book, we can see that the capaciousness of soul required by the cuts and leaps and interpellations introduced by the film editor are in fact not permanent at all—nor even continual in any sense. They are radically discontinuous and therefore entirely dependent on the viewer's ingenuity. Indeed, in the manner of a theoretical injunction, the dissected and jump-cut whirligig motions of film reveal the precisely protofilmic quality of the Warburgian image tables, which required and continue to require adjustment from one gestural inscenation to another in the manner of a multilinear filmstrip.

We can speculate into the Warburgian afterlife by reading Panofsky in light of parts of Warburg's project that Panofsky may or may not have had access to, but we can also hove closer to the extant record by examining the angles on magnanimity actualized in the work of Frances Yates. Yates was a researcher formally engaged at the Warburg Institute from 1941 until 1967, and she took up Warburg's *Bilderatlas* project by examining the art

107. Panofsky, 101: "die Bewegungen, die sie ausführen und die Stellungen, die sie einnehmen, aus einer *freien Selbstbestimmungskraft* zu entspringen und sich dadurch gewissermaßen selber *Raum zu schaffen* scheinen."
108. Panosky, "On Movies," 9.

of memory in early modern Europe. Integral to this scholarship was the obvious but important recognition that once again ancient rhetoric had been the recurrent point of reference for this early modern reinvention. The idea was that early modern authors took up predictions made by ancient authors that one might perform better in the fourth part of classical rhetoric (*memoria*) if one were to visualize a speech as a building and organize one's recollection of the different parts of that speech by placing particular objects in distinct locations within a structure that one knew well in an embodied way—one's own house, for instance.[109] We then discover a new aspect of the Warburgian magnanimity concept when we pair it with Yates's injunction that "we have to think of the ancient orator as moving in imagination through his memory building, whilst he is making his speech, drawing from the memorized places the images he has placed on them."[110] The memory building is something like an image table for spiritual exercise. One practices in that memory space so that one's transitions from particular parts of the exposition, argument, and mis-en-scène of one's speech will possess a nonchalant and thus unquestionable—or at least unquestioned—ease or suppleness.

In response to Yates's invocation of the imagined motion of the ancient orator, I observe that there is a very particular relationship between seriality and totality in the memory practices of classical rhetoric. On the one hand, the order of speaking is memorized as a sequence of rooms through which one moves and may move. Movement in time in the speech is modeled on movement in space; discursive arrangement, on spatial arrangement. On the other hand, within this structure one's sense of timing (one's sense of an ending or, for that matter, one's sense of a beginning) will be modulated by an ease of movement through this familiar place. Utilizing the Panofskian point just elaborated, we can hypothesize that the variety of movements through this space—fast, slow, hesitant, seigneurial, or deliberately shambolic—constitute a palette of possibilities for performing the hinges of one's speech. Living in a place excavates it as a space and embeds knowledge of that space as a variety of potential movements. These will be movements that give the appearance of freedom because habit makes them all, in a sense, equally possible at each moment.

When we follow Yates's excavations of the early modern *fortuna* of the ancient mnemo-technical tradition, we encounter an emphasis on what we might call "the equidistance architectures" of the memory theater. As Yates traced it, Giulio Camillo's sixteenth-century transformation of the memory

109. Cicero, for example, relayed and discussed the constitutive Simonides topos at *De oratore*, 2.85.350–88.360.
110. Yates, *Art of Memory*, 3.

palace into a memory theater was the transposition of a speech training into a system for grasping, memorizing, and working within a modeling of the cosmos. In her words, Camillo's "theatre is . . . a vision of the world and of the nature of things seen from a height, from the stars themselves and even from the supercelestial founts of wisdom beyond them." She went on to say that "this vision is very deliberately cast within the framework of the classical art of memory, using the traditional mnemonic terminology." Thus, "the Theatre is a system of memory places, though a 'high and incomparable' placing," and "it performs the office of a classical memory system for orators by 'conserving for us the things, words, and arts which we confide to it.'"[111] Confiding here consists in finding a place for something while resting assured that when it is needed it can be summoned at will without delay. And the repeated emphasis on the supercelestial distance from which one surveys the contents of this memory theater was, in effect, a motif for marking (relative) equidistance.

The kind of intellectual historiography that I am practicing licenses a retroactive projection of Yates's work onto the *Bilderatlas*. Making that projection, we see that Yates's characterization of Camillo's theater as a kind of *theatrum mundi* becomes a hypothesis about the connection between magnanimity and the astrological, astronomical, and world-systems preoccupations of Warburg's image atlas. Warburg could not subtend the *Bilderatlas* interest in early modern practices of "finding one's place in the cosmos" under the rhetoric-centered project of the restitution of eloquence. What we have uncovered here in Yates, however, is a reason to suppose that even if Warburg came to this conclusion there were other inferences that were also possible for him given the presuppositions to which he was committed. I am proposing that with the materials available to him, Warburg could equally have investigated the interpenetration of magnanimity practices and "world picturing."

That, as a matter of historical contingency, Warburg did not develop a magnanimity reading of geography and world picturing does not in itself mean we may not do so in his name. If the hypothesis seems willful, simply treat it as a prediction that this is an inference one will encounter expressed in a Warburgian idiom. Consider this prediction partially vindicated when we hear from Yates that when asked about the meaning of his theater "Camillo spoke of it as representing all that the mind can conceive and all that is hidden in the soul—all of which could be perceived at one glance by the inspection of the images."[112] In this moment, we see both that the theater was to be a kind of exteriorizing of the mind and a kind of ordering of it

111. Yates, 144.
112. Yates, 341.

in such a way that the entirety of that mental universe would be available within the near simultaneity of "the glance." Mapping a cosmos and one's position in it can be simultaneously a projecting of the soul into the stars and an introjection of the stars into the soul.

In the context of Yates's invocation of "at-a-glance-ness" in relation to Camillo's theater, the abstraction of "equidistance" that I have been using at various points in this book takes on a new architectural specificity. Note an example relayed by Yates. When he spoke of Francis Bacon's home (at what is now Old Gorhambury House), John Aubrey called attention to a gallery with painted windows where "every pane [was adorned] with severall small figures of beast, bird, and flower." Aubrey, the seventeenth-century English antiquary, was hypothesizing that "perhaps his Lordship might use them as topiques for local use."[113] With this early modern license, we may conceive of the image table (or the "image pane") as a local topics, and this entails regarding it as a seedbed of argument and not simply the convening of a usually scattered visual topos.

If the painted window seems too close to the image table to count as a genuinely architectural feature, then consider Yates's account of the Globe Theatre—yes, Shakespeare's Globe. This theater was one regulatory idea in the memory tradition she was examining.[114] The specific architecture of the Globe was optimized for both seeing and being seen. As a result, there was an optically embodiable sense of equidistance within the various sight lines of the theater. The particular propinquities and distances of the theater may certainly have constituted a hierarchy of differences, but at the same time the near simultaneity of the glance underwrote the possibility of a perceiving together that remains the prime vehicle of *ingenium*. A theater like this would be precisely the Arendtian space of appearance in which the greatest diversity of social roles would be exhibited with the greatest concision and proximity. Akin to Rahel's salon, the Shakespearean theater was precisely the space in which the circulation and modulation of poses within a gestural community became most intense.

In the context of the theater, intensity would entail what we might call "shared intelligibility" as well as frequency of appropriation, and here again we encounter one of the basic points I have been making: the concept of magnanimity that I identified in the work of Aby Warburg was not in its essence the beginning of a theory of freedom tightly focused on the kind of capaciousness of soul that a single individual might possess. Granted, an individual might exercise in a visual topical gymnasium such as Warburg's *Bilderatlas*. This was a care of the self that, for example, Sloterdijk was taking

113. Yates, 370.
114. Yates, 158.

up when he continued the Heideggerian project of thinking space. That is all true, but there is also a significant sense in which the capaciousness of soul underwriting the theory of freedom I have essayed here was embedded in a social articulateness that finds its emblem more fundamentally in the theater. A stance or mask or role, as I have been invoking the concepts in this book, is not simply a set of coordinates or joint inflections taken up by an individual. Indeed, the athlete of gesture exercising alone and without an audience in a mock Warburgian gymnasium of the imagination would be merely a semaphore, a windmill, a madman. Such gesturing takes up publicly available names, and it uses them in a social tokening that both plays the token and also simultaneously takes up a position relative to the tokening. This was the kind of rhetorical life of the theater theorized by Benjamin, Lacis, and Brecht. Here, too, we encounter one of the basic elements of the *Bilderatlas* being put into practice in an embodied performative space. It was not simply the individualizability of the names that was crucial to the work of social tokening underwritten by the image atlas. Equally important, if not more so, were the tropic relationships to such names that might be suggested by the ambivalent and perhaps ironic gesture that signified its allegiance to two postures together with an inferred motion between them.

SURFACING

In the course of the myriad paraphrases pursued in this book, a number of interrelated problematics have emerged. Sequencing those paraphrases in this chapter, a line of inquiry has come to the surface. Indecision certainly can be a form of intense anxiety and political debilitation, but it is also a potentially rich zone of investigation in which possibilities can be discerned for the first time. The faculty of such discernment should be understood in relation to judging, which as "distinguishing" (*krinein*) and associated processes is not simply approving or disapproving or evaluating in any superficial sense. The distinguishing I am emphasizing was a practice of eliciting characteristics from appearances in such a way that one might articulate new predicates into existence. Seen in this way, the work of judging is intimately related to the various kinds of modality that we have examined in this book. The interpretation of everydayness as a kind of de facto necessity that I worked out earlier has led to a sense that discernment is intimately related to organizing memory into what we may call topical fields of attention. Within these fields, similarity and difference render sensation itself more acute, and together they also begin to propose sequences of animation from one incarnation of sense to another. Finally, we have also seen that there are practices and institutions of remembering that counteract the deliquescence of everydayness into some merely precise calculation of a "mean." Moreover, such practices and institutions are not just so many gymnasia designed for the exercise of potentially magnanimous and omnicompetent individuals. They are more properly thought of as topical spaces of appearance shaped by and for communities.

This chapter has walked the tightrope of a paradox. On the one hand, it has been deeply invested in paraphrasing the words and works of others. On the other hand, my own interests and predilections have undeniably structured the text. Very often the intermeshing of these two projects is held to be problematic. "Absent yourself and hold yourself to philologically impersonal criteria of selection and treatment!" Or, "be more concise and focus on justifying the claims you wish to make in your own voice!" Pick one. In the introduction of this book, I made an argument for resisting strict demarcations of, for example, philosophy and the history of philosophy. I argued that having a robust and historically informed sense of the inferential implicatures of particular positions is one legitimate and important way of discovering for oneself the positions one is willing to take up. There is no strict division between thinking and the history of thought. In the next chapter, we move beyond this zone of indeterminacy, and I surface out of paraphrase into assertion. Surfacing in the present is neither an afterthought to a primarily historical project nor some overdetermining terminus ad quem overshadowing everything that has come before. The historical inquiry is an end in itself, and the theoretical inquiry is also an end in itself. Both are pursued. In the next and final chapter, I turn to articulating the Weimar origins of rhetorical inquiry in a contemporary idiom, and there I take up a simple question: how may the tradition I have articulated in this book be thought today?

8: THE POSSIBILITIES NOW

AN ARISTOTELIAN SPYGLASS IN WEIMAR AND NOW

The task of this book has been to discern a new array of Weimar origins for rhetorical inquiry. The claim has not been that rhetorical inquiry finds its only or true origin in Weimar between 1918 and 1933. Such a claim would be ludicrous. Rhetorical inquiry has many origins—ancient and medieval, some early modern, some modern, some European, many extra-European. If rhetorical inquiry is to be a vibrant field of inquiry, then a lively sense of the multiplicity of its origins is important. As I have argued in a number of ways in the course of this book, the history of a field's emergence and reinvention will sketch possible lines of investigation. Some of these will have been explored; many will not. Among other things, the past is a repertoire of unpursued possibilities. The book's true claim has been that, although Weimar has been disproportionately important in intellectual histories written in the last half century or so, there is a rhetorical dimension to Weimar that we have not perceived. I have argued that perceiving this dimension is illuminating not just historically but also at the level of theoretical presupposition.

As I have indicated, I think it is useful to organize the Weimar inheritance in terms of an inquiry sequence running through Weber, Schmitt, Strauss, Baron, and Adorno, and the purpose of the book has been to lay out an alternative sequence. I have argued for the existence of lines of inquiry that change our thinking about a number of the basic presuppositions underpinning what I have called "the standard received version." The alternative I have traced has nodal points in Heidegger, Arendt, Benjamin, and Warburg. These are anything but neglected authors. Of course, I am not discovering these authors, nor am I discovering their rhetoricity. The claim is instead that we have not perceived these thinkers as an inquiry sequence in the history and theory of rhetoric. In particular, we have not perceived the parts of their work that unfold a series of arguments about the rhetorical dimensions of appearance, appearance against a background, appearance against a background exhibiting dialectical tensions, appearance against a background exhibiting dialectical tensions that may be splayed onto an image table. The book has been centrally focused on articulating these dimensions as a sequence.

No one in the sequence Heidegger-Arendt-Benjamin-Warburg could be accurately described as a rhetorician pure and simple. In each case, however, it has been possible to generate a minority report that opens up important lines of inquiry. Thinking these oeuvres together and thinking them together by supplementing them with elements from the rhetorical tradition is valuable. It reveals something about each corpus that we have ignored to this point. It also opens up new possibilities for rhetorical inquiry itself. The specification of a new tradition makes new initiatives possible. For this reason, flanking the four central chapters dedicated to each of the key individuals, there have been sketches of both the idioms of rhetorical inquiry available in Weimar Germany and the afterlives of Heideggerian, Arendtian, Benjaminian, and Warburgian lines of rhetorical inquiry in the post-Weimar and postwar periods.

As I indicated in chapter 1 (and then emphasized again in chapter 7), I am particularly interested in the borderlands between paraphrasing the assertions of others and making assertions in one's own voice. The inferentialism of Robert Brandom is one contemporary philosophical initiative that informs my understanding of this borderland. As an intellectual historian, I find Brandom's central idea extremely pertinent: the meaning of any assertion will not be transparent at the moment in which it is uttered because generally speaking the meaning of an assertion is a function of its inferential implications when combined with other assertions against the background of other situations. Intellectual history, one might say, is the process in which protoassertoric practices as well as clusters of assertion encounter new situations. Brandom's insight has been to see—or rather to see anew and express precisely—the sense in which a commitment's entailments become manifest only when that commitment is tested in some way. What does one do when a sentence to which one has committed oneself comes into conflict with a situation? Does one abandon the sentence? Does one remain true to the sentence and turn a blind eye to the situation? Or, alternatively, does one amend the sentence by attaching to it some aspect of the situation at hand in the manner of an annotation, digression, redefinition, qualification, or exception? In their pure forms, both "abandoning" a sentence and "remaining true to" a sentence are more difficult than perhaps it seems. Between these two extremes, one has a historiography of transformation in which the old becomes new amid processes of shunting, inverting, coupling, mirroring, and transposing.

There is, I contend, no great qualitative difference between reconstructing encounters between sentences and situations in the past and imagining encounters between sentences and situations in the present, and this concluding chapter takes that claim as foundational. On my account, reconstruction is itself a highly imaginative endeavor because semantics is itself very basically virtual. That is, given a situation and an array of discursive commitments, semantics is orientated to questions not only of what *was* said in response but also what *could* have been said in response. Equally, imagination is constitutive. Imagination conjures new possibilities simply by placing inheritances in the context of new, unanticipated, nonsubsumed situations. For these and other related reasons, this conclusion does not seek simply to summarize the findings of the book. It seeks instead to relocate some of the book's core conceptual preoccupations into a contemporary twenty-first-century landscape. The task is to think these inheritances now. What emerges is not some surprising denouement but rather a recrafting in a contemporary idiom of various preoccupations that have recurred in this book. The aim is to rewrite the Weimar origins of rhetorical inquiry in such a way that they can be more readily quoted today and taken up as theoretical presuppositions in contemporary research.

If one wishes to think the Heidegger-Arendt-Benjamin-Warburg line as an iterated unity (as I do), there is no more succinct contraction of their shared interests than one of the most famous sentences in the history of rhetoric. I am thinking of *estō dē rhētorikē dunamis peri hekaston tou theorēsai to endechomenon pithanon* from Aristotle's *Rhetoric*. Jonathan Barnes provides a commonly cited translation: "rhetoric," says Aristotle, "may be defined as the faculty of observing in any given case the available means of persuasion."[1] If we fragment the Greek in order to prepare it for twentieth- and twenty-first-century reinvention, we find that there are five moments in Aristotle's assertion. We have the *dunamis* (the power, capacity, faculty, practice, possibility), the *theorēsai* (the seeing, finding, surveying, considering), the *peri hekaston* (the in-any-given-case, in-a-particular-situation, in-a-certain-finding-of-oneself), the *endechomenon* (the possible, permissible, admissible, available), and the *pithanon* (the persuasive, persuasion, persuadedness, belief). Each of these Greek terms is creatively indeterminate, and I have tried to hint at this by listing several English approximations.

The task in what follows is to use these indeterminacies as opportunities to think. Each of the four core chapters of this book has been centered on a figure who takes up different moments from this Aristotelian sentence. On my account, Martin Heidegger reworks *dunamis*, Aby Warburg glosses

---

1. Aristotle, *Rhetoric*, 1355b27–28. Compare Aristotle, *Topics*, 149b26–28, where a similar definition is cited as an example of defining something in its ideal state.

theorēsai, Hannah Arendt recasts both *peri hekaston* and *endechomenon*, and Walter Benjamin configures *pithanon*. I am not claiming that these "takings up" were intentional in any strong sense. Nevertheless, they do constitute important inflections of the rhetorical tradition. If we want to be able to use this Aristotelian sentence creatively today, then we need to take up and rethink its conceptual presuppositions. Here in this final chapter, I use this Aristotelian sentence as a heuristic in answering the following question: what remains conceptually alive today in this Weimar reinvention of the rhetorical inheritance?

FACULTY

Let us begin with the word "faculty"—rhetoric as faculty. Faculty is not an art. *Dunamis* is not *technē*. A *facultas* is a modulation of *facere*, "making" or "doing." Speculative Vichian etymology is useful here: *facultas* may be derived from *facilitas*.[2] This is faculty simply as a facility or an ease of doing. A faculty can be understood as originating in a facility, an ease of performing that derives from practice. Faculty is a habit, and, just so, in his 1565 paraphrase of Aristotle's sentence, Alessandro Piccolomini declared that rhetoric was "an art or, more truly, a faculty, on account of which we become habituated [*habituati*] and capable in knowing how to see and find in reference to whatever matter in which persuasion is possible all that which can be turned to achieve persuasion and transform it [the merely persuadable] into belief."[3] Note immediately the concern for habit expressed here. Rhetoric is an art, or better a faculty—that is, a practice—by means of which we become habituated and powerful in a particular kind of knowing how to see and find. Repeated, the deed becomes repertoire. A facility is eventually reified as a faculty. Faculty is, thus, a kind of "institutionalization."

To be situated amid a repertoire is to be an actuality in the midst of possibilities or an indeterminacy amidst an array of potential actualizations. *Dunamis* here is not so much capacity as, simply, possibility. If habituation is also a matter of responding in a number of different ways to the same input, then possibility is also the array of habituations that one has sequenced. Possibility here is a groove one has carved out for oneself. At this point, we may recall the Heideggerian gloss of Aristotle's sentence that stood at the center of chapter 3: "in relation to what is given in each case," says Heidegger, "rhetoric is the possibility of seeing what speaks for a thing that

---

2. Vico, *De antiquissima Italorum sapientia*, 113.

3. Piccolomini, *Copiosissima parafrase*, 45: "un'arte ò vero una facoltà, per la qual diveniamo habituati, & potenti a saper vedere, & trovare intorno à qual si voglia materia persuasibile, tutto quello che esser possa accommodato à persuaderla, & a farne fede."

is the topic of discussion, in each case to see what *can* speak for a thing."[4] Not a power or a faculty (Heidegger did not speak of *Vermögen*), not even a practice, rhetoric is simply a possibility (*Möglichkeit*) on this account. Rhetoric is a possible mode of being to which situated presencing (*Dasein*) could find itself inclined. And this, said Heidegger, is the *genuine* definition of rhetoric. Inauthentic for him was the more common stipulation that rhetoric be thought of as an "art" (*technē*). On the genuine account, rhetoric would be a disposing of oneself, a "putting-oneself-in-the-midst-of-or-toward." What is distinctive in the Heideggerian rendition of the Aristotelian topos is the sense in which rhetoric is a mode of being-civic, of placing oneself in the midst of possibilities that are intensively connected to the public thing and its diversity of perspectives, narrativizations, and passions. Being amid this maelstrom of tensions disperses being into possibility out in front of all its actualizations. Moreover, as we saw, possibility is constitutive of actuality for Heidegger. This means, for example, that the mere possibility of an action may already be said to exist as an emotion—as fear, for instance. Rhetoric is one of the primary zones for the somewhat indeterminate variegation of being as possibility.

Witnessing novel actions from a third-person perspective will be more common than undertaking them in one's own "first-personal" body if we assume that capacities for novel action are relatively evenly distributed among the members of a community. Granting these assumptions, we find that—insofar as they are understood at all—actions will be more often grasped as passions. The dissemination of a faculty thus does not derive simply from a capacity to invent those actions oneself. More often, the faculty develops out of a capacity to reenact the actions of others by inverting the experience of a passion. Patient becomes agent. Thus, the "possibility" of something is not only a question about whether it can or cannot appear within a particular frame of reference. It is also a question about whether it can be imitated. If we entrust ourselves for a moment to the etymology of the term, "possibility" is simply "do-ability." Possibility is "a something of which one is capable."

Understood as do-ability, possibility's opposite becomes not simply incapacity but more particularly captivation. Captivation, as I understand it here, is an apotropaic incapacity to complete a motion qua imitation. One sees the outer limits of a motion. Perhaps one can follow and reenact parts of its sequence. But one is not able to perform that motion as a totality either physically or imaginatively. There are patterns that one can recognize as patterns without being able to grasp and deploy them as totalities. Here, I am thinking of Alfred Gell's riveting discussion of South Indian kolam,

4. Heidegger, *Grundbegriffe*, 114: "*rhētorikē* ist die *Möglichkeit*," according to Heidegger, "am jeweils Gegebenen zu sehen das, was für eine Sache, die Thema der Rede ist, spricht, jeweilig zu sehen das, was für eine Sache sprechen kann."

where complex patterns are produced by the serial rotation of closed curves that are not symmetrical in any simple sense.[5] Captivation can thus emerge as a form of being trapped by a sensory field because one has grasped its intrinsic patternedness even as one is constantly frustrated in one's attempts to reproduce that pattern in one's own mind or body.

The capacity to complete something as a totality depends in part on extrapolating from a part to a whole. Capacity, thus, is a form of synecdoche. Indeed, *dunamis* itself is also a supplementing in the form of a bringing to completion or provisional completion. As we saw in Agamben's discussion of the "kairological saturation" rendered visible by Bill Viola's *Passions*, *dunamis* can be understood as an extrapolation machine. Each moment in the slow-motion unfolding of the emotion proposes a completion that, it subsequently emerges, is tangential to the curved continuation that actually follows. *Dunamis* is both means and end, because it is both the cause and the effect of extrapolation. Discussing the assertion from Dionysius Thrax that "*dunamis* is the <sound (*phōnē*)> that results from and completes the *stoicheia* [the elements]," James Porter explains, with an eye to the paradox, that *dunamis* "designates the audible, aesthetic, and prosodic value or quality of *stoicheia* once they are 'realized' in a given context."[6] Phrasing is a matter of musical interpretation as well as modern punctuation because it is an analogue of a fully embodied breathing in which one orients oneself to the totality of a performance. Phrasing organizes stance qua reenactability.

Inferred totality is the means by which one gives a kind of balance to one's actions or passions, and such inference establishes a center of gravity from which one cannot easily be shifted. A faculty, on this account, is something like a capacity to remain in the middle of a motion or to find the stations in its course, just as Domenico da Piacenza proposed in the context of dance. The motion itself will have its extremes (and at times we may like to record those extremes statistically), but the subject characterized by a faculty for that motion will not find itself overshooting these extremes. Indeed, the shifting of weight back to the center will already have begun before an extremity is reached. Equally, faculty is something like the fixing solution used to arrest the development of photosensitive materials because it deals with continua of change and fixes on particular stations—or stopping points—amid that change. These stations may also be understood through the metaphor of joint-like inflection points, because these are places in which possibility gathers and concentrates. Despite the robust promise of kairological saturation, not every moment may be variegated into an equal number of potential futures.

We seem to be in the presence of an institutionalization of "the

---

5. Gell, *Art and Agency*, 68–72.
6. Porter, *Origins of Aesthetic Thought*, 214.

subject"—as if that subject were to be generated as a congeries of capacities to act, to be acted on, and to imitate—but the situation is not so straightforward. Capacities do seem to license an agent. And it does seem therefore as if a faculty is an ease of performance that experiences no—or decreasing—difficulty. In fact, however, the ease with which an action can be performed underscores the unavoidability of a question about whether that action *will* be performed. We should say that indecision characterizes rhetoric as a capacity (that is, as a power), because a *dunamis* cannot be understood except as an ability either to do or not to do. As Giorgio Agamben has expressed it, "an experience of power [*potenza*] as such is possible only if power is always also power not to (do or think something)."[7] The existence of a power is synonymous with the genuineness of the question of whether it is to be deployed or not. For this reason, the automation of power deployments is in fact a destruction of power. Such automation transforms power into something inert like weight.

Questions of power and questions of ontology are interrelated, and here we have the incipient ambivalence of the Heideggerian attitude toward actualization. "Activation" (*energeia*) does bring being into a state of greater determination in comparison with being in the mode of possibility qua *dunamis*, which is absent but only in the degree of its vagueness. Yet *energeia* is always already on its way toward completion (*entelecheia*) understood as a kind of end point at which all potential continuations have been organized around a node of indeterminacy. Power depends on the possibility of its being or not being. It depends on the possibility of its restraint but also on the incalculability of the continuations that may ensue. Let us, then, think about rhetoric not simply as a faculty or a capacity but more precisely as a contingency, a nonnecessity or underdetermination that has its central experience in indecision.

"Contingency," however, has a special place in the discourses of so-called modernity. We should be careful about how we handle that word and its connotations. There are senses in which contingency has displaced the *dunamis* that in Aristotle had been counterposed to *energeia*. The word "contingency" now tends toward the semantic zones of the nonnecessary, the chancy, and the "that-which-could-be-otherwise." Of course, in recent centuries, radical expansions of instrumental reason have broadened the horizons of human artifice. In turn, one can understand this expansion of instrumentality as so many demonstrations of the manifold ways in which any given something can be otherwise. A thing's manifestation is but one of the ways in which it might be. One cultivates the earth, one manipulates

7. Agamben, "Bartleby," 55: "un'esperienza della potenza come tale è possibile solo se la potenza è sempre anche potenza di *non* (fare o pensare qualcosa)."

genes, and nature reveals the degrees and pathways of its acculturability. Alongside this attachment of the contingent to the artificial, however, there has also been a decoupling of the natural from the necessary. If, per Darwin, nature was itself "on the move" (albeit relatively slowly), then the realm of the possible broadened radically. It became possible to think of the laws of nature not only as contingent (in the sense that they could have been otherwise) but also, with Peirce, as genuinely historical (in the sense that laws themselves might evolve and might even become more or less regular, more or less statistical).[8] Indeed, underlying this vision was an account of how chance anomalies might assume the role of setting down "rules" for natural forms such as species.

Nonnecessity has taken up a central place in political consciousness too. So much more has become possible and, indeed, so much more has become natural. Expressing the thought a little more precisely, we may observe that it is now possible for political argumentation to be focused on questions of how narrowly specifiable the natural qua the necessary really is. Thus, the emergent post-eighteenth-century split between conservatives and radicals has been in significant ways—as Willibald Steinmetz and others have emphasized—a disagreement about what is possible in the sense of nonnecessary, that is, in the sense of contingent.[9] At the root of this political disagreement between radicals and conservatives was a historiographic disagreement about the possibility of radical and systemic change.

In the wake of opening politics up to historical time, rhetoric as a postmodern political project that focused on contingency threatened to become an endless repetition of the verbal gesture "yes, but you see, if we analyze the mode of its constitution in discourse, we become aware that this state of affairs could have been—and therefore presumably still can be—otherwise." Rhetoric, on this account, seemed to become a professionally deformed optimism, a mere voluntarism. If reality is constituted by language, went the refrain, then we can make and unmake reality as easily as we write and rewrite a sentence. As if it were not true, comes the rejoinder, that some things once said cannot be unsaid. Or as if, comes the material rejoinder, language itself were not a merely provincial idiom with which to analyze life.

The version of rhetorical inquiry emerging from my account of the Weimar thinkers treated in this book is different. As I see it, the *dunamis* offered to us by Weimar is not the *dunamis* of contingency that says simply and continually, "this could have been different." The Weimar *dunamis* that is or should be alive for us is the *dunamis* of indecision. It is a tension

8. I am grateful to Danielle Follett for underscoring the specificity of "contingency."
9. Steinmetz, *Das Sagbare und das Machbare*.

between an always somewhat indeterminate actuality and the variety of possibilities that are its indeterminacy. Under this particular specification of its work, rhetoric simply *is* politic. Again, the thought has a Heideggerian provenance: "rhetoric makes the claim to be itself politic."[10] To denote the intersection of *rhetorikē* and *politikē*, I use the somewhat unusual term "politic" as a substantive—a substantive denoting the *dunamis* operant in what Anglophones commonly refer to as "the field of politics." Politic makes explicit the preoccupation in rhetoric with questions of collective undertaking. Politic is thus to be thought of as a susceptibility. It is a sensitivity to the indeterminateness of situations that raises the question of *which* deployment of a faculty. Politic is so intractable because it is intractability itself. That is, politic occurs where rules have no immediate torsion on cases. Bureaucracy—in its purest, perhaps unattainable, form where rules subsume cases without remainder—is not politic but one of its opposites.

In the twenty-first century, the statisticalization of life to which Heidegger was in part responding in the 1920s has become far more ubiquitous, precise, and collectable. Contemporary forms of statisticalization are radically different from the relationships to possibility qua *dunamis* involved in Aristotle's definition of rhetoric, but this is a difference that enables us to think. When we specify these differences between ancient *dunamis* and contemporary statisticalization, we understand the specificity of ancient and early modern rhetorics. We also gain an ability to apply rhetorical interests to a broader range of phenomena in the contemporary world. Heidegger's Weimar project remains one that is capable of helping us manage this pivoting of attention. His investigations of *dunamis, energeia,* and *entelecheia* as modes of presencing that were by turns vague, definitional, and archiving make it possible to see how contemporary structurations of possibility partake in the constitution of what is.

SENSING

I am rethinking the ways in which rhetoric is a possibility of seeing in situations characterized by either realizable consensus or realizable dissent. I want now to think more precisely about the second element of what I have called "the Aristotelian spyglass"—namely, the element of "seeing." In particular, I want to claim that the particular kind of seeing in question here can be helpfully understood as a kind of carving out. Almost any given sensory field—certainly those that are analogue in their sensitivities—will contain either an infinity of possible sensations or a number of possible sensations in excess of that sensory field's capacity for distinguishing.

10. Heidegger, *Grundbegriffe*, 135: "die Rhetorik macht den Anspruch, selbst Politik zu sein."

Sensory perspicacity is not a matter of pure sensitivity. Indeed, the result of ever-greater sensitivity might be ever-greater indistinctness: absolute sensitivity never rises above the absolutely particular. On the contrary, we may understand the education of a sense in terms of the isolation of particular notes, shapes, sequences, or patterns. One finds, for example, an outline on one's palate and in one's memory for the particular taste of Brettanomyces, which is a highly distinctive yeast used in the brewing of some beers. One empties out a space for this sensation. For a time, this emptiness may itself be palpable. The possibility of a sensation is the carving out of a space, an emptiness and pattern that having been carved is more distinctly actualizable than the increments surrounding it.

In this way, possessing an educated sense is not synonymous with being a reliable responder. That is, being a connoisseur is not simply a matter of saying "yes, Brett," when Brettanomyces has been used in the brewing process. To be sure, although Brett itself is quite distinctive, such reliability of response is a nontrivial skill. Nevertheless, possessing an educated sense is also, and more basically, a matter of being able to sense the presence and the absence of a sensation simultaneously. It is, one might say, a capacity to perceive the edge of a sensation, something that is quite intuitive when one is thinking of vision but less so when one is thinking of taste. Important here is Warburg's emphasis on the silhouette as the unit of identification that permits a figure to pull free from its ground and circulate in an emotional or gestural community. Let a purely digital sensory field be one in which a sensation is simply a binary distinction between "on" and "off" within a framework of discrete and noncontinuous values. Within a sensory field that is more than minimally digital, what one senses is the presence of a quality in its differentiation from the qualities that surround it. Sensation, thus, is basically concerned with relationships between note and harmony, foreground and background, phenomenon and context.

Take the fifth of Georges Braque's *Atelier* paintings, for instance. The point I am making about carving out is vividly instantiated there. This work is a study of the site of painterly invention itself—namely, the studio. It is focused on a kind of differential of distinctiveness: palette, brushes, vase, easel (?), "detritus." It is a kind of visual topics. Indeed, the fact that this painting is part of a sequence of works honed over the course of decades suggests that the process of carving out visual possibilities will itself be an iterated one. Achieved visual possibilities bring new possibilities into being. Or such achievement brings possibilities into a kind of half being. It places them on the edge of being. What I want to emphasize, however, is the carved-out quality of the most figuratively distinct component in Braque's painting, the "bird" inscribed just above the center of the canvas. In Braque's words, what continually preoccupied him was the cultivation of "tactile space" (*l'espace tactile*) in contradistinction to "visual space" (*l'espace visual*).[11] Braque thought that whereas visual space organizes relationships between objects tactile space establishes distances between objects and viewers. The tactility of the bird in his image lies in its two-dimensional cut out quality. It is as if the surface of the painting has been gouged. One wants to know the outline of the object by running one's fingers along the edge of this "wound." What one sees, I am saying, is the possibility of an action of touching. Standing on the edge of a possibility of touching is analogous to the position that Heidegger has put us in while glossing Aristotle's definition of rhetoric as the possibility of a seeing. The possibility of a sensing puts us in a kind of no-man's-land between sensation and imagination. As I have reconstituted them both, Warburg refines what remained merely an intuition in Heidegger. In my reconstruction of the logic of his thought, Warburg works on the assumption that the "possibility of seeing" is also a matter of the body-kinetic reproduction of a silhouette in one's own body. And we should understand this kind of reproduction as a "touching of that pose from within" by means of the borderline tactile senses of balance and kinesthesia.

A widely distributed theoretical presupposition holds that sensation can be analyzed in isolation from imagination, but Warburg helps us to see that this presupposition is optional. In doing so, he opens up a wide range of investigative opportunities in contemporary rhetorical inquiry. Insisting on being able to deal with sense without dealing with imagination, we may infer, is a case of the broader supposition that dealing with reality is a matter of dealing with actualities rather than possibilities. Sensing the shape of the bird in Braque's painting is quite distinct from the, on this account, necessarily subsequent impulse to trace its form with one's fingers. The possibility of touching cannot be understood as constituting the actuality of seeing in any essential way. One senses actualities, and one imagines possibilities. In chapter 6, we grew accustomed to the contrary thought that seeing could be understood more deeply as itself an anticipation of the taking up of a pose. Warburg prepared us simultaneously for the twin notions that possibility is do-ability qua performability and that seeing is implicated in such possibility.

Some scholars desire to maintain a clear distinction between sensation and imagination, and in some articulations of this desire we see an affirmation of the value of noncontinuation in and of itself rather than a positivist injunction against permitting possibility to bleed into and structure actuality. At various points in this book, the term "narrativization" has intruded. This has happened in moments when a single image, pair, or sequence of

11. Braque, *Cahier de Georges Braque*, 78.

images has suggested inferences that might put that exposure or sequence of exposures in motion. Another term for narrativization is "narratocracy." As the political theorist Davide Panagia deployed "narratocracy" in *The Political Life of Sensation*, the term denotes a subsuming of visualizable moments into established hegemonic plots. Specifying the phenomenon, he notes that narratocracy "offers the narrative line which is the story line that determines the trajectory of an action, but it is also the stenographic mark that traces a figure (of speech, of thought, of script, etc.) across a blank page," thereby eliciting the form of that figure.[12] On Panagia's account, we should prize moments that resist narratocracy or forms of standard received narrativization. These are antinarratocratic moments that Benjamin might have attached to experiences of *Staunen*, the kind of "wondering" or "astonishment" that occasions inarticulateness. In Panagia's version, this is a Rancierian "dissensus."

There is certainly something arresting in the sensory artifact that resists immediate continuation. On the account I am building in this book, however, this is the less interesting moment. The denial of continuation can take different forms. It can be the denial of a continuation expressed in either the choreographies of reciprocal gesture and stance or the explicitly discursive domains where the nameability of an image contributes to its secondment as a prop into a script. In both forms, such noncontinuation is aporetic in the sense that there is no immediately obvious way through it. Nevertheless, the more brilliant word that Panagia uses to describe the moment in which narratocracy is derailed is "disarticulation." Taking up and then departing from Panagia's initiative, I would say that disarticulation can be more richly understood as the moment in which multiple continuations appear equipossible rather than the moment that resists narrative continuation as such. Not blankness but rather confusion is the point of departure for disarticulation. Confusion exists at the edge of discourse or testifies to the multiplicity of discourses that appear to have traction on a given case, and confusion is itself to be understood as a motion and not a stasis. The confused being either acts erratically or is brought up short. Starting and stopping are both motions, and there is a motive relation between the beholder and the beheld that belies what we might refer to as a "snapshot" theory of sensation.

Take, for example, Caravaggio's Cerasi Chapel *Conversion of St. Paul*. In that painting, there is an illuminating alternative to the path taken by Panagia. Channeling a reading by the French thinker Louis Marin, Panagia has suggested that there is no motion to be seen in Caravaggio's painting. The hypothesis is that this painting short-circuits narrative continuation

12. Panagia, *Political Life of Sensation*, 12.

and that it is genuinely "a snapshot moment of frozen action."[13] To Panagia's Louis Marin, I counterpose an Aby Warburg whose constant task, as a theorist of *theōrein* (seeing, looking, gazing, considering, theorizing), was to sharpen our sensitivities to stations embodying motion. In the spirit of Warburg, I attend to the hands and forearms of St. Paul as depicted by Caravaggio. In the presence of the original in Rome, comparing left and right reveals—I wager—a tension between two moments: in the left hand and forearm an accent of musculature and finger extension; on the right, the most minimal releasing of tensions. One can perhaps reverse the sequence as one wishes—either shock and then release, or release and then shock. And these are two quite distinct protonarratives, the one divine, the other devilish. The one is Christian-propagandistic perhaps; the other—less likely, to be sure—possesses an as yet indeterminate function.

Caravaggio's painting thematized conversion by taking up the originally rhetorical notion of *metanoia* (the changing of a mind that could be signaled by cutting off and starting again), and certainly that artwork does appear to privilege a divine over a devilish protonarrative, but this vindicates the point I am making. Perceptually, the painting places one always already within a trajectory or complex of trajectories, and it elides any radical disjunction between sensation and imagination.[14] A seeing of the actual that wholly excludes a simultaneous "seeing" of the possible, I am inferring, is either rare or nonexistent. Disattention is a kind of living in the absence of possibility, it is true, but one should note that such disattention is also a living in the absence of actuality. One does this all the time, of course.

The reinterpretation of Heideggerian everydayness offered in this book emphasizes a distinction that sharpens our sense of attention and disattention. On the one hand, there is a kind of coding in the absence of attention where the objects of one's classifying gaze do not write themselves into the taxonomic system in any way. These objects are simply classified and forgotten. They dissolve amid calculations of the mean. On the other hand, there is the kind of everydayness that collects experiences and stores them by means of a sensory topics. Disattention is precisely a matter of not attending to the actual. But the inverse does not follow. It is not the case that attention is precisely an attending *only* to the actual. Attending is, instead, a kind of reenacting of a sensation in the presence of a number of its alternatives, alternatives that are activated in imagination by memory. Insofar as one is genuinely sensing at all, one is attending, and one's attention is to be understood as a kind of opening up of tensions between the actual and the possible, the sensed and the imagined.

13. Panagia, 101.
14. See Marin, *Détruire la peinture*. Note, however, that some scholarship has emphasized Caravaggio's investment in the temporality of narrative: see Pericolo, *Caravaggio and Pictorial Narrative*, esp. 5–7. I am indebted to Gyöngyvér Horváth for this reference.

The carving out of a possibility is also to be understood as the specification of a span between past and future. There are myriad ways in which one can understand such spanning. Visual cognition operates in some sense by means of the imitability of a datum. In the context of computer vision, this becomes an operationalization of the hypothesis that objects are computationally distinguishable qua objects when those objects replicate their own motions. This is a way of saying that one can construct an algorithm capable of scanning for shapes that display degrees and kinds of self-similarity or symmetry. The wing silhouette that mirrors another wing silhouette is algorithmically predictable.[15] In other versions, a datum becomes perceivable as an action insofar as it is reenactable. That is to say, the Protagorean, Aristotelian, and Vichian accounts of mimesis—together with their Collingwoodian, Warburgian, and Benjaminian cousins—may have a continuation in contemporary research. Contemporary cognitive scientists also offer a line of inquiry into what they call "the complementary nature" whereby the coding of an action proceeds by specifying its antistrophe—its complement or contrary.[16] Self-completing, mimetic, and contrappostal, such sensings operate at the grammatical level of the action, where the moment is folded into a possibility existing as a duration in time.

Perhaps speaking of seeing as an anticipation of reenactment seems hopelessly premodern, and one might infer that this is not the way to rethink Aristotle's *dunamis* definition of rhetoric through the prism of Weimar for renewal in the twenty-first century. Caravaggio cannot really gloss the last hundred years, can he? Actually, perhaps he can. His instants are fictions and, as we have seen, perhaps not instants at all. Nevertheless, they anticipate the stills of photography and the anatomies of motion presented by sequences of discrete stills—namely, film. Moreover, we can say that photography and film share a fundamentally statistical attitude toward time. They sample continuity, privileging the discrete. They are de- and recontextualization machines that constantly exercise capacities for inference. There is almost no *visual* similarity between Caravaggio's portraits and the composite portraits of Francis Galton, but they share in a sense the grammar of the sampled and then superimposed instant.[17] Once we make this transition, we are in the distinctively modern terrain of statistical inquiry. Possibility takes on a whole new structure within this frame of reference. Instead of being simply a conceptualization of range, possibility now becomes a science of distribution. It becomes a reckoning of probabilities and deals with the almost always and the almost never.

The rise of statistics was a taming of chance (as Ian Hacking said),

---

15. Pizlo et al., *Making a Machine*, 6: "our new definition [of shape] uses the similarity of the object to itself."

16. See Kelso and Engstrøm, *Complementary Nature*.

17. Galton, "Composite Portraits," 97–100.

because statistical analysis revealed regularities where previously none had been perceptible, and such analysis did this by gazing at things from what we might describe as a statistical distance.[18] In what sense could an accident be genuinely accidental if it exhibited annual frequencies that were stable or changed in what appeared to be a mathematically plottable or historically narratable fashion? It is perhaps here that arguments for the radical separability of sensation and imagination have received their strongest and most insistent articulation. Transposed into a statistical domain, sensation and imagination become measurement and hypothesis. Experimental procedure constructs a situation in which senses or sensors can record values in what seems like a nonhypothetical manner. And the statisticalization of experiment then permits a broader application of the procedure to situations that are less purely constructable because the multiplication of chance incursions into "the laboratory" means that errors can cancel each other out.[19]

If Stephen Ziliak and Deirdre McCloskey are right, though, the apparent mutual independence of sensation and imagination in experimental statistical analysis is a myth—or, at least, a problem. For them, the ultimate fantasy-less decontextualized sensor is the test of statistical significance, which estimates the likelihood that chance is responsible for the divergence between a group of particular observed results and a group of projected null results. For Ziliak and McCloskey, blanket and thoughtless use of the test of statistical significance as a criterion for concentrating on some experimental results and ignoring others amounts to a dangerous and self-inflicted blindness. What is the alternative they suggest? They advocate emancipation from the binary code of "statistically significant/statistically insignificant." And, in effect, they call for continual nurturing of a power of hypothesizing a plenitude of potential explanations for any given set of experimental results.[20] We may conclude that even—and yes, especially—in the age of statistical scientific inquiry, data are occasions for the embedding of actualities in possibilities. We call this "hypothesizing."

The Warburgian line of inquiry that I have been calculating through Weimar and into the present emphasizes the cultivation of organs of sense in particular, and such cultivation is rhetorical in at least two ways. One perceives possibilities on account of one's own access to a community store of shared intelligibilities cast, as it were, in the "plasticine" of sense. But this capacity to perceive with others is simultaneously a capacity to see what others are capable of perceiving. On the basis of this capacity, one

18. Hacking, *Taming of Chance*.
19. Fisher, *Design of Experiments*.
20. Ziliak and McCloskey, *Cult of Statistical Significance*.

can participate in the generation of new names within the communities of passion and gesture discerned by Warburg. Rhetorical performance is deeply immersed in the *sensus communis* of received forms, but that common sense is similarly a feel for the hitherto unnamed poses that may become stations of belief within a community. One's ability to see processes of replication and variation in the motions of others is intimately connected with one's capacity to replicate and vary those motions oneself. For that reason, these twin capacities are also capacities to estimate likelihoods of change. We might call the sum total of such capacities the gestural suppleness, inventiveness, or magnanimity of a community.

CASE

How may we think creatively about a phrase such as "in any given case" (*peri hekaston*), and how may we apply that thinking to contemporary analogues of the *peri hekaston* such as "for any given set of experimental results"? Here, we are concerned with the question of perspicacity with regard to the possible ways of approaching a state of belief in the context of a specific situation. There are at least three different attitudes to the "situatedness" named in this question. One can say that this situation is an opportunity for autonomy, where one understands "autonomy" literally as the process of giving a rule to oneself. Or one can say that the specificity of the situation is such that autonomy has been suspended. The given case is exceptional, and the belief arrived at to resolve the doubt raised by the case is, thus, exceptional as well. Broadly speaking, these first two options are, respectively, Kantian and Schmittian responses to the moment of "in any given case."

Understood as conceptual extremes, neither the Kantian nor the Schmittian attitude toward the case is particularly plausible as a description of the general grammar of "caseness." From a historical point of view, it is improbable that any given case will be transformable into a durable principle of action on account of containing enough of the complexity of either the world in which it occurred or the world in which it will be applied in the manner of a precedent. From a psychological point of view, what is more, it is equally improbable that any given decision context will have precisely no afterlife in muscle memory, individual habit, or culture. This does not mean that it will not be highly instructive to attend to the modes in which principles emerge from situations and the modes in which exceptioning is administered. Kantian and Schmittian routines *do* sharpen the analytical gaze. What I am claiming is that these routines are extremes and do not really suit the majority of situations in which they may be applied.

The third possibility here is, once again, possibility itself. That is, between rule and exception, one has something like a loosely bound habit. With the phrase "loosely bound habit," I mean to denote a regularity of response to situations in which neither the nature of the situation nor the nature of the response is fully or finally described. On this account, when it is not either beginning or being thrown off, a habit is always undergoing a process of further specification. Accretion is the basic mode of habit's historicity. An action becomes a habit by accreting to itself a variety of similar actions taken under similar circumstances, a process akin to annotating. The action is an implicit and perhaps somewhat explicitated rule, and its memorization alongside comparable actions is a kind of cumulative sensitivity to the myriad microexceptions, open questions, and indeterminacies that present themselves within the subroutine. Sometimes accretion will rise to the level of crisis where an explicit decision must be made about the relationship between a case and a rule, but often it will not.

The accretion of habit that is annotation bears a certain similarity to hypotaxis. We can clarify the point with an example. On April 19, 2013, a Department of Justice official was reported as indicating that authorities intended "to invoke the public safety exception to Miranda" in the case of Dzokhar Tsarnaev.[21] "Miranda" designated the reading of rights to a suspect upon arrest, and Tsarnaev had been arrested in connection with the 2013 Boston Marathon bombing. The intention to invoke the public safety exception was an iteration of a 2010 FBI memo, a memo that sought to expand an exception forged by a 1984 Supreme Court ruling in *New York v. Quarles*, an exception that qualified a 1966 Supreme Court specification of Miranda rights in *Miranda v. Arizona*, a specification that itself ultimately derived from constitutional stipulations, stipulations for which—one presumes—a prehistory could also be written.[22]

We see that the language of the law is replete with both "rules" and "exceptions," but we must recognize that neither rule nor exception functions in a fully Kantian or Schmittian fashion. In this case, the rule is not genuinely a rule because its applicability is too indeterminate. Similarly, the exception is not genuinely an exception because it can be claimed as a precedent that articulates a protorule of its own. Attending to examples such as this, we begin to grasp that the true life of the law is its historicity, which is to be understood in relation to its capacity to accrete piecemeal explicitations. And the law's historicity is also future oriented. The exits from indecision that are decisions in particular cases are also understood as potential precedents. As Robert Brandom has said, the common law is a model for how the piecemeal explicitation of concepts is foundational

21. Beuttler, "No Miranda Rights."
22. Federal Bureau of Investigation, "Custodial Interrogation."

for meaning itself.[23] What are the potential construals of the particular suppressions of doubt that permitted a Department of Justice official to announce a suspension of Miranda in the case of Dzokhar Tsarnaev? We do not know. What we can say is that we feel ourselves thrust into a new space of possibilities by this case and its various accumulating contextualizations.

Here is the point I really wish to underscore: the perception of a context as a whole is the creativity that begins an action. At the same time, however, the perception of a case is the perception of a contexture that may or may not be spatially and temporally contiguous, and the weaving that constitutes contexture makes for multiplicity in continuation. The perception of a case is, thus, very often a process of de- and recontextualization by means of cropping and nesting. Only in the context of frames dating from 2010, 1984, 1966, and 1789 can one understand the non-Mirandarizing of Dzokhar Tsarnaev in April 2013. Each of these frames constitutes a node, and to each of these nodes we can attach some other context that changes the implicatures of the whole. The law is particularly sophisticated in its capacity to memorize, recall, and redescribe contexts that oscillate in their specificity because it is an attempt to specify infraction—to identify its kinds or species—even though as a system law remains open to historical change and thus never completes its project of specification.

Attending to contextualization and its modes helps us to see what is, I think, a strange and momentous mistake at the heart of one of the classic considerations of the rhetorical situation. Together with the responses it elicited from other rhetoricians (such as Richard Vatz, Barbara Biesecker, and Jenny Rice), Lloyd Bitzer's 1968 article "The Rhetorical Situation" raised questions about the role orators might play in constituting the contextures to which their speeches were addressed. Did orators simply respond to situations, did they construct them, or were situations and the subject positions of orators mutually constitutive? What I want to say is that these preoccupations covered over an important question: to what degree might a context be specified in the first place? Bitzer did mention the senses in which a situation might be "highly structured or loosely structured," and more recently scholars have examined the nature of more loosely structured contexts and their contemporary media ecologies. Embedded in his original essay, though, was another version of the obsession with situations that permit only one continuation. Warburg's deity of extreme interpellation (*Augenblicksgott*) haunts one of the scenes from which contemporary rhetoric has sought to free itself. "In the best of all possible worlds," Bitzer said, "there would be communication perhaps, but no rhetoric—since exigences

---

23. Marshall, "Implications," 1–31.

would not arise."[24] That is, exigencies or contextures demanding decisions are "imperfections" because they are ambiguities that can be responded to in a variety of ways. Paradoxically, the situation that is so completely delineated and so seamlessly coded that it determines its own resolution is both perfect and, ultimately, no situation at all. The situation materializes, commands, and is worshipped as a deity that vouchsafes one and only one cultic response. Rhetoricians worship that god at their peril.

The law has a talent for contextualizing, but other sensory fields also participate in this process even as they have different parameters and different strengths. Compare, for instance, photography and documentary cinema in terms of their capacities to manifest context. In *Standard Operating Procedure* (2008), the documentary filmmaker Errol Morris argued it was the very manifestness of the Abu Ghraib photographs that, paradoxically, facilitated the work of covering up the crimes that had been committed there. The images foregrounded what we might term the causal extremes of patients and agents (or implied agents) and the actions (or implied actions) that mediate between them. In one sense, the hypervisibility brought into being by the controversial photographs made the "scene" of potential crimes at Abu Ghraib viscerally public. In another sense, however, the visual grammar of the photograph privileged the depiction of, to use a phrase bandied about at the time, "a few rotten apples." Photographic cropping around an instant inhibited the presentation of chains of command. The medium of photography would tend to represent "cases" as tightly bound spatial and temporal contiguities. Documentary film would be more capacious in its potential representations of "cases," and this was Morris's wager in *Standard Operating Procedure*. Nevertheless, my point remains the same: although the word "case" connotes the point-like unity of an instance (a snapshot), its true being lies in the tensions it establishes between an instance and the variety of contexts to which it can be attached and into which it cannot be resolved without remainder.

The rhetorician Daniel Gross has argued that objects of inquiry in the humanities are distinguished by the relative complexity of their contextualizations, and I think that the rhetorical injunction to understand anything as "a given case" plays a significant role here.[25] To Gross's project I would append the following line of thinking: there is a mutually constitutive relationship between the perception of a contexture and the perception of an array of possible responses to a contexture. The moment in which someone genuinely sees a situation is the moment in which that person becomes an actor or a potential agent in that situation. In this way, gestalt psychology

24. Bitzer, "Rhetorical Situation," 13.
25. Gross, "Defending the Humanities."

glosses a golden line from the seventeenth century that we have already encountered: "the Imagination," says Hobbes, "is the first internall beginning of all Voluntary Motion."[26] Expressed here in a more contemporary idiom, we can say that initiative will be an anticipation of the provisionally complete gestalt brought into being once I have successfully rounded out a situation by responding to it.

The Weimar origin of rhetorical inquiry that I have routed through the early thought of Hannah Arendt and then into her later work on judgment points to the discussion of the case and its contexts that I have been staging in this section. Within the tradition of discernment that I emphasized in chapter 7, judgment became a capacity to understand the case in terms of the *differentiae* it might exhibit relative to similar cases. In the vicinity of that thought, the concatenation of contexts that I exemplified with the case of Dzokhar Tsarnaev becomes a narratival capacity to suture cases together for the purpose of presenting a complex contexture of argumentation. Arendtian judgment thus participates in the specification of situation that also came to approach "actualization" (*energeia*) within the Heideggerian tradition, which was not simply presencing but also the determining of a situation in a way that avoided mere classification of it among the repetitions of everydayness. In this way, Arendt and Warburg specify Heidegger. Together, they propose that the "image table" of cases brought together by "wit" (*ingenium*) and held at a distance from each other by "discernment" (*iudicium*) becomes a site of potential narrativization. Such narrativization embeds itself in moves of the following kind: "whereas stance X is to be understood in the context of situation Y, I specify the impulse of that stance by adding permutation Z and enacting pose A." In essence, this is one mode of the variegating practice of naming. In this practice, any given name becomes an ecosystem of differences holding within itself the possibility of new names.

PROXIMITY

When we deal with the possible itself—the adjacent, the available, the admissible, the "that-which-can-be-taken-in" (*to endechomenon*)—we must say immediately and once again that we live in a world of possibility that is radically different from Aristotle's. The difference between Weimar's world of possibility and ours today is less radical, but it is still very significant. We can understand such a "world of possibility" as a choice architecture in which a given set of continuations are on offer. Ours is an age of intensified, specified, culturally particular choice architecture: we have our T9 functionalities, autofills, autocorrects, templatings; desktop and online

26. Hobbes, *Leviathan*, 38.

environments; the "others-liked-you-might-like" algorithm and the "are-you-friends-with-the-friends-of-your-friends" prompts; dropdown menus, left clicks, and right clicks. Moreover, we have the dystopia of our filter bubbles, where the tailoring of possibility to each category of consumers poses fundamental challenges to the continued existence of what we might reasonably call "public life." We have our decision engines and our statistically based prediction softwares; our focus group, city guide, and Siri advisors; our Google Map, virtual or enhanced reality, Street View, pin drop, SatNav, foursquare, and online-dating approximators. Our motion-capture technologies can partner with randomizers in order to fertilize choreographic imaginations. Jazz-playing robots can be asked to imitate Thelonious Monk, Charlie Parker, and whomever they are playing with by working through Markov chain sequences of musical performance. And these algorithmic modulations of both dance and music can be thought of as applications of "personal stylization" algorithms that are at the heart of contemporary capitalism.[27]

Despite the apparent possibilities for diversity built into such systems, the geosociological equivalent of these technologies of proximity in the United States may well be what Bill Bishop famously called the "Big Sort," in which like seeks out like and a high rate of overall diversity breaks down into a series of enclave homogeneities. One can run models in which homogeneous enclaves emerge out of random initial distributions with only minimal homophily, where "homophily" denotes either desire for identity or aversion to alterity. And one can treat such models as reassuring either because they seem to reveal that enclave life need not be fueled by, for example, explicit racism or because they seem to propose that even minimal heterophily can reverse the trend. But Wendy Chun's response at this point is to say that the fiction of "random initial distribution" turns a blind eye to the histories of structural inequality just as "machine learning is like money laundering for bias": it allows one to ignore origins.[28]

The adjacencies (*endechomena*) proposed by homophily and heterophily are, indeed, a panoply of Heideggerian availabilities for use, but at this point the Aristotelian spyglass has us examine the subtly different proximities of our rational choice theory, game theory, social choice theory, and our behavioral economics together with the "nudges" of behavioral economics applied to politics.[29] Moreover, we have our risk assessments, insurance

27. Fdili Alaoui, Bevilacqua, and Jacquemin, "Interactive Visuals"; Wilf, "Computer-Mediated, Algorithmic Forms of Sociality"; David L. Marshall, "Search" (unpublished manuscript).
28. Chun, "Queering Homophily," 62–63 (where she discusses the line from Pinboard quoted above), 82–83, 86–87.
29. Kahneman, *Thinking, Fast and Slow*; Thaler and Sunstein, *Nudge*. I take the phrase "choice architecture" from Thaler and Sunstein.

policies, and contingency plans.[30] Indeed, before being too deeply impressed by Bergson's insight that there are senses in which the possible does not exist before it is real, we should consider the ways in which the preparation of a "menu" of particular futures brings those futures into being or can specify them once they appear to be underway.[31] Nor is this simply a question of where to place the salad in high school cafeterias if one wishes to improve public health. What kind of "targeting packages" for drone strikes does the CIA have on file?[32] Disposition is readiness, and readiness self-fulfills.

We ought to understand these availabilities for use as tissues of disposition. That is, Arendt glosses Heidegger. Attendant possibilities stake out a world by opening up distances. In the early Arendtian idiom that chapter 4 set out, solidarity emerges out of a tension between desire and love. That is, there is a tension between *appetitus* (understood as a desiring that tends to obliterate the distinction between subject and object) and *caritas* (understood as a divine love that is out of proportion to and hence infinitely distant from the particularities of the world). From that tension emerges *dilectio proximi*, which is a love of neighbor that pushes out of the actual into a world of proximate but distinct possibilities. In the late Arendtian idiom, this would be *sensus communis* as the array of tenable opinions clustered around an issue. In turn, Warburg glosses Arendt. A disposition is the ease with which a particular motion begins out of a particular form of rest. Even as a greater imposition of force will open up other possibilities, a cube resting on one of its sides is predisposed to the motion of tipping in four very particular directions. In a Warburgian manner, we might say that possibility is a shadow cast by the actual. Or, better, actuality is the prism that refracts time into its constituent possibilities.

As in a game of chess, however, the space of possibility brought into being by contexture is rarely specifiable to the point that all of its permutations are enumerable. As Warburg himself observed, chess is a beautiful combination of highly specified paused actualities, a limited number of highly distinguishable and proximate possibilities, and an almost infinite number of possibilities further downstream that cannot be distinguished. The construction of a possible world to which no further permutations could be added without contravening or repeating some other aspect of the world—a "complete novel" as Jaakko Hintikka, following Richard Jeffrey, termed it—is thinkable only for extremely simple systems.[33] Heidegger's

30. At precisely this juncture, one finds a growing subliterature within the field of rhetoric— namely, the "rhetoric of risk."
31. Bergson, "Le possible et le réel." I am grateful to Adi Efal for emphasizing Bergson's essay.
32. Dilanian and Bennett, "CIA."
33. Hintikka, "On the Logic of Perception," 153–54.

gloss of Nietzschean eternal recurrence as the "clocking of a system" by running through all of its variations in an excess and consummation of "will to power" was a very similar idea, but it was notional only because it could never be run—not for "the universe." It is very difficult to clock even a relatively simple game such as chess, where the rules are few and now, it seems, historically invariant.[34] Despite the computational power of the latest processors, it seems that we have still not "solved" chess by enumerating and mapping all possible games. We have not identified paths of invulnerability. We have not been able to show that, in chess as in tic-tac-toe, a well-played game should always end in a draw.

The individuation of possibilities is a rigorous imaginative task that is not to be addressed by Llullian or Leibnizian combinatorials alone. Nor is such individuation to be achieved by brute force computational methods that seek to achieve the "complete novelization" of a rule space. Like Descartes's thousand-sided figure, the art of invention proposed by Leibniz is not genuinely imaginable. Given a language with a finite number of stable individual terms and a set of fully explicit rules of permissible combination, one can, in theory, generate a set of all the sentences possible within that language. But such a language is radically dissimilar to any natural language. The closer one gets to a natural language, the less surveyable its list of permutations becomes. The reason for this is that at the semantic if not at the syntactic level the rules of the game are not stable. These rules are genuinely historical, and it is likely that natural languages—that is to say, historical languages—are unsolvable *in principle*. The specification of individual possibilities thus remains, at this point, a human task, because if one cannot explicitate all the possibilities of a given system, then one must have reasons to explicitate some of them.

As we saw in chapter 6, a Warburgian image table can be the birthplace of names. The latticework of similarity and difference set out by those image tables reveals how to attend more closely to a particular appearance not simply by gazing on it longer and harder but by surrounding it with a palette of "related images." Excising images from one image table and using them as seed images for another table is part of the work of articulating a more refined visual vocabulary. More generally, the history of vocabulary reveals social need (or would do so in a just society). And we can hypothesize that the algorithmic imagination of computationally identified "related images" constitutes one machine for the production of image tables. There are computational means to be mobilized for the purpose of differentiating more precise visual vocabularies. For instance, computational processes can highlight whether certain parts of the color spectrum are semantically underrepresented.

34. Rasskin-Gutman, *Chess Metaphors*, 151.

At the same time, there are humanist alternatives to the computational presentation of possibility. At this point, the Al Swearengen character conjured by Ian McShane in David Milch's *Deadwood* television series (2004–2006) and in the film of the same name (2019) becomes a kind of emblem for the perception of possibilities. Stylistically, Swearengen exists at the intersection of soliloquy, *enargeia*, and possibility. His are the wide staring eyes of political visualization in a constant state of annotation. Just so, the HBO series was an allegory of American beginnings. On this account, beginning is a process by which highly unstructured fields with highly unspecifiable potentials come to take on degrees of calculability. In this process, they become increasingly constricted game spaces. Al Swearengen is at his zenith in season 2 of *Deadwood*. Why? Because this is the moment when the game space set out by the series strikes its most delicate and generative balance between open potential and closed calculability. Soliloquy—the weighing of alternatives—is destroyed equally by too many or too few possibilities. Al Swearengen had to become a much diminished and more highly circumscribed figure by the end of the series because the show itself was arguing that civilization was a corralling of potential.[35] On this reading, we should say in response to the recent film denouement that the Deadwood universe dies with Swearengen. A lawful universe is no place for him and no place for possibility either. In this context, "lawful" means "dead."

Within a human frame of reference, the identification of new patterns within fundamentally limited parameters is something like dance. Within such identification, we recognize several capacities: the ability to discover a motion but also the abilities to appreciate and copy it. James Porter suggests that rhythm is "less a sensation than the shape of one."[36] In its broadest sense, rhythm is a practice that is honed by technologies of the self. The pattern recognitions of possibility rely on a constant training. Patterning is a keeping fit in matters of perception. To practice variation is to practice a way of remaining in the center of a sequence of motions that is coming to a point of bi- or multifurcation. Biomechanically, variation is a kind of paradiastolic redescribability of motion in the moment before its differentiation. In the more balletic moments of some sports, such moments appear when one forces an opponent to choose a response before one has committed one's own body to a particular future. As an offensive player, making a defender choose first is one of the most effective means of generating an opening.

Creativity, natality, or beginning can be understood as the unpredicted actualization of something within a set of underdetermined parameters, and this actualization can then itself function as a condition of possibility for a distinctive set of variations in the future. In this case, Bergson was

35. See also Milch, *Deadwood*.
36. Porter, *Origins of Aesthetic Thought*, 221.

right: there is a real sense in which such an actualization had not previously existed in the mode of a specified possibility. The best plans are unlaid. Here we have Arendt's aversion to blueprints in politics. Here, too, we have her interest in reflective judgment, which was concerned with the new principles that might be implicit in particular actions. Arendtian judgment at this point becomes something like the antistrophe of Peircean abduction. Abduction seeks a past-oriented explanation for a surprising fact, while reflective judgment seeks the future-oriented principle implicit in a distinctive act. Here, too, we have Havel's politics as the "art of the impossible" realizing the previously unimaginable.[37] And note Wittgenstein's antiphilosophical witticism: "when does one have the thought: the possible movements of a machine are already there in some mysterious way?—Well, when one is doing philosophy."[38] Some systems have an established range of possibilities. Others do not.

The individuum that is an unpredicted, unpredictable, and properly speaking natal incursion into a system brings its own array of fresh adjacencies with it. Whether in the philological work of establishing critical editions or in the controlled museum environments in which we envelop art objects, the curatorial attitude toward works of art is in part a function of the belief that—qua individua—such works are enduring points of departure. In order to be conditions of possibility for innovation and change, such works must themselves remain static. In committing ourselves to such editorial and museum practices, we seem to be saying that attendant possibilities will be richer and less predictable when an actualization is more precise, specific, and vivid. This thought ligature proposes a hypothesis: a world in which one could only sample a melody, translate a passage, or follow an example by destroying the original would be a world dominated by regression to the mean.

Originality can be understood as a kind of interpolation, for originality is also something like a generation of spaces between historically contingent proximities. Amid the detritus of the given, there are inordinate gaps, possible combinations, iterations, permutations. Call such gaps "opportunities" if you will. Some have called this "the adjacent possible," and others have built accounts of entrepreneurship around the notion. Do not forget, though, that these gaps were Proustian and Benjaminian first.[39] Recall from chapter 5 the example of Proust's famous galleys. These were texts composed metastatically from the inside out by continually finding inferential or descriptive occlusions between sentences where new sentences might be inserted. And recall also Benjamin's comparison of the

37. Havel, *Art of the Impossible*.
38. Wittgenstein, *Philosophical Investigations*, nos. 193–94.
39. Kauffman, *Investigations*, 142ff. For his part, Steven Johnson then builds on Kauffman's notions of the adjacent possible in *Good Ideas*.

work of "imagination" (*Phantasie*) to the opening of a fan, which creates an arc where only a point had existed. When Nancy Struever instructs us to follow Burckhardt's account of *Phantasie* as "supplementing" or "completing" (*ergänzen*), I respond by appending Benjamin's account of *Phantasie* as "interpolating" or "transforming a point into a line extending between two poles" (*interpolieren*). At stake, ultimately, is a capacity to perceive that which *is* not but *could* be. Irony, happy or not, is the process of locating a coherence in the apparently incoherent. Alternatively, it is the discovery of distance between proximities that had seemed contiguous. The point is that the possible emerges from the given like a highly selective thief.

The Arendt of chapter 4 provided an emblem for the various adjacencies that I have traced very briefly into the twenty-first century, and that emblem was Rahel. I contended that the Arendtian space of appearance might be thought more creatively by taking Rahel's salon to be its more genuine point of origin rather than the democratic institutional spaces of ancient Athens. In that moment, we found that spaces of appearance were the various stages generated by postures offering opportunities for response. We found that Rahel was the key performer here precisely on account of her ability to engage multiple interlocutors and arrange them in the salon as so many letters of an alphabet. The eclecticism of the salon was something like a randomization function where patterns of behavior changed and morphed as all manner of discombobulated connections had to be smoothed. If the salon seemed less serious than the polis (less august and lacking its blanched-white classicism), this was also because its quality as a game space was more palpable. And the rhetorical adjacencies of game spaces are precisely the kinds of indirect structuration to which we should be attending now.

BELIEF

We have grown accustomed in English to thinking of *pithanon* as "persuasion," and we tend to imagine persuasion as a process. We think it is a movement from a state of nonbelief to a state of belief. On the basis of this assumption, rhetoric becomes a matter of identifying means of achieving the end of persuasion. We repeat the refrain that rhetoric is a capacity to see in any given case the available *means* of persuasion. As I indicated in chapter 2, though, the Greek has no placeholder for "means" as such. In order to think the phrase afresh, we can consult its early construal into Latin. According to Quintilian, what Aristotle said in his famous sentence was that *rhetorice est vis inveniendi omnia in oratione persuasibilia.*[40] As in the Greek, the Latin has no direct equivalent for what has customarily become

40. Quintilian, *Institutio oratoriae*, 2.15.13.

"means" in English. *Pithanon* and *persuasibilia* denote, simply, the persuasive. Continually interpolating the word "means," we eventually find it more difficult to think rhetoric beyond instrumentality.

Nonbelief, what we might call "skepticism," is one of the antonyms of belief but not the only one. Understood in the context of persuasion, the more genuine antonym of "belief" is "confusion." Confusion distinguishes itself from skepticism insofar as it is not a state in which no beliefs obtain. Confusion is a state in which *multiple* incompatible beliefs are taken up simultaneously or in swift succession. One might add that contexts of persuasion are those in which there is no possibility of a true abstention. Persuasion pertains to situations of action. In such situations, refusing to decide means choosing inaction, and inaction is itself a particular form of action—as Benjamin confirmed with his discussion of Julien Green's protagonist in *The Strange River*. We need to enrich our field of possible translations for the placeholder *pithanon*. Not simply persuasion, it is also the plausible, the credible, and the believable. Beyond that, it is also a mode of excessive believing, the credulous. Understood not only as a process but also as a state (a move licensed by the *Oxford English Dictionary*), persuasion is persuadedness, conviction. That is, persuasion is a state of indifferentiation with respect to oneself or a group.[41]

As Benjamin argued in a line of inquiry running from his *Trauerspiel* work through occasional pieces like "Russian Debate in German" and the "Manifesto of a Proletarian Children's Theater" to late classics like the "Work of Art" essay, politic is the possibility of entering and exiting states of collective indecision. Benjamin's deep fascination with immobilization was thus essentially political. On this account, politic becomes an orientation to indecision. Politic comes into being when a community emerges out of shared habit into a state of indeterminate self-differentiation. Not Schmitt, the decisionist; Benjamin, the indecisionist—there is a Weimar origin for rhetorical inquiry. Benjaminian politic is a capacity to see proclivities to motion, mutabilities or persuadabilities. It attends to points at which changes in input would precipitate changes in output. It asks, "what are the points at which an entity's weight is balanced at the edge of its position?" Such politic is a capacity to see in any given case possible motions from habit to attention and from attention to habit. The pendulum swings from doubt to consensus to doubt. Or more precisely a phenomenon photographed from multiple points of view appears or does not appear as one continuous crowdsourced image.

Here we encounter a double movement in the form of a rhetorical inquiry that is focused less on the means of persuasion and more on the degrees and

41. At this juncture, consider Michelstaedter, *La persuasione e la rettorica*.

kinds of persuadedness, for the seeing of possibilities clustered around a juncture both undermines belief and aims at it. The practices of possibility will entail techniques for questioning confidence. Thus, Atul Gawande's *Checklist Manifesto* is a site-specifiable mnemonic aid for medical professionals forever posing variations of the prompt, "what have you forgotten?"[42] One should understand that manifesto as a kind of twenty-first-century *ars topica* specializing in a "local topics" (as John Aubrey termed it in chapter 7). The so-called premortem method of the psychologist Gary Klein asks each member of a community about to undertake a major new initiative to spend a few minutes sketching out in writing a future perfect conjectural history of why that initiative ultimately failed.[43] An entity with only one belief is monstrous. An entity forever in the grip of multiple incompatible beliefs is also monstrous. Here we have particular ways of moving away from each of these extremes.

Between monomania and multiple personality disorder, there is a process that psychologists have taken to calling "judgment under uncertainty."[44] The 1997 showdown between Garry Kasparov and the IBM supercomputer Deep Blue was such an interesting event because it brought distinctive modes of judging under uncertainty into direct contact at a point in history when neither human nor machine decision making within the field of possibilities called chess was clearly superior. As we have seen, chess is a system that remains "uncertain" for both human and machine to this day. It is uncertain in the sense that it generates more possibilities that can be made computationally explicit and surveyed. The moves that can be made in the immediate future are clear enough, but the consequences of those moves become untrackable very quickly. The true value of most moves is therefore opaque.

Although Kasparov and Deep Blue were in the same epistemic situation, they certainly "experienced" doubt differently and had different ways of coping with it. It seems as if Deep Blue was a sophisticated brute force machine equipped with protocols designed to prevent it from attempting to calculate incalculable lines of inquiry. The machine was tactically superior during tight and highly calculable exchanges. Without yet reaching it, such situations were on their way toward Bitzer's perfect situation of the forced move—which, of course, was actually dystopian. Adopting a novel strategy against IBM's computational superpower, Kasparov strove to keep the board vague (to avoid calculability) and unusual (to avoid databases of past games). If he was pursuing vagueness as such, was Kasparov turning

42. Gawande, *Checklist Manifesto*.
43. Klein, "Performing a Project Premortem," 18–19.
44. See, for instance, Tversky and Kahneman, "Judgment under Uncertainty," 1124–31.

a blind eye to the calculation of paths to an endgame? There is evidence suggesting that Kasparov was evaluating patterns instead of calculating sequences. The best human chess players are said to have memorized a repertoire of 50,000–100,000 patterns. They are said to be surveying the board as a whole and differentiating between broadly good and broadly bad patterns.[45] This is desire and aversion at work in pattern recognition.

We seem to be a long way from *pithanon*. We are not. We are right on top of it. We are thinking about indecision, and I am claiming that indecision is both the best way to approach *pithanon* and the principal orientation of politic. In fact, Kasparov versus Deep Blue is a kind of repetition of the tension that Benjamin observed between the figures of the sovereign (or would-be sovereign) and the intriguer in baroque *Trauerspiel*. Iago is the myth of calculability incarnate. He moves characters on the stage like pieces on a board. But the fact of incalculability is debilitating. Indeed, we may advert at this point to the hypothesis that Kasparov ultimately lost the match to Deep Blue because he was confused and then debilitated by one of the computer's moves in the first game of the match. He was brought up short and undone when he was completely unable to reproduce the move's rationale. As it turned out, the move had been produced by a failsafe mechanism according to which, if the computer found itself getting lost in the exponentiality of its own brute force calculations, it might simply time itself out by choosing a move at random.[46] In place of the Schmittian miracle, one had a randomizer.

To some degree, the Kasparov versus Deep Blue match also replicated one of the long-standing debates within the field of judgment under uncertainty. In Paul Meehl's phrasing of the question, can we say whether generally speaking "clinical" or "statistical" prediction is more accurate?[47] That is, in situations where one must judge under conditions of uncertainty, will humans with expertise in the relevant area produce better predictions than algorithms that extrapolate from some basic statistical observations? There are a host of situations in which human beings make reliably bad predictions. The discipline of behavioral economics continues to map and trace these cognitive biases. And Philip Tetlock has confirmed that predictions in politics are really *very* bad.[48] Nevertheless, expert intuition is not a complete myth.[49] Daniel Kahneman and Gary Klein are representatives of the debate between, respectively, the "heuristics and biases" and the "naturalistic decision making" schools of thought. What is most remarkable

45. Kasparov, *How Life Imitates Chess.*
46. Silver, *Signal and the Noise,* 288.
47. Meehl, *Clinical versus Statistical Prediction.*
48. Tetlock, *Expert Political Judgment.*
49. Gladwell, *Blink.*

about their engagement is that they failed to disagree on the subject of "conditions for intuitive expertise."[50]

Perhaps we still live in an age when the balance between humans and computers is such that the best decisions are on average made by hybrid assemblages. For this reason, the contemporary pop statistician Nate Silver has called for a truce between baseball scouts and Moneyball analysts.[51] And, having lost to Deep Blue, Kasparov himself went on pioneer experiments with hybrid human/computer chess players. Humans playing with assistance from chess programs are superior to both human players and computers when they each play unassisted.[52] The point to emphasize is that like Gawande's checklists all of these various possibility engines are essentially topical. In the context of indecision, site-specific topical orientations to possibility are essential. They are more important than predictions per se because they orient to possibility and suggest lines of inquiry.

Finally, Warburg also glosses Benjamin. That is, the processes of moving from decision to indecision and back again are to be understood in terms of the way in which a soul may hold within itself a variety of possibilities even as it actualizes some specific possibility. I am claiming that Warburg recoursed to magnanimity (as greatness or capaciousness of soul) in order to specify a rhetorical dimension in the Mnemosyne project. He did so because magnanimity described the sense in which any actualized emotional commerce would carry with it an array of possible variations. Expert actualization, on this account, is a kind of determinate being-in-the-midst of an array of equidistant possibilities. And if the actualization that is persuasion, qua belief, is a state of indivision with regard to oneself (that is, an absence of doubt), then persuasion can be a certain kind of immunity to the permutations of the world. If politic is a possibility of seeing in any given situation the possible persuasions, then it is a capacity to perceive the different points of indifference to chance. What are the positions, one asks oneself, that will remain well chosen even in retrospect irrespective of outcome? Which stances are maximally impervious? Politic is not only a genius for finding the eye of the storm but also the liability that one's positions will be blindsided and revealed as basically misdirected.

In chapter 5, we saw Benjamin concerned with investigating how one might stand at a distance from the stance one had adopted without thereby implying a generic skepticism. Iago, the choreographic intriguer, found multiplicity in the selfsame pose by embedding the stances of other actors in alternative plotlines. The proletarian children working with Asja Lacis

50. Kahneman and Klein, "Conditions for Intuitive Expertise," 515–26.
51. Silver, *Signal and the Noise*, 74–107.
52. Kasparov, "Chess Master and the Computer."

were training themselves to find responses that marked awareness of and thus distance from explicit challenge and complete obeisance. Not detained by interpellation and continuing to walk the streets of Paris, Green's protagonist was interpolating an extension between himself and the hail he had not heeded, and along this extension there emerged scenes of divergent reactions registering on the bodies of various characters. Belief would be something approaching an isomorphism between oneself and the mask one chose to wear. Potentially, however, it would also be simply the clarity and perspicacity of any given pose irrespective of the psychologistic substrates "over" which it hovered in any given soul. And perspicacity here would be focused on relations to the positions taken up by other parties to a scene. Belief, thus, became a function of distinctness in the midst of an ensemble.

CONCLUSION

The sentence "rhetoric may be defined as the faculty of observing in any given case the available means of persuasion" is but one of a cluster of related sentences, each of which reveals a slightly different aspect of rhetoric's being and task. In order to multiply the investigative possibilities issuing from the sentence, I have deliberately fractured each of the key terms in Aristotle's definition. The point is not simply to multiply these possibilities until we find ourselves in a position of undecidability, stranded equidistant amid a multitude of equipossible alternatives. The point is to facilitate a particular attitude to the definition. This attitude emphasizes a nonexclusivity in which the use of any one of its variations stands out against the background of other nonactualized sentences. This, we might say, is topical sensitization. The differential between the deployed and that which could have been deployed is a kind of protection against the reification of a theoretical idiom. In this way, the rewriting of intellectual inheritances in novel contexts that is intellectual history becomes a process of constant discovery.

The Weimar reinvention of rhetorical inquiry that I have paraphrased here by refracting an Aristotelian sentence was preoccupied with generating tensions. This was a plastic enterprise. Within the Heideggerian frame, actuality was expressed in terms of possibility, and the dereification of "faculty" implied a relentless adjusting of spannedness. The Warburgian initiative was genuinely a seeing of possibilities. No matter how tightly a sculpture or a painting might appear to attach itself to a static moment, that stasis was always to be sensed by means of its possible origins and possible continuations. From the Arendtian perspective, the actualizations that were actions in the political sphere were fully present to themselves in the moment of their being carried out rather than dispersed among an array of ends-for-the-sake-of-which. Returning to the modality of possibility, however, such actualizations regenerated spaces of indeterminacy almost immediately. Exemplary actions became possibilities for imitation. They became elements of a splayed *sensus communis*. Equally, the principle inarticulately instantiated by any particular action would almost always be indeterminate and multivalent. As a result, it would require further specification in subsequent contexts by reflective judgment. Just so, cases were crystallizations of contexture. Cases worked out from instances of conspicuousness like cracks in a pane of glass. And, on my account, the Benjaminian gambit was to interpose a zone of elasticity between points and persuasions. This zone might be a somewhat elastic rope extending between the performance that had been requested and the performance that had been given. Alternatively, it might be the work of fantasy driving apart contiguities that had given the impression of being all-of-a-piece— that is, persuaded.

The vision of rhetorical inquiry that emerges from this Weimar line of inquiry is distinctive and unusual, and it is a possibility for us. In contrast to standard received versions of Weimar intellectual history, this line of inquiry does not focus on decision. Neither the decidedness of the rule nor the decisiveness of the exception is paramount. This vision of rhetorical inquiry is centered on indecision. It sees indecision as the space of indeterminacy in which rhetoric has its true existence as possibility, visualizability, situatability, metabolizability, and convincibility. The task of describing political communities becomes, simply, a matter of revealing with the greatest possible perspicacity the ways in which they register, articulate, and end indecision. This vision remains a possibility for us because it focuses on the ways in which the world manifests itself. This phenomenological attention to ways of appearing remains just as central as it ever was even as the media modulating appearance continue to change in radical ways. The modes of indecision in which the world manifests itself have changed as the scenes codifying risk and choice have morphed, but rhetorical inquiry returns again to articulate these scenes.

ACKNOWLEDGMENTS

Conceived in Baltimore, proposed in Michigan, researched in Germany, and finished in Pittsburgh, this work would not have been possible without the support of several different communities. Rüdiger Campe, Peter Jelavich, J. G. A. Pocock, and Nancy Struever read and recommended the original research plan, and the Alexander von Humboldt-Stiftung supported that proposal with a two-year fellowship for postdoctoral researchers. This book would not exist without the Humboldt Foundation. Their fellowship made it possible to spend two years in Germany between 2011 and 2013 working in the history department at Bielefeld University. Willibald Steinmetz was an extremely gracious, generous, and sharp host, and I am grateful to both the Studiengruppe Historische Semantik and the Freitagskolloquium in Bielefeld for reading drafts of material from this book.

Bielefeld is a special place in the world for me. A group of close friends lives there, and among them Boris Ender made especially important contributions to this project. I had originally gone to Bielefeld for a year during graduate school with a Deutsche Akademische Austauschdienst collaboration that supported exchanges between the history department at the Johns Hopkins University and its counterpart in Bielefeld. Claudius Torp had come to Baltimore a few years earlier on the same program. He and those responding to his genius for friendship made Bielefeld a real home. I would also like to recognize Martina Engelns and Hedda Gramley.

I am extremely grateful to the interlibrary loan service at Bielefeld University and also to those at Kettering University and the University of Pittsburgh. At Kettering and at Pitt, assistant professor writing groups took up different pieces of the project, and I express my thanks to them, as I do to members of the department of communication's agora at Pitt for discussing a chapter from this project. Similarly, graduate students in three seminars at Pitt heard and sharpened many of the ideas contained in this book.

In the course of myriad trips, I became grateful for the generosity and criticism of many scholars, including Richard Blum, Robert Brandom,

Randall Bush, Ross Carroll, Christopher Celenza, Mary Dietz, James Farr, Dilip Gaonkar, Daniel Gross, Robert Hariman, Uli Hoefer, Bonnie Honig, Theodor Kisiel, Joachim Knape, Jerome Kohn, Matthew Maguire, Ursula Marx, John Monfasani, Terukazu Morikawa, Arndt Niebisch, Nobutaka Otobe, Maria Robaszkiewicz, Rocco Rubini, Philippe Salazar, Peter Simonson, Christopher Swift, Yannik Thiem, Helene Tieger, Dietmar Till, Anne Ulrich, and Ronald Witt.

There is perhaps only one person with whom I worked through each and every chapter before submission, and I am extremely grateful to Christopher Nygren for his energy, imagination, and solidarity. At the University of Chicago Press, I would like to thank Doug Mitchell, Dylan Montanari, Adriana Smith, and Kyle Wagner as well as two anonymous readers. My thanks also to C. Steven LaRue for copyediting, Susan Olin for proofreading, and Marta Steele for producing the index.

Finally, I would like to express my gratitude for contributions to the Warburg chapter made by a number of different scholars and scholarly communities: Tom Willette for guiding my first forays into the area; Guido Giglioni, Eckart Marchand, and Claudia Wedepohl, who made my stay at the Warburg Institute a generative one; Jonathan Arac and the Humanities Center at Pitt; Horst Bredekamp, Jürgen Trabant, Tullio Viola, and the whole Symbolische Artikulation group in Berlin; Caroline van Eck, Ruth Webb, and Caitlin Bruce for workshops in Leiden and Maryland; and especially Adi Efal for a genuinely inspiring conversation one afternoon in Cologne. Perhaps this book will find its continuation in the project intuited there.

BIBLIOGRAPHY

TRANSLATIONS

No translation can substitute for the original, but some of the texts cited in this book are available in English, and those who do not read German may wish to consult the following: Arendt's *Love and Saint Augustine* (Chicago: University of Chicago Press, 1996), edited with an interpretive essay by Joanna Vecchiarelli Scott and Judith Chelius Stark; Arendt's *Rahel Varnhagen: The Life of a Jewess* (Baltimore: The Johns Hopkins University Press, 1997), edited by Liliane Weissberg and translated by Richard and Clara Winston; Benjamin's *Origin of the German Trauerspiel* (Cambridge, MA: Harvard University Press, 2019), translated by Howard Eiland; Heidegger's *Basic Concepts of Aristotelian Philosophy* (Bloomington: Indiana University Press, 2009), translated by Robert D. Metcalf and Mark B. Tanzer; and Warburg's *Renewal of Pagan Antiquity: Contributions to the Cultural History of the European Renaissance* (Los Angeles: Getty Research Institute, 1999), translated by David Britt. All translations from modern European languages are my own, but I have used translations from the Loeb Classical Library for ancient texts.

MANUSCRIPT COLLECTIONS

The Hannah Arendt Papers. Manuscript Division, Library of Congress, Washington, DC. Warburg Institute Archive. Warburg Institute. University of London.

WORKS CITED

Ackermann, Friedrich. "Das Pithanon bei Sophokles." Diss., Friedrich-Alexanders-Universität Erlangen, 1910.
Adorno, Theodor W. *Gesammelte Schriften*. Edited by Rolf Tiedemann with assistance from Gretel Adorno, Susan Buck-Morss, and Klaus Schultz. 20 vols. Frankfurt am Main: Suhrkamp, 1970–.
———. "Parataxis: Zur späten Lyrik Hölderlins." *Die neue Rundschau* 75 (1964): 15–46.
Adorno, Theodor W., Else Frenkel-Brunswik, Daniel J. Levinson, and R. Nevitt Sanford. *The Authoritarian Personality*. New York: Harper, 1950.
Agamben, Giorgio. "Aby Warburg e la Scienza senza Nome." *Aut Aut* 199/200 (1984): 51–66.

———. "Bartleby o della Contingenza." In *Bartleby: La formula della creazione*, 47–92. Macerata: Quodlibet, 1993.

———. "Experimentum Linguae." In *Infancy and History: Essays in the Destruction of Experience*, translated by Liz Heron, 3–10. London: Verso, 1993.

———. *Infanzia e storia: Distruzione dell'esperienza e origine della storia*. Turin: Einaudi, 1978.

———. *Ninfe*. Turin: Bollati Boringhieri, 2007.

———. "On Potentiality." In *Potentialities: Collected Essays in Philosophy*, 177–84. Stanford, CA: Stanford University Press, 2000.

———. *Stato di eccezione*. Turin: Bollati Boringhieri, 2003.

Ammon, Georg. "Bericht über die Literatur zu Ciceros rhetorischen Schriften aus den Jahren 1918–1923." *Jahresbericht über die Fortschritte der klassichen Altertumswissenschaft* 204 (1925): 1–58.

Arendt, Hannah. "About 'Collaboration.'" *Jewish Frontier* 15 (October 1948): 55–56.

———. "Adam Müller Renaissance?" *Kölnische Zeitung*, September 13, 1932, Unterhaltungsblatt.

———. "Approaches to the 'German Problem.'" *Partisan Review* 12 (1945): 93–106.

———. "Aufklärung und Judenfrage." *Zeitschrift für die Geschichte der Juden in Deutschland* 4 (1932): 65–77.

———. "Augustin und Protestantismus." *Frankfurter Zeitung*, April 12, 1930.

———. "Berliner Salon." *Deutscher Almanach* (1932): 173–84.

———. "Concern with Politics in Recent European Philosophical Thought." In *Essays in Understanding, 1930–1954*, edited by Jerome Kohn, 428–47. New York: Schocken, 1994.

———. "The Crisis of Zionism." In *The Jewish Writings*, edited by Jerome Kohn and Ron H. Feldman, 329–37. New York: Schocken Books, 2007.

———. *Denktagebuch, 1950 bis 1973*. Edited by Ursula Ludz and Ingeborg Nordmann. 2 vols. Munich: Piper, 2002.

———. *Der Liebesbegriff bei Augustin: Versuch einer Philosophischen Interpretation*. Berlin: Julius Springer, 1929.

———. "Die Jüdische Armee: Der Beginn einer jüdische Politik?" *Aufbau* 7 (November 14, 1941): 1–2.

———. "Die Tage der Wandlung." *Aufbau* 10 (July 28, 1944): 16.

———. "Für Ehre und Ruhm des jüdischen Volkes." *Aufbau* 10 (April 21, 1944): 1–2.

———. "The Jew as Pariah: A Hidden Tradition." *Jewish Social Studies* 6 (1944): 99–122.

———. "Originale Assimilation: Ein Nachwort zu Rahel Varnhagens 100. Todestag." *Jüdische Rundschau* 38 (April 7, 1933): 143.

———. "Peace or Armistice in the Near East?" *Review of Politics* 12 (1950): 56–82.

———. "Philosophy and Politics." *Social Research* 57 (1990): 73–103.

———. "Portrait of a Period." Review of *The World of Yesterday: An Autobiography*, by Stefan Zweig. *Menorah Journal* 31 (1943): 307–14.

———. *Rahel Varnhagen: Lebensgeschichte einer Deutschen Jüdin aus der Romantik*. Munich: R. Piper, 1959.

———. Review of *Das Frauenproblem der Gegenwart*, by Alice Rühle-Gerstel. *Die Gesellschaft* 10 (1932): 177–79.

———. Review of *Die Entstehung des deutschen Bildungsprinzips*, by Hans Weil. *Archiv für Sozialwissenschaft und Sozialpolitik* 66 (1931): 200–205.

———. "Søren Kierkegaard." *Frankfurter Zeitung 75/76* (January 29, 1932): 2.

———. "Understanding and Politics (The Difficulties of Understanding)." In *Essays in Understanding, 1930–1954,* edited by Jerome Kohn, 307–27. New York: Schocken, 1994.

———. "We Refugees." *Menorah Journal* 31 (1943): 69–77.

———. *Willing.* New York: Harcourt Brace Jovanovich, 1978.

———. "Zionism Reconsidered." *Menorah Journal* 33 (August 1945): 162–96.

Arendt, Hannah, and Hermann Broch. *Hannah Arendt/Herman Broch Briefwechsel, 1946 bis 1951.* Edited by Paul Michael Lützeler. Frankfurt am Main: Jüdischer Verlag, 1996.

Arendt, Hannah, and Martin Heidegger. *Briefe 1925 bis 1975 und andere Zeugnisse.* Edited by Ursula Ludz. Frankfurt am Main: Vittorio Klostermann, 2002.

Arendt, Hannah, and Karl Jaspers. *Hannah Arendt–Karl Jaspers Briefwechsel 1926–1969.* Edited by Lotte Köhler and Hans Saner. Munich: Piper, 1985.

Baron, Hans. *The Crisis of the Early Italian Renaissance: Civic Humanism and Republican Liberty in an Age of Classicism and Tyranny.* Princeton, NJ: Princeton University Press, 1955.

Barthes, Roland. *Éléments de sémiologie.* In *Le degré zero de l'écriture suivi de éléments de sémiologie,* 77–172. Paris: Éditions du Seuil, 1964.

Baumgarten, Alexander Gottlieb. *Ästhetik.* Translated and edited by Dagmar Mirbach. Hamburg: Felix Meiner, 2007.

Baxandall, Michael. *Episodes: A Memorybook.* London: Francis Lincoln, 2010.

———. *Painting and Experience in Fifteenth-Century Italy: A Primer in the Social History of Pictorial Style.* Oxford: Oxford University Press, 1972.

Behnegar, Nasser. *Leo Strauss, Max Weber, and the Scientific Study of Politics.* Chicago: University of Chicago Press, 2003.

Beiner, Ronald. "Hannah Arendt and Judging." In *Lectures on Kant's Political Philosophy,* 89–156. Chicago: University of Chicago Press, 1982.

Belting, Hans. *Anthropology of Images: Picture, Medium, Body.* Princeton, NJ: Princeton University Press, 2011.

Belting, Hans. *Bild-Anthropologie: Entwürfe für eine Bildwissenschaft.* Munich: Fink, 2001.

Benjamin, Walter. *Gesammelte Briefe.* Edited by Christoph Gödde and Henri Lonitz. 6 vols. Frankfurt am Main: Suhrkamp, 1995–2000.

———. *Gesammelte Schriften.* Edited by Rolf Tiedemann and Hermann Schweppenhäuser with assistance from Theodore W. Adorno and Gershom Scholem. 7 vols. Frankfurt am Main: Suhrkamp, 1972–1989.

Bergson, Henri. "Le possible et le réel." In *La pensée et le mouvant: Essais et conférences,* 115–34. Paris: Félix Alcan, 1934.

———. *Matière et mémoire: Essai sur la relation du corps à l'esprit.* Paris: Félix Alcan, 1908.

Bertram, Ernst. *Nietzsche: Versuch einer Mythologie.* Berlin: Georg Bondi, 1922.

Beuttler, Brian. "DOJ Official: No Miranda Rights for Boston Bombing Suspect Yet." *Talking Points Memo,* April 19, 2013. http://livewire.talkingpointsmemo.com/entry /doj-official-no-miranda-rights-for-boston-bombing.

Binswanger, Ludwig, and Aby Warburg. *Die unendliche Heilung: Aby Warburg's Krankengeschichte.* Edited by Chantal Marazia and Davide Stimilli. Zurich: Diaphanes, 2007.

Bitzer, Lloyd. "The Rhetorical Situation." *Philosophy and Rhetoric* 1 (1968): 1–14.

Blumenberg, Hans. "Anthropologische Annäherung an die Aktualität der Rhetorik." In *Wirklichkeiten in denen wir leben,* 104–36. Stuttgart: Reclam, 1981.

————. "Approccio antropologico all'attualità della retorica." *Il verri* 35/36 (1971): 49-72.

Bogost, Ian. *Persuasive Games: The Expressive Power of Videogames*. Cambridge, MA: MIT Press, 2007.

Boni, Giacomo. "Leggende." *Nuova antologia di lettere, scienze ed arti* 126 (1906): 3-39.

Brandom, Robert. "A Hegelian Model of Legal Concept Determination: The Normative Fine Structure of the Judges' Chain Novel." In *Pragmatism, Law, and Language*, edited by Graham Hubbs and Douglas Lind, 19-39. New York: Routledge, 2013.

————. *Tales of the Mighty Dead: Historical Essays in the Metaphysics of Intentionality*. Cambridge, MA: Harvard University Press, 2002.

Braque, Georges. *Cahier de Georges Braque: 1917-1947*. Translated by Bernard Frechtman. New York: Valentin, 1946.

Bredekamp, Horst. "From Walter Benjamin to Carl Schmitt, via Thomas Hobbes." *Critical Inquiry* 25 (1999): 247-66.

————. *Theorie des Bildakts*. Frankfurt am Main: Suhrkamp, 2010.

Breiner, Peter. *Max Weber and Democratic Politics*. Ithaca, NY: Cornell University Press, 1996.

Brik, Osip. "Selected Criticism, 1915-1929." *October* 134 (2010): 75-110.

Bröcker, Walter. *Aristoteles*. Frankfurt am Main: Klostermann, 1935.

————. *Kants Kritik der ästhetischen Urteilskraft: Versuch einer phänomenologischen Interpretation*. Glückstadt: Augustin, 1928.

Buchanan, Scott. *Possibility*. London: Kegan Paul, Trench, Trubner, 1927.

Buchwald, Reinhard. Review of *Rahel Varnhagen: Eine Lebensgeschichte*, by Hannah Arendt. *Das Historisch-Politische Buch: Ein Wegweiser durch das Schrifttum* 8 (1960): 142-43.

Bultmann, Rudolf. "Die Eschatologie des Johannesevangeliums." *Zwischen den Zeiten* 6 (1928): 4-22.

Burns, Timothy W., ed. *Brill's Companion to Leo Strauss's Writings on Classical Political Thought*. Leiden: Brill, 2015.

Büttemeyer, Wilhelm. *Ernesto Grassi: Humanismus zwischen Faschismus und Nationalsozialismus*. Munich: Karl Alber, 2010.

Carlyle, Thomas. *Sartor Resartus*. London: Chapman and Hall, 1831.

Cassirer, Ernst. *Begriffsform im mythischen Denken*. Leipzig: Teubner, 1922.

————. *Sprache und Mythos: Ein Beitrag zum Problem der Götternamen*. Leipzig: Teubner, 1925.

Chacón, Rodrigo. "Reading Strauss from the Start: On the Heideggerian Origins of 'Political Philosophy.'" *European Journal of Political Theory* 9 (2010): 287-307.

Chen, Chung-Hwan. "The Relation between the Terms *Energeia* and *Entelecheia* in the Philosophy of Aristotle." *Classical Quarterly*, n.s., 8 (1958): 12-17.

Chun, Wendy Hui Kyong. "Queering Homophily." In *Pattern Discrimination*, edited by Clemens Apprich, Wendy Hui Kyong Chun, Florian Cramer, and Hito Steyerl, 59-97. Minneapolis: University of Minnesota Press, 2018.

Civai, Mauro, and Marilena Caciorgna. *Il tema della* Magnanimitas *nell'arte italiana*. Siena: Protagon, 2008.

Clark, Kenneth. "Pathos." In *The Nude: A Study in Ideal Form*, 225-72. New York: Pantheon Books, 1956.

Curtius, Ernst Robert. *Europäische Literatur und lateinisches Mittelalter*. Berne: Francke, 1948.

Cysarz, Herbert. *Deutsche Barockdichtung: Renaissance, Barock, Rokoko*. Leipzig: H. Haessel, 1924.

Damaschke, Adolf. *Geschichte der Redekunst*. Jena: Fischer, 1921.

Darwin, Charles. *The Descent of Man and Selection in Relation to Sex*. 2 vols. London: John Murray, 1871.

David, Eduard. *Referenten-Führer: Anleitung für sozialistische Redner*. Berlin: P. Ginger, 1919.

Derman, Joshua. *Max Weber in Politics and Social Thought: From Charisma to Canonization*. Cambridge: Cambridge University Press, 2012.

Derrida, Jacques, "Force de loi: Le fondement mystique de l'autorité/Force of Law: The Mystical Foundation of Authority." *Cardozo Law Review* 11 (1990): 920–1045.

———. "*Ousia* et *Grammē*: Note sur une note de *Sein und Zeit*." In *L'endurance de la pensée: Pour saluer Jean Beaufret*, 219–66. Paris: Plon, 1968.

Didi-Huberman, Georges. "*Dialektik des Monstrums*: Aby Warburg and the Symptom Paradigm." *Art History* 24 (2001): 621–45.

Diels, Hermann. *Die Fragmente der Vorsokratiker*. Berlin: Weidmann, 1903.

———. "Etymologica." *Zeitschrift für vergleichende Sprachforschung* 47 (1916): 193–210.

Dilanian, Ken, and Brian Bennett. "CIA Begins Sizing up Islamic Extremists in Syria for Drone Strikes." *Los Angeles Times*, March 15, 2013. http://articles.latimes.com/2013/mar/15/world/la-fg-cia-syria-20130316.

Dilthey, Wilhelm. *Gesammelte Schriften*. 26 vols. Leipzig: Teubner, 1921–.

Dockhorn, Klaus. "Die Rhetorik als Quelle des vorromantischen Irrationalismus in der Literatur- und Geistesgeschichte." *Nachrichten der Akademie der Wissenschaften zu Göttingen, Philologisch-historische Klasse* 5 (1949): 109–50.

———. Review of *Wahrheit und Methode: Grundzüge einer philosophischen Hermeneutik*, by Hans-Georg Gadamer. *Göttingen Gelehrte Anzeigen* 218 (1966): 169–207.

Eagleton, Terry. *Walter Benjamin, or Toward a Revolutionary Criticism*. London: Verso, 1981.

Efal, Adi. *Figural Philology: Panofsky and the Science of Things*. London: Bloomsbury, 2016.

Fdili Alaoui, Sarah, Frederic Bevilacqua, and Christian Jacquemin. "Interactive Visuals as Metaphors for Dance Movement Qualities." *ACM Transactions on Intelligent Design Systems* 5, no. 3 (2015): 1–24.

Federal Bureau of Investigation. "Custodial Interrogation for Public Safety and Intelligence-Gathering Purposes of Operational Terrorists Inside the United States." *New York Times*, March 25, 2011. http://www.nytimes.com/2011/03/25/us/25miranda-text.html?_r=1&.

Fichte, Johann Gottlieb. *Reden an die deutsche Nation*. Berlin: Deutsche Bibliothek, 1912.

———. "Über den Gebrauch der Regeln der Dicht- und Redekunst: Abschiedesrede Fichtes." In *Neue Fichte-Funde aus der Heimat und Schweiz*, edited by Maximilian Runze, 31–78. Gotha: F. A. Perthes, 1919.

Fisher, Ronald A. *The Design of Experiments*. Edinburgh: Oliver and Boyd, 1935.

Fleckner, Uwe, Martin Warnke, and Hendrik Ziegler, eds. *Handbuch der politischen Ikonologie*. Munich: Beck, 2011.

Gadamer, Hans-Georg. *Die Lektion des Jahrhunderts: Ein Interview mit Riccardo Dottori*. Münster: Lit, 2002.

———. "Replik." In *Hermeneutik und Ideologiekritik*, 283–317. Frankfurt am Main: Suhrkamp, 1971.

Galton, Francis. "Composite Portraits." *Nature* 18 (May 23, 1878): 97–100.

Gawande, Atul. *The Checklist Manifesto: How to Get Things Right*. New York: Metropolitan Books, 2009.

Geißler, Ewald. *Rhetorik: Anweisungen zur Kunst der Rede*. Leipzig: Teubner, 1914.

——. *Sprachpflege als Rassenpflicht*. Berlin: Deutsche Sprachverein, 1937.

Gell, Alfred. *Art and Agency: An Anthropological Theory*. Oxford: Clarendon, 1998.

Gerathewohl, Fritz, and Siemens-Studien-Gesellschaft für Praktische Psychologie. *Überlegenheit durch Suggestive Redekunst*. Bad Homburg: Siemens, 1933.

Gerber, Gustav. *Sprache als Kunst*. 2 vols. Bromberg: H. Heyfelder, 1871.

Giddens, Anthony. *Politics and Sociology in the Thought of Max Weber*. Oxford: Polity, 1972.

Giehlow, Karl. "Dürers Stich *Melencolia I* und der maximilianische Humanistenkreis." *Mitteilungen der Gesellschaft für Vervielfaltigende Kunst* 27 (1903): 29-41; 28 (1904): 6-18, 57-78.

Ginzburg, Carlo. "Da A. Warburg a E. H. Gombrich (Note su un Problema di Metodo)." *Studi Medievali*, ser. 3, 7 (1966): 1015-65.

Gladwell, Malcolm. *Blink: The Power of Thinking without Thinking*. New York: Little, Brown, 2005.

Goethe, Johann Wolfgang. *Sprüche in Prosa: Maximen und Reflexionen*. Edited by Herman Krüger-Westend. Leipzig: Insel, 1908.

Gomperz, Heinrich. *Sophistik und Rhetorik*. Leipzig: Teubner, 1912.

Gomperz, Theodor. *Griechische Denker: Eine Geschichte der antiken Philosophie*. 3 vols. Leipzig: Veit, 1903.

Gonzales, Francisco J. "Whose Metaphysics of Presence? Heidegger's Interpretation of *Energeia* and *Dunamis* in Aristotle." *Southern Journal of Philosophy* 44 (2006): 533-68.

Gordon, Peter Eli. *Adorno and Existence*. Cambridge, MA: Harvard University Press, 2016.

Gottsched, Johann Christoph. *Ausfürliche Redekunst*. Leipzig: Breitkopf, 1739.

Grassi, Ernesto. "G. B. Vico und das Problem des Beginns des modernen Denkens: Kritische oder topische Philosophie?" *Zeitschrift für philosophische Forschung* 22 (1968): 491-509.

——. "Über das Problem des Wortes und des individuellen Lebens: Erwägungen aus der italienischen Überlieferung." *Geistige Überlieferung* 2 (1942): 7-23.

——. *Verteidigung des individuellen Lebens: Studia humanitatis als philosophische Überlieferung*. Bern: A. Franke, 1946.

——. *Vico and Humanism: Essays on Vico, Heidegger, and Rhetoric*. New York: Peter Lang, 1990.

——. *Vom Vorrang des Logos: Das Problem der Antike in der Auseinandersetzung zwischen Italienischer und Deutscher Philosophie*. Munich: Beck, 1939.

——. "Vom Wahren und Wahrscheinlichen bei Vico." *Kant-Studien* (1942/1943): 48-63.

Grassi, Ernesto, and Thure von Uexküll. *Von Ursprung und Grenzen der Geisteswissenschaften und Naturwissenschaften*. Munich: Lehnen, 1950.

Gross, Daniel M. "Being-Moved: The Pathos of Heidegger's Rhetorical Ontology." In *Heidegger and Rhetoric*, edited by Daniel M. Gross and Ansgar Kemmann, 1-45. Albany: State University of New York Press, 2005.

——. "Defending the Humanities with Charles Darwin's *The Expression of Emotions in Man and Animals* (1872)." *Critical Inquiry* 37 (2010): 35-59.

——. *The Secret History of Emotion: From Aristotle's Rhetoric to Modern Brain Science*. Chicago: University of Chicago Press, 2006.

Güde, Fritz. "Der Schiffbrüchige und der Kapitän: Carl Schmitt und Walter Benjamin auf stürmischer See." *Kommune* 3 (1985): 61–67.

Gundolf, Friedrich. *Andreas Gryphius.* Heidelberg: Weiss, 1927.

Gusy, Christoph. *Weimar—Die Wehrlose Republik? Verfassungsschutzrecht und Verfassungsschutz in der Weimarer Republik.* Tübingen: J. C. B. Mohr, 1991.

Hacking, Ian. *The Taming of Chance.* Cambridge: Cambridge University Press, 1990.

Hankamer, Paul. *Die Sprache: Ihr Begriff und ihre Deutung im sechzehnten und siebzehnten Jahrhundert; Ein Beitrag zur Frage der literaturhistorischen Gliederung des Zeitraums.* Bonn: F. Cohen, 1927.

Hankins, James. "The 'Baron Thesis' after Forty Years and Some Recent Studies of Leonardo Bruni." *Journal of the History of Ideas* 56 (1995): 309–38.

Hankins, James, ed. *Renaissance Civic Humanism: Reappraisals and Reflections.* Cambridge: Cambridge University Press, 2000.

Havel, Václav. *The Art of the Impossible: Politics as Morality in Practice.* New York: Knopf, 1997.

Hegel, G. W. F. *Wissenschaft der Logik.* Edited by Georg Lasson. 2 vols. Hamburg: Meiner, 1923.

Heidegger, Martin. "Andenken." In *Hölderlin: Gedenkschriften zu seinem 100. Todestag,* edited by Paul Kluckhohn, 267–324. Tübingen: J. C. B. Mohr, 1944.

———. *Aristoteles, Metaphysik Theta 1–3, Von Wesen und Wirklichkeit der Kraft* (Summer Semester 1931). Vol. 33 of *Gesamtausgabe,* edited by Heinrich Hüni. 2nd ed. Frankfurt am Main: Vittorio Klostermann, 1990.

———. *Augustinus und der Neuplatonismus* (Summer Semester 1921). In *Phänomenologie des religiösen Lebens,* edited by Claudius Strube, vol. 60 of *Gesamtausgabe,* 160–299. Frankfurt am Main: Vittorio Klostermann, 1993.

———. *Becoming Heidegger: On the Trail of His Early Occasional Writings, 1910–1927.* Edited by Theodore Kisiel and Thomas Sheehan. Evanston, IL: Northwestern University Press, 2007.

———. "Dasein und Wahrsein (nach Aristoteles)." In *Vorträge, Teil 1: 1915 bis 1952,* edited by Günther Neumann, vol. 80 of *Gesamtausgabe,* bk. 1, 55–101. Frankfurt am Main: Vittorio Klostermann, 2016.

———. "Der Begriff der Zeit (1924)." In *Der Begriff der Zeit,* edited by Friedrich-Wilhelm von Herrmann, vol. 64 of *Gesamtausgabe,* 1–103. Frankfurt am Main: Vittorio Klostermann, 2004.

———. "Der Begriff der Zeit (Vortrag 1924)." In *Der Begriff der Zeit,* edited by Friedrich-Wilhelm von Herrmann, vol. 64 of *Gesamtausgabe,* 105–25. Frankfurt am Main: Vittorio Klostermann, 2004.

———. *Der Satz vom Grund.* Pfullingen: Neske, 1957.

———. *Die Frage nach dem Ding: Zu Kants Lehre von den transzendentalen Grundsätzen.* Tübingen: Niemeyer, 1962.

———. *Die Kunst und der Raum.* St. Gallen: Erker, 1969.

———. "Einblick in Das Was Ist: Bremer Vorträge 1949." In *Bremer und Freiburger Vorträge,* edited by Petra Jaeger, vol. 79 of *Gesamtausgabe,* 1–77. Frankfurt am Main: Vittorio Klostermann, 1994.

———. *Einführung in die phänomenologische Forschung* (Winter Semester 1923/1924). Vol. 17 of *Gesamtausgabe,* edited by Friedrich-Wilhelm von Herrmann. Frankfurt am Main: Vittorio Klostermann, 1994.

———. *Einleitung in die Phänomenologie der Religion* (Winter Semester 1920/1921). In

Phänomenologie des religiösen Lebens, edited by Matthias Jung and Thomas Regehly, vol. 60 of *Gesamtausgabe*, 1–156. Frankfurt am Main: Vittorio Klostermann, 1995.

———. "Gelassenheit." In *Martin Heidegger zum 80. Geburtstag von Seiner Heimatstadt Messkirch*, 16–30. Frankfurt am Main: Vittorio Klostermann, 1969.

———. *Grundbegriffe der aristotelischen Philosophie* (Summer Semester 1924). Vol. 18 of *Gesamtausgabe*, edited by Mark Michalski. Frankfurt am Main: Vittorio Klostermann, 2002.

———. *Grundprobleme der Phänomenologie* (Winter Semester 1919/1920). Vol. 58 of *Gesamtausgabe*, edited by Hans-Helmuth Gander. Frankfurt am Main: Vittorio Klostermann: 1993.

———. "Hölderlin und das Wesen der Dichtung." *Das innere Reich* 3 (1936): 1065–78.

———. *Holzwege.* Frankfurt am Main: Vittorio Klostermann, 1950.

———. *Kant und das Problem der Metaphysik.* Bonn: Friedrich Cohen, 1929.

———. *Martin Heidegger im Gespräch.* Edited by Richard Wisser. Freiburg: Karl Alber, 1970.

———. *Nietzsche.* 2 vols. Pfullingen: Neske, 1961.

———. *Ontologie (Hermeneutik der Faktizität)* (Summer Semester 1923). Vol. 63 of *Gesamtausgabe*, edited by Käte Bröcker-Oltmanns. Frankfurt am Main: Vittorio Klostermann, 1988.

———. *Phänomenologie der Anschauung und des Ausdrucks* (Summer Semester 1920). Vol. 59 of *Gesamtausgabe*, edited by Claudius Strube. Frankfurt am Main: Vittorio Klostermann, 1993.

———. *Phänomenologische Interpretationen ausgewählter Abhandlungen des Aristoteles zu Ontologie und Logik* (Summer Semester 1922). Vol. 62 of *Gesamtausgabe*, edited by Günther Neumann. Frankfurt am Main: Vittorio Klostermann, 2005.

———. "Phänomenologische Interpretationen zu Aristoteles (Anzeige der hermeneutischen Situation)." *Dilthey-Jahrbuch für Philosophie und Geschichte der Geisteswissenschaften* 6 (1989): 237–69.

———. *Phänomenologische Interpretationen zu Aristoteles: Einführung in die phänomenologische Forschung* (Winter Semester 1921/22). Vol. 61 of *Gesamtausgabe*, edited by Walter Bröcker and Käte Bröcker-Oltmanns. 2nd ed. Frankfurt am Main: Vittorio Klostermann, 1994.

———. *Phänomenologie und transcendentale Wertphilosophie* (Summer Semester 1919). In *Die Bestimmung der Philosophie*, edited by Bernd Heimbüchel, vol. 56/57 of *Gesamtausgabe*, 119–220. Frankfurt am Main: Vittorio Klostermann, 1987.

———. "Platons Lehre von der Wahrheit." *Geistige Überlieferung* 2 (1942): 96–124.

———. "Platons Phaidros. Übungen im Sommersemester 1932." In *Seminare: Platon, Aristoteles, Augustinus*, edited by Mark Michalski, vol. 83 of *Gesamtausgabe*, 83–148. Frankfurt am Main: Vittorio Klostermann, 2012.

———. *Platons Lehre der Wahrheit: Mit einem Brief über den Humanismus.* Bern: A. Francke, 1947.

———. *Platon: Sophistes* (Winter Semester 1924/25). Vol. 19 of *Gesamtausgabe*, edited by Ingeborg Schüßler. Frankfurt am Main: Vittorio Klostermann, 1992.

———. *Sein und Zeit.* Halle: Max Niemeyer, 1927.

———. *Selbstbehauptung der deutschen Universität.* Breslau: W. G. Korn, 1933.

———. "Über 'Die Linie.'" In *Freundschaftliche Begegnungen: Festschrift für Ernst Jünger zum 60. Geburtstag*, 9–45. Frankfurt am Main: Vittorio Klostermann, 1955.

——. *Überlegungen II–VI (Schwarze Hefte 1931–1938)*. Vol. 94 of *Gesamtausgabe*, edited by Peter Trawny. Frankfurt am Main: Vittorio Klostermann, 2014.

——. *Überlegungen VII–XI (Schwarze Hefte 1938/39)*. Vol. 95 of *Gesamtausgabe*, edited by Peter Trawny. Frankfurt am Main: Vittorio Klostermann, 2014.

——. *Überlegungen XII–XV (Schwarze Hefte 1939–1941)*. Vol. 96 of *Gesamtausgabe*, edited by Peter Trawny. Frankfurt am Main: Vittorio Klosterman, 2014.

——. *Unterwegs zur Sprache*. Pfullingen: Neske, 1959.

——. *Vom Wesen der Wahrheit*. Frankfurt am Main: Klostermann, 1943.

——. *Vom Wesen des Grundes*. Halle: Max Niemeyer, 1929.

——. *Was ist Metaphysik?* Bonn: Friedrich Cohen, 1929.

——. *Wegmarken*. Frankfurt am Main: Vittorio Klostermann, 1967.

——. "Wilhelm Diltheys Forschungsarbeit und der gegenwärtige Kampf um eine historische Weltanschauung." Edited by Frithjof Rodi. *Dilthey-Jahrbuch für Philosophie und Geschichte der Geisteswissenschaften* 8 (1992/1993): 143–80.

Hennis, Wilhelm. *Politik und praktische Philosophie*. Neuwied am Rhein: Luchterhand, 1963.

Hensel, Thomas. *Wie aus der Kunstgeschichte eine Bildwissenschaft wurde: Aby Warburgs Graphien*. Berlin: Akademie, 2011.

Herder, Johann Gottfried. "Bruchstücke einer Abhandlung über die Grazie in der Schule." In *Poetische Werke*, edited by Carl Redlich, vol. 30 of *Sämtliche Werke*, edited by Bernhard Suphan, 29–35. Berlin: Weidmann, 1889.

——. "Die Kritischen Wälder zur Ästhetik." In *Schriften zur Ästhetik und Literatur, 1767–1781*, edited by Gunter E. Grimm, vol. 2 of *Werke in Zehn Bände*, edited by Günter Arnold et al., 9–442. Frankfurt am Main: Deutscher Klassiker, 1993.

——. "Sollen Wir Ciceronen auf den Kanzeln Haben?" In *Sämtliche Werke*, edited by Bernhard Suphan, 1:502–13. Berlin: Weidmann, 1877.

——. "Ursachen des Gesunknen Geschmacks." In *Schriften zu Philosophie, Literatur, Kunst, und Altertum, 1774–1787*, edited by Jürgen Brummack and Martin Bollacher, vol. 4 of *Werke in Zehn Bände*, edited by Günter Arnold et al., 898–929. Frankfurt am Main: Deutscher Klassiker, 1994.

Herrmann, Gustav. *Die Kunst der politischen Rede*. Leipzig: Dürr & Weber, 1920.

Herzl, Theodor. *The Tragedy of Jewish Immigration: Evidence Given before the British Royal Commission in 1902 by Theodor Herzl*. New York: Zionist Organization of America, 1920.

Hessen, Johannes. Review of *Der Liebesbegriff bei Augustin: Versuch einer philosophischen Interpretation*, by Hannah Arendt. *Kant-Studien* 36 (1931): 175.

Hinks, Roger. *The Gymnasium of the Mind: The Journals of Roger Hinks, 1933–1963*. Edited by John Goldsmith. Salisbury: Michael Russell, 1984.

Hintikka, Jaako. "On the Logic of Perception." In *Models for Modalities: Selected Essays*, 151–83. D. Reidel: Dordrecht, 1969.

Hobbes, Thomas. *Leviathan*. Edited by Richard Tuck. Cambridge: Cambridge University Press, 1991.

Hofmannsthal, Hugo von. *Das Schrifttum als geistiger Raum der Nation*. Munich: Bremer, 1927.

——. *Gesammelte Werke*. 10 vols. Frankfurt am Main: S. Fischer, 1986.

Honig, Bonnie. *Emergency Politics: Paradox, Law, Democracy*. Princeton, NJ: Princeton University Press, 2009.

———, ed. *Feminist Interpretations of Hannah Arendt.* University Park: Pennsylvania State University Press, 1995.

Horkheimer, Max. *Anfänge der bürgerlichen Geschichtsphilosophie.* Stuttgart: Kohlhammer, 1930.

———. *Kants Kritik der Urteilskraft als Bindeglied zwischen theoretischer und praktischer Philosophie.* Stuttgart: W. Kohlhammer, 1925.

Horkheimer, Max, and Theodor Adorno. *Dialektik der Aufklärung: Philosophische Fragmente.* Frankfurt am Main: Suhrkamp, 1984.

Howse, Robert. *Leo Strauss, Man of Peace.* Cambridge: Cambridge University Press, 2014.

Hume, David. *A Treatise of Human Nature.* Edited by David Fate Norton and Mary J. Norton. Oxford: Oxford University Press, 2000.

Husserl, Edmund. *Briefwechsel.* Edited by Karl Schuhmann. 10 vols. Dordrecht: Kluwer, 1994.

Jaeger, Werner. *Aristoteles: Grundlegung einer Geschichte seiner Entwicklung.* Berlin: Weidmann, 1923.

———. "Der Großgesinnte." *Die Antike: Zeitschrift für Kunst und Kultur des klassischen Altertums* 7 (1931): 97–105.

———. *Paideia: Die Formung des griechischen Menschen.* Berlin: De Gruyter, 1934.

Janitschek, Hubert. Introduction to *Kleinere Kunsttheoretische Schriften,* by Leone Battista Alberti, i–xliii. Edited by Hubert Janitschek. Vienna: Wilhelm Braumüller, 1877.

Jaspers, Karl. *Die geistige Situation der Zeit.* Berlin: De Gruyter, 1932.

———. "Gutachten." In *Hannah Arendt-Karl Jaspers Briefwechsel 1926-1969,* edited by Lotte Köhler and Hans Saner, 723–24. Munich: Piper, 1985.

———. *Max Weber: Deutsches Wesen im politischen Denken, im Forschen und Philosophieren.* Oldenburg: Gerhard Stalling, 1932.

Jay, Martin. "Les extrêmes ne se touchent pas: Eine Erwiderung auf Ellen Kennedy: Carl Schmitt und die Frankfurter Schule." *Geschichte und Gesellschaft* 13 (1987): 542–58.

Jochmann, Carl Gustav. *Über die Sprache.* Heidelberg: Winter, 1828.

Johnson, Christopher D. *Memory, Metaphor, and Aby Warburg's Atlas of Images.* Ithaca, NY: Cornell University Press, 2012.

Johnson, Steven. *Where Good Ideas Come From: The Natural History of Innovation.* New York: Riverhead, 2010.

Jünger, Ernst. "Die totale Mobilmachung." In *Krieg und Krieger,* 9–30. Berlin: Junker & Dünnhaupt, 1930.

Kahn, Victoria. *The Future of Illusion: Political Theology and Early Modern Texts.* Chicago: University of Chicago Press, 2014.

Kahneman, Daniel. *Thinking, Fast and Slow.* New York: Farrar, Straus and Giroux, 2011.

Kahneman, Daniel, and Gary Klein. "Conditions for Intuitive Expertise: A Failure to Disagree." *American Psychologist* 64 (2009): 515–26.

Kant, Immanuel. *Kritik der Urteilskraft.* Leipzig: Felix Meiner, 1924.

Kasparov, Garry. "The Chess Master and the Computer." *New York Review of Books,* February 11, 2010.

———. *How Life Imitates Chess.* London: William Heinemann, 2007.

Kauffman, Stuart. *Investigations.* Oxford: Oxford University Press, 2000.

Kelly, Duncan. *The State of the Political: Conceptions of Politics and the State in the Thought of Max Weber, Carl Schmitt, and Franz Neumann.* Oxford: Oxford University Press, 2003.

Kelso, J. A. Scott, and David A. Engstrøm. *The Complementary Nature.* Cambridge, MA: MIT Press, 2006.

Kennedy, Ellen. "Carl Schmitt und die 'Frankfurter Schule': Deutsche Liberalismus Kritik im 20. Jahrhundert." *Geschichte und Gesellschaft* 12 (1986): 380–419.

Kierkegaard, Søren. *Entweder/Oder*. In vol. 1 of *Gesammelte Werke*, translated by Wolfgang Pfeiderer and Christoph Schrempf. Jena: Diederich, 1911.

Kim, Sung Ho. *Max Weber's Politics of Civil Society*. Cambridge: Cambridge University Press, 2004.

Kisiel, Theodore. *The Genesis of Heidegger's* Being and Time. Berkeley: University of California Press, 1993.

———. "Situating Rhetorical Politics in Heidegger's Protopractical Ontology. 1923–25: The French Occupy the Ruhr." *International Journal of Philosophical Studies* 8, no. 2 (2000): 185–208.

Klein, Gary. "Performing a Project Premortem." *Harvard Business Review* 85 (2007): 18–19.

Klein, Jacob, and Leo Strauss. "A Giving of Accounts." In *Jewish Philosophy and the Crisis of Modernity: Essays and Lectures in Modern Jewish Thought*, edited by Kenneth Hart Green, 457–66. Albany: State University of New York Press, 1997.

Kleist, Heinrich von. *Über das Marionettentheater: Aufsätze und Anekdoten*. Leipzig: Insel, n.d.

———. "Über die Allmähliche Verfertigung der Gedanken beim Reden." In *Erzählungen, Anekdoten, Gedichte, Schriften*, vol. 3 of *Sämtliche Werke und Briefe*, edited by Klaus Müller-Salget, 534–40. Frankfurt am Main: Deutscher Klassiker, 1990.

Klemperer, Victor. *LTI: Notizbuch eines Philologen*. Berlin: Aufbau, 1949.

Knape, Joachim. "Gibt es Pathosformeln? Überlegungen zu einem Konzept von Aby M. Warburg." In *Muster im Wandel: Zur Dynamik topischer Wissensordnungen in Spätmittelalter und Früher Neuzeit*, edited by Wolfgang Dickhut, Stefan Manns, and Norbert Winkler, 115–37. Göttingen: V & R, 2008.

Kommerell, Max. *Der Dichter als Führer in der Deutschen Klassik: Klopstock, Herder, Goethe, Schiller, Jean Paul, Hölderlin*. Frankfurt am Main: Vittorio Klostermann, 1982.

Kopperschmidt, Josef. "Endlich Angenommen im Westen; oder, Über das Ende des rhetorischen Sonderweg des Deutschen." In *Hitler der Redner*, edited by Josef Kopperschmidt, 455–79. Munich: W. Fink, 2003.

Koselleck, Reinhart. "Krise." In *Geschichtliche Grundbegriffe: Historisches Lexicon zur politisch-sozialen Sprache in Deutschland*, edited by Otto Brunner, Werner Conze, and Reinhart Koselleck, vol. 3, 617–50. Stuttgart: Klett, 1982.

———. *Kritik und Krise: Ein Beitrag zur Pathogenese der bürgerlichen Welt*. Freiburg: Karl Alber, 1959.

Kracauer, Siegfried. *Ornament der Masse*. Frankfurt am Main: Suhrkamp, 1963.

Krockow, Christian Graf von. *Die Entscheidung: Eine Untersuchung über Ernst Junger, Carl Schmitt, Martin Heidegger*. Stuttgart: F. Enke, 1958.

Kroll, Wilhelm. "En Éthei." *Philologus* 75 (1919): 68–76.

———. "Rhetorik." In *Real-Encyclopädie der klassischen Altertumswissenschaft*, edited by August Pauly and Georg Wissowa, supplement vol. 7, 1039–138. Stuttgart: J. B. Metzler, 1940.

Krüger, Gerhard. "Die Herkunft des philosophischen Selbstbewußtseins." *Logos: Internationale Zeitschrift für Philosophie der Kultur* 22 (1933): 225–72.

Kuki, Shūzō. *The Structure of Detachment: The Aesthetic Vision of Shūzō Kuki, with a Translation of* Iki no kōzōi. Honolulu: University of Hawai'i Press, 2004.

Lacis, Asja. *Revolutionär im Beruf: Berichte über proletarisches Theater, über Meyerhold,*

Brecht, Benjamin und Piscator. Edited by Hildegard Brenner. Munich: Rogner & Bernhard, 1971.

Landauer, Gustav. *Anarchismus*, in *Ausgewählte Schriften*, edited by Siegbert Wolf, vol. 2. Lich: Edition AV, 2009.

Landgrebe, Ludwig. *Über einige Grundfragen der Philosophie der Politik*. Cologne: Westdeutscher, 1969.

Landshut, Siegfried. "Über einige Grundbegriffe der Politik." *Archiv für Sozialwissenschaft und Sozialpolitik* 54 (1925): 36–86.

Leibniz, Gottfried Wilhelm. *Nouveaux essais sur l'entendement humain*. In *Philosophische schriften*, ser. 6, vol. 6. Berlin: Akademie, 1962.

Linfert, Carl. "Die Grundlagen der Architekturzeichnung." *Kunstwissenschaftliche Forschungen* 1 (1931): 133–246.

Loos, Alfred. "Ornament und Verbrechen." In *Ornament und Verbrechen: Ausgewählte Schriften*, edited by Adolf Opel, 192–202. Vienna: G. Prachner, 2000.

Löwith, Karl. *Das Individuum in der Rolle des Mitmenschen*. Munich: Drei Masken, 1928.

———. "Les implications politiques de la philosophie de l'existence chez Heidegger." *Les temps modernes* 14 (1946): 343–60.

——— [Hugo Fiala, pseud.]. "Politischer Dezisionismus." *Revue Internationale de la Théorie du Droit* 9 (1935): 101–23.

Lübbe, Hermann. *Theorie und Entscheidung: Studien zum Primat der praktischen Vernunft*. Freiburg: Rombach, 1971.

Lukács, Georg. *Die Theorie des Romans: Ein geschichtsphilosophischer Versuch über die Formen der großen Epik*. Neuwied: Hermann Luchterhand, 1974.

Magnes, Judah L. "Toward Peace in Palestine." *Foreign Affairs: An American Quarterly Review* 21 (1943): 239–49.

Mali, Joseph. "Retrospective Prophets: Vico, Benjamin, and Other German Mythologists." *Clio* 26 (1997): 426–48.

Mann, Thomas. *Betrachtungen eines Unpolitischen*. Frankfurt am Main: Fischer, 2009.

Mannheim, Karl. *Ideologie und Utopie*. Bonn: Friedrich Cohen, 1929.

———. *Ideology and Utopia*. Translated by Louis Wirth and Edward Shils. London: Routledge & Kegan Paul, 1936.

Marin, Louis. *Détruire la peinture*. Paris: Galilée, 1977.

Marshall, David L. "The Afterlife of Rhetoric in Hobbes, Vico, and Nietzsche." In *The Making of the Humanities*, vol. 2, *From Early Modern to Modern Disciplines*, edited by Rens Bod, Jaap Maat, and Thijs Westersteijn, 337–53. Amsterdam: Amsterdam University Press, 2012.

———. "Giambattista Vico, Aphorism, and Aphoristic Machines." *The Italianist* 37 (2017): 324–47.

———. "The Implications of Robert Brandom's Inferentialism for Intellectual History." *History and Theory* 52 (2013): 1–31.

———. "Intellectual History, Inferentialism, and the Weimar Origins of Political Theory." *Journal of the Philosophy of History* 11 (2017): 170–95.

———. "The Intrication of Political and Rhetorical Inquiry in Walter Benjamin." *History of Political Thought* 34 (2013): 702–37.

———. "The Origin and Character of Hannah Arendt's Theory of Judgment." *Political Theory* 38 (2010): 367–93.

———. "The Polis and Its Analogues in the Thought of Hannah Arendt." *Modern Intellectual History* 7 (2010): 123–49.

——. "Rhetorical Trajectories from the Early Heidegger." *Philosophy and Rhetoric* 50 (2017): 50–72.

——. "The Transformation of Rhetoric in G. B. Vico's *De nostri temporis studiorum ratione*." *Italian Quarterly* 46 (2009): 123–37.

——. *Vico and the Transformation of Rhetoric in Early Modern Europe*. Cambridge: Cambridge University Press, 2010.

——. "Warburgian Maxims for Visual Rhetoric." *Rhetoric Society Quarterly* 48 (2018): 352–79.

Meehl, Paul E. *Clinical versus Statistical Prediction: A Theoretical Analysis and Review of the Evidence*. Minneapolis: University of Minnesota Press, 1954.

Meier, Heinrich. *Carl Schmitt and Leo Strauss: The Hidden Dialogue*. Translated by J. Harvey Lomax. Chicago: University of Chicago Press, 1995.

Meyers, Peter Alexander. "Notes on 'Now': Benjamin's Vico and Vico's Benjamin." In *Il mondo di Vico/Vico nel mondo: In ricordo di Giorgio Tagliacozzo*, edited by Franco Ratto, 383–408. Perugia: Guerra, 2000.

Meyers, Peter Alexander, and Nancy S. Struever. "Esquisse sur la modernisation de la rhétorique comme enquête politique." *Littérature* 149 (2008): 4–23.

Michelstaedter, Carlo. *La persuasione e la rettorica*. Florence: Vallecchi, 1922.

Milch, David. *Deadwood: Stories from the Black Hills*. New York: Bloomsbury, 2006.

Mitchell, W. J. T. "What Do Pictures 'Really' Want?" *October* 77 (1996): 71–82.

Mommsen, Wolfgang. *Max Weber und die deutsche Politik, 1890–1920*. Tübingen: Mohr, 1959.

Monrad, Olaf Peder. *Sören Kierkegaard: Sein Leben und Seine Werke*. Jena: Diederich, 1909.

Most, Glenn, and Thomas Fries. "Die Quellen von Nietzsches Rhetorik-Vorlesung." In *"Centauren-Geburten": Wissenschaft, Kunst und Philosophie beim jungen Nietzsche*, edited by Tilman Borsche, Federico Gerratana, and Aldo Venturelli, 17–46. Berlin: De Gruyter, 1994.

Müller, Adam. *Zwölf Reden über die Beredsamkeit und deren Verfall in Deutschland*. Edited and with a foreword by Arthur Salz. Munich: Drei Masken, 1920.

Müller-Doohm, Stefan. *Adorno: A Biography*. Cambridge: Polity, 2005.

Nancy, Jean-Luc. *Être Singulier Pluriel*. Paris: Galilée, 1996.

Nietzsche, Friedrich. *Gesammelte Werke*. 23 vols. Munich: Musarion, 1920–29.

Norbrook, David. *Writing the English Republic: Poetry, Rhetoric and Politics, 1627–1660*. Cambridge: Cambridge University Press, 1999.

Novalis [Georg Philipp Friedrich Freiherr von Hardenberg]. *Schriften*. Edited by Richard Samuel, Hans-Joachim Mähl, and Gerhard Schulz. 6 vols. Stuttgart: W. Kohlhammer, 1960.

Panagia, Davide. *The Political Life of Sensation*. Durham, NC: Duke University Press, 2009.

Pangle, Thomas L. *Leo Strauss: An Introduction to His Thought and Intellectual Legacy*. Baltimore: Johns Hopkins University Press, 2006.

Panofsky, Erwin. "Der Begriff des Kunstwollens." *Zeitschrift für Ästhetik und allgemeine Kunstwissenchaft* 14 (1920): 321–39.

——. *Die Gestaltungsprincipien Michelangelos, besonders in Ihrem Verhältnis zu denen Raffaels*. Edited by Gerda Panofsky. Berlin: De Gruyter, 2014.

——. "On Movies." *Bulletin of the Department of Art and Archaeology of Princeton University* (June 1936): 5–15.

———. "Über das Verhältnis der Kunstgeschichte zur Kunsttheorie: Ein Beitrag zu der Erörterung über die Möglichkeit 'kunstwissenschaftliche Grundbegriffe.'" *Zeitschrift für Ästhetik und allgemeine Kunstwissenschaft* 18 (1925): 129–61.

———. "Zum Problem der Beschreibung und Inhaltsdeutung von Werken der bildenden Kunst." *Logos* 21 (1932): 103–19.

Panofsky, Erwin, and Fritz Saxl. *Dürers "Melencolia I": Eine Quellen- und Typen-Geschichtlichen Untersuchung.* Leipzig: Teubner, 1923.

Parens, Joshua. *Leo Strauss and the Recovery of Medieval Political Philosophy.* Rochester, NY: University of Rochester Press, 2016.

Paul, Jean. *Vorschule der Aesthetik.* 3 vols. Hamburg: Friedrich Berthes, 1804.

Pecchioli, Renzo. *Dal "Mito" di Venezia all'"Ideologia Americana": Itinerari e modelli della storiografia sul repubblicanesimo dell'età moderna.* Venice: Marsilio, 1983.

Pericolo, Lorenzo. *Caravaggio and Pictorial Narrative: Dislocating the Istoria in Early Modern Painting.* London: Harvey Miller, 2011.

Philippi, Adolf. *Die Kunst der Rede: Eine deutsche Rhetorik.* Leipzig: Grunow, 1896.

Piccolomini, Alessandro. *Copiosissima parafrase di M. Alessandro Piccolomini, nel primo libro della Retorica d'Aristotele.* Venice: Giovanni Varisco, 1565.

Pizlo, Zygmunt, Yunfeng Li, Tadamasa Sawad, and Robert M. Steinman. *Making a Machine That Sees Like Us.* Oxford: Oxford University Press, 2014.

Plessner, Helmut. *Die Stufen des Organischen und der Mensch.* Berlin: De Gruyter, 1975.

Pocock, J. G. A. Afterword to *The Machiavellian Moment: Florentine Political Thought and the Atlantic Republican Tradition,* 553–83. Princeton, NJ: Princeton University Press, 2003.

———. "Machiavelli, Harrington and English Political Ideologies in the Eighteenth Century." In *Politics, Language, and Time: Essays on Political Thought and History,* 104–47. New York: Atheneum, 1971.

———. *The Machiavellian Moment: Florentine Political Thought and the Atlantic Republican Tradition.* Princeton, NJ: Princeton University Press, 1975.

Porter, James I. "'Don't Quote Me on That!': Wilamowitz contra Nietzsche in 1872 and 1873." *Journal of Nietzsche Studies* 42 (2011): 73–99.

———. *The Origins of Aesthetic Thought in Ancient Greece: Matter, Sensation, and Experience.* Cambridge: Cambridge University Press, 2010.

Preuss, Ulrich K. "Anmerkungen zu dem Aufsatz von Ellen Kennedy." *Geschichte und Gesellschaft* 13 (1987): 400–418.

Radkau, Joachim. *Max Weber: Die Leidenschaft des Denkens.* Munich: Carl Hanser, 2005.

Rasskin-Gutman, Diego. *Chess Metaphors: Artificial Intelligence and the Human Mind.* Cambridge, MA: MIT Press, 2009.

Reisig, Christian Karl. *Vorlesungen über lateinische Sprachwissenschaft.* Leipzig: Lehnhold, 1839.

Rensmann, Lars, and Samir Gandesha. *Arendt and Adorno: Political and Philosophical Investigations.* Stanford, CA: Stanford University Press, 2012.

Richter, Werner. *Liebeskampf 1630 und Schaubühne 1670: Ein Beitrag zur deutschen Theatergeschichte des siebzehnten Jahrhunderts.* Berlin: Mayer & Müller, 1910.

Rickert, Thomas. *Ambient Rhetoric: The Attunements of Rhetorical Being.* Pittsburgh: University of Pittsburgh Press, 2013.

Ringer, Fritz. *Max Weber: An Intellectual Biography.* Chicago: University of Chicago Press, 2004.

Roller, Herrmann. *Die Griechischen Sophisten zu Sokrates und Plato's Zeit und Ihr Einfluß auf Beredsamkeit und Philosophie.* Stuttgart: Metzger, 1832.

Romilly, Jacqueline de. *Les Grands Sophistes dans l'Athèns de Péricles.* Paris: Éditions de Fallois, 1988.

Rosello, Mireille. *Declining the Stereotype: Ethnicity and Representation in French Cultures.* Hanover, NH: University Press of New England, 1998.

Rubini, Rocco. *The Other Renaissance: Italian Humanism between Hegel and Heidegger.* Chicago: University of Chicago Press, 2014.

———. Review of *Ernesto Grassi: Humanismus zwischen Faschismus und Nationalsozialismus,* by Wilhelm Büttemeyer. *Intellectual History Review* 20 (2010): 538–40.

Rumpf, Michael. "Radikale Theologie: Walter Benjamins Beziehung zu Carl Schmitt." In *Walter Benjamin Zeitgenosse der Moderne,* edited by Peter Gebhardt, 37–50. Kronberg im Taunus: Scriptor, 1976.

Scheler, Max. "Das Ressentiment im Aufbau der Moralen." In *Abhandlungen und Aufsätze,* vol. 1, 39–274. Leipzig: Weisse Bücher, 1915.

———. *Späte Schriften.* Edited by Manfred S. Frings. Bern: Franke, 1976.

Schiller, Kay. "Hans Baron's Humanism." *Storia della Storiografia* 34 (1998): 51–99.

Schlegel, Friedrich. "Über die Unverständlichkeit." In *Charakteristiken und Kritiken I (1796–1801),* edited by Hans Eichner, 363–72. Munich: F. Schöningh, 1967.

Schmitt, Carl. *Der Begriff des Politischen.* Munich: Duncker & Humblot, 1932.

———. *Die Diktatur: Von der Anfängen des modernen Souveränitätsgedankens bis zum proletarischen Klassenkampf.* 2nd ed. Munich: Duncker & Humblot, 1928.

———. *Die geistesgeschichtliche Lage des heutigen Parlamentarismus.* Munich: Duncker & Humblot, 1923.

———. *Glossarium: Aufzeichnungen der Jahre 1947–1951.* Edited by E. Freiherr von Medem. Berlin: Duncker & Humblot, 1991.

———. *Politische Theologie: Vier Kapitel zur Lehre von der Souveränität.* Munich: Duncker & Humblot, 1922.

———. "Vorbemerkung (über den Gegensatz von Parlamentarismus und Demokratie)." In *Die geistesgeschichtliche Lage des heutigen Parlamentarismus,* 5–23. Berlin: Duncker & Humblot, 1926.

Schmitt-Dorotić, Carl. *Politische Romantik.* Munich: Duncker & Humblot, 1919.

Schoel-Glass, Charlotte. "Warburg's Late Comments on Symbol and Ritual." *Science in Context* 12 (1999): 621–42.

Schopenhauer, Arthur. *Die Welt als Wille und Vorstellung.* In *Sämtliche Werke,* edited by Paul Deussen, vol. 2. Munich: Piper, 1911.

Seigel, Jerrold. "'Civic Humanism' or Ciceronian Rhetoric? The Culture of Petrarch and Bruni." *Past and Present* 34 (1966): 3–48.

Semon, Richard. *Die Mneme als erhaltendes Prinzip im Wechsel des organischen Geschehens.* Leipzig: Wilhelm Englemann, 1920.

Semper, Gottfried. *Über die Formelle Gesetzmäßigkeit des Schmuckes und dessen Bedeutung als Kunstsymbol.* Zurich: Meyer & Zeller, 1856.

Silver, Nate. *The Signal and the Noise: Why So Many Predictions Fail—But Some Don't.* New York: Penguin, 2012.

Simmel, Georg. "Über Kunstausstellungen." In *Soziologische Ästhetik,* edited by Klaus Lichtblau, 45–52. Bodenheim: Philo, 1998.

Skinner, Quentin. *Liberty before Liberalism.* Cambridge: Cambridge University Press, 1998.

———. "Meaning and Understanding in the History of Ideas." *History and Theory* 8 (1969): 3–53.

Sloterdijk, Peter. *Blasen, Mikrosphärologie*. Vol. 1 of *Sphären*. Frankfurt am Main: Suhrkamp, 1998.

Smith, A. William, trans. *Fifteenth-Century Dance and Music: Twelve Transcribed Italian Treatises and Collections in the Tradition of Domenico da Piacenza*. Hillsdale, NY: Pendragon, 1995.

Söllner, Alfons. "Jenseits von Carl Schmitt: Wissenschaftsgeschichtliche Richtungstellungen zur politischen Theorie im Umkreis der 'Frankfurter Schule.'" *Geschichte und Gesellschaft* 12 (1986): 502–29.

Solmsen, Friedrich. "The Aristotelian Tradition in Ancient Rhetoric." *American Journal of Philology* 62 (1941): 35–50, 169–90.

———. *Die Entwicklung der aristotelischen Logik und Rhetorik*. Berlin: Weidmann, 1929.

Sontag, Susan. *Under the Sign of Saturn*. New York: Farrar, Straus and Giroux, 1978.

Spengel, Leonhard. "Die Definition und Eintheilung der Rhetorik bei den Alten." *Rheinisches Museum für Philologie* 18 (1863): 481–526.

Spiel, Hilde. "Rahel Varnhagen oder das sublimierte Leben." Review of *Rahel Varnhagen: Eine Lebensgeschichte*, by Hannah Arendt. *Süddeutsche Zeitung* 15, no. 171 (July 18–19, 1959).

Steinmetz, Willibald. *Das Sagbare und das Machbare: Zum Wandel politischer Handlungsspielräume England 1780–1867*. Stuttgart: Klett-Cotta, 1993.

Strauss, Leo. "Anmerkungen zu Carl Schmitt, *Der Begriff des Politischen*." *Archiv für Sozialwissenschaft und Sozialpolitik* 67 (1932): 732–49.

———. "The Living Issues of German Postwar Philosophy." In *Leo Strauss and the Theologico-Political Problem*, by Heinrich Meier, 115–39. Cambridge: Cambridge University Press, 2006.

———. *The Political Philosophy of Hobbes: Its Basis and Genesis*. Oxford: Clarendon, 1936.

Struever, Nancy S. *Rhetoric, Modality, Modernity*. Chicago: University of Chicago Press, 2009.

Sulzer, Johan George. *Allgemeine Theorie der schönen Künste*. 2 vols. Leipzig: Weidemann, 1771–1774.

Summers, David. "Contrapposto: Style and Meaning in Renaissance Art." *Art Bulletin* 59 (1977): 336–61.

———. "*Maniera* and Movement: The *Figura Serpintinata*." *Art Quarterly* 35 (1973): 269–301.

Taminiaux, Jacques. "The Platonic Roots of Heidegger's Political Thought." *European Journal of Political Theory* 6 (2007): 11–29.

Taubes, Jacob. *Ad Carl Schmitt: Gegenstrebige Fügung*. Berlin: Merve, 1987.

Tetlock, Philip E. *Expert Political Judgment: How Good Is It? How Can We Know?* Princeton, NJ: Princeton University Press, 2005.

Thaler, Richard H., and Cass Sunstein. *Nudge: Improving Decisions about Health, Wealth, and Happiness*. Penguin: London, 2009.

Theremin, Franz. *Die Beredsamkeit eine Tugend*. Berlin: Galfeld, 1814.

Turk, Horst. "Politische Theologie? Zur Intention auf die Sprache bei Benjamin und Celan." In *Juden in der deutschen Literatur: Ein deutsch-israelisches Symposion*, edited by Stéphane Moses and Albrecht Schöne, 330–49. Frankfurt am Main: Suhrkamp, 1986.

Tversky, Amos, and Daniel Kahneman. "Judgment under Uncertainty: Heuristics and Biases." *Science*, n.s., 185 (1974): 1124–31.

Usener, Hermann. *Götternamen: Versuch einer Lehre von der Religiösen Begriffsbildung*. Bonn: Friedrich Cohen, 1896.

Varnhagen, Rahel. *Rahel: Ein Buch des Andenkens für Ihre Freunde*. Edited by Karl August Varnhagen. Berlin: Duncker & Humblot, 1834.

Vico, Giambattista. *De antiquissima Italorum sapientia*. In *Opere filosofiche*, edited by Paolo Cristofolini, 55–168. Florence: Sansoni, 1971.

——. *Princìpi di scienza nuova d'intorno alla comune natura delle nazioni (1744)*. In *Opere*, edited by Andrea Battistini, 1:411–971. Milan: Arnoldo Mondadori, 1990.

Viesel, Hansjörg. *Jawohl, der Schmitt: Zehn Briefe aus Plettenberg*. Berlin: Support, 1998.

Vignoli, Tito. *Mito e scienza*. Milan: Fratelli Dumolard, 1879.

Vischer, Robert. *Über das optische Formgefühl: Ein Beitrag zur Aesthetik*. Leipzig: Hermann Credner, 1873.

Volkmann, Richard. *Die Rhetorik der Griechen und Römer in systematischer Übersicht*. Berlin: Ebeling & Plahn, 1872.

Vossler, Karl. *Gesammelte Aufsätze zur Sprachphilosophie*. Munich: M. Hueber, 1923.

Wackernagel, Wilhelm. *Poetik, Rhetorik, und Stilistik*. Halle: Weisenhauses, 1873.

Walker, Jeffrey. *Rhetoric and Poetics in Antiquity*. Oxford: Oxford University Press, 2000.

Warburg, Aby. *Der Bilderatlas Mnemosyne*. Edited by Martin Warnke and Claudia Brink. Berlin: De Gruyter, 2012.

——. *Die Erneuerung der heidnischen Antike: Kulturwissenschaftliche Beiträge zur Geschichte der europäischen Renaissance*. 2 vols. Leipzig: Teubner, 1932.

——. *Fragmente zur Ausdruckskunde*. Edited by Ulrich Pfisterer and Hans Christian Hönes. Berlin: De Gruyter, 2015.

——. *Heidnisch-antike Weissagung in Wort und Bild zu Luthers Zeit*. Heidelberg: Carl Winter, 1920.

——. *Sandro Botticellis "Geburt der Venus" und "Frühling": Eine Untersuchung über die Vorstellungen von der Antike in der italienischen Frührenaissance*. Hamburg: Leopold Voss, 1893.

——. *Tagebuch der Kulturwissenschaftlichen Bibliothek Warburg, mit Einträgen von Gertrud Bing und Fritz Saxl*. Edited by Karen Michels und Charlotte Schoell-Glass. Berlin: Akademie, 2001.

——. *Werke in einem Band*. Edited by Martin Treml, Sigrid Weigel, and Perdita Ladwig. Frankfurt am Main: Suhrkamp, 2010.

Weber, Max. "Der Sozialismus." In *Gesammelte Aufsätze zur Soziologie und Sozialpolitik*, 492–518. Tübingen: Mohr, 1924.

——. *Geistige Arbeit als Beruf*. Munich: Duncker & Humblot, 1919.

——. *Gesammelte politische Schriften*. Munich: Drei Masken, 1921.

——. *Wirtschaft und Gesellschaft: Grundriss der verstehenden Soziologie*. Edited by Johannes Winkelmann. 3 vols. Tübingen: Mohr, 1976.

——. "Zur Lage der bürgerlichen Demokratie in Rußland." *Archiv für Sozialwissenschaft und Sozialpolitik* 22 (1906): 234–353.

Weber, Samuel. "Taking Exception to Decision: Walter Benjamin and Carl Schmitt." *Diacritics* 22 (1992): 5–18.

Wedepohl, Claudia. "Pathos, Polarität, Distanz, Denkraum: Ein archivarische Spurensuche." In *Warburgs Denkraum: Formen, Motive, Materialien*, edited by Martin Treml, Sabine Flach, and Pablo Schneider, 17–49. Munich: Fink, 2014.

——. "'Wort und Bild': Aby Warburg als Sprachbildner." In *Ekstatische Kunst, Besonnenes Wort: Aby Warburg und die Denkräume der Ekphrasis,* edited by Peter Kofler, 23–46. Innsbruck: Studien, 2009.

Wehler, Hans Ulrich. *Deutsche Gesellschaftsgeschichte.* Vol. 4, *Vom Beginn des Ersten Weltkrieges bis zur Gründung der beiden deutschen Staaten 1914–1949.* Munich: Beck, 2003.

Weinstein, David, and Avihu Zakai. *Jewish Exiles and European Thought in the Shadow of the Third Reich: Baron, Popper, Strauss, Auerbach.* Cambridge: Cambridge University Press, 2017.

Weise, Christian. *Politische Redner.* Leipzig: J. Gerdesius, 1694.

Weiss, Helene. "The Greek Conceptions of Time and Being in the Light of Heidegger's Philosophy." *Philosophy and Phenomenological Research* 2 (1941): 173–87.

——. *Kausalität und Zufall in der Philosophie des Aristoteles.* Basel: Haus zum Falken, 1942.

Wilamowitz-Moellendorf, Ulrich von. "Asianismus und Atticismus." *Hermes* 35 (1900): 1–52.

Wilf, Eitan. "Toward an Anthropology of Computer-Mediated, Algorithmic Forms of Sociality." *Current Anthropology* 54 (2013): 716–39.

Wind, Edgar. "II. Contemporary German Philosophy." *Journal of Philosophy* 22 (1925): 516–30.

——. "On a Recent Biography of Warburg." In *The Eloquence of Symbols: Studies in Humanist Art,* 106–13. Oxford: Clarendon, 1983.

——. "Warburgs Begriff der Kulturwissenschaft und seine Bedeutung für die Ästhetik." *Beilageheft zur Zeitschrift für Ästhetik und allgemeine Kunstwissenschaft* 25 (1931): 163–79.

Winograd, Terry, and Fernando Flores. *Understanding Computers and Cognition: A New Foundation for Design.* Norwood, NJ: Ablex, 1986.

Wittgenstein, Ludwig. *Philosophical Investigations.* German text with English translation by G. E. M. Anscombe, P. M. S. Hacker, and Joachim Schulte. Edited by P. M. S. Hacker and Joachim Schulte. 4th ed. Chichester: Wiley-Blackwell, 2009.

Yates, Frances. *The Art of Memory.* Chicago: University of Chicago Press, 1966.

Zepf, Max. Review of *Der Liebesbegriff bei Augustin: Versuch einer philosophischen Interpretation,* by Hannah Arendt. *Gnomon* 8 (1932): 101–5.

Zerilli, Linda. *A Democratic Theory of Judgment.* Chicago: University of Chicago Press, 2016.

Ziliak, Stephen T., and Deirdre N. McCloskey. *The Cult of Statistical Significance: How the Standard Error Costs Us Jobs, Justice, and Lives.* Ann Arbor: University of Michigan Press, 2008.

Zuckert, Michael P., and Catherine H. Zuckert. *The Truth about Leo Strauss: Political Philosophy and American Democracy.* Chicago: University of Chicago Press, 2006.

INDEX

abstraction, 43–44; and concatenation (Warburg), 214–15

Abwehrphantasie (defensive imagination): vs. *Denkraum* (Warburg), 229; vs. *geistige Tat* (Warburg), 209

Ackermann, Friedrich, on *eikos* and *pithanon*, 79

action: and inaction, 169–70, 322; as *praxis* (*Handlung*), 69–70, 132. *See also* indecision

actor (in theater), 55, 180; and acting, 189. *See also* theater; tragedy; *Trauerspiel*

actuality: and possibilities, 317; seeing as, *vs.* touching (Warburg), 306. *See also* possibility (*Möglichkeit*)

actualization, 113, 232, 273, 274, 277, 315, 320, 325; Bergson on, 319–20; as *energeia*, 278, 315; Heidegger on, 302; and possibility, 103, 106, 164, 276, 283, 299, 300; and possibility, Arendt on, 326–27; Warburg on, 325

adjacencies (*endechomena*): and homophily/heterophily, 315; Rahel as emblem for, 321. *See also* Arendt, Hannah; salon, Rahel Varnhagen's

Adorno, Theodor: agreeing with Hegel's "historical concretion," 69; aphorisms of and parataxis, 42; on authoritarian personalities, 17; *Dialectic of Enlightenment*, 41, 69; *Dialectic of Enlightenment*, on modernity and rule procedures, 17; "The Essay as Form," 43–44; *Jargon of Authenticity*, 276; on Kierkegaardian existentialism, 41; *Minima moralia*, 29–30, 43; on music, as trove for aphorisms, 42–43; on music, notation as dictatorship, 18; and redescription, 27

aestheticism, and the metropolis (Adorno), 19

aesthetics, 56, 59, 268; political (Arendt), 145; and politics (Benjamin), 185, 186–88, 201; on self-summation and tragic character, 170; Warburg's, 206–51. *See also* art (*Kunst*); artist; dance; film; photography

Agamben, Giorgio: "Aby Warburg and the Nameless Science," 258–59; *Infancy and History*, 259; on "kairological saturation," 277; on potentiality, 275–76, 302; on Schmitt's definition of "sovereign," 11. *See also* sovereign, Schmitt's definition of

agency (*Kraft*), as *dunamis* (Heidegger), 122

aisthēsis (sensing), 70, 92

Ajax, silence of, 59–60

Alberti, Leon Battista, 220

alētheia (truth), 126; and appearance (Heidegger), 88; Grassi on, 269; as unconcealedness (Heidegger), 106, 109. *See also* truth

algorithms: and capitalism, 316; as predictors, 324; for producing image tables, 318

being-with-one-another (*Miteinander-sein*) (*continued*)
of (Heidegger), 111–12; meanings of (Heidegger), emotions and, 131. *See also* Heidegger, Martin
belief: antonyms of, 322; and persuasion/ *pithanon*, 321–26; and rhetoric, 77–84. See also *pithanon, to*
Belting, Hans: *Anthropology of Images*, 262–63; on images, 285
Benhabib, Seyla, on *Rahel Varnhagen*, 141
Benjamin, Walter, 30; Agamben invokes, 259–60; *Arcades Project* of recreating culture, 199; and Arendt, 150; on Brecht and "dialectics at a standstill," 191–92; "Club of Friends to the New Russia" debate, 184–87; *The Concept of Art Criticism in German Romanticism*, 173; "Disputation at Meyerhold's," 188; "Experience and Poverty," 194, 195–96, 259; influence on Adorno, 43; "Manifesto for a Proletarian Children's Theater," 190, 194; preference for allegory over symbolic, 170; radio work of, and *Konfrontation*, 193; "Russian Debate in German," 184; "The Sociology of Language," 198; "Vichian," regarding photography and language, 196–202; "What a Russian Theater Hit Looks Like," 188–89; "The Work of Art in the Age of Its Technological Reproducibility," 194, 198, 200–202, 203, 204, 322
Benjamin, Walter, *The Origins of German Tragic Drama*, 194, 202; as early thematic, 168–75; gifting Schmitt with copy of, 165; reformulated baroque obsession with *concetto*, 41; Schmitt's *Hamlet or Hecuba* responding to, 166; Weimar relevance of, 165–66
Beredsamkeit. See eloquence (*Beredsamkeit*)
Bergson, Henri: influence of on Heidegger, 90; on the possible, 317, 319–20
Bertram, Ernst, 236

Bestimmung (determination). *See* determination (*Bestimmung*)
Bildungsroman, heritage of (Arendt), 143
Bing, Gertrud, 238, 239, 245
Bishop, Bill, on the "Big Sort," diversity/homogeneity within, 316
Bismarck, Otto von, rules basis of nation-state of (Weber), 5–6
Bitzer, Lloyd, 313–14
Blumenberg, Hans, on insufficiency of reason, 257
Botticelli, Sandro, *Primavera* and *Birth of Venus* (Warburg on), 225, 235. *See also* aesthetics; art (*Kunst*)
bourgeoisie, as "*endlessly* discussing" class (Benjamin), 186
Brandom, Robert: on common law, 312–13; on context, 46–47
Brandom, Robert, inferentialism of: application of concept, 125; appropriating Frege, 24; and genres of historiography, 23, 25–30; on meaning, 22, 297; on nonmonotonicity, 22–23, 252
Braque, Georges, *Atelier* paintings, 305–6
Brecht, Bertolt: "alienation effects" of and Benjamin on theater, 191; Belting's analysis continues Benjamin's on, 262–63
Bredekamp, Horst, *Image Acts*, 285
Brik, Osip M., 201; on art and propaganda, 184; on film, 197–98
Broch, Hermann, on Arendt's Rahel manuscript, 150
Bröcker, Walter: *Aristoteles* flattening Heidegger, 273; on art as communicating a concept, 270–71; Heidegger notes, 112
Bruni, Leonardo: Baron's obsession with misportrays, 16; as lifelong rhetorician (Seigel), 40
Buchanan, Scott, *Possibility*, on Warburg, 249
Bühler, Karl, on origins of language, 198
Bultmann, Rudolf, "The Eschatology of the Gospel of John," 137
Bureaucracy, and rules (Schmitt), 7

contradiction (*Gegensatz*), Benjamin on, 176

contrapposto: of human figure (Warburg), 215; involves image and viewer (Warburg), 247. *See also* art (*Kunst*)

conversation: dictatorship and, 36; eternal, 27, 34–35, 173, 254, 255; at Rahel's salon (Arendt), 144, 145, 149, 152; universe as (Müller), 35

cornucopia (*Fülle*), breeds newness (Benjamin), 176, 180

Cortés, Juan Donoso, contempt for discussion of, 185, 186

cosmic, the, and cosmetic (Semper), 233. See also *kosmos*

cosmos. See *kosmos*

creativity: and actualization, 319–20; must risk derivativeness (Warburg), 220; unintelligibility and, 67. *See also* aesthetics; art (*Kunst*)

crisis, and modernity (Koselleck), 263–64

critic, genuine, tasks of (Benjamin), 173

criticism: art, "continuation" as only genuine (Benjamin), 173; art, endless (Benjamin), 173 (*see also* criticism [*Kunstkritik*]); as *krinein*, task of, 262, 267; revolutionary (Eagleton), on rhetoric, 267. *See also* art (*Kunst*)

Croce, Benedetto, 183

Cukor, George, cinematography of, and Heidegger's space/time differentials, 94

culture: endless task of (Benjamin), and Arendt on political space, 174–75; European, swings between cult and mathematics (Warburg), 249–50; language excels, 50

Curtius, E. R., 247

Cushing, Frank Hamilton, on Pueblo Indians, 227

Cysarz, Herbert, on baroque imitating classical rhetoric, 183

Da: Greeks on (Heidegger), 116; Heidegger on, 112, 117; Nietzsche on, 91; Sloterdijk's as space, 280. See also *Dasein*

dadaism: decomposed centuries of habit (Benjamin), 197; montages anticipate film (Benjamin), 197

Damaschke, Adolf: on history of rhetoric, 56; importance of rhetoric spread widely, 54

dance: and absence of verbal predication (Warburg), 231; marionettes and, 55; materialized by knotwork, 233; new patterns relate to, 319; as serial isolation of poses (da Piacenza), 277. *See also* music; performance

Darstellungsfähigkeit (capacity to make the absent present), works against centeredness, 68

Darwin, Charles, 229, 303

Dasein: historicity of (Löwith), 254; as *Möglichsein* (Heidegger), 98; oratory and (Heidegger), 105; as "situated presencing," 88, 90, 94, 111, 136; temporality of rewritten, 280

David, Eduard, tactics of for socialist orator, 61

Deadwood (television show), Swearengen and corralling of possibility in, 319

debate, as indecision (Benjamin), 185. *See also* argument(s)

decisionism, Schmittian: *vs.* Heideggerian existentialism, 254; lacks past and future, 263; opposition to, 254–57; and politics (Lübbe), 255; Strauss examines, 13; Wind on, 260. *See also* indecision; Schmitt, Carl

de dicto/de re distinction, Brandom appropriates from Frege, 24

de dicto exercising, 28

definition, story necessary for (Heidegger), 91

deixis, *Geste* as (Benjamin), 198

delivery (*pronuntiatio*): and *deixis* (Benjamin), 181–82; as element of rhetoric, 179. *See also* rhetoric

democracy: annihilates heterogeneity (Schmitt), 10; empty formalism of parliament in (Schmitt), 8; preemptive war and (Strauss), 14. *See also* politics

democratization, relocates

decision-making (Benjamin), 185. *See also* indecision; politics; sovereign baroque (Benjamin)

Denkraum, 222, 249; as decontextualization (Warburg), 229–30; as freedom from fear (Warburg), 231; mistaken interpretation of, 285–86

depoliticization, moment of, as closure *vs.* source of motion, 200. *See also* politics; theory, political

de re redescription: and embedding at level of term, 27; at level of sentence, 27–28, 297

Derrida, Jacques, 275; on *auctoritatis interpositio*, 10

Descartes, René, on magnanimity, 244

desire (*appetitus*): and Aristotle's *orexis* (conation), 132; and *caritas* (Augustine, Arendt), 131, 317; Christian abstention from (Arendt), 132; and dispersion (*dispersio*), 132–33; to narrativize, 285

detachment (*iki*), Kuki on, 277–78

determination (*Bestimmung*): distinct from determinism, 101; possibility and, 101

Deutungsbedürftigkeit (being in need of interpretation), 83

dialectic, Socratic, Heidegger extends beyond formalities, 138. *See also* rhetoric

dictatorship, feigns populism (Weber), 33. *See also* politics; sovereign, baroque (Benjamin); sovereign, Schmitt's definition of

Didi-Huberman, Georges, on multiplicities of indecision (Freudian), 263

Diels, Hermann: on *entelecheia*, 96; *Fragments of the Presocratics*, 84

difference, Augustine's *vs.* Arendt's, 139–40, 152. *See also* assimilation

dilectio proximi (love of neighbor/solidarity): in Augustine's concept of love, 131; as *Dasein* and *Befindlichkeit*, 136; as rhetorical capacity (Arendt), 138–39

Dilthey, Wilhelm: on *contextus*, 72; definitions of "trope," 74; on rhetoric

as unchanged, 74; on understanding, 68; on wide reaches of rhetoric, 56

Dionysian/Apollonian, the, 218, 242, 285–86; as activity/passivity (Warburg), 236; body habits of (Warburg), 214–15; both elements of magnanimity, 261; imagination and (Warburg), 220; nature and (Warburg), 218. *See also* Nietzsche, Friedrich

Dionysius Thrax, on *dunamis*, 301. See also *dunamis*

disarticulation, as motion and confusion, 307

discernment, compared with connoisseurship, 70

dispositio (arrangement), in painting and drama, 182–83

Dockhorn, Klaus, 86–87; on rhetoric and the irrational, 257

Dossi, Dosso, *Apollo and Daphne* (painting), 194–95, 197

doubt, opposite of belief, 82

Dudow, Slatan, *Kuhle Wampe*, 201; perspectives on indecision in, 202

dunamis: defined, 301; and *energeia*, 98, 163; energy and capital underlie (Heidegger), 118; Heidegger's transformation of, 125–26; "liquidating" (Heidegger), 117–25; as *Möglichsein* (Heidegger), 97–98; and possibility (Heidegger), 99, 101, 103, 299–300; rhetoric as, 52; rhetoric as, Heidegger on, 107, 256; rhetoric as, Nietzsche on, 60; Weimar, as indecision, 303–4

Dürer, Albrecht, *Melencolia I* of: Saxl and Panofsky on, 176–77, 219, 288–89; Warburg on, 219–20

Eagleton, Terry, and "revolutionary criticism," 267

Ebert, Friedrich, 33

education, political: nation-state omitted (Weber), 6; theater as organ of (Benjamin), 175, 189–92, 194. *See also* politics

Eichmann, Adolf, Arendt distinguishes evilness of, 266, 271, 272

eikos (probable), Ackermann on, 79

exempla, collection of leads to magnanimity (Baumgarten), 60
exhibitions, art, analogized with modern city (Simmel), 58–59
existentialism: Heideggerian, 254; Kierkegaardian, desires freedom from idealism, 41
Existenzphilosophie (philosophy of existence), and renewed interest in Christian theorists, 134
experience (*Erfahrung*), and the present (Heidegger), 91
Exzentrizität (eccentricity), 68

facticity, 117, 254
faculty: defined, 301; etymology of, 299
failure, Arendt on, in Rahel book, 152
fate, as techno-scientific during WWI (Warburg), 214
fear: and nonbeing (Heidegger), 100, 112; and possibility (Heidegger), 300
Fichte, Johann Gottlieb, 65–66
film: Caravaggio anticipates, 309; dadaism anticipates, 197; juxtaposed with photography (Agamben), 276–77; and magnanimity, motion, 290; photography excels in Abu Ghraib case, 314; positive barbarism in (Benjamin), 197–98; relationship to time (Benjamin), 201–2. *See also* photography
flaneur, Kierkegaard as (Adorno), 19
Flores, Fernando, *Understanding Computers and Cognition*, 279
fragmentation, quotations as, in new contexts, 29
fragments (*Bruchstücke*): aphorisms and, 276; art as (Benjamin), 173; in Benjamin's Arcades project, 199; generative capacity of (Adorno), 41; Heidegger on, 274; and indecision (Benjamin), 177; photography as, of film (Benjamin), 198; Warburg's, 213
freedom: artworks and, 289; Blumenberg on, 257; *Denkraum* as (Warburg), 231; *elocutio* as, 232–33; eloquence as practice of (Warburg), 250; and *Erfindungskraft* (Warburg), 220–21;

and inhibition (Warburg), 208; and magnanimity (Warburg), 237; and ornamentation (Warburg), 210; redescribed (Warburg), 235
Freud, Sigmund, speech-imagery analogies in film, 202
friend-enemy distinction (Schmitt's), Arendt draws on, 155–56
future, past and (Heidegger), 90
futurity, Heidegger on, 90, 98

Gadamer, Hans-Georg, on rhetoric, 256–57
Galton, Francis, 309
Gandesha, Samir, 41
Gasparri, Cardinal Pietro, 239
Gawande, Atul, 323, 325
Gehlen, Arnold, 68
Geißler, Ewald: on conditions for rhetoric, 64–65; on eloquence and possibility, 54; on Esperanto, 51
Gell, Alfred, on South Indian kolam, 300–301
gender roles, in Arendt, 146–47
genius: Goethe's, 67, 150–51; melancholy and, 177; and Romanticism (Arendt), 151; and *Witz*, 219. *See also ingenium*; *Witz* (wit)
genre: as nonidentity (Benjamin), 170; replete with fillable spaces (Benjamin), 171
Gerber, Gustav, 75; *Language as Art*, 69–70
Gerede (idle talk): and genuine speech, 105, 272; poets *versus* (Grassi), 268–69
Geselligkeit (sociability), Schmitt and Müller on, 36
Gesinningsethik, "ethic of conviction" (Weber), 6
gesture (*Geste*): action becomes (Brecht), 191; analysis of in theater (Benjamin, Warburg), 189, 191, 294; Benjamin on, 176, 198; and power (Warburg on de' Medici), 249; reciprocity and (Warburg), 215–16
Gewohnheit (habit): in Benjamin, 195; rhetoric as (Nietzsche), 53

Ghirlandaio, Domenico: *Birth of the Baptist*, 289; fresco by depicts de' Medici power (Warburg), 248–49; magnanimity of (Warburg), 248; Warburg's lecture on, 237–38

Gide, André, 202, 203

Giehlow, Karl, 219

Ginzburg, Carlo, on Warburg's *Bilderatlas*, 284

Giotto di Bondone, *Kiss of Judas*, interfacial configurations in (Sloterdijk), 281–82

Globe Theatre, sight-lines in and *ingenium*, 293. *See also* Shakespeare, William

Goethe, Johann Wolfgang von: *vs.* Benjamin on art, 173; influence on Arendt, 150; on mathematics and superstition, 214; on Shakespeare's *Henry IV*, 67

Goetz, Walter, 15; on Northern Renaissance, 16

Gomperz, Heinrich, on Protagoras's dictum on "human being as measure," 83

Gomperz, Theodor: on anger (*Zorn*), 81; on Protagoras's dictum on "human being as measure," 83

Gordon, Peter, on Adorno on Kierkegaard, 41

Gottsched, Johann Christoph, 72–73; and "master tropification," 75

Gracián, Balthasar, *Art of Ingenium* of, 177

Grassi, Ernesto: *Defense of Individual Life*, 268, 269; on differentiation, 267–68; reception of Heidegger, 273–74

gratia (grace), *caritas* and (Arendt), 133

Green, Julien, *The Strange River*, indecision/inaction in (Benjamin), 192, 193, 322, 326

Gross, Daniel, 113, 314

Gryphius, Andreas, *Leo Arminius* of taken up by Benjamin, 170

Gundolf, Friedrich, 151; on rhetoric as baroque and earlier, 183

habit, 53, 116, 137, 205, 299; alienation from (Augustine), 134; always a possibility (Heidegger), 115; as *Gewohnheit*/

ethos/ēthos, eviscerated during war (Benjamin), 195; "loosely bound," 311–12

Hamlet, 166, 167–69, 171, 218

Handbook of Political Iconology, 285–86

Hankamer, Paul, on rhetoric and Roman grammar, 183

Hankins, James: on Baron and Bruni, 16; on Baron's vision of republicanism, 39–40

Havel, Václav, 320

Hegel, Georg Wilhelm Friedrich, 151, 191; "historical concretion" of, 69; on reflective judgment, 265–66

Heidegger, Martin: Adorno's critique of, 276; "The Basic Concepts of Aristotelian Philosophy," 100, 102, 128; *Being and Time*, 93, 111, 117, 118, 134; *Being and Time*, as apex of his thought, 86–87; *Being and Time*, on *das Man*, 137, 272; Bremen lectures of, 123; "The Concept of Time," 89–90, 100, 114, 116; "*Dasein und Wahrsein (nach Aristoteles)*" ("Ruhr-Speech"), 103, 104; "Equanimity" essay of, 123–24; on humans and being, 95; *The Individual in the Role of Fellow Human Being*, Löwith on, 272; influence of on Strauss, 38; on "liquidating" *dunamis*, 117–25; misreading of, 104–7; and National Socialism, 123; "The Origin of the Work of Art," 97, 119, 122–23; problem with, 125–26; "The Question Concerning Technology," 119, 124; "Rector's Address" (*Rektoratsrede*) 119, 125; on refashioning vocabularies via fragments, 26; on rhetoric, 88–126 (*see also* rhetoric); on "situatedness," 95–102; on temporality, 89–95; Weimar project of, 304

Heine, Heinrich, as pariah, 161

Hennis, Wilhelm, on *ars topica* (topics), 255–56

Herder, Johann Gottfried: dissociates rhetoric from aesthetics, 56; on rhetoric's decline, 64

hermeneutic (practice): Heidegger on, 116–17; rhetoric as (Heidegger), 89

hermeneutics (art): of everydayness, 110–17; Heidegger on, 117
heroism, and art (Grassi on), 268
Herrmann, Gustav, *The Art of Political Speech*, 82–83
Herzfelde, Wieland, 184
Herzl, Theodor, Arendt on, 156
Hindenburg, Paul von, rule by decree of, 10, 165
Hinks, Roger, 279
historian, intellectual, tasks of, 47, 251
historicism, Burns defines, 37
historicity (*Geschichtlichkeit*): of *Dasein*, 254; as potentialization of life (Heidegger), 119; as true life of the law, 312–13
historicization, as "first principle of all hermeneutics" (Heidegger), 117
historiography: Brandom on, 252; Heidegger's on Nazi crimes, 123
historiography, intellectual: afterlife important within, 252–53; Brandom on, 25, 125, 252; as constant discovery, 326
history, 295; *vs.* ahistoricity (Heidegger), 121; Arendt uses more than Grassi, 271; event-centered rather than linear (Arendt), 159; as infinite (compared with tragedy) (Benjamin), 172; Napoleon as (Hegel), 151; as process of de- and recontextualization, 66; and religiosity (Benjamin), 171; Romantics and (Schmitt), 35
history, intellectual, 3, 250–51, 256; *de traditione* perspective on regarding *fragmentation*, 29; of rhetoric before Renaissance, 39–40. *See also* history
Hitler, Adolf: Grassi associated with, 269; as orator, 66. *See also* Eichmann, Adolf, Arendt distinguishes evilness of
Hobbes, Thomas: on conatus, 200; on contexture, 72, 150, 314–15; on freedom, 250; on imagination, 250, 315; on magnanimity and virtue (Strauss), 39, 244; pessimism of influenced by Aristotle, 38; rhetorical inheritance of, 37–38, 40

Hofmannsthal, Hugo von, 50
Hölderlin, Friedrich, Heidegger and, 109, 268, 276
homelessness, as human condition, 68
homonym/synonym distinction (Brandom), 24
Honig, Bonnie, on *Rahel Varnhagen*, 141
Horkheimer, Max, 17, 41, 68–69; accuses Benjamin of plagiarism, 203
hubris, in tragedy and among German teachers (Benjamin), 172
humanism, civic: as rhetorical performances (*contra* Baron), 40; rhetoric at core of, 39, 40
Humboldt, Wilhelm von, on Rahel Varnhagen, 149
humor, *Witz* produces, 218. See also *Witz* (wit)
Husserl, Edmund, Heidegger distances himself from, 87, 91–92
hypotaxis, 71, 72, 210, 274
hypothesis, positions as no more than, Müller and Schmitt agree on, 173
hypothesizing, as preferable to statistical either/or, 310

Iago: as intriguer, 182, 325; as manipulator, 324
ideology, fear of history bent to, 20
Illés, Béla, 184, 201
images: incite desire, 284; play games with viewers, 285, 286. *See also* art (*Kunst*); film; Warburg, Aby
imagination (*Phantasie*), 298; defined (Benjamin), 200; Hobbes on *vs.* modern rephrasing, 314–15; and sensation, 306–7, 310; as twin with memory (*anamnēsis*), 134
imitatio Christi (emulation of Christ), Weber on, 11
imitation (*Nachahmung*): completion as endless (Sloterdijk), 281; as mimesis (Aristotle), 69; and symbolism (*Symbolismus*) (Warburg), 226; Warburg on, 212–13, 226
immobility: and *entelecheia* (Heidegger), 96; and *Stillstand* (Benjamin/Brecht and), 192

Nazi Party, Schmitt joins (1933), 7
Nazism, Arendt imputes to Strauss, 14
necessitarianism, and being/manifesta-
    tion, 227
necessity (*Notwendigkeit*): absolute *vs.*
    relative, 102; as determination of
    being (Heidegger), 101-2; and possi-
    bility (Heidegger), 101
New Testament, 12
Nietzsche, Friedrich, 35, 48, 214, 236,
    240; on Aristotle on rhetoric, 52-53; on
    Ciceronian excess, 77; on Greek tragic
    speech distinct from action, 169;
    Heidegger on ideas of, 121, 317-18;
    on language (in Heidegger), 109; on
    pithanon, 79-80; on speech (*Rede*), 49;
    on tropes, 76; on Wagner, 50. *See also*
    Dionysian/Apollonian, the
nonassimilation: Arendt's *Rahel Varnha-
    gen and*, 139-53; Zionists and anti-
    Semites champion, 154, 163
nonbeing, and fear (Heidegger), 100
nonnecessity, as contingency, 303. *See
    also* contingency; necessity
Norbrook, David, on rhetoric and speech
    act theory, 40
nothing (*Nichts*), as "being-possible"
    (Heidegger), 100
Notwendigkeit (necessity), as "require-
    ment of the ought" (Heidegger). *See*
    necessity (*Notwendigkeit*)
Novalis, Georg Philipp Friedrich, 63; on
    language, 51

ontology, and simplicity (Winograd and
    Flores), 279
ontology, Greek: Heidegger inverts, 116;
    modalities of, 96-100; from necessary
    to possible (Heidegger), 88-126
orator: approaches rhetoric as "beautiful
    soul" (*schöne Seele*), 55; Grassian, and
    naming, 270; Lenin and Hitler exem-
    plify, 66; memory building of (Yeats),
    291; tactics for socialist (David), 61.
    See also oratory; rhetoric; speech
oratory: and *Dasein*, 105; irrelevant
    to children (Benjamin), 190; as

synonymous with rhetoric, 187; in
    Weimar film, 201. *See also* orator;
    rhetoric; speech
origin, as node vital to its future, 22,
    153-54
originality, and interpolation of spaces,
    320-21. *See also* creativity; possibility
    (*Möglichkeit*)
ornament: as crime (Loos), 78; mask
    freed from body becomes (Belting),
    263; origins of (Cicero et al.), 77-78;
    and repetition of movement (War-
    burg), 233; as *Schmuck* (Warburg),
    232-33
ornamentation: action as (Warburg), 234;
    exhibiting or not (Warburg), 222-37;
    as mannerism (Warburg), 233-34;
    perception of and *Augenblicksgott*,
    236-37
ousia, as presence (Derrida), 275
overpreparation, dangers of, 55
Ovid: on Marsyas and Apollo, 262; on
    Medea and oxymoronic emotions
    (Warburg), 217-18
oxymoron, in art (Warburg), 216

Panagia, Davide, on narratocracy and
    narrativization, 307
Panofsky, Erwin, 176-77; on artist's
    creative possibilities, 287; on Michel-
    angelo's *Moses*, 216; on space and
    gesture, 289-90; as "Warburgian,"
    290-91; on "worldview" (*Weltan-
    schauung*), 288. *See also* art (*Kunst*)
parataxis: and circumstance, 71, 72;
    as freedom from Cicero's hyper-
    structuration, 42; Hölderlin and
    (Adorno), 276; *vs.* hypotaxis (Cicero's),
    276
Parens, Joshua, on political thought, 14
pariahs, conscious, Arendt's list of,
    161-62
parliament: and democratic crisis,
    Schmitt and Benjamin on, 8, 174;
    suspended in Germany, 10
parliamentarism, and liberalism
    (Schmitt), 9

parousia: and *kosmos* (Heidegger), 96; and Mussolini, 241; and the second coming (Heidegger), 91

passion: as *Leidenschaft* (Grassi on), 270; as *pathēsis*, in Heidegger and Arendt, 131

past, and future (Heidegger), 90

pathē (passions, emotions), and motion (Heidegger, Clark), 112–13, 286

Paul, Jean, 236; on "constitutive wit" (Warburg cites), 218–19. See also *Witz* (wit)

Pecchioli, Renzo, on Venice as mythical/ ideal republic, 16

Peirce, Charles Sanders, 23, 303, 320

performance, 145–46, 149, 327; and debate (Benjamin), 188–89; *energeia* and, 97; importance of (Arendt), 152; judgment of, 164; and language, 50; language, *vs.* art (Grassi), 268; lecture as (Warburg), 238; Mussolini's (Warburg), 239, 241; and nonperformance, 60; and *pithanon* (Nietzsche), 80; and possibilities, 54–55; and *pronuntiatio* (Nietzsche), 80; in Rahel's salon (Arendt), 141, 143–44, 148; rhetoric and, 48–49, 51–52, 55, 311; style in, 222; synonymous with being (Native Americans), 227, 228, 231; theatrical (Benjamin), 181, 189. See also language; rhetoric

persuasio, as "at-oneness" with great deed, 60

persuasion: as actualization, 325; Benjamin's definition of, 187; as beyond *pithanon*, 322; in modern politics (Benjamin), 190; and rhetoric, 299, 321–22. See also *pithanon, to*; rhetoric

Petrarch, compared with Bruni, 40

Phänomen, Heidegger on, 91

Phänomenologie, Heidegger on, 87

Phantasie (imagination): in Adorno, 43; Benjamin's concept of, 200, 320–21; Benjamin's concept of, *vs.* Vico on *ingenium*, 204

Philippi, Adolf: on prose succeeding

poetry, 76; on rhetoric and modern culture, 56

philosophy, 260; compared to rhetoric (Benjamin), 176; role of (Wind), 260; Wittgenstein on, 320

photography: juxtaposed with film, 276–77, 314; more advanced than film (Benjamin), 198. See also film

phronēsis: Heidegger borrows from Plato's *Sophist*, 92; judgment as Aristotelian (Arendt), 162, 264; as rewriting of solidarity, 139

Piacenza, Domenico da, *On the Art of Dancing and Moving*, 277

Piccolomini, Alessandro, defines *rhetoric*, 299

pithanon, to: and belief, 128; and indecision, 321–26; Nietzsche's translation of (from Aristotle), 53; Nietzsche et al. on, 79–80

Pius XI, Pope, 238

Plato: on *dunamis*, 97; *Gorgias*, 106; *Phaedrus*, 106, 108; *Sophist*, Heidegger on, 87, 92, 106, 107–8, 138

Plessner, Helmut, 68

Pocock, J. G. A.: on Cicero's legacy, 40; *Machiavellian Moment*, transforms Baron's civic humanism, 17

"poeming," as language/rhetoric (Heidegger), 109

poetics, rhetoric as, 74. See also poetry

poetry: as art of invention (Benjamin), 179; as mimesis (Aristotle), 69; and naming (Heidegger et al.), 271; rhetoric and (Heidegger), 49, 108–9

poets, *vs. Gerede* (idle talk) (Grassi on), 268–69

poiēsis (making), and acting (*praxis*) (Arendt on), 256

polis: Arendt's concept of, 130, 146; Arendt's concept of, and Rahel as original analogue of, 144–45 (*see also* salon, Rahel Varnhagen's); Arendt's concept of, as space for political action, 162; in Heidegger, 111; theory of and Italian culture (Pocock), 17. *See also* politics

politic: defined, 325; and indecision (Benjamin), 322; rhetoric as (Heidegger), 303–4. *See also* indecision; politics; rhetoric

politics: and aesthetics (Benjamin), 185, 187–88, 201; Arendt on, 158–59; as art of the impossible (Havel), 320; as contingent on rules (Weber), 4; decisionmakers' importance in (Weber), 7; differs from law, 9; drama as education in (Benjamin), 175, 189–92; as *dunamis* (Arendt), 163–64; and friend/enemy distinction (Schmitt), 9; importance of for refugees (Arendt), 157–58; Lübbe on, 255; presentists and, 20–21; Schmittian, as "eternal conversation," 173; Scipio topos and (Poussin), 245–46; Strauss on, 13. *See also* education, political; rhetoric; sovereign, baroque (Benjamin); sovereign, Schmitt's definition of

politics, identity, exiting (Arendt), 155, 164. *See also* Jewishness

Porter, James, on *dunamis*, 301. See also *dunamis*

possibility (*Möglichkeit*): actuality *vs.* (Warburg), 306; and actualization, 320; barbarism breeds (Benjamin), 196; care/appetite and (Arendt), 135–36; chess as infinite (Warburg, Kasparov), 317–18, 323–24; in context of statistics, 309; defined in modern terms, 315–16; and *dunamis* (Heidegger), 99–100, 107, 273; etymology of, 300; freedom and (Warburg), 208, 221–22; Heidegger's critiques of, 124–25; and indecision, 325; and indecision, Benjamin on, 192, 257–58; life as (Heidegger), 99; modern world of, 315–16; naming and (Arendt), 267; and necessity (*Notwendigkeit*) (Heidegger on), 101; politics and (Arendt), 159; refracts reality (Warburg), 249; rhetoric and (Heidegger), 112–13, 300; seeing as, 168, 254, 294, 306; and situatedness (Heidegger et al.), 95–96, 311–12; as vague future in present

(Heidegger), 97–98; and *Weltanschauung*, 287–88

Potenz (potency), as possibility of determination (Heidegger), 101. *See also* possibility (*Möglichkeit*)

Poussin, Nicolas, visualization of Scipio's *magnanimitas*, 245–46

power: de' Medici's depicted by Ghirlandaio (Warburg), 249; deployed or not, 302; in drama, 324; as *dunamis*, rhetoric as, 52–53, 72; as *dunamis*, speech and, 49; as *dunamis*, will to (Nietzsche/Heidegger), 121; as *Macht* (Heidegger), 122; as potential-to-be (Weiss on Heidegger), 274; self-implodes, 302

powerlessness: conation leads to (Arendt), 132; Heidegger fetishizes, 120. *See also* power

predication: activation and (Heidegger), 99; applied to Eichmann (Arendt), 266, 271; in art (Warburg), 234; and dance, 231; defined, 108; and interpolation, 271; making "is" transitive (Arendt), 265–66

presencing: and beauty (Heidegger), 110; and *Parousia* (Heidegger), 91

present, the, Heidegger on, 90–91

presentism: as history based on ideology, 20; obliterates alterity of past, 21

pre-Socratics: fragmentary formulations of essential to posterity, 26; quotation of, 26–27, 274

pronuntiatio (delivery): as element of rhetoric, 179; as performance (Nietzsche), 80; pointing as paradigmatic form of, 181. *See also* rhetoric

prosopopoeia, 82, 262–63, 281

Protagoras, dictum on human being as a measure, 83

Proust, Marcel, and discovery of spaces, 200, 320. *See also* space

psuchē (soul), and movement (Heidegger), 92

Pueblo Indians: and humans as imperfect among animals (Cushing), 227; Warburg's ideas on, 223–24, 226–27

rhetoric, Arendt and: from epideixis to deliberation, 156; largely overlooks, 127–28, 153

rhetoric, Aristotle on: definition of (per Quintilian), 321–22, 326; Heidegger on, 128; as Heidegger's main authority, 107 (*see also* Aristotle, *Rhetoric*)

rhetorico-politics, Arendt on, 1940s, as historical/presentist, 157–62. *See also* history; politics

rhythm, 319. *See also* dance; music

Richter, Werner, on early modern drama and rhetoric/art, 175

Rilke, Rainer Maria, 94–95, 281

Roller, Herrmann, 83

Romanticism, political, Schmitt on: attributes to Weber, 34–36; considers dangerous, 36; considers risible, 185–86. *See also* Schmitt, Carl

Romilly, Jacqueline de, 172

Rosello, Mireille, *Declining the Stereotype*, 280

Rühle-Gersetel, Alice, *The Women's Question of the Present Age*, Arendt's review of, 140

rules (laws): destructive, per se (Weber), 6–7; dominance of, threatens leadership capacity, 12; as fearful (post-Shoah), 30; judgment needed along with, 6; politics precedes (Schmitt), 9. *See also* law, the

running, of a script, defined, 28

Russian Revolution, Benjamin on, 187

salon, Rahel Varnhagen's: as assimilated milieu, 144; compared with epistle writing, 148–49; compared with political space, 145; conversation as true space of, 145–46, 321; distinction of, 143; distinction of, from polis (Arendt), 141; "*Witz*" as purpose of, 152. *See also* Arendt, Hannah

Salz, Arthur, 50; defending Müller against Schmitt, 35, 56, 186

Sartre, Jean-Paul, *Letter on Humanism*, 118, 225

Saxl, Fritz, 176, 288–89

Scheler, Max, 68; Arendt opposing on

love, 134–35; critiquing Heidegger, 109–10

Schiller, Friedrich, as poetic rhetor (Kommerell), 49

Schlegel, Friedrich: on irony, 82; on sophists, 174; on understanding words, 51; on unintelligibility as a virtue, 67

Schmitt, Carl: appropriating Weber's ideas, 8, 35–36; Benjamin opposes, 185–86; binaries of, 13; on bureaucracy fixated on rule, 7–8; *The Concept of the Political*, 13, 36; *Freund/Feind* distinction of (in politics), 36; *Hamlet or Hecuba*, 166; on Müller as political Romantic, 34–35; *Political Romanticism*, 34, 173, 185, 186; *Political Theology*, 7–8, 185, 204; quotability/simplicity of, 9–10; sent copy of Benjamin's book, 165; state-philosophy of *vs.* Benjamin's art-philosophy, 165, 169, 170–71

Schopenhauer, Arthur, on eloquence, 50, 54

science, empirical: as depersonalization of myth (Vignoli), 229; and policy (Strauss), 12–13

science, political: Behnegar defines, 13–14; can't defend democracy from enemies (Behnegar), 13. *See also* politics

Scipio Africanus (in Livy), as topos for *magnanimitas*, 244–46

sculpture, Heidegger on, 94

seeing, rhetoric as, 304–11

Seigel, Jerrold, on Bruni's milieu and practice, 40

Sein, das (being), Heidegger on, 95

self-awareness (*Ichgefühl*): and play as repetition (Warburg), 234; in *Trauerspiel* (Benjamin), 181

semantics, and possibility, 298. *See also* language

Semon, Richard, 244

Semper, Gottfried, 77, 233

Seneca, on eloquence, 235

sensus communis (common sense): as collective sensitivities (Vico), 195–96; and judgment (Kant), 164; as opinions around an issue (Arendt), 317; and rhetorical performance, 311; as shared syllogisms, 57

sentences, and situations, reconstruction of, 296–327

Shakespeare, William, 40, 67, 74, 151, 166, 169, 293. *See also* Hamlet; Iago

silhouette, 309; and sensation (Warburg), 305, 306

Silver, Nate, 325

Simmel, Georg, on psychology of exhibitions, 58–59, 60

Sinn (sense), and *Bedeutung* (reference) (Frege), 24

Sistine Madonna (Raphael), 58

situatedness: "in any given case" (*peri hekaston*), Kantian/Schmittian responses, 311; modal dimensions of (Heidegger), 95–102; rhetorical, 65–66. See also *Befindlichkeit* (situatedness)

skepticism, 260, 325; as antonym of belief, 322; about presentist historiography, 20; religiosity and, 171

Skinner, Quentin: on Hobbes's political theory and rhetoric, 37; on political theory, *vs.* history of political thought, 21; on practice of intellectual history, 21–22, 45–46; on rhetorical legacy of Cicero, in Hobbes and Shakespeare, 40

Sloterdijk, Peter, 293–94; "ontotoplogy" of, 280; *You Must Change Your Life, anthropogenesis* in, 281, 282; *You Must Change Your Life, anthropotechnics* in, 280–81

Socrates, influence of, on Nietzsche, 236. *See also* Plato

solidarity. See *dilectio proximi* (love of neighbor/solidarity)

Solmsen, Frederick, on marginalization of Aristotle's *Topics*, 62–63

Sontag, Susan, against depictions of Benjamin as aphoristic, 258

sophistic: Benjamin's, in Late Weimar, 184–94; rhetoric as, 83–84

sophists: antilogies of, as endless (Benjamin), 174; Schlegel defines, 174

soul: "affective topics of" (Warburg), 242; *appetitus* and *caritas* as movements of (Arendt), 135; Aristotle on, 92, 93; "beautiful," 55; equilibrium within (Warburg), 248–49; Ghirlandaio/Warburg on, 248; imagination and (Benjamin, Vico), 204; and *krinein/kinein* (Heidegger), 92, 95, 267; magnanimity and, 60, 237, 243, 249, 290, 292–94, 325; magnanimity and, Strauss on, 14, 18, 39 (*see also* magnanimity [*magnanimitas*]); movements of (Arendt), 135; and possibilities, 325; rhetoric as leading (Heidegger), 106; struggle of (*Seelenkampf*), 217; therapy for (Warburg), 246; *Witz* and (Paul), 218

sovereign, baroque (Benjamin): decision-making process of (Benjamin), 176–79; and indecision, 183–84

sovereign, Schmitt's definition of: Agamben on, 11; as controller of constitution, 8; decides "state of exception," 10–11; as decisionist, 253–54

sovereignty, in terms of quotation (Warburg), 248

space: of appearance (Arendt), 145–46, 155; at archeological sites, 199; in art, 216 (*see also* art [*Kunst*]); *Denkraum* as (Warburg), 230; discovery of, as Benjamin's task, amid extremes, 175; discovery of, as Benjamin's task, new, where not previously detected, 200; originality and, 320–21; as potential movements (Panofsky), 289–90; Rahel Varnhagen and, 145–46, 148; rhetoric as movement through, 291; Sloterdijk's sphere and, 280; and spanning of time (Heidegger), 94; tradition as a (Arendt), 161

speech: Augustine's metaphorical, 138; *Gerede* and genuine, 105; Heidegger defines, 128; listener to as enemy of orator (Schmitt), 36–37; and performance, 55; political, bureaucratization of (Weber), 32–33; political, oral and mute, 32. *See also* orator; oratory; politics; rhetoric

speech act theory: preserves alterity of
past (Skinner), 21; as reinvention of
rhetoric (Norbrook), 40
Spengel, Leonhard, on rhetoric and the
particular, 64
Stadtstaatsburger (city-state citizen), as
"retina" for city (Adorno), 19
state, Weber *vs.* Schmitt on, 8–9. *See also*
polis; politics
statisticalization, contemporary: and
dunamis (per Aristotle), 304; and
separability of sensation from imagination, 310
statistics: and prediction, 324; as taming
of chance, 310
Stillstand, as possibility of motions
(Benjamin et al.), 191–92. *See also*
motion; movement
Strauss, Leo: Aristotle's *Rhetoric* crucial
to, 38; breaks with Schmitt, 13; compared to Weber and Schmitt, 12; as
conservative/neoconservative, 14;
on defeating Nazis from right, 14; on
Hobbes's use of Aristotle's *Rhetoric*,
38; influence of rhetorical tradition
on, 37–38; on magnanimity, 38–39,
244; *The Political Philosophy of Thomas
Hobbes*, 37
Struever, Nancy, on everydayness, 114
style (*elocutio*): Asiatic within baroque
(Benjamin), 181; definition of, 222,
232–33, 242–43; Goethe's constancy
of, 150–51; Goethe's constancy of,
ineffective in politics (Arendt), 159;
impossibility of constant (Arendt),
149–50; of the "sublime" (Benjamin),
178
Sulzer, Johann Georg, 71; on eloquence,
49; on rhetoric, 75
syllogism, 104
symbolism (*Symbolismus*), as a collision
or question (Warburg), 226
synecdoche, 301

Tacitus, baroque revision of, 30
technē (art): nonbeing of (Heidegger),
106; rhetoric as, 52. *See also* art
(*Kunst*): rhetoric as (Müller/Clark)

technology, Heidegger denounces,
123–24
temporality, Heidegger on, 89–95. *See
also* time
temporalization (*Zeitigung*), and situatedness (Heidegger), 95–96
Tetlock, Philip, 324
theater: as education in Soviet Union
(Benjamin), 190–91; gesture and
indecision in (Benjamin), 189; as
view of world from cosmos (Camillo),
291–92. *See also* education, political;
Trauerspiel
theory, democratic, and representation, 9
theory, political: differs from history of
political thought, 21; on emergency
(Schmitt), *vs.* emergence (Benjamin),
200; Hobbes's and rhetoric, 37; Weimar origins of, 4–20. *See also* politics
thought, political: as "architectonic anthropology" (Parens), 14; differs from
political theory, 21. *See also* politics
time: and *Augenblicksgott* (Cassirer,
Usener), 228; Heidegger on, 90, 93–
94; as motions (Heidegger), 93–94;
points of interpolation in (Benjamin),
202; rhetoric as (Heidegger), 108; and
space (Sloterdijk), 280
topics: defined (Hennis), 256; figural
topoi as (Vico), 284; Grassi on, 270;
local, 293, 323; sensory and everydayness, 308; of the soul (Warburg),
242; spatialization and (Sloterdijk),
282; visual (Braque), 305. See also *ars
topica* (topics); topos/topoi
topos/topoi: artistic, Simmel *vs.*
Baumgarten on, 59; baroque as
mundane, 180; cultivating, 279–80;
defined, 61–62, 162, 280; Emperor
Trajan as, 246; figural as visual
(Ginzburg), 284; related to idea of
polis (Arendt), 162; Scipio Africanus
as, 244–46; as source for arguments,
162; traditions as (Arendt), 162. See
also *ars topica* (topics); topics
tradition: defined, 30, 161; as space
between exemplars (Arendt), 161, 162